Thinking About Art

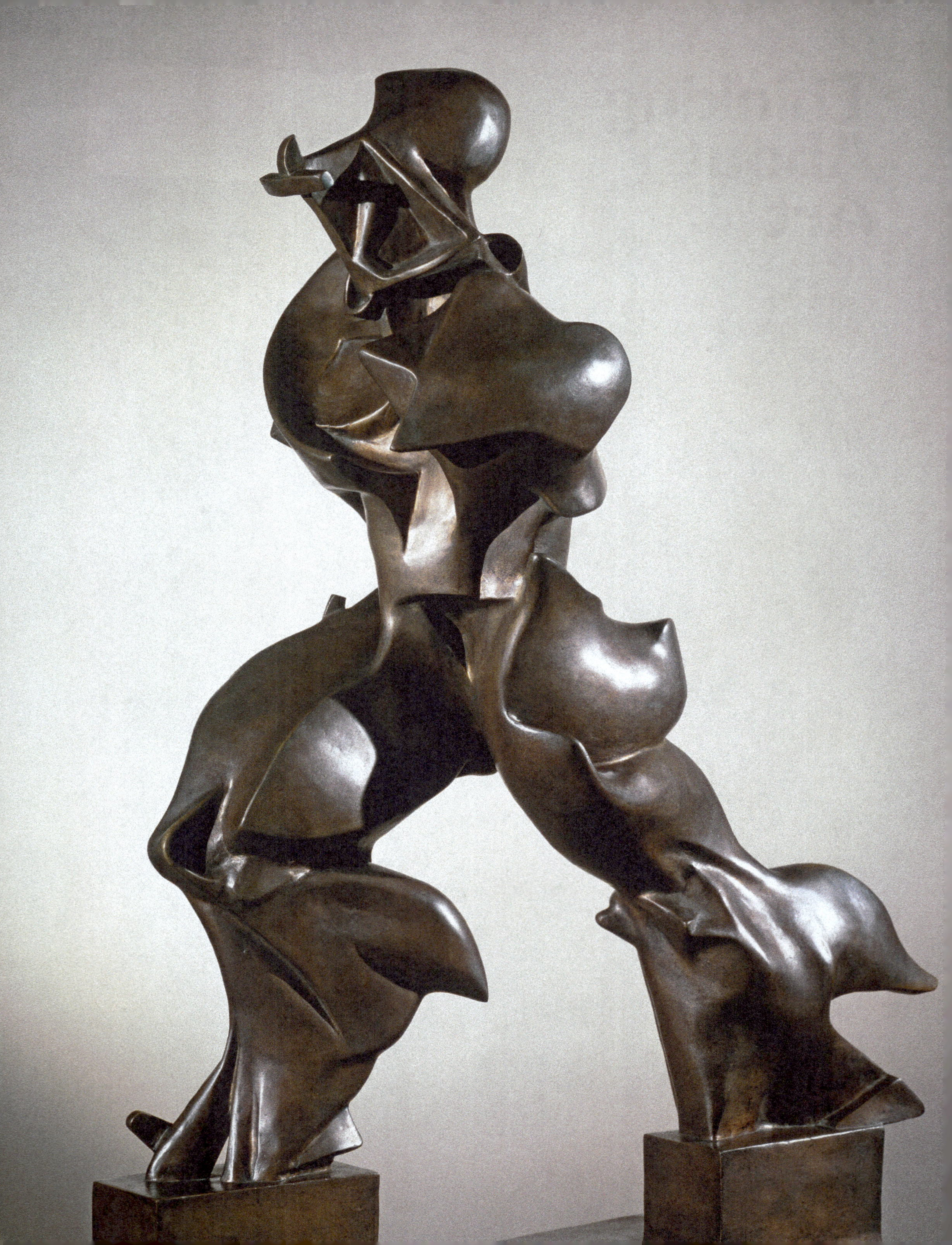

Thinking About Art

A Thematic Guide to Art History

Penny Huntsman

Umberto Boccioni,
Unique Forms of Continuity in Space,
1913, bronze, 1175 × 876 × 368 mm, cast
1972. London, Tate.
Source: © Tate, London 2015.

WILEY Blackwell
AAH ASSOCIATION OF ART HISTORIANS

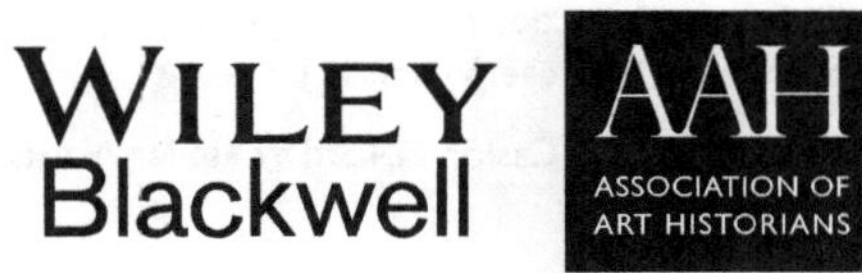

This edition first published 2016

Registered Office
John Wiley & Sons Ltd,
The Atrium, Southern Gate, Chichester,
West Sussex, PO19 8SQ, UK

Editorial Offices
350 Main Street, Malden, MA 02148-5020, USA
9600 Garsington Road, Oxford, OX4 2DQ, UK
The Atrium, Southern Gate, Chichester,
West Sussex, PO19 8SQ, UK

For details of our global editorial offices, for customer services, and for information about how to apply for permission to reuse the copyright material in this book please see our website at www.wiley.com/wiley-blackwell.

Library of Congress Cataloging-in-Publication Data
Huntsman, Penny.
Thinking about art : a thematic guide to art history / Penny Huntsman.
pages cm
Includes index.
ISBN 978-1-118-90517-3 (cloth) -- ISBN 978-1-118-90497-8 (pbk.) 1. Art--History. 2. Art--Themes, motives. I. Association of Art Historians (Great Britain) II. Title.
N5303.H86 2015
700.9--dc23 2015021567

A catalogue record for this book is available from the British Library.

Cover image: Jackson Pollock, 1949. Photo © Martha Holmes / LIFE Picture Collection / Getty Images
Cover design by Atelier Works LLP

Set in 10/14pt ITC Caslon 224 Std by Atelier Works LLP

1 2016

Contents

Companion Website

Please visit the companion website at **www.wiley.com/go/thinkingaboutart** to view additional, freely available content for this title.
– Exam Practice Questions for each chapter
– Other useful books and references for each chapter

Acknowledgements

Five years ago, I sat in my back garden with Caroline Osborne, former Chair of the Association of Art Historians Schools' Group, and together we decided that an A-level textbook must be written to support art history in further education. We decided upon its plain-speaking tone and easy-to-follow form.

I devised a 10,000-word outline; over the next couple of years this contribution would grow more than ten-fold and, before I knew it, I had an entire manuscript. In order to satisfy the current A-level demands, it was decided that, alongside the thematic chapters, an additional section would be provided as a stand-alone or complementary 'Toolbox'. This is essentially a list of questions or prompts which aids the reading of any given work of art or architecture. I am particularly indebted to Caroline Osborne for having a list of questions far more exhaustive and well-structured than mine. I give her thanks for sharing these invaluable points, for collating all of the many school reviews and for proof-reading the manuscript with an expert eye.

I also owe thanks to Tamara Trodd, a former AAH trustee at the start of the project, who really helped me to refine my initial ideas, and to my friend and a highly respected English teacher, Jane Lewis, who spent many an hour in my study proof-reading and offering constructive grammatical criticism. As the manuscript began the long process to publication, the staff at Wiley Blackwell offered invaluable support. The staff over in Boston provided technical assistance and emotional strength when the pedagogy of the book became the focus. Towards the end of a long process, I called upon the help of Graham Whitham. I have held Graham in very high regard for many years; indeed, I wrote the book in response to the dynamism of the AS Specification that he wrote. Graham provided indispensable expert knowledge and tidied many a loose end that I simply did not have the energy to face. Graham, along with Caroline Osborne and current AAH trustee Chrissie Bradstreet, reviewed the entire manuscript; I thank them all individually for such a protracted undertaking.

I did not set out to write a book; the book found me in many ways. For that reason, especial heartfelt thanks go to the headmistress, Louise Higson, and her leadership team, Alison Binns and Mandy Higgs, at Farlington School for their constant support and enthusiasm. Most importantly, I must thank my husband, Mark, and my children, Hannah, Laurence and William, for the thousands of hours I shut myself away to bring the manuscript to completion. I could not have completed the task without their support.

This book was written with heart and with a desire to facilitate art teachers – indeed, any teachers – to pick this subject up and introduce it into their schools and colleges – something less likely to occur without a textbook of sorts to guide them. In terms of the support they offered, a couple of individuals meant more to me than they could have imagined at the time: Tom Christopherson, Head of Art and Law Studies at Sotheby's Institute of Art, London, and Michael Casartelli, then Procurement Manager at the V&A (now Head of Procurement, Tate), both of whom offered me very timely support and encouragement. I first met Michael on the staircase at the V&A where I singled him out as a member of staff to berate about the fact that the V&A's wonderful 'lost-wax process' clip was not available to those students who could not make it to London. The next time we spoke, he told me the DVD had been uploaded onto YouTube for everyone to enjoy – that single gesture reminded me that even busy people care about making art history more inclusive. Both of these individuals actively support the inclusivity of the subject, and make time to listen to voices as unimportant as mine.

I would like to thank the following for allowing me private tours and detailed information on their respective buildings: MCC (Lord's Cricket Ground) London; James Breslin, former keeper of William Morris' Red House, Bexleyheath; and David Beever, keeper of the Royal Pavilion, Brighton.

Of course, this book would not have been possible without the AAH. Under the aegis of former Chair Evelyn Welch, the organisation supported a brave new schools-based project which relentlessly pursued a plain-speaking approach to the subject in order to make its scholasticism accessible to all. At a time when visual literacy has never been more important, the AAH has advocated the inclusivity of the subject and enabled non-specialists to introduce it into the Maintained Sector. Personal thanks must go to the current Chair, Christine Riding, for making the project a priority upon her arrival and for the forward-thinking approach she has taken towards the project ever since. Pontus Rosén, Chief Executive Officer at the AAH, has endured rather than enjoyed my highs and lows, and I thank him for the perpetual optimism and forbearance he has shown throughout the process. The AAH has taken the boldest of steps in championing such a long-awaited guidebook to the A-level and in acknowledging the mainstream audience to whom this book is really dedicated.

Penny Huntsman, June 2015

In the interest of space I will refrain from listing the individuals Penny has mentioned in her acknowledgements, but I wholeheartedly add my thanks, on behalf of the Association, to hers. There are, however, a few people I would like to add.

First and foremost I would like to thank AAH members for supporting and encouraging publication of this textbook as part of our mission to promote the professional practice and public understanding of art history.

Given the size of this project compared to the size of our office, all AAH staff have been involved and I thank them all for their professionalism and good sense. Rose Aidin, Education Officer, has gone beyond the call of duty in project managing the last 11 months of the book's gestation period, skilfully coordinating the design, production and publication process.

I want to thank Alison Yarrington, AAH Chair between the project's initiation under Evelyn Welch and its conclusion under Christine Riding, for her trust in and encouragement of Penny and others involved in the project during this time.

AAH trustee Grischka Petri was part of all legal negotiations with our publishers – negotiations that were greatly aided by solicitor Bunmi Durowoju, who gave generously of her time to find the best legal structures for a publication with so many stakeholders and interested parties.

Jacky Klein, AAH trustee and noted professional art editor, gave freely of her time and advice. Her knowledge of the Association and publishing allowed her to see practical solutions that suited both us and our publishing partners, benefiting the project immensely.

Designers Quentin Newark and Matt Hannah of Atelier Works worked with limitless patience and skill. They never failed to turn divergent stakeholder opinions into strong and beautiful designs.

There were many other professionals involved, working for the AAH and/or Wiley, and I wish I could mention them all.

Special thanks go to Jayne Fargnoli, Executive Editor at Wiley, whose business sense and enthusiasm for this project have kept us all focused and motivated, and Julia Kirk, Project Editor at Wiley, who cheerfully helped us at every corner while coordinating the project from the publisher's side.

Last but not least, on behalf of the whole Association, I would like to thank all students and teachers of history of art for disseminating this important discipline far and wide into the twenty-first century and beyond.

Pontus Rosén, Association of Art Historians, June 2015

Introduction

The book you are holding is not a history of art and architecture. It is a guide to understanding, interpreting and, ultimately, appreciating works of art and architecture. Of course, it includes some history, but its fundamental purpose is to help you 'read' a work of art or a building so that you can explain and discuss it in an informed and meaningful way and recognise its significance and the value of its qualities.

Unlike many books about art and architecture, this one is not organised in a chronological way. Although art and architecture's sequential development is an important part of understanding the subject, and this book does not ignore that, a thematic organisation has been adopted. In part, this is because it allows for effective relationships to be made that really assist understanding and interpretation, such as when examples from different art-historical periods are compared and contrasted. Since works of art and architecture are products of time and place, social and political systems, individual aspirations and so on, a thematic approach also demonstrates how the study of them is inescapably related to other disciplines and knowledge bases, from history to sociology, mathematics, science and technology to economics, psychology and beliefs, let alone to other cultural pursuits such as literature, music, theatre, dance, film and so on.

Another reason for the thematic arrangement lies in the book's dual purpose. Not only is it intended to serve as an effective guide for both lay readers and those who want to extend and expand their knowledge and understanding, but it is also a helpful and constructive 'tool' for students and prospective students of the AQA A-level examination in History of Art (Art of the Western World).

In general, there are two fundamental approaches (we might call them methodologies – that is, procedures applied to exploring and examining) in the history of art. Essentially, one is concerned with what we see and the other with what we know.

When we look at works of art and architecture we see a number of elements. In a painting it would be such things as colours, lines and shapes, the way the artist has applied the paint, the size of the painting and so on. These are the formal features and we would hope to understand and interpret the painting as a result of identifying and deciphering these.

The other methodology may be prompted by what we see but is more about the knowledge we already have or seek to have. This concerns the historical, social, cultural, psychological and other circumstances of a work's production and subsequent reception; in other words, the contexts of the work of art or architecture.

Although they appear to consider different things, these methodologies are not independent of each other. It would be fatuous to think that we could look at the formal characteristics of a work of art or architecture and hope to gain anything approaching a reasonable understanding of its purpose and meaning. Equally, even a thorough acquaintance with its subject matter (or its function, in the case of architecture), the circumstances of its creation, the personality of its creator and so on, would only take us so far in understanding and appreciating the work's aesthetic qualities or its capacity to 'move' us. In fact, the two methodologies outlined above must be 'used' alongside each other in order to develop a richer, more nuanced understanding and appreciation of art and architecture.

This book has been organised so that you can use these two methodologies – formal analysis and contextual knowledge – side by side. The shorter, but no less important, section is the Formal Analysis Toolbox, designed as a comprehensive list of questions that may be posed in relation to any work of art or architecture. The greater part of the book, which is organised thematically, applies contextual knowledge and analysis, as well as formal analysis, to examples selected as appropriate illustrations of the themes of each chapter.

Formal Analysis Toolbox

The Formal Analysis Toolbox is a series of questions that you would ask when looking at works of art and architecture. Each question focuses your attention on a particular feature of a work, and your 'answers' will lead to a thorough understanding of the way it has been created and how it communicates on a formal level, that is, by the way it looks.

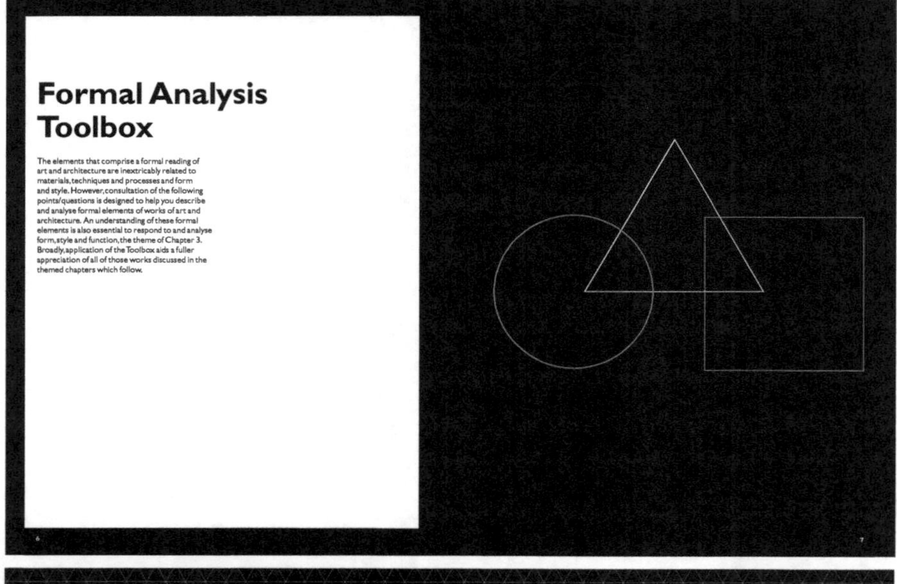

Formal Analysis Toolbox

The elements that comprise a formal reading of art and architecture are inextricably related to materials, techniques and processes and form and style. However, consultation of the following points/questions is designed to help you describe and analyse formal elements of works of art and architecture. An understanding of these formal elements is also essential to respond to and analyse form, style and function, the theme of Chapter 3. Broadly, application of the Toolbox aids a fuller appreciation of all of those works discussed in the themed chapters which follow.

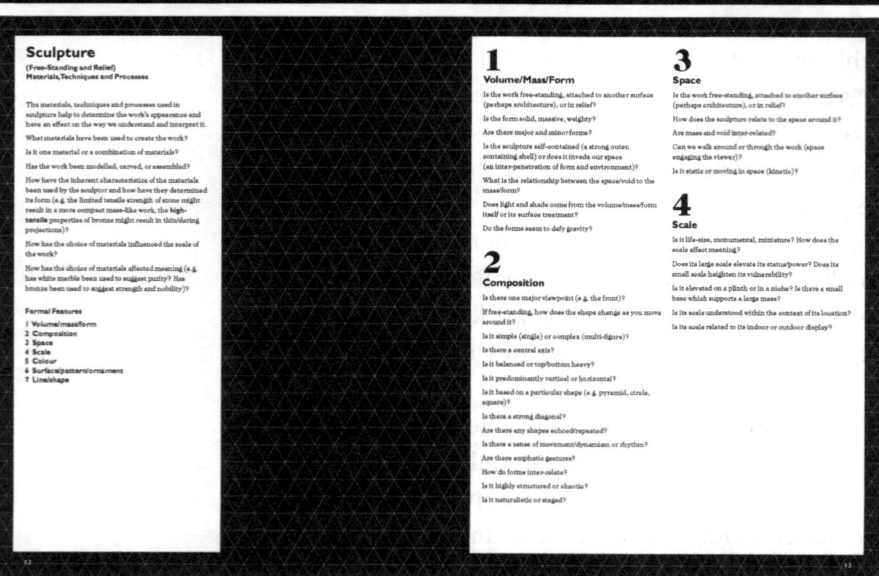

Sculpture

(Free-Standing and Relief)
Materials, Techniques and Processes

The materials, techniques and processes used in sculpture help to determine the work's appearance and have an effect on the way we understand and interpret it.

What materials have been used to create the work?

Is it one material or a combination of materials?

Has the work been modelled, carved, or assembled?

How have the inherent characteristics of the materials been used by the sculptor and how have they determined its form (e.g. the limited tensile strength of stone might result in a more compact mass-like work, the **high-tensile** properties of bronze might result in thin/daring projections)?

How has the choice of materials influenced the scale of the work?

How has the choice of materials affected meaning (e.g. has white marble been used to suggest purity? Has bronze been used to suggest strength and nobility)?

Formal Features

1 Volume/mass/form
2 Composition
3 Space
4 Scale
5 Colour
6 Surface/pattern/ornament
7 Line/shape

1 Volume/Mass/Form

Is the work free-standing, attached to another surface (perhaps architecture), or in relief?

Is the form solid, massive, weighty?

Are there major and minor forms?

Is the sculpture self-contained (a strong outer, containing shell) or does it invade our space (an inter-penetration of form and environment)?

What is the relationship between the space/void to the mass/form?

Does light and shade come from the volume/mass/form itself or its surface treatment?

Do the forms seem to defy gravity?

2 Composition

Is there one major viewpoint (e.g. the front)?

If free-standing, how does the shape change as you move around it?

Is it simple (single) or complex (multi-figure)?

Is there a central axis?

Is it balanced or top/bottom heavy?

Is it predominantly vertical or horizontal?

Is it based on a particular shape (e.g. pyramid, circle, square)?

Is there a strong diagonal?

Are there any shapes echoed/repeated?

Is there a sense of movement/dynamism or rhythm?

Are there emphatic gestures?

How do forms inter-relate?

Is it highly structured or chaotic?

Is it naturalistic or staged?

3 Space

Is the work free-standing, attached to another surface (perhaps architecture), or in relief?

How does the sculpture relate to the space around it?

Are mass and void inter-related?

Can we walk around or through the work (space engaging the viewer)?

Is it static or moving in space (kinetic)?

4 Scale

Is it life-size, monumental, miniature? How does the scale affect meaning?

Does its large scale elevate its status/power? Does its small scale heighten its vulnerability?

Is it elevated on a plinth or in a niche? Is there a small base which supports a large mass?

Is its scale understood within the context of its location?

Is its scale related to its indoor or outdoor display?

Implicit in the Toolbox questions is the proposition that the analysis may be developed from mere description of how something looks to one that points to interpretation. For instance, asking if the composition (the organisation and arrangement of elements) of a painting might be unstructured, or informally arranged, or dynamic and exciting, or harmonious, well-balanced and rigid, suggests that any of these is important to understanding the work and would, in all likelihood, contribute to our interpretation of it. Equally, identifying what materials are visible in a building and whether the choice of material affects a building's structure is not just about describing what you see; the implication is that distinguishing such things may facilitate a more meaningful interpretation of the building.

The Toolbox is particularly useful for those new to art-historical analysis. It provides a starting point, a way 'into' looking at works of art and architecture, which, after all, are frequently complex, difficult and challenging things, at least if we want to get something more than a superficial experience from looking at them.

Although the Toolbox can be used as a standalone guide to 'reading' works of art or architecture, used alongside the examples discussed in the thematic sections of this book, it will provide you with a comprehensive and effective means of understanding and lead you to meaningful interpretation.

The Formal Analysis Toolbox has also been designed to meet the requirements of the first teaching and assessment unit of the AQA's A-level History of Art (Art of the Western World) Specification (curriculum). Entitled 'Visual Analysis and Interpretation', this unit is about how to describe the formal features, subjects and themes of works of art, and the formal features, building types and functions of architecture. It is also concerned with how to discuss, interpret, comment on and evaluate works of art and architecture.

Themes in art and architecture

Each of the six chapters of this book discusses and interprets a range of examples in relation to fundamental art-historical themes. However, you must not think that simply because a particular work of art appears, let's say, as an example of how patronage operates, that this is the only way you should understand it. It is well to remember that there are countless interpretations of a work of art or architecture since different people at different times and in different places have looked at, written and spoken about it. Some of these provide us with valuable, helpful and effective ways of looking, interpreting and evaluating, but however perceptive, no one of them is definitive simply because there is no such thing as the definitive interpretation. Therefore, many of the examples in this book that have been interpreted in relation to a particular theme can also be interpreted in relation to other themes, and this point is made throughout the six thematic chapters. Moreover, once you have grasped the way that works of art and architecture can be thematically interpreted, you might substitute the given examples for some of your own.

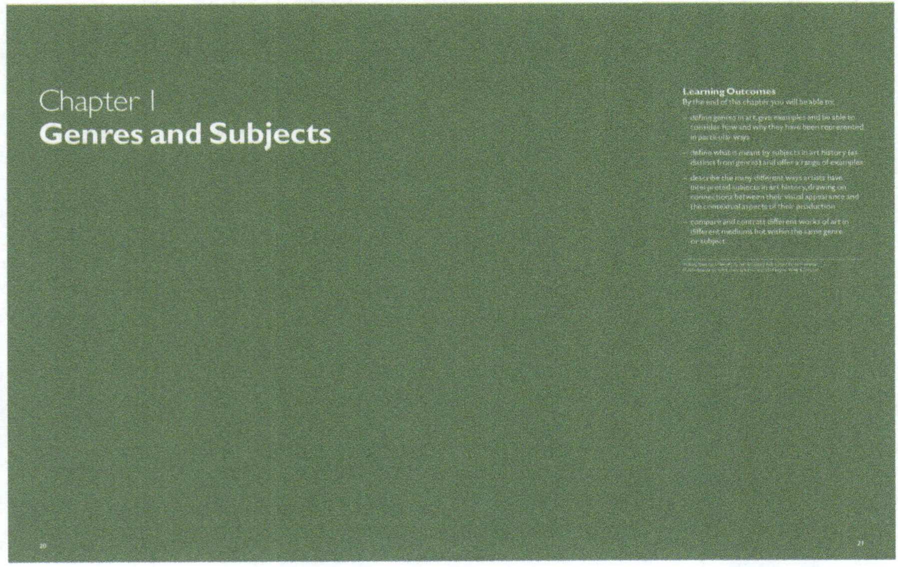

Chapter 1

Genres and Subjects

Learning Outcomes

By the end of this chapter you will be able to:

- define genres in art, give examples and be able to consider how and why they have been represented in particular ways
- define what is meant by subjects in art history (as distinct from genres) and offer a range of examples
- describe the many different ways artists have interpreted subjects in art history, drawing on connections between their visual appearance and the contextual aspects of their production
- compare and contrast different works of art in different mediums but within the same genre or subject

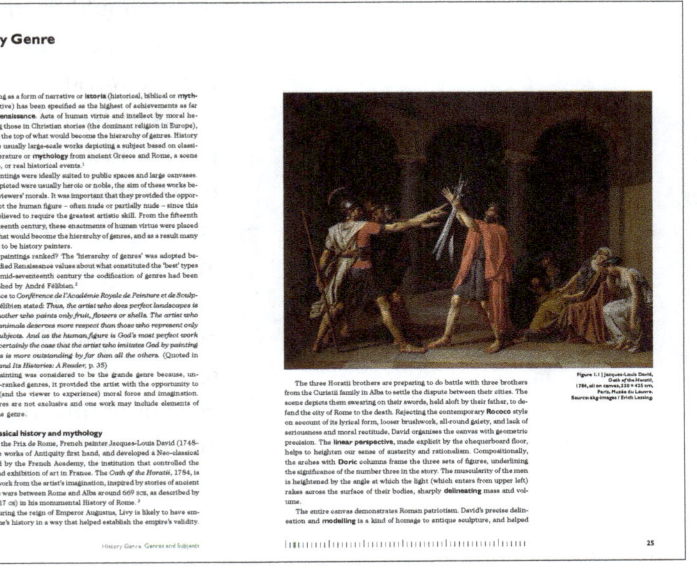

History Genre

History painting as a form of narrative or **istoria** (historical, biblical or **mythological** narrative) has been specified as the highest of achievements as far back as the **Renaissance**. Acts of human virtue and intellect by moral heroes, including those in Christian stories (the dominant religion in Europe), were placed at the top of what would become the hierarchy of genres. History paintings were usually large-scale works depicting a subject based on classical history, literature or **mythology** from ancient Greece and Rome, a scene from the Bible, or real historical events.[1]

History paintings were ideally suited to public spaces and large canvases. The scenes depicted were usually heroic or noble, the aim of these works being to elevate viewers' morals. It was important that they provided the opportunity to depict the human figure – often nude or partially nude – since this subject was believed to require the greatest artistic skill. From the fifteenth until the nineteenth century, these enactments of human virtue were placed at the top of what would become the hierarchy of genres, and as a result many artists aspired to be history painters.

Why were paintings ranked? The 'hierarchy of genres' was adopted because it embodied Renaissance values about what constituted the 'best' types of art. By the mid-seventeenth century the codification of genres had been firmly established by André Félibien.[2]

In his Preface to *Conférence de l'Académie Royale de Peinture et de Sculpture* (1669), Félibien stated: *Thus, the artist who does perfect landscapes is superior to another who paints only fruit, flowers or shells. The artist who paints living animals deserves more respect than those who represent only still, lifeless subjects. And as the human figure is God's most perfect work on earth, it is certainly the case that the artist who imitates God by painting human figures is more outstanding by far than all the others.* (Quoted in Edwards, *Art and Its Histories: A Reader*, p. 35)

'History' painting was considered to be the grande genre because, unlike the lower-ranked genres, it provided the artist with the opportunity to demonstrate (and the viewer to experience) moral force and imagination. However, genres are not exclusive and one work may include elements of more than one genre.

Ancient Classical history and mythology

After winning the Prix de Rome, French painter Jacques-Louis David (1748–1825) saw the works of Antiquity first hand, and developed a Neo-classical style favoured by the French Academy, the institution that controlled the production and exhibition of art in France. The *Oath of the Horatii*, 1784, is a large-scale work from the artist's imagination, inspired by stories of ancient Rome and the wars between Rome and Alba around 669 BCE, as described by Livy (59 BCE–17 CE) in his monumental History of Rome.[3]

Writing during the reign of Emperor Augustus, Livy is likely to have embellished Rome's history in a way that helped establish the empire's validity.

1 Although the Bible is a unified book, there is an important distinction to be made between the Old Testament, which relates to the laws of God and the prediction of the coming of Christ, and the New Testament, which reveals Christ and provides an account of his ministry.

2 In accordance with André Félibien's hierarchy of genres, the ranking in descending order of importance is: History, Portraiture, Genre, Landscape and Still-Life. The 2010 AQA Specification arranges the order as: History, Portraits, Landscape, Still-Life, Genre.

3 David's *Oath of the Horatii*, 1784, was also inspired by Pierre Corneille's play *Horace* (1640).

24

History Genre Genres and Subjects

Figure 1.1 | Jacques-Louis David, *Oath of the Horatii*, 1784, oil on canvas, 330 × 425 cm, Paris, Musée du Louvre. Source: akg-images / Erich Lessing.

The three Horatii brothers are preparing to do battle with three brothers from the Curiatii family in Alba to settle the dispute between their cities. The scene depicts them swearing on their swords, held aloft by their father, to defend the city of Rome to the death. Rejecting the contemporary **Rococo** style on account of its lyrical form, looser brushwork, all-round gaiety, and lack of seriousness and moral rectitude, David organises the canvas with geometric precision. The **linear perspective**, made explicit by the chequerboard floor, helps to heighten our sense of austerity and rationalism. Compositionally, the arches with **Doric** columns frame the three sets of figures, underlining the significance of the number three in the story. The muscularity of the men is heightened by the angle at which the light (which enters from upper left) rakes across the surface of their bodies, sharply **delineating** mass and volume.

The entire canvas demonstrates Roman patriotism. David's precise delineation and **modelling** is a kind of homage to antique sculpture, and helped

25

The first three thematic chapters – Genres and Subjects; Materials, Techniques and Processes; Form, Style and Function – discuss examples using both formal and contextual methodologies in relatively equal part. The final three chapters – Social and His-

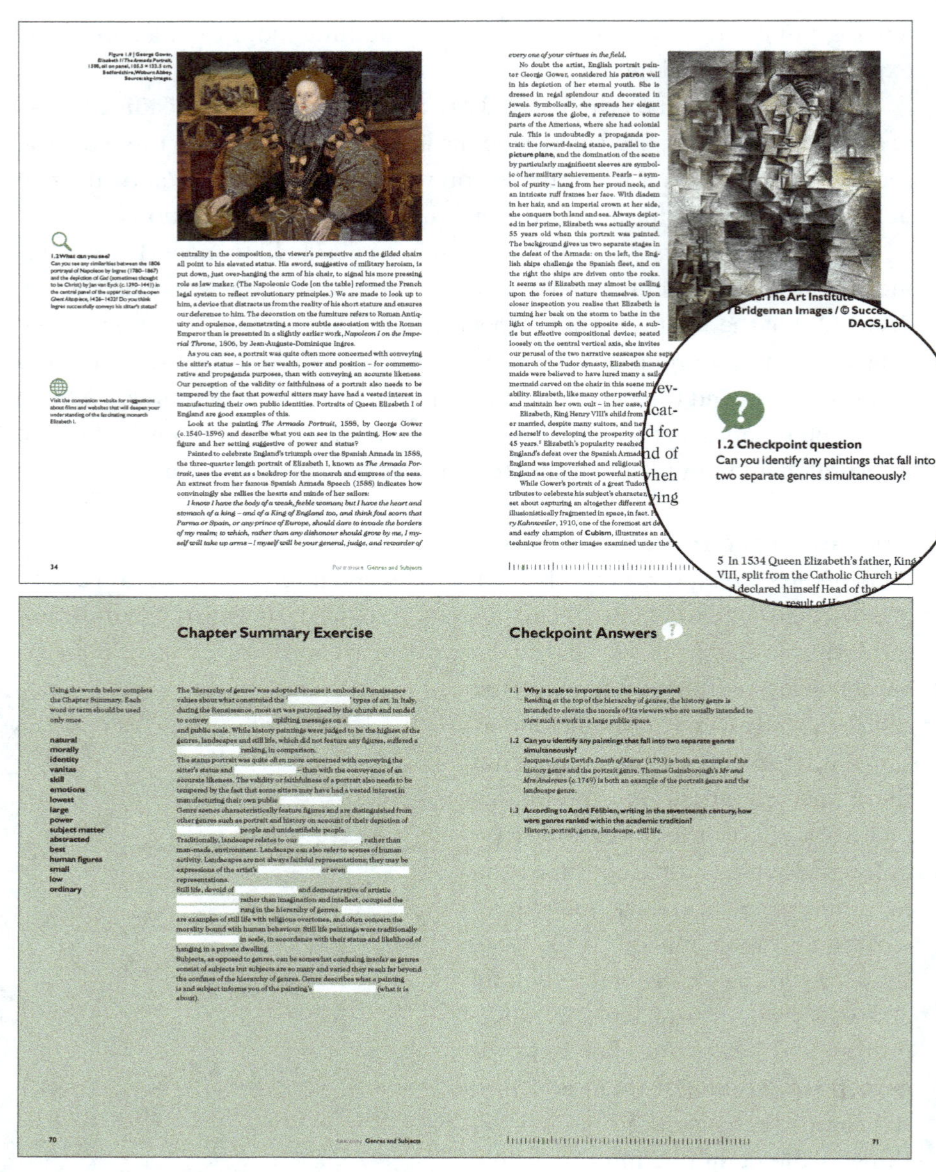

torical Contexts; Patronage and the Status of the Artist; Gender, Nationality and Ethnicity – almost exclusively employ a contextual methodology. But the point should be made again that these methodologies are not independent of one another and a fuller and richer understanding will result from interpreting the works from both positions.

As with the Formal Analysis Toolbox, the six chapters that discuss themes in art and architecture meet the requirements of the AQA's A-level examination in History of Art (Art of the Western World). The second teaching and assessment unit is called 'Themes in History of Art' and is about understanding and interpreting specific examples in relation to these themes.

The third and fourth teaching and assessment units of the AQA Specification require both formal and contextual analysis of works of art and architecture, the only difference being that these are now selected from specific periods of time (generally a century) and discussion should be in more depth and detail than for the first two units.

Other features of this book

This book offers a number of other important features. It has a Glossary of terminology (art-historical and other), with a pronunciation guide where necessary. Terms in the Glossary are emboldened when they first appear in each chapter. At the end of each chapter there is a Summary Exercise that tests how well you have understood what the chapter has been about. There are also questions similar to those found in the AQA History of Art examination, and Checkpoint Answers ❓ that pick up on important points made in the chapter. Finally, the companion website directs you to reading, websites, DVDs and other resources, as well as listing some useful books that have not already been referenced.

This book offers an approach to the discipline that will not be beyond criticism – far from it – but its aims are simple: to provide an accessible text for anyone interested in art and architecture, however knowledgeable they may or may not be; to offer a constructive and, hopefully, helpful guide for students, prospective students and teachers of the AQA History of Art Specification; to inspire inquiry, encourage links with other subject areas and add fuel to the AQA's Extended Project Qualifications (EPQ). Finally, the book's definitive aim is to make history of art interesting, enjoyable and fulfilling.

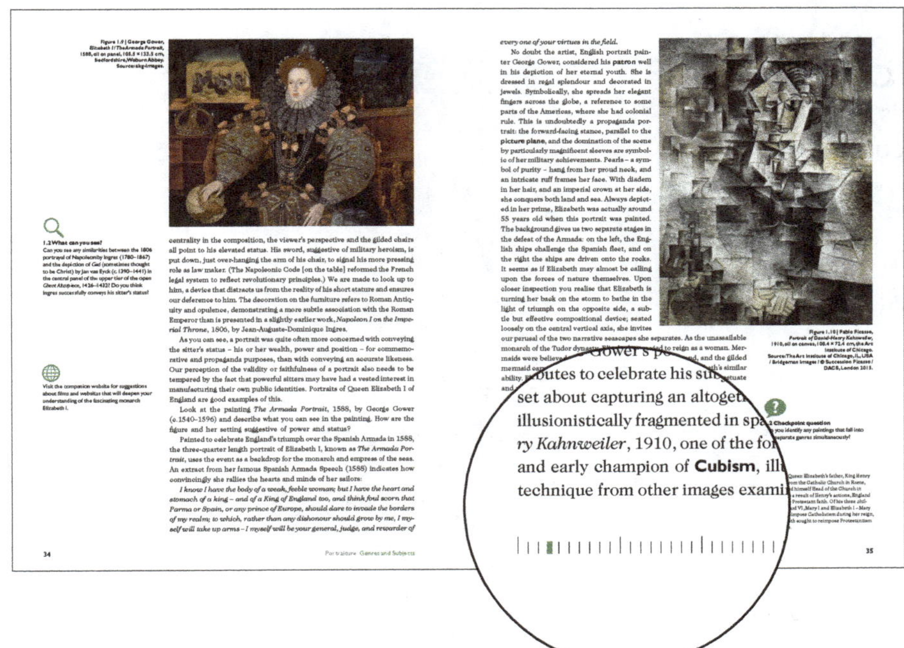

centrality in the composition, the viewer's perspective and the gilded chairs all point to his elevated status. His sword, suggestive of military heroism, is put down, just over-hanging the arm of his chair, to signal his more pressing role as law maker. (The Napoleonic Code [on the table] reformed the French legal system to reflect revolutionary principles.) We are made to look up to him, a device that distracts us from the reality of his short stature and ensures our deference to him. The decoration on the furniture refers to Roman Antiquity and opulence, demonstrating a more subtle association with the Roman Emperor than is presented in a slightly earlier work, *Napoleon I on the Imperial Throne*, 1806, by Jean-Auguste-Dominique Ingres.

As you can see, a portrait was quite often more concerned with conveying the sitter's status – his or her wealth, power and position – for commemorative and propaganda purposes, than with conveying an accurate likeness. Our perception of the validity or faithfulness of a portrait also needs to be tempered by the fact that powerful sitters may have had a vested interest in manufacturing their own public identities. Portraits of Queen Elizabeth I of England are good examples of this.

Look at the painting *The Armada Portrait*, 1588, by George Gower (c.1540–1596) and describe what you can see in the painting. How are the figure and her setting suggestive of power and status?

Painted to celebrate England's triumph over the Spanish Armada in 1588, the three-quarter length portrait of Elizabeth I, known as *The Armada Portrait*, uses the event as a backdrop for the monarch and empress of the seas. An extract from her famous Spanish Armada Speech (1588) indicates how convincingly she rallies the hearts and minds of her sailors:

I know I have the body of a weak, feeble woman; but I have the heart and stomach of a king – and of a King of England too, and think foul scorn that Parma or Spain, or any prince of Europe, should dare to invade the borders of my realm; to which, rather than any dishonour should grow by me, I myself will take up arms – I myself will be your general, judge, and rewarder of every one of your virtues in the field.

No doubt the artist, English portrait painter George Gower, considered his **patron** well in his depiction of her eternal youth. She is dressed in regal splendour and decorated in jewels. Symbolically, she spreads her elegant fingers across the globe, a reference to some parts of the Americas, where she had colonial rule. This is undoubtedly a propaganda portrait: the forward-facing stance, parallel to the **picture plane**, and the domination of the scene by particularly magnificent sleeves are symbolic of her military achievements. Pearls – a symbol of purity – hang from her proud neck, and an intricate ruff frames her face. With diadem in her hair, and an imperial crown at her side, she conquers both land and sea. Always depicted in her prime, Elizabeth was actually around 55 years old when this portrait was painted. The background gives us two separate stages in the defeat of the Armada: on the left, the English ships challenge the Spanish fleet, and on the right the ships are driven onto the rocks. It seems as if Elizabeth may almost be calling upon the forces of nature themselves. Upon closer inspection you realise that Elizabeth is turning her back on the storm to bathe in the light of triumph on the opposite side, a subtle but effective compositional device; seated loosely on the central vertical axis, she invites our perusal of the two narrative seascapes she separates. As the unassailable monarch of the Tudor dynasty ... to reign as a woman. Mermaids were believed ... d, and the gilded mermaid ... th's similar ability ... etuate and ...

Gower's p...
...butes to celebrate his su...
set about capturing an altoget...
illusionistically fragmented in sp...
ry *Kahnweiler*, 1910, one of the fo...
and early champion of **Cubism**, ill...
technique from other images exami...

34 Portraiture: Genres and Subjects 35

Formal Analysis Toolbox

The elements that comprise a formal reading of art and architecture are inextricably related to materials, techniques and processes and form and style. However, consultation of the following points/questions is designed to help you describe and analyse formal elements of works of art and architecture. An understanding of these formal elements is also essential to respond to and analyse form, style and function, the theme of Chapter 3. Broadly, application of the Toolbox aids a fuller appreciation of all of those works discussed in the themed chapters which follow.

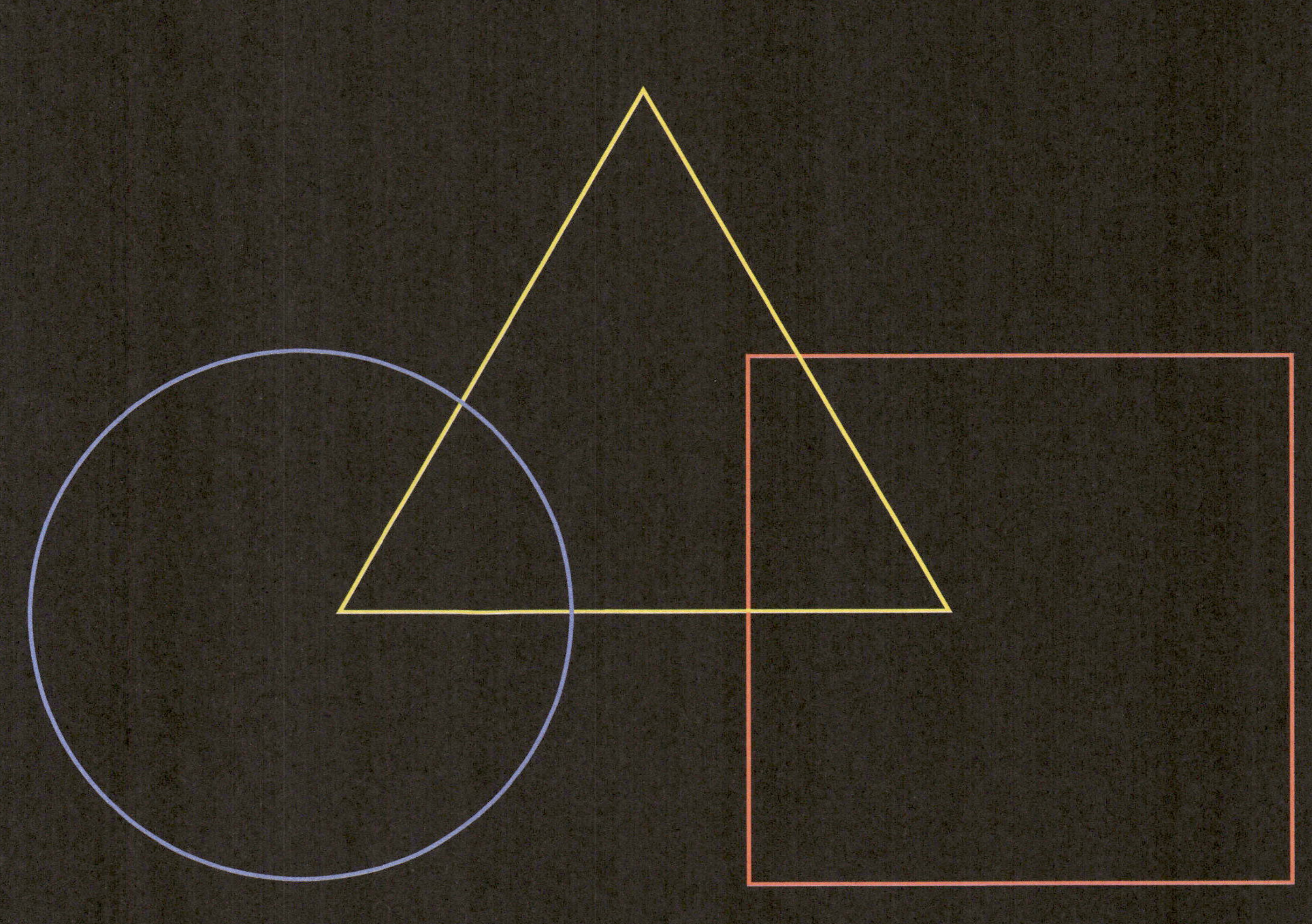

Painting

Materials, Techniques and Processes

The materials, techniques and processes used in a painting help to determine the work's appearance and have an effect on the way we understand and interpret it.

What materials have been used to create the work?

How have the inherent characteristics of the materials been used by the artist (e.g. watercolour's transparency, the quick-drying property of **tempera** that does not allow colour to be blended easily, other than by **hatching**, oil paint's versatility to create translucent layers (**glazes**) to thick **impasto**)?

What is the painting's support (the surface on which the paint is applied)?

Is there evidence of what tools has the painter used?

Have the **medium**, support and/or tools used helped to determine the painting's scale?

Formal Features

1 **Composition**
2 **Colour**
3 **Pictorial space**
4 **Light and tone**
5 **Form**
6 **Line**
7 **Scale**
8 **Pattern/ornament/decoration**

1

Composition

(Relates to the organisation and arrangement of elements in the work into a whole.)

What is the format (portrait or landscape)?

What is the dominant structure of the painting? Where is the focal point? Where are our eyes directed?

Is it formally arranged? Is there a central axis? Is it symmetrical or asymmetrical? Is it balanced? Does it appear random?

Does it use certain shapes (squares, rectangles, pyramids) or forms in a particular manner? What effect does this have? Are any elements repeated or echoed? What effect does this create?

Does the composition create movement? How – using a curvilinear composition (circles) or moving from one side to the other, from top to bottom?

Is it seemingly unstructured? Is it informally arranged? Is it dynamic and exciting? Is it harmonious, well-balanced and rigid?

Has the artist used the **Golden Section**?

Is the image 'open' with elements continuing beyond the frame? Or, is the image 'closed' with elements confined within the frame? Has the image been cropped?

How have the colours been organised?

How does the composition link with the subject matter?

2

Colour

What hues (colours based on wavelengths) are used? Are the hues saturated (the most vivid form of the colour)? Do the colours show lustre (a brightness that exceeds surface colour), like silk? Are the colours luminous (i.e. brighter than the surrounding visual field), like a flame?

Has the painter used a wide range of colours or a limited palette (range of colours)? Are prismatic colours (colours of the rainbow: red, orange, yellow, green, blue, indigo, violet) used?

Are there **primary colours**? Or, have **secondary colours** (orange, green, violet – mixtures of primary colours) been used?

Have **complementary colours** been used?

Are earth colours (e.g. ochre, burnt umber, burnt sienna) used?

Are the colours descriptive (represented as it is seen)? Have the 'natural' colours of the objects been used?

Are the colours warm (e.g. red, orange, yellow) or cool (e.g. green, blue, violet)?

Are shades (a darker **tone**) of one colour used?

Are tints (a lighter tone) of one colour used?

Are tones varying in hue and lightness used?

Are colours used to suggest distance (e.g. become paler/ bluer)?

Are colours painted in blocks or blended?

How important is colour in the painting? Is it more important than line? What is its relationship to light (e.g. the Impressionists used colour as light so generally they did not use black)?

How is colour used? Is it used expressively to create a feeling or sensation? Does it create mood? Is it used:

– for psychological effect (blue for emotional coolness/ melancholy),

– symbolically (as an established convention – e.g. blue for heaven),

– spiritually (blue for transcendental – e.g. Wassily Kandinsky, Yves Klein),

– for compositional unity,

– to suggest volume or weight,

– atmospherically

– as a means of decoration?

Does the colour create harmony or disharmony?

Is there optical mixing (e.g. as in Neo-impressionism such as paintings by Georges Seurat and Paul Signac)? Are there colour patches (e.g. as in paintings by Paul Cézanne)?

Is it monochrome? If so, to what effect? Do the colours create a sense of calm, excitement, anxiety?

3

Pictorial Space

(The illusion of three-dimensional space on a flat picture plane/surface.)

Is there a convincing sense of depth in the painting (an illusion of real three-dimensional space)? Does the illusion of space look realistic or unrealistic?

Are the objects/figures located in the pictorial space or just piled on top of each other, or flat on the surface?

Do the objects/figures diminish in size to suggest space?

Does the ground plane tilt naturalistically or non-naturalistically?

Is our viewpoint high or low?

Is our viewpoint close or far away? Do we have a narrow view or a panoramic view?

Is the space detached from us or connected to ours?

How do these points relate to the painting's original location?

Has perspective been applied to an individual/object (i.e. **foreshortening** rather than throughout)?

Is there a clear foreground, middle ground and background? Where is the focus? Does the compositional arrangement lead the viewer into the picture?

How is the sense of space achieved?

– Through colour (warm colours recede, cool colours advance)?
– Through the use of light and shade?
– Through overlapping planes?
– Through a winding path that leads the eye?

Has a system of perspective been used? Which system of perspective has been used?

– Mathematical one-point perspective, where lines converge at one point on the horizon to give an illusion of space.
– Mathematical two-point perspective.
– Linear perspective, with diagonal lines reaching into the picture space but not necessarily converging.
– **Atmospheric** (or **aerial**) **perspective** in which colours in a distant landscape fade and forms dissolve with distance (first used by Leonardo da Vinci).

4

Light and Tone

Is the painter's illusion of light used naturalistically?

Is the light source depicted in the painting? Where is it? Is there more than one light source? Are there any shadows cast? Are they cast in a naturalistic way (e.g. in the correct direction)? Is the source natural (e.g. sun, window) or unnatural (e.g. candle)?

Does the light heighten realism? Is it used symbolically? Is light used dramatically (with strong contrasts, of highlights and shadows (i.e. **chiaroscuro**)?

Is shading used to model form? What is highlighted and why?

Are the gradations from light to dark subtle?

Does the light emphasise texture?

Is the effect three-dimensional or flat?

Is light and shade used to create space?

Does light and shade modify colour? Are colours deflected, absorbed, reflected, refracted?

Does light pick out the most important elements of the composition or is symbolism or narrative more important? Does light make details clearer? Does light create mood or atmosphere?

5

Form

(Can be related to light/tone.)

Are the forms convincingly three-dimensional or do flat shapes dominate?

Do the forms of objects or figures have solidity and mass? Do they seem weighty/sculptural?

Has tonal **modelling** been used?

Are the forms soft/curved/hard/angular?

Are forms depicted through shading/outline/colour?

Can the complete form/figure be seen or is it lost in shadow or obliterated by light?

Are forms depicted as naturalistic, realistic, abstracted?

6

Line

Is the image constructed through line?

Do outlines dominate?

Describe the line (e.g. straight, curved or chaotic)?

Does the line contain colour and/or form?

Are forms flat or three-dimensional?

Are the outlines of the figures/objects naturalistic or distorted?

7

Scale

Is the scale of the work itself monumental/ life-size/ miniature?

Is there a **hierarchical scale** within the work in which the most important figures are larger?

How is size and scale related to meaning?

8

Pattern/Ornament/Decoration

Is pattern of primary or secondary importance?

Is pattern created with line or colour?

Is the pattern as a result of materials, techniques and processes? Has the painting incorporated **gold leaf** which has been **tooled**?

Sculpture

(Free-Standing and Relief)
Materials, Techniques and Processes

The materials, techniques and processes used in sculpture help to determine the work's appearance and have an effect on the way we understand and interpret it.

What materials have been used to create the work?

Is it one material or a combination of materials?

Has the work been modelled, carved, or assembled?

How have the inherent characteristics of the materials been used by the sculptor and how have they determined its form (e.g. the limited tensile strength of stone might result in a more compact mass-like work, the **high-tensile** properties of bronze might result in thin/daring projections)?

How has the choice of materials influenced the scale of the work?

How has the choice of materials affected meaning (e.g. has white marble been used to suggest purity? Has bronze been used to suggest strength and nobility)?

Formal Features

1 **Volume/mass/form**
2 **Composition**
3 **Space**
4 **Scale**
5 **Colour**
6 **Surface/pattern/ornament**
7 **Line/shape**

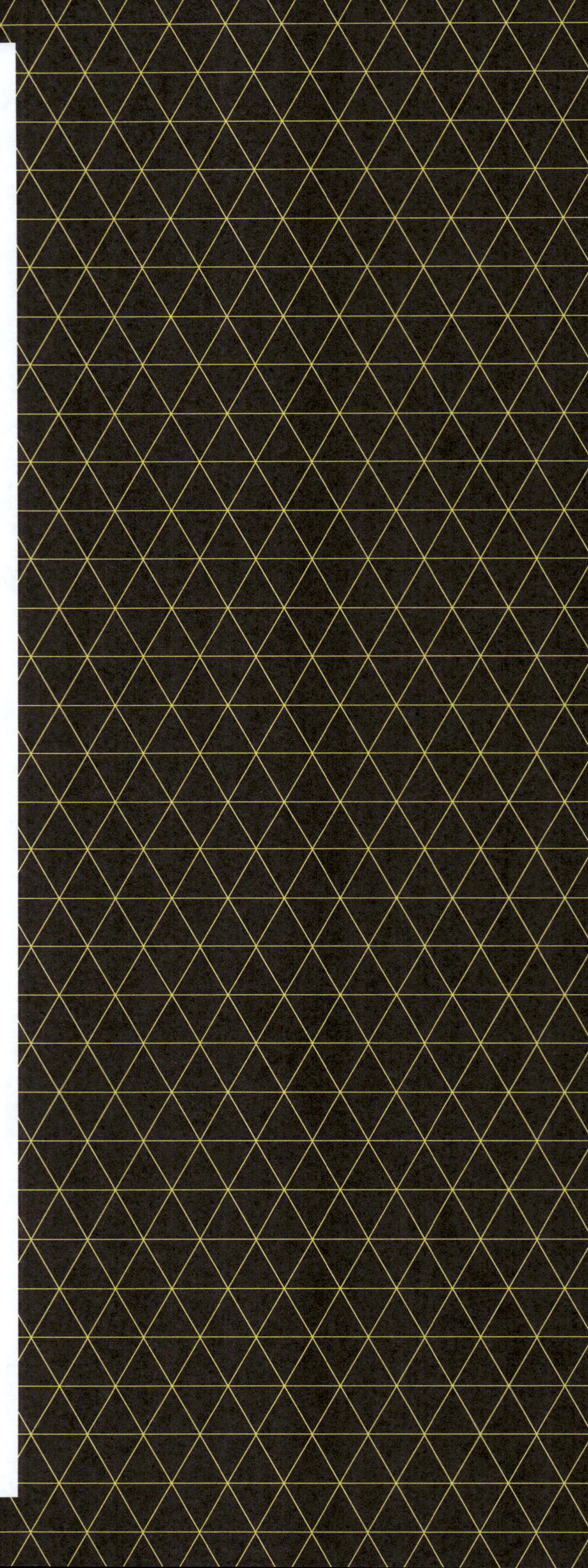

1

Volume/Mass/Form

Is the work free-standing, attached to another surface (perhaps architecture), or in relief?

Is the form solid, massive, weighty?

Are there major and minor forms?

Is the sculpture self-contained (a strong outer, containing shell) or does it invade our space (an inter-penetration of form and environment)?

What is the relationship between the space/void to the mass/form?

Does light and shade come from the volume/mass/form itself or its surface treatment?

Do the forms seem to defy gravity?

2

Composition

Is there one major viewpoint (e.g. the front)?

If free-standing, how does the shape change as you move around it?

Is it simple (single) or complex (multi-figure)?

Is there a central axis?

Is it balanced or top/bottom heavy?

Is it predominantly vertical or horizontal?

Is it based on a particular shape (e.g. pyramid, circle, square)?

Is there a strong diagonal?

Are there any shapes echoed/repeated?

Is there a sense of movement/dynamism or rhythm?

Are there emphatic gestures?

How do forms inter-relate?

Is it highly structured or chaotic?

Is it naturalistic or staged?

3

Space

Is the work free-standing, attached to another surface (perhaps architecture), or in relief?

How does the sculpture relate to the space around it?

Are mass and void inter-related?

Can we walk around or through the work (space engaging the viewer)?

Is it static or moving in space (kinetic)?

4

Scale

Is it life-size, monumental, miniature? How does the scale affect meaning?

Does its large scale elevate its status/power? Does its small scale heighten its vulnerability?

Is it elevated on a plinth or in a niche? Is there a small base which supports a large mass?

Is its scale understood within the context of its location?

Is its scale related to its indoor or outdoor display?

5

Colour

Is the original material coloured (e.g. marble, onyx, granite, mahogany, wood)? Was the material chosen because of its colour?

Has it been coloured, painted, stained, etc?

Is it single-coloured or **polychromatic**?

Is the colour used naturalistically, symbolically, decoratively, or in some other way?

6

Surface/Pattern/Ornament

Is there a dominant pattern of repeated forms and shapes? Is it fundamental to the work's meaning?

Has pattern been created through the form or by surface treatment?

Is pattern used decoratively or to capture light?

Is its purpose decorative, ornamental or symbolic?

What is the treatment of the surface texture? Is it rough or highly polished? Is it in its natural, unworked state or significantly altered? Does the treatment of the surface affect the meaning of the work? Has the surface **patina** been changed?

7

Line/Shape

Is there a clear outline shape/silhouette?

Is line and shape more important than form and mass?

Are the shapes recognisable (e.g. as human or suggestive of a figure)?

Are the shapes flat or abstract?

Are the shapes fixed or do they change (kinetic – i.e. moving parts)?

The Nude Figure

Is the figure naked? Is the figure male/female/gender ambiguous? Is the figure naturalistic? Idealised? Distorted? Expressive?

What are the proportions of the figures, of head to body, and limbs to body?

Is the pose static or animated (**contrapposto**)?

What gestures are used? Are they natural or dramatic?

What are the facial expressions? Are they connecting with the viewer or is their gaze averted, blank?

If part of a multi-figured composition, what's the relationship between the figures?

Is there any drapery? What is its purpose? Does it cover modesty? Does it breathe life, like its wearer? What is the body/drapery relationship? Does it reveal or conceal?

The Clothed Figure

Is their clothing contemporary to the period of the art or not? Does it identify the figures (e.g. wealth/status/occupation)?

Do the clothes reveal or conceal the body?

Do they enhance masculinity or femininity?

Architecture

Materials, Techniques and Processes

The materials, techniques and processes used in architecture help to determine the building's appearance and have an effect on the way we understand and interpret it.

What materials have been used to create the building?

What materials are visible?

Is it one material or a combination of materials?

How do the materials contribute to the building's appearance?

How does the choice of material affect the building's structure?

Is the exterior clad or **rusticated**, rendered, pebble-dashed?

Are the materials **vernacular**?

Is the building style vernacular or derived from vernacular styles?

Have the materials been selected for their functional properties more than their aesthetic qualities?

Formal Features

1 Structure/form
2 Volume/mass
3 Architectural elements
4 Composition
5 Site/location
6 Scale
7 Colour
8 Pattern/ornament/decoration

1

Structure/Form

How is it constructed (how does it stay up)? Is it a load-bearing construction (e.g. with solid walls) or a skeletal (frame) construction (e.g. **curtain wall**)? Does it look **prefabricated**?

Is it a **trabeated** construction? Are the columns load-bearing or decorative? Is it arcuated (arch-based) architecture? Are there any vaults?

Is there a dome?

Is there buttressing?

How many storeys are there?

What is the relationship between the structure and the decoration?

Are there smaller structures within the main structure (e.g. an **aedicule**)?

2

Volume/Mass

Is the building symmetrical or asymmetrical?

Are there recessions and projections? Are spaces based on squares or another shape? Is the space contained/ constricted by a roof?

Is the building based on solids and voids?

Is it airy or claustrophobic?

3

Architectural Elements

Has the classical language of architecture been used (e.g. dome, **columns**, **pediment**)?

Are there features associated with castles (e.g. turrets)? Or features associated with churches (e.g. spires)?

How many architectural elements can you identify?

4

Composition

Is there a single mass or an arrangement of parts?

Is the building symmetrical or asymmetrical? Is there a formal or informal arrangement? A regular or irregular arrangement?

Is it a unified design or did it develop over time?

Is there an obvious entrance?

Is the **façade** balanced horizontally? Vertically?

Are a set of proportions used (e.g. the Classical Orders, or Golden Section)?

How is the building articulated (how do the parts relate to one another)? Is it divided into bays? Are some recessed or projected?

Are elements repeated for rhythm? What effect does spacing have on the composition (e.g. intercolumniation)?

Is there interplay between curved and straight elements?

Does the exterior suggest the arrangement of the interior (e.g. a number of storeys, chimneys, tall windows)?

What is the arrangement of the windows (fenestration)? What sort of windows are there – dormer, rose, etc. Are they large in relation to the wall mass? Are they pedimented?

Does the building suggest movement? In what direction and using what elements (**volutes**, solids/voids, undulation)?

5

Site/Location

Is it rural or urban? Look at the surrounding buildings; is it part of a complex? Does it stand out?

Is there a main façade? Is there a processional approach to add grandeur? Are the gardens landscaped/formal?

Does the structure have a relationship with its surrounding space/environment?

How does the site affect our interpretation of the building?

6

Scale

What has determined the building's scale?

Is it a monumental scale or a private domestic space?

How does its scale relate to its function?

How does it impact on the viewer?

7

Colour

What colour are the materials? Does the colour affect our interpretation of the building or help define its style (e.g. white-painted concrete is synonymous with the International Modern Movement)?

Is colour used for decoration?

Have materials been used in their natural state/colour or have they been altered/painted?

8

Pattern/Ornament/Decoration

Are the features of the building standardised (e.g. classical language, Gothic) or individualised?

Are features decorative, structural or both (e.g. the use of caryatids)?

Are features hand crafted or mass produced? How does this affect the style (appearance) of the building? Is the decoration associated with a particular style (e.g. a hand-crafted building may appear vernacular and individual such as the Arts and Crafts style).

Has the material been used decoratively (e.g. **herringbone brickwork**, **rustication**)? What affect does this have?

Is the decoration coherent or eclectic?

Works Consulted

Clarke, M. *Oxford Concise Dictionary of Art Terms*, Oxford University Press, 2010.

Curl, J.S. *Oxford Dictionary of Architecture and Landscape Architecture*, Oxford University Press, 2006.

Fleming, J, Honor, H. and Pevsner, N. *The Penguin Dictionary of Architecture and Landscape Architecture*, 4th ed., Penguin, 1991.

Other Useful Sources

Acton, M. *Learning to Look at Painting*, Routledge, 2007. This is an excellent source of detailed discussion on the following formal elements: composition, space, form, tone and colour.

Pooke, G. and Whitham, G. *Understand Art History*, Hodder, 2010. This book explains the various meanings of formalism and examines the different art periods and styles using easy-to-understand illustrations and well-known examples.

Chapter 1
Genres and Subjects

Learning Outcomes

By the end of this chapter you will be able to:

- define genres in art, give examples and be able to consider how and why they have been represented in particular ways
- define what is meant by subjects in art history (as distinct from genres) and offer a range of examples
- describe the many different ways artists have interpreted subjects in art history, drawing on connections between their visual appearance and the contextual aspects of their production
- compare and contrast different works of art in different mediums but within the same genre or subject.

Thinking About Art: A Thematic Guide to Art History, First Edition. Penny Huntsman.

Chapter Map

This chapter map provides a visual overview of Chapter 1 – 'Genres and Subjects' – together with its key works.

History Genre

Ancient Classical history and mythology

– Jacques-Louis David (1748–1825), *Oath of the Horatii*, 1784
– Titian (1488/90–1576), *Bacchus and Ariadne*, 1520–1523

Biblical scenes: narrative in fresco

– Masaccio (1401–1428/29), *The Tribute Money*, c.1425–1428

Modern history: heroes and villains

– Francisco de Goya (1746–1828), *The Third of May 1808*, 1814
– Pablo Picasso (1881–1973), *Guernica*, 1937

Bridging two genres: 'history' and 'portraiture'

– Jacques-Louis David, *The Death of Marat*, 1793

Portraiture

Single portraiture: the portrait as power

– Jacques-Louis David, *The Emperor Napoleon in his Study*, 1812
– George Gower (c.1540–1596), *The Armada Portrait*, 1588
– Pablo Picasso, *Portrait of Daniel-Henry Kahnweiler*, 1910

Group portraiture: relationships between sitters

– Jan van Eyck (c.1390–1441), *The Arnolfini Portrait*, 1434
– David Hockney (born 1937), *Mr and Mrs Clark and Percy*, 1970
– Edgar Degas (1834–1917), *The Bellelli Family*, 1858–1867

Self-portraiture: suffering and confrontation

– Frida Kahlo (1907–1954), *The Broken Column*, 1944
– Caravaggio (1571–1610), *David with the Head of Goliath*, 1609–1610

Genre

'Genre' scenes: everyday life

– Johannes Vermeer (1632–1675), *The Milkmaid*, 1657–1658
– William Maw Egley (1826–1916), *Omnibus Life in London*, 1859
– Edgar Degas, *L'Absinthe*, 1875–1876
– Edward Hopper (1882–1967), *Nighthawks*, 1942

Landscape

Owning and working the land

– Thomas Gainsborough (1727–1788), *Mr and Mrs Andrews*, c.1750
– Meindert Hobbema (1638–1709), *The Avenue at Middelharnis*, 1689

Landscape as emotional expression

– Vincent van Gogh (1853–1890), *Wheatfield with Crows*, 1890
– Georgia O'Keeffe (1887–1986), *Deer's Skull with Pedernal*, 1936

Still Life

Memento mori

– Harmen Steenwyck (1612–1656), *An Allegory of the Vanities of Human Life*, c.1640
– Frida Kahlo (1907–1954), *Viva la Vida*, 1954
– Audrey Flack (born 1931), *Marilyn (Vanitas)*, 1977

Subjects

Religious subjects

Madonnas

– Elisabeth Frink (1930–1993), *Walking Madonna*, 1981
– Michelangelo (1475–1564), *Pietà*, 1498–1499

Representations of Christ

– Caravaggio, *The Entombment of Christ*, 1602–1604

The nude

Religious and mythological nudes

– Myron, *The Discus-Thrower (Discobolus)*, c.450 BCE
– Titian, *Resting Venus (Venus of Urbino)*, c.1538

Modern nudes

– Édouard Manet (1832–1883), *Olympia*, 1863
– Jenny Saville (born 1970), *Branded*, 1992

Motherhood: mother and child

– Paula Modersohn-Becker (1876–1907), *Kneeling Mother Nursing a Baby*, 1907
– Barbara Hepworth (1905–1975), *Mother and Child*, 1934
– Käthe Kollwitz (1867–1945), *Woman with Dead Child*, 1903

Animals

War: heroisation and protest

– Jacques-Louis David, *Oath of the Horatii*, 1784
– Francisco de Goya, *The Third of May 1808*, 1814
– Jenny Holzer (born 1950), *Lustmord*, 1993
– Pablo Picasso, *Guernica*, 1937

Introduction

This chapter introduces you to two important categories in the description of art-historical works that comprise the theme: subjects and genres. It explains the distinctions between and sub-categories within the terms, and the innumerable ways in which artists have interpreted them. This chapter covers the most ground in the book, and many of its examples can be used as a basis for study under the other five chapter headings.

Genre means 'type' or 'category'. Examples include 'still life', 'landscape', 'portrait' and 'history painting'. However, genre can also refer to a specific type of painting known as 'genre', which depicts scenes from everyday life. There was a system for ranking art in terms of its cultural value known as the 'hierarchy of genres'. The most well-known formulation was provided in 1667 by André Félibien (1619–1695), a historiographer, architect and honorary consultant to the French Royal Academy of Painting and Sculpture. The history of art tended to follow this ranking until the twentieth century, and knowledge of the hierarchy of genres is very important for the understanding of Western painting, as it provides insight into the scale and treatment of many works.

The **subject** of a work might be something like 'fruit', 'mountains', 'family group' or 'war' and this might help to define the work's genre. Some works fall into two or more genres, or between subjects and genres. This chapter will provide you with the knowledge and understanding to make these judgements, and the multiple placements of works will be made clear within the text.

In addition, this chapter will enable you to compare and contrast works of art of a common genre, noting points of similarity and difference in relation to both formal and interpretational aspects of the works chosen. Formal aspects might include: composition, scale, use of colour and **tone**, depiction of light and space, technique and materials and degrees of finish and detail. Interpretational aspects might include: aesthetics (the branch of philosophy which relates to beauty and taste), **ideology** (a particular set of ideas or values related to certain social groups) or **iconography** (formal and symbolic elements in relation to their wider social and historical context). The social and historical context of visual representation is examined explicitly in *Chapter 4*.

History Genre

History painting as a form of narrative or **istoria** (historical, biblical or **mythological** narrative) has been specified as the highest of achievements as far back as the **Renaissance**. Acts of human virtue and intellect by moral heroes, including those in Christian stories (the dominant religion in Europe), were placed at the top of what would become the hierarchy of genres. History paintings were usually large-scale works depicting a subject based on classical history, literature or **mythology** from ancient Greece and Rome, a scene from the Bible, or real historical events.[1]

History paintings were ideally suited to public spaces and large canvases. The scenes depicted were usually heroic or noble, the aim of these works being to elevate viewers' morals. It was important that they provided the opportunity to depict the human figure – often nude or partially nude – since this subject was believed to require the greatest artistic skill. From the fifteenth until the nineteenth century, these enactments of human virtue were placed at the top of what would become the hierarchy of genres, and as a result many artists aspired to be history painters.

Why were paintings ranked? The 'hierarchy of genres' was adopted because it embodied Renaissance values about what constituted the 'best' types of art. By the mid-seventeenth century the codification of genres had been firmly established by André Félibien.[2]

In his Preface to *Conférence de l'Académie Royale de Peinture et de Sculpture* (1669), Félibien stated: *Thus, the artist who does perfect landscapes is superior to another who paints only fruit, flowers or shells. The artist who paints living animals deserves more respect than those who represent only still, lifeless subjects. And as the human figure is God's most perfect work on earth, it is certainly the case that the artist who imitates God by painting human figures is more outstanding by far than all the others.* (Quoted in Edwards, *Art and Its Histories: A Reader,* p. 35)

'History' painting was considered to be the grande genre because, unlike the lower-ranked genres, it provided the artist with the opportunity to demonstrate (and the viewer to experience) moral force and imagination. However, genres are not exclusive and one work may include elements of more than one genre.

Ancient Classical history and mythology

After winning the Prix de Rome, French painter Jacques-Louis David (1748–1825) saw the works of Antiquity first hand, and developed a Neo-classical style favoured by the French Academy, the institution that controlled the production and exhibition of art in France. The *Oath of the Horatii*, 1784, is a large-scale work from the artist's imagination, inspired by stories of ancient Rome and the wars between Rome and Alba around 669 BCE, as described by Livy (59 BCE–17 CE) in his monumental History of Rome.[3]

Writing during the reign of Emperor Augustus, Livy is likely to have embellished Rome's history in a way that helped establish the empire's validity.

1 Although the Bible is a unified book, there is an important distinction to be made between the Old Testament, which relates to the laws of God and the prediction of the coming of Christ, and the New Testament, which reveals Christ and provides an account of his ministry.

2 In accordance with André Félibien's hierarchy of genres, the ranking in descending order of importance is: History, Portraiture, Genre, Landscape and Still-Life. The 2010 AQA Specification arranges the order as: History, Portraits, Landscape, Still-Life, Genre.

3 David's *Oath of the Horatii*, 1784, was also inspired by Pierre Corneille's play *Horace* (1640).

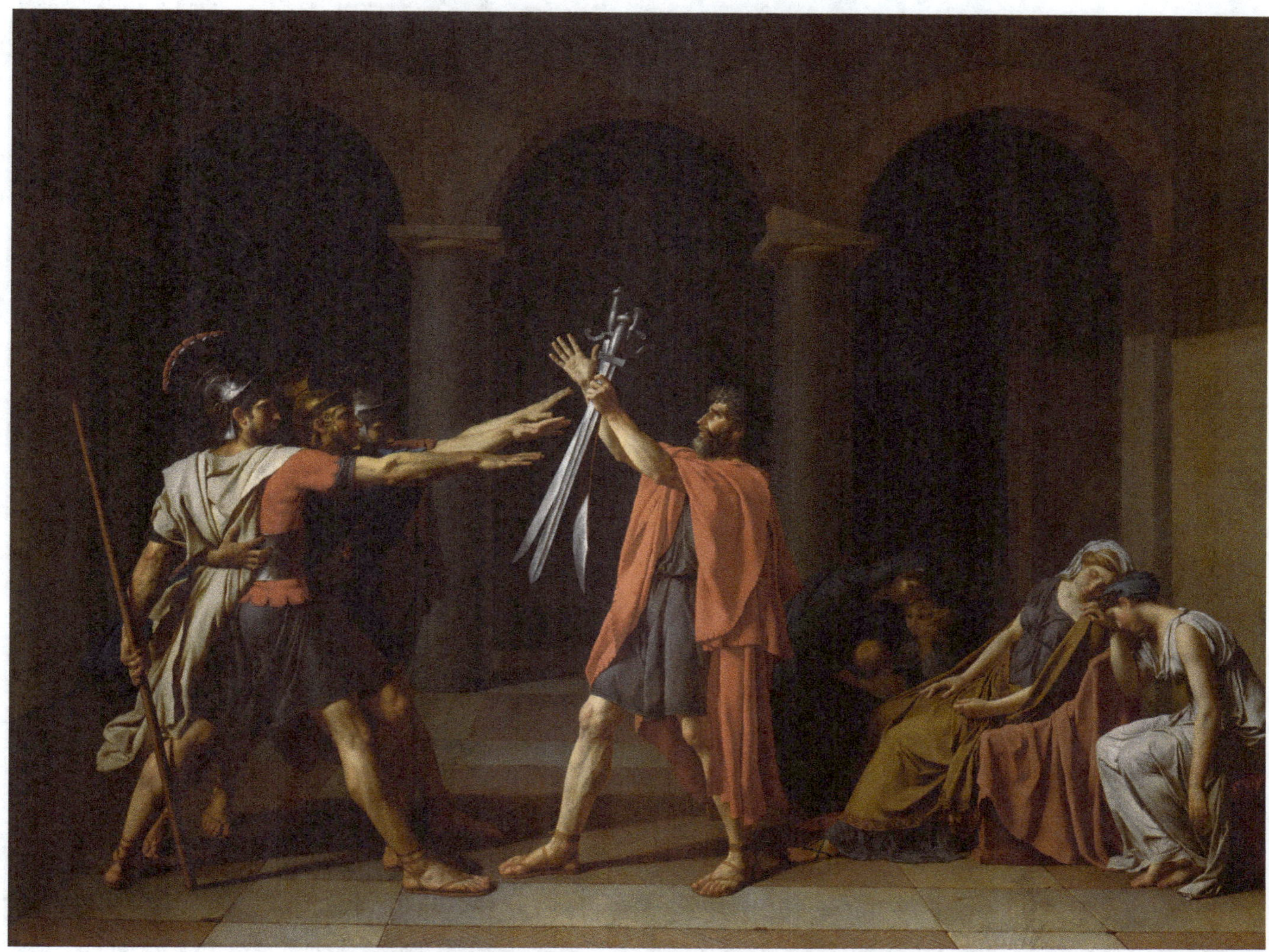

Figure 1.1 | Jacques-Louis David, ***Oath of the Horatii,*** **1784, oil on canvas, 330 × 425 cm, Paris, Musée du Louvre. Source: akg-images / Erich Lessing.**

The three Horatii brothers are preparing to do battle with three brothers from the Curiatii family in Alba to settle the dispute between their cities. The scene depicts them swearing on their swords, held aloft by their father, to defend the city of Rome to the death. Rejecting the contemporary **Rococo** style on account of its lyrical form, looser brushwork, all-round gaiety, and lack of seriousness and moral rectitude, David organises the canvas with geometric precision. The **linear perspective**, made explicit by the chequerboard floor, helps to heighten our sense of austerity and rationalism. Compositionally, the arches with **Doric** columns frame the three sets of figures, underlining the significance of the number three in the story. The muscularity of the men is heightened by the angle at which the light (which enters from upper left) rakes across the surface of their bodies, sharply **delineating** mass and volume.

The entire canvas demonstrates Roman patriotism. David's precise delineation and **modelling** is a kind of homage to antique sculpture, and helped

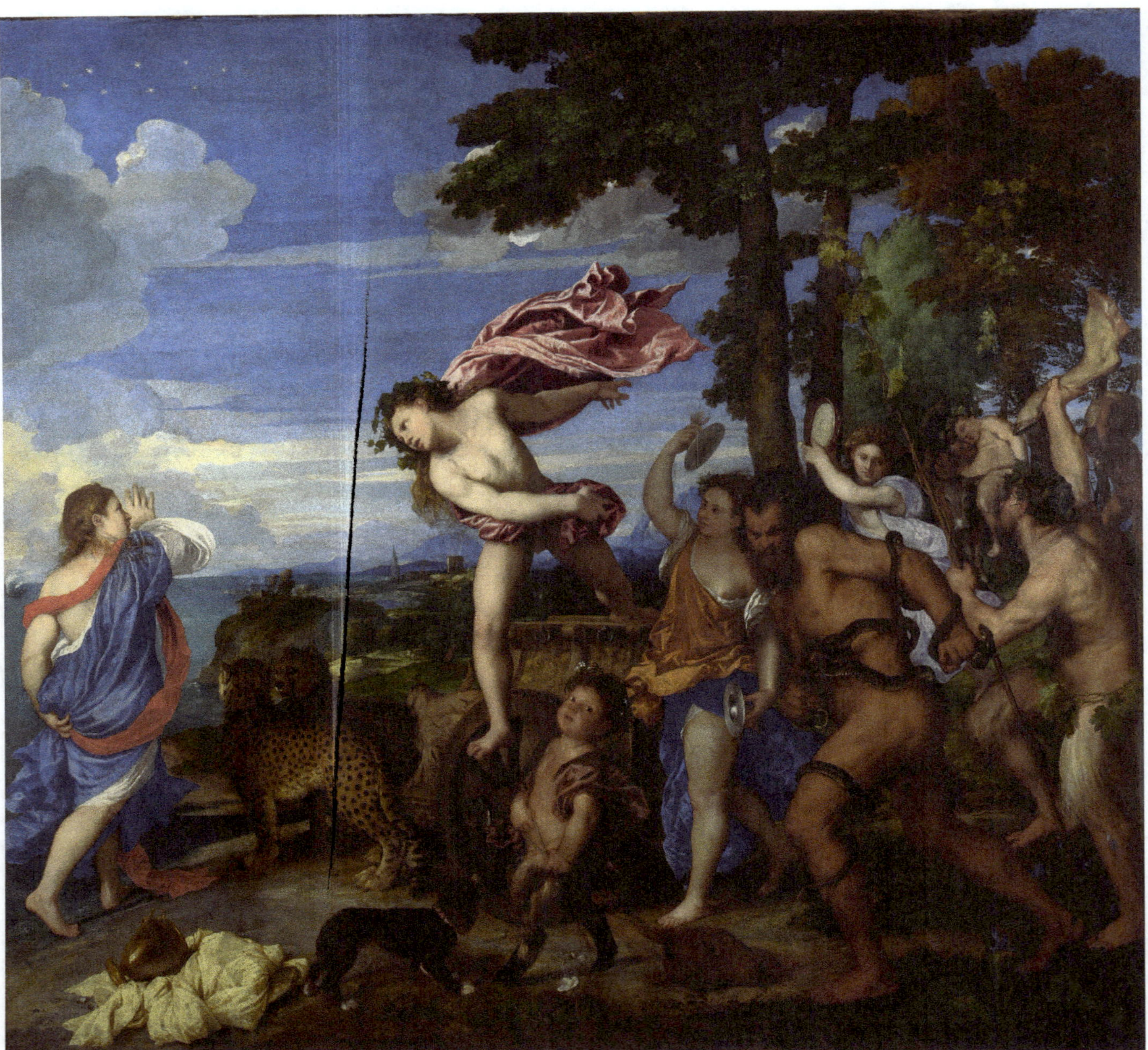

Figure 1.2 | **Titian,** ***Bacchus and Ariadne,*** **1520–1523, oil on canvas, 176.5 × 191 cm, London, National Gallery.**
Source: © 2015. Copyright The National Gallery, London / Scala, Florence.

ensure that this monumental and moralising work perpetuated and maintained the political ideology of revolution on the eve of the French Revolution (1789–1799). While the painting does not depict a real historical event, the *Oath of the Horatii* presents a form of narrative or istoria in its enactment of stoic bravery. The painting is also examined in *Chapter 6*, in relation to the theme of '**gender**'.

Large-scale mythological scenes, especially multi-figured ones, were also categorised under the history genre. For example, the mythological painting *The Rape of Europa*, 1559–1562, by Italian painter Titian (originally Tiziano Vecelli/o, 1488/90–1576), demonstrates the way in which some history paintings used classical iconography and antique literary sources as inspiration. Europa's rape by Zeus is one of many mythological themes taken from the Roman poet Ovid's narrative poem *Metamorphoses*, a text that had become widely read among the educated classes during the period. Ovidian myth is also the inspiration for Titian's painting *Bacchus and Ariadne*, 1520–1523.

In the painting, Bacchus, god of wine, is leaping into the air from his chariot upon sight of princess Ariadne, with whom he has fallen in love. Ariadne had been abandoned on the Greek island of Naxos by her lover, Theseus, whose ship is shown in the distance. Bacchus offers Ariadne the sky in return for becoming his immortal wife. His promise to transform her into a constellation is signalled by the stars above her head. Think about the way Titian has used the formal device of composition to enhance his story telling.

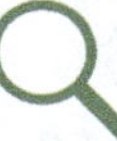

1.1 Explore this example
A further example of the history genre is David's later painting *Intervention of the Sabine Women*, 1799, depicting an episode from Roman history that would have been well-known to his audience. The Sabine women are trying to stop the Sabine men from fighting the Romans. Note the date of the painting – what message do you think David is trying to convey to his contemporaries?

Biblical scenes: narrative in fresco

As well as subjects from classical history and mythology, the history genre also included revered religious istoria epitomised by the work of the **Early Renaissance** Italian painter Masaccio (originally Tommaso di Ser Giovanni di Simone, 1401–1428/29). His biblical **fresco** painting *The Tribute Money*, 1425–1428, depicts a scene from the Gospel of St. Matthew. It is part of Masaccio's famous fresco cycle depicting the life of St. Peter commissioned by the Brancacci family for their chapel in Santa Maria del Carmine in Florence.

Not all biblical works need to tell a story; however, this **continuous narrative** tells the story of St. Peter being asked to pay tax. Grey-haired St. Peter appears three times in this monumental scene: first, positioned in the central group among the apostles, during Christ's instruction to find a coin from the mouth of a fish; second, kneeling down at the water's edge to retrieve a coin from the mouth of a fish; third, handing over the coin to the Roman tax collector on the far right. We can read the story as three separate moments unfolded in time: an innovative device made easier to follow by St. Peter's unaltered costume and facial features. Also, notice that the tax collector appears twice for the purpose of continuity. This particular Gospel story would have been a sympathetic subject for the Florentines, who paid high and unpopular taxes to defend the city. The issue of taxation was particularly culturally specific in relation to this work because the Florentine castasto (income tax) was introduced in 1427.

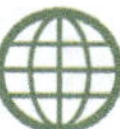

See the companion website for a link to a video clip relating to Masaccio's use of innovative formal devices in *The Tribute Money*.

Figure 1.3 | Masaccio, *The Tribute Money*, c.1425–1428, fresco, 247 × 597 cm, Florence, Santa Maria del Carmine, Cappella Brancacci. Source: akg-images / Rabatti – Domingie.

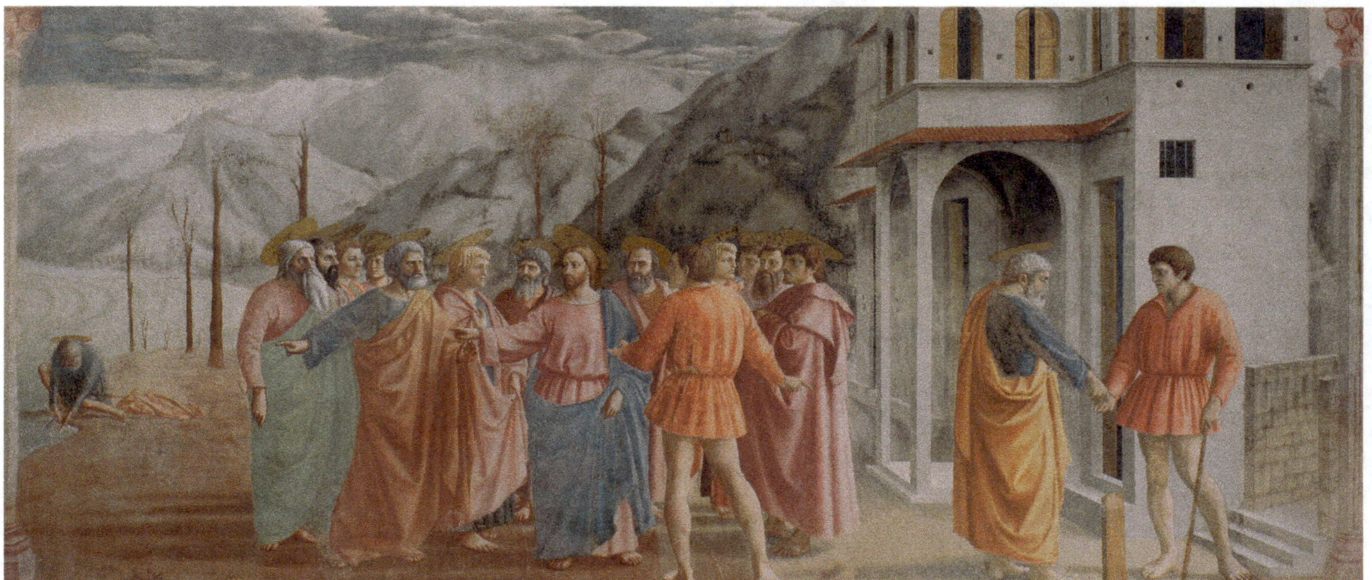

Modern history: heroes and villains

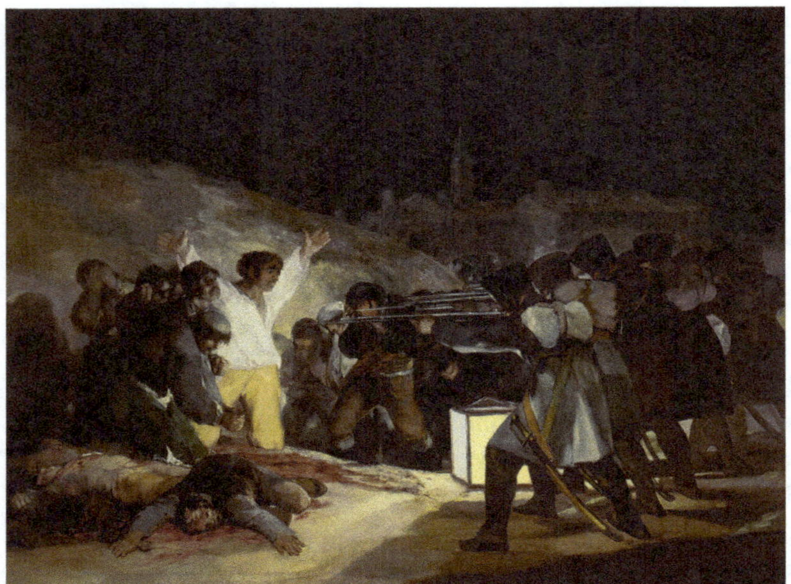

Figure 1.4 | Francisco de Goya, *The Third of May 1808*, 1814, oil on canvas, 268 × 347 cm, Madrid, Museo del Prado. Source: akg-images / Album / Oronoz.

The history genre is also applied by art historians to representations of modern historical events. For example, *The Third of May 1808*, 1814, by Spanish artist Francisco de Goya (1746–1828) depicts invading French troops, under Napoleon I's command, executing a group of Spanish civilians (see *1.1 Let's connect the themes: historical perspectives – the Peninsular War)*. It conveys Goya's response to Napoleon's substitution of the Spanish king for Napoleon's own brother, Joseph, an act of favouritism that led to the Spanish resistance and war.

The Spanish, trapped against a hill, confront their deaths at the hands of a faceless firing squad. The squad, unified in similar dark colours, echoes the resolute and unified stance of the equally determined brothers in David's *Oath of the Horatii*; David's heroes become Goya's anti-heroes. Goya's soldiers are machine-like and anonymous, in contrast to the individual faces of the illuminated Spaniards. The central figure stands out in a white shirt and yellow trousers, thereby advancing compositionally. Despite the fact that he is kneeling, he becomes a powerful and oversized presence. The **cruciform** shape of his emphatically raised hands echoes Christ's posture at the Crucifixion and the **stigmata** on his palms are a further reference. The hand furthest from us leads us to the church in the distance. The corpse in the foreground has fallen towards us, arms also outstretched, to forge a connection between the two: the fate of the central figure appears sealed. The formal aspects of Goya's *The Third of May 1808* are examined in more detail in *Chapter 4*.

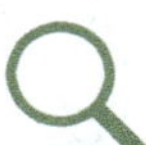

1.1 What can you see?

Using the Toolbox at the start of the book to help you, compare the formal similarities and differences between Goya's *The Third of May 1808* and David's *Oath of the Horatii* on page 25. What do the two paintings say about the artists' attitude to war? Do you think Goya held Napoleon in the same high esteem as did his contemporary David in France?

1.1 Let's connect the themes: historical perspectives – the Peninsular War

The Third of May 1808 and many other works in Goya's **oeuvre** were completed during the Peninsular War (1808–1814), fought between France and the allied powers of Spain, Portugal and Britain. Napoleon's troops crossed Spain to invade Portugal in 1807 and then in 1808 turned on its former ally, Spain. Napoleon's bother, Joseph Bonaparte, was placed on the Spanish throne. There was a fierce uprising by the Spanish people. On 2 May 1808, there was a violent clash in the streets of Madrid, and on 3 May the French troops carried out a series of brutal reprisals for the previous day's resistance. The Peninsular War provides a social and historical background which could be used to support the use of Goya's painting as an example to use in relation to the theme explored in *Chapter 4*. *The Third of May* is an image of rebellion captured in a style as resistant to tradition as the Spanish civilians became to French invasion.

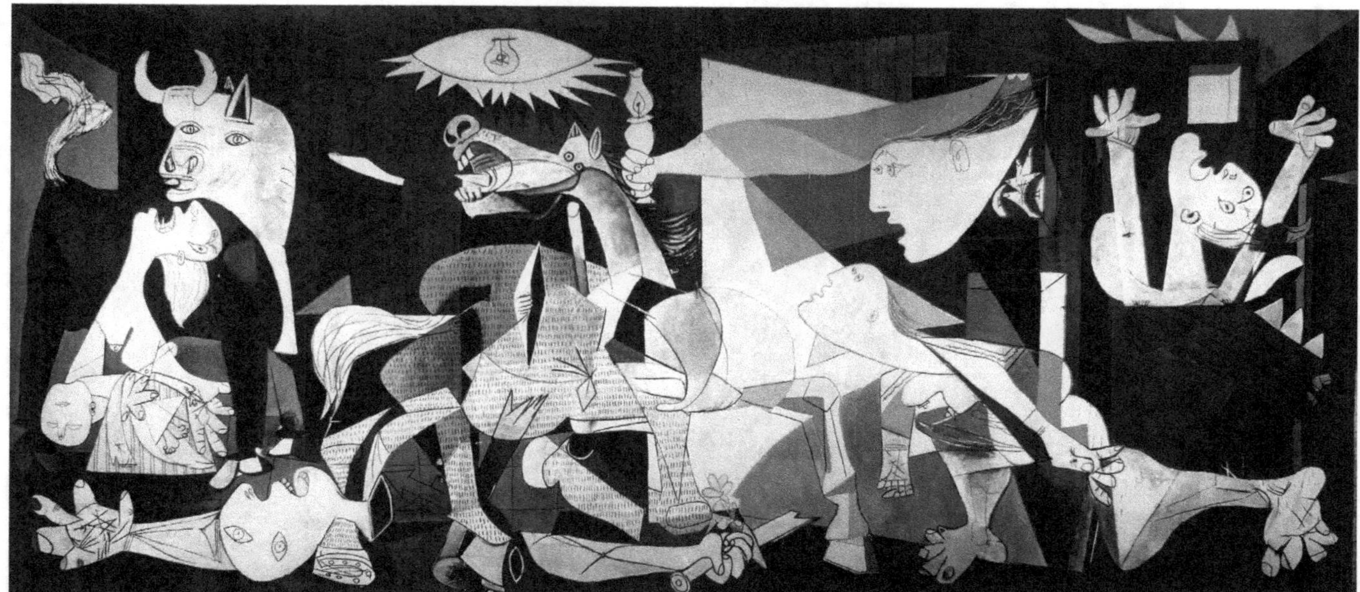

Figure 1.5 | Pablo Picasso, *Guernica*, 1937, oil on canvas, 349.3 × 776.6 cm, Madrid, Museo Nacional Reina Sofia. Source: Photo: akg-images / Erich Lessing / Artwork: © Succession Picasso / DACS, London 2015.

Perhaps the most famous twentieth-century example of modern history paintings is Guernica, 1937, by Spanish artist Pablo Picasso (1881–1973). History paintings are often large in scale and Guernica is no exception. Its physical monumentality reinforces its epic anti-war message.

Based on the tragedy of the bombing of a small Basque town in Spain, Picasso's *Guernica* employs the visual language of distortion, angularity and fragmentation. The latter appears in **planes** of shallow projection and recession as if **collaged**. These devices help to convey the chaos of war. The town was bombed by 28 German Bombers (under Hitler's command and in alliance with Spain's fascist leader General Franco) during the Spanish Civil War (1936–1939). This was among the first aerial bombardments in which civilians were deliberately attacked and among the many casualties were women and children. The scene of ruination (see Figure 1.6) clearly had an unprecedented effect upon Picasso as he began his epic portrayal within 15 days of the attack.

A **formal analysis** of the painting shows the composition moving from right to left, focusing our attention on the bull that looms large in the left-hand corner (which maybe we are meant to interpret as a symbol of Spain), while, just beneath, a mother shrieks with terror as she mourns her dead child; the dismembered corpse of a soldier lies in the foreground, and a panic-stricken horse (possibly representing suffering) gesticulates towards the woman. Their postures are angst-ridden, the engulfing flames signify destruction, the sword in the foreground symbolises defeat, and daggers replace tongues. The eye-like light bulb at the top of the image is reminiscent of the torturer's cell, but we may also read it as a reminder of the advanced technology that helped bring about destruction, or as a symbol of the all-seeing eye of God, passing judgement.

The horror of the event is represented in *Guernica* in such a way that it becomes universal. The painting's **monochromatic** scheme is reminiscent of the newspaper from which Picasso learnt about the attack, but may also be interpreted as showing the life-destroying meaning of war: draining the emotion, humanity and colour out of life. When we see the cathedral-like ruins shown in photographs of the devastation of Guernica, it heightens the poign-

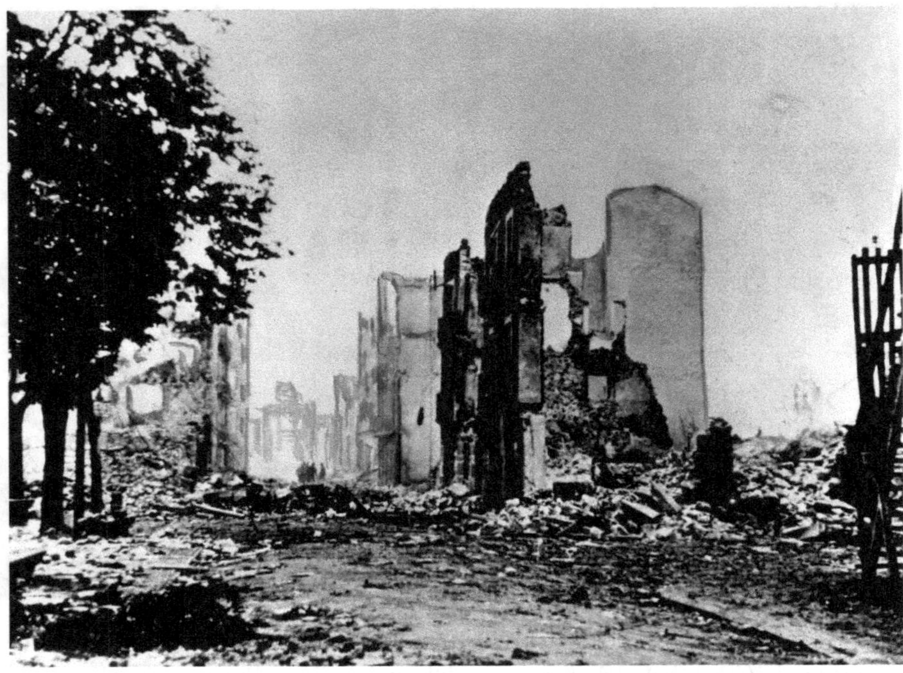

Figure 1.6 | Bombing of Guernica, air attack, 1937, Spanish Civil War, 1936–1939. Bombing of the North Spanish town Guernica by the German Luftwaffe 'Legion Condor' on 24 April 1937. Guernica was completely destroyed after the attack. Ruins of destroyed houses after the attack. Photo, retouched, 6/5/1937. Source: akg-images.

ancy of the historical event and provides us with a sense of empathy with the town's inhabitants and with Picasso. The photograph shown here could be of any decimated town at any time in history, but this tragedy prompted Picasso to make possibly the most famous artistic anti-war declaration of all time (see *1.1 Critical debates: Guernica's 2003 cover-up*).

1.1 Critical debates: Guernica's 2003 cover-up

The United Nations Building in New York City has a tapestry copy of *Guernica* at the entrance to the Security Council room. On 5 February 2003, the work was covered by a blue curtain so that it would not be visible in the background when US Secretary of State Colin Powell gave a press conference concerning the war with Iraq. In his presentation to the UN Security Council on the US case against Iraq, Powell stated, *Iraq has now placed itself in danger of the serious consequences called for in UN Resolution 1441. And this body places itself in danger of irrelevance if it allows Iraq to continue to defy its will without responding effectively and immediately* (Powell, 'US Secretary of State's Address to the United Nations Security Council').

Controversy ensued, although official sources claimed that the curtain was necessary as an appropriate backdrop for television. Picasso's masterpiece was considered to be too 'busy' (i.e. distracting) for TV viewers. What is your political view on this? Was a curtain purposely placed over *Guernica* to hide it?

Bridging two genres: 'history' and 'portraiture'

Some works of art can belong to two or more genres simultaneously. *The Death of Marat*, 1793, by Jacques-Louis David is both a portrait of the French political revolutionary Jean-Paul Marat and a record of a historical event – his murder – thereby encompassing two positions in the hierarchy of genres.

In 1789, the storming and destruction of the Bastille (a fortress-prison in Paris) publicly marked French King Louis XVI's loss of control over Paris and the beginning of the French Revolution. A national assembly was formed to take over the monarch's leadership and there were riots throughout the region. Every citizen of France was forced into making a political choice. The painter, David, chose to join ranks with the extremist pro-revolutionaries, the Jacobins. David was himself elected to the National Convention in 1792 and voted for the king's execution. He then devoted his artistic talents to the revolutionary cause and cultivated a severe Neo-classical style that was well suited to the depiction of revolutionary 'martyrs', such as the French journalist Marat, associated with the Reign of Terror. From the eve of the French Revolution to the last days of the French Empire, David provided the French state with epic portrayals of the French people. He conveyed great moral lessons to ordinary citizens.

Marat fought the royalists and the bourgeoisie, making many enemies. It was during one of Marat's many baths – taken to alleviate the irritation of his chronic skin disease – that the young aristocrat and counter-revolutionary Charlotte Corday murdered him with a knife. In the painting, David depicts

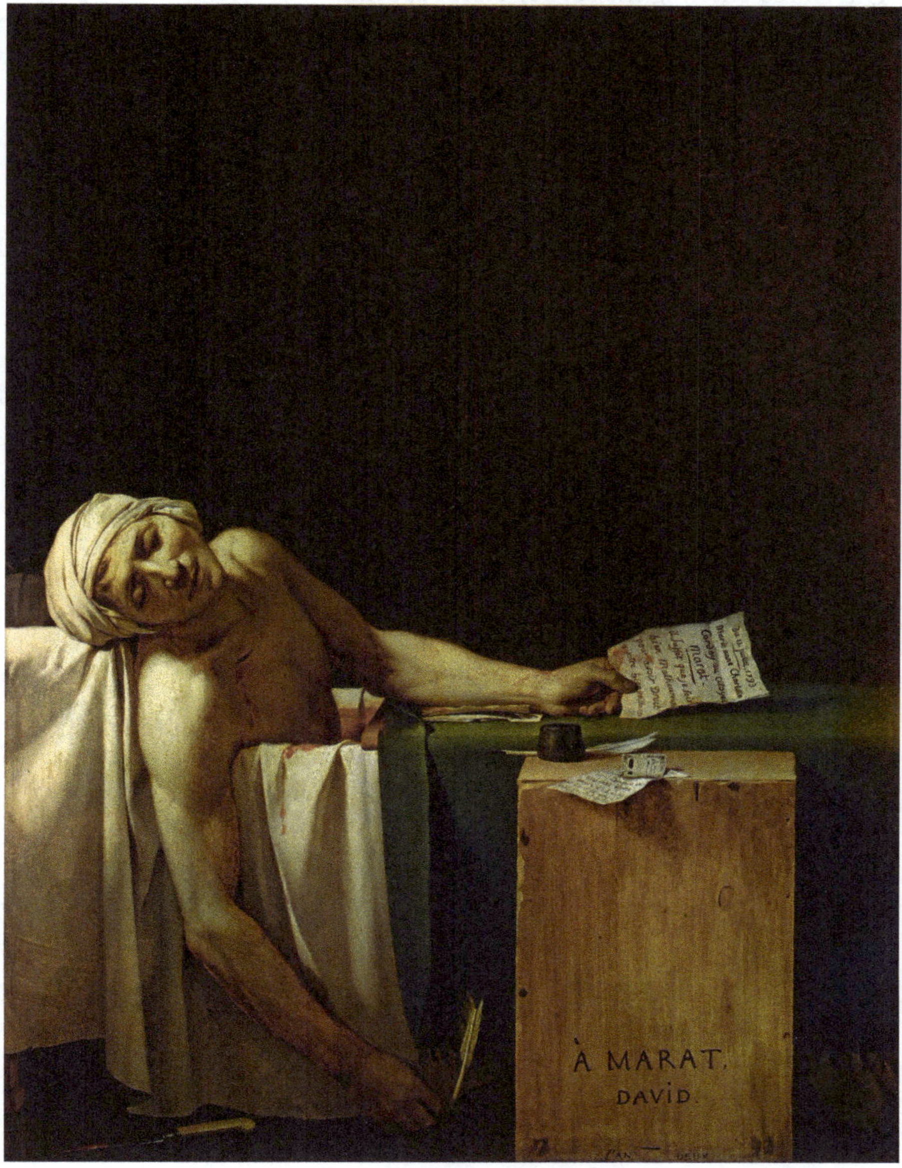

Figure 1.7 | Jacques-Louis David, *The Death of Marat*, 1793 (stabbed in his bath by Charlotte Corday, Paris, 13 July 1793), oil on canvas, 165 × 128 cm, Brussels, Musées Royaux des Beaux-Arts. Source: akg-images / André Held.

Marat holding the blood-stained letter by which Corday gained her entry into his apartment. Marat is represented as a modern-day Christ lying in a watery tomb. How does the fact that the artist was both a friend and political ally of the martyred Marat affect his depiction and our interpretation of the work?

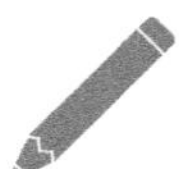

1.2 Explore this example
More than 60 years after the event, Paul-Jacques-Aimé Baudry (1828–1886) also depicted the moment of Marat's death in his painting *Charlotte Corday*, 1860. Unlike David, Baudry places the victim to one side and focuses our attention on the emotions expressed by the murderer. Which of the two people in Baudry's painting are we expected to empathise with? What techniques do Baudry and David use to influence our interpretation of this historical event?

With the revolution as its backdrop, and Marat as a political martyr, this image may also be explored in terms of its social and historical context. David was commissioned by the National Convention to turn this horrific murder scene into an idealised and pro-revolutionary image; its purpose was pure propaganda. Ironically, Marat, a tyrant to so many, became more powerful when he was dead – a martyr to the revolutionary cause, arguably, aided by David's depiction of his death.

The work's style and technique reinforce its content; the naturalistic rendering of the moment of Marat's death is aided by David's crisp delineation, **chiaroscuro**, limited colour palette and static composition. The starkly divided composition focuses our attention: half open (with the void at the top of the composition), half closed (occupied by the figure and his attributes at the bottom). How do you suppose the artist wants us to interpret the unnatural light source entering the scene? Marat appears as the friend of the people, thwarted and dying. He has just finished sending money to a soldier's widow, the letter he has written on the table reads 'give this banknote to the mother of five whose husband died defending the fatherland'.

1.1 Checkpoint question
Why is scale so important to the history genre?

Certain key compositional features in David's painting also aid the suggestion that Marat, the revolutionary hero, may be seen as a secular Christ – his hanging arm, outstretched like those in representations of Christ deposed from the Cross, draws on centuries of biblical association. Two notable examples you can compare it with are Michelangelo's (originally Michelangelo di Lodovico Buonarroti Simoni, 1475–1564) sculpture *Pietà*, 1498–1499, and Rogier van der Weyden's painting *Deposition of Christ* or *The Descent from the Cross*, 1435.[4] Both invest the hanging arm of Christ with the metaphorical weight of sacrifice, and thus this pose has become emblematic of sacrifice throughout the centuries.

I killed one man to save a hundred thousand; a villain to save innocents; a savage wild-beast to give repose to my country.
(Charlotte Corday)

Arguably, Picasso's *Guernica* is a more perceptive portrayal of the horrors of human suffering than David's historical **idealisation**; although both Picasso and David worked to their own agendas: pacifist and extremely pro-revolutionary, respectively. David's portrait of the political journalist Marat and the event in history to which it alludes provides an informative bridge between the history genre examined so far and the genre of portraiture which we are about to examine.

4 **Pietà** refers to the Virgin Mary holding the body of her dead son – Christ – in her lap.

Portraiture

Portraits are, fundamentally, pictures of people. That of the assassinated journalist Marat is one example. The genre includes **self-portraits**, group and individual portraits (these may be face only, head and shoulders or full length), and also includes sculptural portraits, including portrait busts, equestrian monuments and portraits of standing figures such as the life-size bronze portrait/monument to French author Honoré de Balzac, *Monument to Balzac*, 1891–1898, cast 1939, by French sculptor Auguste Rodin (1840–1917). Portraiture dates back to ancient civilisations, but it emerged as an important discipline in its own right during the Renaissance, when the concept that man was made in God's image gave rise to the celebration of important figures and their individual achievements. Commonly, portraits aimed to depict the external physical features and the character of a person, and provided an important motivation for patronage for centuries (see *Chapter 5* for a full exploration and definition of patronage). Private images of less important people tended to be overlooked until the early twentieth century, by which time the hierarchy of genres had lost its significance.

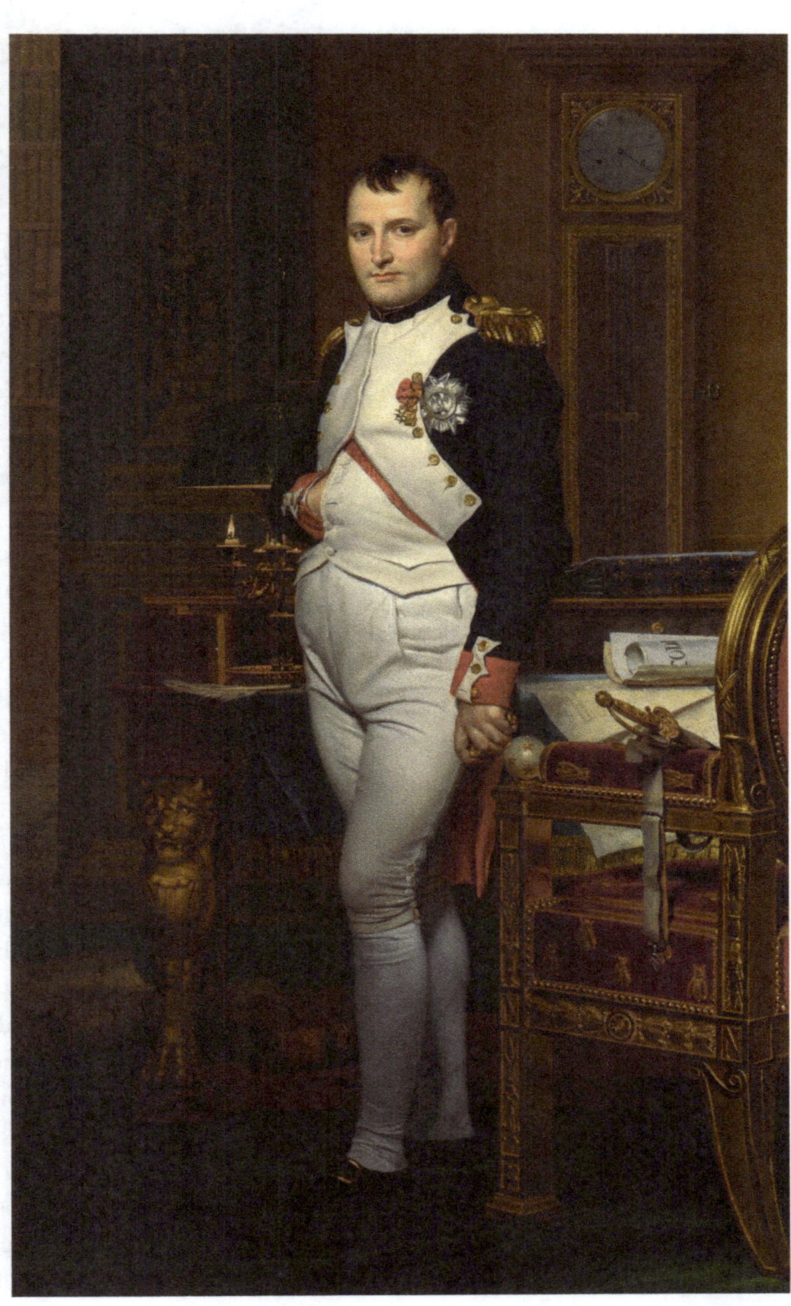

Figure 1.8 | Jacques-Louis David, *The Emperor Napoleon in His Study at the Tuileries*, 1812, oil on canvas, overall: 204 × 125 cm, Washington, National Gallery of Art, Samuel H. Kress Collection, 1961.9.15. Source: Courtesy National Gallery of Art, Washington.

Single portraiture: the portrait as power

Napoleon Bonaparte crowned himself Napoleon I, Emperor of France, in 1804 and would govern the nation for a decade. He befriended artists who helped him to promote his image – one might say his myth – and after he became Emperor, images of him in the imperial tradition multiplied.

In his portrait of Napoleon, *The Emperor Napoleon in His Study at the Tuileries*, 1812, David disguises every brushstroke and executes every line with the accuracy of a skilled draughtsman. What effect does such a smooth finish have on our interpretation of the painting? Is it leading us to respond to the image in any particular way? Decorative accessories surrounding the Emperor serve a symbolic function. For example, the books signify learning, the early morning hour on the clock represents the long hours he labours for the people. Consider how the figure and his setting suggest status. His pose, posture, gaze and attributes along with his

Figure 1.9 | George Gower, *Elizabeth I / The Armada Portrait*, 1588, oil on panel, 105.5 × 133.5 cm, Bedfordshire, Woburn Abbey. Source: akg-images.

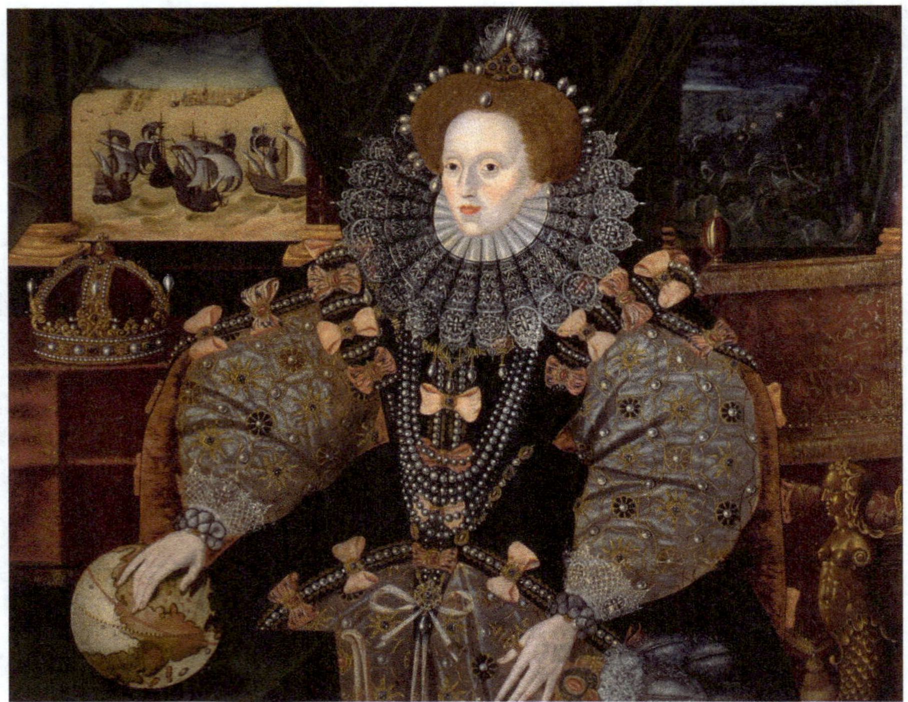

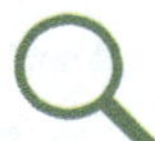

1.2 What can you see?
Can you see any similarities between the 1806 portrayal of Napoleon by Ingres (1780–1867) and the depiction of *God* (sometimes thought to be Christ) by Jan van Eyck (c.1390–1441) in the central panel of the upper tier of the open *Ghent Altarpiece*, 1426–1432? Do you think Ingres successfully conveys his sitter's status?

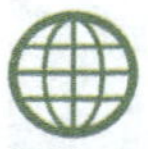

Visit the companion website for suggestions about films and websites that will deepen your understanding of the fascinating monarch Elizabeth I.

centrality in the composition, the viewer's perspective and the gilded chairs all point to his elevated status. His sword, suggestive of military heroism, is put down, just over-hanging the arm of his chair, to signal his more pressing role as law maker. (The Napoleonic Code [on the table] reformed the French legal system to reflect revolutionary principles.) We are made to look up to him, a device that distracts us from the reality of his short stature and ensures our deference to him. The decoration on the furniture refers to Roman Antiquity and opulence, demonstrating a more subtle association with the Roman Emperor than is presented in a slightly earlier work, *Napoleon I on the Imperial Throne*, 1806, by Jean-Auguste-Dominique Ingres.

As you can see, a portrait was quite often more concerned with conveying the sitter's status – his or her wealth, power and position – for commemorative and propaganda purposes, than with conveying an accurate likeness. Our perception of the validity or faithfulness of a portrait also needs to be tempered by the fact that powerful sitters may have had a vested interest in manufacturing their own public identities. Portraits of Queen Elizabeth I of England are good examples of this.

Look at the painting *The Armada Portrait*, 1588, by George Gower (c.1540–1596) and describe what you can see in the painting. How are the figure and her setting suggestive of power and status?

Painted to celebrate England's triumph over the Spanish Armada in 1588, the three-quarter length portrait of Elizabeth I, known as *The Armada Portrait*, uses the event as a backdrop for the monarch and empress of the seas. An extract from her famous Spanish Armada Speech (1588) indicates how convincingly she rallies the hearts and minds of her sailors:

I know I have the body of a weak, feeble woman; but I have the heart and stomach of a king – and of a King of England too, and think foul scorn that Parma or Spain, or any prince of Europe, should dare to invade the borders of my realm; to which, rather than any dishonour should grow by me, I myself will take up arms – I myself will be your general, judge, and rewarder of every one of your virtues in the field.

No doubt the artist, English portrait painter George Gower, considered his **patron** well in his depiction of her eternal youth. She is dressed in regal splendour and decorated in jewels. Symbolically, she spreads her elegant fingers across the globe, a reference to some parts of the Americas, where she had colonial rule. This is undoubtedly a propaganda portrait: the forward-facing stance, parallel to the **picture plane**, and the domination of the scene by particularly magnificent sleeves are symbolic of her military achievements. Pearls – a symbol of purity – hang from her proud neck, and an intricate ruff frames her face. With diadem in her hair, and an imperial crown at her side, she conquers both land and sea. Always depicted in her prime, Elizabeth was actually around 55 years old when this portrait was painted. The background gives us two separate stages in the defeat of the Armada: on the left, the English ships challenge the Spanish fleet, and on the right the ships are driven onto the rocks. It seems as if Elizabeth may almost be calling upon the forces of nature themselves. Upon closer inspection you realise that Elizabeth is turning her back on the storm to bathe in the light of triumph on the opposite side, a subtle but effective compositional device; seated loosely on the central vertical axis, she invites our perusal of the two narrative seascapes she separates. As the unassailable monarch of the Tudor dynasty, Elizabeth managed to reign as a woman. Mermaids were believed to have lured many a sailor to their end, and the gilded mermaid carved on the chair in this scene might allude to Elizabeth's similar ability. Elizabeth, like many other powerful rulers, deployed art to perpetuate and maintain her own cult – in her case, the cult of 'Virgin Queen'.

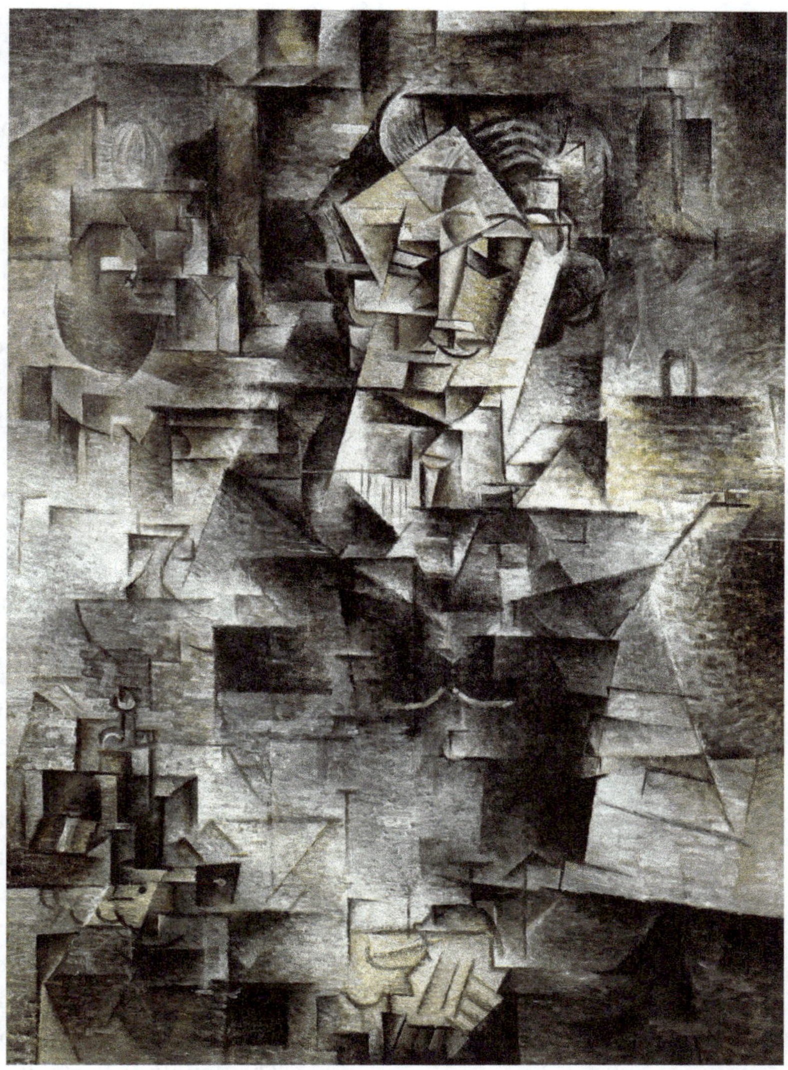

Figure 1.10 | Pablo Picasso, *Portrait of Daniel-Henry Kahnweiler*, 1910, oil on canvas, 100.4 × 72.4 cm, the Art Institute of Chicago. Source: The Art Institute of Chicago, IL, USA / Bridgeman Images / © Succession Picasso / DACS, London 2015.

Elizabeth, King Henry VIII's child from his second wife, Anne Boleyn, never married, despite many suitors, and never produced an heir. She dedicated herself to developing the prosperity of England, the country she ruled for 45 years.[5] Elizabeth's popularity reached its zenith during her command of England's defeat over the Spanish Armada. She ascended to the throne when England was impoverished and religiously divided; she died, adored, leaving England as one of the most powerful nations in the world.

1.2 Checkpoint question

Can you identify any paintings that fall into two separate genres simultaneously?

While Gower's portrait of a great Tudor monarch uses accessories and attributes to celebrate his subject's character, some four centuries later, Picasso set about capturing an altogether different side to his sitter – multiple sides, illusionistically fragmented in space, in fact. Picasso's *Portrait of Daniel-Henry Kahnweiler*, 1910, one of the foremost art dealers of the twentieth century and early champion of **Cubism**, illustrates an altogether different style and technique from other images examined under the 'portraiture' genre. Unlike

5 In 1534 Queen Elizabeth's father, King Henry VIII, split from the Catholic Church in Rome, and declared himself Head of the Church in England. As a result of Henry's actions, England adopted the Protestant faith. Of his three children – Edward VI, Mary I and Elizabeth I – Mary sought to reimpose Catholicism during her reign, and Elizabeth sought to reimpose Protestantism during hers.

any of the other portraits examined so far, Picasso's has dissolved the form of the figure, fragmenting the lines which conventionally contain it. This half-length frontal portrait epitomises a style known as **Analytical Cubism** (1909–1912). Linear perspective and chiaroscuro are replaced by **faceted** planes and a complex tonality; we see the subject from multiple viewpoints simultaneously, and tone is not used descriptively but rather to lend a sense of volume – the picture's surface has been shattered, disrupting the flat, two-dimensional picture plane, and yet the various tones and overlapping forms still suggest three-dimensional depth. Kahnweiler's form is fragmented to the point of being nearly unrecognisable, save for details such as his moustache, watch-chain and lush hair. He is at one with his background, which includes the effect of perpetually shifting spatial planes; the traditional distinction between foreground, middle ground and background has been eliminated. The tension created between two- and three-dimensional spaces is quite deliberate on Picasso's part. Picasso, together with his partner in Cubist invention, Georges Braque, sets forth a 'new reality'– a reality so ground-breaking that to use colour in this painting, or any other analytical works, might be too distracting.

Group portraiture: relationships between sitters

Group portraiture, which includes two or more individuals, may be especially interesting for the viewer to scrutinise, given the added dimension of the relationship between the sitters. Although it only depicts two individuals, the northern Renaissance masterpiece *The Arnolfini Portrait*, 1434, by Netherlandish painter Jan van Eyck (c.1390–1441), is one of the most complicated of all portraits.

Look at the painting *The Arnolfini Portrait* by Jan van Eyck and describe what you think is happening in the scene. Do you think the female figure on the right-hand side of the painting is pregnant?

The Arnolfini Portrait, a double portrait, is naturalistically and meticulously painted of a man and a woman standing slightly turned towards each other. This three-quarter view would have been considered more effective than a frontal or profile view in showing their physical volume. This famous painting was, until recently, unanimously agreed to depict the marriage of Giovanni Arnolfini to Giovanna Cenami. However, it has recently been claimed that this could be his cousin and an unknown wife. Multiple readings plague this work while simultaneously maintaining interest in it, and *1.2 Critical debates: matrimony or betrothal?* examines some of the different interpretations which have been offered. Whichever Mr. and Mrs. Arnolfini this is, a symbolic reading of the work seems to be the one that many viewers find the most compelling. That question of whether Mrs. Arnolfini is or is not pregnant seems to have been one of the painting's most alluring features; it's the first in a sequence of puzzles for the viewer. As well as being fashionable at the time, the abundance of heavy green fabric gathered at her waist becomes an emblem of her cloth merchant husband's wealth. The chair on the back wall is carved in the image of Saint Margaret, a patron of childbirth and fertility. The dog, whose two-tone hair is painted with such a high degree of **verisimilitude**, is commonly understood to represent loyalty and provides a fitting comparison with his counter-symbol, the cat, whose appearance as a symbol of infidelity we will discuss later in the chapter.

Until recent alternative interpretations, this work was fairly simple to read in terms of gender roles. She stands away from the window and adjacent to the bed, in keeping with her 'feminine' role as housewife. He, bathed in natural light, is closer to the outside sphere, symbolic of his active role in the commercial world. Mr. Arnolfini's direct gaze confronts the viewer while his wife looks passively and obediently at her husband. His emphatically raised hand signals authority. However, even this gender-based reading has been disputed by a number of art historians and historians, who suggest that she was probably of equal ranking to him under the Burgundian court system (at this time, this region of the Netherlands was ruled by the Duke of Burgundy).

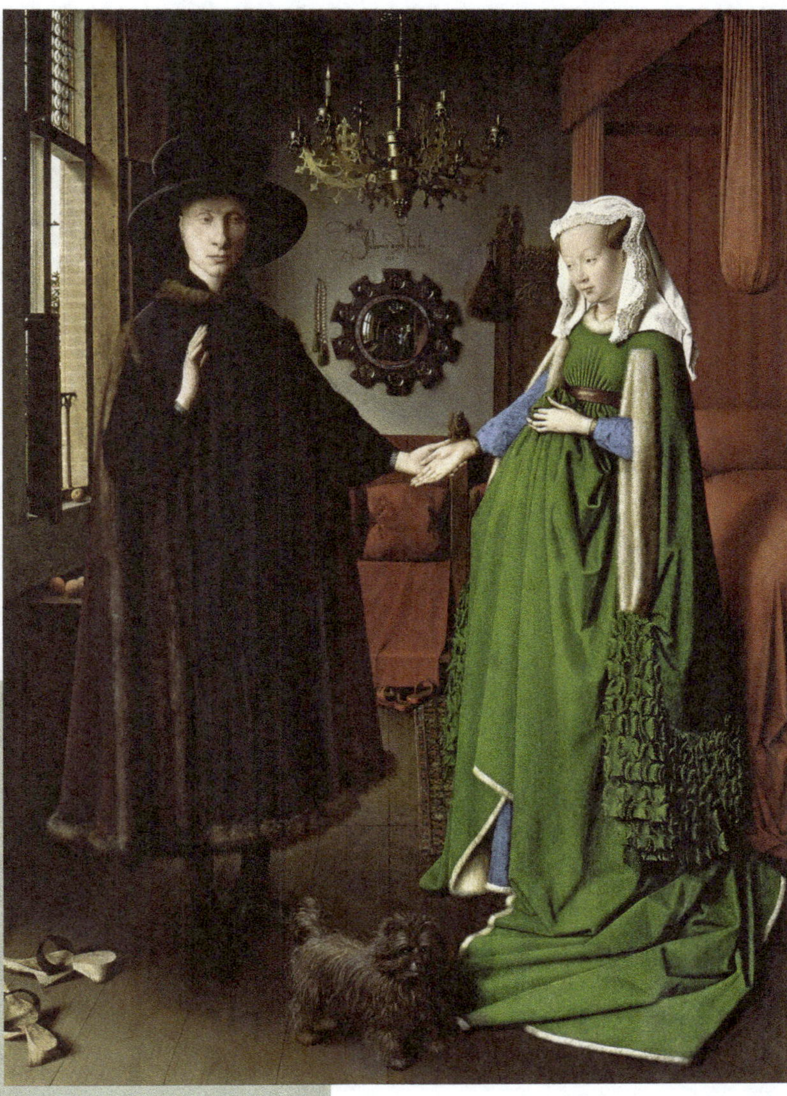

Figure 1.11 | Jan van Eyck, *The Arnolfini Portrait*, 1434, portrait of Giovanni (?) Arnolfini and his wife Giovanna Cenami (?), oil on oak panel, 82.2 × 60 cm, London, National Gallery. Source: National Gallery, London, UK / Bridgeman Images.

1.2 Critical debates: matrimony or betrothal?

According to the website of the National Gallery, London, where the work is housed: *This work is a portrait of Giovanni di Nicolao Arnolfini and his wife, but is not intended as a record of their wedding. His wife is not pregnant, as is often thought, but holding up her full-skirted dress in the contemporary fashion. Arnolfini was a member of a merchant family from Lucca living in Bruges.* (National Gallery, *The Arnolfini Portrait*)

Whether or not the scene represents an act of matrimony or a betrothal is debatable. In 1934, art historian Erwin Panofsky published a seminal article entitled 'Jan van Eyck's *Arnolfini* Portrait' in the *Burlington Magazine* in which he described the work in terms of 'a man and a woman represented in the act of contracting matrimony' (p. 117). While Panofsky points to the artist's signature on the back wall as evidence to support the suggestion that it was painted as a legal document recording a marriage, art historian Edwin Hall later disagreed with Panofsky's reading when he suggested that the painting represents a betrothal, rather than the act of matrimony. At about the same time, art historian Margaret D. Carroll argued that the painting is a portrait of an already married couple and she suggested, in a rather less romantic vein, that it documents Mr. Arnolfini granting his wife the equivalent of 'power-of-attorney' in his business affairs (Carroll, 'In the Name of God and Profit: Jan van Eyck's *Arnolfini* Portrait', p. 101). Scholarly debate concerning the couple's identity is regularly stoked, and the latest interpretations see the scene as an artist's self-portrait in which Jan van Eyck publicises his own wealth with a meticulous depiction of his own bourgeois interior. What do you think? What evidence can your eyes draw upon to support your interpretation of the scene?

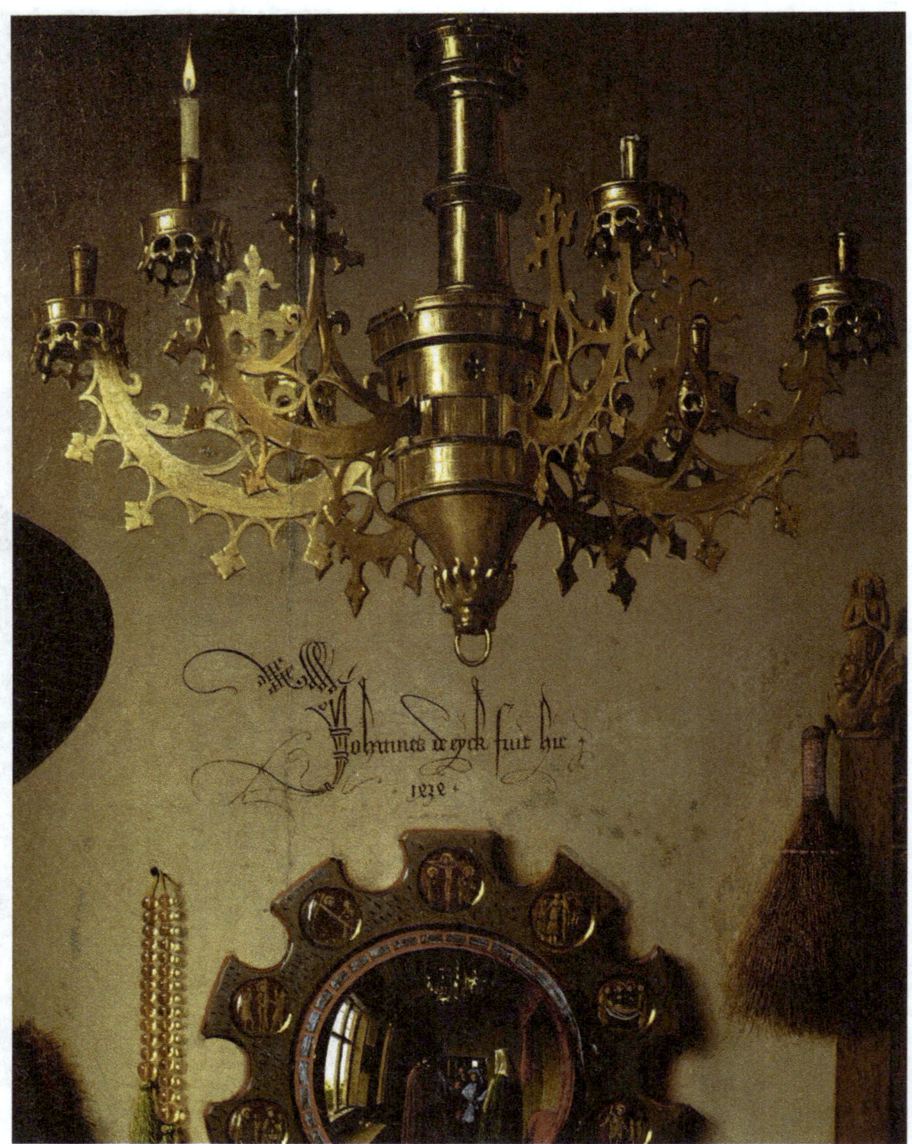

Figure 1.12 | Jan van Eyck, *The Arnolfini Portrait*, 1434, detail of chandelier and Van Eyck's signature on back wall, oil on oak panel, 82.2 × 60 cm, London, National Gallery. Source: National Gallery, London, UK / Bridgeman Images.

That the painting portrays an 'event' is supported by the artist's rather florid statement on the back wall. It is the Latin equivalent of 'Jan van Eyck was here'. This is testimony not only to the matrimonial act which may have been documented in the painting but also to the changing status of the artist towards the middle of the fifteenth century. Jan van Eyck's self-publicising '**graffito**', coupled with what is believed to be the artist's reflected image in the mirror, marks a more general move towards the recognition of artists in their own right, and is a topic for further discussion in *Chapter 5*.

Another double portrait, this time from the twentieth century, is *Mr and Mrs Clark and Percy,* painted between 1970 and 1971 by British artist David Hockney (born 1937). Mr. and Mrs. Clark are, in fact, fashion designer Ossie Clark and the textile designer Celia Birtwell. They had only recently married and Hockney, a long-standing friend of the couple, was best man at their wedding. It has been suggested that Hockney drew on *The Arnolfini Portrait* for his use of symbolism and compositional arrangement. Birtwell and Clark present a reverse formation from Van Eyck's, with the added predominance of Birtwell over Clark. Hockney presented the work to his friends as a wedding present, suggesting perhaps a further point of comparison with *The Ar-*

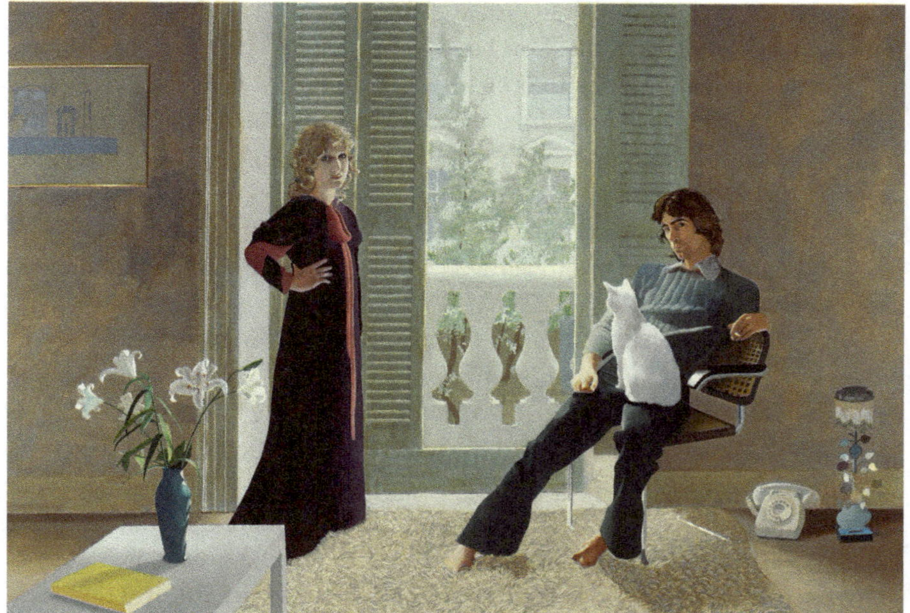

Figure 1.13 | David Hockney,
Mr and Mrs Clark and Percy,
1970, acrylic on canvas, 213.4 × 304.8 cm, London, Collection Tate.
Source: © Tate, London 2015 / © David Hockney.

nolfini Portrait (formerly known as *The Arnolfini Wedding*).

The lilies in the foreground are positioned close enough to Birtwell to suggest a symbolic association. Lilies, at least since the fourteenth century, appeared in depictions of the Annunciation (the announcement by the archangel Gabriel to the Virgin Mary that she would become the mother of Jesus Christ, the Son of God) as a symbol of the Virgin's purity. The Angel Gabriel offers a lily to Mary as he announces that she will bear the Christ Child. At the time of this work, Birtwell was pregnant. Compare the symbolic function of the lilies in Hockney's scene with those in Pre-Raphaelite artist Dante Gabriel Rossetti's *The Annunciation*, 1849–1850, for example.

In the same way that the Virgin Mary possessed an immaculate soul there is something of the immaculate in Hockney's style. The **acrylic medium**, which dries rapidly, suits the purity and minimalism of the couple's environment. Interestingly, it also helps to create a certain mood. The clarity of the **contre-jour** light, together with the cool colour-palette, drains warmth out of the room, and arguably contributes to the 'coolness' we detect in their relationship: the pair are separated compositionally and stare at us, the viewer,

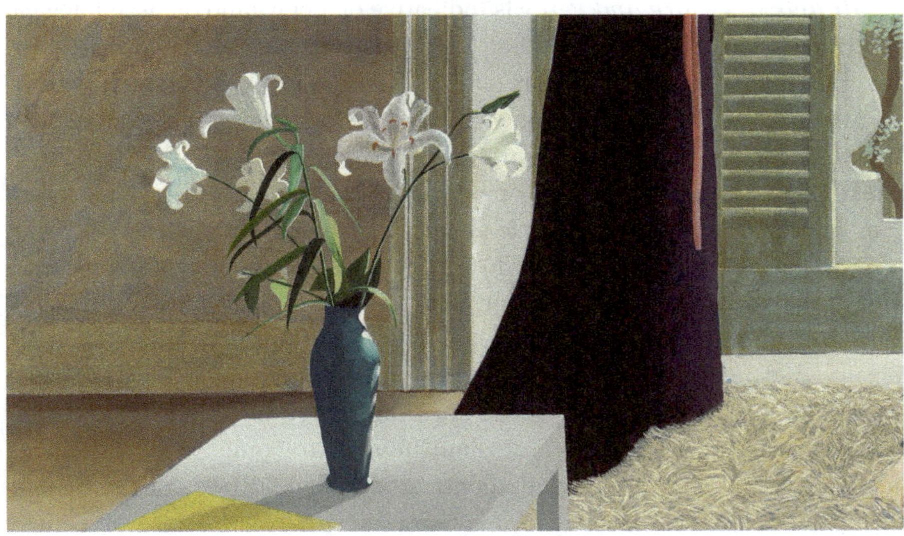

Figure 1.14 | David Hockney,
a detail from *Mr and Mrs Clark and Percy,*
1970, acrylic on canvas, 213.4 × 304.8 cm, London, Collection Tate.
Source: © Tate, London 2015 / © David Hockney.

rather than at each other. Could the carefully positioned unplugged telephone indicate a lack of communication between the pair? Their designer objects and clothes are rendered with a distinctly flat quality. Could this reveal as much about their lack of emotional connectivity as it does their celebrity lifestyle? Mrs. Clark stands erect, hand on hip: he sits, leaning back on his chair, in a way that may be interpreted as equally defiant and in opposition to traditions of gendered representation. Consider how this room and the figures' positions within it compare to Jan van Eyck's *Arnolfini Portrait*, examined previously.

Percy, the white cat on Clark's lap, could be a symbol of infidelity: his carefree disengagement from his environment may be suggestive of his owner's attitude to extra-marital affairs. Percy follows a long line of symbolic pets in art history. Perhaps the highly charged tail and arched back of the cat in *Olympia*, 1863, by French painter Édouard Manet (1832–1883) is a pertinent comparison here. Clark was bisexual, and the continuation of affairs during his time with Birtwell is said to have contributed to the breakdown of their marriage in 1974. Knowledge of these facts aids *an* interpretation of the work, although it can never provide a defining or singular one.

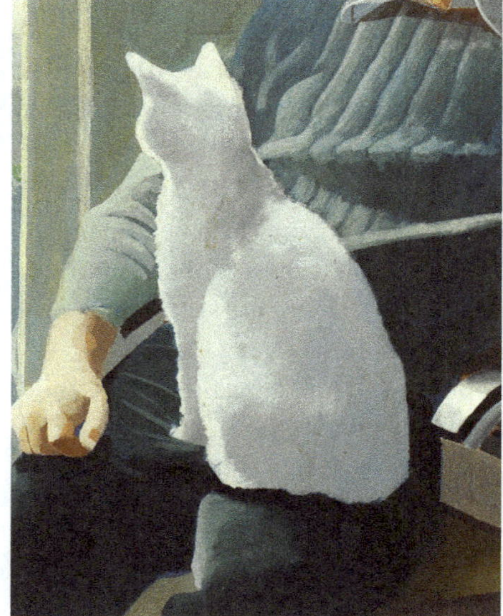

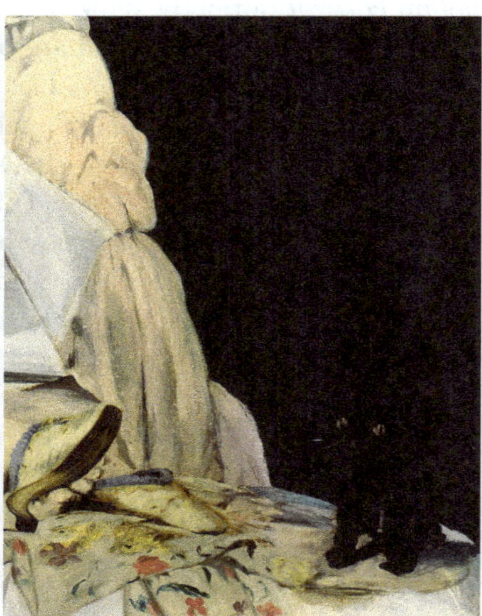

Figure 1.15 | David Hockney, *Mr and Mrs Clark and Percy*, 1970, detail of Percy, acrylic on canvas, 213.4 × 304.8 cm, London, Collection Tate. Source: ©Tate, London 2015 / © David Hockney.

Manet, *Olympia*, 1863, detail of the black cat, oil on canvas, 130.5 × 190 cm, Paris, Musée d'Orsay. Source: Musée d'Orsay, Paris, France / Bridgeman Images.

Mr and Mrs Clark and Percy is indicative of a new kind of 'psychological interior' that art historian Jonathan Harris suggests pervaded twentieth-century portraiture. In such interiors, objects become 'signs' of personality (Harris, *Art History: The Key Concepts*, p. 242). The kind of psychological tension found in Hockney's double portrait was captured centuries earlier by French artist Edgar Degas (1834–1917) in his group portrait featuring the Bellelli family, with whom Degas lodged for a period of time in Italy.

The Bellelli Family, c.1858–1860, by French Impressionist Edgar Degas shows the artist's much-loved aunt, Laura Degas, with her husband, Baron Bellelli, and their daughters Giulia and Giovanna. This detailed and acutely observed scene reminds us of Degas' classical training at the École des Beaux-Arts, and only the hasty exit of the dog from the bottom right-hand corner signals the looseness of his impressionistic-style to come. In fact, the dog's movement provides an energetic contrast with the stillness of the figures. Compositionally reminiscent of a camera shot, the figures are off-centre.

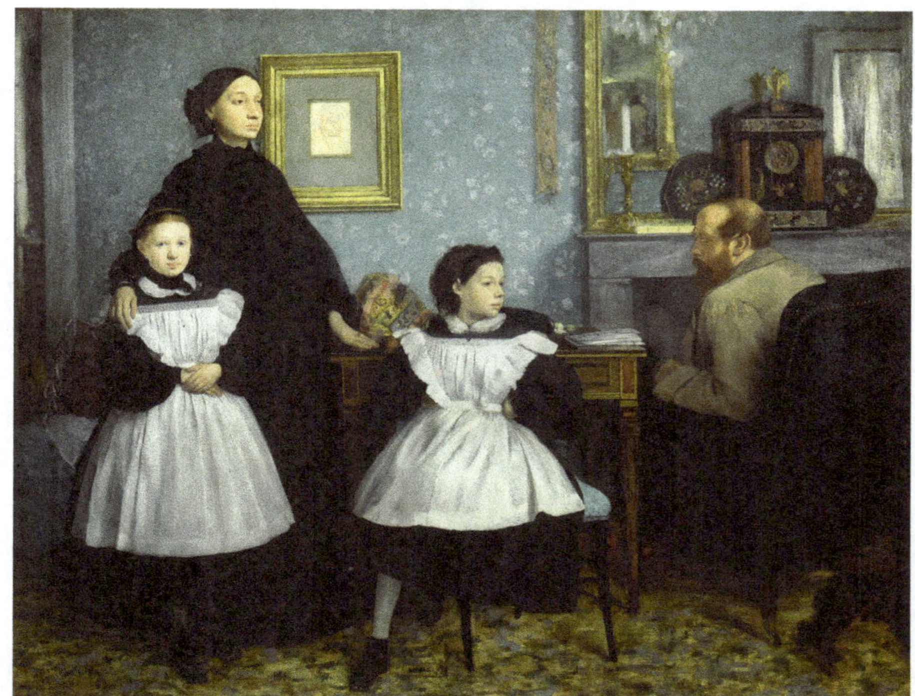

Figure 1.16 | Edgar Degas, *The Bellelli Family*, c.1860, 2 × 2.5 m, Paris, Musée d'Orsay. Source: The Art Archive / Musée d'Orsay Paris / Gianni Dagli Orti.

Could this formal element have been used by the painter to convey the family's dynamic? Find out more about the Bellelli family and look again at the painting in order to reach your own conclusions.

Mrs. Bellelli forms a dark and austere pyramid to the left of the composition, and we perhaps follow her fixed gaze beyond her sedentary and rather disconnected husband to a window, a space beyond the one she occupies. Mrs. Bellelli appears to be supported by her eldest daughter Giovanna, who, aged only ten at the time, already mimics her mother's restraint and formality. A further, less obvious, support is achieved by Mrs. Bellelli's tensely arched hand which props itself on the table's top to reveal a clearly visible wedding band. Her black dress reminds us that she is mourning for her late father, Hilaire Degas, whose portrait hangs next to her on the wall. Hilaire, alive only in the red lines that depict him, appears to stare purposefully at the baron. How should we interpret this?

While Giovanna is buttoned up to the neck and well-groomed like her mother, the youngest daughter, Giulia, reveals a subtle unwillingness to conform for the sake of social responsibility and hides one leg under her chair. How can this deliberate disruption to the formality of the scene be understood? Giulia occupies the centre of the composition – caught between two warring factions perhaps. What do you think? Whose kindred spirit is she?

By virtue of the multiple figures present in group portraiture, the sub-genre is often rich in detail and symbolism. Spanish artist Diego Velázquez's *Las Meninas*, c.1656, is certainly no exception. *See 1.3 Explore this example.*

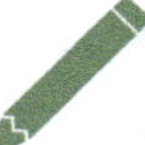

1.3 Explore this example
Examine *Las Meninas* by Spanish artist Diego Velázquez. Why is it considered to be such an unusual group portrait? What other categories of portraiture does it fall into? How has the artist subverted the conventions of portraiture at this time?

Self-portraiture: suffering and confrontation

A self-portrait may be a portrait of the artist by himself or herself, or included in a group. Self-portraits have a long history, although it was not until the mid-fifteenth century that painters took themselves as their subjects in earnest. The self-portrait can also be used for the purpose of self-promotion. Mexican painter Frida Kahlo (1907–1954) is probably best known for her

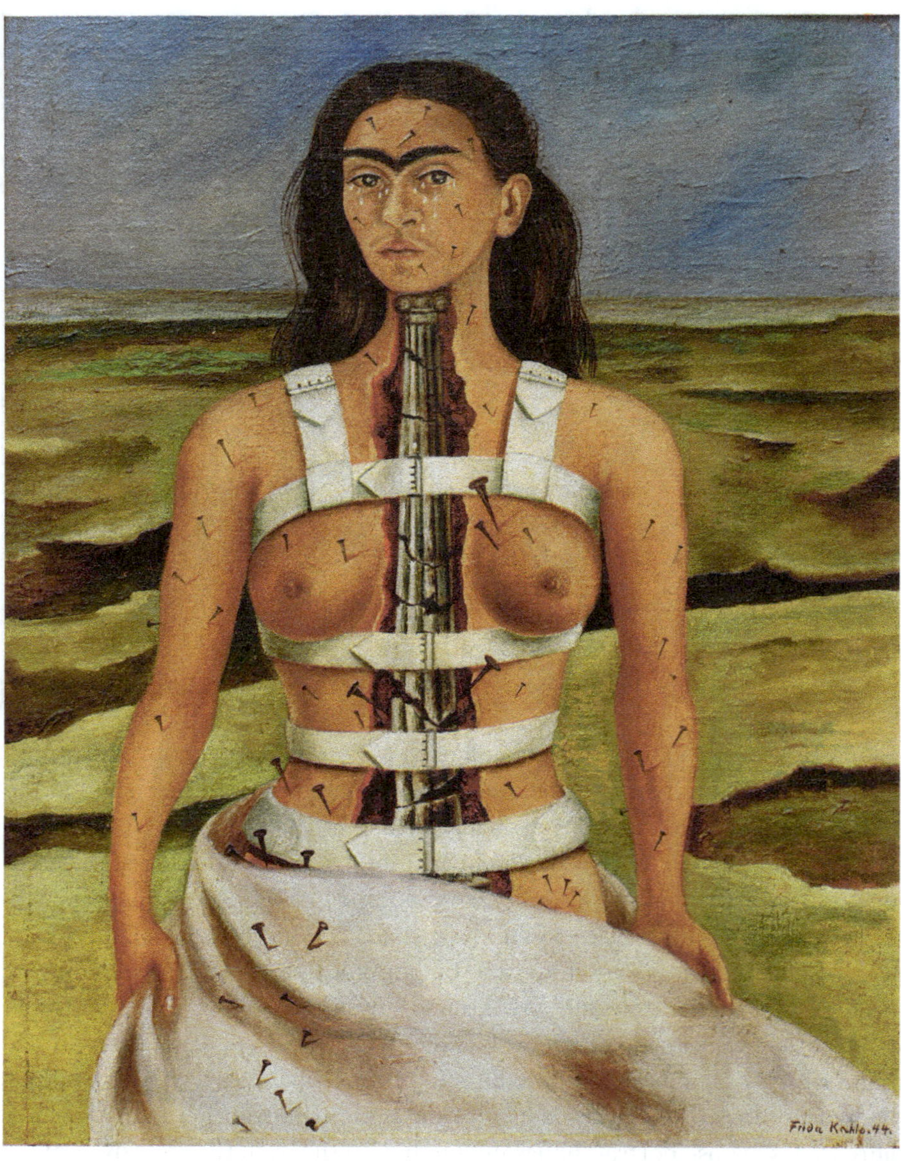

Figure 1.17 | Frida Kahlo, *The Broken Column*, 1944, oil on canvas, mounted on hardboard, 40 × 30.7 cm, Mexico City, Museo Dolores Olmedo Patiño, Xochimilco. Source: akg-images / © 2015. Banco de México Diego Rivera Frida Kahlo Museums Trust, Mexico, D.F. / DACS.

I paint self-portraits because I am so often alone, because I am the person I know best.

(Frida Kahlo)

self-portraits, many of which art historians have read as depictions of her suffering from the physical pain of long-term health problems and the emotional pain associated with her marriage to prominent Mexican painter, Diego Rivera.

A metal rod pierced Kahlo's abdomen in a horrific tram accident when she was a teenager, fracturing her spine and destroying any chance of her later bearing children. *The Broken Column*, 1944, is confessional of the life-long pain she experienced following the accident. Her sense of isolation is conveyed in this vast, barren landscape and her physical suffering conveyed in tears like those of the *mater dolorosa* (a Christian title used for the Virgin Mary, meaning 'our lady of sorrows'). Her body is visibly broken open, and the splintered, **Ionic** column represents her broken spine and the brace which supported her back. This self-portrait, like so many others in her oeuvre, depicts the artist in a frontal pose, maintaining direct eye-contact with the viewer under a heavy and distinguishing mono-brow.

Her nakedness only heightens her vulnerability although, arguably, Kahlo's shroud-like drapery is an allusion to religious suffering. Her eyes express courage, and her depiction is more than faintly reminiscent of the *Ecce Homo* or the martyrdom of St. Sebastian, her nails a substitute for his arrows. A good comparison might be to *The Martyrdom of St. Sebastian*, 1473–1475 by Italian Early Renaissance painters Antonio del Pollaiuolo (1432/3–1498) and Piero del Pollaiuolo (1441–1496).

Complicating Kahlo's representation of herself as a brave and tragic figure is the frequently suggested idea that the artist consciously forged a strong and schematic identity, which aided the perpetuation of her own fame and status as an artist. Kahlo's artistic self-preoccupation finds a parallel with that displayed by other artists, as seen for example in the Christ-like *Self-Portrait*, 1500, by German artist Albrecht Dürer (1471–1528) (see Figure 5.4). Dürer epitomises the theme of the changing status of the artist; his ambition, declared almost blasphemously, in this self-portrait, represents unprecedented self-aggrandisement on the part of the artist. We could argue that Dürer's *Self-Portrait* as Christ marked the start of the artist as celebrity.

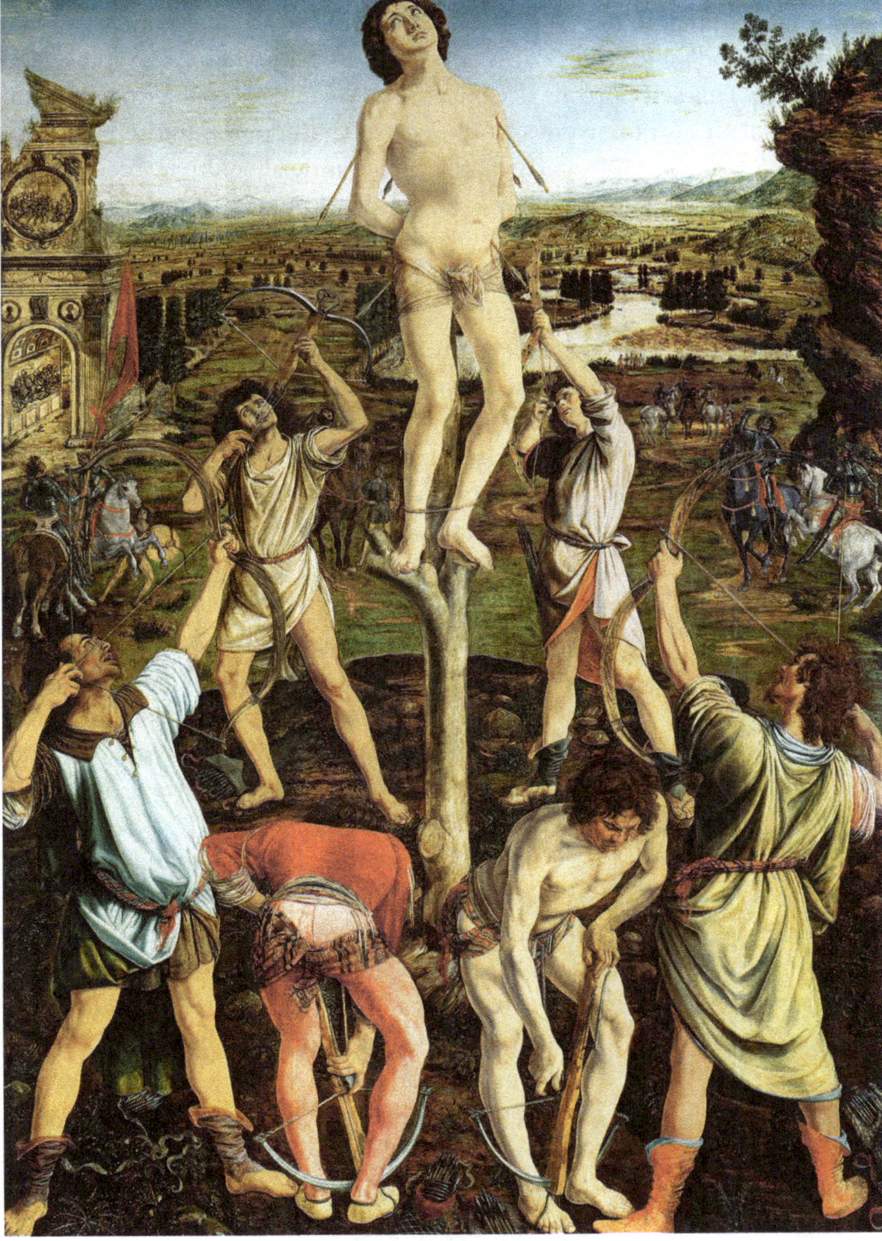

Figure 1.18 | Antonio del Pollaiuolo and Piero del Pollaiuolo, *The Martyrdom of St. Sebastian*, 1475, oil on poplar, 291.5 × 202.6 cm, London, National Gallery. Source: National Gallery, London, UK / Bridgeman Images.

Dürer's *Self-Portrait* (see Figure 5.4) is best understood in the context of **humanism**. Humanism emerged in **Classical Antiquity** and focused on people's intellectual capacity and ability to achieve great things. It was resurrected in Italy during the Renaissance, where it became a sign of progress and development. Religion had by no means lost its significance during the Renaissance, but humanism was a parallel concern that celebrated the achievements of God's creation in the form of humankind. Dürer was heavily influenced by the Italian Renaissance and played a key role in the development of something like a northern equivalent in Germany. During the Renaissance it was still uncommon for artists to sign their works and even less common for artists to paint themselves as their subjects. In this sense, Dürer's *Self-Portrait*, which appears to imitate Christ, is ground-breaking on a number of levels.

The severed head in *David with the Head of Goliath*, 1609–1610, by Caravaggio (originally Michelangelo Merisi da Caravaggio, 1571–1610) is a rather atypical self-portrait of the artist. In May 1606, Caravaggio was accused of murdering a young Roman, Tomassoni, following a trivial argument. With a price on his head for murder, Caravaggio fled Rome, travelling to Naples, Sicily and Malta. This self-portrait as Goliath's severed head demonstrates an unconventional plea for forgiveness. Although the pardon was granted, tragically, Caravaggio was dead before he received the news. Maybe David's loose grip on his sword and his piteous face prophesy a tragic ending? The narrative unlocks the artist's use of a number of devices. David's expression of sad resignation fosters sympathy in the viewer for an artist ruined by his own tempestuous nature. David's face is illuminated from the **tenebristic** background, possibly providing both a divine authority for Goliath's execution and a guarantee that we understand the **sub-text**. Is Caravaggio emerging from the darkness and awaiting judgement? *David with the Head of Goliath* is, according to journalist and art **critic** Jonathan Jones, *perhaps the truest painting ever done of death* (Jones, 'The Complete Caravaggio Part 3'). What was painted as a gesture of apology becomes a tragedy of Shakespearean proportion.

Figure 1.19 | Caravaggio, *David with the Head of Goliath (with Self-Portrait of the Artist as the Dead Goliath)*, 1609–1610, oil on canvas, 125 × 100 cm, Rome, Galleria Borghese. Source: akg-images / Nimatallah.

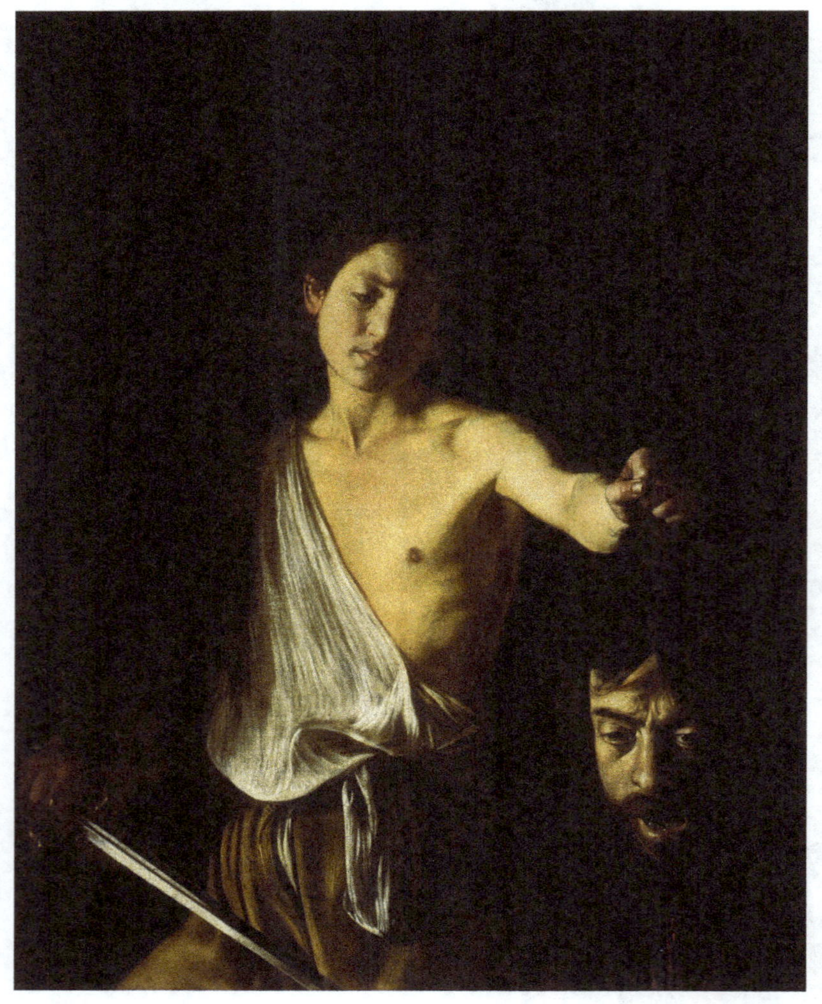

Self-portraiture became increasingly less naturalistic from the end of the nineteenth century, and artists such as Vincent van Gogh (1853–1890) found ways to reveal their personal states of mind using interior and landscape settings, expressive brushwork, arbitrary colour and other devices. Mark Quinn's *Self*, 1991, made with the artist's own blood, is a self-portrait in twentieth-century terms.

Genre

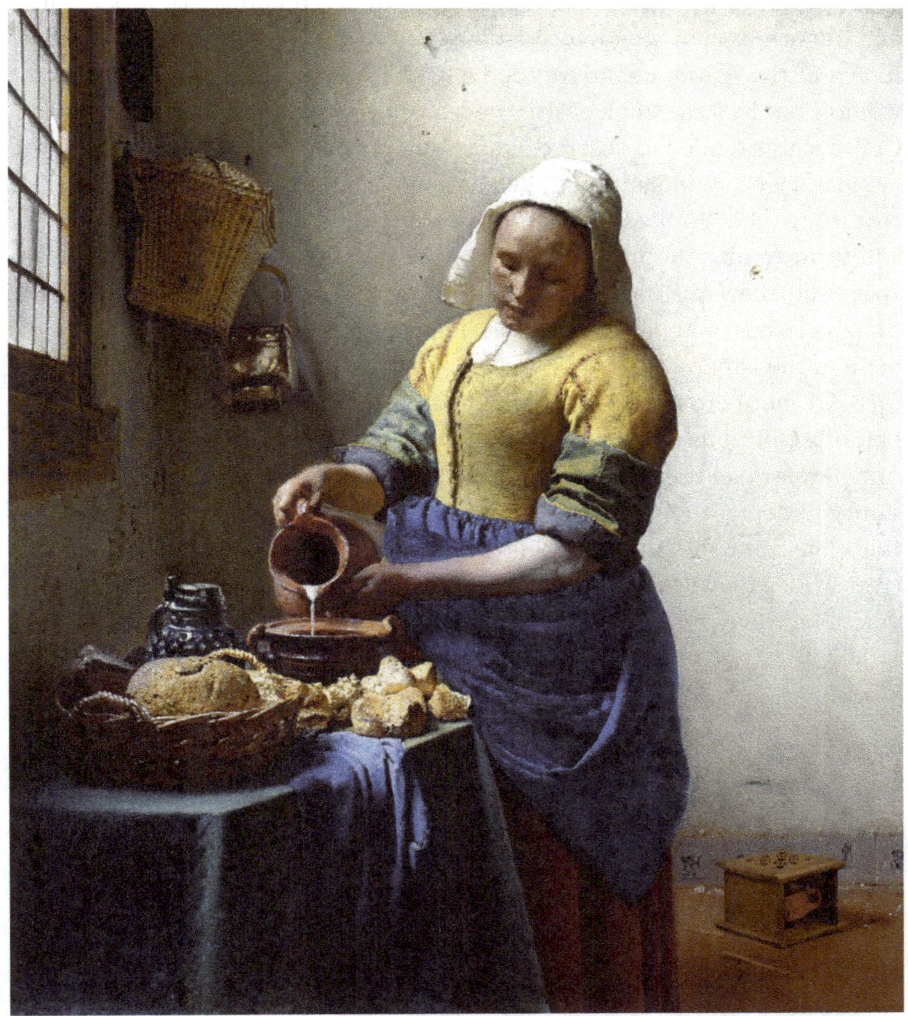

Figure 1.20 | Jan (Johannes) Vermeer, *The Milkmaid*, c.1660, oil on canvas, 45.5 × 41 cm, Amsterdam, Rijksmuseum. Source: Rijksmuseum, Amsterdam, The Netherlands / Bridgeman Images.

As well as meaning 'type', the word 'genre' also refers to scenes depicting the everyday life of people. Thus, in accordance with the 'hierarchy of genres' outlined by Félibien in the seventeenth century, the **genre-genre** suffered a low ranking, following the history and portraiture genres previously examined. Genre paintings often provided a counterpoint to the more serious and academic history genre. Genre works are a category of art that tends to depict realistically scenes of everyday life such as street scenes, markets or domestic interiors as shown in *The Milkmaid*, 1660, by Dutch artist Johannes Vermeer (1632–1675). Genre scenes characteristically feature figures and are distinguished from other genres such as portrait and history on account of their depiction of ordinary people and unidentifiable people. Genre scenes flourished in northern Europe, and Vermeer specialised in their perfection.

'Genre' scenes: everyday life

Demonstrating a characteristically introspective study of a milkmaid at work, the artist's mastery of light brings every conceivable texture of this scene to life. Employing a variety of **impasto** effects, we almost feel the roughness of the bread's crust scratching our mouths and sense the milk slipping over the glazed rim of its terracotta vessel. The maid appears unaware of us and yet we feel as if we were right there with her, due to the artist's technical verisimilitude and realistic quality of light. This mundane, low-life scene testifies to the represented woman's virtue: she is making a pudding to nourish others and her strength of character is reinforced by her physical mass. We could interpret the grainy quality of the light which enters the room through the window on the left, coupled with the heavenly blue of her apron, as spiritual. Genre works tended to observe objects and people as though through a virtual microscope, demonstrating the meticulous attention to detail and surface texture, to the clothing and setting. Vermeer masterfully demonstrates his ability to render the intangible quality of natural daylight in this intimate space: he shows us light reflected in the glazed pot, light absorbed by the maid's clothes, and light as a quasi-religious shaft pouring through a broken pane in the window.

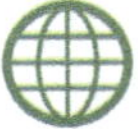

The Tate Gallery website categorises many of the objects in *Omnibus Life in London* in order to suggest their significance in society.

A far more crowded 'genre' scene is provided by the nineteenth-century painting *Omnibus Life in London*, 1859, by William Maw Egley (1826–1916). As a new form of transport, the (horse-drawn) omnibus gave Egley the opportunity to depict the social and historical context of the Victorian era within this claustrophobic interior. This genre scene, comically packed to capacity, provides the viewer with an insight into the social hierarchy of London's emerging travel system.

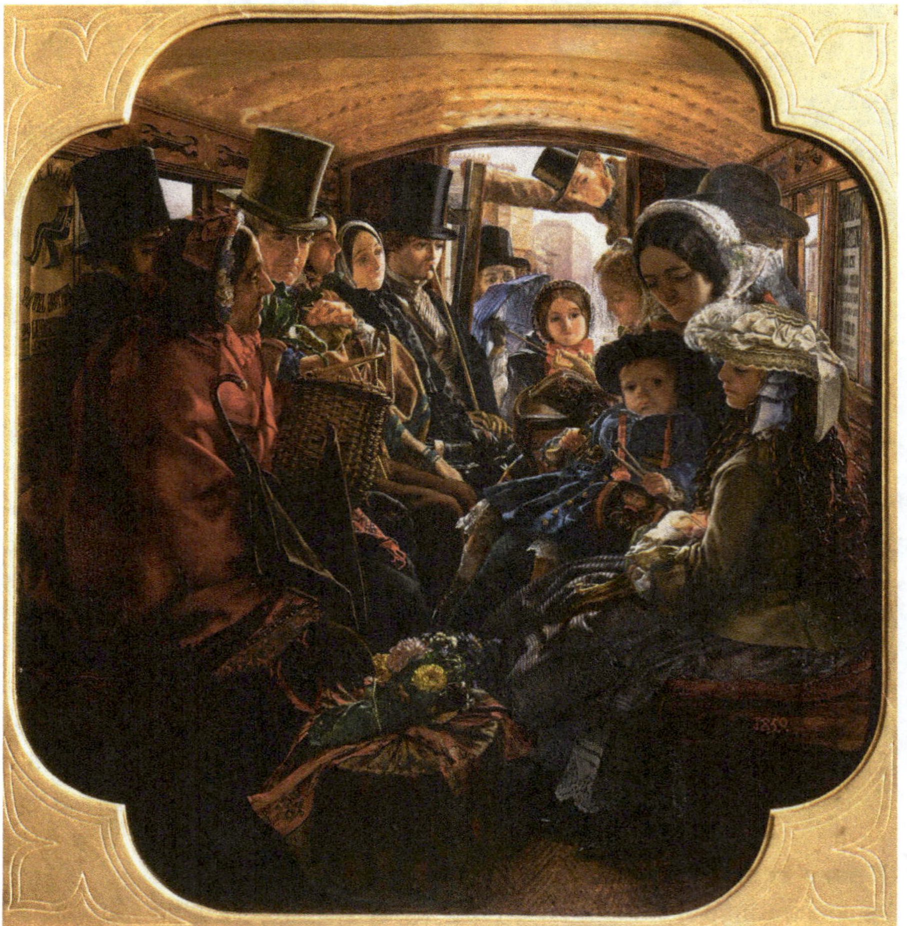

Figure 1.21 | William Maw Egley, *Omnibus Life in London*, 1859, oil on canvas, 44.8 × 41.9 cm, London, Tate Britain. Source: © Tate, London 2015.

The viewpoint the artist has chosen makes it seem almost as though we are entering the carriage ourselves, a probability made more likely by the quizzical glare of the fashionable little boy wriggling in his mother's arms. Every object is rendered with meticulous detail and is suggestive of meaning in some way. What do you think the objects say about social class and status? The carriage has been described as conveying 'a variety of social types'; however, omnibus travel was still relatively expensive and tended to attract middle-class commuters (Treuherz, *Victorian Painting*, p. 109).

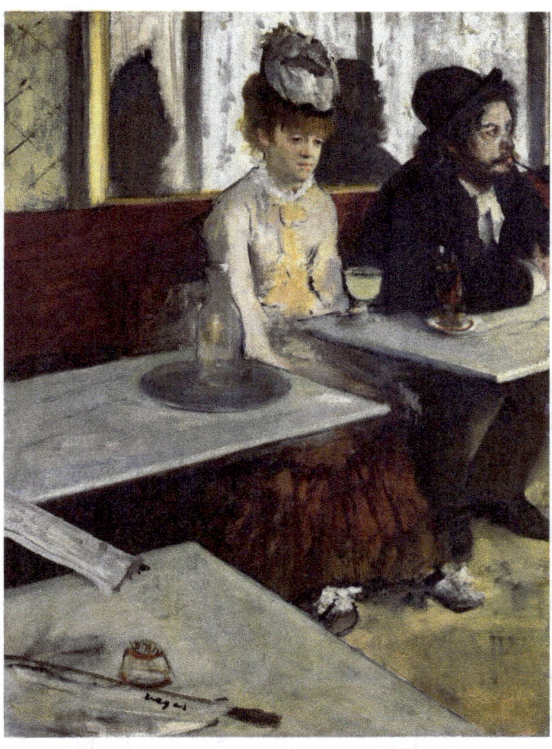

Figure 1.22 | Edgar Degas, *In a Cafe* or *L'Absinthe*, c.1875–1876, oil on canvas, 92 × 68 cm, Paris, Musée d'Orsay.
Source: Musée d'Orsay, Paris, France / Bridgeman Images.

There is also the suggestion that the coach represents a series of binary oppositions which provide a form of sub-text prevalent in British society at this time. For example, the juxtaposition of young and old, male and female, and, more subtly, exterior and interior, and watched or being watched. This is precisely the kind of societal contrast being acutely observed by some of the most famous writers and playwrights of the nineteenth century.

The crowds of people represented in microcosm in Egley's omnibus embody a duality that would fascinate nineteenth-century artists. The crowd was both a depraved and gleeful source of life itself – *[f]or Baudelaire the phenomenon of the crowd is the manifestation of modernity itself* (Schnapp and Tiews, *Crowds*, p. 345). Charles Baudelaire (1821–1867), poet, critic and the ultimate spectator of modern life, embraced the epic quality of contemporary living and championed the 'new reality' depicted by Manet and the **Impressionists**. In his 1845 **Salon** Review, Baudelaire describes the modern artist's ability to capture the transience and **modernity** of the times in a manner which rivals the 'epic' works of the ancients: *There is no lack of subjects, or of colours, to make epics. The painter, the true painter for whom we are looking, will be he who can snatch its epic quality from the life of today* (Baudelaire, *Art in Paris 1845–62: Salons and Other Exhibitions*, p. 32). Baudelaire wrote about, and Manet and the Impressionists painted, both sides of modern life: the socially enjoyable and the socially and economically deprived.

In *L'Absinthe*, 1875–1876, a genre scene of Parisian life by Edgar Degas, two miserable absinthe drinkers represent a significant aspect of urban life. During the nineteenth century, hordes of people migrated into the metropolis in search of work. The 'phenomenon of the crowd' was born together with, ironically, a new and modern sense of isolation. Life in the city was overcrowded and squalid; unsurprisingly, alcohol consumption, particularly absinthe, had become the recreational pastime of the working-classes. Photographic techniques had been honed by the 1850s and the camera's ability to capture the immediate and the real is evident here. The composition of the painting is cropped almost like a photograph, helping the work seem modern and up to date, and perhaps contributing to its sense of realism and actuality. It heightens our sense of the transient and, in so doing, captures a Baudelairian sense of modernity. Degas' *L'Absinthe* and the social and historical context of mid-nineteenth-century France is examined in more detail in *Chapter 4*.

As well as being an example of the genre-genre in a later era, *Nighthawks*, 1942, by Edward Hopper (1882–1967), offers an equally sombre insight into the period of its production and, for that reason, also appears in more detail in *Chapter 4*.

Look at the painting *Nighthawks* by Hopper and describe the figures and their setting. What type of mood has the artist conveyed in the painting and how has he achieved this?

This scene of American life, painted in 1942, characterises Hopper's haunting style. Muted tones compromise its realism and signal its sub-text. An airless quality seems aided by the superficially rendered space and graphic quality of the painted surface. The physical window that separates the diners from the area outside appears to mirror the psychological barrier that distances them from us as viewers, locking the depicted figures deeper into a helpless and parallel plane. Ironically, the figures are isolated from one another, despite occupying a social space, and this contributes to the 'eeriness' of the scene.

Figure 1.23 | Edward Hopper, *Nighthawks*, 1942, oil on canvas, 84.1 × 152.4 cm, Friends of American Art Collection, 1942.51, the Art Institute of Chicago. Source: Photography ©The Art Institute of Chicago.

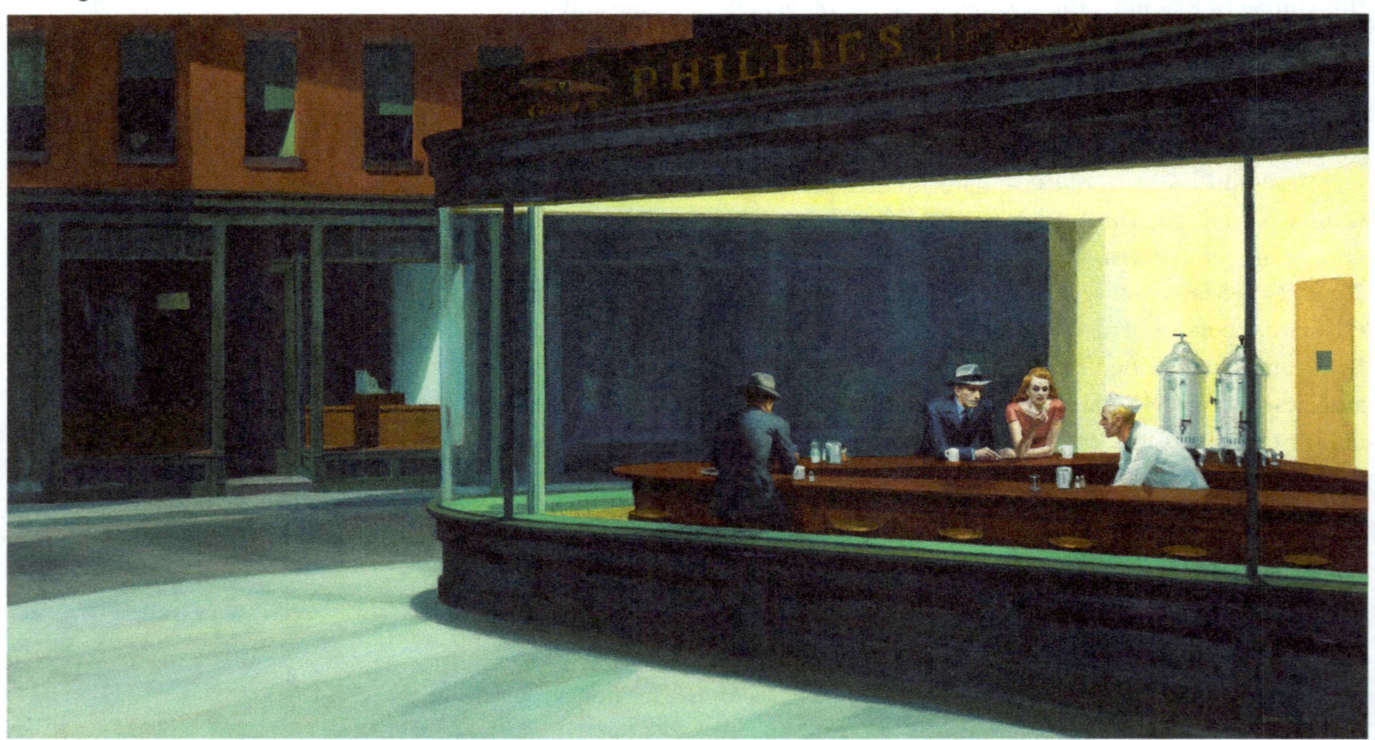

Landscape

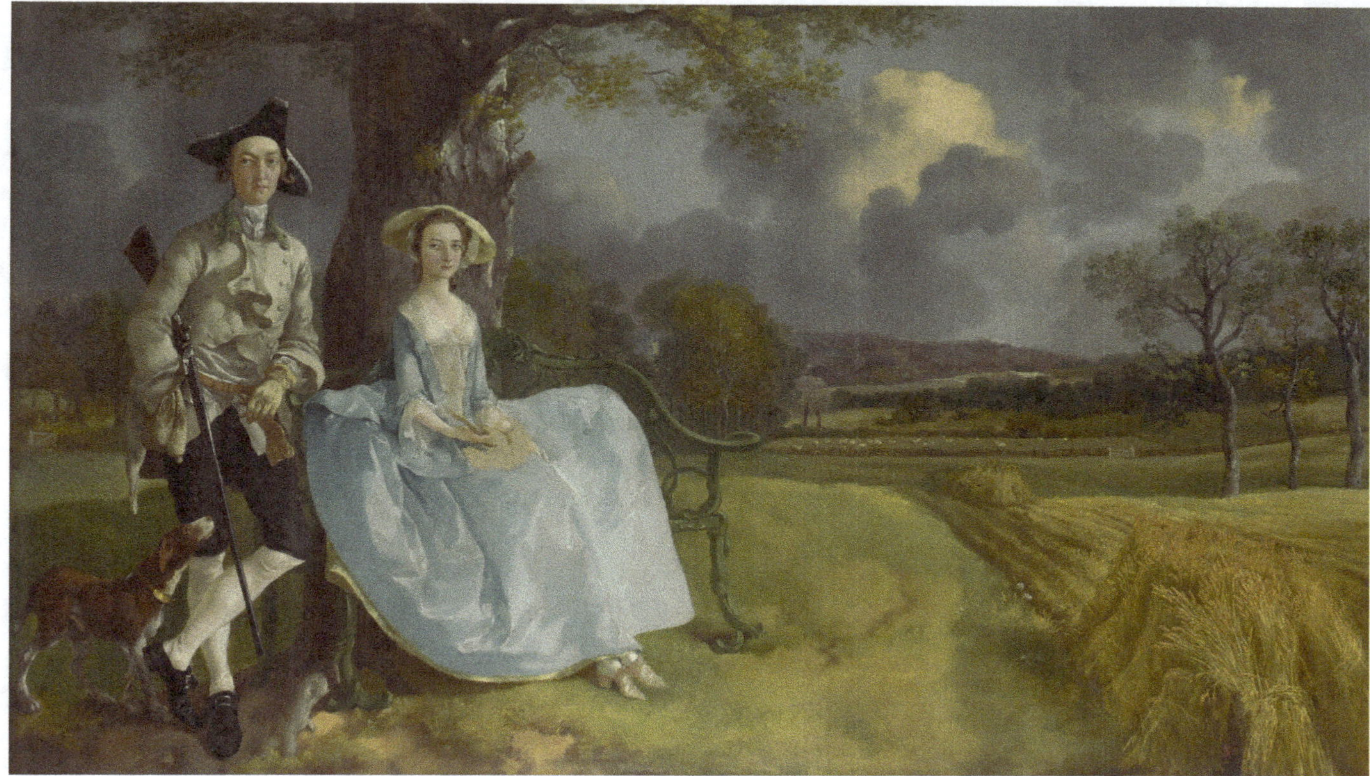

Figure 1.24 | Thomas Gainsborough, *Mr and Mrs Andrews*, c.1750, oil on canvas, 69.8 × 119.4 cm, London, National Gallery. Source: The National Gallery, London / akg-images.

Landscape is a broad term, especially in the hands of artists, and its low ranking in the hierarchy of genres established in the seventeenth century, bears little or no relevance today. Traditionally, it relates to our natural, rather than man-made environment, although these categories are not always easily distinguished. Landscape can also include scenes of human activity. Landscapes are not always faithful representations. Depending on the period of their creation, landscapes can represent an idealised 'myth' of the land, or an expression of national pride, or perhaps subjective emotional and even **abstracted** representations.

Owning and working the land

The double portrait of *Mr and Mrs Andrews*, c.1750, by English painter Thomas Gainsborough (1727–1788) is unusual as it is also a landscape. More complex landscapes can represent two or more genres when they incorporate figures, especially recognisable ones. The Suffolk squire, Robert, and his wife, Mary, look incredibly pompous in the knowledge that we are made to survey their land. His casually crossed legs and slightly raised brow imply he's brimming with rural-aristocratic complacency – he owns the land and has the ability to control it with use of the latest technology of that time.

In his *The Avenue at Middelharnis*, 1689, Dutch artist Meindert Hobbema (1638–1709) offers us a view of a quintessential Dutch avenue. Weathered poplars guard man-made tracks in the broad Dutch landscape, leading our

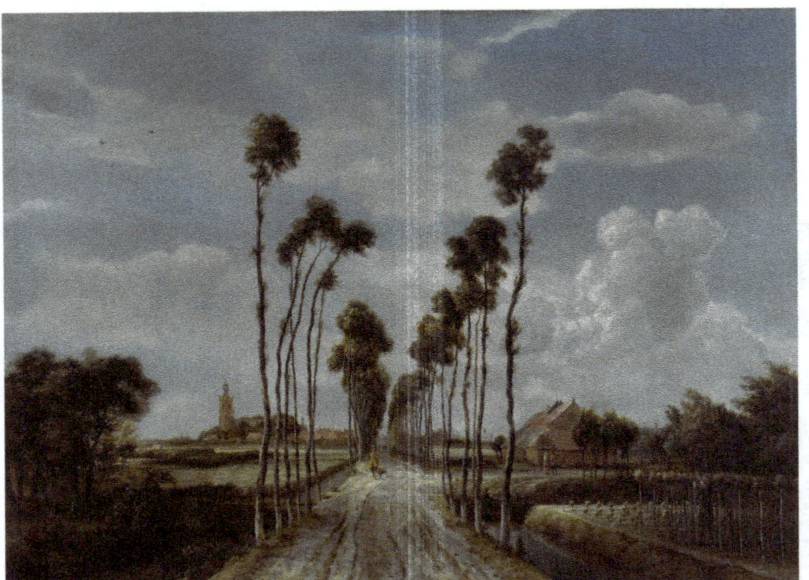

Figure 1.25 | Meindert Hobbema, *The Avenue at Middelharnis*, 1689, oil on canvas, 103.5 × 141 cm, London, National Gallery.
Source: The National Gallery, London / akg-images.

gaze to a villager on the path and beyond him to the horizon line (where the sky meets the land). Compositionally, the land is divided into two parts by the central road which we appear to be travelling along too, albeit in a slightly elevated position. The left-hand side is slightly more unkempt and natural: the right-hand side is highly structured and ordered by man's honest labour. The low horizon line is typical of seventeenth-century Dutch landscape, as is the panoramic view; both devices remind the viewer of humans' relationship with their natural environment and its importance to the Dutch Republic at this time. (See *1.2 Let's connect the themes: historical perspectives – land reclamation project*.)

Landscape can also convey a sense of national pride. In this sense, landscape could be said to express prevailing ideology and social values. It certainly expressed the dominant social control of the bourgeois landowners in Gainsborough's *Mr and Mrs Andrews*.

1.2 Let's connect the themes: historical perspectives – land reclamation project

Landscape scenes abound in seventeenth-century Dutch art. Due to topography and politics, the Dutch had a unique relationship with their land, one that differed from those of other European countries. After gaining independence from Spain, the Dutch undertook an extensive land-reclamation project that lasted almost a century. Dikes and drainage systems cropped up across the countryside. Because of the effort expended on these endeavours, people developed a very direct relationship to the land. Further, the reclamation affected Dutch social and economic life. The marshy and swampy nature of much of the land made it less desirable for large-scale exploitation, so the extensive feudal landowning system that existed elsewhere in Europe never developed in the United Provinces (as the Netherlands was then known). Most Dutch families owned and worked their own farms, cultivating a feeling of closeness to the terrain (Kleiner, *Gardner's Art Through the Ages: The Western Perspective*, p. 606).

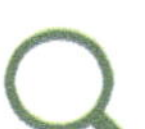

1.3 What can you see?
Look at the painting *The Avenue at Middelharnis* by Meindert Hobbema. How has the artist depicted nature in the scene? Why do you think the figures are so small in relation to the land?

Landscape as emotional expression

Landscape is as much born from its context as any other genre in the history of art. Whether seen through a scientific lens in the seventeenth century, or through an expressionistic and individualistic one in the nineteenth century, it never fails to provide an insight into the times of its production. In 1883, German philosopher Friedrich Wilhelm Nietzsche famously professed 'God is dead' as part of his increasingly pessimistic view of the world. The Nietzschean belief that life lacks purpose could be related to Vincent van Gogh's *Wheatfield with Crows*, 1890, for example.

Dutch **Post-Impressionist** Vincent van Gogh (1853–1890) used landscape and, most notably, colour to express his feelings. In viewing *Wheatfield with Crows*, 1890, we become a part of the 'topsy-turvy world' he depicts. Painting in the nineteenth century, Van Gogh was one of the first to express his interior as opposed to his exterior view of the world; however, in the twentieth century, the landscape was often used as a conduit for the communication of artists' suffering and angst. Although the region of Auvers, France, where this painting was made, initially offered him peace, towards the end of his time he was increasingly prone to bouts of temper, possibly as a consequence of a form of epilepsy from which he appears to have been suffering. It appears that the artist shot himself in a lonely field on 27 July 1890 and died the morning of the 29th.[6]

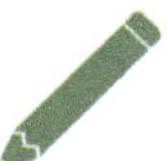

1.4 Explore this example
Cityscapes such as Johannes Vermeer's *View of Delft* (1660–1661) are included as landscape genre. Vermeer's scene shows how the artist perceives the serenity of this city despite the fact that the north-east section of Delft (located in the Netherlands) had been devastated in the gunpowder store explosion of 1654.

Van Gogh's technique involved the rapid application of paint, in thick impasto, and each stroke carries a sense of urgency: the wheat seems to thrash about in various directions and the paths seem to move just as organically, suggesting instability and uncertainty. We sense that those menacing crows, age-old symbols of doom, may encircle us soon. In this painting, the turbulence of the artist's mind manifests itself in the violence of his brushwork. Characteristically, colour is the artist's main symbol of expression: the uppermost sky turns from blue to black, creating an ominous mood over the field. *Wheatfield with Crows* is arguably the most agitated of his works and it is tempting to read it as his suicide note given its execution so close to his death. Although some have suggested that this was the 'last' work the artist painted, what we know for certain is that it was *one* of his last. Van Gogh painted a series of landscapes leading up to his death about which he wrote, rather prophetically:

They are vast stretches of wheat under troubled skies, and I did not need to go out of my way to express sadness and extreme loneliness. (Roskill, *The Letters of Vincent van Gogh*, p. 338)

Landscape may also be a reminder of nature's power to inspire awe and metaphysical wonder. American painter Georgia O'Keeffe (1887–1986) be-

6 There is recent speculation about who was responsible for shooting Van Gogh, although the view that he shot himself is the one most commonly adhered to.

Figure 1.26 | Vincent van Gogh, *Wheatfield with Crows*, 1890, oil on canvas, 50.5 × 103 cm, Amsterdam, Van Gogh Museum. Source: Van Gogh Museum, Amsterdam, The Netherlands / Bridgeman Images.

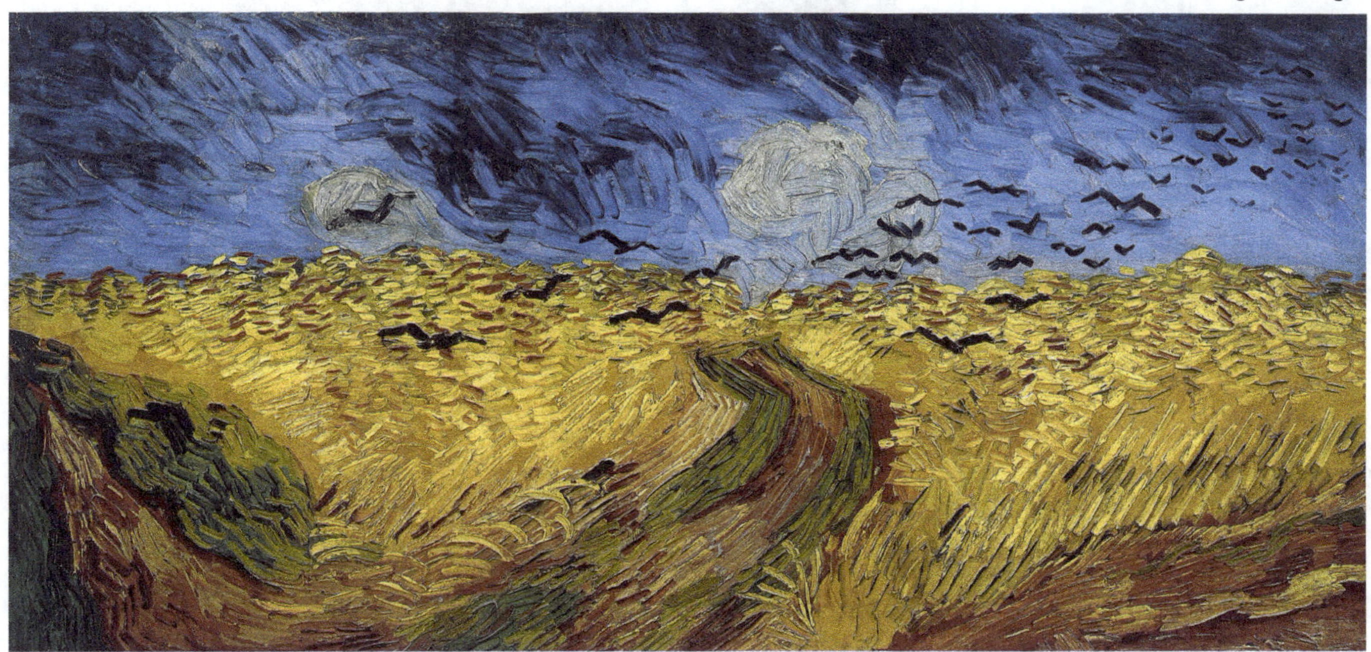

came interested in anti-academic, non-traditional art and was increasingly concerned with nature in its purest form; she attempted to represent the underlying essence of things. We know that O'Keeffe read Wassily Kandinsky's 1911 publication *Concerning the Spiritual in Art*, which proposed that artists could lead humanity to spiritual enlightenment.

Deer's Skull with Pedernal, 1936, set in an infinite and barren landscape, may be seen as reminiscent of the Crucifixion. The viewer is provided with a low perspective which forces our gaze upwards in an act of veneration – these are the bones of once-living creatures bleached white under the searing heat of nature's sun; to the artist, these are the bones indicative of nature's wondrous power. O'Keeffe travelled to New Mexico in 1929 and its vast space overwhelmed her. The interminable blue sky and swollen rhythms of the hills are as significant as the bones themselves. In the same way that **synaesthete** Kandinsky's blindingly colourful compositions were designed to affect our very soul, O'Keeffe's oeuvre became increasingly bound up with the idea of its Almighty creation – and the search for a quasi-religious universalism in her art. O'Keeffe's painting is an atypical landscape insofar as it is also a form of exterior still life; however, it is the might of God's nature, a nature evident in the landscape, that O'Keeffe observes.

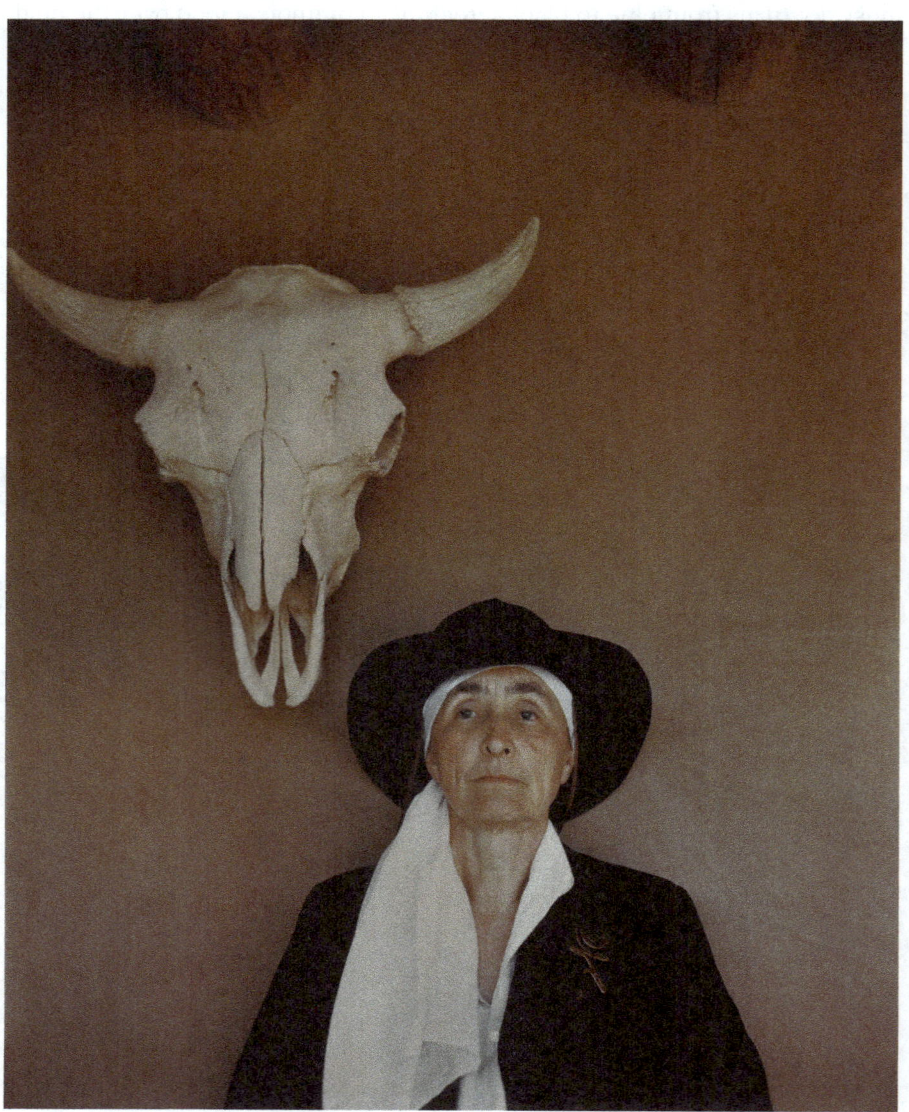

Figure 1.27 | Philippe Halsman: Georgia O'Keeffe at her desert ranch, 1948, Abiquiu, New Mexico. Source: © Philippe Halsman / Magnum Photos.

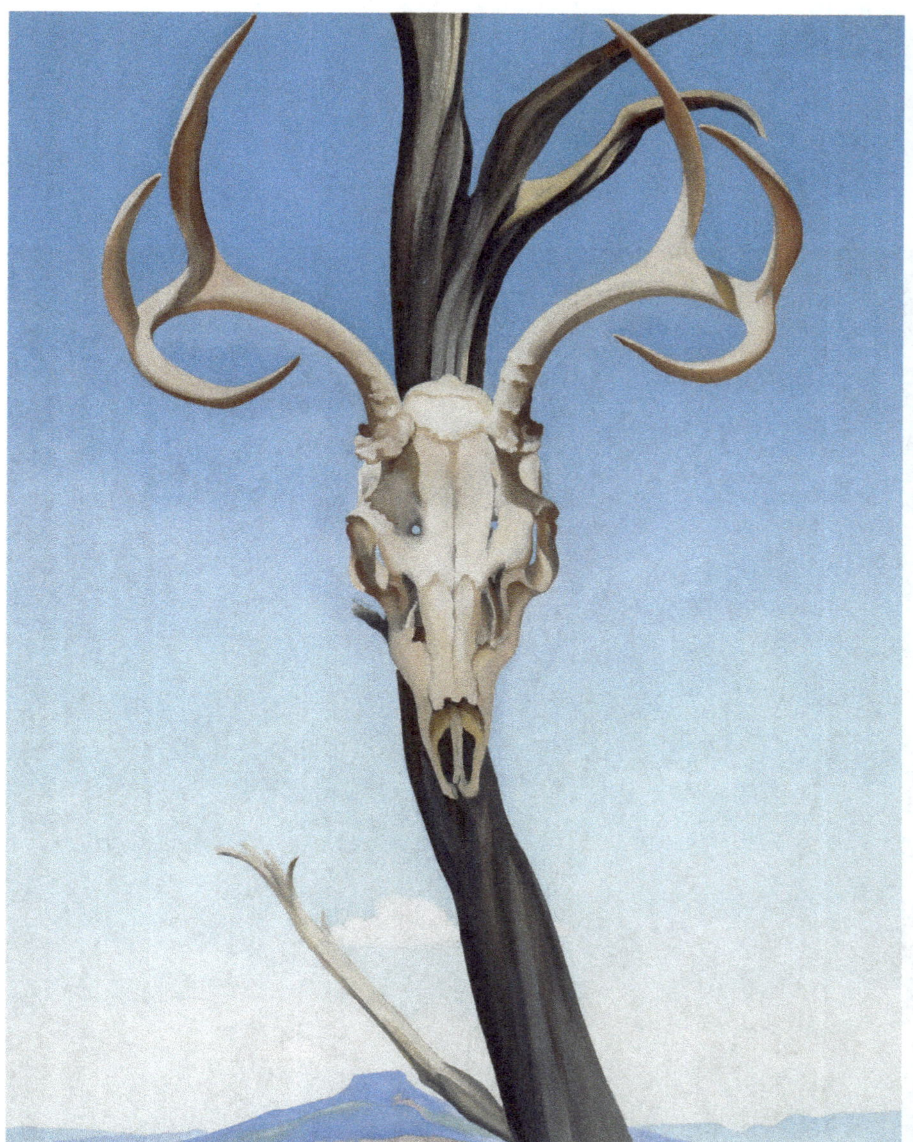

Figure 1.28 | Georgia O'Keeffe, *Deer's Skull with Pedernal*, 1936, oil on canvas, 91.4 × 76.5 cm, Museum of Fine Arts, Boston, Gift of the William H. Lane Foundation, 1990.432.
Source: Photograph © 2015 Museum of Fine Arts. Boston / © Georgia O'Keeffe Museum / DACS, 2015.

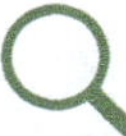

1.5 Explore this example
How does the **German Expressionist** artist Gabriele Münter (1877–1962) express her view of the world in her painting *Landscape with Church*, 1910? What were her influences? How can this landscape be described as a reaction to the **formalism** of traditional landscape painting?

The landscape genre, in common with every other genre, has evolved a great deal over the centuries. While it has been used to reveal the status of its landowners and the relationship between man and nature's infinite might, it has also been used by modern artists unconventionally, even as a form of self-portraiture, as is the case with Sam Taylor-Johnson's (formerly Sam Taylor-Wood) photograph *Self-Portrait as a Tree*, 2000.[7]

The landscape in Western art seems to have fallen in and out of favour over the centuries. It emerged during the Renaissance as a convincing backdrop to scenes enacted from the Bible or from mythology, and continued to grow in stature during the sixteenth century. By the seventeenth century, landscape was recognised as being a valuable genre in its own right. In the nineteenth century, the landscape provided experimental ground for a variety of **avant-garde** movements.

7 Sam Taylor-Johnson's *Self-Portrait as a Tree*, 2000, is a photograph and therefore less suitable as an example for examination purposes, although it is highly illustrative of the loose interpretation of the genre in contemporary times.

Still Life

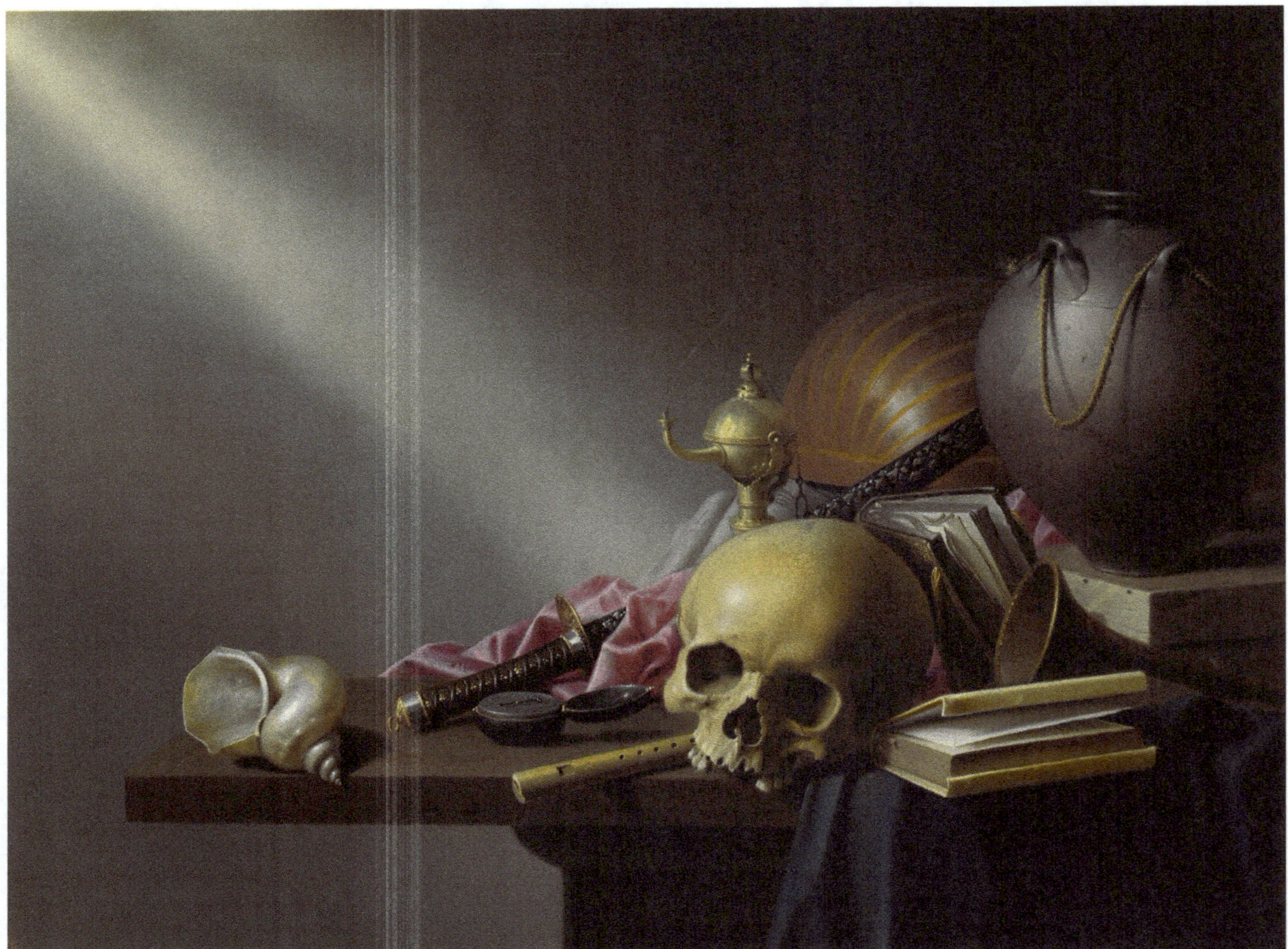

Figure 1.29 | Harmen Steenwyck, *An Allegory of the Vanities of Human Life*, c.1640, oil on oak, 39.2 × 50.7 cm, London, National Gallery.
Source: The National Gallery, London / akg-images.

Still life, devoid of human figures and more demonstrative of artistic skill than imagination and intellect, was considered relatively unimportant in the hierarchy of genres. Still life commonly refers to paintings depicting a selection of everyday objects such as fruit, flowers, utensils and collectors' items, which may have been painted both for the intrinsic value of their form and in order to infuse the objects with symbolism (often religious). Still life paintings were traditionally small in scale, in accordance with their status and likelihood of hanging in a private dwelling.

Memento mori

Seventeenth-century Flemish and Dutch painting, such as *An Allegory of the Vanities of Human Life*, c.1640, by Harmen Steenwyck (1612–1656), excelled in this genre. Objects were carefully chosen for the senses they evoked. Delicate materials such as the paper and the shell were common, not least for their reference to the fragility of human life. The skull acts as the ultimate reminder of mortality also known as **memento mori**. Thus, this painting is essentially a religious work in the guise of a still life. **Vanitas** are examples of still life with religious overtones, and often are concerned to point the viewer towards an awareness of his or her own mortality. Vanitas paintings prick the viewer's moral conscience and warn them to be careful about placing too much importance on the materiality and pleasures of this life, as they could prevent salvation in the next, so communicating the message summarised in the Gospel of Matthew: *Do not store up for yourselves treasures on earth, where moth and rust destroy, and where thieves break in and steal. But store up for yourselves treasures in heaven, where moth and rust do not destroy and where thieves do not break in and steal. For where your treasure is, there your heart will be also* (Matthew 6:18–21).

Viva la Vida, 1954, is one of Frida Kahlo's last works. Having endured multiple surgeries spanning many years, in 1953 gangrene set into her right foot and her leg had to be amputated below the knee. The impact of this final surgery was devastating. The event precipitated this image as a diary entry, and with the usual and humorous tone she writes *Pies para que los quiero, si tengo alas pa' volar?* (Feet, what do I need them for when I have wings to fly?) The blood-red fruit in this painting may reflect the pain she suffered, and the jagged cuts in the watermelon suggest the numerous surgeries she endured. The fruit lays bare its fleshy interior, ripped open, as she was. She died the same year *Viva la Vida* was painted, seven days after her 47th birthday.

Viva la Vida is often discussed as a vehicle for the artist's national pride. By selecting only locally grown produce, she made the fruits of the earth symbols of her. The red, green and white colour scheme represents the national

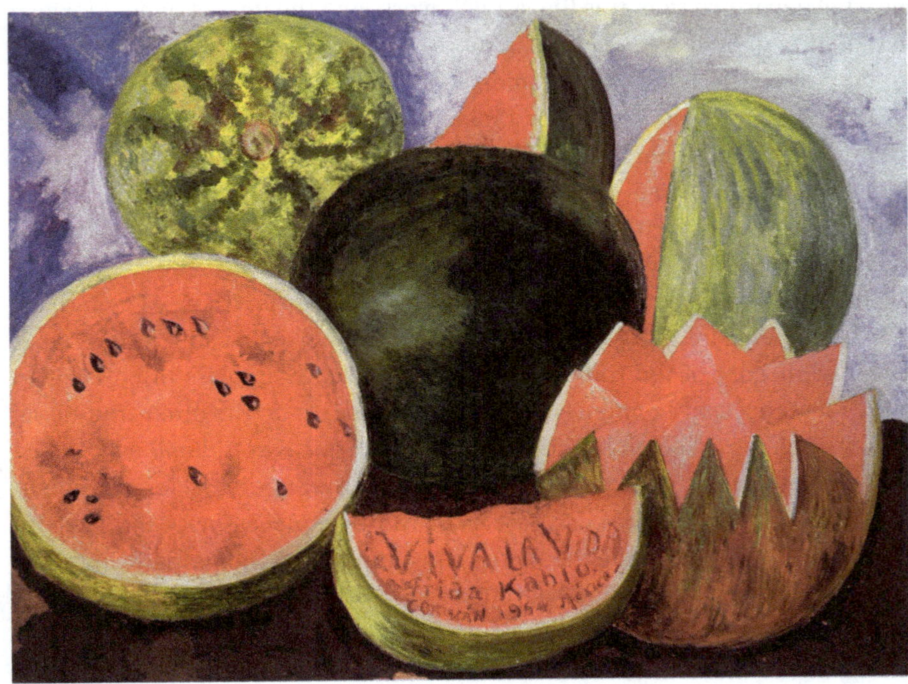

Figure 1.30 | Frida Kahlo, *Viva la Vida*, 1954, print, Private Collection. Source: Private Collection / Bridgeman Images / © 2015. Banco de México Diego Rivera Frida Kahlo museums Trust, Mexico, D.F. / DACS.

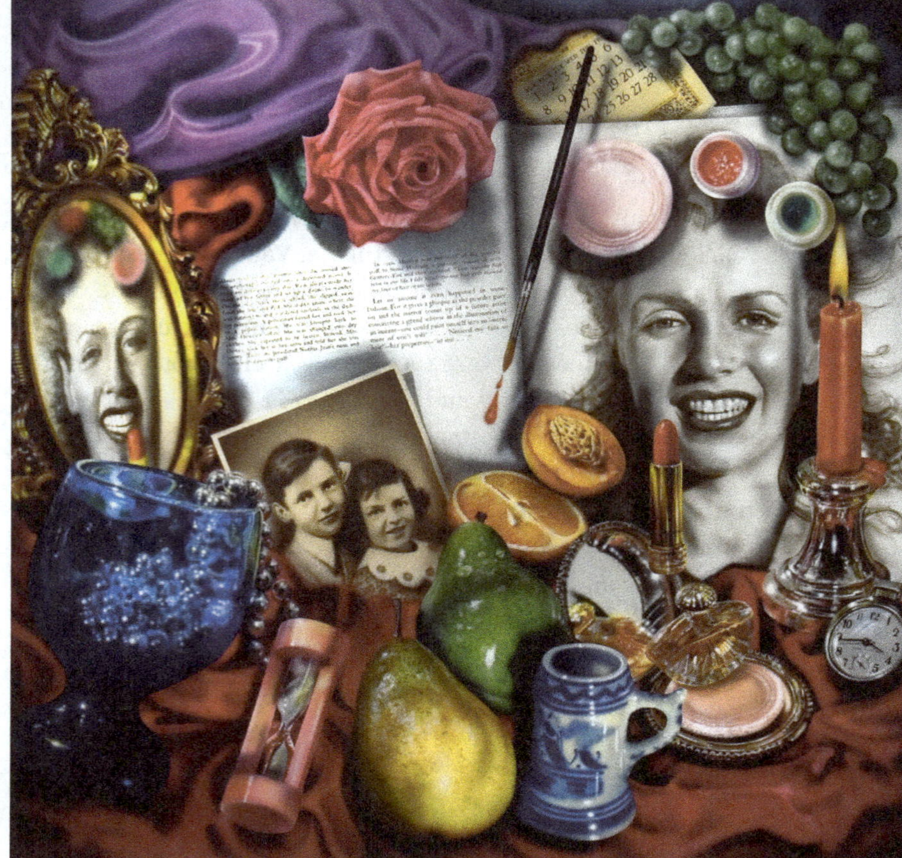

Figure 1.31 | Audrey Flack, *Marilyn (Vanitas)*, 1977, oil over acrylic on canvas, 244 × 244 cm, the University of Arizona Museum of Art. Source: Collection of the University of Arizona Museum of Art; Museum Purchase with Funds Provided by the Edward J. Gallagher, Jr. Memorial Fund. / Courtesy of Louis K. Meisel Gallery.

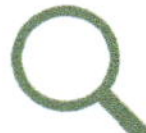

1.4 What can you see?
Look at the painting *Marilyn (Vanitas)* by Audrey Flack (Figure 1.31). Why has the artist selected these particular objects? How has the artist chosen to represent these objects to the viewer? What message do you think the artist is trying to convey?

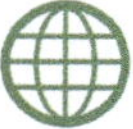

Consult the companion website for more information on hyperrealism.

colours of Mexico and their intensity echoes the national pride felt by an artist who changed her birth date to coincide with that of the Mexican Revolution. This work makes a fruitful comparison with Steenwyck's, a connection only made clear with an autobiographical reading of Kahlo's work. Both are memento mori; Steenwyck's overtly, in relation to its metaphorical objects; Kahlo's covertly in relation to her deteriorating health and sense of her own nearing departure from this life. Kahlo's work, and the impact of her Mexican nationality upon it, is examined in more detail in *Chapter 6*.

Superrealism is a style that emerged in the United States in the 1960s and 1970s, and is synonymous with (sometimes also called) Photorealism and Hyperrealism. It is characterised by an unnerving and incredible level of realism. Superrealist artists often imitate photographs in paint, and many of the qualities associated with a photographic image are replicated in Superrealist images, such as varying focus and a frozen image effect.

One of the pioneers of photorealism, American artist Audrey Flack (born 1931), presents in *Marilyn (Vanitas)*, 1977, a Superrealist still life as a modern-day allegory of the transience of life: a kitsch hour-glass in bubblegum pink metaphorically reminds us of time's passing, as do the other traditional vanitas objects: the candle and the fruit. The latter is so ridiculously waxed and obviously fake, it forces us to think beyond the superficial for a moment. The fruit, the lipstick, the pearls are all adornments, accessories and 'signs' of our modern age – an age defined by its consumption and commodification. As well as alluding to traditional seventeenth-century vanitas paintings, Flack updates the genre with the inclusion of a calendar, a modern object, although suitably symbolic of the transience of life and referring back to traditional images of the labours of the months.

The work's main subject, the American icon Marilyn Monroe (1926–1962) smiles as if for a publicity shot, possibly reminding us that she was consumed by her own media-made persona. Typecast as a 'dumb blonde', packaged and sold, she wound up as a 'probable suicide' victim. Little wonder that Andy Warhol used her image in the 1960s in one of a series of 'mass produced' images of celebrities. Marilyn's image is surrounded by the kinds of luxury objects that denoted her life, and yet this work becomes almost commemorative of her death. Some objects appear in sharper focus than others and this is as a result of Flack's technique: she projects the image onto the canvas and paints over it, creating an exact replica of the photographed image. How does the inaccurate perspective alter your perception of the scene? A sepia-toned photograph of the artist and her brother nestle among the objects, forging a connection between the transience of Monroe's life and the artist's. The main image of Marilyn on the right depicts her beauty but is reflected and distorted in the mirror on the left. What do you think this could mean?

1.3 Checkpoint question
According to André Félibien, writing in the seventeenth century, how were genres ranked within the academic tradition?

Flack's technique of projecting her image onto canvas and then painting it may reinforce a lack of authenticity theme. Photorealism is all about illusion after all. The paradoxical relationship between the 'false' and 'true' elements of this picture – the real Marilyn: the false persona; the real photographs: the false fruit – remind us that the hierarchy of genres and fixed rules in art were laid to rest in the early twentieth century by a series of avant-garde pioneers, most notably Picasso. Once relegated to the lowest rung in the hierarchy of genre, 'still life' has proven to be an enduring subject for artists. Despite being three centuries apart, the technical expertise of Flack's twentieth-century *Marilyn* (*Vanitas*) has much in common with Steenwyck's seventeenth-century *Vanitas*, and both paintings challenge the viewer on a number of moral and intellectual levels.

Subjects

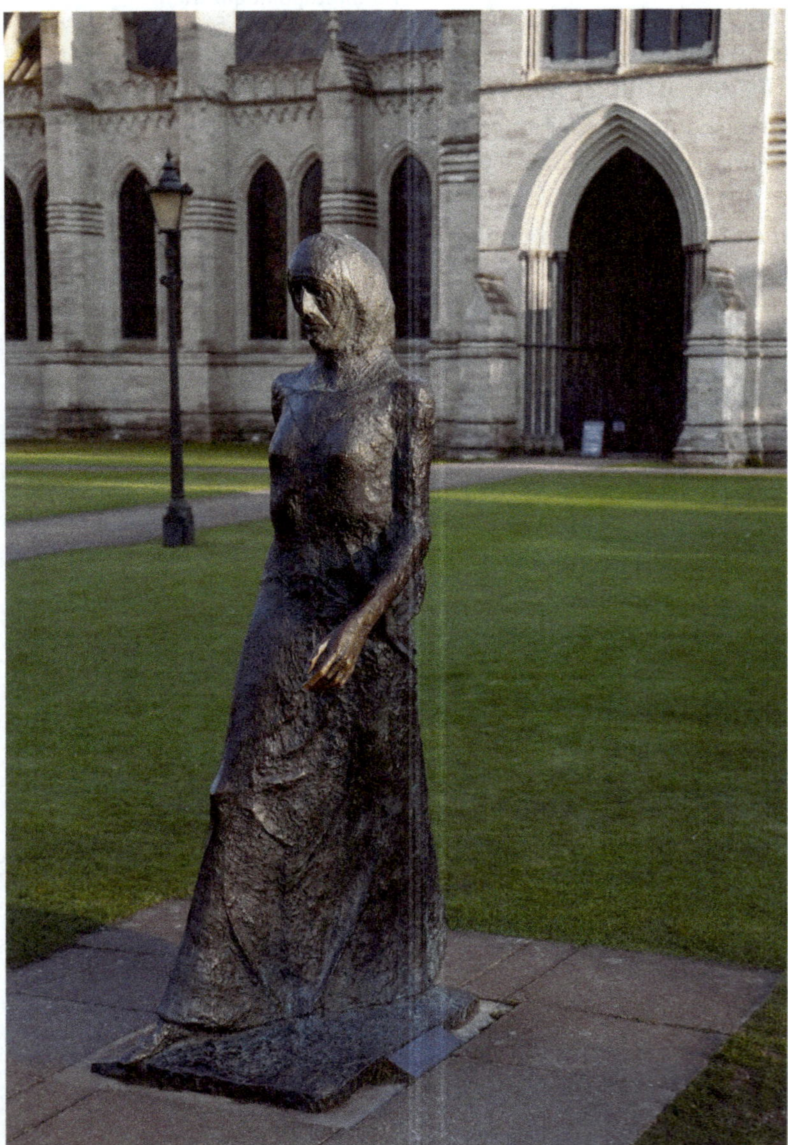

Figure 1.32 | Elisabeth Frink, *Walking Madonna*, 1981, bronze, height 182 cm, Salisbury Cathedral. Source: © Kevin George / Alamy / © Estate of Elisabeth Frink. All Rights Reserved, DACS 2015.

Subjects as a category may seem slightly confusing in its relation to genre, since genres consist of subjects, but there are so many varied subjects that they reach far beyond the confines of the hierarchy of genres. Perhaps the easiest way to settle their distinction is to view the genre as describing what a painting *is* (its category) and the subject as what it is about, or what it depicts.

Religious subjects

In this context, religious subjects are drawn from the Western world where Christianity was historically the dominant religion. Images are commonly drawn from Christian stories in the New Testament, such as the Crucifixion and Entombment of Jesus, together with other narrative scenes from His life; however, not all biblical works are based on narrative. Images of the Virgin Mary tended to be most widely depicted in the art of Catholic countries such as Italy. Christian images are almost as old as Christianity itself and it was not until the Italian Renaissance in the early fifteenth century that secular subjects became more commonplace. In modern times, religious art has tended to be less motivated by devotion than by aesthetics. As mentioned previously, stories and figures from the Bible can be included under the 'history' genre; however, they can also be treated as a subject in terms of having religious subject matter.

Madonnas

Unexpectedly positioned walking away from Salisbury Cathedral, the *Walking Madonna*, 1981, is the sole female in English sculptor Elisabeth Frink's (1930–1993) oeuvre. A strong female type, based on Frink's own face, strides away from the security of the church, her emphatic arms providing a sense of dynamism and self-reliance. She exudes a purposefulness that may be interpreted as intimidating. Atypically, this is a post-resurrection Madonna, perhaps an exemplar for the guidance of faith in a new and often doubting world. The sculpture is perhaps also semi-autobiographical, depicting the artist's strength of character and artistic independence. Look at photographs of the artist's distinguishing features and see what you think.

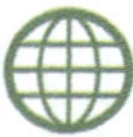

See the companion website for details of an audio interview with Elizabeth Frink.

Portrayed as striding, strong and self-reliant, perhaps one only recognises the extent of Frink's innovation on an age-old theme when we compare her Madonna with the iconic *Pietà*, 1498–1499, by Michelangelo (1475–1564). Commissioned for St. Peter's Basilica in Rome, the most important church in Christendom, Michelangelo carved his name onto the Virgin's sash to ensure he received credit for the masterpiece. This Madonna is widely regarded as an idealised beauty whose serenity is unparalleled. Her tiny frame supports the adult Christ with exquisitely carved drapery. This Virgin is dignified in mourning and her upturned-hand gesture signals the stoic resignation of her loss; she makes her own sacrifice of her son in counterpart to Christ's greater sacrifice. In this sense she provides a stark contrast with Frink's *Walking Madonna* in terms of material, technique, process, demeanour and effect on the audience. Not least, Frink expresses her interpretation of Christ's mother as symbolic of all powerful women, real women; in contrast, the Renaissance biographer Vasari congratulated Michelangelo's *Pietà* on its idealised representation of Mary: *To be sure, there are some critics, more or less fools,*

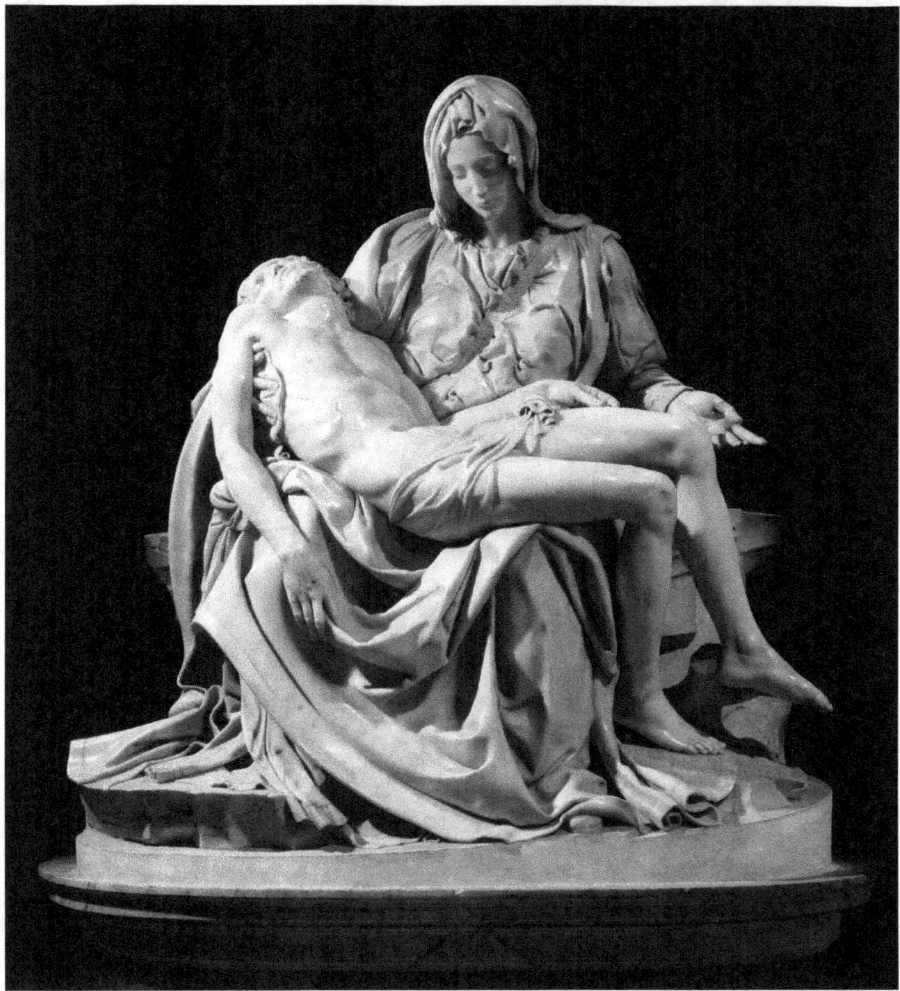

Figure 1.33 | Michelangelo, *Pietà*, 1498–1499, marble, height 174 cm, base 195 cm, depth 69 cm, Rome, St. Peter's Basilica.
Source: © 2015. White Images / Scala, Florence.

who say that he made Our Lady look too young. They fail to see that those who keep their virginity unspotted stay for a long time fresh and youthful (Vasari, *Lives of the Artists*, p. 337).

The gender of the respective artists, together with the contexts within which they made their works, is bound to have influenced these polarised representations of the same religious subject. Reverential religious iconography prevailed throughout the Renaissance; not until the arrival of Caravaggio in Rome did it become controversial.

Representations of Christ

Having already established that scenes from the Bible such as the Crucifixion, Entombment and Resurrection could be used in so-called 'history' painting, it may be surprising to learn that Caravaggio's *Entombment*, 1602–1604, has been categorised as a religious subject here. However, it may be that the

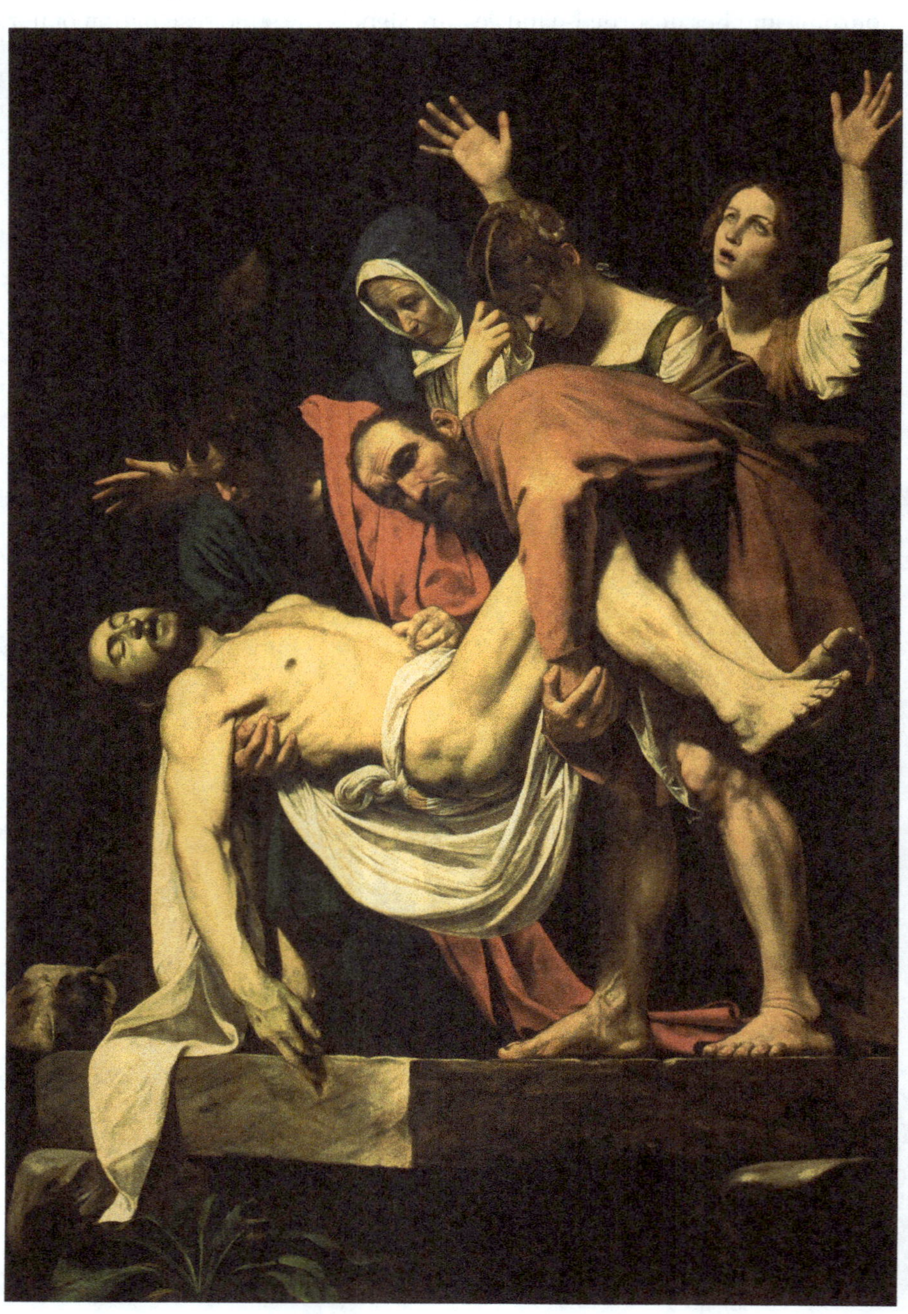

Figure 1.34 | Caravaggio, *The Entombment of Christ*, 1602–1604, oil on canvas, 300 × 203 cm, Rome, Pinacoteca Vaticana. Source: akg-images.

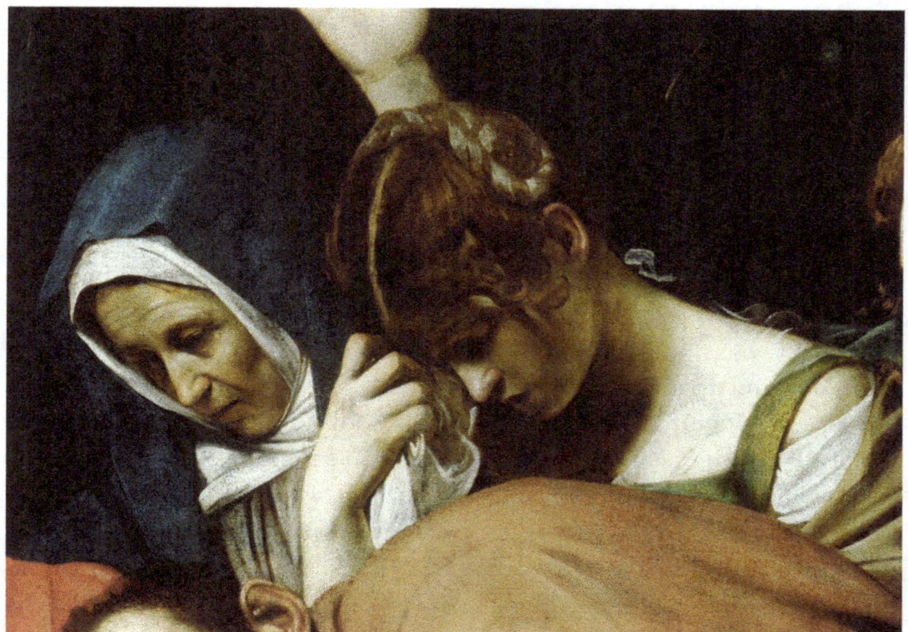

Figure 1.35 | Caravaggio, *The Entombment of Christ*, detail of Mary's face, 1602–1604, oil on canvas, 300 × 203 cm, Rome, Pinacoteca Vaticana.
Source: © 2015. Photo Scala, Florence.

artist's somewhat controversial interpretation of the scripture undermined any claims this image might have to occupancy of the highest genre. Commissioned as a monumental altarpiece for Santa Maria Vallicella, the painting typifies the form of **Baroque** style which can be referred to as naturalistic. A pyramid formation liberates it from the strict equilateral triangle typical of the Renaissance (exemplified by Michelangelo's *Pietà*), to form a diagonal composition from the splayed fingers of Mary of Cleophas (whether this figure is Mary Magdalene or Mary of Cleophas is debated), top right, to Christ's equally illuminated white shroud trailing over the stone slab, bottom left. The figures emerge theatrically from a tension-filled and tenebristic background. Christ's mourners are bent over in an undignified way, and the painting is cropped at the top, perhaps to heighten their claustrophobic sense of grief. English journalist and art critic Jonathan Jones observes:

The actors in his paintings are recognisable as actual people – often you can follow the same model from one canvas to another, posing now as Cupid, now as Saint John. They are not well-to-do people either. They are the scum of the city – prostitutes, rent boys, beggars. Caravaggio's marginal existence is fully reflected in his art, its drama conveyed by his extreme optical style, all brightness and blackness. (Jones, '*The Complete Caravaggio Part 1*') With Caravaggio's characteristic realism, the Virgin's face is depicted as old (see detail) and bears no resemblance to the unsullied beauty of Renaissance Virgins.

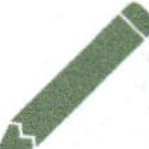

1.6 Explore this example
Ofili's religious work *The Holy Virgin Mary*, 1996, nearly caused the closure of the museum housing its exhibition. Why do you think this was? Ofili's work is examined in more detail in *Chapter 2*.

The image of Christ by American photographer Andres Serrano (born 1950) would have been inconceivable in Caravaggio's seventeenth century, and it was still considered controversial in the more secular 1980s. Serrano created the transcendental and visually spectacular photographic image *Piss Christ*, 1987, by submerging a small plastic image of Christ in a glass of his own urine, and photographing it from a close-up and raking angle. The work caused public outrage, which is something it has in common with *The Holy Virgin Mary*, 1996, by British artist Chris Ofili (born 1968), which mixes holy iconography with pornography in order to make a powerful social statement.

The nude

The nude has become one of art history's most enduring subjects and is rich terrain for exploring themes of gender and racial **stereotypes**, as well as culturally specific ideals of beauty. While the female nude has been invested with iconic status and has become synonymous with gallery visits and perhaps even art history itself, the civilisations of ancient Greece and Rome had an unparalleled aesthetic appreciation for the beauty, musculature and strength of the naked male form, and heroes, athletes and gods were commonly depicted unclothed.

Religious and mythological nudes

The Greek sculptor Myron of Eleutherae is known to have created a bronze sculpture of *The Discus-Thrower* in about 450 BCE, but all that remains are copies made in Roman times. Caught in the flush of youth, the figure is an idealised male nude captured in athletic **contrapposto** and rendered anatomically correct, if idealised, by its sculptor. His limbs, positioned in perfect equilibrium, suggest a restrained dynamism and overall harmony. *Discobolus* is one of many male nudes that comprise the masculine statuary of Antiquity.

Figure 1.36 | *The Discus-Thrower (Discobolus)*, Roman copy of a bronze original of the fifth century BCE, 152 cm high, from Hadrian's Villa in Tivoli, Lazio, Italy. London, British Museum. Source: ©The Trustees of the British Museum.

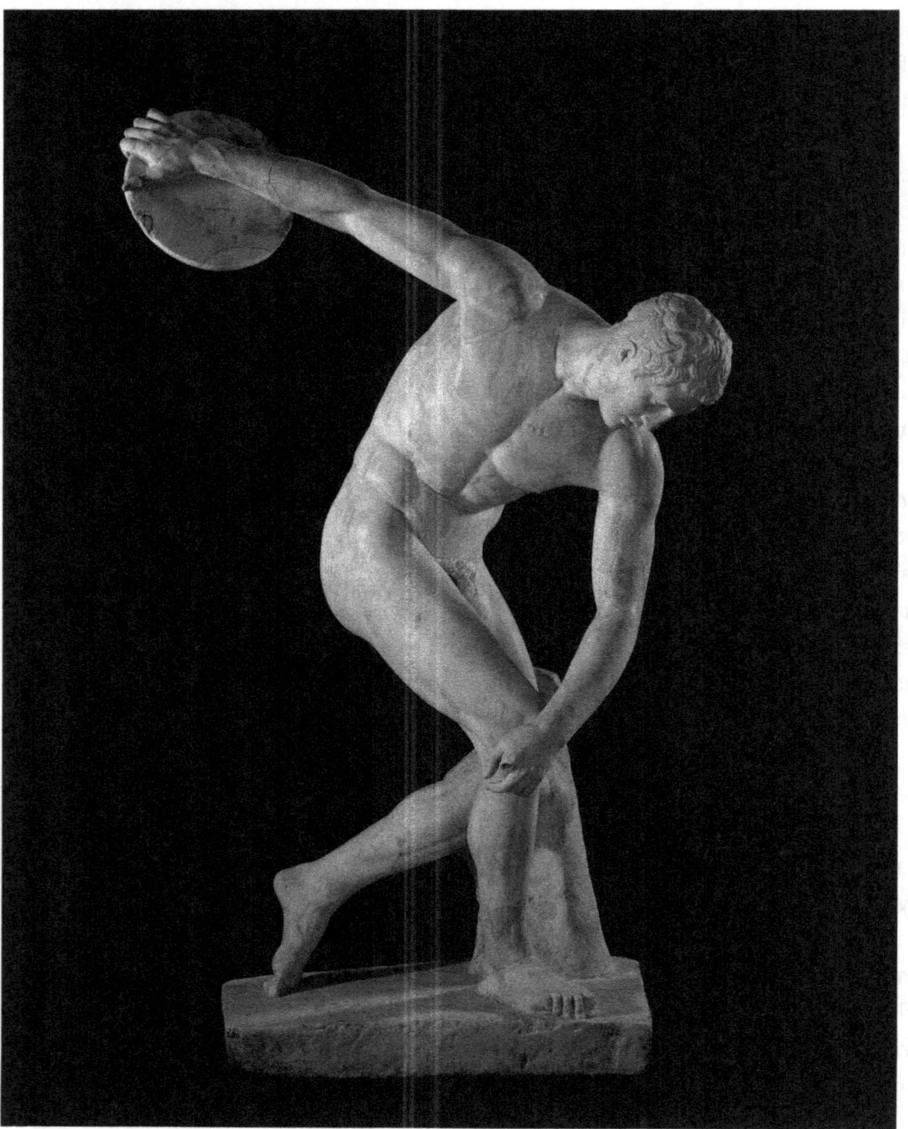

Athletes who took part in the games at Olympia (the site of the Olympic Games in Classical Greece) were said to compete naked (gymnastics comes from the word *gymos*, which means 'naked' in Greek). These men, considered the acme of male beauty, often doubled as soldiers and defenders of the *polis* (the state).

An aesthetic appreciation of the male nude is certainly not confined to Antiquity; its revival during the Renaissance reached its zenith in Michelangelo's *David*, 1501–1504, which is examined in *Chapter 5* and *Chapter 6*. There is a wide range of examples to choose from, especially from the seventeenth century to the present day: Ron Mueck's small but unnervingly realistic sculpture *Dead Dad*, 1996–1997, and his frighteningly oversized *Big Man*, 2000, are examples of the male nude made in modern materials for consumption in modern (or **postmodern**) times. Both are examined in *Chapter 2*. The work of nineteenth-century sculptor Antonio Canova exemplifies the idealised female nude. His mythological sculpture, *The Three Graces*, 1815–1817, which is based on a Classical Greek prototype, is examined in de-

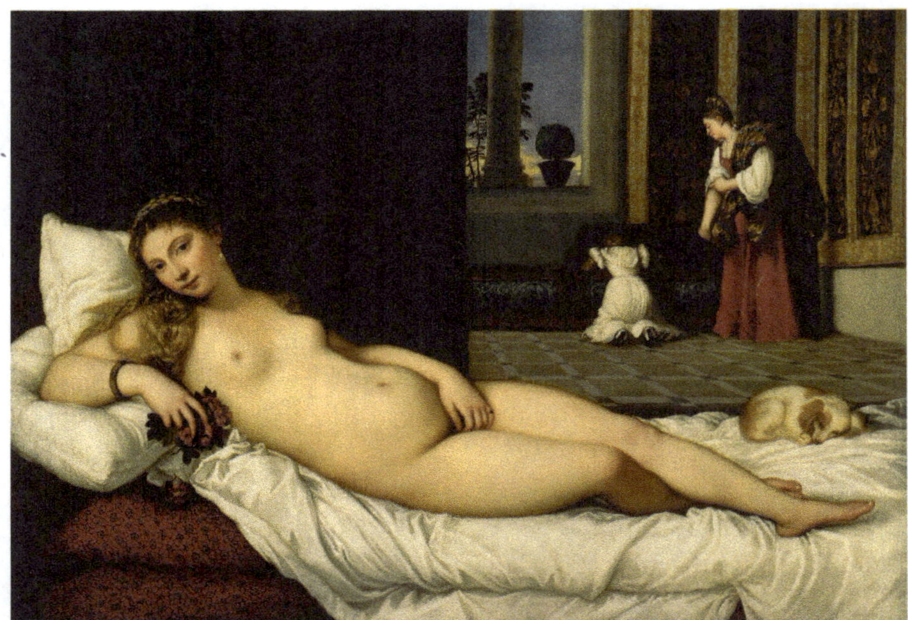

Figure 1.37 | Titian, ***Resting Venus (Venus of Urbino),*** **c.1538, oil on canvas, 119 × 165 cm, Florence, Galleria degli Uffizi. Source: akg-images.**

tail in *Chapter 3*. The nude has evolved through a number of phases, although *Mary Magdalen in the Grotto*, 1876, by French artist Jules Joseph Lefebvre (1836–1911) depicts a stereotypically languid and desirable form. Lefebvre depicts a sexually charged 'sinner' who appealed to the voyeuristic audiences of the male-orientated Salon in nineteenth-century France. See *1.7 Explore this example*.

Male control over the female nude is evident in Zoffany's *The Tribuna of the Uffizi*, 1772–1777, in which Titian's *Venus* is being honoured as the epitome of beauty by an exclusively male audience of British politicians, aristocrats and artists. Arguably, this is a manifestation of artistic 'taste'; these men represent the authority of the Western tradition in art, an authority based on the continuing reverence for Antiquity (Perry, *Gender and Art*, pp. 90–91). It would appear that mythological treatment of the female nude sanitised its eroticism.

Modern nudes

The history of art has offered up many paintings of nudes disguised as mythological Venus-types in order to satisfy the aesthetic censors in operation during their respective periods of production. Manet's *Olympia*, 1863, is no exception. She is often compared with Titian's *Venus of Urbino,* c.1538, in order to expose Manet's daring modernity. While the woman in Titian's *Venus* is depicted as gazing up coyly alongside those locks of free-flowing hair, in Manet's *Olympia* the central figure is depicted as a modern prostitute who locks onto the viewer with a confrontational stare. Titian's *Venus* cups her genitals coyly, at the same time titillating the viewer in a tickling fashion, the dog a sign of her faithfulness to one lover at a time. Manet's *Olympia* clamps a firm hand over hers, implying her ownership over her own sexuality. Olympia's flesh is tonally unmodelled and pale, unidealised in contrast to that of Venus, who looks peachy and soft. The nude in Manet's painting is depicted in a style which is avant-garde, the nude in Titian's in a style that is wholly **canonical**.

Manet's iconic nude, *Olympia*, translates Titian's canonical nude into the language of modernity – which is examined in more detail in *Chapter 4*. Its

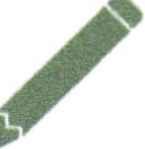

1.7 Explore this example

Examine Jules Joseph Lefebvre, *Mary Magdalen in the Grotto*, 1876. Does this strike you as a painting likely to appeal to a religious audience? Or do you think the artist was painting it with a different kind of audience in mind?

Figure 1.38 | Édouard Manet, *Olympia*, 1863, oil on canvas, 130 × 190 cm, Paris, Musée d'Orsay. Source: Musée d'Orsay, Paris, France / Bridgeman Images.

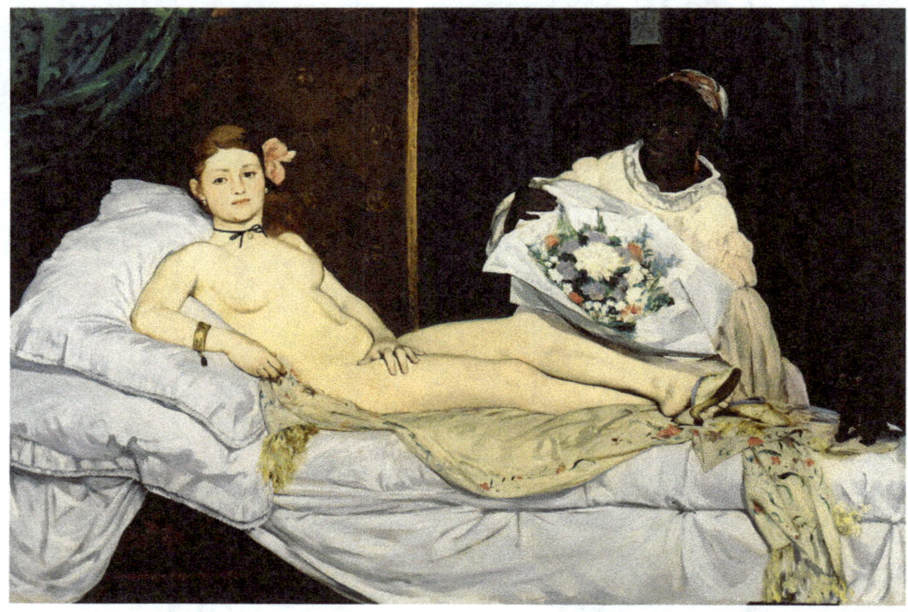

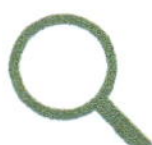

1.5 What can you see?
Look at the painting *Branded* by Jenny Saville. How has the artist represented herself? What do you think could be her motive for depicting herself in such an unexpected way?

lack of precision, direct return of the **male gaze** and pale anatomy provoked a storm of reaction when the painting was exhibited at the Paris Salon of 1865. The stark juxtaposition of her white leg against the dark background was considered too modern. The influence of **Japonisme**, particularly its propensity for unmodulated areas of paint, is probably responsible for *Olympia*'s controversial thigh. While Japonisme was considered to be avant-garde in landscape and genre, it proved to be a step too far when rendering the staple of Western art – the female nude. *Olympia* was deemed so outrageous that she was guarded by policemen at the Salon, probably because she represented a well-toned young courtesan, despite her dubiously mythological title. Her maid presents her with flowers, presumably from a client, but, so accustomed is the woman to receiving gifts, their arrival does not interrupt her glare at us. Manet's 'modern' technique and Japanese-inspired simplification of form, according to art historian Linda Nochlin, gave *a salutary jolt to the notion of the nude as timeless and elevated*, so 'problematizing' it thereafter (Nochlin, *Representing Women*, p. 219). The nineteenth-century context of *Olympia*'s production – modernity – is examined in more detail in *Chapter 4*.

A large female body has a power, it occupies a physical space, yet there's an anxiety about it. It has to be hidden.

(Jenny Saville quoted in Mackenzie, 'Under the Skin')

Best known for her large-scale modern nudes, British artist Jenny Saville (born 1970) has used herself as the model for *Branded*, 1992 – illustrating that the nude 'subject' may also feature in the 'portrait' genre, specifically, the self-portrait, in this instance. Her flesh fills the picture; this woman is monumental, and we are made to look up to her. Saville literally *brands* words such as 'decorative' and 'precious' into her painted flesh, almost as an act of self-harm. She leans back, heightening our exposure to her breasts and stomach, cropped at the hips, and so framing our attention.

We are judging her – and she knows it – but she is also judging us. Saville claims her own body by grabbing her stomach and accentuating her weight in a way which might be interpreted as cathartic. Consider a comparison with

Caravaggio's self-portrait as *David with the Head of Goliath* examined earlier in the chapter – Caravaggio confronts the 'ugly' truth – his, an epitaph, an apology: hers a rebuttal, an exorcism of body consciousness. Both artists share the ability to communicate a visceral reality that compels and repels the viewer at the same time. The composition of *Branded* is important, as Saville slants the perspective of the painting and adopts a low, close-up viewpoint. This makes the body seem to be rising above us.

The depiction of Saville's body is unidealised and verging on the monstrous. Interestingly, this photograph of the artist reveals the extent to which the self-portrait has reversed the 'idealisation-of-self' sought by earlier artists such as Dürer. In reality she is physically representative of the average woman and the discrepancy between the real Saville and her painted and mountainous self makes clear the message: to exaggerate is to confront. Saville is challenging the perpetuation of an ideological discourse by fighting flesh with flesh: an effective method – she makes us sorry for being 'fattist' in the same way that some artists examined in later chapters make us examine our own, potentially racist attitudes.

The nude is commonly associated with the female figure and, in recent decades, the examination of images of the nude throughout the centuries has tended to attract analysis from a primarily **feminist** perspective; however, *Chapter 6* returns explicitly to 'gendered' representation in art and seeks to establish a greater degree of balance in its examination of the depiction of both the male and female nude in what is a contentious area of art history.

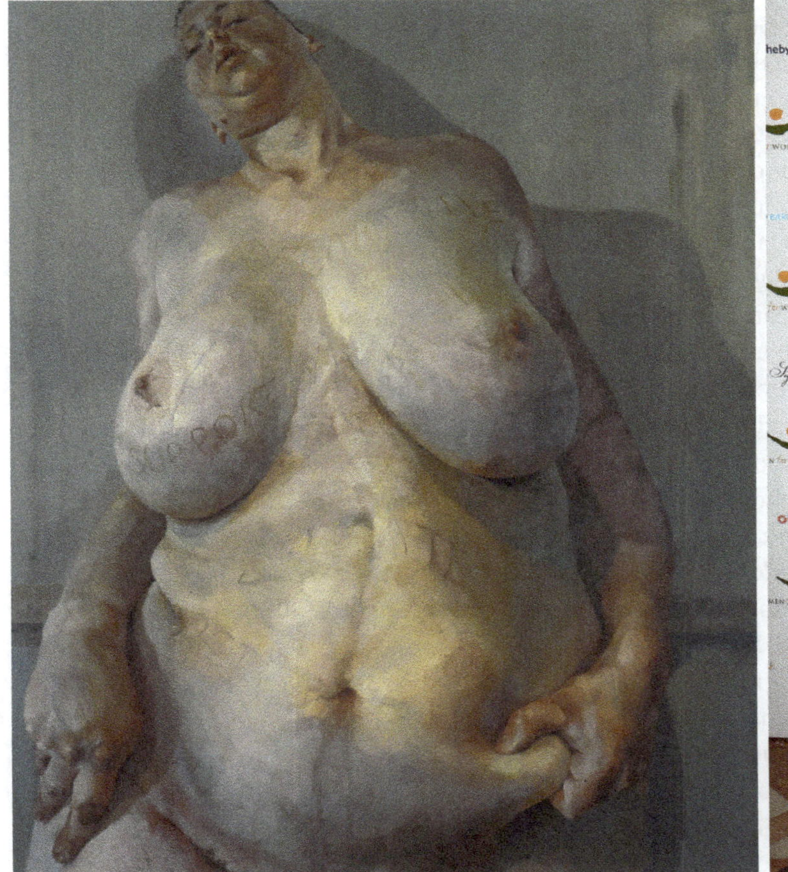

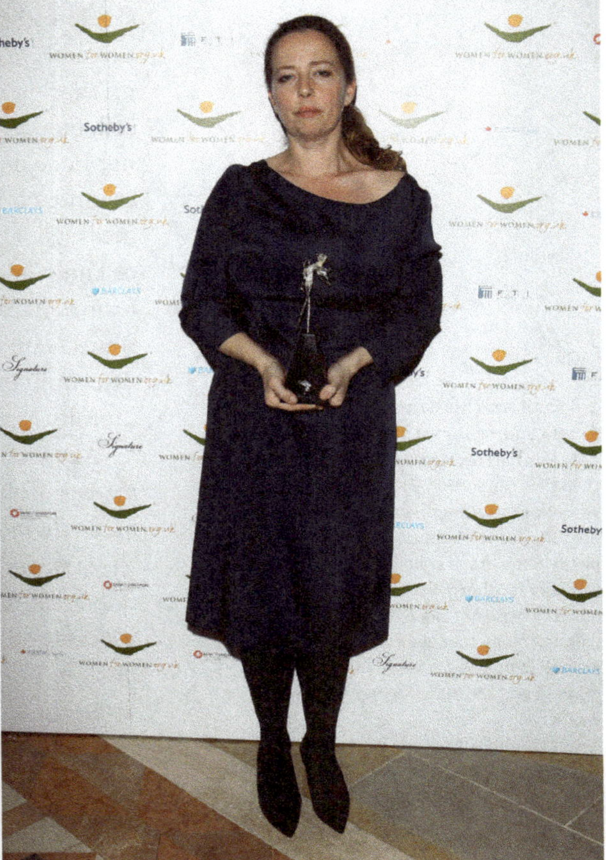

Left to right:
Figure 1.39 | Jenny Saville, *Branded*, 1992, oil on canvas, 209 × 179 cm. Source: Photo courtesy Gagosian Gallery. © Jenny Saville. All rights reserved, DACS 2015.

Figure 1.40 | Jenny Saville poses with her award at the Women for Women International Gala dinner in association with *Harper's Bazaar*, The Guildhall, London, 3 May 2012. Source: Dave M. Benett / Getty Images.

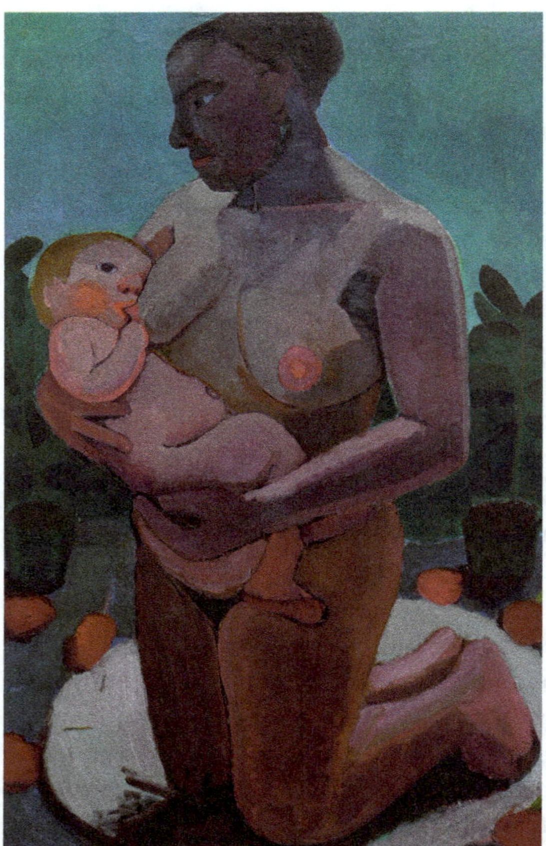

Figure 1.41 | Paula Modersohn-Becker, ***Kneeling Mother Nursing a Baby,*** **1907, oil tempera on canvas on wood, 113 × 74 cm, Berlin, SMB, Nationalgalerie. Source: akg-images.**

Motherhood: mother and child

The subject of motherhood is long-standing in the history of art, and images of maternity have featured across cultures and centuries. In the Western tradition, the Virgin Mary, mother of Christ, has often been viewed as symbolic of a mother's love, endurance and sacrifice. These qualities seem manifest in the dignified strength of Elisabeth Frink's *Walking Madonna,* and are made monumental in paint by German painter Paula Modersohn-Becker (1876–1907), an early exponent of **Expressionism**.

German painter Paula Modersohn-Becker foreshadowed German Expressionism and remained rooted to **primitivism** and the embrace of nature it entailed. In 'volkish' or folk-art fashion, her 'earth mother' is monumental and fills our field of vision. Her gaze is directed and reflected in the suckling child. Kneeling, she is physically rooted to the earth, her huge cupping hands emblematic of Mother Nature. The fruit in the background, coupled with the natural earthy colour palette, further reinforce this message. Flat blocks of colour remind us of the contemporaneous technique of Paul Gauguin – although Gauguin's arguable objectification of the female form is negated in Modersohn-Becker's treatment of the same subject. Sometimes Gauguin's young subjects are positioned and objectified by the doubly discriminatory Western, and male, gaze simultaneously; conversely, we are literally made to look up to Modersohn-Becker's image of dignified maternity.

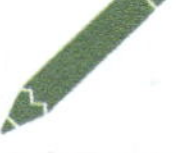

1.8 Explore this example
American-born artist Mary Cassatt depicts a far less harrowing scene of motherhood than that rendered by Kollwitz. Cassatt, who worked alongside the nineteenth-century French Impressionists, developed a particularly loose style quite fitting with the scene of motherly love depicted in *Mother about to Wash her Sleepy Child*, 1880. Despite painting many scenes of private and 'feminine' domesticity, Cassatt was an independently minded and socially progressive working woman.

American art historian Whitney Chadwick observes that *[t]he immobility, monumentality, and generalised surfaces of these self-portrait nudes place them within conventions that work to universalize the female nude as a transcendent image* (Chadwick, *Women, Art and Society*, p. 289). It is this universal image of motherhood which is rendered all the more poignant on account of Modersohn-Becker's premature death only a few days after giving birth to her first child, Mathilde.

In the same way that Modersohn-Becker used visual forms to suggest universality, another female artist, Barbara Hepworth (1905–1975), used simplification to convey a deeply maternal relationship between two abstracted forms (see Figure 1.43). This most elemental communication of motherhood is equally powerful, despite its **essentialism**, perhaps even more so. These **biomorphic** forms, one smaller and enveloped protectively by the other, represent the very essence of the maternal bond. The interplay between void and mass is **symbiotic**, and the soft, swollen forms seem distinctly female.

Käthe Kollwitz (1867–1945) was a German graphic artist and sculptor who is associated, like Modersohn-Becker, with the Expressionists. Her subjects were often tragic and always expressive of her social conscience. The etching *Woman with Dead Child*, 1903, is possibly the most poignant expression of a mother's love for a child ever expressed in such modest means. The moment of grief is raw. Her pain has reduced her to a primitive state. She morphs animalistically, almost dripping into her dead child, as if in a moment to consume the child's last breath, last smell – suggesting an unspeakable life-cycle. Like Picasso's *Guernica*, the monochrome palette of this work focuses – even forces – our attention; we feel a sense of tangible loss and grief through the most expressive use of line. There are countless images of motherhood in art history and not all of them depict the subject in association with sacrifice and endurance. Some alternative readings of motherhood will be examined in *Chapter 6*.

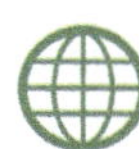

To hear an audio interview, recorded in 1961, with Barbara Hepworth discussing the influence of the Cornish landscape on her work, visit the companion website.

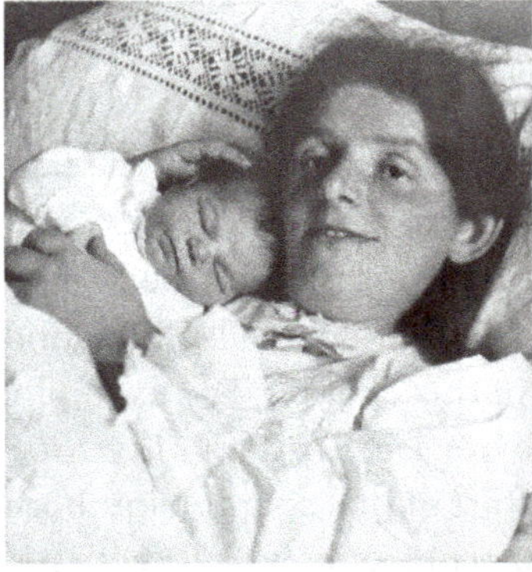

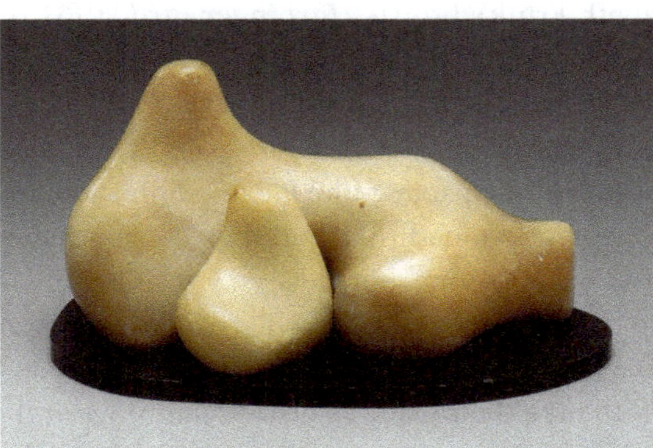

Left to right:
Figure 1.42 | Hugo Erfurth: Paula Modersohn-Becker with her daughter Mathilde, November 1907, Paula-Modersohn-Becker-Stiftung, Bremen.
Source: Paula-Modersohn-Becker-Stiftung, Bremen / © DACS 2015.

Figure 1.43 | Barbara Hepworth, *Mother and Child*, 1934, alabaster, height 230 cm, Private Collection.
Source: Private Collection / Photo © Christie's Images / Bridgeman Images / © Bowness, Hepworth Estate.

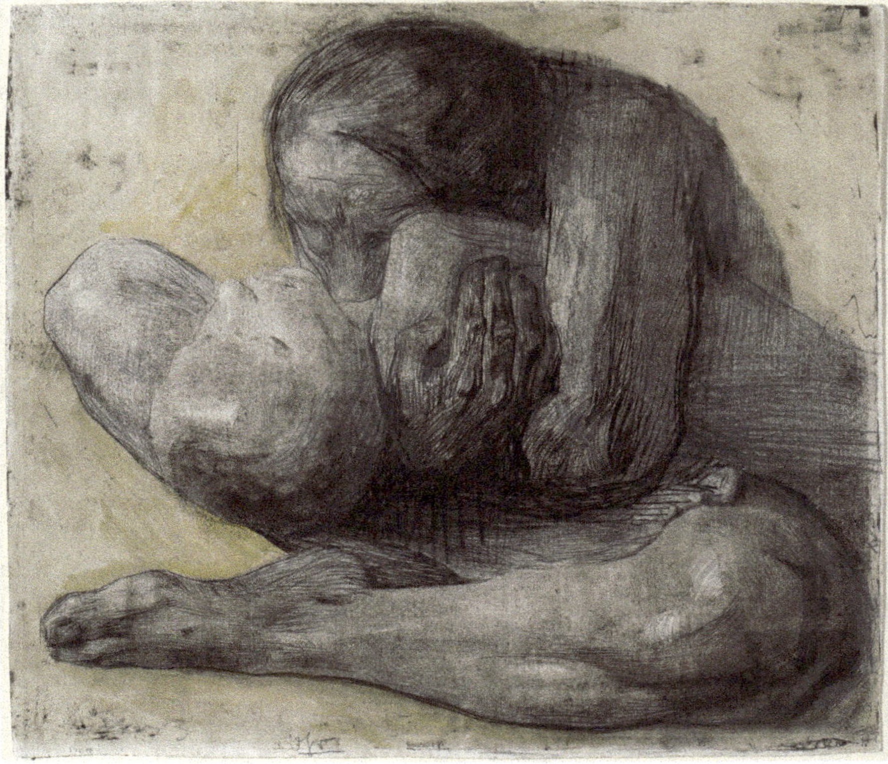

Figure 1.44 | Käthe Kollwitz, *Woman with Dead Child*, 1903, engraving and softground etching retouched with black chalk, graphite and metallic gold paint on heavy wove paper (trial proof), sheet (trimmed to and within plate mark), 41.7 × 47.2 cm, Washington, National Gallery of Art, Gift of Philip and Lynn Straus, in Honor of the 50th Anniversary of the National Gallery of Art 1988.67.1.
Source: Courtesy National Gallery of Art, Washington / © DACS 2015.

Animals

Animals have appeared in art history throughout the centuries, from ancient cave paintings 40,000 years ago to the present day. Perhaps on account of their long-standing, if changing, relationship to humankind, the subject is a frequently revisited one. They have appeared as sacred objects, as mythological beasts and as much-loved companions and champions. English painter Sir Edwin Landseer's *The Monarch of the Glen*, 1851, is an animal painting that replicates a history painting. The artist gives the deer the same saintly expression as Renaissance artist Raphael (Raffaello Sanzio da Urbino, 1483–1520)'s *Saint Catherine*, c.1507, for example; and the canvas is certainly on the scale of a history painting too. The spectrum of animal depiction is as vast as any other subject – ranging from extreme **naturalism** to near abstraction. The subject of animals may also be examined using examples from elsewhere in the book. For example, George Stubbs' painting *Whistlejacket*, c.1762 (*Chapter 5*), Constantin Brancusi's bronze *Bird in Space*, c.1928, and Elisabeth Frink's bronze *Harbinger Bird*, 1961 (*Chapter 2*).

War: heroisation and protest

War is also a long-standing subject in art. War may be depicted from the perspective of a pacifist like Picasso in his iconic anti-war manifesto, *Guernica*, or commissioned to accurately and meticulously depict military personnel and events. Some subjects may stand alone while others may also be found in the hierarchy of genres discussed at the start of this chapter. For example, David's *Oath of the Horatii* and Francisco de Goya's *The Third of May 1808* both take their place as history paintings at the start of this chapter, but both may also be discussed as images which depict the subject of war. David's heroic figures painted in the Neo-classical style arguably fuelled the authority of the prevailing political regime in France, while Goya's Romanticism seems to blend with the passion of his protest against the brutality of Napoleon's troops in Spain.

Similarly protesting against violence, but in a twentieth-century context, American artist Jenny Holzer (born 1950) worked in the male-dominated world of TV, advertising and billboards before becoming an award-winning artist. The German word *Lustmord* translates as 'sex murder' and is the title of a controversial project of 1993 that addresses the taboo issues of rape and murder of women during times of war. The project comprised LED signs, photographs of tattooed skin (shown here) and the remains of human bones, both male and female, inscribed with text. Collectively, the work relates to the Bosnian war in Yugoslavia (1992–1995) and, specifically, the artist's response to sexual violence against women.

With characteristic candour, Holzer invades the flesh of women with the language of violence. Her subjects gave their blood, which was mixed with ink, voluntarily, to the project. The textual element of the project is divided into three voices: Perpetrator, Victim and Observer (someone who may or may not intervene). Each one describes a scene of a murderous rape. In presenting us with three positions, the artist hopes that the viewer will feel compelled to *take a stance* (Joselit, Simon and Salecl, *Jenny Holzer,* p. 48).[8] The perpetrator describes the woman's submission to him: *I step on her hands*. The victim responds: *with you inside me comes the knowledge of my Death*. Holzer takes the viewer to the darkest, hidden side of war. Helplessness, inno-

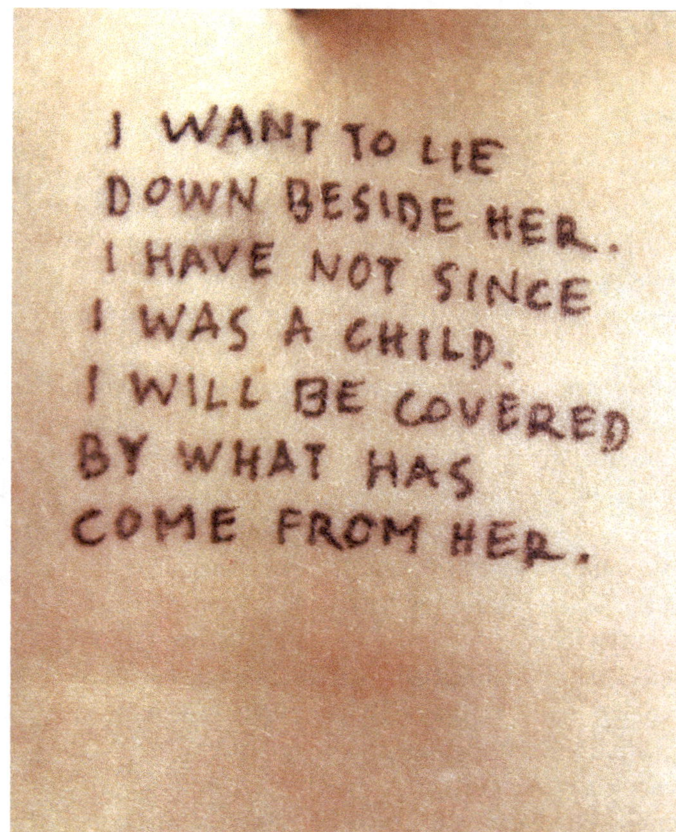

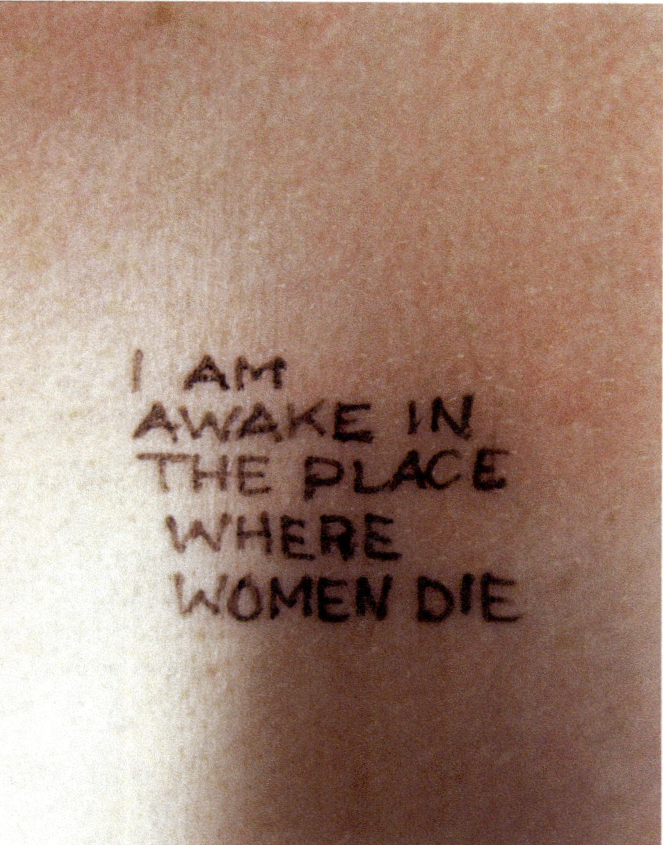

Figure 1.45 | Jenny Holzer, *Lustmord*, 1993, ink on skin: cibachrome print, 33 × 50.8 cm. Source: Photo: Alan Richardson / Courtesy: Jenny Holzer / Art Resource, NY / © Jenny Holzer. ARS, NY and DACS, London 2015.

cence and suffering pervade the entire project. The body is the scene of violation and so becomes Holzer's means for expression. There may, as the artist herself concedes, be elements of autobiography in her work: *My mother, Virginia Holzer, died in 1993. Thoughts about her appeared in* Lustmord, *but I could not describe the size and import of her death … My mother's death was especially difficult because she may have suffered sexual assault of which she did not speak. I was attacked by the man who may have harmed her* (Joselit, Simon and Salecl, *Jenny Holzer*, p. 111).

Artists' depictions of war and violence have prevailed throughout the centuries; the heroic aspect of the battle exemplified in works such as David's *Oath of Horatii* are no longer fit for purpose in a society where mass literacy and critical engagement are heavyweight challenges to the status quo (the existing state of things). Art has always had the power to persuade; the question is, do artists have a moral duty to respond to politics and particularly war? Early twentieth-century expressionist Käthe Kollwitz certainly thought so, as did twenty-first-century mixed-media artist Jenny Holzer. With the subject of war's continued relevance today, people's inhumanity to each other appears to be an aspect of human existence that continues to provide one of many subjects for the artist to represent.

8 Holzer's oeuvre is gripping and deeply uncomfortable viewing at times. Only a fraction of her *Lustmord* project is revealed here and her work is worthy of far greater consideration.

Chapter Summary Exercise

Using the words below complete the Chapter Summary. Each word or term should be used only once.

natural
morally
identity
vanitas
skill
emotions
lowest
large
power
subject matter
abstracted
best
human figures
small
low
ordinary

The 'hierarchy of genres' was adopted because it embodied Renaissance values about what constituted the '__________' types of art. In Italy, during the Renaissance, most art was patronised by the church and tended to convey __________ uplifting messages on a __________ and public scale. While history paintings were judged to be the highest of the genres, landscapes and still life, which did not feature any figures, suffered a __________ ranking, in comparison.

The status portrait was quite often more concerned with conveying the sitter's status and __________ – than with the conveyance of an accurate likeness. The validity or faithfulness of a portrait also needs to be tempered by the fact that some sitters may have had a vested interest in manufacturing their own public __________.

Genre scenes characteristically feature figures and are distinguished from other genres such as portrait and history on account of their depiction of __________ people and unidentifiable people.

Traditionally, landscape relates to our __________, rather than man-made, environment. Landscape can also refer to scenes of human activity. Landscapes are not always faithful representations; they may be expressions of the artist's __________ or even __________ representations.

Still life, devoid of __________ and demonstrative of artistic __________ rather than imagination and intellect, occupied the __________ rung in the hierarchy of genres. __________ are examples of still life with religious overtones, and often concern the morality bound with human behaviour. Still life paintings were traditionally __________ in scale, in accordance with their status and likelihood of hanging in a private dwelling.

Subjects, as opposed to genres, can be somewhat confusing insofar as genres consist of subjects but subjects are so many and varied they reach far beyond the confines of the hierarchy of genres. Genre describes what a painting is and subject informs you of the painting's __________ (what it is about).

Checkpoint Answers

1.1 Why is scale so important to the history genre?
Residing at the top of the hierarchy of genres, the history genre is intended to elevate the morals of its viewers who are usually intended to view such a work in a large public space.

1.2 Can you identify any paintings that fall into two separate genres simultaneously?
Jacques-Louis David's *Death of Marat* (1793) is both an example of the history genre and the portrait genre. Thomas Gainsborough's *Mr and Mrs Andrews* (c.1749) is both an example of the portrait genre and the landscape genre.

1.3 According to André Félibien, writing in the seventeenth century, how were genres ranked within the academic tradition?
History, portrait, genre, landscape, still life.

References

The AQA A-level History of Art Specification has been used to form chapter introductions, definitions of themes, concepts and exam practice.

Baudelaire, C. *Art in Paris 1845–62: Salons and Other Exhibitions*, Phaidon, 1965.

Carroll, M.D. 'In the Name of God and Profit: Jan van Eyck's *Arnolfini* Portrait', *Representations*, No. 44, 1993.

Chadwick, W. *Women, Art and Society*, 4th ed., Thames & Hudson, 2007.

Edwards, S. *Art and Its Histories: A Reader*, Yale University Press / Open University, 1999.

Harris, J. *Art History: The Key Concepts*, Routledge, 2008.

Jones, J. 'The Complete Caravaggio Part 1', *The Guardian*, 16 February 2005, http://www.theguardian.com/culture/2005/feb/17/1.

Jones, J. 'The Complete Caravaggio Part 3', *The Guardian*, 16 February 2005, http://www.theguardian.com/culture/2005/feb/17/3.

Joselit, D. , Simon, J. and Salecl, R. (ed.) *Jenny Holzer*, Phaidon, 2003.

Kleiner, F.S. *Gardner's Art Through the Ages: The Western Perspective*, 13th ed., Wadsworth, 2009.

Mackenzie, S. 'Under the Skin', *The Guardian*, 22 October 2005, http://www.theguardian.com/artanddesign/2005/oct/22/art.friezeartfair2005.

National Gallery, 'The Arnolfini Portrait', n.d., http://www.nationalgallery.org.uk/paintings/jan-van-eyck-the-arnolfini-portrait.

Nochlin, L. *Representing Women*, Thames & Hudson, 1999.

Panofsky, E. 'Jan van Eyck's *Arnolfini* Portrait', *The Burlington Magazine for Connoisseurs*, Vol. 64, No. 372, 117–119, 122–127.

Perry, G. (ed.) *Gender and Art*, Yale University Press / Open University Press, 1999.

Powell, C. 'US Secretary of State's Address to the United Nations Security Council', *The Guardian*, 5 February 2003.

Roskill, M. (ed.) *The Letters of Vincent van Gogh*, Flamingo, 1963.

Schnapp, J. and Tiews, M. *Crowds*, Stanford University Press, 2006.

Treuherz, J. *Victorian Painting*, Thames & Hudson, 1997.

Vasari, G. *Lives of the Artists*, Vol. 1, Penguin, 1987. (First published 1550.)

Other Useful Sources

Baudelaire, C. 'On the Heroism of Modern Life', in *The Painter of Modern Life and Other Essays*, Phaidon, 1995. (First published 1846.)

Belsey, A. and Belsey, C. 'Icons of Divinity: Portraits of Elizabeth I' in Gent, L. and Llewellyn, N. (eds.) *Renaissance Bodies: The Human Figure in English Culture, c.1540–1660*, Reaktion Books, 1990.

Berger, J. *Ways of Seeing*, Penguin, 2008. (First published 1972.)

Blazwick, I. and Wilson, S. *Tate Modern: The Handbook*, Tate Publishing, 2000.

Clark, K. *Landscape into Art*, John Murray, 2008. (First published 1949.)

De Leeuw, R. (ed.) *The Letters of Vincent van Gogh*, trans. Pomerans, A., Penguin, 1997.

Honour, H. and Fleming, J. *The World History of Art*, 6th ed., Laurence King, 2002.

Montias, J.M. *Vermeer and His Milieu: A Web of Social History*, Princeton University Press, 1989.

Ovid, *Metamorphoses*, books I–VIII, trans. Justus Miller, F., rev. by Goold, G.P., Loeb Classical Library, 2004.

Panofsky, E. *Perspective as Symbolic Form*, trans. Wood, C., Zone Books, 2009. (First published 1927.)

West, S. *Portraiture*, Oxford University Press, 2004.

Chapter 2
Materials, Techniques and Processes

Learning Outcomes

By the end of this chapter you will be able to:

- define the concepts of materials, techniques and processes in relation to painting, sculpture and architecture
- outline the qualities of various materials
- describe the many different ways in which artists and architects have used the properties of their chosen mediums to help them determine the appearance and interpretation of painting, sculpture and architecture
- analyse the ways in which artists have overcome the apparent limitations of different media
- compare and contrast different works of art and architecture of similar or different types which have been made using different materials, techniques and processes.

Thinking About Art: A Thematic Guide to Art History, First Edition. Penny Huntsman.

Chapter Map

This chapter map provides a visual overview of Chapter 2 – 'Materials, Techniques and Processes' – together with its key works.

Painting: Timeless and Honoured

Fresco: all in a day's work

– Giotto di Bondone (c.1267–1337), *The Lamentation of Christ*, c.1305

Tempera: jewel-like Madonnas

– Duccio di Buoninsegna (c.1255/60 – c.1318/19), *Maestà (Enthroned Madonna and Child with Angels and Saints)*, 1311
– Masaccio (1401–1428/29), *The Virgin and Child*, 1426

Oil: versatile and enduring

– Jan van Eyck (c.1390–1441), *The Arnolfini Portrait*, 1434

Acrylic: modern detachment

– David Hockney (born 1937), *Mr and Mrs Clark and Percy*, 1970–1971
– Marcus Harvey (born 1963), *Myra*, 1995

Other Media

Modern mixed media

– Chris Ofili (born 1968), *The Holy Virgin Mary*, 1996

Spray-paint: anti-art rebellion

Screen printing: the language of signs

– Barbara Kruger (born 1945), *Untitled (Thinking of You)*, 1999–2000

Sculpture

Marble: traditional aesthetics

– Gian Lorenzo Bernini (1598–1680), *Apollo and Daphne*, 1624

Bronze: timeless and dark

– Constantin Brancusi (1876–1957), *Bird in Space*, c.1928
– Elisabeth Frink (1930–1993), *Harbinger Bird IV*, 1961

Wood: in the service of devotion and expression

– Gregorio Fernández (1576–1636), *Dead Christ*, c.1625–1630
– Georg Baselitz (born 1938), *Untitled (Figure with Raised Arm)*, 1982–1984

Non-traditional art materials: deceptive perfection

– Ron Mueck (born 1958), *Dead Dad*, 1996–1997

Readymade: courting controversy

– Tracey Emin (born 1963), *My Bed*, 1998

Architecture

Wood, masonry and tile construction

– Filippo Brunelleschi (1377–1446), Dome of Florence Cathedral, 1420–1436
– Philip Webb (1831–1915), Red House, 1859–1860

Steel, concrete and glass

– Richard Rogers (born 1933), Lloyd's Building, 1978–1986

Introduction

This chapter introduces you to the various materials, techniques and processes used by artists and architects. It will allow you to compare and contrast art and architecture in various materials spanning more than five centuries, although examples may be drawn from the entire book, and beyond, from the time of **Classical Antiquity**. The term **material** is used interchangeably with **medium** to describe the physical elements used by artists and architects in the creation of works of art and architecture.

Painters have used a variety of painting materials through the ages, such as natural and, later, chemical pigment in **fresco**, egg **tempera**, watercolour and oil. More contemporary materials include **acrylics**, household emulsions and 'mixed media' – a range of different materials all in one work. Sculptors have traditionally used materials such as wood, marble and bronze, but contemporary artists also use 'non-art' materials, such as cardboard, plastic and everyday household items. In architecture, the form of a building is often dictated by an architect's choice of materials, such as stone, brick, concrete, cast or wrought iron, **reinforced concrete**, steel, glass and aluminium. Various materials have been used to clad buildings such as glass, cedar shingles (thin wooden tiles which overlap) and titanium.

Techniques and processes describe the various methods used in the creative process. In painting, knowledge that oil can be applied thickly in **impasto** or thinly in **glazes** affects our understanding of the artwork. Brushwork may be fine and disguised, thickly applied with a palette knife or stencilled. In sculpture, it is important to know the differences between carving and modelling, and about the **subtractive**/reductive processes (removal of stone and wood) in direct carving, the **additive process** (modelling in a soft medium such as clay), and casting (**lost-wax process**), **assemblage**, and the lack of process involved in **readymades** and **found objects**. In architecture, we should be able to recognise whether a building has been erected brick by brick or largely **prefabricated** off site and moved to the location where they are assembled.

Painting: Timeless and Honoured

Painting is typically paint applied to a flat surface and comprises **pigment** mixed with a **binder**, to hold the particles of the pigment together, and a **thinner** (or vehicle), to render the substance liquid so that it can flow from the brush. The type of paint used, or its combinations with other materials, has a tremendous effect on the look of a painting and on our interpretation of it. The range of coloured pigments available during earlier centuries (before the advent of the chemical industry and when only natural materials were used) was limited and so the colour palette and relatively muted tones of fourteenth-century paintings are in stark contrast to the extensive colour range and vibrant tones of the early twentieth century. Every material has its own characteristics, but the effects of a material such as paint can vary, depending on the artist's choice of technique and even the size and type of brush they use.

Fresco: all in a day's work

Fresco, a method of painting rather than a material, has been around since before the time of Christ. Fresco is made using **lime-proof pigments** and water, and is painted into the surface of a freshly lime-plastered wall. The paint is then absorbed into the wall itself as the plaster (which serves as the binder) dries. This makes the finished artwork extremely durable and sufficiently stable to last for centuries. Part of its charm, though it may perhaps appear a disadvantage to an art-loving public, is that true fresco is not portable; we must make a pilgrimage to view the work in its original site.[9] The particular materials, techniques and processes of fresco make it particularly susceptible to damage from damp, earthquake and subsidence. True fresco (**buon**), as opposed to dry fresco (**secco**), is a more time-consuming technique. The artist was able to paint the wet plaster only in sections, which became known as **giornate**, or a day's work, because once dry the plaster would fail to absorb the pigment. Timing errors would have to be removed ready for the next giornate.

Close examination of *The Lamentation of Christ* by Florentine artist Giotto di Bondone (c.1267–1337) reveals the lines that distinguish one day's work from another. It appears that one day equated, loosely, to one angel. Giotto has tried to match the blue colour of the sky in each section but the process was beyond his capability or that of science; the only pure blues available to him in fourteenth-century Italy were the minerals **lapis lazuli** and **azurite**. Lapis was too expensive for large areas and azurite reacted with the lime in the plaster and changed colour, so Giotto had to apply the blue azurite *secco* fresco, meaning he mixed the pigment with egg yolk and water and applied it to the wall when the plaster dried. Consequently, it has deteriorated more than the **buon fresco** areas, creating more of a 'jigsaw puzzle' than **celestial** effect. The painting's imperfections provide us with tremendous insight into the processes and techniques behind its production. The limited colour palette available at this time (largely earth colours), coupled with the lime

9 There are examples where frescos have been removed from the wall; the National Gallery in London has some by Pintoricchio (originally Bernardino di Betto (Benedetto)) and Domenichino, (originally Domenico Zampieri) for example.

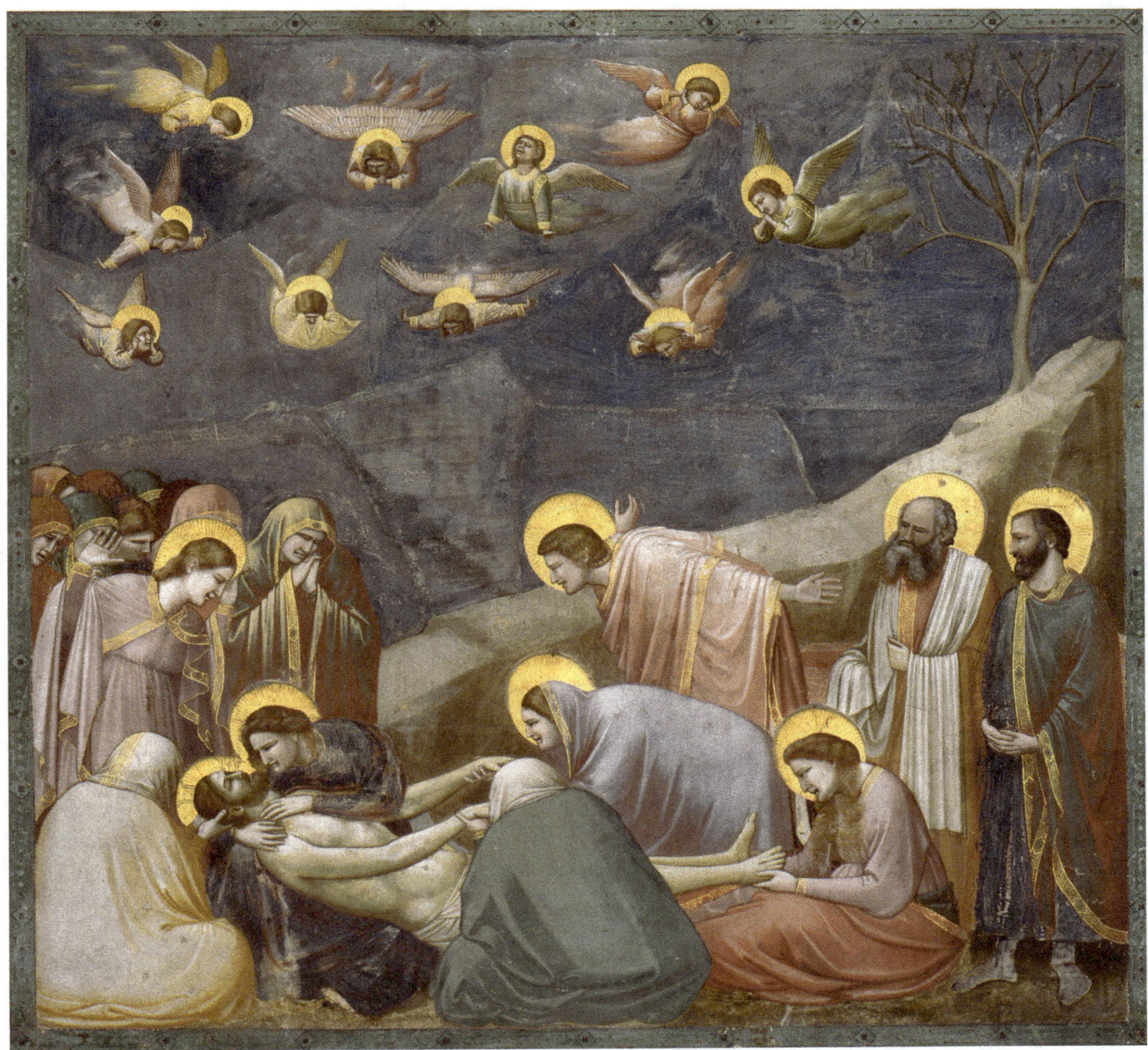

Figure 2.1 | Giotto di Bondone, *The Lamentation of Christ*, c.1305, from the series with scenes from the life of Mary and Christ, fresco, approx. 185 × 200 cm, Padua, Cappella degli Scrovegni. Source: akg-images / Cameraphoto.

plaster, producing slightly insipid and pastel effects, may be regarded as detrimental, but fresco's subtle chalkiness and prized longevity distinguish it from other mediums.

Tempera: jewel-like Madonnas

Sienese artist Duccio di Buoninsegna (c.1255/60–c.1318/19) painted the central panel, *Maestà (Enthroned Madonna and Child with Angels and Saints)*, of the altarpiece for Siena Cathedral on poplar wood, a tree indigenous to central Italy. Wood panels were glued together, planed smooth and the surface stabilised using layers of **gesso**, sanded between coats. This acted as a primer for the application of tempera. The use of **gold leaf** was prevalent at this time and entirely fitting as a medium to mirror the status of the Virgin Mary. The artist's use of gold, an expensive material, to represent the majesty of the scene would have caught nearby candlelight and made the image gleam with a seemingly divine light. Befitting the Virgin's status, Duccio paints the

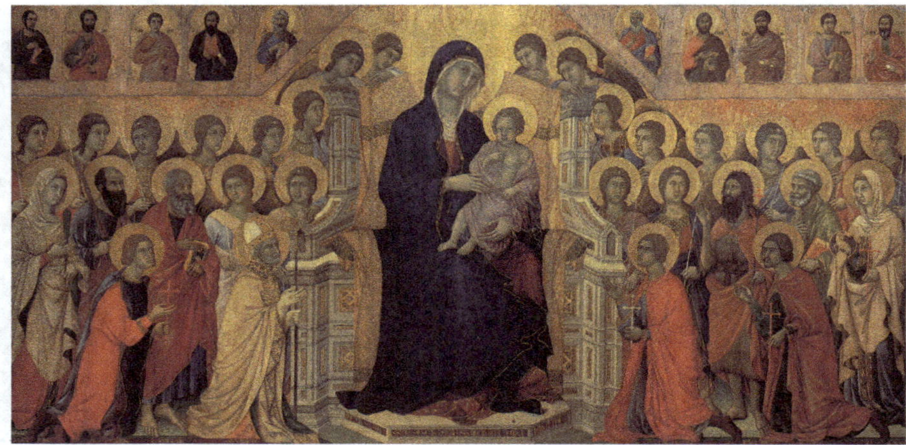

Figure 2.2 | Duccio di Buoninsegna, *Maestà (Enthroned Madonna and Child with Angels and Saints)*, 1311, formerly the high altar of the Duomo in Siena, tempera and gold ground on wood panel, 211 × 426 cm, Siena, Museo dell'Opera Metropolitana. Source: akg-images / MPortfolio / Electa.

Duccio has made the Madonna and Christ Child larger than the surrounding figures to indicate their importance. What other techniques has he used to show this?

Virgin's blue-black robe using the ground material of the semi-precious stone, lapis lazuli.

Highly valued as an expensive and rare material, gold was commonly reserved for use in the creation of sacred objects. Gold leaf application, known as gilding, was undertaken prior to painting on a dark red clay substance known as 'bole'. The thinly beaten (and fragile) gold leaf adheres to the 'bole' and creates a warm marriage of colour. The gilded area is then burnished to a polish and also allows for the further adhesion to the bole underneath. At this point the surface is **tooled** or incised for decoration.

Tempera uses the yolk of an egg mixed with water and, like modern acrylic paint, it dries very quickly, making **modelling** particularly difficult. Shading is indicated by juxtaposing two slightly different tones using **hatching** and **cross-hatching**, and the outcome can be fairly two-dimensional and stiff. Tempera needs to be applied in thin layers, as impasto techniques are not suited to the medium. The flatness of the medium in Duccio's work lacks **verisimilitude** but heightens its decorativeness.

2.1 Let's connect the themes: form and style – formal characteristics of the Gothic style (see also Chapter 3)

A work of art's materials, techniques and processes are inextricably linked with its form and style. Many of the formal elements present in Duccio's painting comprise its **Gothic** style. The form of Duccio's Madonna is revealed through her drapery; however, her fleshy realism is held at bay by the artist who is, on balance, more interested in her devotional purpose. Scale is used to signal importance, known as **hierarchical scale**, rather than render three-dimensional space realistic; and the arrangement of colour and line provides a balance which constitutes a highly ordered composition far more decorative than naturalistic. The blaze of gold and use of gold leaf is a signature of the Gothic style, as are the elongated figures. Similarly, in Gothic architecture, scale is vast in accordance with the glory of God; and God – who is light – is made manifest in monumental stained-glass windows which dazzle like jewels to create an otherworldly experience for the worshipper.

Duccio uses a range of techniques to indicate the status of the Virgin and the Christ Child, including making them proportionally larger than other figures in the painting, positioning them on the central vertical axis, and making the Madonna's head the apex of a compositional pyramid that is pointing heavenwards. The Madonna is flanked on either side by an equal number of heavenly bodies, every repeated face only enhancing the overall feeling of symmetry and balance.

Although the rules of **linear perspective** had not yet been codified, some attempt is evident in the Virgin's throne, although the effect is quite illusory on the corners: unintentionally, they appear either to recede or to advance, according to the individual viewer's perception. This lack of linear perspective, along with the incorrect anatomical proportion and **foreshortening**, make the work appear quite rigid and unnatural. However, as Duccio's *Maestà* was primarily a sacred object intended to inspire devotion, its lack of **naturalism** was not considered a failing. In fact, Duccio was one of the first artists to aspire to naturalism, evident in the drapery of the figures in the foreground, which give the impression of falling away softly and naturally. And while the figures in the top row all face the front, those in the foreground move more realistically around the seated Virgin. The materials, techniques and processes render it so decorative, symbolic and compelling that even in these increasingly secular times their images endure, especially in the form of Christmas cards.

Figure 2.3 | Masaccio, *The Virgin and Child*, 1426, egg tempera on wood, 134.8 × 73.5 cm, London, National Gallery. Bought with a contribution from The Art Fund, 1916. Acc. no.: 1772. Source: © 2015. Copyright The National Gallery, London / Scala, Florence.

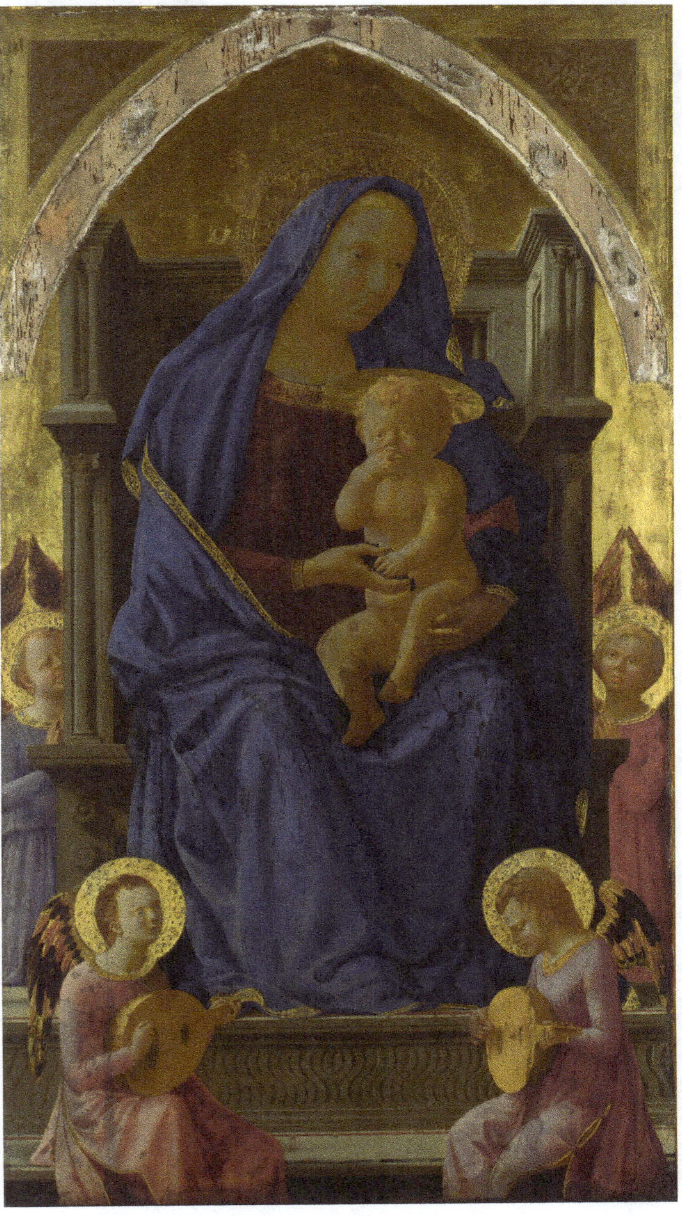

Duccio's style was influenced by the rich and decorative pattern of **Byzantine mosaic**. Its aesthetic is largely due to the artist's use of a strong, clear line to define mass. A tempera and gilded version of a mosaic icon, the Virgin sits in an 'otherworldly' and hierarchical realm. Her symbolic might is not weakened by her two-dimensional simplicity. Duccio uses line rather than modelling to achieve the faint illusion of drapery.

Masaccio (originally Tommaso di Ser Giovanni di Simone, 1401–1428/29), a painter of the **Early Renaissance**, became well known for the **polyptych** altarpiece for a church in Pisa, of which this is the central panel. He uses a traditional pyramidal composition, symbolic colours and gold leaf applied to the surface, all of which are legacies of the style known as **International Gothic**. The gold has been tooled to provide a decorative pattern, in contrast to the **ultramarine** (lapis lazuli) of the Virgin's robes. If you look carefully at Masaccio's work, you can see the subtle variation of texture created in the halo and decorative trim of the Virgin's robes. Tooling and possibly a **stylus** have been used to incise the gold surface (although not an innovation) and this decorative technique enables light to reflect off the small indentations and provide the impression of illumination.

Masaccio has used tempera, a quick-drying medium, which may account for the rather flat appearance

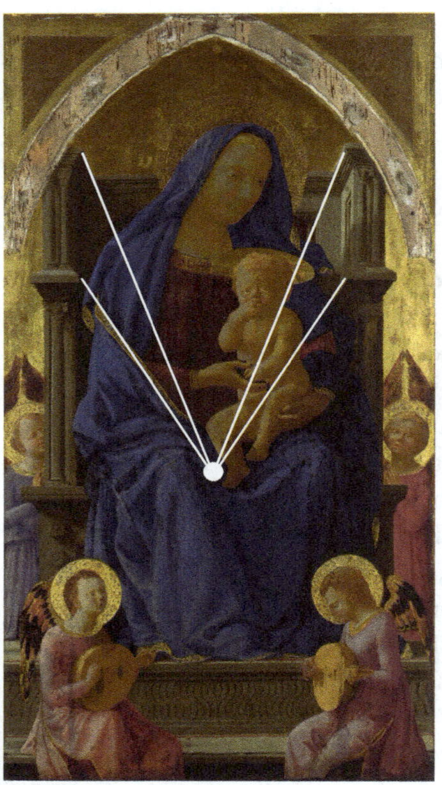

Figure 2.4 | Masaccio, *The Virgin and Child*, 1426, egg tempera on wood, 134.8 × 73.5 cm, with converging lines of single-point perspective on vanishing point, London, National Gallery. Bought with a contribution from The Art Fund, 1916. Acc. no.: 1772. Source: © 2015. Copyright The National Gallery, London / Scala, Florence.

of Mary's face and neck. The tempera has been applied to create a smooth surface with crisply defined edges, providing the image with a characteristically enamel-like quality, well suited to the devotional nature of the scene. However, despite tempera's limitations, Masaccio has managed to create a more naturalistic work than Duccio's *Maestà*, painted 100 years earlier. Masaccio demonstrates the early use of linear perspective – evident in the realistic recession of the Virgin's foreshortened throne, and Christ's elliptical halo. The artist owed this technical accomplishment to the newly discovered laws of linear perspective.

The Madonna's weight is made more tangible by the shadow she casts within her throne, which convinces us that she is occupying a real three-dimensional space. The artist's use of foreshortening – particularly in the lutes played by the angels in the foreground – aids the deception and is a technical change from the Gothic past. It makes the scene seem dramatically close. The Christ Child appears to have been drawn from a real baby, since he is shown realistically sucking his fingers and interacting with his mother. Do you think there is a family resemblance? The Christ Child's body is anatomically correct, especially in comparison to Duccio's. Masaccio has achieved this new level of realism using **chiaroscuro** – light and shade – to create a convincing roundness in the form of the body.

Artists during the Early Renaissance sought to emulate the art of **Antiquity** and increasingly aspired to achieve a realistic representation of the human form. This included persistent experimentation in the quest for three-dimensional realism. Early developments towards a greater realism were expressed in the works of Giotto and Duccio; however, it was Masaccio in the Early Renaissance who was one of the first to triumph in single-point linear perspective, daring foreshortening and chiaroscuro. When combined, these techniques gave his work an unprecedented level of realism. Effectively, however, Duccio and Masaccio are using the same materials, processes and techniques; however, they achieve different styles: broadly Gothic and Early Renaissance, respectively. The stylistic differences are largely as a result of Masaccio's look back at Antiquity, and a shift in intention, towards naturalism, rather than significant technical developments.

Perspective relates to the fact that the size of an object appears to decrease with increasing distance from the eye. This is the phenomenon that makes the throne in Masaccio's *The Virgin and Child* appear to recede in an illusory three-dimensional space. Foremost architect and engineer of the **Renaissance** Filippo Brunelleschi (1377–1446) is credited with formulating the first accurate rules of linear perspective (a formula based on the convergence of parallel lines to a single vanishing point). It is thought that Brunelleschi's discoveries in perspective manifested themselves in Masaccio's work because the pair were artistic contemporaries and friends. The lines of the throne converge on the vanishing point and locate our eye to create the illusion of a real, three-dimensional space.

Masaccio can be given the credit for originating a new style of painting; certainly everything done before him can be described as artificial, whereas he produced work that is living, realistic, and natural.

(Vasari, *Lives of the Artists*, p. 125)

Masaccio's *The Virgin and Child* offers points of comparison and contrast with contemporary British artist Chris Ofili's *Holy Virgin Mary*, 1996, examined later in this chapter: both represent religious subjects in a highly decorative manner.

The artistic limitations of tempera were not particularly problematic in the **Middle Ages** or in the Early Renaissance because artists were creating representations of the Madonna and saints for people to address their prayers to, rather than accurate portrayals of their likeness. However, the development of oil painting and its refinement in the fifteenth century allowed artists to achieve new levels of realism and likeness to the sitter.

Oil: versatile and enduring

In *Chapter 1*, we examined Jan van Eyck's *The Arnolfini Portrait*, 1434, as an example of the portrait genre, and in this chapter it can be re-examined in relation to its materials and techniques. Jan van Eyck (c.1395–1441) did not invent oil paint, as suggested by the Renaissance biographer Giorgio Vasari in the sixteenth century and Dutch biographer Karel van Mander in the seventeenth century, although he can be credited with mastering its blend and application. The artist painted the double portrait on an oak panel – as was popular in the Netherlands – and its surface was treated with warm animal-skin glue and a chalk ground primer to provide a smooth surface and hide the wood grain. Van Eyck applied oil in thin layers from an opaque base to a translucent finish; shading is aided by paint layering insofar as the paint is thickest where it is darkest and thinnest where it is lightest – look at the original painting in the National Gallery, London, and see for yourself. Jan van Eyck has used the technique of glazing because when light travels through the transparent glaze and bounces back off the opaque layer it produces a brilliance and a glow unachievable in tempera painting.

Figure 2.5 | Jan van Eyck, *The Arnolfini Portrait*, 1434, portrait of Giovanni (?) Arnolfini and his wife Giovanna Cenami (?), oil on oak panel, 82.2 × 60 cm, London, National Gallery. Source: National Gallery, London, UK / Bridgeman Images.

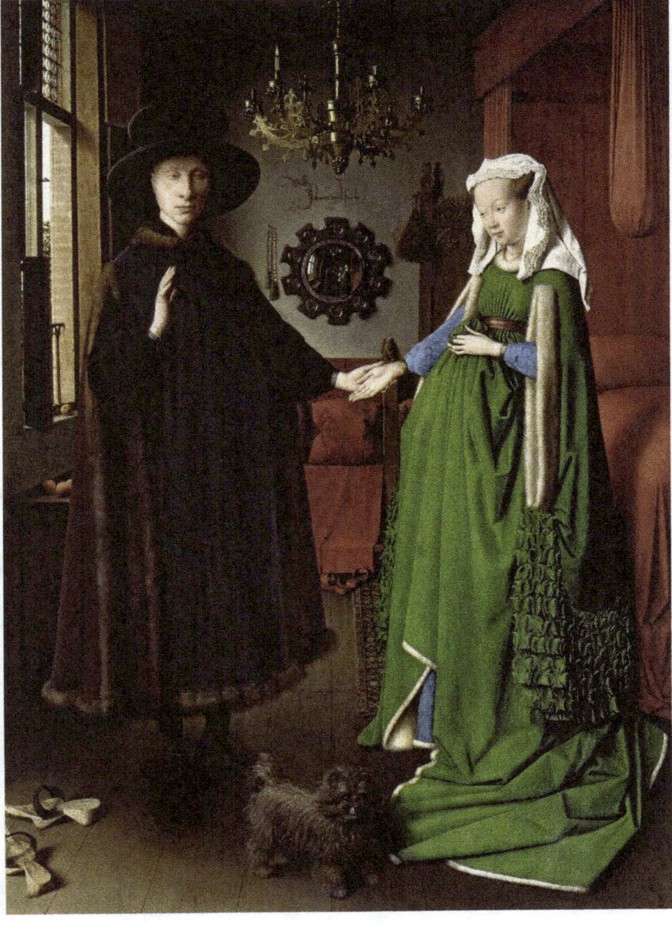

The Arnolfini Portrait depicts its patron's status so convincingly because the slow-drying medium of oil has allowed the artist to depict a catalogue of perfectly modelled material objects in meticulous detail and render their textures so believable that our disbelief is suspended upon sight of every object. The thick pile of the rug on the floor is easily distinguished from Mr. Arnolfini's fur-trimmed coat, for example. Oil allows for smooth transitions in colour and tone, such as is evident in the believable folds of Mrs. Arnolfini's green gown. The artist has painted this diminutive work using a small brush, probably made with squirrel or weasel fur, and painstakingly blended the medium in order to disguise his brush marks (unachievable in tempera). Van Eyck used the finest pigments to display the couple's status. Mrs. Arnolfini's sleeves are painted in lapis lazuli, her **verdigris** gown from ground copper and the rich red of the interior drapery from a mixture of silver and sulphur (Hicks, *Girl in a Green Gown*, p. 194).

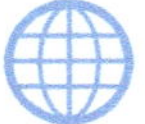

Consult the companion website for the opportunity to discover more information about Van Eyck's materials, techniques and processes.

All art works are made using materials, techniques and processes, and so any art work (whether featured in this book or a work of your choosing) can be worthy of examination under the heading of this chapter. The nineteenth-century **Impressionists** used oil paint in a very different way from northern Renaissance artist Van Eyck; not least, their centuries apart allowed for a revolution in chemical pigments. Look ahead to *Chapter 3* where Impressionist painting *Autumn Effect at Argenteuil*, 1873, by Claude Monet is discussed in relation to its form and style. This time, however, you need to focus on its materials, techniques and processes. Discussion of oil also features in the next section, where its properties and application are compared to acrylic paint.

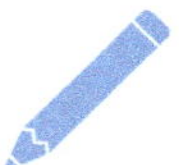

2.1 Explore this example
The works discussed in *Chapter 1* have all been made using materials, techniques and processes, and so any one of them, or a limitless choice of your own, is worthy of examination under the heading of this chapter. Jenny Saville's *Branded*, 1992 (examined in *Chapter 1* as an example of the portrait genre), subverts our traditional sense of the female nude in terms of its fleshy quality of beauty in part through Saville's use of materials, techniques and processes.

What technique does she use to mimic the puckering and dimpling of fat? How does she achieve the appearance of 'branding' on her body? Her body appears very close to us, the viewer. How does she achieve that in her use of perspective?

Acrylic: modern detachment

You may recall that in *Chapter 1* we saw that the use of acrylic paint in David Hockney's *Mr and Mrs Clark and Percy* gave the work a modern, graphic feel, entirely fitting for the fashionable lifestyle the couple led.

Acrylic paint was first used in the 1940s and made commercially available in the 1950s and while it is assumed to have greater durability than oil and a reduced tendency to discolour, its permanency is yet to be tested. Acrylic also dries much faster than oil, and so is less suited to images that require modelling or chiaroscuro. Acrylic paint, which uses an acrylic polymer emulsion as a binder, dries to a flexible paint film because it is comprised of interlocking molecules which shift without causing damage during expansion and contraction. While oil paint is referred to as 'oil-based' on account of its mix with linseed oil, acrylic is referred to as water-based on account of its dilution with water, if desired, although it is most commonly applied thickly to give an opaque finish.

2.1 What can you see?
Hockney used diluted acrylic in *Mr and Mrs Clark and Percy* which gives a slightly more transparent appearance in places. Nonetheless, the use of acrylic medium in unmodulated blocks of colour produces a graphic quality, evident on Mrs. Clark's two-dimensional looking dress, and the sharp **planes** of the coffee table in the foreground (Ione, *Innovation and Visualization: Trajectories, Strategies, and Myths*, p. 170). How does this flat appearance affect our interpretation of their relationship?

Acrylic is also quite flat in terms of its light absorption which can render its subject fairly stark in contrast to the light-reflective qualities of oil.

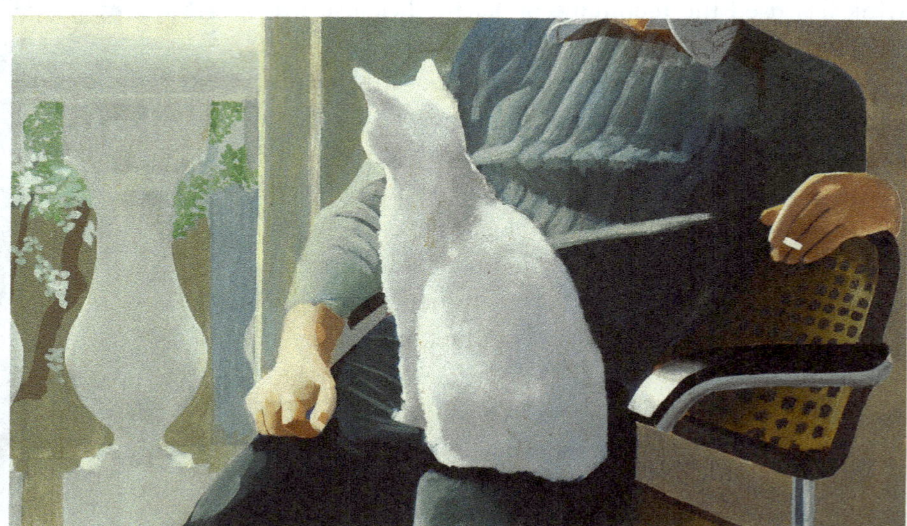

Figure 2.6 | David Hockney, a detail from *Mr and Mrs Clark and Percy*, 1970–1971, acrylic on canvas, 213.4 × 304.8 cm, London, Collection Tate. Source: © Tate, London 2015 / © David Hockney.

Consider Vermeer's *View of Delft*, 1660–1661, for example; if this work had been executed in acrylic, then the atmosphere, the reflected sparkle, and the richness would all be lost. The Prussian Blue that Van Gogh described as 'heavenly' in the *View of Delft*, is not even possible in acrylic on account of a chemical incompatibility (De Leeuw, *The Letters of Vincent van Gogh*, p. 401). Vermeer's renowned depiction of sunlight in some works, and the 'spiritual' glow in others, was achievable through his use of Indian Yellow, an oil paint made from the urine of cows fed upon mango leaves. Conversely, as liberating as the medium of oil was for artists like Vermeer, the acrylic paints exploited in Ofili's contemporary works (examined later in this chapter) are not available in oils. Every material brings its own range of possibilities and limitations.

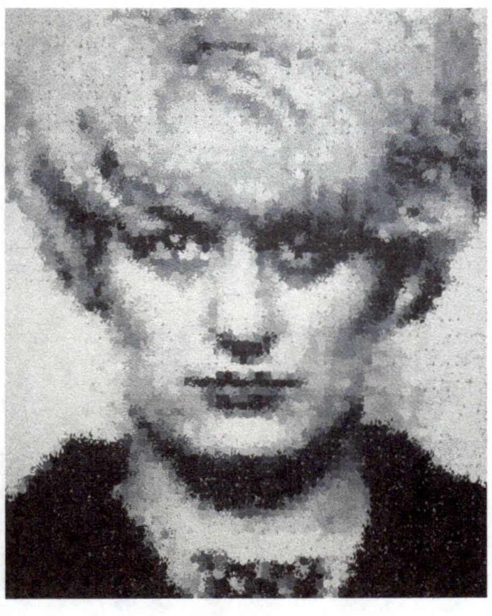

Figure 2.7 | Marcus Harvey, *Myra*, 1995, acrylic on canvas, 396 × 320 cm. Source: Image courtesy of Marcus Harvey and Vigo Gallery. © Marcus Harvey. All Rights Reserved, DACS 2015.

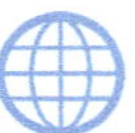

Consult the companion website for the opportunity to discover more information about the acrylic medium.

Oil paintings are prone to cracking over time, while acrylic paintings maintain a stable surface. This is because the binders (liquids mixed with the pigment) in oil and acrylic paint are different. Oil paint binders, such as linseed oil, dry to an inflexible, weak film that may crack as it expands and contracts with changes in external temperature.

Young British Artist (YBA) Marcus Harvey (born 1963) uses the medium of acrylic in a similar way to that of Hockney insofar as he shows an awareness of the limitations of the medium and uses the graphic properties of acrylic to lend a further dimension of meaning to his painting of child murderer Myra Hindley. How do you think the qualities of acrylic help to convey a sense of Hindley's character?

Harvey's large-scale portrait *Myra* uses acrylic with a hand-printing technique to create a mosaic effect, which, when seen from a distance, is reminiscent of her black and white police mug-shot on which the painted image is based. That Harvey used the plaster cast of a child's hand to print the portrait catapults an already emotive image to new levels of explosive controversy. Primary school children, innocent and untutored, make perhaps their first personalised creations like this, only usually they adorn our kitchen walls and later become memories in parents' scrapbooks. However, Harvey implements an unorthodox technique, causing the handprints to appear pixelated and mechanically detached from us.

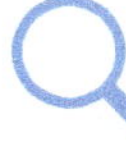

2.2 What can you see?

In 1966 Ian Brady and Myra Hindley were convicted of the murder of five children. How does the form and content of Harvey's *Myra* intensify the shock of this terrible act? Why do you think the artist has focused on Hindley rather than Brady?

Like so many artists before him, in a lineage that started with Caravaggio (originally Michelangelo Merisi da Caravaggio, 1571–1610) in the seventeenth century, Harvey paints the 'ugly truth': pointing directly to an unspeakable crime. While it has been argued that this work is astonishingly insensitive, others consider that children are too often without a voice in an adult world, and that in noting their tiny handprints, we become poignantly aware of their vulnerability.

Other Media

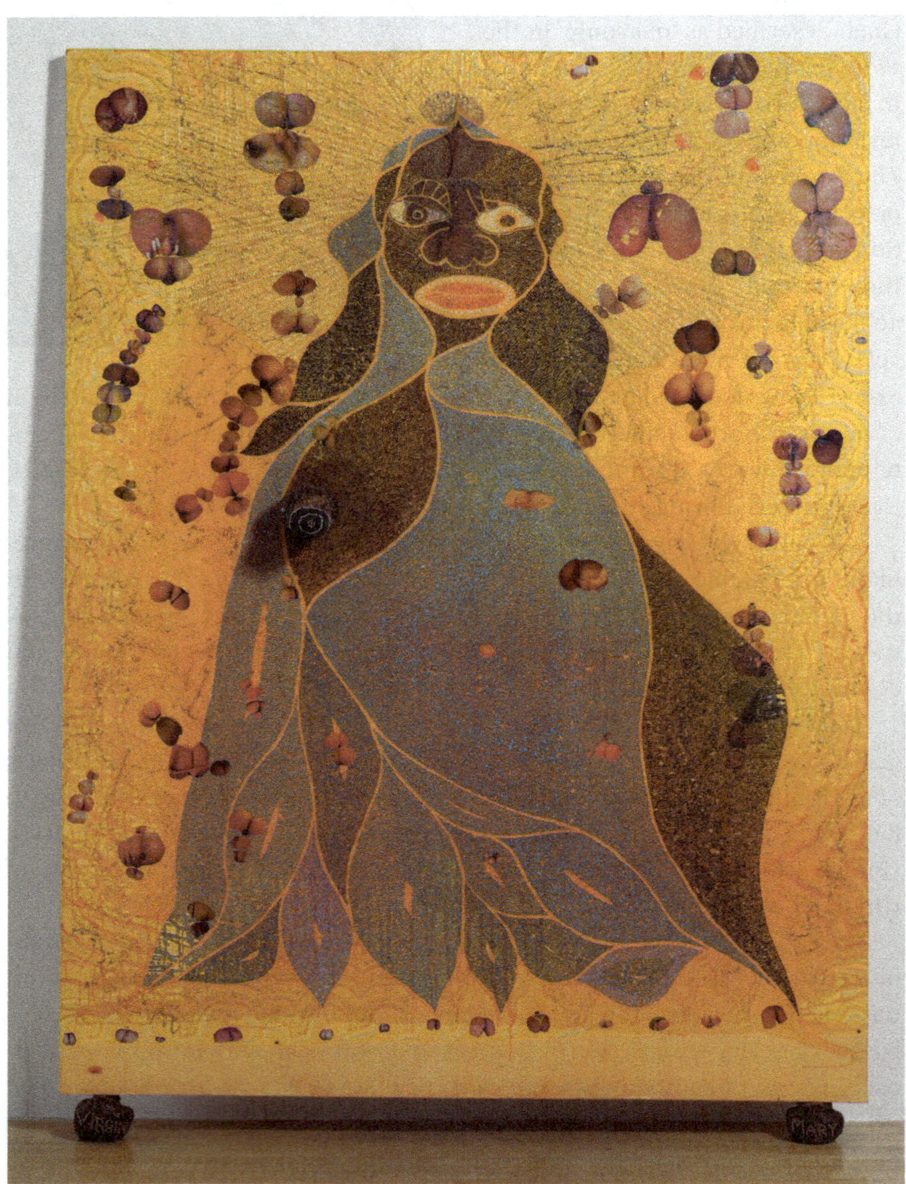

Figure 2.8 | Chris Ofili, *The Holy Virgin Mary*, 1996, acrylic, oil, polyester resin, paper collage, glitter, map pins and elephant dung on linen, 243.8 × 182.8 cm. Source: Courtesy the Artist and Victoria Miro, London. Copyright: © Chris Ofili.

Modern mixed media

The materials used by Chris Ofili (born 1968) in *The Holy Virgin Mary* include paper **collage** (such as pages from pornographic magazines), acrylic, oil paint, glitter, polyester resin, map pins and elephant dung, built up in layers upon linen. Dried spherical lumps of elephant dung are applied directly onto the surface and used as foot-like supports to elevate the canvas. Arguably, the glittering rays that emanate from Ofili's Black Virgin mimic those of Masaccio's some five centuries earlier.

The versatility of acrylic paint, and particularly its enhanced adhesive qualities in comparison to oil, coincides with the extensive range of experimental materials, techniques and processes employed by artists from the second half of the twentieth century. Chris Ofili's *Holy Virgin Mary* is depicted using acrylic paints that had only been developed in the early 1980s. The timing was perfect for Ofili, who exploited the properties of acrylic as a twentieth-century alternative to gold leaf; it's certainly reminiscent of medieval icons, albeit with added 'gangsta bling'.

Fast-drying and permanent, acrylic paint can easily be over-painted. Like oil, it can be applied straight from the tube or simply thickly if **opacity** is desired. Equally, it can be diluted with water and used like watercolour. Its fast drying time makes blending difficult in comparison to oil. In this sense Ofili uses the medium in its purest form, creating a highly decorative and vibrant effect. Its adhesive nature is also useful to a work like Ofili's, where the technique of collage is used to create a multi-layered surface of imported materials. The rather unlikely combination of materials underlines the artist's experimental perspective on materials, techniques and processes in art.

The sexually explicit close-ups of female genitalia are cut out from magazines and rather irreverently stuck onto an otherwise ethereal surface. Controversially, the close-ups of female genitalia are positioned swooping around the head of the Virgin, in the position traditionally assigned to seraphim – the highest order of angels. Here, Ofili uses them to refer to **blaxploitation** imagery in a bid to question racial and sexual **stereotypes**. The richly decorated complexity of Ofili's surfaces may relate to the myriad references he makes to Black identity. However, because Ofili's work draws attention to stereotypes and issues of ethnic hybridisation (the mixing of ethnic elements), we need to approach the compartmentalisation of the artist's **oeuvre** cautiously, avoiding a simplistic and stereotyped reading.

2.3 What can you see?
In *The Holy Virgin Mary*, Ofili deliberately referred to some of the stereotypes about Black culture – bling, pimps, gangstas, drugs. Why do you think he did this? Does it counteract racist stereotypes, or does it risk confirming them? Conduct some research into the audience's reception and review of this work.

Spray-paint: anti-art rebellion

Many artists in the twenty-first century have used modern materials and techniques to confront prejudice and expectation. French street artist JR (born 1983) and British artist Banksy (born c.1974) are notable examples. Arguably, Banksy is responsible for our changed perception of **graffiti** in the UK. A predominantly urban art, graffiti was initially dismissed as lacking in artistic merit, and practised by ignorant law-breakers, but it has recently been reassessed as an art form that is satirical, intelligent and relevant to contemporary society. As part of the Bristol graffiti scene, Banksy turned, like so many other graffiti artists, to stencils in order to speed up the process and create more **precisionist** images. Paint was added to aerosol technology in 1949, and in the decades that followed, the portability of the spray-can and its speed of application became an obvious medium for the illicit work of street artists; the link between technological advancement and artistic practice also became an obvious one.[10] The anti-art materials and techniques Banksy uses are fitting for the anti-establishment statements his works convey. In Banksy's case, even the site and location of his works – very often on the walls of public buildings – reinforce his intention to create an art accessible to us all.

10 The link between technological invention and art is a historical one. It was just as clearly felt when the invention of tube paints and the camera impacted the work of the nineteenth-century Impressionists.

Figure 2.9 | Barbara Kruger, *Untitled (Thinking of You)* 1999–2000, photographic silk screen print on vinyl, 312.4 × 256.5 cm, New York, Mary Boone Gallery MBG#7969. Source: Copyright: Barbara Kruger. Courtesy: Mary Boone Gallery, New York.

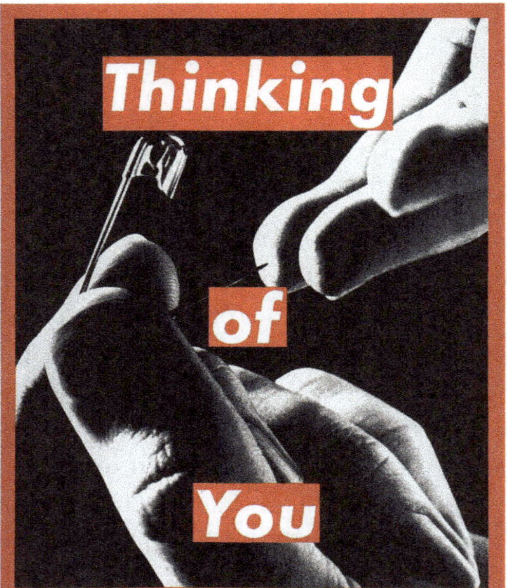

Screen printing: the language of signs

American feminist Barbara Kruger (born 1945) drew on her political values and experience as a graphic designer to produce a series of works juxtaposing photographic images with aggressive or ironic text. Her hard-hitting combinations raise issues of power, control and injustice. Her conscious borrowing of the traditionally male-dominated medium of advertising provides authoritative simplicity. You can stop, look and ultimately reflect upon her message. She overlays black and white photographs with white writing on a red background. *Thinking of You*, 1999–2000, has a similar effect to the monochromatic power of Picasso's *Guernica*, only Kruger has achieved a powerful statement by juxtaposing the hard edges of Futura Bold Italic font (a common advertising font) with recognisably human conditions, such as being the victim of an abusive partner. Through her choice of material and technique she manages to destabilise the process of constructing identities. She challenges **patriarchy** and convention, if only for as long as we look at her work. So striking are her methods, we can hardly look anywhere else. Kruger's work plays on the **kitsch** of greeting-card sentiment. 'Thinking of you' – a caring message – abruptly becomes ironic in juxtaposition with the suggestion of imminent male aggression: it is a recognisably male hand that is about to pierce the more passively positioned and upturned hand of what appears to be a female recipient. In this sense, the image may also be interpreted as suggestive of psychological control. The technique of photo-**screen printing** that Kruger uses is essentially a stencil method of printing which may be used to print on a variety of surfaces, including paper, fabric, wood and vinyl. A fine mesh fabric is stretched over a frame to form the screen. Then the screen is coated in a photopolymer emulsion (light-sensitive liquid). The film positive (in this case, the hands in this image) is then placed over the screen and exposed to UV light which burns the photopolymer emulsion, creating a stencil on the mesh screen (a further stencil would need to be used to create Kruger's red border). Finally, Kruger has pushed ink through the mesh using a squeegee onto the vinyl to create the image. Kruger's choice of materials and techniques created a signature style – red-framed text in a media-style font, printed across a black and white photograph – which tended to convey a powerful and satirical commentary on contemporary issues. Consider how **Pop Art** painter Andy Warhol used the screen printing technique in *Marilyn Diptych*, 1962, to signal the mass consumerism sweeping American culture (the social and historical context of this image is discussed in *Chapter 4*).

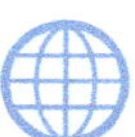

Consult the companion website for the opportunity to discover more information about the silkscreen printing technique.

2.1 Checkpoint question
Which paint medium would be most effective for tonal modelling of form and why?

In the same way that Ofili's *Holy Virgin Mary* examines racial prejudice, Kruger's art forces the viewer to confront gender inequality and issues of patriarchy.

Sculpture

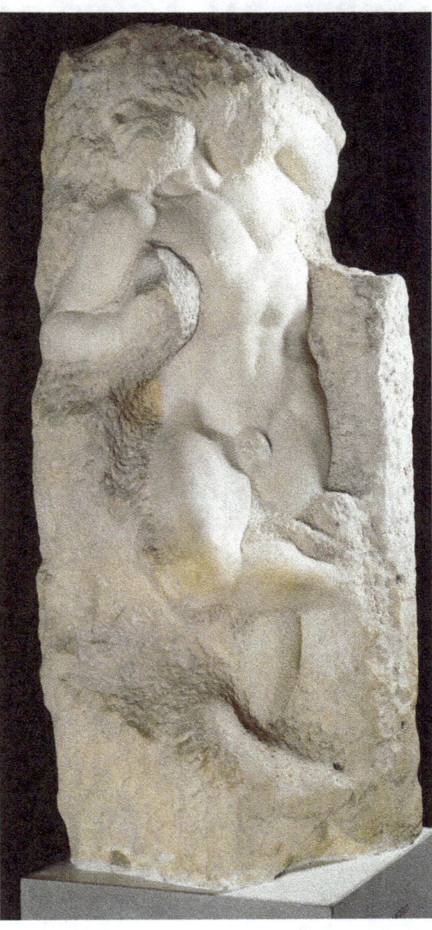

Figure 2.10 | Michelangelo, *The Awakening of a Slave*, 1525–1530, marble, height 267 cm, Florence, Galleria Dell'Accademia. Source: akg-images / De Agostini Picture Library / G. Nimatallah.

Marble and bronze are the traditional materials of the sculptor within the Western **canon**, and the entire Renaissance was based upon the perceived elegance and purity of the figures and buildings of Antiquity. It is ironic therefore that the classical white marbles of ancient Greece upon which the Renaissance based its style were, in fact, originally painted in many colours, and only became white as their ancient paint flaked and peeled away over time. Marble has been used for centuries and continues to impart connotations of nobility, purity and status to its subject.

Sculptural techniques tend to be either subtractive (taking stone, wood or plaster away) or additive (building up a soft material, often prior to casting in bronze). The subtractive technique (sometimes referred to as the reductive technique) involves the direct or indirect carving of a block of stone, marble or wood. The actual process involved is evident in one of the unfinished *Prisoners* by Michelangelo (originally Michelangelo di Lodovico Buonarroti Simoni, 1475–1564), where the subtractive process is clearly visible. As if held captive by the stone, the figure appears to have emerged from the medium with every blow of Michelangelo's skilfully led chisel.

Marble: traditional aesthetics

When viewing a sculpture it is helpful to consider how the sculptor has exploited the medium to represent the object, or been limited by it. Italian master of the **High Baroque** Gian Lorenzo Bernini (1598–1680) created such dynamic sculptures that they appear to have been moulded out of wax, rather than carved out of marble. His sculpture *Apollo and Daphne*, 1624, created by the subtractive technique, shows the **mythological** God Apollo chasing the nymph Daphne, as described in Ovid's *Metamorphoses*. The life-likeness of this mythological duo is also examined from the perspective of their **Baroque** form and style in *Chapter 3*.

The moment is grippingly fleeting: the nymph Daphne transforms into a laurel tree before our eyes rather than face Apollo's desire for her. She

Figure 2.11 | Gian Lorenzo Bernini, *Apollo and Daphne*, 1624, marble, height 243 cm, Rome, Borghese Gallery. Source: akg-images / Andrea Jemolo.

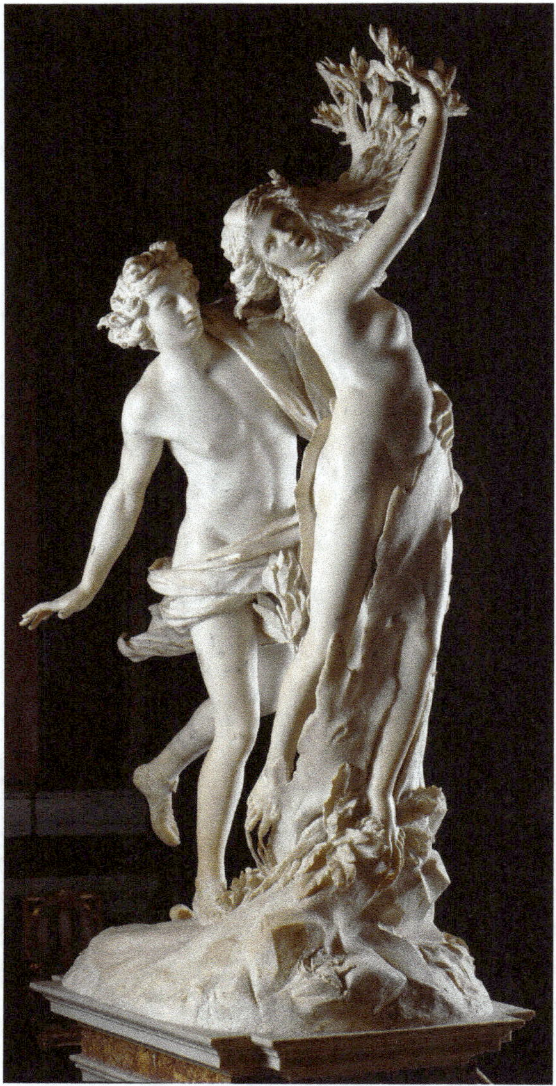

2.4 **What can you see?**
Simon Schama describes *Apollo and Daphne* as *the greatest tease in all of sculpture* (Schama, *The Power of Art*, p. 94).
What do you think he means?

eludes him, her fleshy fingers metamorphosing into branches of laurel, a feat never before depicted in stone. Marble's low-tensile properties are exploited to their limit in the delicate leaves between Daphne's fingertips, but their carefully planned structure ensures their durability. Even her emphatically raised arms have their weight over the centre of gravity – a necessary counter-balancing technique that also aesthetically enriches the composition.

Bernini's technique for engaging the viewer was an innovative synthesis of pure theatre and sculpture; it is as if these figures are reaching out to us, physically and emotionally interacting with us. The highly polished stone renders flesh appealing to the touch; this provides a stark contrast with the rough-textured bark that sheaths Daphne's lower body from Apollo's grip. Their vitality contrasts with the inanimate and unfinished base they spring from. This allows us to see the reductive (or subtractive) process from which a block of rough marble is carved and polished. The stages are increasingly delicate, and finalised with a polish that creates a realistic portrayal of flesh.

Bernini had discovered a way to make marble movies.
(Schama, *The Power of Art*, p. 92)

The drapery around Apollo's groin seems alive with his passion and billows unrealistically around him. The deeply carved folds lend dynamism to the scene and display Bernini's miraculous technical skill. Take a closer look at Daphne's long locks of hair which find volume in the gust that carries her aloft; it becomes leaf-like as it extends away from her. Her breasts and her cheeks are soft and voluminous with a sheen that is both enticing and wondrous, especially when seen in comparison to other sculpture of the time. Her scream seems almost audible from one of the most deeply hollowed mouths in sculpture.

A supreme master of the medium of marble, Bernini's oeuvre is overflowing with examples for study in terms of materials, techniques and processes. The basic tools of the sculptor are the mallet (usually a hammer with a broad, barrel-shaped head) and chisel (a pointed metal tool with a sharp end). The pointed end of the chisel is placed against the marble at the desired angle, and the sculptor hits the blunt end with the hammer, with appropriate force.

Various weights and shapes of tool are used, depending on the amount of marble to be removed with each blow. For splitting off large pieces of marble the sculptor might use a flat 'pitching tool'. Claw chisels, with notched 'teeth', may be used to add texture, and flat chisels provide a smoother finish. Rasps or files are used after the chiselling stage to render the chisel marks invisible, and sandpaper, wet or dry, is used to achieve varying degrees of polish.

The marks of Bernini's tools are evident on the rough stone beneath Apollo and Daphne, but quite invisible on their highly polished bodies. It's likely he sanded their flesh smooth using paper and marble dust from the floor of his workshop.

Bronze: timeless and dark

Metallurgy – the understanding of the properties of metal – has evolved over thousands of years, with different combinations of metals used to create **alloys** such as bronze, a mixture of tin and copper. Bronze sculptures are usually made initially using the additive process, which involves building up and modelling a form from a soft substance such as clay, plaster or sculptor's wax (a malleable wax) before it is cast into bronze. The casting is done in a foundry by craftsmen, rarely by the artist, although the artist will oversee the process.

Bronze sculptures were considered prestigious in ancient Greece and the Riace bronzes (Riace Warriors), *which date from around the fifth to the fourth century* BCE, *are considered to be among the finest examples of bronze casting we know*. (Penny, *The Materials of Sculpture*, p. 226)

Despite centuries of bronze sculpting and changes in the precise composition of the alloy used, most bronze sculpture is today created using the same cast-metal processes as those employed for the life-size warriors of Antiquity. The twentieth-century bronzes of Romanian-born artist Constantin Brancusi (1876–1957) are arguably as exploitative of the medium and as timeless as those of ancient Greece.

Brancusi felt that traditional ways of representing forms could not satisfy the need for spiritual truths in art, and believed that purity in medium and form would provide the answer. In *Bird in Space* he therefore abandoned the realistic form of a bird and its characteristic attributes and concentrated instead on its form. Reduced to the swell of a chest and the aerodynamic form of an oval plane, this form is reduced to the essential idea of a bird.

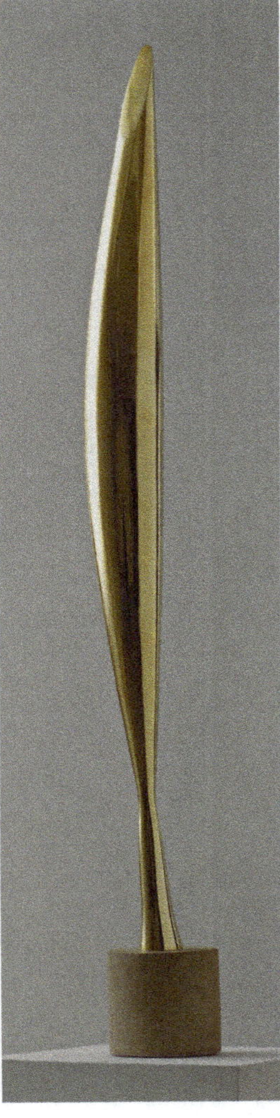

Figure 2.12 | Constantin Brancusi, *Bird in Space*, 1928, bronze (unique cast), 137.2 × 21.6 × 16.5 cm, New York, Museum of Modern Art (MoMA). Given anonymously. Acc. no.: 153.1934. Source: © 2015. Digital image, The Museum of Modern Art, New York / Scala, Florence / ©ADAGP, Paris and DACS, London 2015.

Brancusi's aesthetic of **essentialism** reveals the fundamental 'essence' of the subject to the point of its quasi-religious form in nature. All extraneous detail is omitted to leave only an elemental outline. In

> **What is real is not the external form, but the essence of things. Starting from this truth it is impossible for anyone to express anything essentially real by imitating its exterior surface.**
>
> (Brancusi quoted in Hamilton, *Painting and Sculpture in Europe, 1880–1940*, p. 426)

this instance, Brancusi's bird is devoid of details such as eyes and feathers, but it is universally emblematic of the idea of a bird, any bird. He was fascinated by flight and the nearness of God's creatures to the spiritual realm, and he sought to capture only the most universal and fundamental elements of a bird in this work: its vertical form is organically rhythmic and soaring.

Brancusi's use of his medium, which may be described as 'truth to materials' (**truth to medium**), further aids his aesthetic ideal. Bronze is hard and easily made into a flawless and aerodynamic surface such as this. The 'bronzeness of bronze' is visible in the sculpture's flawless, reflective surface, which lacks the usual **patina** that results from weathering. Although the surface appears to have all of the perfection of a machine-made object, Brancusi painstakingly polished this by hand with a fine emery board (see Lydiate, 'What Is Art?', p. 125).

Its extreme tapering and top-heavy form is only achievable using a metal substance that can endure elongation and load-bearing without breaking. At its uppermost point, the tip reminds us of the material's ability to produce the sharpest of edges. Swords are made of metal compounds after all, and this bird looks capable of soaring through the air like a blade. So very thin, the bird's base is reminiscent of legs on the one hand, and the **high-tensile** properties of the medium on the other.[11] Its colour is important too: gold, signifying majesty. Brancusi has juxtaposed this metal with the matt, porous stone of its elegant base, serving as another reminder of the distinction between his materials, techniques and processes.

Figure 2.13 | Dame Elisabeth Frink, *Harbinger Bird IV*, 1961, bronze, 483 × 213 × 356 mm, London, Tate. Source: ©Tate, London 2015 / © Estate of Elisabeth Frink. All Rights Reserved, DACS 2015.

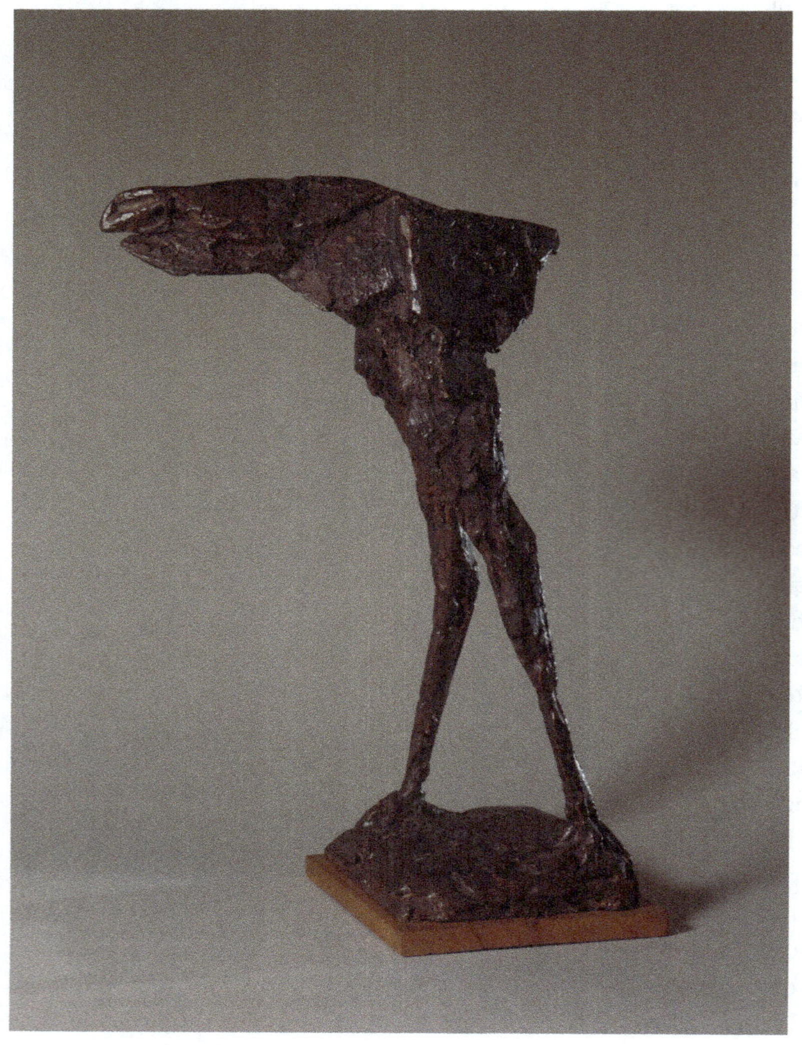

Brancusi's treatment of the subject of the bird in these materials can be compared and contrasted with the treatment and materials offered in Elisabeth Frink's *Harbinger Bird*, 1961. While classical bronze prototypes and their resurgence during the Renaissance tended to disguise the materials and processes of their making by **chasing** or creating a patina on the surface after casting, many sculptures of the twentieth and twenty-first centuries have consciously revealed them.

British artist Elisabeth Frink (1930–1993) often began a sculpture using a light, chicken-wire construction. She then used a modelling technique, an additive process, applying wet plaster in layers as an initial process. The building up of plaster onto an **armature** is a technique called **applied plaster** and Frink attributes her use of it to the Swiss artist Alberto Giacometti (1901–1966), who was in her opinion *the greatest artist of the twentieth century*

(Stevas, 'Norman St. John Stevas in Conversation | Elisabeth Frink'). The spindly legs of so many of her works are clearly indebted to his post-1945 style.

Once modelled, Frink's plaster was carved and scarred to achieve a rougher surface when it was subsequently cast in bronze. She would then further work the bronze sculpture with chisels, scrapers, rasps, even mallets, to distress its surface. The haunting texture that characterises her oeuvre functions on a number of levels; not least, it generalises the subject and reduces the form to a similar kind of essentialism that Brancusi achieved, although the aerodynamic grace of Brancusi's *Bird in Space* offers an expressive contrast to the agitated surface of Frink's *Harbinger Bird*.

2.2 Checkpoint question
What is meant by 'truth to material/medium'?

This bird emanates a sense of the jerky, pecking dynamic associated with its species, and is likely to make anyone who shares Frink's phobia of birds anxious. The degree of emaciation in *Harbinger Bird's* demonic-looking legs can only be achieved in a high-tensile material such as bronze. Its dark colour suggests something sinister, unlikely to have been achievable in a light coloured or more malleable material such as wood. The low-tensile properties of stone would not have been compatible with the gravity-defying mass atop those emaciated legs. Its oversized beak, spindly legs and threatening aura provide a form quite different from Brancusi's but, nonetheless, both reside on the spectrum of essentialism.

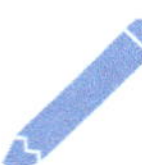

2.2 Explore this example
The work of Alberto Giacometti is rich with examples of how the technical possibilities of the bronze medium can be employed to enhance our understanding of the human condition. Look at the form and texture of Giacometti's *Man Pointing*, 1947, bronze, height 178 cm. How do the qualities of bronze contribute to the impact of the sculpture?

Turning a creation modelled in plaster or similar substance into a bronze replica is highly skilled, and is most commonly achieved by the lost-wax process. A negative plaster mould is made from the original wax, clay or plaster sculpture. This is frequently made in pieces, rather than one piece, unless the original is a simple, small form. Hot wax is poured in to form a layer inside each of the plaster moulds. The hollow wax copies are then removed from the negative plaster mould and joined to create a wax copy of the original sculpture. Foundry sand, a liquid mixture of sand and plaster that will set, is poured inside this copy to create a solid core. Wax rods are attached to the copy at one end and a wax funnel at the other. Small metal pins are inserted through the wax copy and into the solid core to hold it in place. A plaster mould is then put around the wax model and the wax rods, but not to the base of the funnel. The whole thing is then heated in a kiln, to melt the wax which flows out through the funnel. The wax areas are now empty, the core still held in place by the pins. Molten bronze is poured through the funnel, flowing through the channels vacated by the wax rods and into the space left where the wax copy was. When the bronze cools, the mould is broken open and the copy and rods are now bronze. The bronze rods are cut off, the metal pins are removed and the holes plugged with bronze, and the imperfections and details of the sculpture are filed and smoothed.

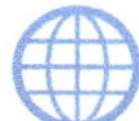

Consult the companion website for more information and video links showing the lost-wax process and other casting techniques being employed.

The advantage of the lost-wax process, used by both Frink and Brancusi, is that the surface texture of the finished sculpture is not limited by the bronze medium; through modelling, the artist can achieve a range of finishes. This is evident in the surfaces of Frink's and Brancusi's bird sculptures. Brancusi's precisionist and light-reflective surface disguises human intervention, while Frink's shows the physical impression made by her bare hands as she modelled and scarred the original plaster surface.

11 Brancusi's *Bird in Space* may taper to the point of defying gravity (a large mass is supported by a small base); however, more impressive perhaps is the fact that the artist made a marble version of this form.

Figure 2.14 | Gregorio Fernández, *Dead Christ*, c.1625–1630, polychromed wood, horn, glass, bark, and ivory or bone, length 191 cm, Valladolid, National Sculpture Museum. Source: Photography: © Imagen M.A.S.

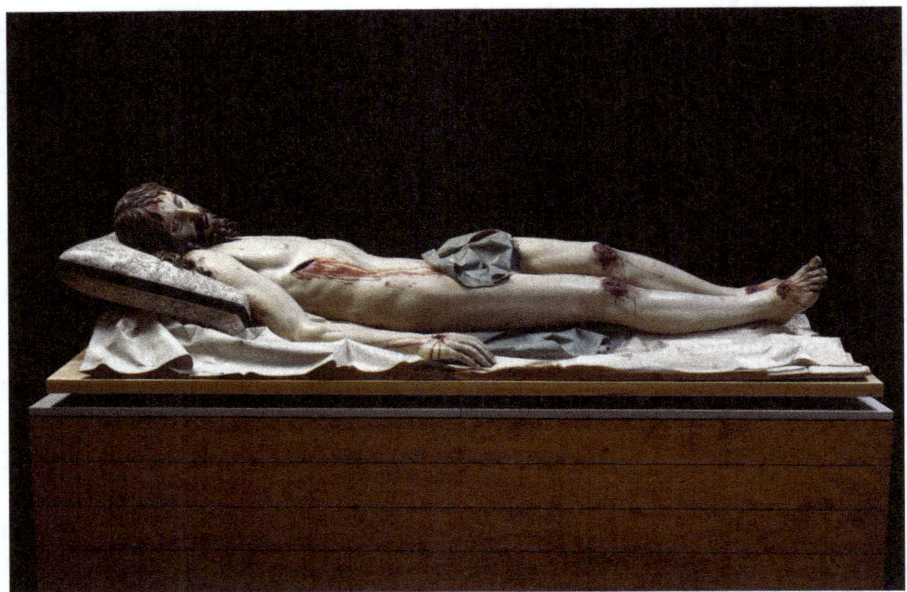

Wood: in the service of devotion and expression

Unlike bronze, wood is carved through a subtractive process that involves material being taken away during the artwork's creation. Like Giacometti, Spanish sculptor Gregorio Fernández (1576–1636) shows, in his life-size *Dead Christ*, c.1625–1630, a physically tortured body, but in this case the texture and colour of the flesh appears almost real. The Spanish were known for a more visceral level of realism than their Italian counterparts and this is evident not only in the congealed blood on Christ's knees, achieved with a mixture of pigment and cork, but also in the **polychromatic** finish of this tortured cadaver.

The work of sculptor and **polychromer** were quite separate at this time. Although we have no documentation for the latter in this instance, Fernández often worked with the painter Valentín Diaz (Bray, *The Sacred Made Real: Spanish Painting and Sculpture, 1600–1700*, p. 64).

According to the National Gallery Exhibition Guide 'The Sacred Made Real', the preparation for the painting of the sculpture was as follows: *Sawdust was removed, wood knots were pierced to expel sap and rubbed with garlic to enhance adhesion, and several coats of glue* ***size*** *and white ground applied* (Bray, *The Sacred Made Real: Spanish Painting and Sculpture, 1600–1700*, p. 51). The polychromer used one of two types of flesh texture at this time: glossy or matt. *Dead Christ's* flesh is a realistic matt finish, in contrast to the gloss (wet-looking) texture of his gaping wounds. The artists of Seville preferred matt finishes, and the latter is certainly closer to flesh than its highly polished counterpart (Bray, *The Sacred Made Real: Spanish Painting and Sculpture, 1600–1700*, p. 51).

The realism of the sculpture is arguably heightened with the use of glass eyes, horn nails and ivory teeth. It's a technical and multi-media approach to verisimilitude but one that may appear vulgar from the perspective of certain artistic traditions. Painted sculpture was characteristic of the Spanish Baroque and yet presents quite a shock to unaccustomed eyes. Christ's lifeless body feels contained upon its platform, giving it a restrained effect. Yet the work also feels theatrical, with Christ's mouth hanging ajar in death and eyes lifelessly glossed over. Christ is presented as dying alone without his usual mourners – his mother and Mary Magdalene – we, the viewers, are the only witnesses to his sufferings. Fernández created this work to be prayed over, touched and kissed, and it was positioned close to the congregation in order to inspire piety. Fernández's wooden Christ, his modesty protected by a loin cloth, can be compared to Ron Mueck's work (Figure 2.16), in which the artist's own father is laid bare in a miniaturised replica created using modern industrial media.

> When I took up a piece of wood, it was not to go with the grain but against it.
>
> (Duby and Daval, *Sculpture from Antiquity to the Present Day*, p. 1087)

A sculptor's technique can be so effective, as in the case of Fernández's Christ that it disturbs our sense of what is real, or it can be so expressive that it forces a very real and urgent response from the viewer. *Untitled (Figure with Raised Arm)* by German artist Georg Baselitz (born 1938) is strong, vertical, emphatic and primitively carved. Indeed, the carving is so crude it appears forged by axe or chain saw. The angularity and wide-eyed appearance of the figure might be interpreted as threatening.

The form of the figure is proportionate, but with little anatomical detail: rather than being **hyperrealistic**, the style is expressionistic. In fact, Baselitz contributed to a revival of Expressionism in the 1970s that shared the same subjective focus as the early twentieth-century German movement but was more self-reflective. His figure embodies the rawness of **Neo-Expressionism**, and the combination of direct carving and bold colour is both immediate and thought-provoking. The figure is clearly based on the human body, but even its gender is ambiguous. The splashes of **primary colour** may appear tribal but, from a Western cultural perspective, are also reminiscent of the two distinct circuits that carry blood around the body: one depicted in red, the other in blue in medical diagrams.

In a manner comparable to Brancusi's essentialism, Baselitz also responds to the natural and inherent properties of the medium, demonstrating a certain truth to the medium of wood: the 'woodness of wood'. The tree from which the wood was formed has a strong vertical emphasis and a natural roughness on account of its splintering, jagged qualities.

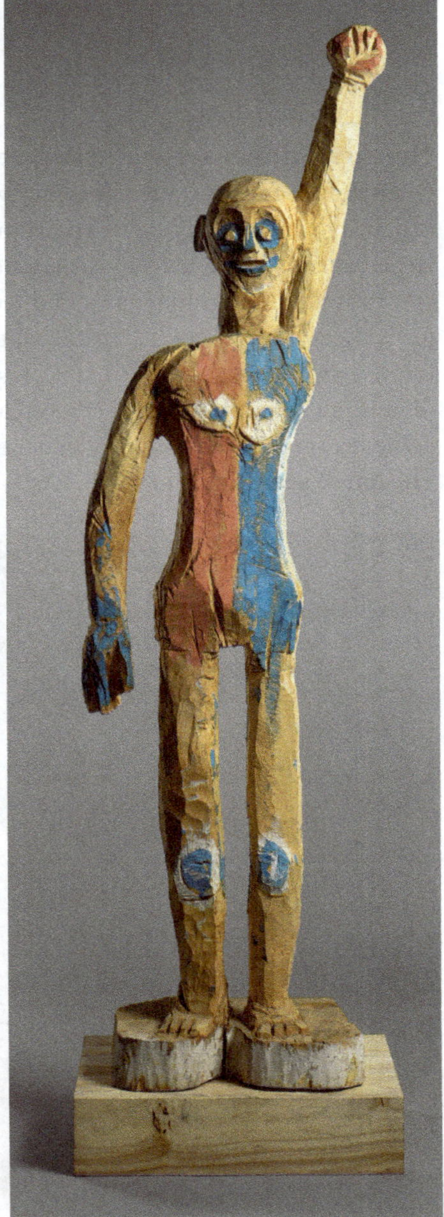

Figure 2.15 | Georg Baselitz, *Untitled (Figure with Raised Arm)*, 1982–1984, lime wood and oil paint, 253 × 71 × 46 cm, Edinburgh, National Galleries of Scotland.
Source: © Georg Baselitz 2015. Photo by Jochen Littkemann, Berlin.

2.5 What can you see?

It has been suggested that Baselitz's *Untitled (Figure with Raised Arm)* is a reflection on our essential selves; that this person, in these colours, represents the very lifeblood of human existence. If so, how might the materials, techniques and processes used be said to match the intention? Compare the sculpture with biological models of the human form found in science laboratories. What do they have in common?

2.3 Checkpoint question

Explain why bronze statues are able to have protruding limbs and a small base supporting a larger mass, which is not possible in wooden sculptures.

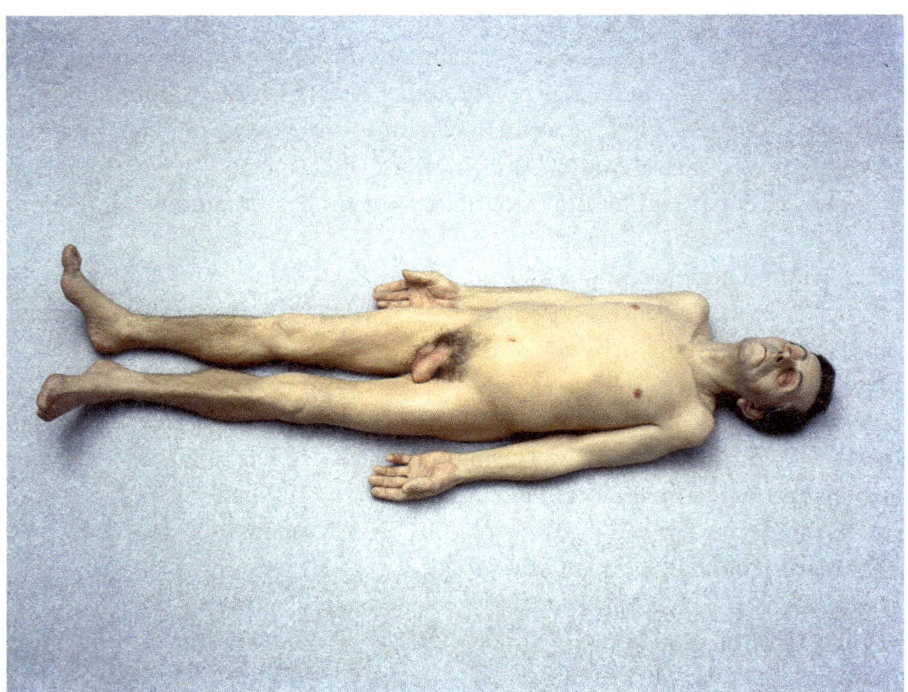

Figure 2.16 | Ron Mueck, *Dead Dad,* 1996–1997, mixed media, 20 × 38 × 102 cm, Stefan T. Edlis Collection. Source: © Ron Mueck, Courtesy the artist, Anthony d'Offay, London and Hauser & Wirth. Photo: Anthony d'Offay, London.

Non-traditional art materials: deceptive perfection

Over three centuries after Fernández's wooden sculpture *Dead Christ*, Australian-born contemporary artist Ron Mueck (born 1958) offers the viewer hyperrealism with a level of verisimilitude unobtainable by Fernández on account of its modern materials and techniques. That this diminished human form is a copy of Mueck's own dead father draws a response similar to, if not as intense as, that evoked by *Christ*. Despite their polarity in style, material and technique, grief may be interpreted as resonating from both works and each achieves tremendous psychological effect.

The small scale of *Dead Dad*, 1996–1997, certainly has some effect on our interpretation of such a life-like naked male. A full-scale dead body has the potential to repel the viewer. However, Mueck's use of diminished scale heightens the figure's vulnerability and feebleness; we feel compelled to kneel down beside him, laid bare on the gallery's floor.

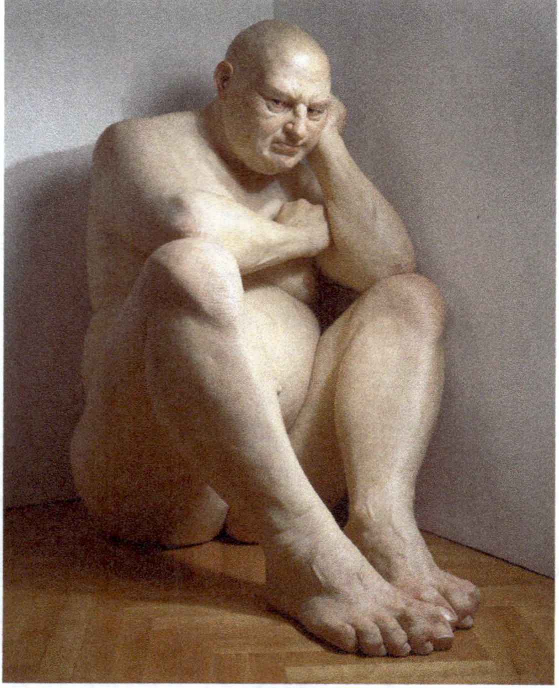

Figure 2.17 | Ron Mueck, *Big Man,* 2000, mixed media, 205.1 × 117.4 × 209 cm, Hirshhorn Museum and Sculpture Garden, Smithsonian Institution, Washington DC Museum, the Joseph H. Hirshhorn Bequest Fund, 2001. Source: © Ron Mueck, Courtesy the artist, Anthony d'Offay, London and Hauser & Wirth. Photo: Anthony d'Offay, London.

The process of the making of *Dead Dad* is more technical than Frink's chicken wire followed by plaster on an armature, but it provides a level of special effect found hitherto only in films and life-like dolls; indeed Mueck had worked as a model maker for television and film productions before becoming a professional artist. The diminutive *Dead Dad* was first sculpted in clay, in every tiny detail, before being cast in silicone, carefully tinted layers of which were hand painted into the mould to create the colour and translucency of skin and flesh. Finally each hair was individually inserted to complete the verisimilitude. A later work, the larger than life *Big Man*, 2000 (Figure 2.17), was made in a similar way but cast in resin.

Readymade: courting controversy

The artist's choice of medium and its treatment is inextricably bound to its representation, and our subsequent interpretation of it. This is evident in the work of contemporary British artist Tracey Emin (born 1963) whose use of materials, techniques and processes supports the content of her work and enhances our understanding of its meaning on a number of different levels.

My Bed, 1998, is the infamous **installation** that Emin contributed to the 1999 Turner Prize Exhibition. It's a readymade in the sense that it's a real wooden bed; however, the assemblage has been constructed and, therefore, altered. This is a very literal work. Its space, its lighting and its close proximity to the viewer are all unrelenting.

Taking a look at *My Bed*, we read the debris slowly, almost chronologically, like the lines of a poem. We are drawn, perhaps despite ourselves, to noticing

Figure 2.18 | Tracey Emin, *My Bed*, 1998, mixed media (mattress, linens, various memorabilia), maximum width 234 cm. Source: ©Tracey Emin. All rights reserved, DACS 2015. Image courtesy Saatchi Gallery, London. Photo: Prudence Cuming Associates Ltd.

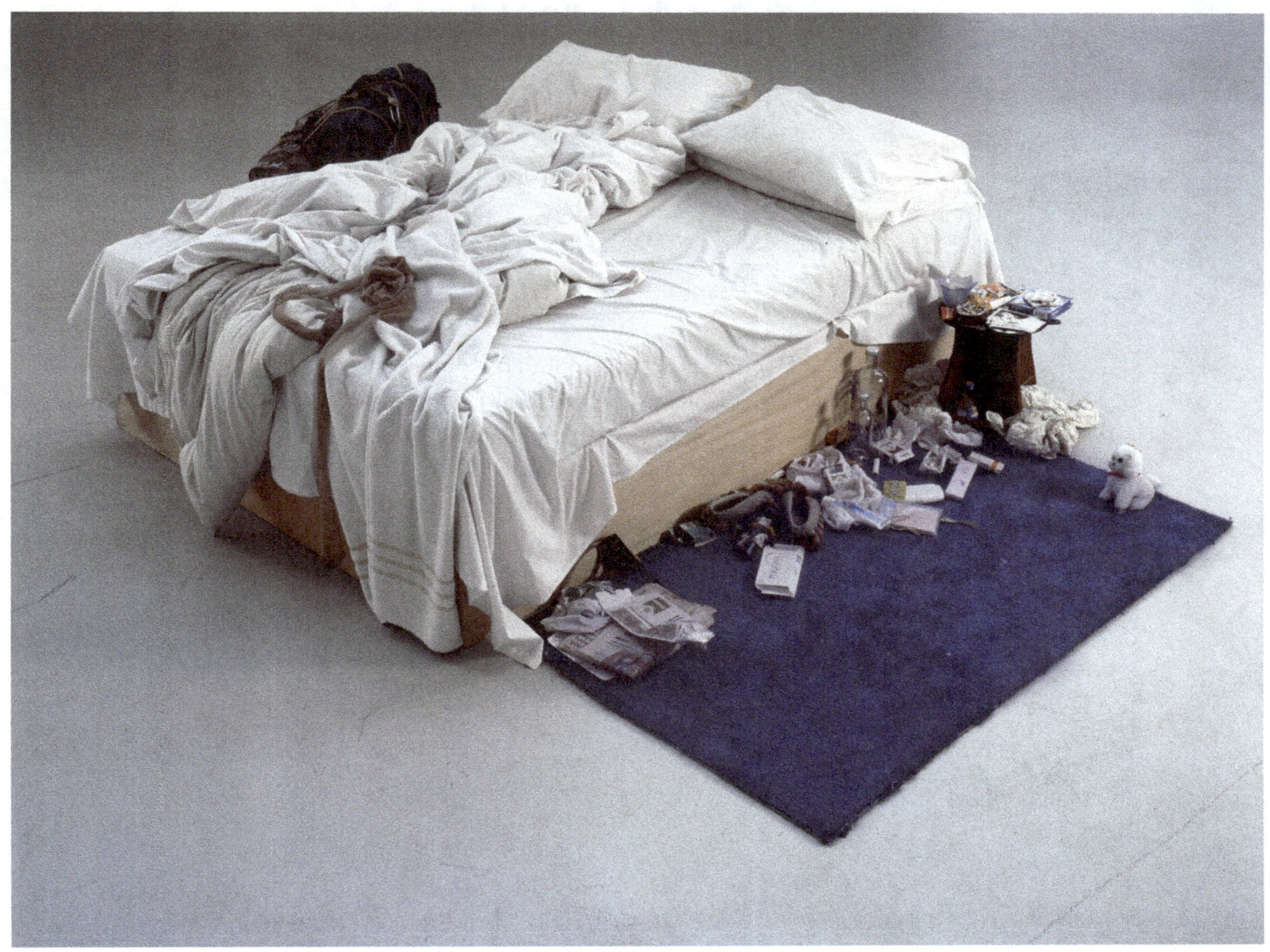

the most personal items that litter the crudely cut carpet to the bed's side. We see the KY jelly, packet of cigarettes, dirty knickers, Tampax applicator, vodka bottles (empty, of course), and a used and bloodied condom. Furthermore, the apparently authentically worn slippers lend credence and perhaps a further pathos to the whole construction. The assemblage is powerfully evocative and suggests memories of past, emotionally loaded events. The floor is so cluttered with taboo objects that it may be hard to tear our eyes away, but finally our gaze is drawn up to those sheets stained with the full spectrum of bodily fluids. This is 'scratch and sniff' art – it is uncultured and indecent but our senses applaud it. The material – all of the above-mentioned objects, plus the bed itself – is 'readymade', but also made, constructed and layered by Emin's assembly of them. The duvet, thrown back to reveal a space, implies her physical presence. The use of space is particularly effective in *My Bed* because it's not illusionistic – we could indeed lie down where the artist lay.

Unlike Andres Serrano's use of urine as a medium to show Christ awash in sublime and ephemeral matter (see *Chapter 1*), Emin's bed appears to be simply urine-stained and distasteful. Arguably, the work's materials and techniques are highly effective in the extrapolation of our reflective engagement with the work. The closeness to someone's personal detritus, self-harm, isolation and desperation feels like an uncomfortable invasion, akin to reading someone else's love letter or secret diary entry. The question is: are we insulted by its coarseness or moved by gaining privileged insight into the artist's psyche? Emin has described the work as looking like a 'crime scene', where someone had been *fucked to death* (Brown, *TE: Tracey Emin*, p. 99).

An hour later I was still there –
Talking on neat vodka –
A full ashtray by my side –
I reluctantly put the receiver down –
Drunk, spinning, I made my way
To bed –
My Bed –
It smelt like I should change the
sheets –
but I kind of liked it –

(Emin, *Always Glad to See You*)

The very idea is repugnant and yet it provides an insight into the process of its construction: the meticulous placing of objects in the overall composition of the work. It all seems to be deeply encoded with autobiographical details. In a further possible layer of interpretation, the unprecedented level of her confession demonstrates courage; the courage to lay it all bare, under bright lights, and allow us to see and possibly feel this artistic construction of her pain. If the work is intended to provoke self-reflection in the viewer, do you think it successfully meets the objective?

Architecture

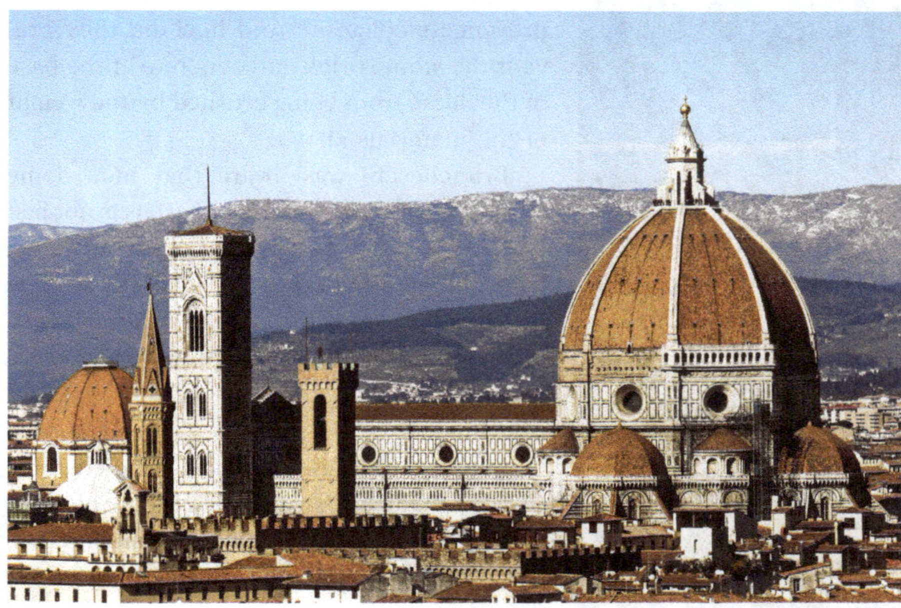

Figure 2.19 | Filippo Brunelleschi, Dome of Florence Cathedral, 1420–1436. Source: © santof / iStockphoto.

The materials, techniques and processes used in architecture often have a significant relationship with the building's form, style and function. It is important to recognise the materials and methods used to construct a building because they so often affect a structure's form, style and function (the thematic title of *Chapter 3*)

Wood, masonry and tile construction

Traditional materials such as brick and stone may be a thing of the past as new technologies enable buildings to double the height of skyscrapers in the future. However, the Florentine architect, goldsmith and sculptor Filippo Brunelleschi (1377–1446) became a major name in the architecture of Early Renaissance Italy when, in a remarkable feat of engineering, he managed to erect what is still the largest **masonry** dome in the world.

In 1418 a competition was announced for the construction of a huge dome to be raised for the partially built cathedral of Florence. The proposed dome would be the highest and the widest ever built, an unprecedented architectural challenge that called for an unprecedented architectural solution.

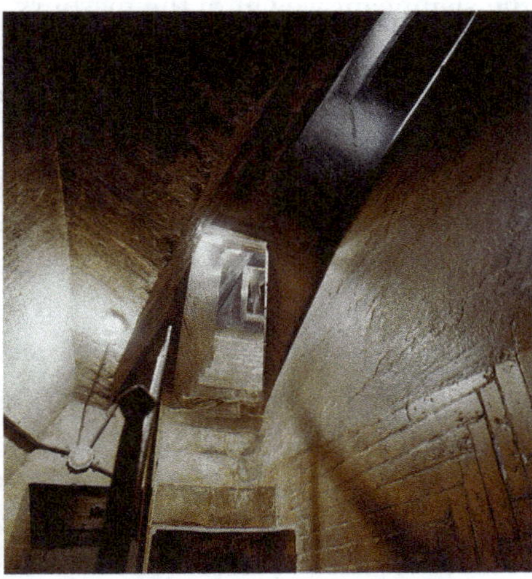

Figure 2.20 | Filippo Brunelleschi, Air space between the shells of the Dome of Florence Cathedral. The herringbone brickwork visible here on the inner and outer shell of the dome is self-supporting. The technique is borrowed from the Pantheon in Rome. Source: © 2015. Photo Scala, Florence.

Renaissance biographer Giorgio Vasari wrote that in order to solve the problem of how to build the dome on the cathedral in Florence, Brunelleschi familiarised himself

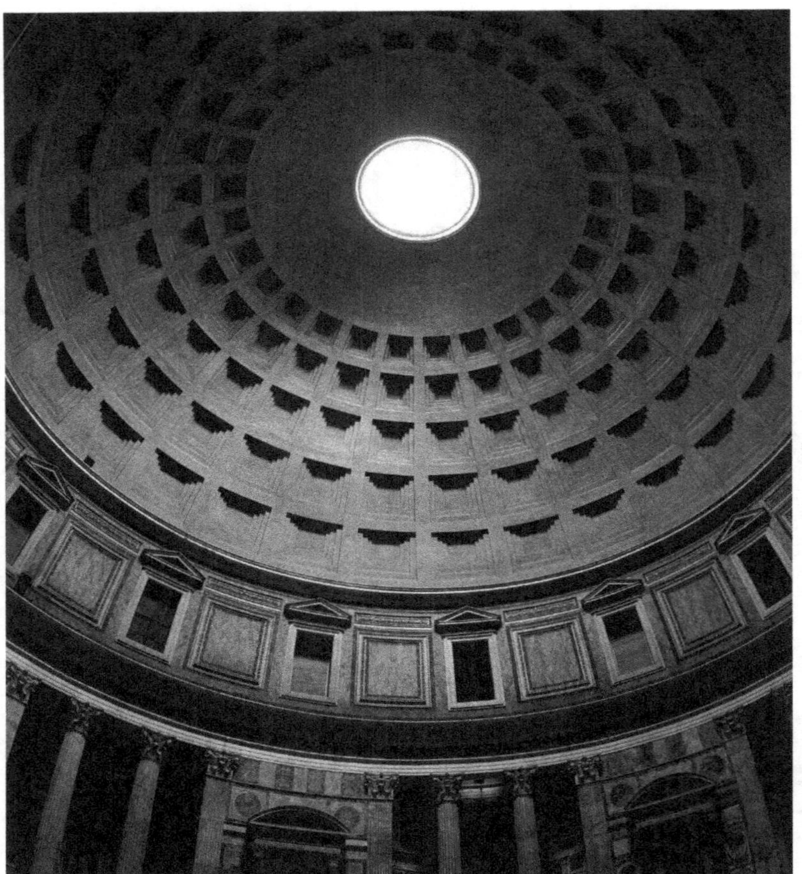

Figure 2.21 | Pantheon, Rome, 118–128 CE, interior of dome. Source: © ROMAOSLO / iStockphoto.

with Roman construction techniques and, in particular, investigated the colossal span and height of the dome of the Pantheon in Rome (125 CE), which had no visible means of support. How did the Roman builders counteract the 'push' and 'pull' forces on the dome and prevent its collapse? And how did they prevent the stone, brick and concrete at the base of the dome from being crushed by the weight of the materials above?

Brunelleschi was aware that in a dome structure the weight of the materials is not just transmitted downwards, but also outwards, by a pull energy known as 'hoop stress'. The Pantheon showed that a perfect hemispherical dome was possible, but only with massive **abutment**. (The Pantheon walls are 7.5 metres thick.)

Florence Cathedral's double-skinned dome (used in medieval Islamic structures), coupled with its self-supporting brickwork and innovative **hoop-tie**, eliminated the need for Gothic **flying buttresses**; a welcome formula given the Italians' disdain for them. The stone and wooden chains which encircle the belly of the dome like a giant belt are buried deep in the masonry and remain invisible to this day. Perhaps Brunelleschi's greatest feat of engineering was raising the dome without the need for wooden **centring**. It was only with the use of modern industrial materials like plastic and high-carbon steel that wider vaults were raised some six centuries later, such as the Millennium Dome (now the O2) in London, the largest dome in the world, albeit a mast-supported structure.

The dome's vault was seated on existing walls nearly 52 metres high and Brunelleschi developed an ox hoist, a ground-breaking innovation, to carry incredible weights up to the builders. The dome itself consisted of two layers. Four sandstone bands encircled the inner dome, linked by iron clamps. Their tensile strength prevented the bottom of the dome being forced outwards by the significant weight of the masonry. The **herringbone brickwork** used for the interior layer was ingenious in that it was self-supporting, with the weight of the bricks being transferred down onto the circumference. Brunelleschi resurrected the great and long-forgotten achievements of Roman engineering in this interlocking masonry technique. The outer layer becomes thinner as its rises, as do its eight vertical **ribs**. To dissipate the force exerted on the dome by the wind Brunelleschi included 72 small round windows on the outer skin of the dome, which not only prevent damage but bring light and air into a cramped and claustrophobic space. The dome is almost Gothic in outline and rib structure, thereby having stylistic integrity with the older Gothic cathedral.

The form of a building is largely dependent upon the architect's understanding of the qualities of materials, the limitations, and the possibilities of techniques and processes. The most successful architects, at least in the past, had to be simultaneously structural engineers and artists willing to take risks. The next building looks back in time to the same Gothic period Brunelleschi was keen to leave behind.

Across the English Channel, and more than 400 years after Brunelleschi's dome, William Morris (1834–1896), founder of the nineteenth-century **Arts and Crafts Movement**, commissioned the architect Philip Webb (1831–1915) to design a home for himself and his new wife, Jane Burden, in Bexleyheath, Kent. (See *2.2 Let's connect the themes: historical perspectives – the politics of Arts and Crafts.*) Both men were committed to the resurrection of the **applied arts**. The result of their collaboration is Red House, constructed using masonry and exposed common red brick in a traditional, **vernacular** style.

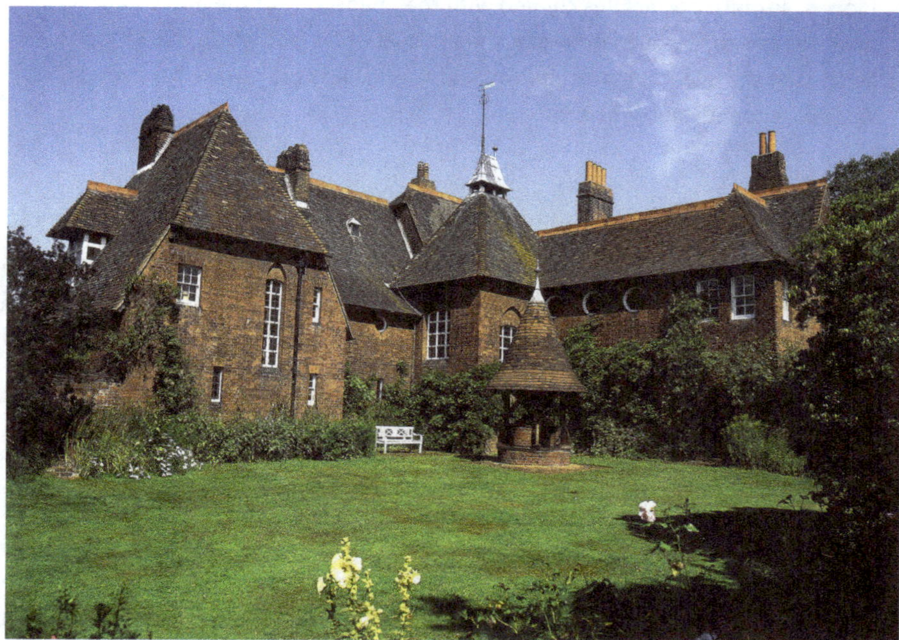

Figure 2.22 | Philip Webb, Red House, Bexley Heath, 1859–1860, east view with well. Source: © David Ball / Alamy.

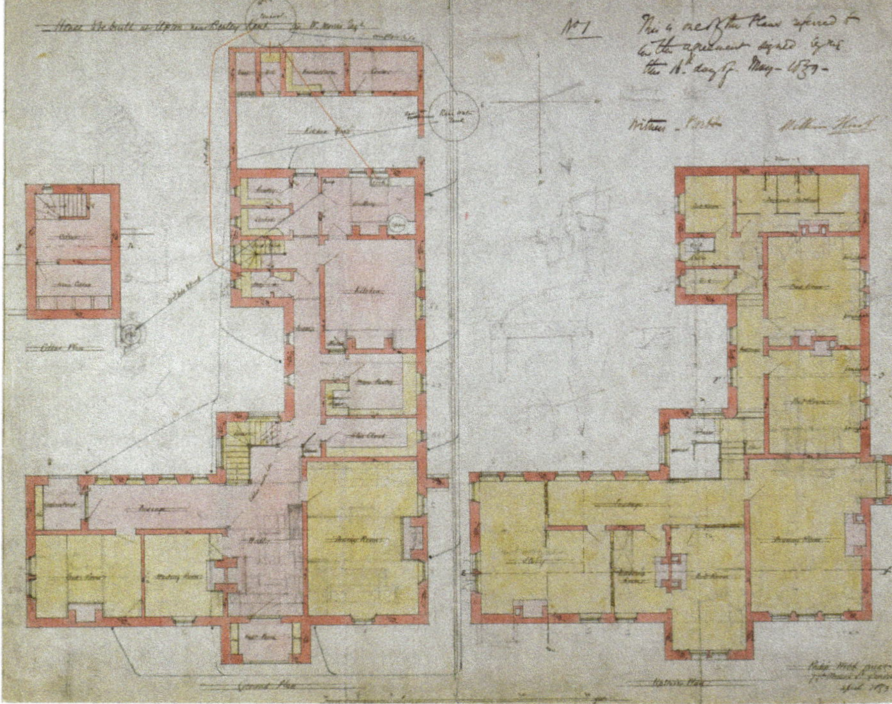

Figure 2.23 | Philip Webb, Red House, Bexley Heath, 1859–1860, L-shaped plan. Source: © Heritage Image Partnership Ltd / Alamy.

Philip Webb used a wide variety of different window shapes in Red House, including round ones for a passage-way on the first floor. How many other shapes can you see?

2.2 Let's connect the themes: historical perspectives – the politics of Arts and Crafts

Along with fellow members of the Arts and Crafts Movement, Morris reacted strongly to the new industrialised trends in mechanical production and harked back to a period in history when materials were worked by hand, and every brick and tile was an individual artefact invested with its own intrinsic value. Morris' **socialist** principles chimed with the philosophy of the movement – man was not to feel alienated from the product of his labours. In 1885 Morris addressed the question of 'useful work versus useless toil' in a lecture which was subsequently published.

A domestic dwelling set in approximately one acre and built in plain red brick, Red House is robust, perhaps even a little austere. Its ground-hugging and horizontal two-storey construction is counterbalanced by the striking vertical emphases provided by the steeply pitched **gables** and chimneys. The 'L' shaped plan is irregular, as is the building's roofline, **fenestration**, hand-made clay tiles and individual bricks, but the uniform red of its exterior, the repetition of triangular shapes, and the undisguised nature of its materials combine to make a unified whole out of the disparate parts.

Upon closer inspection the building is surprisingly detailed and entirely organic, 'home-made' and warm. The entrance to Red House is approached from the side and has been described as hugged by the wide, low arch of the porch. Its pointed Gothic shape reminds us of the medieval period when craftsmanship was celebrated, something Webb and Morris were keen to return to in an age increasingly defined by **modernity**, as exemplified in new industrial materials and techniques. The twinned **lancet** arches of the **oriel** window on the northwest side epitomise the hand-crafted, labour-intensive construction of Red House. The lancet enjoyed resurgence during the **Gothic Revival** of Victorian times, when Augustus Pugin and his successors advocated the Gothic as a style capable of 'moral reform'. The diamond detail in the leaded-light window is repeated in the series of triangular roof shapes and the **corbels** that support the oriel itself. However, the match is less poetic than it first appears because the leaded lights are in fact later substitutes for the original sash windows.

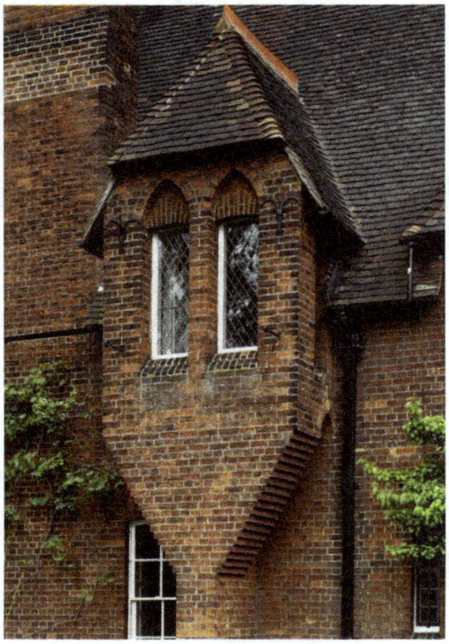

Figure 2.24 | Philip Webb, Red House, Bexley Heath, 1859–1860, detail of oriel window, west front of Red House, designed in 1859 by Philip Webb for William Morris. Built of red brick laid in 'English Bond' with a red tiled roof. Source: © National Trust Images / Andrew Butler.

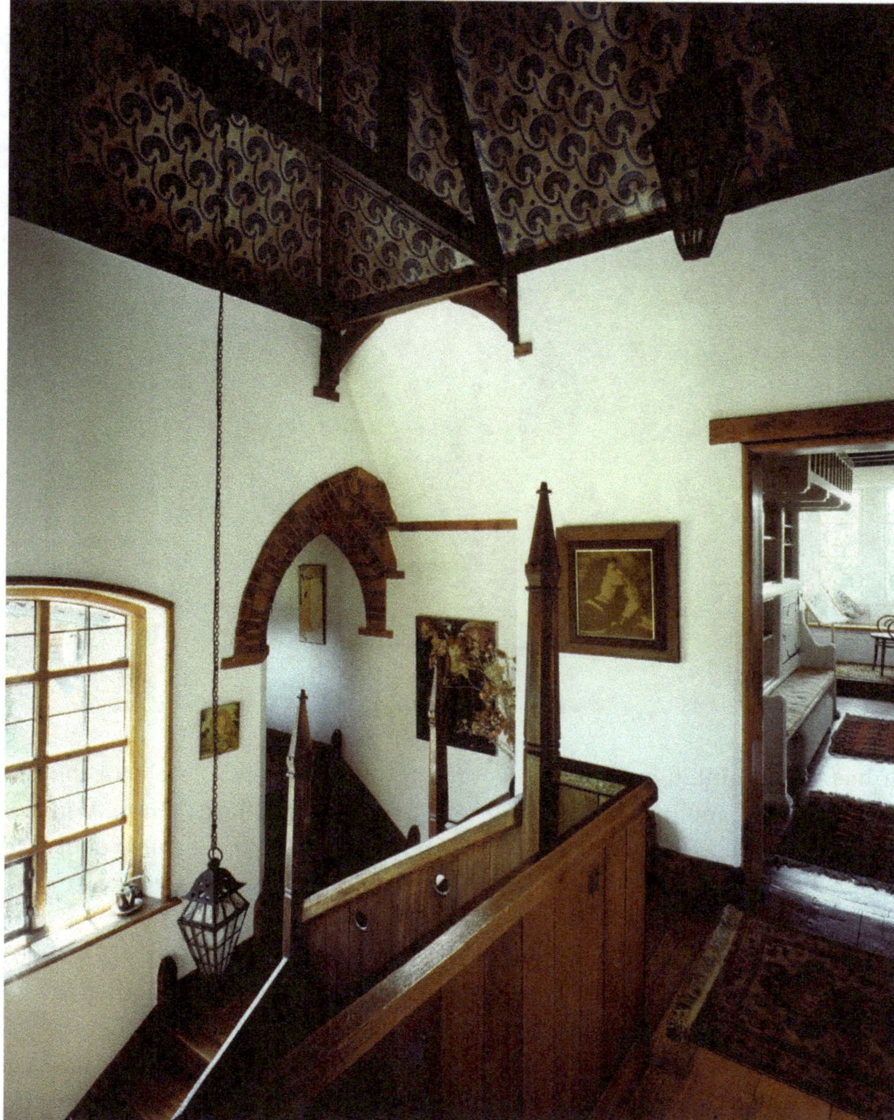

Figure 2.25 | Philip Webb, Red House, Bexley Heath, 1859–1860, oak staircase landing. Source: © Arcaid Images / Alamy.

The furniture, textiles, wall hangings, bespoke door handles and hand-painted glass panes all contribute to the holistic and collaborative nature of Red House. Its fireplaces are all undisguised brick, possibly a reaction to the Victorian preference for disguising fireplaces and façades with plaster, paint and **stucco**. Red House's staircase, with its exposed underside revealing the very mechanics of its joinery, deviates from the trend for 'boxing-in' and making neat. It is a feature that echoes the wooden-framed construction of the well situated between its wings. Another design feature of the close-boarded **balustrade** is its portholes, anecdotally described as 'peeping holes' for the Morris children.

Apart from the vernacular materials, techniques and processes employed in the construction of Red House, its form is arguably said to follow its function too: most rooms are orientated north, probably because Victorians disliked exposure to the sun. Sunlight pours into the hall through a series of windows and it *diminishes as the day and season progresses, keeping the main rooms cool in the heat of the summer* (Marsh, *William Morris and Red House: A Collaboration Between Architect and Owner*, p. 29). However, despite the building's vernacular style, and Webb's desire to use local materials,

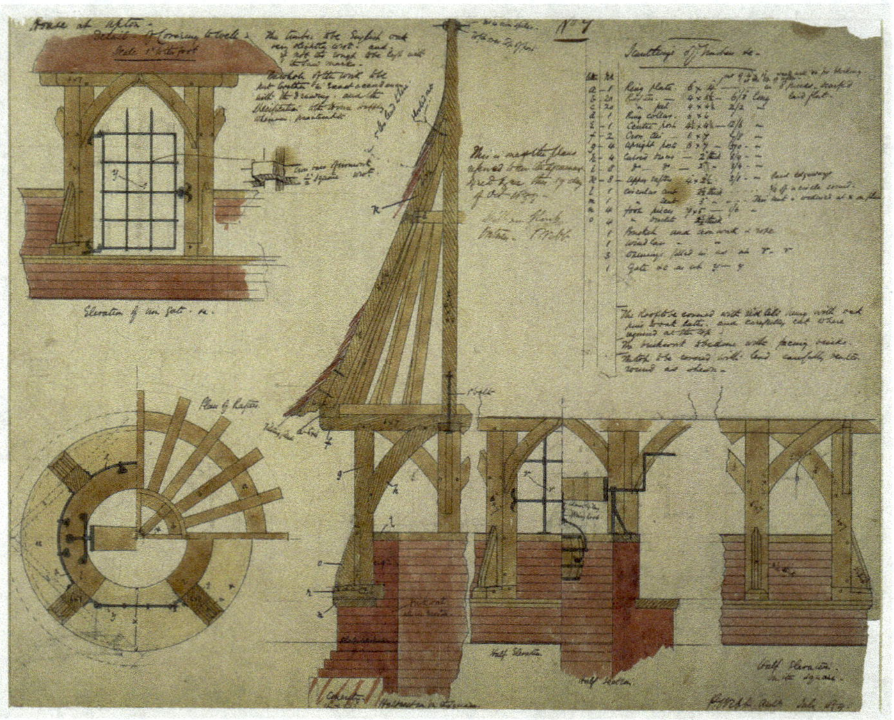

Figure 2.26 | Philip Webb, 1858, pen, ink and watercolour on paper, original architectural drawings for the conical wellhead at Red House, based on local Kentish oast houses, situated close to the house, in the east garden at Red House, Bexley Heath. Private Collection. Source: Private Collection / The Stapleton Collection / Bridgeman Images.

it has been pointed out that he ignored the yellow-brown bricks of the immediate area, and purchased red bricks from further afield (Marsh, *William Morris and Red House: A Collaboration Between Architect and Owner*, p. 30). Why do you think he chose red over yellow bricks if he desired to use local materials?

The English Victorian art critic and theorist John Ruskin (1819–1900) wrote extensively on architecture, and his advocacy of the Gothic Revival style had a significant influence on Morris. In Ruskin's essay *The Seven Lamps of Architecture* (published in book form in 1849), he set down seven principles ('lamps') of good architecture. Each 'lamp' has its own chapter, and the second of these was entitled 'Truth'. This related to Ruskin's belief that a good building was good if it was 'honest' to its materials. This effectually expounded a celebration of the natural and unchanged state of materials. Ruskin described the unnecessary cladding, painting or covering-up of the natural state of a material as an '[a]rchitectural deceit' (Ruskin, *The Seven Lamps of Architecture*, p. 35). Morris and Webb's Red House responds to Ruskin's demand for 'truth to materials' in every irregular-shaped and multi-tonal brick and tile, although it was anathema to those who preferred the stuccoed villas of London that Webb and Morris saw as symptomatic of the 'degradation' of architecture. Where else does Red House reveal its materials and construction methods?

Red House embodies many of the architectural precepts set out by John Ruskin, including the functionality and desirability of steeply pitched roofs and gables. Various compositional elements of the house direct our gaze heavenward: those pointed arches, defining chimneys, conical wellhead in the east garden lead us to the weathervane carrying the owner's initials 'WJM 1859' (William: Janey: Morris).

Continuing with the legacy of the medieval, Morris tops his home, or castle, with a medieval-style pennant. Its wrought iron frame supports a copper flag with a horse's head and three horseshoes: his father's coat of arms. This feature, coupled with the turreted newel posts of the staircase and minstrels' gallery of the north reception room upstairs, suggests that Morris proclaimed this house his realm.

The house and garden were conceived as one, and the pilgrim's rest (bench seat) accessed from the pointed arch leading from the east garden links the two. The wellhead is treated with the same materials and techniques as the house and they have a symbiotic relationship. Indeed, viewed from the east, the witch's hat shape of the wellhead echoes the pyramid-roofed stair tower which acts like a hinge between the two wings of the main house. The well was a necessity and functioned to provide water but, in accordance with the philosophy of this entire conception, it was an object of value and beauty in itself. Red House was not just a family home but a space where the **Pre-Raphaelites**, with whom Morris was associated, gained inspiration and where local craftsmanship was celebrated

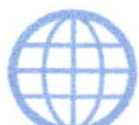

See the companion website for details relating to the history of Lloyd's buildings and their locations since the company's beginning in 1688.

Steel, concrete and glass

The crafts-based materials, techniques and processes employed at Red House can be contrasted to those that epitomise the height of mechanisation in the Lloyd's Building (1978–1986), designed by Richard Rogers (born 1933). Yet, in their distinctive ways, both are examples of the vernacular.

Lloyd's Insurance is a commercial building (not open to the public) and a global beacon for commerce. Lloyd's commissioned Rogers to redevelop their existing site. The building cost £75 million – in exchange for which Lloyd's got one of London's most iconic buildings.

Its skeletal frame and glass **curtain-wall** construction would not have been achievable without the use of steel. The windows have triple-layered solar-controlled glass, and there is a ventilated cavity to allow for the maximum refraction of artificial light into the interior – a functional and environmentally friendly feature. This 12-storey manifestation of engineering and industrial design draws a close comparison with Joseph Paxton's Crystal Palace, 1851. Both represent great London buildings that were modular in construction and served the demands of British industry.

Left to right:

Figure 2.27 | Richard Rogers, Lloyd's Building, City of London, 1978–1986, City of London, façade with atrium. Source: © Robert Harding Picture Library Ltd / Alamy.

Figure 2.28 | The modular, prefabricated iron sections of the Crystal Palace, London, 1851, are discernible in this drawing, as is its inspirational role in the Lloyd's atrium. Source: © FALKENSTEINFOTO / Alamy.

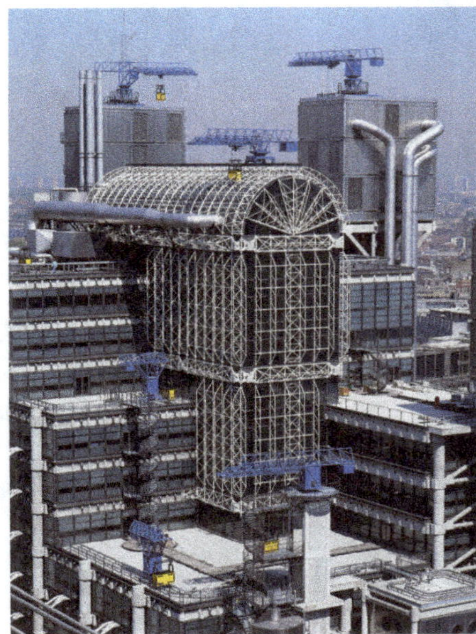

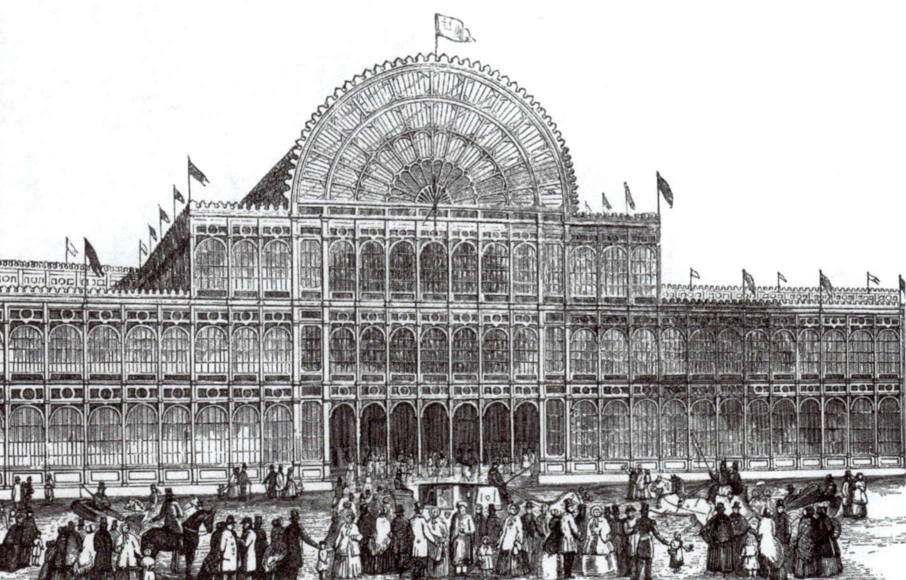

Lloyd's Crystal Palace-inspired **atrium** draws inspiration from the Victorian period in the same way that Red House drew inspiration from medieval architecture. Despite being built of very different materials, both are truthful to their respective mediums. Lloyd's effects proclaim the 'metalness of metal' – hard, durable, mechanised, light-reflective, futuristic and urban – while Red House proclaims the 'clayness of clay', seeming friable, perishable, handmade, light-absorbing, traditional and rural.

The Crystal Palace, London, 1851, designed by Joseph Paxton, a gardener and greenhouse builder, was constructed from cast iron, wrought iron, glass and timber to house the Great Exhibition, held to celebrate the achievements of the British Empire under one 'temporary' roof. It was symbolic of all that was deemed great about the Industrial Revolution and the emergence of new technologies.

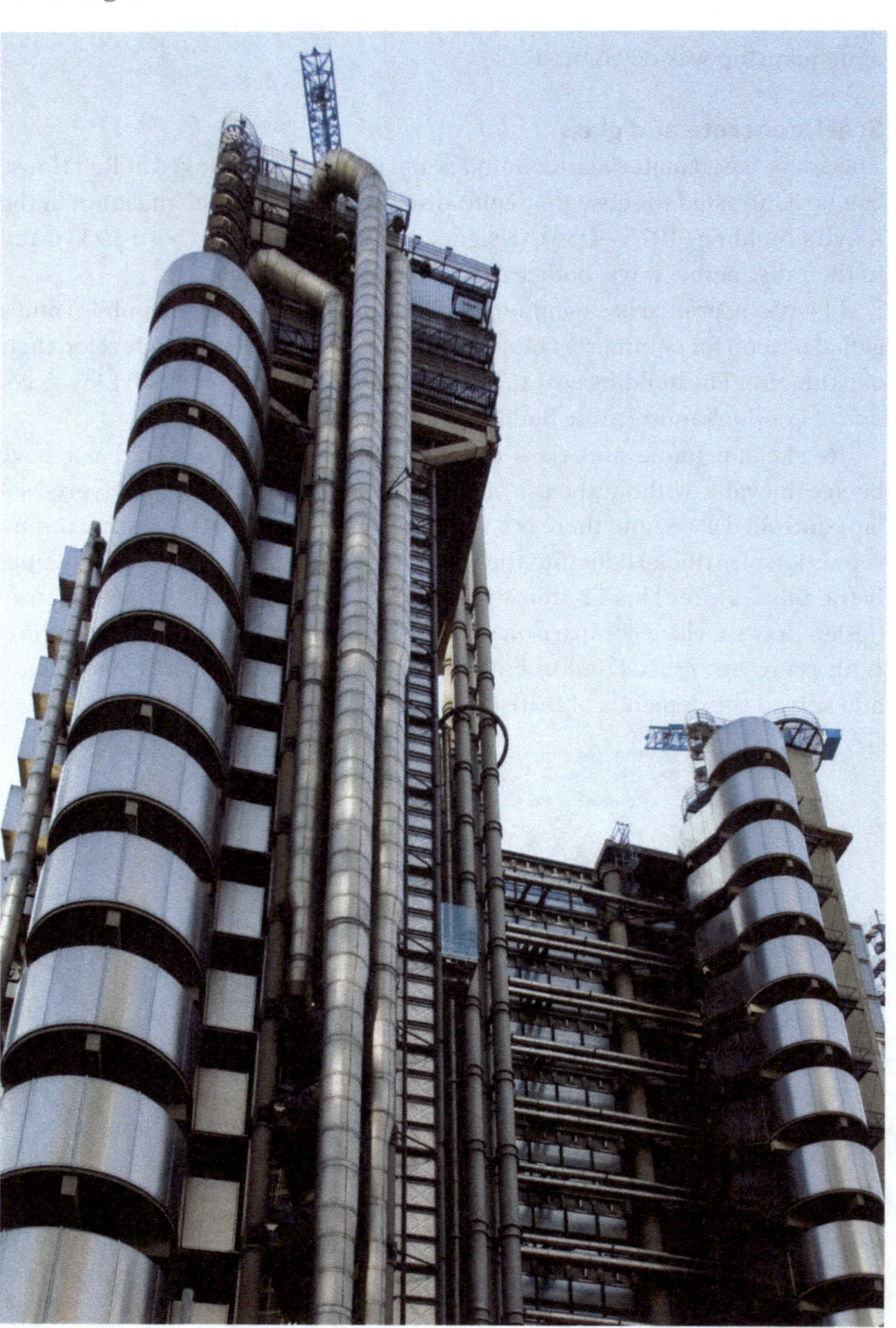

Figure 2.29 | Richard Rogers, Lloyd's of London, exterior ducts. Source: Images from www.lloyds.com have been reproduced with the kind permission of Lloyd's of London.

The building was a kit-building project on a giant scale and testament to the ability to mass-produce metal modules or units that could be quickly and cost-effectively assembled on location. An innovative, steam-powered machine developed by Paxton standardised elements of the construction, enabling the building to be designed and constructed in eight months. It was *hailed as the first architectural application of Adam Smith's principle of the division of labour* and became a crowd-drawing feat that would ultimately inspire Henry Ford's automobile assembly lines of the future (Parkyn, *Wonders of World Architecture*, p. 136).

The Lloyd's Building has its staircases, lifts, electrical power conduits and water pipes on the outside, enabling maintenance workers to easily access toilets, lifts, kitchens and fire-escapes. The prefabricated and modular construction offers a degree of flexibility to the interior design, highly suited to

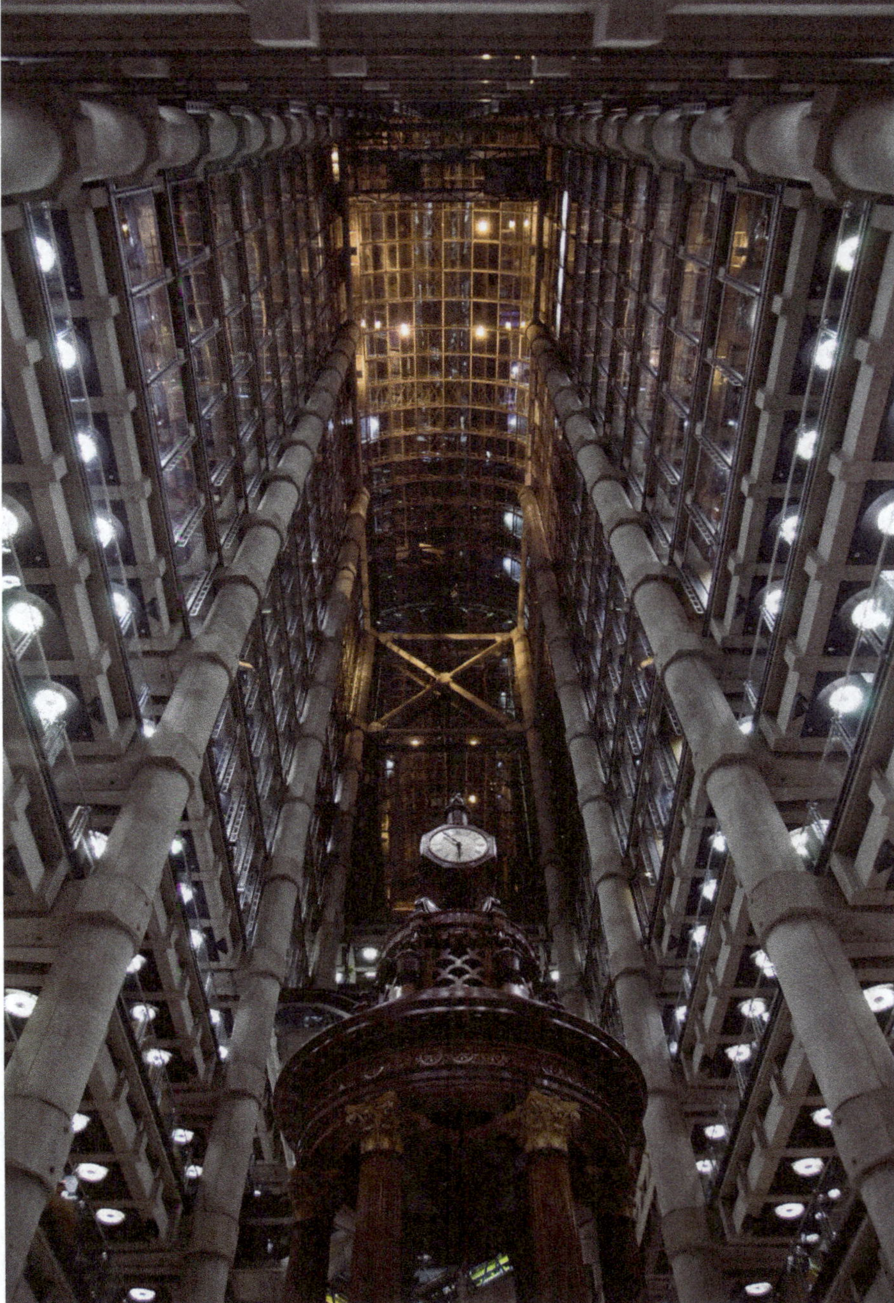

Figure 2.30 | Richard Rogers, Lloyd's of London, interior of atrium. Source: Images from www.lloyds.com have been reproduced with the kind permission of Lloyd's of London.

the demands of modern industry.

Its style is modern and '**high-tech**' on the one hand, and skeletal and unfinished on the other. Its steel frame allows for an open-plan interior and exposed exterior. It has been described as 'a building on life-support', 'an oil refinery' and 'the inside-out building'. The brightly coloured cranes that crown the building are both decorative and functional (they serve as hoists for the window cleaning gantries). Lloyd's choice of Richard Rogers as the architect and the fact that the 12 glass lifts were the first of their kind in the UK contribute to the value of the building as a high-status assertion.

Reinforced concrete columns soar through the cathedral-like space of the atrium some 200 feet to its glass roof and the exposed mechanics of the escalators criss-cross between two sides of the building (Figure 2.30). Their undisguised nature is reminiscent of the underside of Webb's staircase in Red House: both buildings expose us to the materials and techniques and processes of their construction.

The focal point of the ground floor is the underwriting room: a large, open-plan interior with a cathedral-like space rising up to the summit, visible on the outside as the segmental **pediment** of the atrium. As the escalators carry insurance brokers to every floor, their ascent and descent is visible for 360 degrees. In the Lloyd's Building we can sense that the need for transparency in business is a philosophy that has manifested itself in its very materials, techniques and processes: its skeletal, see-through structure echoes its function as one of the few insurance trading floors remaining in the world where business deals are negotiated face-to-face.

Despite the human element of Lloyd's face-to-face trading, the skeletal structure is a product of the kind of corporate evolution – **automation** – that Morris had so feared and rejected when he was having Red House built. Described as a beacon of capitalism within the city of London, and in Honor and Fleming's *A World History of Art* as *one of 'High Tech's finest achievements to date*', this approach to, and celebration of, precision engineering is evidently at odds with the emphasis on individuality and craftsmanship guarded

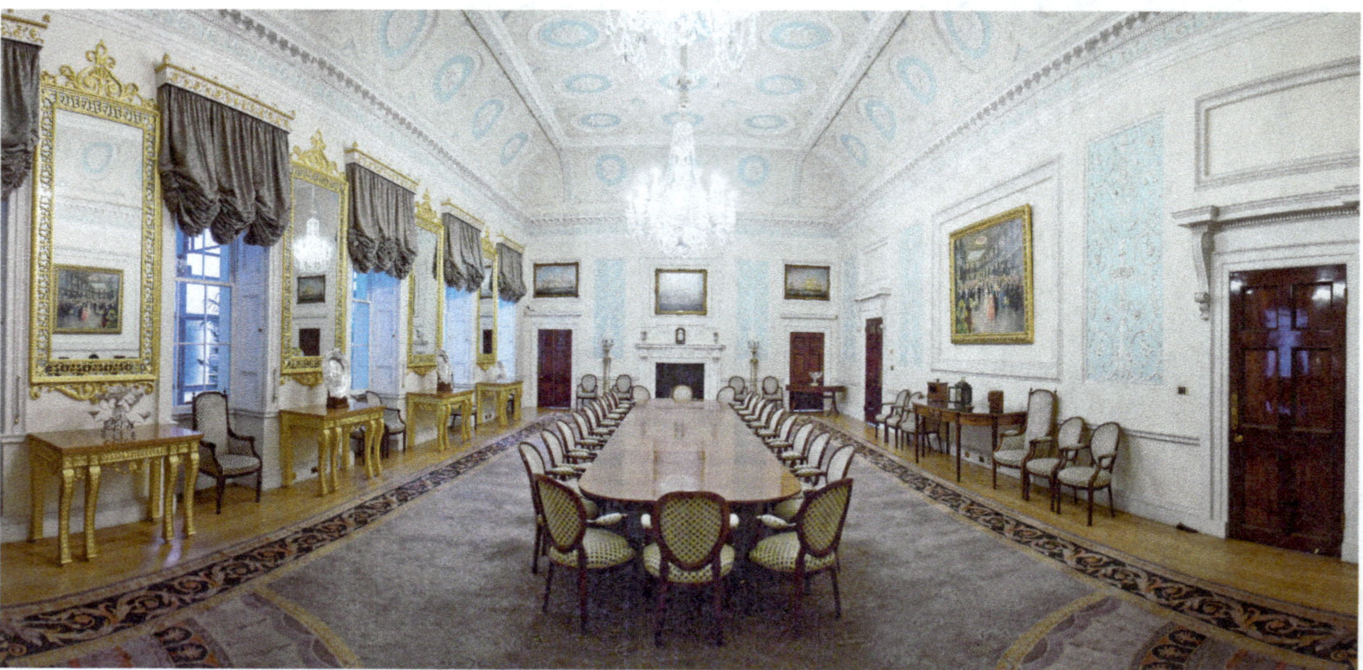

Figure 2.31 | Richard Rogers, Lloyd's of London, elaborate plasterwork in Committee Room designed by Robert Adam, 1763.
Source: Images from www.lloyds.com have been reproduced with the kind permission of Lloyd's of London.

by Philip Webb and others in the Arts and Crafts Movement (Honor and Fleming, *A World History of Art*, p. 869).

Lloyd's, along with architectural writers, describe the building as fundamentally **postmodern**; however, in architectural terms the Lloyd's Building is modern because of its intrinsically functionalist design. Where it incorporates older elements, these are not pastiche, as in Postmodernism, but actual/real older elements. For example, there remain many physical relics of the old Lloyd's Building, including a preserved wood-panelled Committee Room designed by Robert Adam in 1763 (see Figure 2.31) and the historic Lutine Bell on the ground floor relocated in its entirety. Lloyd's subsidiary entrance on 12 Leadenhall Street (Figure 2.32) boasts a classical triangular pediment with richly decorated **tympanum**, juxtaposed with its twentieth-century polished steel body. These significant nods to Classicism clash with its predominantly high-tech exterior. Lloyd's controversial design statement, eclectic ensemble and tremendous expense were all deemed risky at the time, but if Lloyd's, the giant insurer, could not take a risk, then who could?

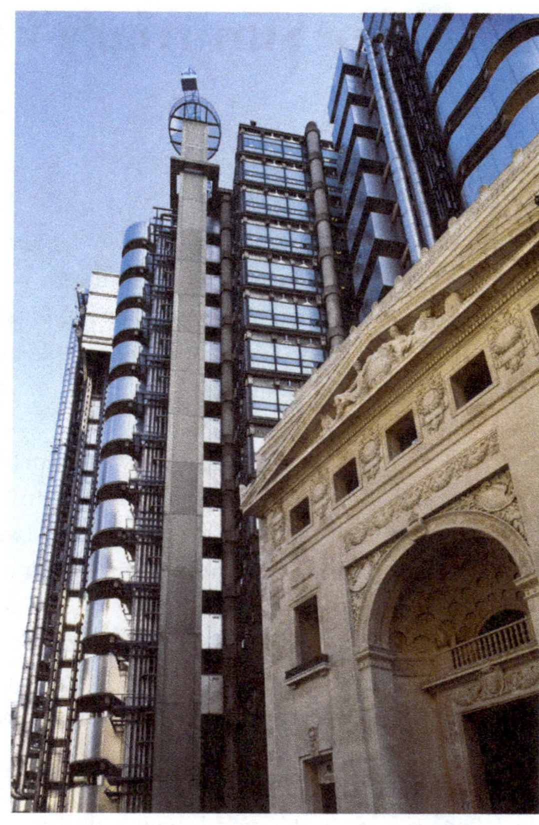

Figure 2.32 | Entrance to Lloyd's Building, 12 Leadenhall Street, London, with classical triangular pediment.
Source: © Gregory Wrona / Alamy.

The term Postmodernism is far from straightforward and is used in many different ways. **Marxist** social theorist Fredric Jameson, in his essay *Postmodernism, or, The Cultural Logic of Late Capitalism*, describes the term as parasitical on all of the other 'isms' – Classicism and Modernism, for example (Jameson, *Postmodernism, or, The Cultural Logic of Late Capitalism*, p. xii).

Postmodernism is not pure, neither is it a break from the past, he suggests, but rather it is a continuum of late capitalism, *a simple prolongation of more of the same under different sheep's clothing* (Jameson, *Postmodernism, or, The Cultural Logic of Late Capitalism*, p. xiii).

2.4 Checkpoint question
What kind of structure replaced load-bearing walls to support a roof in the twentieth century?

In fact, Jameson warns us against using the term altogether. Paradoxically, Postmodernism, in its rebuttal of any one true 'ism', such as Jameson's Marxism incidentally, finds its position as a theory, or 'ism' itself, arguably untenable.

Chapter Summary Exercise

Using the words below complete the Chapter Summary. Each word or term should be used only once.

high-tensile
elongation
giornate
chiaroscuro
reveal
style
glass
steel
disguise
lime-proof
subtractive
egg yolk
wall
fast drying
low-tensile
Renaissance
form
gold leaf

Fresco is made using ________ pigments and water, and is painted into the surface of a freshly lime-plastered ________. The medium is then absorbed into the wall itself as the plaster dries. During the fresco method the artist is able to paint the wet plaster only in sections. This is known as a day's work or ________, because once dry the plaster would fail to absorb the pigment.

________, prevalent in the fourteenth century, was often used in paintings to reflect the status of the Virgin Mary or other religious scenes.

Egg tempura uses ________ mixed with water, and, like modern acrylic paint, it dries very quickly, making modelling particularly difficult. The development of ________ would create a more realistic modelling effect and heighten the realism of painted images.

Acrylic paint, which is a relatively recent medium, is very ________ in comparison to oil paint. It is less suited to images that require modelling.

Marble is a ________ medium which means it is liable to breakage if exploited beyond the capability of its properties. The process from which a block of marble is carved is called ________ because stone is removed.

While classic bronze prototypes and their resurgence during the ________ tended to ________ the materials and processes of their making, many twentieth and twenty-first-century sculptures have consciously tried to ________ them. Bronze is a ________ medium because it can withstand ________ without breaking.

The materials, techniques and processes used in architecture often have a significant relationship with the building's ________ and ________. Commercial buildings often use modern industrial materials such as ________ and ________.

Checkpoint Answers

2.1 Which paint medium would be most effective for tonal modelling of form and why?
Traditional glazing technique of oil paint with subtle build up from shadows to highlights.

2.2 What is meant by 'truth to material/medium'?
When an artist respects and enhances the qualities inherent in the material rather than making it imitate something else (e.g. marble looking like a stone rather than like flesh or hair).

2.3 Explain why bronze statues are able to have protruding limbs and a small base supporting a larger mass, which is not possible in wooden sculptures.
The metal alloy bronze has high-tensile strength which allows for horizontal extensions as well as high compressive strength which is able to support a heavy weight.

2.4 What kind of structure replaced load-bearing walls to support a roof in the twentieth century?
Skeletal frame and hanging or curtain wall.

References

Bray, X. *The Sacred Made Real: Spanish Painting and Sculpture, 1600–1700,* National Gallery / Yale University Press, 2009.

Brown, N. *TE: Tracey Emin,* Tate Publishing, 2006.

De Leeuw, R. (ed.) *The Letters of Vincent van Gogh,* trans. Pomeranz, A., Penguin, 1997.

Duby, G. and Daval, J.-L. (eds.) *Sculpture from Antiquity to the Present Day*, Taschen, 2010.

Emin, T. *Always Glad to See You,* Tracey Emin, 1996.

Hamilton, G.H. *Painting and Sculpture in Europe, 1880–1940,* 6th ed., Yale University Press, 1993.

Hicks, C. *Girl in a Green Gown: The History and Mystery of the Arnolfini Portrait,* Chatto & Windus, 2001.

Honor, H. and Fleming, J. *A World History of Art,* 6th ed., Laurence King, 2002.

Ione, A. *Innovation and Visualization: Trajectories, Strategies, and Myths,* Editions Rodopi, 2004.

Jameson, F. *Postmodernism, or, The Cultural Logic of Late Capitalism,* Duke University Press, 1991.

Lydiate, H. 'What Is Art? A Brief Review of International Judicial Interpretations of Art in the Light of the UK Supreme Court's 2011 Judgement in the *Star Wars Case: Lucasfilm Limited v. Ainsworth', Journal of International Media Law,* Vol. 4, No. 2, 2012–2013, http://www.swlaw.edu/pdfs/jimel/4_2_lydiate.pdf.

Marsh, J. *William Morris and Red House: A Collaboration Between Architect and Owner,* National Trust Books, 2005.

Parkyn, N. *Wonders of World Architecture,* Thames & Hudson, 2009.

Penny, N. *The Materials of Sculpture,* 3rd ed., Yale University Press, 2005.

Ruskin, J. *The Seven Lamps of Architecture,* Dover Publications, 1989.

Schama, S. *The Power of Art,* Bodley Head, 2006.

Stevas, N. St. J. 'Norman St. John Stevas in Conversation | Elisabeth Frink', 1981, http://www.bbc.co.uk/ archive/sculptors/12803.shtml.

Vasari, G. *Lives of the Artists*, Vol. 1, Penguin, 1987. (First published 1550.)

Other Useful Sources

Ayres, J. *The Artist's Craft: A History of Tools, Techniques and Materials,* Phaidon, 1985.

Blazwick, I. and Wilson, S. (eds.) *Tate Modern: The Handbook,* Tate Publishing, 2000.

King, R. *Brunelleschi's Dome: The Story of the Great Cathedral in Florence,* Pimlico, 2000.

Mathieson, E. and Tapies, X.A. *Street Artists: The Complete Guide*, Graffito Books, 2009.

Mayer, R. *The Artist's Handbook of Materials and Techniques,* Faber & Faber, 1991.

Nesbitt, J. *Chris Ofili,* Tate Publishing, 2010.

Rosenthal, N. and Stone, R. *Sensation: Young British Artists from the Saatchi Collection,* Thames & Hudson, 2009. (First published 1997.)

Chapter 3
Form, Style and Function

Learning Outcomes

By the end of this chapter you will be able to:

- define the concepts of form, style and function in relation to painting, sculpture and architecture and show how these help to determine our interpretation
- describe the formal characteristics that comprise different styles/movements in the history of art
- compare and contrast different works of art and architecture of similar or different styles.

Thinking About Art: A Thematic Guide to Art History, First Edition. Penny Huntsman.

Chapter Map

This chapter map provides a visual overview of Chapter 3 – 'Form, Style and Function' – together with its key works.

The Beginning of Western Art

Classical style

– Polykleitos, *Doryphoros (Spear Bearer)*, 450–440 BCE
– Iktinos and Kallikrates, the Parthenon Temple, 447–438 BCE

Discovery of Antiquity and Development of Sacred Art

The Early Renaissance

– Masaccio (1401–1428/29), *The Virgin and Child*, 1426
– Donatello (c.1386–1466), *David*, 1440

The High Renaissance

– Raphael (1483–1520), *Alba Madonna*, c.1510

The Baroque

– Artemisia Gentileschi (1593–1656), *Judith Slaying Holofernes*, c.1620
– Gian Lorenzo Bernini (1598–1680), *Apollo and Daphne*, 1624
– Pietro da Cortona (1596–1669), Santa Maria della Pace, 1656–1657

Neo-classicism

– Jacques-Louis David (1748–1825), *Death of Marat*, 1793

A Move Towards Individualism

Romanticism

– Francisco de Goya (1746–1828), *The Third of May 1808*, 1814
– Théodore Géricault (1791–1824), *The Raft of Medusa*, 1819
– Eugène Delacroix (1798–1863), *The Death of Sardanapalus*, 1827

Impressionism and after

– Claude Monet (1840–1926), *Autumn Effect at Argenteuil*, 1873
– Mary Cassatt (1844–1926), *Lydia at the Tapestry Loom*, c.1881
– Edgar Degas (1834–1917), *Dancer Looking at the Sole of her Right Foot*, c.1900, cast 1920
– Vincent van Gogh (1853–1890), *Wheatfield with Crows*, 1890

New and Divergent Ways of Seeing in the Twentieth Century

Cubism

– Pablo Picasso (1881–1973), *Portrait of Daniel-Henry Kahnweiler*, 1910

Futurism

– Umberto Boccioni (1882–1916), *Unique Forms of Continuity in Space*, 1913

European Modernism: In Search of an Elemental Truth

Modernism and abstract art

– Piet Mondrian (1872–1944), *Composition with Yellow, Blue and Red*, 1937–1942

Form, style and function in architecture

In search of purer forms

– Gerrit Thomas Rietveld (1888–1965), Schröder House, 1924

Form follows function: Modern Movement

– Le Corbusier (1887–1965), Villa Savoye, 1928–1931

The Classical vocabulary in architecture

– Sir Herbert Baker (1862–1946), the Bank of England, 1929–1935

A style of its own

– Frank Lloyd Wright (1867–1959), Fallingwater, 1935–1938

New forms from new technologies

– Future Systems, J.P. Morgan Media Centre, Lord's Cricket Ground, London, 1999

Introduction

This chapter introduces you to the concepts of form and style in relation to painting and sculpture, and form, style and function in relation to architecture. For ease of reference some of the most recognised styles or movements in the history of art, for example, Classical, Renaissance and Neo-classical will be examined chronologically in terms of the individual formal elements – line, colour, **tone** and texture – that constitute their respective style. Your teacher may decide to teach you the skills of **formal analysis** separately – perhaps before examining the six chapter themes – or may use each thematic example as an opportunity to pause and complete a formal analysis first. Help with conducting a formal analysis is provided explicitly in the 'Formal Analysis Toolbox' section at the start of the book. While it is beneficial for you to have an awareness of the evolution of styles in art history, only a partial and therefore unrepresentative sample of works has been selected for examination within this chapter.

Form

When conducting an analysis of form (in this context, a formal analysis in relation to the appearance of a work, be it two or three-dimensional), readers should pay attention to the following features:

- composition in painting, sculpture and architecture
- colour in painting, sculpture and architecture
- pictorial space in painting and relief sculpture
- light and tone in painting
- pattern, ornament or decoration in painting, sculpture and architecture
- line and shape in painting; line, shape and three-dimensional form in sculpture; three-dimensional form and space in architecture
- scale in painting, sculpture or architecture
- architectural elements or features in buildings
- structures in architecture
- volume and mass in architecture and sculpture
- site or location in architecture
- materials, **techniques and processes** in painting, sculpture and architecture, particularly as this theme overlaps with form, style and function.

Many of these formal elements are inter-related; for example, the arrangement of line, shape and colour may give us effects such as rhythm, balance and pattern which constitute the composition. In reality, most of us find it difficult to separate *what* is represented (the subject, and its deeper meaning, the content) from how it's represented (form).

Style

Style can be easily understood when describing our clothes, furniture or domestic interiors because it denotes the features that they have in common.

The same is true of paintings, sculptures and architecture. Perhaps it is easiest to think of style as relating to the way an artist arranges formal elements and the recognisable look these take.

Style is the distinctive visual appearance of a work of art or architecture. However, we cannot always ascribe a particular label to the set of visual characteristics with which we are presented. For example, Frank Lloyd Wright's Fallingwater, examined later in this chapter, has a distinctive visual appearance but it is not distinctive enough to be identified strongly with a specific style; instead, it is discussed here as representing a variant on the **Modern Movement** style; although essentially, it has an individual style.

While the collective styles of artists are sometimes associated with a movement, before the twentieth century it was not all that common for artists to group together either to produce consciously crafted manifestos or to proclaim the characteristics of their artistic style. Most commonly, the history of art has been studied in accordance with a succession of styles: **Gothic**, **Renaissance**, **Baroque**, **Neo-classicism**, Romanticism, Realism, **Impressionism**, Fauvism, **Expressionism**, **Cubism**, Futurism and so on. These broadly correspond to particular historical periods. Art historians adopt these categorisations because it simplifies and clarifies our examination of art history, and the examination of style tends to necessitate a visual formal analysis from which shared or collective characteristics emerge. However, we must guard against the rigidity of this process because it may lead to the omission of some of the most iconic works of art and architecture ever made. Some works fall between styles and some are so innovative they seem to stand alone, such as Antoni Gaudi's fantastical apartment block Casa Batlló, 1904–1906, for example.

Importantly, from the thematic perspective of this book, style creates the overall aesthetic effect, regardless of the subject matter and irrespective of the work's social and historical context. Many of the following images are accompanied by a 'What can you see?' prompt to aid your understanding of the formal elements of art and architecture that comprise a work's 'style'.

Function

Function (purpose) is examined in relation to architecture alone (in addition to an examination of its architectural form and style) since architecture serves specific utilitarian/practical purposes that painting and sculpture do not. Functionalism can suggest a certain prioritising of function over decoration in accordance with the 'form follows function' slogan, which became common currency in the architectural vocabulary of the twentieth-century Modern Movement. However, not every functional building smacks of utilitarianism. Whatever the visual stimulus, we need to consider the relationship between the function of a building and its appearance.

The Beginning of Western Art

Classical style

It is commonly agreed that the tradition of Western art began in ancient Greece, and, although the term Classical can be a broadly used concept within an art-historical context, as a stylistic category, Classical refers to the culture of ancient Greece and Rome, with the period around c.480–323 BCE, when Greece, and especially the Athenian state, achieved cultural and artistic supremacy, as the apogee of Classicism. During this period, Classical sculptors noted the way real humans stand – their pelvises tilt with unequal weight distribution, and that the human form can twist around its central axis. Translated into statuary, this counter-balancing is known as **contrapposto**, and it characterises the more naturalistic style of Classical sculpture, separating it from its more rigid and 'unrealistic' Egyptian and earlier Greek predecessors. Because harmony was believed to be found in nature, it was reasoned that it should be replicated in sculpture.

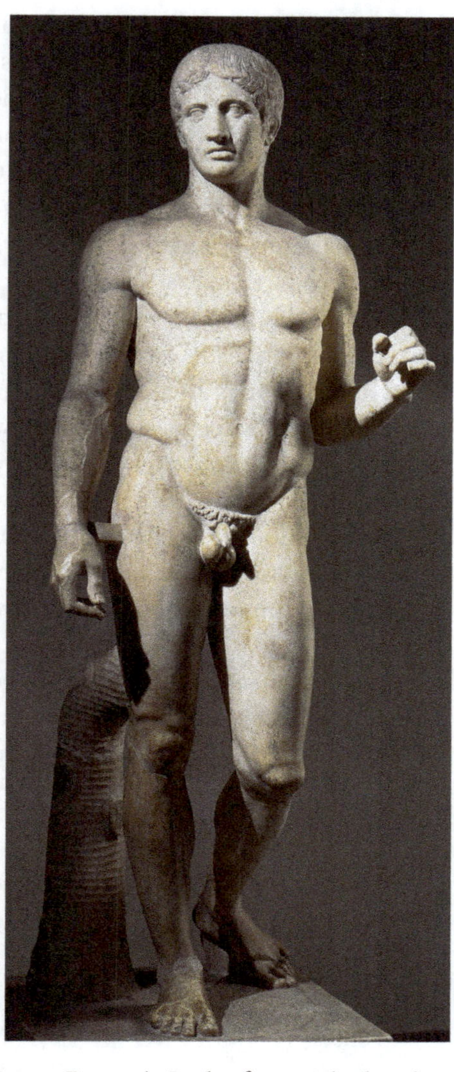

Figure 3.1 | Polykleitos, *Doryphoros (Spear Bearer)*, 450–440 BCE, copy of a Greek original, marble, height 212 cm, Roman, Naples, Museo Archeologico Nazionale. Source: Museo Archeologico Nazionale, Naples, Italy / Photo ©Tarker / Bridgeman Images.

Look at Polykleitos' *Doryphoros (Spear Bearer)*. Is the figure idealised or anatomically correct? How is it posed? Is it contrapposto? What is the facial expression? Is it gesturing? Is it static or animated? Consider materials, techniques and processes in your analysis. You may want to refer to the discussion of marble sculpture in *Chapter 2*.

In terms of formal elements such as line, form, colour and texture, the appearance of Polykleitos' *Doryphoros (Spear Bearer)*, 450–440 BCE, has a distinctive and rhythmically balanced outline; line contains the figure's mass; that is to say, his body form is not disturbed by extended limbs or any other protuberances, which contrasts with modern works such as Boccioni's *Unique Forms of Continuity in Space*, 1913 (mentioned in greater detail later in this chapter). These formal features help to convey a sense of harmony and stillness. His anatomical correctness and well-defined musculature is characteristic of the Classical style, a combination of realism and an **idealisation** of the human form. His pelvis tilts realistically in keeping with his bent knee and unequal weight distribution. Contrapposto is evident in the head turning in one direction and the hips in the other. The marble has been polished to mimic the smooth flesh of its subject and enhance the figure's athletic form. His left arm is raised at waist level but maintains a reserved closeness to his body. His head tilts realistically, but despite his slightly parted lips – which lend a hint of animation – his face is idealised and sets a standard for natural beauty. Indeed, *Doryphoros* epitomises the ideal nude male and the **anthropocentrism** characteristic of the Classical style. This 'type' of nude figure would become a prototype for the Renaissance ideal nearly 2,000 years later. Also bequeathed to the Renaissance was **humanism** that led artists in the Western tradition to celebrate the virtues of humankind; in the renewed perspective of the Renaissance *man would become the measure of all things*.

Just as there was an ideal of the perfect human body, there was an ideal of a perfect proportional ratio used in art and architecture. Known as the **Golden Section**, it is thought to have originated in ancient Greece from the sixth century BCE. The exact proportion cannot be expressed as a finite number but it approximates to 1:1.618. The proportions of the Parthenon Temple, 447–438 BCE, Athens, were designed with tremendous precision to create a building whose separate parts achieve a perfect, mathematical harmony with its whole; the ratio of its height to its width is a Golden Section. The Golden Section was thought to have an inherent visual harmony and beauty and the Classical buildings of Antiquity that first used the formulae have become a blueprint for numerous architects throughout the history of Western architecture.

Classical art and architecture has been historically imbued with authority and beauty. Temples like the Parthenon in Athens have come to represent the pinnacle of Classical aesthetics and have established an architectural

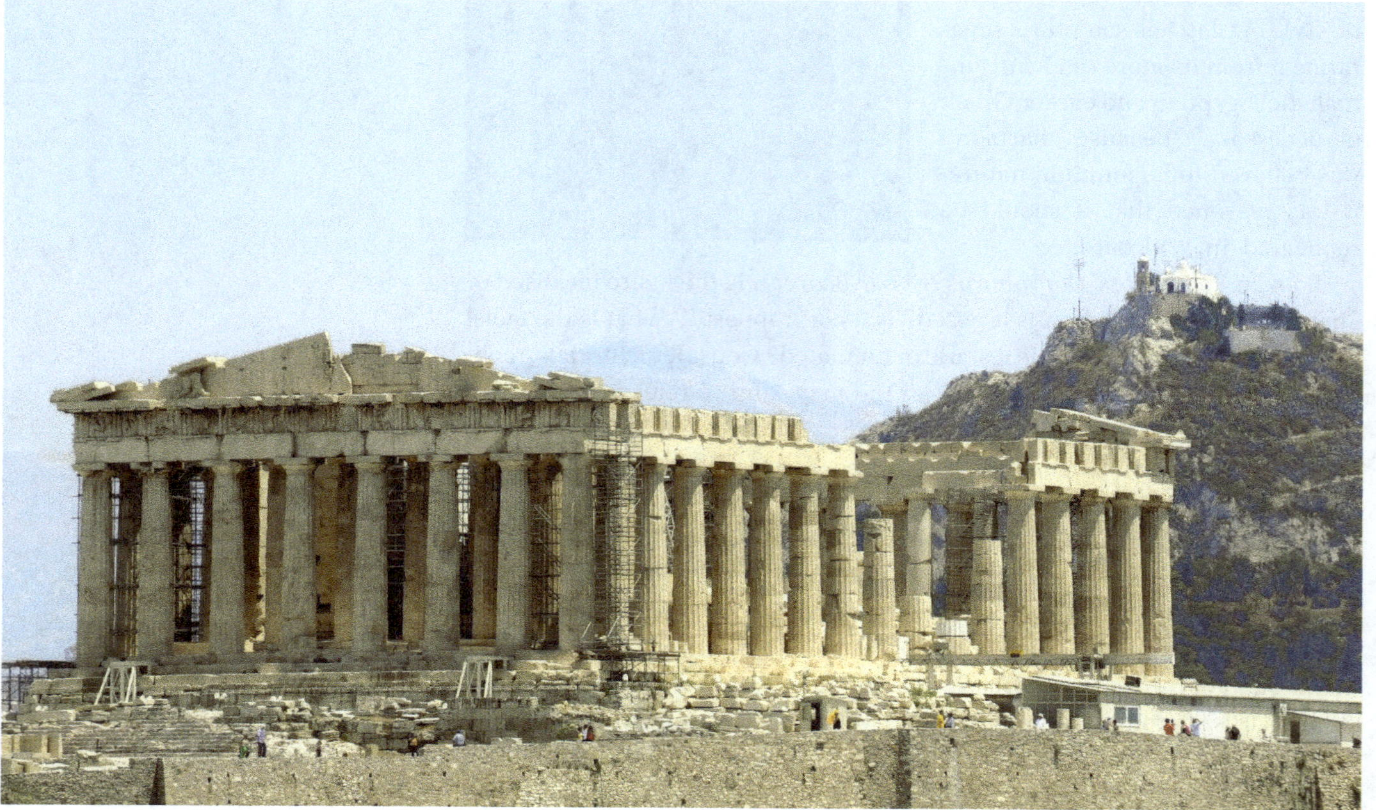

Figure 3.2 | The Parthenon Temple, 447–438 BCE.
Source: © krechet / iStockphoto.

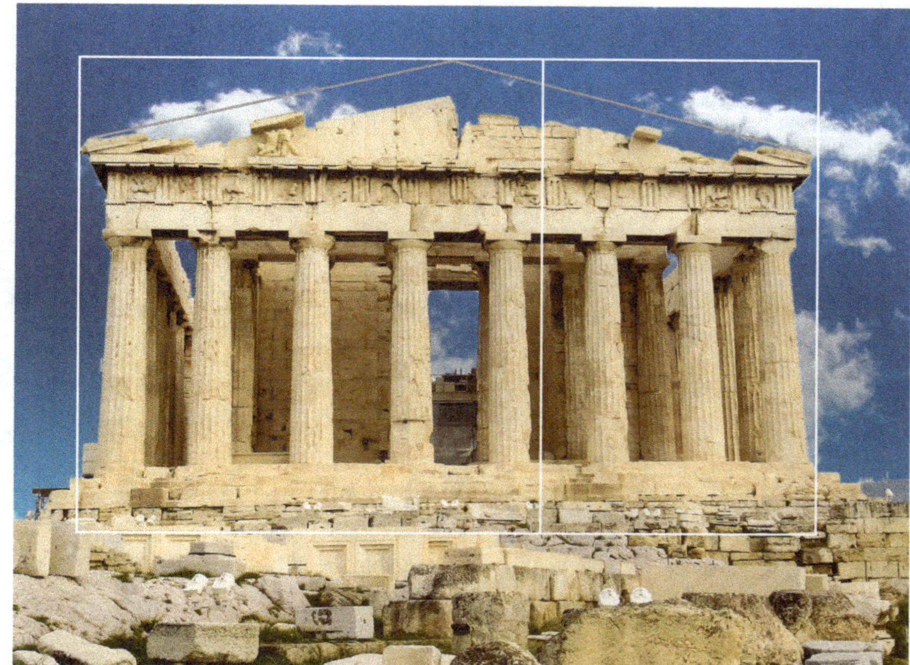

Figure 3.3 | The Parthenon Temple with Golden Section overlay. Source: © Sergio Bettino / Shutterstock.

grammar in terms of scale, proportion and symmetry that has been imitated repeatedly over the last 2,000 years. Greek buildings are **trabeated** – that, is a post and lintel structure (the arch was a later, Roman invention). In the case of the Parthenon, the **columns** support the **entablature**, which in turn supports the roof beams. The sloping roof (now destroyed) has **gables** at each end (known as **pediments**). In Classical architecture (Greek and Roman) each different style of column, with its base, shaft and **capital**, and entablature, architrave, **frieze** and **cornice**, is known as an **Order**.

Much of a Classical building's style comes from its choice of Order. Part of the Parthenon's austerity and authority comes from its plain **Doric** Order. The Doric frieze is divided by alternating triglyphs (three vertical grooves) and metopes (the spaces between the triglyphs that could be decorated). The proportions of the Doric Order differ from the more delicate **Ionic** Order (the capitals of which have **volutes**) and, later still, the flamboyant **Corinthian** Order (with capitals based on acanthus leaves). The height of the Doric column is between four and usually six times its diameter; the slimmer Ionic column eight to ten times its diameter in height (Woodford, *The Parthenon*, p. 14).

Artists and architects in later periods used Classicism as an exemplary foundation for their work. For example, the revival of all things classical would characterise the Renaissance across Europe during the fifteenth and sixteenth centuries.

Discovery of Antiquity and Development of Sacred Art

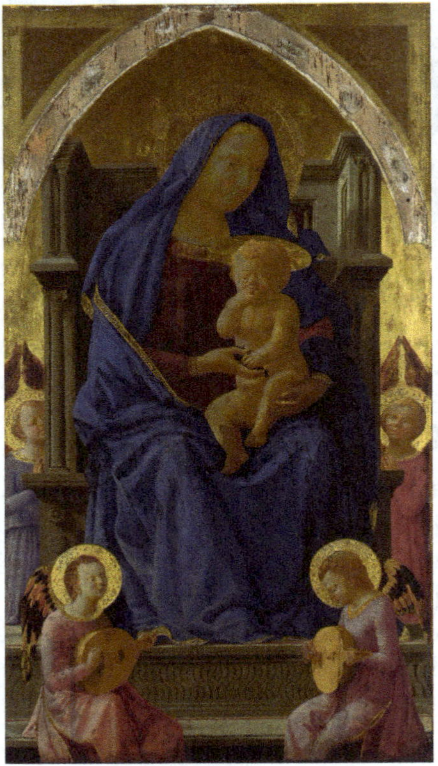

Figure 3.4 | Masaccio, *The Virgin and Child*, 1426, egg tempera on wood, 134.8 × 73.5 cm, London, National Gallery. Bought with a contribution from The Art Fund, 1916. Acc. no.: 1772. Source: © 2015. Copyright The National Gallery, London / Scala, Florence.

The Early Renaissance

The Renaissance is best understood when it is divided between the **Early Renaissance** (essentially the fifteenth century) and the **High Renaissance** (specifically in Rome in the early sixteenth century, although it might be seen as having a longer existence in other locations, such as Venice, for example).[12] The stylistic development from one to the other was noted by the Renaissance biographer Giorgio Vasari in his *Lives of the Artists*. While it is generally agreed that the Early Renaissance in art began in the 1420s with Masaccio (originally Tommaso di Ser Giovanni di Simone, 1401–1428/29) and ended, roughly speaking, at the close of that century, the High Renaissance that followed it drifted into a style called Mannerism around the time of the Sack of Rome in 1527. The prefix 'high' describes the height of Rome's artistic and cultural ascendency under the guidance of Pope Julius II (1503–1513) and Pope Leo X (1513–1527) and, from the perspective of Vasari, marks the achievement of a long-awaited perfection.

The Early Renaissance in Italy marked a new beginning in art history and became characterised not only by the revival of Classicism but also the artists' greater understanding of anatomical correctness and new ways to achieve **naturalism**. *The Virgin and Child*, 1426, by Masaccio, which has already been examined in *Chapter 2*, is widely considered to epitomise the aspirations of this period.

3.1 What can you see?

In Masaccio's *The Virgin and Child* is the composition formally arranged? Is it symmetrical or asymmetrical? Does it use certain forms (shapes) for a particular effect? Is colour used naturalistically? Is colour used symbolically (as part of a recognised convention)? Has the artist created an illusion of three-dimensional space? Is there tonal **modelling**? Do lines provide the edge of forms? See *Chapter 2* for a full discussion of the materials, techniques and processes involved in the creation of this work.

The Early Renaissance is often identified stylistically by its greater attention to anatomical detail in comparison to the Gothic period that preceded it, and its use of **chiaroscuro** and single-point **linear perspective**. The Virgin sits on the central vertical axis in a pyramidal composition (used by earlier artists such as Duccio di Buoninsegna (c.1255/60–c.1318/19) (see *Chapter 2*) with her head at the apex. Colour is used both naturalistically and symbolically – for example, flesh is recognisable as such, while blue and gold symbolise heaven; the use of **gold leaf** is one sign of the Gothic legacy from which the Early Renaissance style had developed. Linear perspective has been used to **foreshorten** Christ's elliptical halo and the Virgin's throne so that both appear to recede naturalistically. Chiaroscuro is used to develop the anatomical correctness of the figures, particularly evident in the musculature of the

12 Arguably, there is no such thing as Renaissance style; rather, there are styles and there are elements/features that can be recognised as characteristics of the Renaissance in general.

naked Christ Child's torso, and the Virgin's robes. Masaccio's treatment of the Virgin's drapery can be described as tonal insofar as the juxtapositions of dark, mid and light blues provide a convincing modelling effect. **Tempera** was not able to blend shades of colour indiscernibly and so the placing of varying tones side by side was the best that could be accomplished with this medium (see *Chapter 2*). The Virgin's body appears solid and 'weighty', despite its depiction on a two-dimensional surface. She appears to sit back in her throne, which itself is a reference to classical prototypes, an illusion made all the more credible by the single light source from our left which casts her shadow to her right. Using perspective to foreshorten her thighs as they recede only heightens her human quality and separates her from countless earlier depictions of seated Madonnas, as noted by the Renaissance biographer, Giorgio Vasari: *Masaccio also made more use than other artists of nude and foreshortened figures, which indeed had rarely been seen before* (Vasari, *Lives of the Artists*, p. 126).

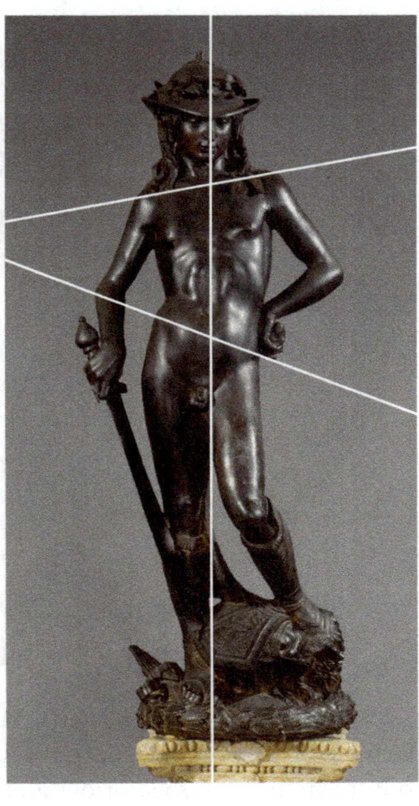

Figure 3.5 | Donatello, *David* (before restoration), 1440, bronze, Florence, Bargello Museum. Source: © 2015. Photo Scala, Florence – courtesy of the Ministero Beni e Att. Culturali.

Is the figure idealised? Is it anatomically correct? How is it posed? Is it contrapposto? What is the facial expression? Is the figure gesturing? Is it static or animated? Consider materials, techniques and processes in your analysis. You may want to refer to the discussion of bronze sculpture in *Chapter 2*.

The Virgin and the Christ Child's physicality are a result of the artist's attention to anatomical detail and the pervading humanism that would mark the beginnings of the Early Renaissance.

The sculptor Donatello (originally Donato di Niccolò di Betto Bardi, c.1386–1466) was Massacio's equal, in terms of his artistic status and embodiment of the Italian Early Renaissance style. A similar attention to anatomical accuracy and the realistic interpretation of form is demonstrated in the sculptor's *David*, 1440.

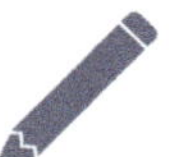

3.1 Explore this example

Compositionally, artists such as Masaccio in the Early Renaissance sought to balance the components of a painting with one another to convey harmony. Masaccio's *The Virgin and Child*, 1426, is formed in a pyramid on the central vertical axis, which establishes a strict symmetrical composition. Make a formal comparison of Masaccio's compositional devices with those employed by seventeenth-century artist Michelangelo Merisi da Caravaggio in his painting of *The Entombment of Christ*, 1602–1604 (discussed as an example of a religious subject in *Chapter 1*)

In relation to the formal element of line, the composition of Donatello's sculpture of the youth David, biblical slayer of the giant Philistine Goliath, loosely follows a vertical line down the central vertical axis of the figure. This grounds him, heightens his self-assurance and gives him a dignified air. His contours are both defined and fluid over his anatomically correct body. The shift in his weight distribution to the right leg is followed through in his tilted pelvis and demonstrates a naturalistic contrapposto derived from Classical sculpture and employed to heighten naturalism. His musculature is reminiscent of the Classical male nude *Doryphoros* by Polykleitos, discussed earlier in the chapter, and, of course, the Early Renaissance was largely inspired by

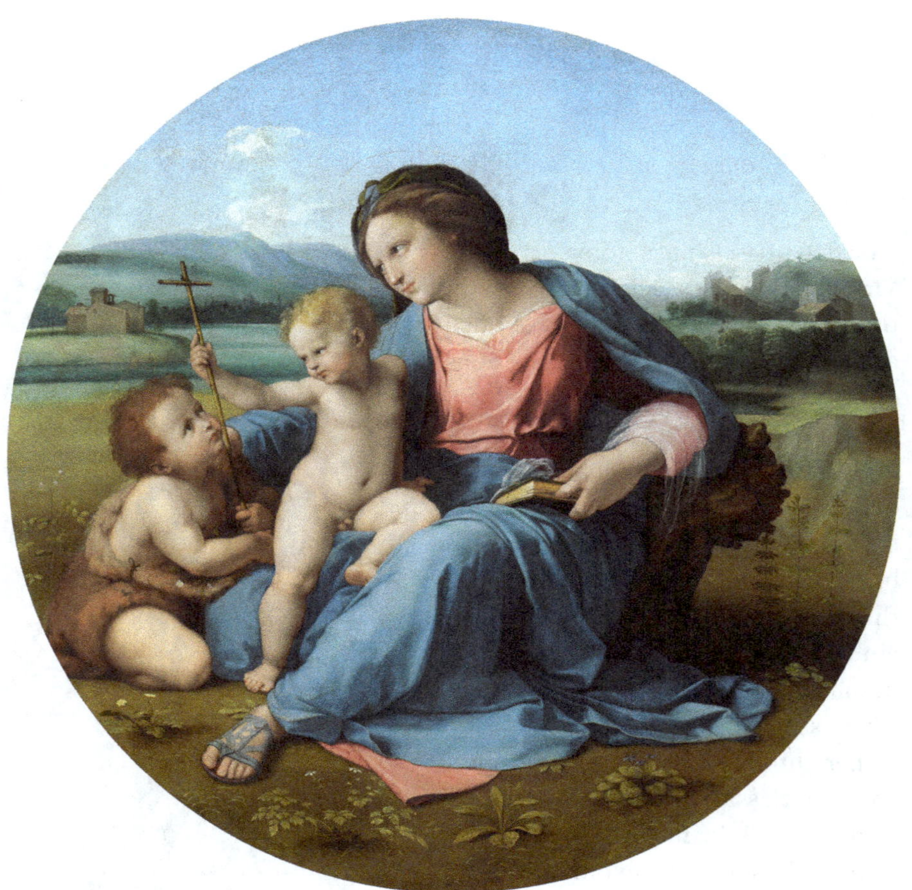

Figure 3.6 | Raphael, *Alba Madonna*, c.1510, oil on panel transferred to canvas, overall (diameter): 94.5 cm, framed: 139.7 × 135.9 × 14 cm, Washington, National Gallery of Art, Andrew W. Mellon Collection, 1937.1.24. Source: Courtesy National Gallery of Art, Washington.

Classical characteristics. The surface texture is smooth and highly light-reflective on account of its dark-bronze medium, the **patina** of which seems to suit the nature of his victorious and heroic stance. Despite the youth's defiant hand on his hip, the overall impression is harmonious and static.

The stylistic developments that demarcated the Early from the High Renaissance can be examined by comparing this Early Renaissance sculpture by Donatello with the High Renaissance sculpture of the same subject by Michelangelo (originally Michelangelo di Lodovico Buonarroti Simoni, 1475–1564), which can be seen in *Chapter 5*.

The High Renaissance

Is the composition of Raphael (Raffaello Sanzio da Urbino, 1483–1520)'s *Alba Madonna*, c.1510, symmetrical or asymmetrical? Do the Virgin and Child form a rigid pyramid shape? What effect does Raphael's colour palette have on the scene? How is pictorial space conveyed? Also, consider materials, techniques and processes in your analysis.

The High Renaissance is distinguishable from the Early Renaissance on account of its greater sophistication, innovation and perfection. For example, the composition of Masaccio's *Virgin and Child with Angels* is a strict pyramid, in contrast to the High Renaissance work the *Alba Madonna*, by Raphael. Both Madonnas are positioned on the central vertical axis, creating compositional symmetry, but Raphael's demonstrates greater naturalism; his *Alba Madonna* twists in realistic contrapposto, creating an illusion of natural movement towards her lively son. This looser, organic pyramid, coupled with this level of interaction between the figures, and a convincing landscape, provides the viewer with an unprecedented sense of realism, as noted by the biographer Vasari, stating, *for in his figures the flesh seems to be moving, they breathe, their pulses beat, and they are utterly true to life* (Vasari, *Lives of the Artists*, p. 304).

The convincing modelling of form was attributable to artists' use of oil paint, which could be manipulated and over-painted easily. The composition of the *Alba Madonna* is fairly complex: the Virgin holds onto Christ while simultaneously directing our gaze beyond St. John, and into the distance on the far left. This allows us to consider her contemplation of the future and empathise with her evident sense of foreboding – a sense underlined by Christ's playful grip of the Cross, which may also be read as his acceptance of the Crucifixion at the end of his life. While Jesus looks at St. John, St. John looks heavenward rather than return his gaze – a complex series of compositional directions that lead us from the Virgin Mary to Christ, from Christ to St. John and from St. John to heaven above. A poetic circularity compositionally suited to its circular shape, known as a **tondo**.

Like Masaccio, Raphael uses colour symbolically to represent the Virgin but, unlike Masaccio, he is also concerned with realistic colouring, particularly in his depiction of flesh tones. The chiaroscuro which lent Masaccio's earlier work an innovative realism has been perfected here to produce a porcelain-like skin quality. The whole scene is bathed in a gentle and diffused light. This device, together with Raphael's clarity of line and execution, lend the entire work a sense of idealised beauty. The tonality is fairly bright and, despite its naturalism, the palette is fairly limited to blues, greens and pinks, and these hues are used repeatedly to create an overall harmony across the composition.

The Virgin's classical dress falls away in a style reminiscent of antique relief sculpture. Raphael was in Rome at the time he painted this work and the influence of Antiquity would have been all around him. Despite the work's naturalism, Raphael expresses divinity not only through the faintest of halos, around each holy figure, but also through the idealised beauty of the figures and their scenery.

A further characteristic of the High Renaissance style, at least in painting done in Rome, is the increasing rationalisation of space. Linear perspective is used to render Mary's Bible foreshortened, and **atmospheric perspective** is evident in the diminishing vibrancy of colour and dominance of blue and green as it approaches the horizon, and in the way the landscape blurs realistically as it recedes. The influence of humanism is evident in the fact that Raphael's Virgin, historically depicted seated on a throne (as in Duccio's *The Madonna Enthroned*, 1311, in *Chapter 2*, or Masaccio's, Figure 3.4), is represented as the Madonna of Humility: sitting on the ground, with only a rock or tree stump as support. In a manner that suggests a complex symbolism, but is nevertheless naturalistically believable, the Virgin's outstretched limbs provide a makeshift throne for the Christ Child – a subtle device, entirely indicative of High Renaissance accomplishment.

3.1 Checkpoint question
Identify three formal elements associated with the Renaissance style.

The Baroque style that emerged in the century that followed the High Renaissance would deepen the palette, disrupt the symmetry and throw a spotlight on its actors to create scenes more theatrical than Western art had ever seen before. The style had its basic dynamic code but it also had a multitude of variants.

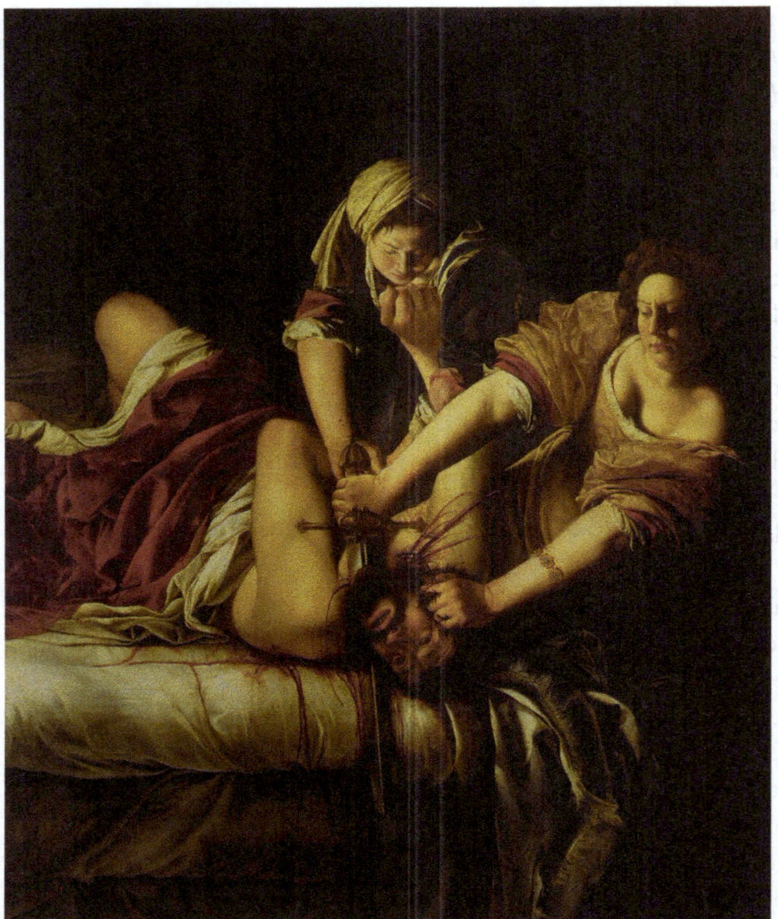

Figure 3.7 | Artemisia Gentileschi, ***Judith Slaying Holofernes,*** **c.1620, oil on canvas, 199 × 162 cm, Florence, Galleria degli Uffizi.**
Source: © 2015. Photo Scala, Florence – courtesy of the Ministero Beni e Att. Culturali.

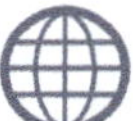

See the companion website for a related comparison exercise.

The Baroque

Baroque is a term used to describe a seventeenth-century style of art and architecture which extended from the late sixteenth to the mid-eighteenth century. The Baroque style originated in Rome, although it found various stylistic variants across Western Europe: from Italy to Flanders, Spain, France, the Dutch Republic and England. In every country the style took on a distinguishing form.

The realism achieved by artists in Spain rivalled the quality achieved by Caravaggio in Italy, and both countries were driven by Catholic **Counter-Reformation** zeal. A comparison of the work of Gregorio Fernández's *Dead Christ*, c.1625–1630 (examined in detail in *Chapter 2*), with Gian Lorenzo Bernini's *Ecstasy of St. Teresa*, 1645–1652 (examined in detail in *Chapter 4*), provides a striking illustration of the different Baroque styles in Spain and Italy, respectively.

As a further illustration of the breadth of the term 'style', the Baroque style in Italy alone expressed itself in two separate ways: first, through the unprecedented realism of Caravaggio and his followers, the **Caravaggisti**, and, second, through the classical Baroque style typified by Italian artist and architect Pietro da Cortona (1596–1669). Cortona's typically theatrical interior fresco *The Glorification of the Reign of Urban VIII*, 1633–1639, emulated the idealised style of Antiquity. Works such as Cortona's experimented safely within the confines of decorum, whereas Caravaggio's boldly innovative art made only the occasional nod to the decorous, but never at the expense of the ugly truth, especially if that truth was evident in scripture. In most manifestations of the Baroque style, dynamism was favoured over the static compositions of its Renaissance predecessor, and many artists set out to stir the emotions of the spectator.

Caravaggio exemplifies the early Baroque style characterised by pure theatre emerging from dark and psychologically charged backgrounds. His *The Entombment*, 1602–1604, was examined in detail in *Chapter 1* as a religious subject, and may also be examined here in terms of the formal features that comprise its Baroque style.

The work of female painter Artemisia Gentileschi (1593–1656) exemplifies the Caravaggisti. Gentileschi's *Judith Slaying Holofernes*, c.1620, is a good example of the way in which the formal elements of a style, in this case Baroque, can become so distinctive that they are instantly recognisable as such.

Gentileschi uses light and tone to render the subject theatrically for the viewer. Gentileschi, who had seen Caravaggio's works, used similar tonal contrasts and **raking light** to create a dramatic atmosphere, in this instance, a haunting, night-time murder scene. Such **tenebrism** creates a psychological void, which focuses our attention on the deed. If the Baroque style was concerned with capturing the transient moment, then Gentileschi delivered. Blood spouts from Holofernes' brutish neck as the gleaming sword slices through a main artery. He seems to take his last breath here, before our eyes. The dynamism of the style is reinforced formally with Judith's arms, like murderous arrows, set on a diagonal which drives in from the right-hand side of the picture, leading us to the point of execution. The diagonals of her arms lend movement and are balanced by Holofernes' less powerful legs, raised pitifully on the left. On the central vertical axis, Judith's accomplice leads us to the point of death with her gaze and her arms to complete a complex intersection of diagonals and pyramid formations; all converge at the point of Holofernes' slaying and provide evidence of the power of formal elements to tell a complex narrative.

3.2 What can you see?
In *Judith Slaying Holofernes*, do the shapes Gentileschi uses affect the composition? Where are our eyes led in the composition? Has the artist used a wide range of colours or is the palette limited? Is colour used symbolically? What type of lighting is used? To what effect is light used?

Directional lighting not only lends a theatrical atmosphere but, more practically, functions to illuminate important elements of the scene: the heroines' determined expressions, their arms, his face and the steely weapon used to bring about his demise. Light is also responsible for modelling the figures' believable forms. Judith's arms are strong and robust enough to carry out the job in hand. The colours, predominantly red, white and black, provide stark contrast with one another, and the blood-red doubles as a symbol for passion and destruction. That this bloodthirsty scene is enacted so close to the **picture plane** draws us unnervingly close to the action; we see his death a fraction before his killers do. According to the biblical Book of Judith, Holofernes was killed with two strikes from his sword, and it would appear that we have just witnessed the moment of the second blow. The scale of the women's violent achievement is conveyed in a single juxtaposition: the mighty fist of Holofernes takes on a terrifying proportion against the maid's comparatively small head.

The striking realism and unprecedented **verisimilitude** of the style is part of its rhetorical character – a truthfulness that was ironically staged. Its compositional dynamism, colour palette and lighting set it firmly apart from its Renaissance predecessors. Many of the formal devices used in Baroque painting are instantly recognisable in Baroque sculpture. The compositional use of the diagonal is a particularly characteristic device used by Baroque artists to create the feeling that we are witness to a dramatic and transient moment. For example, the marble sculpture *Apollo and Daphne*, 1624, by Gian Lorenzo Bernini (1598–1680) is composed on a diagonal axis, skilfully suggesting the thrust of movement and a precise moment in the chase. This dramatic scene is also examined in greater detail in *Chapter 2*.

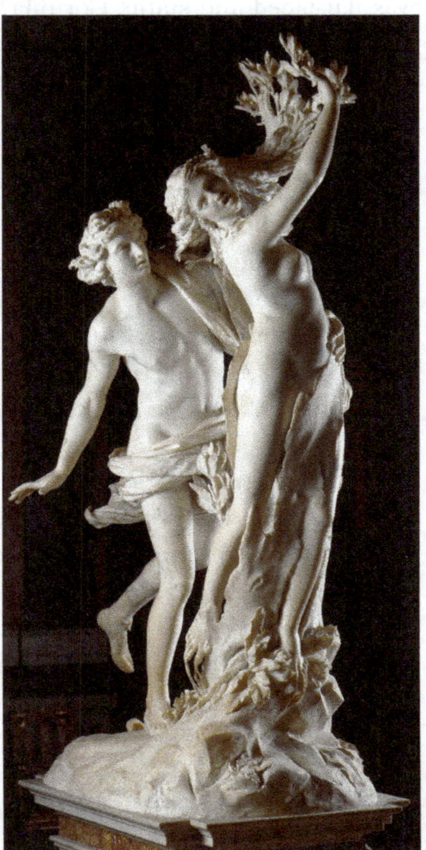

Figure 3.8 | Gian Lorenzo Bernini, *Apollo and Daphne*, 1624, marble, height 243 cm, Rome, Borghese Gallery.
Source: akg-images / Andrea Jemolo.

Is Bernini's sculpted multi-fig-

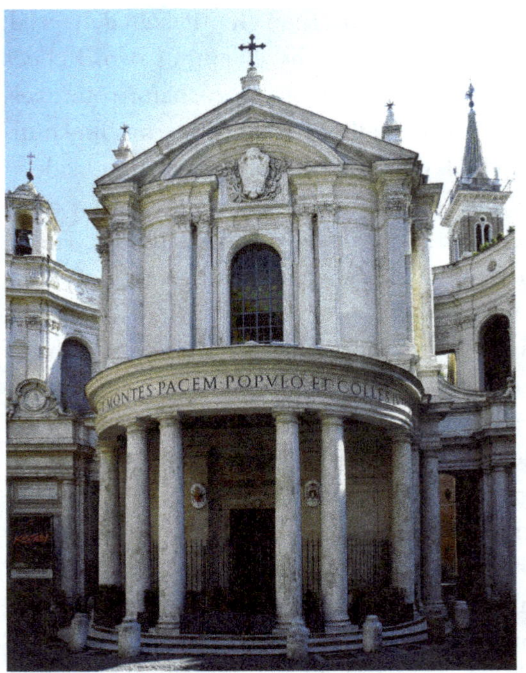

Figure 3.9 | Pietro da Cortona, Church of Santa Maria della Pace, Rome, 1656–1667, view of façade. Source: © 2015. Photo Scala, Florence.

ure composition *Apollo and Daphne* idealised? Are they anatomically correct? How are they posed? Are they in contrapposto? What are their facial expressions? How can we read their gesturing? Are they static or animated? In addition, what is the purpose of the drapery? Does it fall away naturalistically, or does it have a life of its own? Consider materials, techniques and processes in your analysis. You may want to refer to the discussion of marble sculpture in *Chapter 2*.

Baroque architecture of the seventeenth century is as recognisable stylistically as Baroque painting and sculpture. Cortona was one of three great Roman architects of the High Baroque, together with his famous contemporaries, Gian Lorenzo Bernini and Francesco Borromini. Cortona's architectural features are rooted in Antiquity but their alteration and inventive use is characteristically Baroque. The Classical features of Cortona's church include pediment, entablature and columns, but, while the true Classical temple of the Parthenon in Greece, constructed 2,000 years earlier, was flat-faced and static, Cortona's church is voluptuous and dynamic. Its triangular **pediment** houses a segmental one, its frieze is inscribed – deviating from the true Doric Order – its columns are twinned. The convex cornice projects deeply to cast a dramatic strip of horizontal shade, sweeping onto the piazza like the welcoming arms of the Catholic Church, and even its upper tier supports subtle projections squeezed like putty between the **pilasters** and **engaged columns** that frame their swell. We have seen the interplay of light and shade before in great paintings and sculptures of the seventeenth century; here we see the same tonal theatricality played out in stone.

3.2 Checkpoint question

Identify three formal elements that are associated with the Baroque style of painting and/or sculpture and/or architecture.

The classical models from which Bernini and Cortona would draw inspiration reappeared as the finest artistic standard some two centuries later in the style suitably known as Neo-classicism.

Neo-classicism

Neo-classicism was a prevalent artistic style in Europe from the mid-eighteenth to the early nineteenth century, and was characterised by a taste for Antiquity and academic sobriety. The Neo-classical style is epitomised in the painting *Death of Marat*, 1793, by Jacques-Louis David (1748–1825).

Form and style accentuate the narrative of the painting, which was discussed in both the 'history' and 'portrait' genres in *Chapter 1*. The formal elements that could be said to embody the Neo-classical style include crisply delineated forms and disguised brushwork. These elements create an illusion of reality. The painting is an important piece of propaganda and the artist does not intend us to question the version of events that he is portraying. The wooden box in the foreground, which doubles as a makeshift table and metaphorical headstone, is graphically demarcated from its green backdrop. The folds of the cotton sheet fall away so convincingly, so crisply, that we can almost feel their texture. Marat's anatomically correct body appears solid, three-dimensional, as a result of the artist's use of chiaroscuro. Yet, Marat's idealised face is achieved through a classical treatment the artist has borrowed from Antiquity.

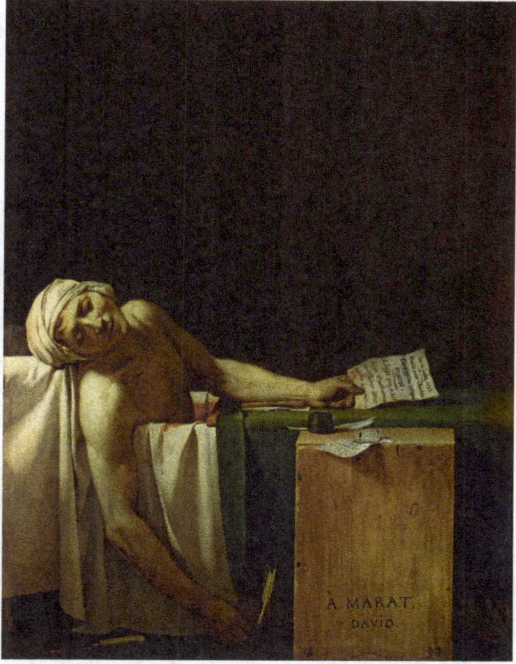

Figure 3.10 | Jacques-Louis David, *The Death of Marat*, 1793 (stabbed in his bath by Charlotte Corday, Paris, 13 July 1793), oil on canvas, 165 × 128 cm, Brussels, Musées Royaux des Beaux-Arts. Source: akg-images / André Held.

Light is used not only to create three-dimensional form but to direct our gaze compositionally towards significant aspects of the work: the illuminated letter in Marat's left hand that his assassin used to gain entry to his apartment, the quill-pen Marat used to send a letter of condolence to a widow of the revolution in his right hand, the assassin's knife on the floor in the foreground and so on. Light is also used symbolically in this painting: Marat seems to bathe in the grainy illumination of a quasi-religious light, referencing historical scenes of martyrdom.

The whole composition is divided in two, and the emptiness of the upper half only focuses our eyes more intently on the murder scene in the lower half. Marat's elevated head forms a diagonal which is used to guide our eye down his left arm to the letter, and a secondary path can be followed from his right arm which over-hangs the bath and acts as an arrow to the quill. In other words, the narrative is revealed through our understanding of the formal elements; the relationship between form and meaning is shown to be **symbiotic**, or complementary. The sum total of these formal elements could be said to comprise the Neo-classical style – a style that sought to suspend our disbelief and made for convincing propaganda images such as *Death of Marat*, which served the French Republic as a pro-Revolutionary icon.

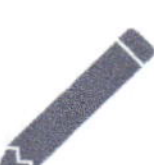

3.2 Explore this example

Look at an image of Antonio Canova's *Three Graces*, 1814–1817. Are the sculpted trio idealised? Anatomically correct? Are they in contrapposto poses? What are their facial expressions? Are they gesturing? Are they static or animated? Does the colour or highly polished surface of the medium affect our interpretation of the Graces? Is there any kind of relationship between the figures?

A Move Towards Individualism

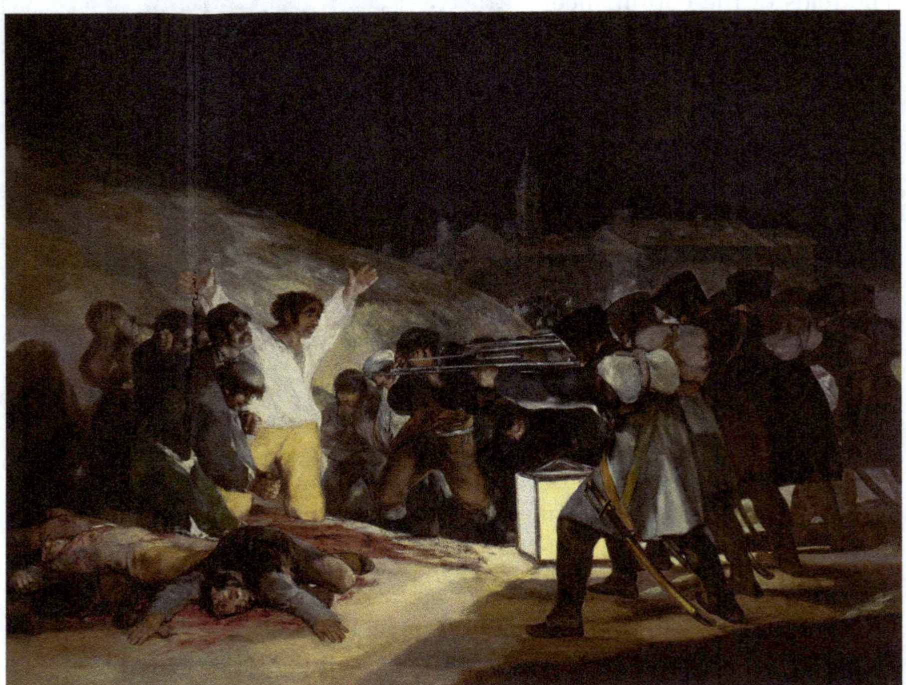

Figure 3.11 | Francisco de Goya, *The Third of May 1808*, 1814 (Execution of the insurgents on the Montana del Principe Pio), oil on canvas, 266 × 345 cm, Madrid, Museo del Prado. Source: akg-images / Album / Oronoz.

Romanticism

Romanticism in the visual arts developed towards the end of the eighteenth century and is commonly understood to be a reaction against the Neo-classical tradition; both of these styles were parallel, if apparently antithetical. The stylistic elements that characterise Romanticism are exemplified in Spanish artist Francisco de Goya's 'history' painting *The Third of May 1808*, already examined in some depth in *Chapter 1*. However, Romanticism took many forms, and styles were frequently more closely linked to individuals. In France, Romanticism represented a rebellion against Neo-classical order and control, and artists set free their imaginations and emotions in canvases such as Théodore Géricault's *The Raft of Medusa*, 1819 and Eugène Delacroix's *Liberty Leading the People*, 1830 (examined in *Chapter 6*). British Romanticism was encapsulated by the expressive skies in Turner's *The Fighting Temeraire*, 1839, and Spanish Romanticism arguably became synonymous with the later work of Francisco de Goya (1746–1828), whose emotions seem to pour through the pigment in his highly individual and emotive take on warfare (Figure 3.11).

How does the composition of Goya's *The Third of May 1808*, 1814, relate to the subject matter? (See *Chapter 1* for help with this.) Is colour used descriptively and/or symbolically? How has the artist used light in the scene? Consider how the artist's brushwork may have impacted the message Goya is trying to convey here?

Unlike his Neo-classical antithesis David, Goya paints modern people in a style as liberated and undisguised as his emotion. He uses light and tone dramatically to indicate the difference between good and evil and, in this sense, uses tonal contrast to convey meaning. The scene is enacted in front of a tenebrous background which sets the mood and silhouettes a church in the distance. The outstretched hand of the central protagonist directs us compositionally towards its spire, which could be interpreted as meaningful in the context of this image: God will judge these men. The flashes of white evident in the group of 'innocents' on the left are absent from the group of executioners on the right, who are painted in tones of grey, black and brown.

The forms (shapes) of the troops are identical, a homogeneity which seems to heighten their seemingly mechanistic and inhuman nature. The palette reserved for them is virtually **monochromatic** in comparison with their victims – the whitest and brightest of which is reserved for the central protagonist: a lone figure invested with the symbolism of innocence and Christ's sacrifice. This is where raw emotion seems to surpass realism and Goya's loose and painterly brushstrokes communicate an intensity of feeling rarely conveyed either before or since. The rapid application becomes a conduit for expressing suffering and the immediacy of the situation in Spain during the French occupation. The artist provides us with a mixture of acutely observed detail and an unfocused blurring, which is more evident in the extreme close-ups provided as a result of Google Earth's collaboration with Spain's Prado Museum, where the work is housed.

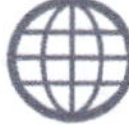

See the companion website for more on this Google Earth project.

A formal analysis of this work suggests it is constructed through a series of binary opposites: light versus dark tonality, faces revealed versus faces concealed; a chaotic huddle of innocents opposed to an orderly group of soldiers; defenceless victims opposed to armed executioners; and so forth. These formal extremes are used by the artist to simplify and heighten the expressive meaning of the painting. The Romanticism represented here by the Spanish artist Goya also developed along similar lines in France, as a movement rep-

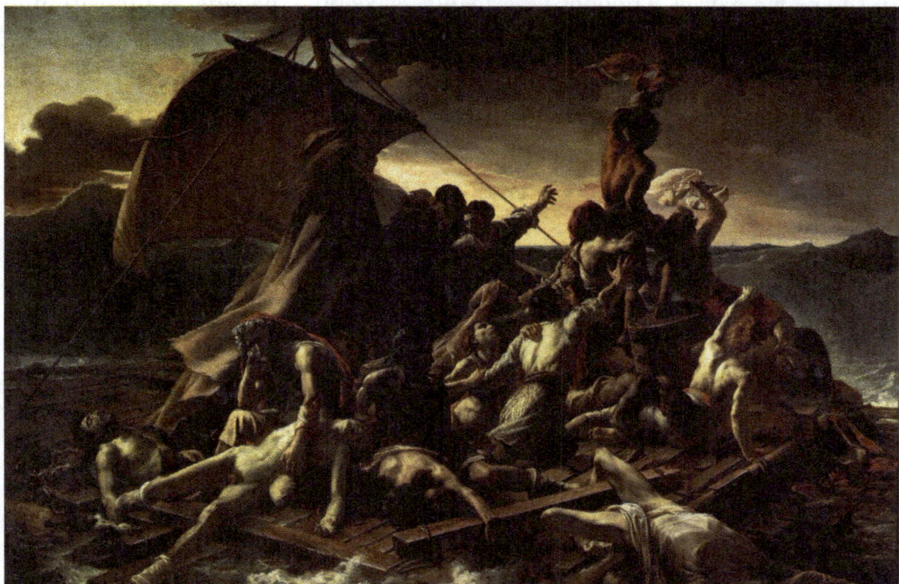

Figure 3.12 | Théodore Géricault, *The Raft of the Medusa*, 1819, oil on canvas, 491 × 716 cm, Paris, Musée du Louvre. Source: akg-images / Album / Joseph Martin.

3.3 What can you see?
In *The Raft of the Medusa* is Théodore Géricault's composition symmetrical or asymmetrical? What is the effect of the pyramidal composition on our interpretation of the work? Does the form symbolically suggest the building up of hope? Are the figures gesturing in such a way to reveal meaning? Where are our eyes led in the composition? Has the artist used a wide range of colours or is the palette limited? Is colour used to create mood? Has a system of perspective been used? Is light used naturalistically? Is light used symbolically? How should we interpret the scale of this work? Is the brushwork disguised or painterly?

resenting artistic freedom and imagination. Consider the form and style of French Romanticism in *The Raft of the Medusa*, 1819, by Théodore Géricault (1791–1824) (Figure 3.12).

In 1816 the French ship *Medusa* sank off the coast of Africa, forcing the 150 passengers to take to a makeshift raft upon which they floated on the open seas for 13 days before they were eventually rescued. By the time help arrived, there were only 15 survivors. Géricault's painting, based on these events, takes a loosely diamond-shaped composition, with the red flag held aloft at its apex and a corner loaded with corpses seemingly about to enter our space at lower left. These elements are balanced by the billowing sail on the left-hand side, sheltering the men from the menacing wave that threatens their already fragile existence. The horizontal or 'landscape' format Géricault chose for this monumental work serves to intensify the never-ending horizontality of the sea from the perspective of those shipwrecked.

Light has been used to model the figures' forms – a particularly important feature given the jumble of bodies on the raft. Their asymmetrical formation creates an overlapping chaos that eschews the rigid order of Neo-classicism. The dark and threatening sky, shot through with light, is also employed to create a foreboding atmosphere, prompting us to wonder, can they survive another night adrift? Light also illuminates an important diagonal in the composition: it leads us from the corpse whose blue/green body hangs humiliatingly naked across an older man's lap (we may perhaps identify this man as the boy's father), bottom left, to the flag-waving men at the top right of the composition. Compare the gesture and facial expression of this grey-haired man in the red cloak (the father) with the gestures of those at the composition's apex. How do their polarised positions help us to interpret their predicament? Perhaps we could describe the raft as rising through a hierarchy from desperate agony to hope – from death to life – which is embodied in the form of a tiny ship on the vast horizon. In actual fact, this ship did not see the raft and the shipwrecked survivors had to endure a further agonising day until they were finally rescued.

The power of form to elicit a response from the viewer has not been lost on contemporary artists, some of whom have referenced historic masterpieces in their own works. Théodore Géricault's sweeping diagonal composition in *The Raft of the Medusa*, 1819, has arguably become the skewed pyramid of all pyramids in art history – if the number of its citations is a measurement. Acclaimed French photographer Gérard Rancinan remade Géricault's epic masterpiece in his *Raft of Illusions*, 2008, and substituted the painter's emaciated sailors with contemporary migrants in pursuit of Western commodities. Rancinan's remake relies on the fact that we are sufficiently familiar with Géricault's pyramid of false hope to make sense of his contemporary political statement about the illusion of wealth and prosperity in developed countries.

Look at all four of these works side by side (opposite). In each case, a turbulent composition sweeps upwards to a climactic apex and the structural skeleton of the work becomes an allegory for the disaster unfolding in each. From top to bottom, we see the false hope of the sailors paralleled in the false hope of the migrants, and the pre-emptive destruction of the king's own court reinterpretation as the allegorical destruction of a woman's life. In each case, the modern reinterpretation uses the same formal structure and jumble of bodies and clothes, similar sharp juxtapositions of light and shade,

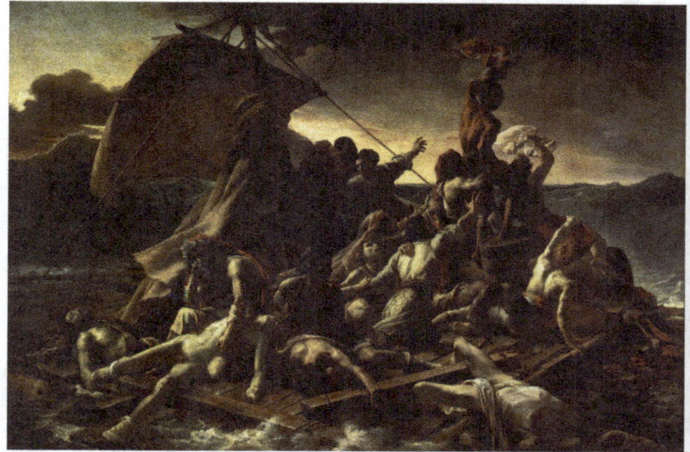
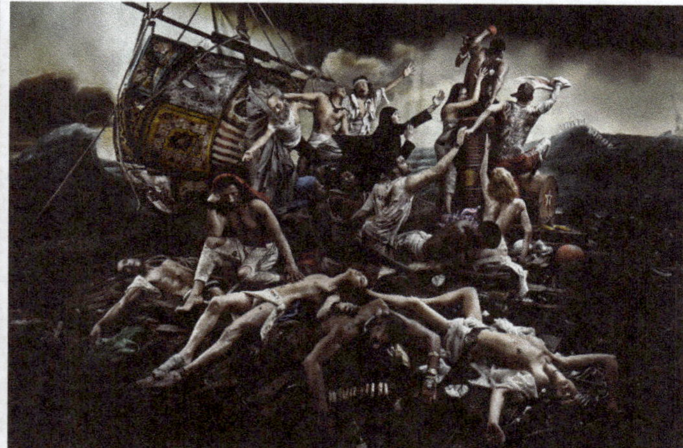
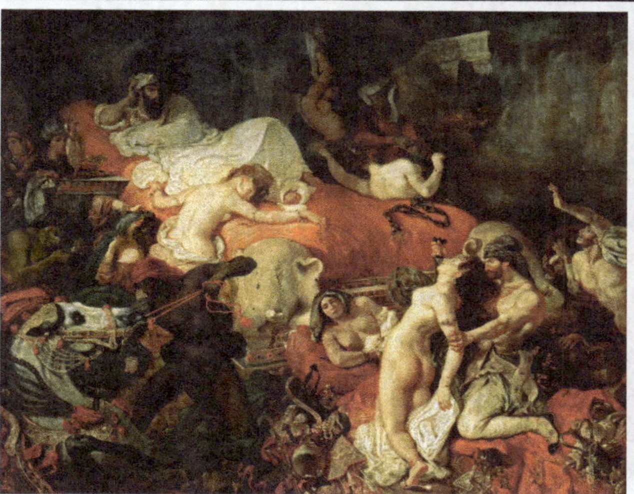
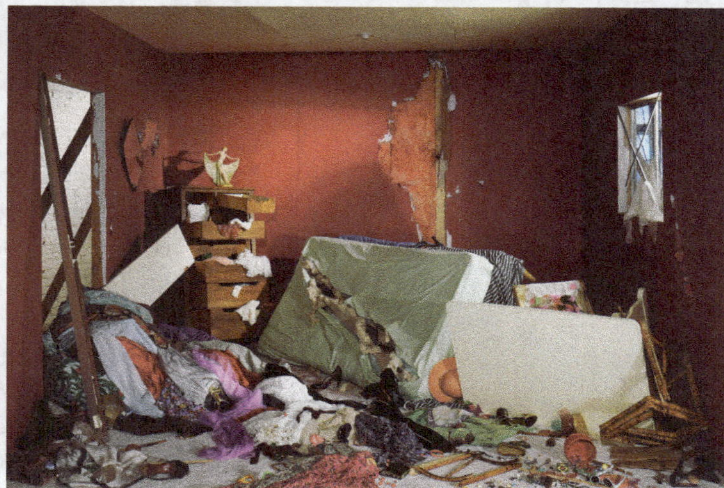

Clockwise from top left:
Figure 3.13 | Théodore Géricault, *The Raft of the Medusa*, 1819, oil on canvas, 491 × 716 cm, Paris, Musée du Louvre. Source: akg-images / Album / Joseph Martin.

Figure 3.14 | Gérard Rancinan, *Raft of Illusions*, 2008, photograph. Source: Fine Art Cube / ©ADAGP, Paris and DACS, London, 2015.

Figure 3.15 | Jeff Wall, *The Destroyed Room*, 1978, transparency in lightbox, 159.0 × 229.0 cm, Collection of National Gallery of Canada, Ottawa. Source: Courtesy of the artist and White Cube.

Figure 3.16 | Eugène Delacroix, *The Death of Sardanapalus*, 1827, oil on canvas, 395 × 495 cm, Paris, Musée du Louvre. Source: akg-images / Erich Lessing.

inertia and turbulence as the historical masterpieces that inspired them. In formal terms, the red-hooded man at the foot of Géricault's raft may be seen as mirroring the Assyrian king in Delacroix's literary subject; both figures remain still with resignation in tumultuous settings.

The loose brushwork that characterised Géricault's Romanticism became an equally defining feature of Impressionism a few decades later; however, the Impressionists' brush touched the canvas with rather less focus on the expression of emotion and rather more focus on capturing the transient effects of light in landscapes and leisure scenes.

Impressionism and after

The art critic Louis Leroy coined the term 'Impressionism', which he intended derisively, when he reviewed the painting *Impression, Sunrise* by Claude Monet (1840–1926) on its first exhibition in 1874. Monet's seascape (a sub-genre of the landscape) neither idealises nature nor, arguably, expresses the artist's emotional feelings towards it; instead, Monet's canvas renders the impression of the artist's visual experience of the scene. Leroy thought that Monet had not presented a finished work, but rather a sketch and, as such, an impression of the subject, not a valid representation of it.

Although the term 'Impressionism' was originally derisory, it stuck and came to describe a style of painting that developed in France from the middle to the end of the nineteenth century. Impressionism became associated with a group of artists including Claude Monet, Pierre-Auguste Renoir

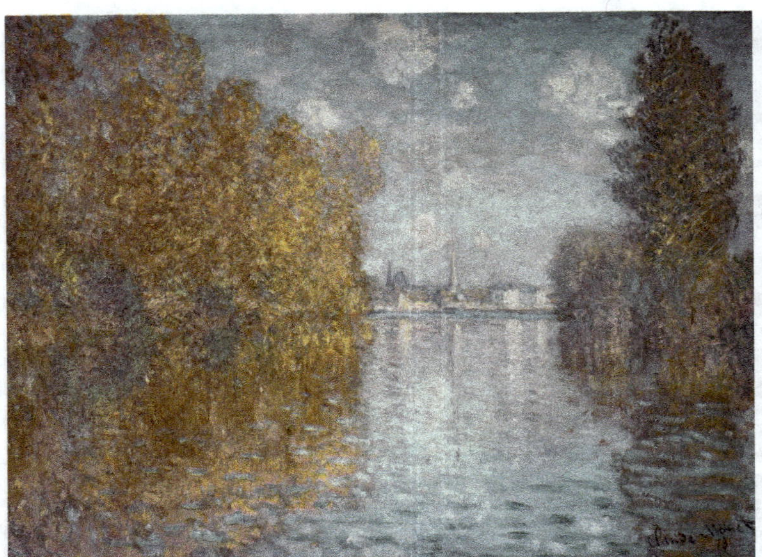

Figure 3.17 | Claude Monet, *Autumn Effect at Argenteuil*, 1873, oil on canvas, 55 × 74.5 cm, London, Courtauld Gallery.
Source: © Samuel Courtauld Trust, The Courtauld Gallery, London, UK / Bridgeman Images.

(1841–1919), Alfred Sisley (1839–1899), Camille Pissarro (1830–1903), Edgar Degas (1834–1917), Berthe Morisot (1841–1895) and Mary Cassatt (1844–1926). They sought to achieve a modern (meaning different from the contemporary conventions) style by rendering the play of light as naturalistically as possible and by blurring at the edges the line which had for centuries defined form and contained colour so rigidly. A high tonality, achieved using contrasting colours close together, and the rapid application of paint with broad visible brushstrokes came to characterise the style.

Impressionism was affected by the invention of new chemical pigments and pre-packaged tubes of oil paint that made painting plein air possible. Painting outdoors allowed the group to capture the fleeting impressions of light upon water or in the landscape, and the typically small scale of Impressionist canvases is largely attributable to the artists' desire to paint in outdoor locations, since smaller canvases were easier to transport. They were also more suited to the domestic market for which the Impressionists painted.

Monet's *Autumn Effect at Argenteuil*, 1873, was exhibited in the first Impressionist exhibition of 1874, and the vibrancy of its unfamiliar palette brought it to the critics' attention. Light is of unprecedented importance in this work: light disintegrates form and alters colour; light, together with the rapid application of paint, is also the means through which the sense of a fleeting and particular moment in time is conveyed.

This landscape imitates the sensory impressions nature makes on us, rather than simply imitating the appearance of the scene. The palette is a blend of cool blues and warm oranges (**complementary colours**), communicating the overall impression of autumn hues. Ask yourself what clothes you would select from your wardrobe were you to enter the scene. Can you gauge the weather? How has Monet used light and colour to create such a tangible temperature? The variegated foliage is rendered through a juxtaposition of yellow and orange dabs, which are not blended on the painting's surface but 'mix in the eye' and consequently seem to vibrate and quiver as autumn leaves do in the wind. The tall tree on the right, perhaps less sheltered, appears to have been whipped by the wind, an effect achieved by scratching through the pigment in diagonal strokes with the sharp end of a brush.

Colour rather than tonal modelling creates light and shade, as conventional shadow effects are abandoned. The artist's free and visible brushwork defines the style as unequivocally Impressionist, each stroke capturing the character of the form it represents, whether ripples on the water or leaves in the tree. Colour can also be muted and turned bluish to convey a sense of recession or atmospheric perspective, as we see in this painting.

The composition is arranged in terms of its balance between the complementary blues of the water and the orangey colours of the trees. The trees also act as a framing device and an anchor point for the dark blue horizon line that forms a compositional bridge, unifying the disparate parts of the arrangement.

3.1 Let's connect the themes: materials and techniques

Monet uses white paint, thickly applied, using the technique known as **impasto** to create the reflection of sunlight on the cobalt blue of the water. Despite the sketchiness of the scene, Monet employs his brush with meticulous accuracy: short, thick strokes convey nearness: longer, thinner strokes convey distance. Forms are largely ignored as light and colour combine to fragment the scene into a series of impressionistic marks. Monet's **wet-on-wet** application of pigment creates an essential transience; myriad marks bustle in a mosaic-like arrangement to remind us that this moment, these reflections and shadows in shifting colours, are only fleeting. The technical aspects of Monet's technique could therefore be examined as an example of the materials, techniques and processes that artists employ.

Mary Cassatt (1844–1926), the American painter who exhibited with the Impressionists from 1879, provides a good example of the way a painting's formal and stylistic elements convey meaning and aid our interpretation in her *Lydia at the Tapestry Loom*, c.1881. The interior scene may be atypical of the Impressionists' **oeuvre** but its style is unequivocally Impressionist in this particular painting of the artist's sister, Lydia.

The physical qualities of the paint itself and the way it is applied are more important than the draughtsmanship (line) which preoccupied the painters of the Neo-classical style, for instance. The leg of Cassatt's loom appears to melt away at the far end and Lydia's skirt's edge is very roughly handled. Lydia's hand is so ill-defined that the viewer needs the context of the whole work to recognise it as such. However, the handling of paint becomes more precise in the sitter's face and informs us of the subject's concentration on her domestic task. Despite the **painterly** nature of this work and the artist's rapid application of paint, the impression of the scene is complete. The way Lydia's floral dress merges with her equally floral chair could be interpreted as referring to the sitter's 'feminine' role in this interior, domestic scene: she literally

3.4 What can you see?
In Mary Cassatt's *Lydia at the Tapestry Loom* where is the light source? What is the effect of light? Do lines provide the edge of forms? How does the artist's application of paint affect our interpretation of the scene? Consider how the compositional elements of this painting affect the representation of the sitter.

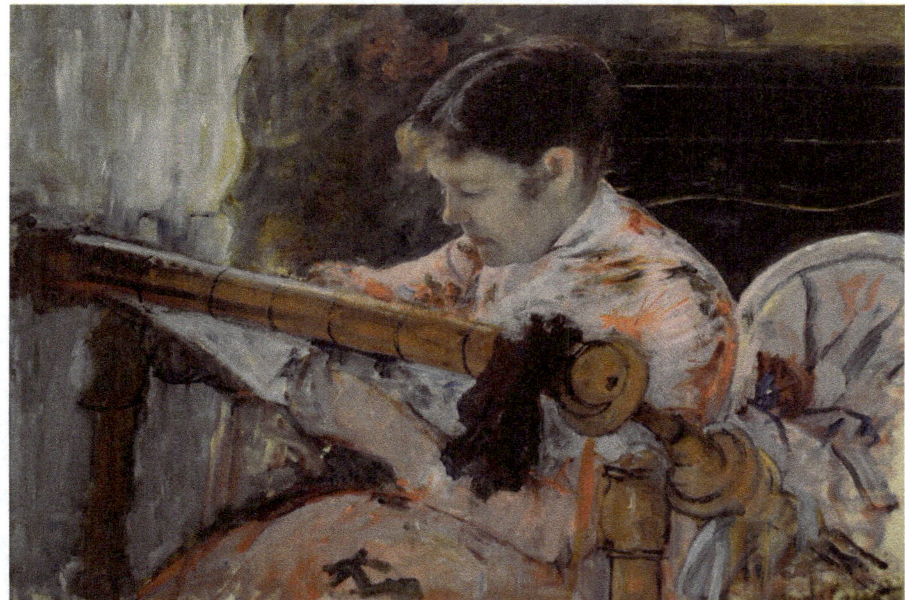

Figure 3.18 | Mary Cassatt, *Lydia at the Tapestry Loom*, c.1881, oil on canvas, 64.7 × 92.7 cm, Collection of the Flint Institute of Arts, Flint, Michigan; Gift of the Whiting Foundation, 1967.32. Source: Flint Institute of Arts, Flint, Michigan.

blends in with her surroundings.

Compositionally, the scene is cluttered and, despite the chest in the background that convinces us of the room's three-dimensional volume, the space is uncomfortably contracted – claustrophobic even. This feeling is heightened by the compositional intrusion of the loom into the viewer's orbit; arguably, it overpowers the scene and acts like a frame, trapping Lydia behind it. The window to the sitter's right is covered over. A multitude of interpretations could be offered as to why. What do you think?

The affiliation of Edgar Degas (1834–1917) with the Impressionists was marked by the free handling of paint and its transient application; he tended not to share their interest in painting plein air. He did, however, share their desire to capture the fleeting aspects of modern life. He was particularly interested in the form (shape) and the movement of dancers – off duty, backstage or rehearsing – and tried to capture their spontaneity. The hallmarks of the Impressionist painterly style – its fleeting sketchiness – may also be seen in Impressionist sculpture. In Edgar Degas' *Dancer Looking at the Sole of Her Right Foot*, the transience of the dancer's form is conveyed by Degas' treatment of the figure's surface.

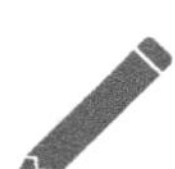

3.3 Explore this example

As a formal comparison focusing on line, compare the draughtsmanship of Raphael's *Alba Madonna*, c.1510, with Mary Cassatt's *Lydia at the Tapestry Loom*, c.1881. The realism of form sought so painstakingly by Italian High Renaissance artist Raphael has clearly been substituted for a different type of realism – the reality of the transience of **'modernity'** – in the nineteenth-century work of Cassatt.

Is Degas' sculpted figure idealised? Is it anatomically correct? How is she posed? Is she contrapposto? Can we see a facial expression? Is she static or animated?

Her body outline is dynamic and indicative of a fleeting moment – she cannot possibly hold this pose for much longer, despite the arm she has hooked up high as a counterbalance. The one grounded foot gives the impression it's about to hop from side to side, and her bent knee seems about to provide the momentum. She is a dancer, full of movement, and the surface of the bronze seems to dance too. Light falling on its dark surface activates the form, and this dynamic is aided by the artist's rough handling of the clay medium before it was cast. The kinetic form of the dancer, preoccupied momentarily and precariously with the inspection of her foot, is far more important than her identity; her face is anonymous, blurred in the Impressionist style.

By the mid-1880s, Impressionism was changing. The term **Post-Impressionism**, invented by the British art critic and painter Roger Fry in 1912, is used to distinguish those artists who both drew upon the Impressionist style and reacted against it by adapting aspects of other contemporary approaches, such as **Symbolism**. The artists most commonly labelled as Post-Impressionists are Vincent van Gogh (1853–1890) – who never exhibited with the Impressionists – and Paul Cézanne (1839–1906) and Paul Gauguin (1848–1903) who did. Since each of these artists exhibits differences in the way they painted, Post-Impressionism is, strictly speaking, not a style. However, the work of these artists may be broadly characterised as tending to render objects more sculpturally, with more structured investigations of form, and using more vigorous and muscular textures than the shimmering light

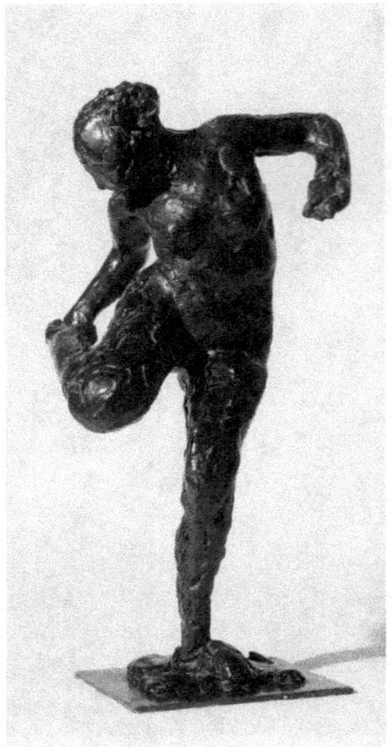

Figure 3.19 | Edgar Degas, *Dancer Looking at the Sole of her Right Foot*, cast 1920 from a plaster cast c.1900, bronze, 476 × 267 × 216 mm, London, Tate. Source: ©Tate, London 2015.

and painterly surface of Impressionism.

Dutch artist Vincent van Gogh's *Wheatfield with Crows*, 1890 (examined in detail in *Chapter 1* as an example of the 'Landscape' genre), also provides a rich study of the formal elements that constitute Post-Impressionism.

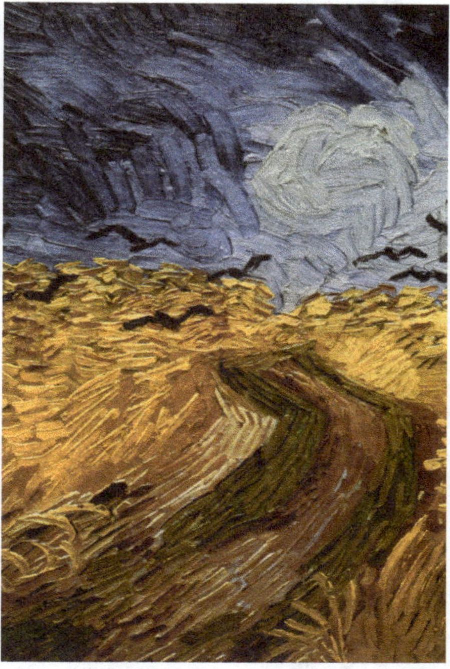

Figure 3.20 | Vincent van Gogh, *Wheatfield with Crows*, 1890, detail, Amsterdam, Van Gogh Museum.
Source: © 2015. Photo Art Media / Heritage Images / Scala, Florence.

In this work, colour is used both as a means of expression and to convey meaning. The vibrancy of the hues energises the work while the addition of black in the blue sky creates a sense of foreboding and anxiety; black crows executed with angular wings intensify that feeling.

Van Gogh used an intense colour palette and a rapid, emotionally charged technique to express his innermost feelings. The formal elements of Van Gogh's work that have categorised him as a Post-Impressionist also make him representative of Expressionism, a fact that illustrates the necessary fluidity required for an analysis of works in terms of their form and style.

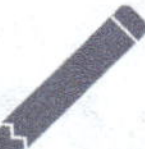

3.4 Explore this example

It is possible to make a formal comparison focusing on colour. Compare for example, the way colour has been employed naturalistically in Meindert Hobbema's *Avenue at Middelharnis*, 1689, with the non-naturalistic use of colour to convey emotion in Van Gogh's *Wheatfield with Crows*, 1890. These two very different landscapes, completed two centuries apart, have already been compared and contrasted in *Chapter 1*, but before you refer back, have a closer look at them now and single out *only* the formal elements that stylistically separate them.

The Formalist approach to *Wheatfield with Crows* seeks to analyse the artist's use of colour, line, texture and so forth. We notice that this menacing landscape tilts up unnaturalistically towards us. The colour intensity achieved is aided by Van Gogh's use of complementary colours: red and green in the paths that lead us nowhere and orangey-yellow in the wheat that thrashes wildly beneath a cobalt-blue and black sky. Colours bulge onto the canvas straight from the tube and heighten our feeling of immediacy.

Characteristically, every single brushstroke can be distinguished, the paint thickly applied and standing proud to create a viscerally textured surface. Line only partially demarcates form; in its wildness, line also conveys the artist's tormented perspective, from which nature has become inimical. Rather than using conventional linear perspective, van Gogh has used brushwork to suggest depth, the strokes of yellow ochre becoming shorter as they recede towards the horizon.

> **instead of trying to reproduce exactly what I see before my eyes, I use colour more arbitrarily, in order to express myself forcibly.**
>
> (Quoted in Chipp, *Theories of Modern Art*, p. 34)

Colour can be used naturalistically and descriptively, as it was in Hobbema's *Avenue at Middelharnis*, 1689; emotionally and psychologically, as it was in Van Gogh's *Wheatfield with Crows*; or reduced to a narrow range of earthy tones, as we will see in the painting we discuss next, *Portrait of Daniel-Henry Kahnweiler*, by Spanish artist Pablo Picasso. Our job is to ask why, and to what effect?

New and Divergent Ways of Seeing in the Twentieth Century

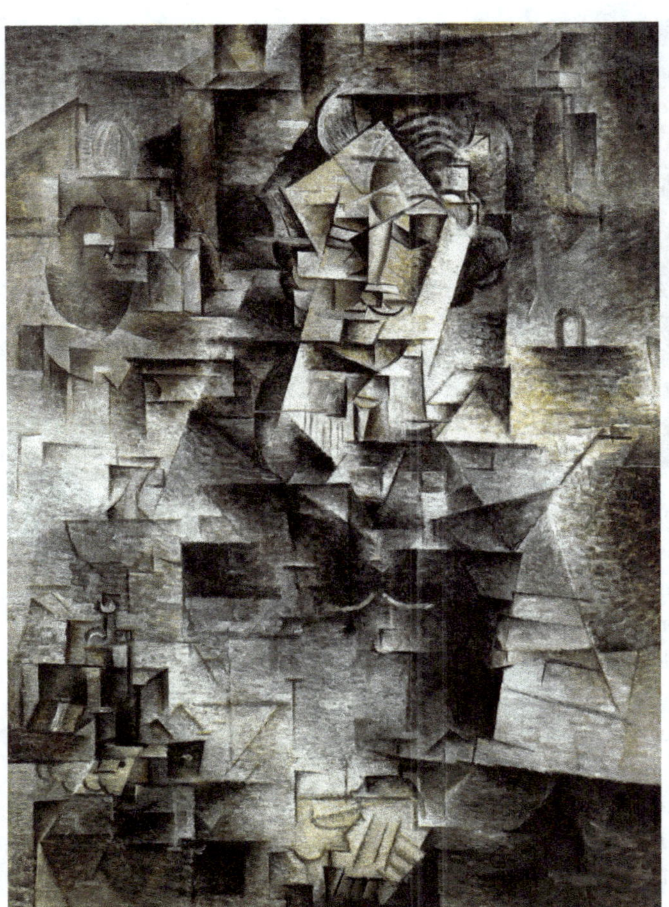

Figure 3.21 | Pablo Picasso, *Portrait of Daniel-Henry Kahnweiler*, 1910, oil on canvas, 100.6 × 72.8 cm, the Art Institute of Chicago.
Source: The Art Institute of Chicago, IL, USA / Bridgeman Images / © Succession Picasso / DACS, London 2015.

Describe the colour palette Picasso uses in his *Portrait of Daniel-Henry Kahnweiler*. Is colour used descriptively? Is colour used to create and model form? Is colour more important than line? Is the subject located in a realistic pictorial space? Is traditional linear perspective used? Does the image appear two-dimensional or three-dimensional?

Cubism

Invented by Pablo Picasso (1881–1973) and French artist Georges Braque (1882–1963), the style known as **Cubism** evolved between c.1907 and 1914. Cubism developed through three distinct phases: **Proto-Cubism**, **Analytical Cubism** and finally, **Synthetic Cubism**. Picasso's *Portrait of Daniel-Henry Kahnweiler*, 1910, exemplifies its Analytical phase.

Daniel-Henry Kahnweiler was one of the foremost art dealers of the twentieth century, and was an early champion of Cubism. In Picasso's portrait of him, the form of the subject seems to have been dismantled, only to be reconstructed using small **faceted planes** to create a sense of shallow three-dimensional space. In a manner characteristic of the Analytical stage of Cubism, the 'contour' lines that traditionally contained the figure have been broken, helping to produce the overall fragmented formal effect of the painting.

Linear perspective has been almost entirely abandoned, and it is as if we see the subject from multiple, contradictory viewpoints simultaneously. Nevertheless, a sense of volume and depth is suggested using isolated portions of shading and modelling. A sense of the fourth dimension (in this case, meaning time) is suggested in perpetually shifting planes. Kahnweiler's form is broken to the point of being nearly unrecognisable save for details such as his moustache, watch-chain and hair. The traditional distinction between foreground, middle ground and background has been eliminated. Just as the Impressionists had done before him, Picasso sets forth a 'new reality' – a reality so ground-breaking that to use colour in this painting, or in any other Analytical work, seemed distracting. The image is drained of colour (with its spatial implications) and light is neither used naturalistically or perspectively to create form or to strategically highlight important elements of the painting. As Daniel-Henry Kahnweiler stated:

Of these paintings one can no longer say, 'the light comes from this or that side', because light has become completely a means. The pictures are almost monochromatic; brick red and red brown, often with a grey or grey green ground, since the colour is meant only to be chiaroscuro. (Quoted in Chipp, *Theories of Modern Art,* p. 248)

Decades later, Picasso's famous black and white anti-war painting, *Guernica*, 1937 (examined in detail in *Chapter 1*), displayed the influence of collage (a characteristic of Picasso's Synthetic Cubism of 1912–1914), which had developed from the faceting of Analytical Cubism. *Guernica* is another example of an iconic painting to which it is quite difficult to ascribe a stylistic label; however, devoid of style it is not. Previously examined in terms of its narrative and response to a real historical event, here the focus has narrowed to an analysis of its formal features.

In this work, the figures are not rendered naturalistically. They are presented as flat, simplified and unmodelled, with a clear linear outline (something that is not a feature of real visual appearances). Instead, a different type of reality has been conveyed using flat, shattered shapes and overlapping forms that heighten the sense of chaos associated with war. In this sense the formal elements that comprise Guernica aid our interpretation of the scene and lend a further layer of meaning to the image.

In this detail of the work, the mother is cartoonishly outlined by the artist, and yet the message Picasso conveys is far from simplistic. Picasso shows the power of line in this work: the mother's dagger-like tongue is forged from two straight lines, so simple and yet so forceful in conveying her agonising, shrill cry. Line is used to distort her body: her head is thrown back as if her neck were on a hinge. We follow the line of her arm, up through her chest and neck until we fall into her gaping mouth and hear her cry. The line of the mother's arm on the left is comprised of relatively straight lines, and these contrast with the curvilinear sweep of the baby's arm, which hangs, lifelessly, limply in a formal syntax we recognise from images of the **pietà**. This line has the power of expression and provocation.

The Futurist movement, founded by writer and poet Filippo Marinetti (1876–1944) in 1909, employed the language of Cubism to express a celebration of speed and power. See *Chapter 4* for more detail on the social and historical context of the Futurist movement, its manifestos and its powerful expression of the modern world.

Futurism

The Futurists embraced technological innovation for its promises of dynamism at the dawning of a new era. Marinetti's fellow Italian Umberto Boccioni (1882–1916), was one of the first to respond to its demands.[13] (see Figure 3.23)

Boccioni's Futuristic creation abandons the traditional use of line used to define and contain the body's form (as seen in Donatello's *David*, 1440, for example). Instead, as in many Cubist paintings, this figure's outline is faceted, opened-up and begins to penetrate the space around it. The way the outside flows in and the inside flows out describes the inter-penetration of form that characterises much of the Futurists' oeuvre. The effect

13 Some art historians have debated as to whether Futurism is a defined style, and argued that it is probably better described as a movement (it has a manifesto). Regardless of the ease with which we may attach a label to it (and some art historians attach the label as easily to Futurism as they do to Cubism or Expressionism and so on) every Futurist work provides us with its own formal features to analyse in terms of form and style.

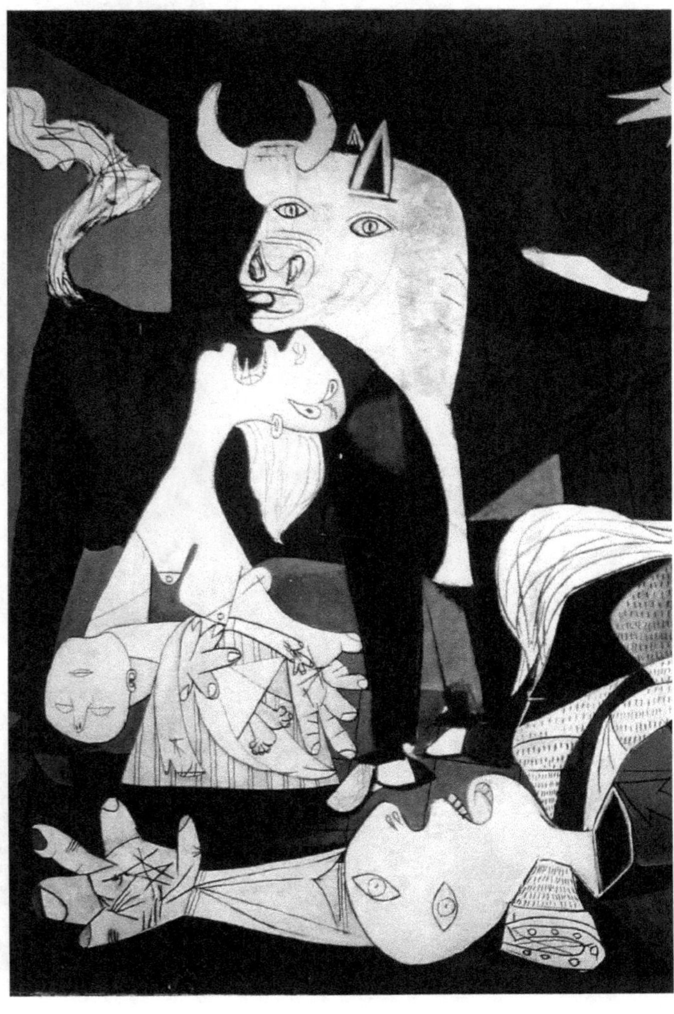

Figure 3.22 | Pablo Picasso, *Guernica*, 1937, detail, oil on canvas, 349.3 x 776.6 cm, Madrid, Museo Nacional Reina Sofia. Source: akg-images / Erich Lessing / © Succession Picasso / DACS, London 2015.

of smashing through the body outline is dynamic, creating flame-like projections from powerful and robotic legs. The figure appears armoured and indestructible. Its swift motion through space is aided by its highly polished surface and sharp, jagged edges; the viewer's eye is made to move ceaselessly over its dynamic form. The figure strides, almost audibly, on block-like bases and strikes a threatening, albeit transient, pose. A loose pyramidal form has been shifted forward to create a diagonal composition which, coupled with the opening between the legs, is further suggestive of force and movement. The play of light over the figure's surface is dramatised by the deep recesses that harbour shade and create an interweaving of tonal contrasts across its body.

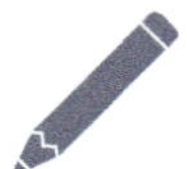

3.5 Explore this example
Compare Boccioni's bronze *Unique Forms of Continuity in Space*, 1913, with the marble **Hellenistic** sculpture, *The Victory of Samothrace*, that it sought to revolutionise. They are fairly antithetical stylistically, but do they share any formal elements?

A close analysis of the formal elements of *Unique Forms of Continuity in Space* tells us a great deal about the Futurist movement it embodies: its militarist aesthetic appears entirely capable of the 'destructive gesture' the movement fostered, and its very dynamism becomes both its subject and its form.

Boccioni's abstracted figure may have been futuristic for the period, but subsequent styles looked to a future based upon the purely **abstract** and the spiritual; a path far more absolute and **avant-garde**.

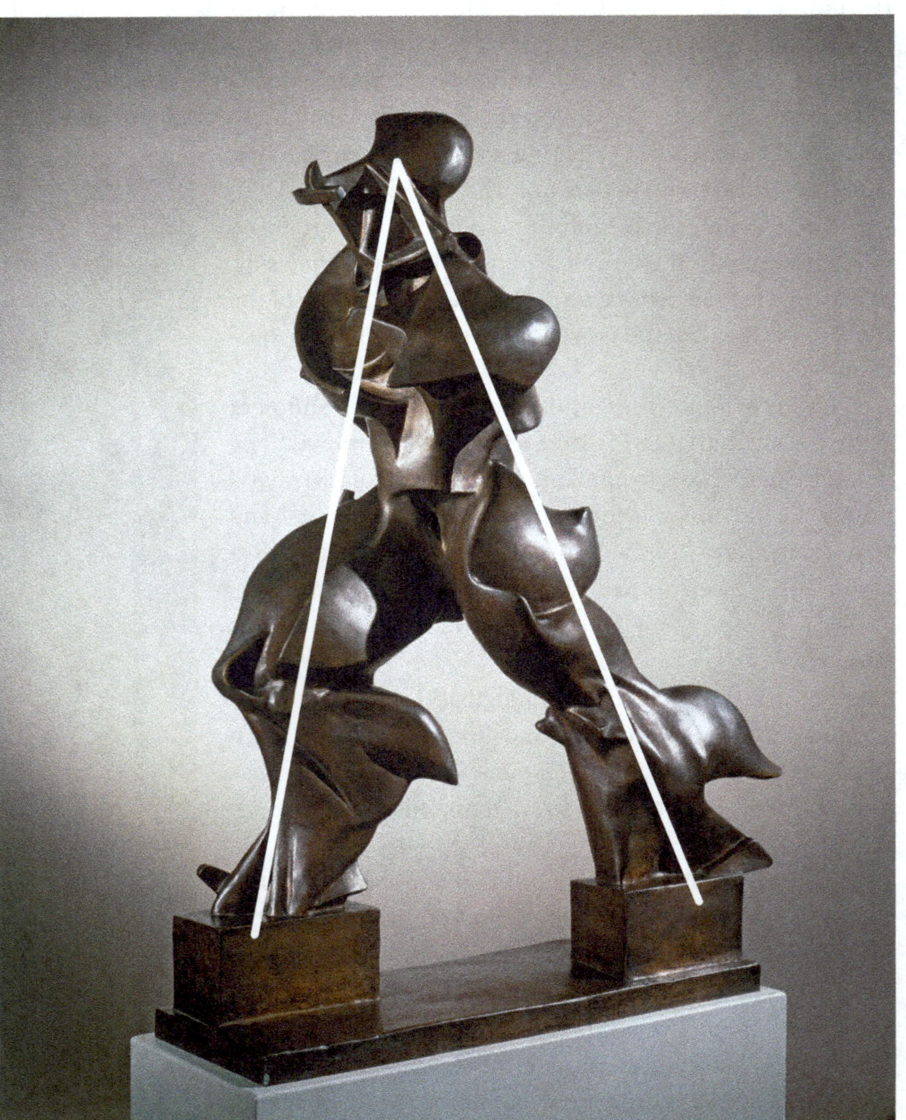

Figure 3.23 | Umberto Boccioni, *Unique Forms of Continuity in Space*, 1913, bronze, 1175 × 876 × 368 mm, cast 1972. London, Tate. Source: © Tate, London 2015.

In Umberto Boccioni's *Unique Forms of Continuity in Space* is the figure idealised? Is it anatomically correct or abstracted? How is it posed? Is it contrapposto? Is there any facial expression? Is it gesturing? Is it static or animated?

European Modernism: In Search of an Elemental Truth

Modernism and abstract art

The turmoil of the early twentieth century caused some artists to seek various ways to model and express utopian ideals in artistic forms. **Suprematism** and **Constructivism** in Russia around the time of the October 1917 revolution, and the **De Stijl** group in the Netherlands sought to eliminate all traces of the external world, sometimes in pursuit of a higher spiritual consciousness. These new styles attempted to reflect the dawn of a new age: a generation emerging from World War I and rejecting imitation and subjectivity in pursuit of an underlying, elementary and objective language. To these artists, imitative art seemed inadequate to express the era and an abstract language seemed better able to express their hopes for a new, universal visual language. Artist Piet Mondrian (1872–1944) christened this approach *Niewe Beeldung*, usually translated as **Neo-Plasticism** but probably better understood as 'new image-making'. This style was intimately associated with the journal *De Stijl* and the like-minded artists and designers based in the Netherlands who contributed to it, including Theo van Doesburg, Bart van der Leck, Georges Vantongerloo and Gerrit Rietveld. Mondrian's art was still about reality, but a deep and underlying reality; below the surface of that with which we are usually preoccupied.

The formal means of neo-plastic expression comprised the primary colours (red, yellow and blue), with the addition of white, grey and black, pure geometric shapes and grids of black vertical and horizontal lines. Together, these elements composed a **formalism** that was thought to correspond to and express the underlying, ideal geometry found in the universe. Dutch painter, Piet Mondrian, stated:

The new plastic idea cannot, therefore, take the form of a natural or concrete representation, although the latter does always indicate the universal to a degree, or at least conceals it within. This new plastic idea will ignore the particulars of appearance, that is to say, natural form and colour. On the contrary, it should find its expression in the abstraction of form and colour, that is to say, in the straight line and the clearly defined primary colour. (Quoted in Chipp, *Theories of Modern Art,* p. 322)

In accordance with Mondrian's neo-plasticity, his paintings are reduced to horizontal and vertical lines interspersed with geometric blocks of primary colour. Thus, these formal elements become the subject matter of the painting, not simply accessories to the content; they alone comprise the style, a style recognised by its pure and abstract form.

3.2 Let's connect the themes: historical perspectives

Abstract art tends to rely on form and colour alone to convey meaning. The idea, while motivated by the newly felt need to liberate art from a tradition that was considered to have become stale, also justified itself by drawing on older principles expressed by Classical Greek philosopher Plato (c.429–c.347 BCE):

I do not now intend by beauty of shapes what most people would expect, such as that of living creatures or pictures, but ... straight lines and curves and the surfaces or solid forms produced out of these by lathes and rulers and squares ... These things are not beautiful relatively, like other things, but always and naturally and absolutely. (Quoted in Murray and Murray, *Dictionary of Art and Artists*, p. 1)

Plato suggested that abstracts and universals of the immaterial realm are to be contrasted with the particular ideas of the material realm. The former are more beautiful and perfect. **Neo-platonic** beauty suggests that which is beyond the imperfection of the material realm. His celebration of the straight line and the purity of basic form is echoed in the principles of Mondrian's new artistic language, which Mondrian hoped would reflect the new direction of modern society.

The development towards abstract form became a universal means of expression for artists such as Mondrian. His individual style sought, through the balance of forms and colour, to establish a unity through relations of equivalence; formal relations quite literally weighed up in accordance with their shape, size and colour values.

Figure 3.24 | Piet Mondrian, *Composition with Yellow, Blue and Red*, 1937–1942, oil on canvas, support: 727 × 692 mm, frame: 917 × 882 × 63 mm, London, Tate. Source: ©Tate, London 2015.

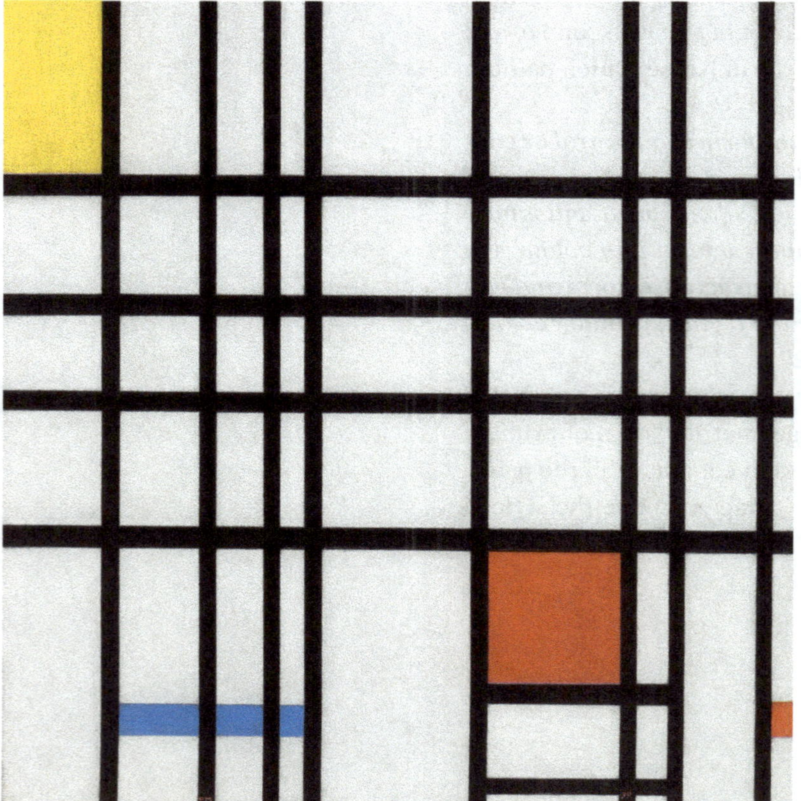

The German chemist Wilhelm Ostwald's book *The Colour Primer*, 1916, influenced the paintings of Piet Mondrian and De Stijl. From a wholly scientific perspective, Ostwald believed that colour needed to be described in quantifiable terms. He found four 'psychological primaries': red, yellow, blue and green. He also examined the complementary pairs: black and white, blue and yellow, green and red (Gage, *Colour and Meaning: Art Science and Symbolism*, p. 258).

Despite the appearance of its flat, unmodulated planes, Piet Mondrian's *Composition with Yellow, Blue and Red*, 1937–1942, does not appear entirely two-dimensional. The colours compete with space in accordance with their various colour values: red advances, blue recedes and the tension between them is held in an overall equilibrium by a black trellis-like grid. The balance of these various forms and primary colours are held in position by black lines of various widths, every formal element playing its part in the whole. The off-white areas balance the intensity of the large red square, smaller blue square and smaller-still yellow rectangle. The yellow area seems to be frustratingly cropped and suggestive of a continuation beyond the confines of the canvas, perhaps into infinity, the ultimate natural phenomenon. Mondrian's 'new' geometric austerity was a style as pure as the promises of the machine age. Yet, this type of formalism also compels us to look inward, towards a higher spiritual reality – Mondrian's highly ordered abstract paintings were about God's highly ordered universe.

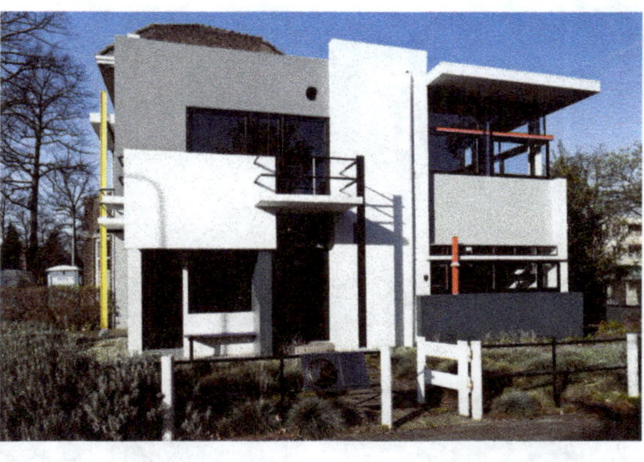

Figure 3.25 | Gerrit Thomas Rietveld, Schröder House, Utrecht, Netherlands, 1924. Source: © Julian Castle / Alamy; © DACS 2015.

Evidently, the various formal elements combine to form a style: the formal elements that comprise Donatello's *David* are recognisable as belonging to the Early Renaissance style, while the formal elements that comprise Goya's *The Third of May 1808* are recognisable as belonging to the style known as Romanticism, and the formal elements that comprise Mondrian's compositions are recognisably a Neo-Plasticist style, and so on. Mondrian's abstract art provided a new formal language for describing the world.

Form, style and function in architecture

In the same way that the formal elements that comprise a painting or a sculpture can be said to have a style, architectural styles are also distinguishable by the common visual language they share. In this chapter, architecture is also examined in terms of its function as well as its form and style, as all three elements are related.

In search of purer forms

As we have seen in our examination of painting and sculpture, in the first quarter of the twentieth century, naturalism was relinquished by artists such as Wassily Kandinsky (1866–1944), Kazimir Malevich (1878–1935) and Piet Mondrian, who each pursued spirituality and purity in the form of abstract composition. Mondrian's belief that pure geometric shapes led to some higher universal consciousness in the viewer filtered into many works of art and architecture at the time. The Schröder House, built in 1924 by Gerrit Thomas Rietveld (1888–1965), is arguably considered to be the finest architectural manifestation of De Stijl, its structure being dominated by planar forms held in perfect equilibrium to achieve an overall unity.

This small domestic dwelling in Utrecht was built for Mrs. Truus Schröder, and it embodies a number of familiar neo-plastic principles: horizontal/vertical lines; a dominant off-white palette combined with grey, black and primary colours. The same primary colours reappear in the interior furnishings to create an overall harmony. The basic design of the house was entirely modern, and as stripped-back as the Netherlandish Calvinism that provided its social context. Its formal purity relates to its functionality – an observation made by architectural historian and critic Kenneth Frampton:

The new architecture is anti-cubic, that is to say, it does not try to freeze the different functional space cells in one closed cube. Rather it throws the

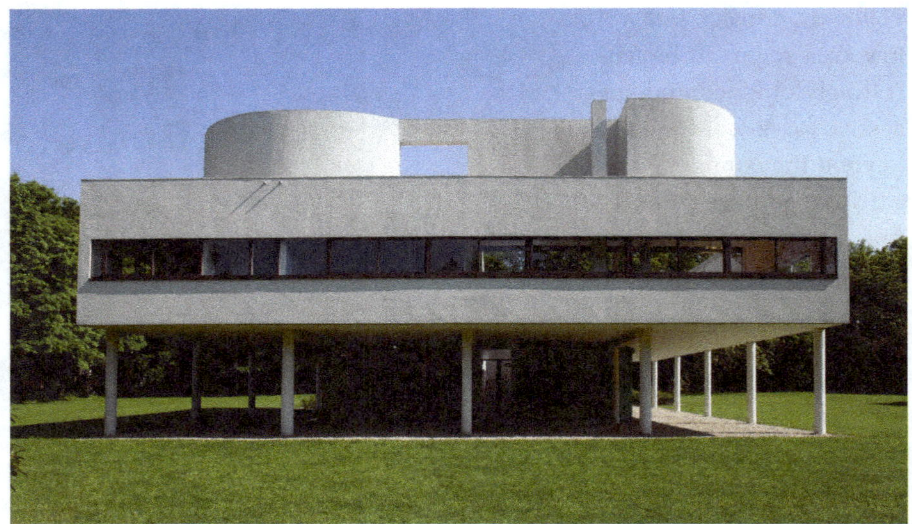

Figure 3.26 | Le Corbusier, Villa Savoye, Poissy, France, 1928–1931, exterior view from the north. Built for Pierre and Eugénie Savoye. Source: akg-images / Schütze / Rodemann; © FLC/ ADAGP, Paris and DACS, London 2015.

Analyse Le Corbusier's Villa Savoye in relation to its formal features such as: composition, colour, volume/mass/void, line/shape, architectural decoration/ features. How does its structure (load-bearing frame) affect its appearance? How do its modern industrial materials affect its appearance? You should also consider the extent to which these formal elements underlie the function of Villa Savoye as a domestic weekend retreat away from Paris for the Savoye family.

functional space cells (as well as the over-hanging planes, balcony volumes, etc.) centrifugally from the core of the cube. And through this means, height, width, depth and time (i.e. an imaginary four dimensional entity) approaches a totally new plastic expression of open spaces. In this way architecture acquires a more or less floating aspect that, so to speak, works against the gravitational forces of nature. (Frampton, *Modern Architecture: A Critical History*, p. 145)

Form follows function: Modern Movement

In the same way that Rietveld's Schröder House is an icon of De Stijl in architecture, the Villa Savoye, 1928–1931, designed by Le Corbusier (1887–1965) may be described as an icon of the Modern Movement, a style that, like the Schröder House, eschewed ornament and decoration and emphasised geometric shapes and forms.

This three-bedroom dwelling designed for the Savoye family in France arguably demonstrates the symbiotic relationship between form, style and function in architecture. Its style is clearly indebted to the materials, techniques and processes of its construction. Stylistically it can be described as modern, minimalist, machine-age, sleek, weightless, open-plan and geometric. Line is an important formal element in its modern syntax: it has a flat roof because a pitched one would spoil its clean hard edges, a geometrical form, and a simplicity that is uninterrupted by surface decoration.

Prefabricated ferroconcrete has been exploited for its appearance as well as the structural freedom it affords to the planning of their interior. The structure of the building is a series of columns (Le Corbusier called them **pilotis**) that support floors and roof. This then allows free positioning of both exterior and interior walls since the columns support the building and the walls are not load-bearing. Moreover, it allows for continuous lines of the **ribbon windows** that allow for the optimum flow of light inside and a view of nature outside. The concrete surface maintains a truth to materials with the addition of brilliant-white paint, which provides a sanitised and pure appearance.

The building has a 'masculine' squareness, set off against the curved lines of its organic form at roof-terrace level. Its predominantly horizontal emphasis is counterbalanced by the vertical pilotis and the upright organic structure on top.

The main living area is on the first floor (a **piano nobile**), allowing the villa's inhabitants to respond to their natural environment. The villa's flat roof maintains the clean geometric lines of the building and also functions as a roof terrace. The villa's functional interior also boasts an open-plan bathroom with built-in recliner for Madame Savoye to rest upon.

The enclosed ground level has a curved glass-end wall (a **curtain wall**) containing a garage and service functions. The Savoye family could drive right under the house and the curve of the wall matched the turning radius of their car. In this respect the house is in tune with a 'machine aesthetic', since the car was seen as the ultimate machine at the time.

The Villa Savoye became the prototype for functional architecture. Its form, style and function are a manifestation of Le Corbusier's 'Five Points of a New Architecture', published in 1926:

1. pilotis – thin columns that support or appear to support a building
2. the 'free plan' for the elimination of load-bearing walls
3. the free **façade** – a non-supporting wall as skin
4. horizontal ribbon windows, to provide maximum illumination
5. the roof garden.

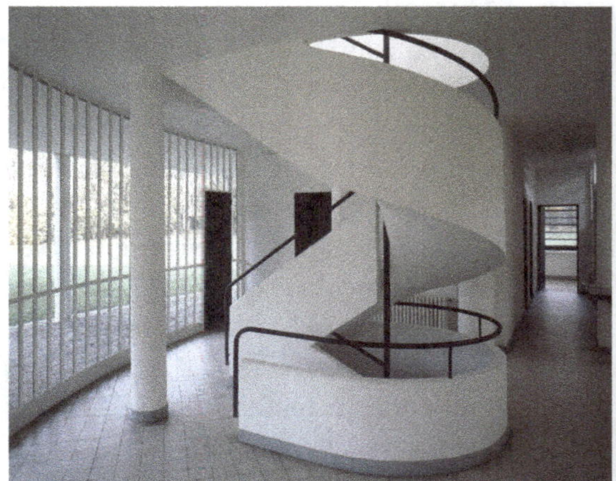

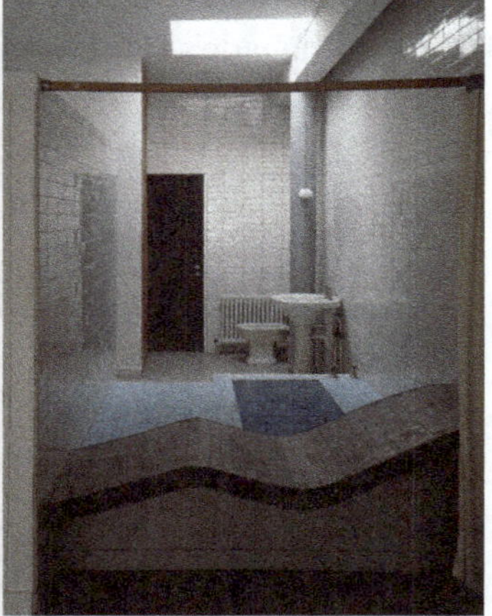

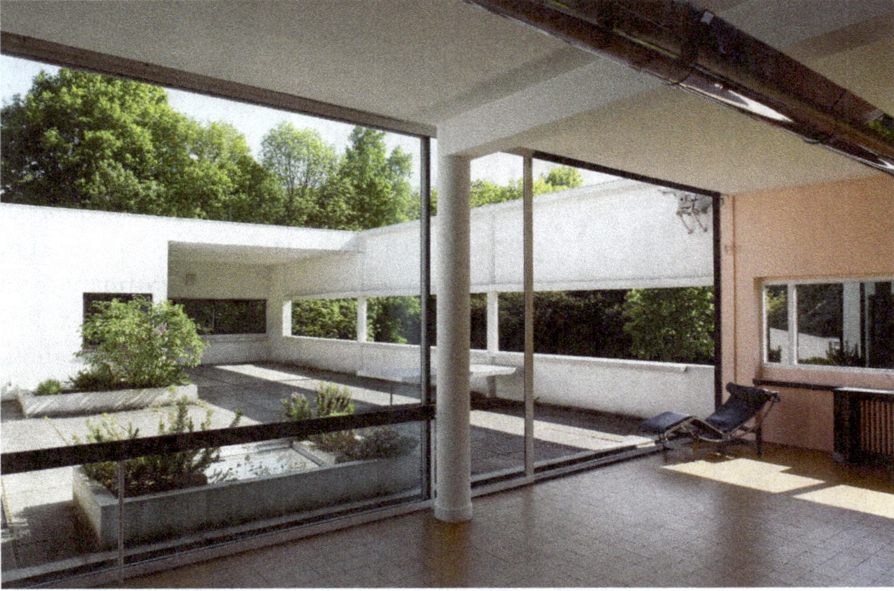

Clockwise from top left:
Figure 3.27 | Le Corbusier, Villa Savoye, Poissy, France, 1928–1931, entrance hall showing pilotis and glass wall.
Source: © Paul Raftery / Alamy; © FLC/ADAGP, Paris and DACS, London 2015.

Figure 3.28 | Le Corbusier, Villa Savoye, Poissy, France, 1928–1931, bathroom with built-in recliner.
Source: © Paul Raftery / Alamy; © FLC/ADAGP, Paris and DACS, London 2015.

Figure 3.29 | Le Corbusier, Villa Savoye, Poissy, France, 1928–1931, interior living space leading onto enclosed terrace.
Source: © Bildarchiv Monheim GmbH / Alamy; © FLC/ADAGP, Paris and DACS, London 2015.

Le Corbusier described houses as 'machines for living' and yet the Villa's stark geometry and industrial construction have been described, perhaps justifiably, as dehumanising. Since the 1960s many architects have deliberately sought to move away from the strict syntax of the Modern Movement (or **International Style** – an alternative style label created after an exhibition of that name in 1932) in favour of more eclectic styles such as that demonstrated in the Lloyd's Building, 1978–1986 (discussed in *Chapter 2*).

3.3 Checkpoint question
What kinds of formal elements are associated with the Modern Movement (International Style)?

The Bank of England was designed at the same time as Villa Savoye but in a completely contrasting style. However, both buildings could be scrutinised in terms of the idea that their form follows their function (i.e. that they were designed primarily for their functional purposes and that their form – appearance/style – was a secondary consideration).

The Classical vocabulary in architecture

Founded in 1694 to act as the government's banker, the Bank of England has performed a variety of functions over its long history. Its role in maintaining the UK's economic stability and public confidence is vital to the effective functioning of the economy itself. The impressive façade of the Bank of England building, constructed between 1929 and 1935 by Sir Herbert Baker (1862–1946), suitably conveys the institution's economic gravitas by adopting elements of Classical architectural vocabulary (not to be confused with the more formalised Neo-classicism of the late eighteenth and early nineteenth centuries). The façade's regular fenestration and equally spaced columns certainly lend a sense of order to a building that is the public face of England's banking. While the lower tier retains its classical elegance, its smooth **rustication** and small-barred windows also establish a secure and slightly uninviting entrance level.

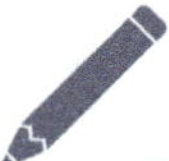

3.6 Explore this example
Make a formal comparison of the curvilinear forms of Donato Bramante's High Renaissance Tempietto, Rome, c.1502–1503, with the straight lines of Le Corbusier's Villa Savoye, built some four centuries later. Their respective form, style and function should provide a rich comparison.

The mass of the building lightens as it ascends above the interrupted **balustrade**, and **caryatids** borrowed from the classical style of Antiquity; they stand like guards either side of the central Roman arch, a feeling heightened by the fact that these features do not perform their traditional load-bearing function. Attending the uppermost story is a bright and airy **loggia** formed with twinned columns. Its form and style suit its function, and yet it is ironic that its rather static façade belies the constant state of flux within.

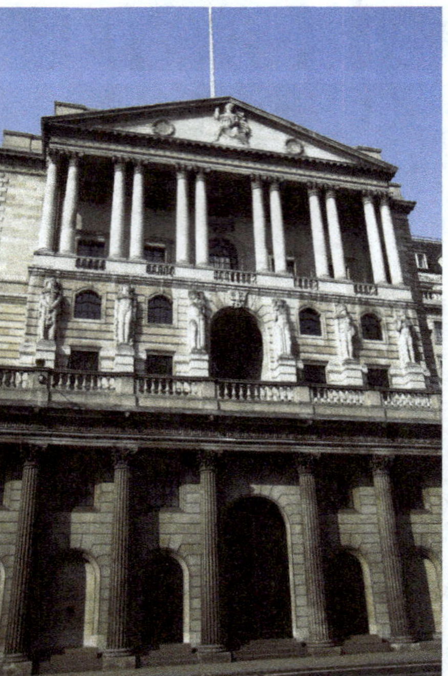

Figure 3.30 | Sir Herbert Baker, The Bank of England, London, 1929–1935. Source: ©TonyBaggett / iStockphoto.

Identify the architectural features on the façade of the Bank of England. Does the decoration have a function? How do these features, together with its stone construction, affect its appearance? Is the Bank on a grand scale? Is the scale of the building functional? Does the decoration have a function? Compositionally, how is the building divided? Is it symmetrical or asymmetrical? We should also consider the extent to which these formal elements underlie the function of the Bank of England as a commercial symbol of the UK economy.

The Bank's architectural decoration is individualistic and symbolic: Britannia, whose image is carved in relief, resides in the **tympanum** of the building's pedimented apex. Britannia is an ancient personification, or symbolic figure, of Great Britain. She has appeared on coinage as far back as Roman Antiquity, on British currency for centuries, and is found on modern bank notes, where she is depicted, as on the building, seated

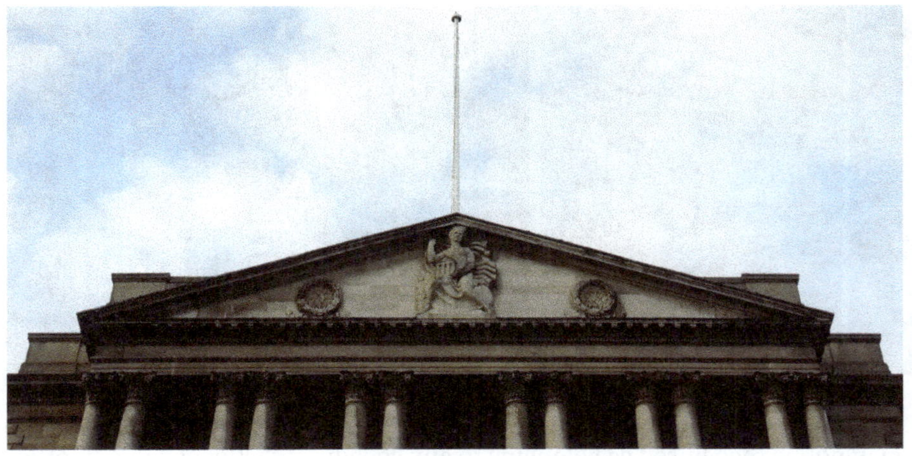

Figure 3.31 | Sir Herbert Baker, The Bank of England, London, 1929–1935, Britannia on tympanum. Source: © BiffBoffBiff / iStockphoto.

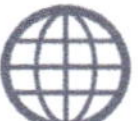

See the companion website for details of the Bank's website, which provides an extensive range of information about its role, history and educational services.

with her shield. The Bank of England is sometimes referred to as the 'Old Lady of Threadneedle Street', where the Bank is located. While Baker used stone to create a grand façade and guard the treasures of the Bank of England within, the American architect Frank Lloyd Wright (1867–1959) designed his Fallingwater building around the pre-existing rock face of a waterfall, opening up its façade as an invitation to nature.

A style of its own

Frank Lloyd Wright's Fallingwater, 1935–1938, conveys a form not all that dissimilar to those expressed in De Stijl or other modern creations, although Wright's infinitely more organic-looking structure is best described as a variant on the Modern Movement. In its sympathetic siting and use of local materials, Fallingwater illustrates aspects of Wright's notion of organic architecture, although its **reinforced concrete** balconies suggest an influence from the European Modern Movement. Its overall appearance, however, is firmly rooted in Wright's desire to create an innovative American architecture, independent of past styles; moreover, Wright created nothing quite like it again, so if it has a style it is its own.

3.5 What can you see?

Is Frank Lloyd Wright's Fallingwater building symmetrical or asymmetrical? Is its composition open or closed? How has Wright tried to blend it in with its surroundings? Are there any clues as to whether its frame is load-bearing?

We should also consider the extent to which these formal elements underlie the function of Fallingwater as a weekend dwelling for a wealthy businessman and his family. One of the idiosyncratic functions of the house is the acoustic purpose of its design, for example.

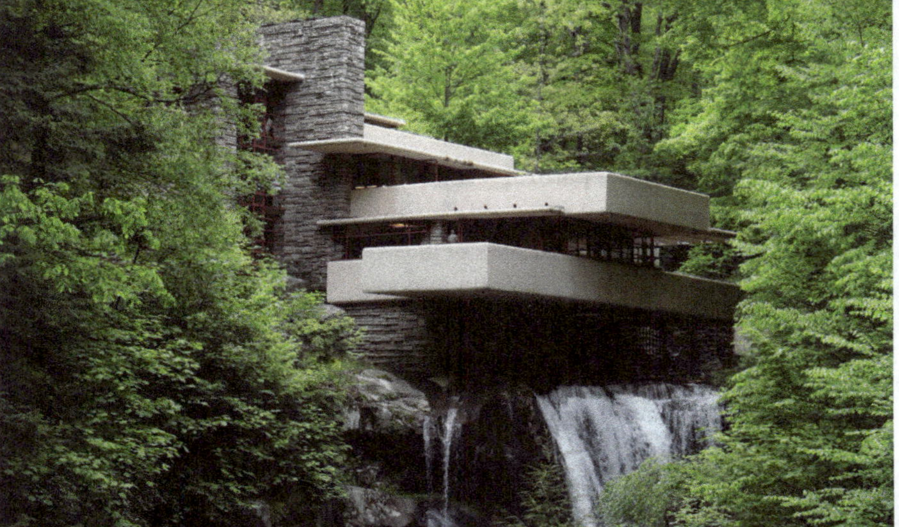

Figure 3.32 | Frank Lloyd Wright, Fallingwater, Mill Run, Pennsylvania, 1935–1938, southwest view with tower acting as cantilever for the over-hanging terraces. Source: © Nick Higham / Alamy; © ARS, NY and DACS, London 2015.

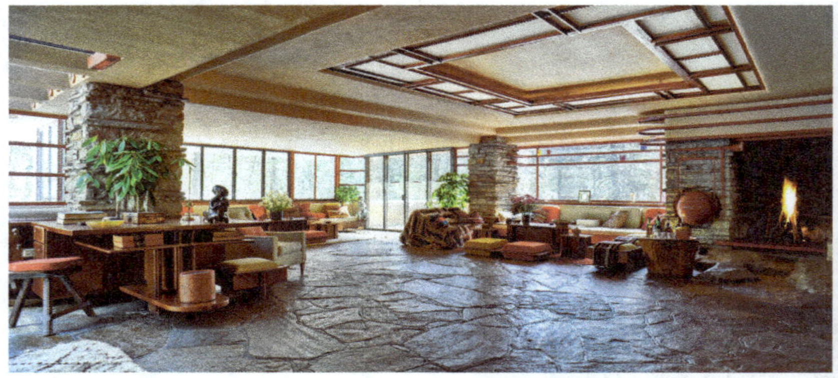
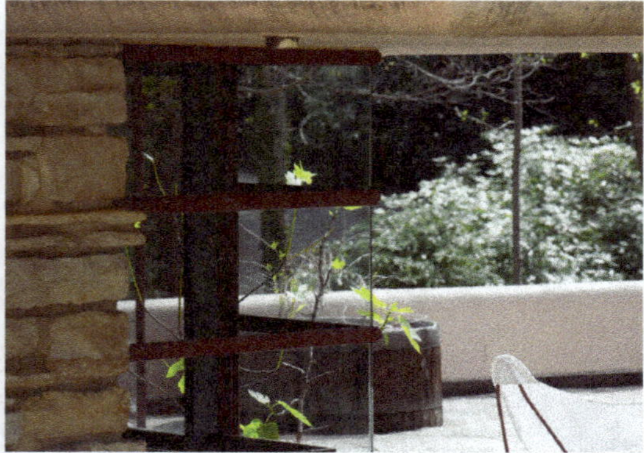

Left to right:
Figure 3.33 | Frank Lloyd Wright, Fallingwater, Mill Run, Pennsylvania, 1935–1938, interior with flagstone flooring.
Source: Christopher Little, courtesy of the Western Pennsylvania Conservancy; ©ARS, NY and DACS, London 2015.

Figure 3.34 | Frank Lloyd Wright, Fallingwater, Mill Run, Pennsylvania, 1935–1938, detail of mitred window.
Source: Christopher Little, courtesy of the Western Pennsylvania Conservancy; ©ARS, NY and DACS, London 2015.

This house, built for the department store magnate Edgar Kaufmann Sr., may not be recognised as belonging to any specific stylistic movement, other than what some have loosely called 'Organic Modernism', but it is certainly recognised as a building brimming with style in terms of its visual appearance.

Fallingwater is both a modern icon and a rejection of Modern Movement principles: Wright valued craftsmanship and truth to material over industrialisation and mass production. While he exploited modern materials such as reinforced concrete in order to achieve the **cantilevered** balconies, he used them less for their minimalist purity and more for their formal resemblance to tree-like structures, entirely at one with their natural environment; he even rounded their edges off, a small but significant detail illustrating Wright's propensity towards organic form. Fallingwater appears to grow out of the rocks, its volume emanating from a natural core into which are embedded massive reinforced concrete supports for the cantilevered balconies and the main body of the house, creating the ultimate synthesis between site and building.

Compositionally, the building is constructed using smooth horizontals and rough-hewn rock verticals. While this house may be described as an extension of Wright's more familiar **Prairie Style** of architecture, it is a unique synthesis between the Modern Movement with its 'industrial' look, and its opposite, the **Arts and Crafts** style (see more on this in *Chapter 2*). Its cave-like interior reveals open-plan living spaces with low ceilings, rough stone columns and flagstone floors that create a comforting level of intimacy, reminding us of nature with our every footstep over their irregularly mortared joins. The floors are treated to provide an almost wet appearance which is reminiscent of the bottom of the river bed itself. This building may be interpreted as sacred, not least in the special and reverent exposure and treatment of its site's materials and natural forms.

Glass is framed in steel painted in a Cherokee red that blends in with its environment. The expansive areas of glass help to create a symbiotic relationship between the inside and the outside.

Fallingwater functions as a reminder to its inhabitants of the importance of a human being's relationship to nature, and of the architect's duty to deliver a dwelling whose form and style respond to its environment. Wright's staircase on the east of the house leads its occupants from outside the main living area directly to the stream below, and literally closer to nature. Its inhabitants are thus able to flow through the house via interconnecting spaces like the rhythmic flow of water itself – humane living in the machine age reconciled in accordance with Wright's **Usonian** vision.

The solidity of Wright's Fallingwater coupled with its inter-penetration of form and space could be interpreted as the antithesis of the closed, lightweight and precarious-looking form of the Lord's Media Centre, in London; however, both buildings represent formal, stylistic and technological innovation, and form appears to follows function in each.

New forms from new technologies

Czech architect Jan Kaplický and his wife Amanda Levete of architectural and design practice Future Systems were commissioned by Marylebone Cricket Club to design Lord's Media Centre (known by various names depending on sponsorship) for a contract price of £5 million. The building had to be finished in time for the 1999 Cricket World Cup – and it was. Future Systems designed a building that innovatively announced the new millennium and heralded a new formal aesthetic – **biomorphic** – potentially alien in the context of a ground steeped in tradition. Seeming to hover 15 metres above the ground, its form appears to defy gravity. Its construction techniques were equally 'blue sky': boat builders were sub-contracted to develop the structure

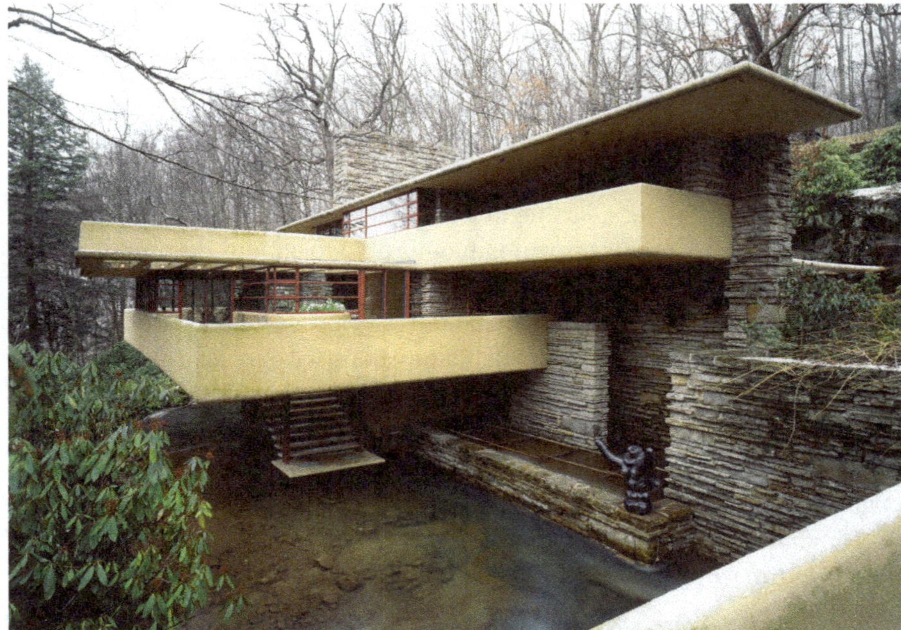

Figure 3.35 | Frank Lloyd Wright, Fallingwater, Mill Run, Pennsylvania, 1935–1938, staircase from living space to stream below. Source: © H. Mark Weidman Photography / Alamy; © ARS, NY and DACS, London 2015.

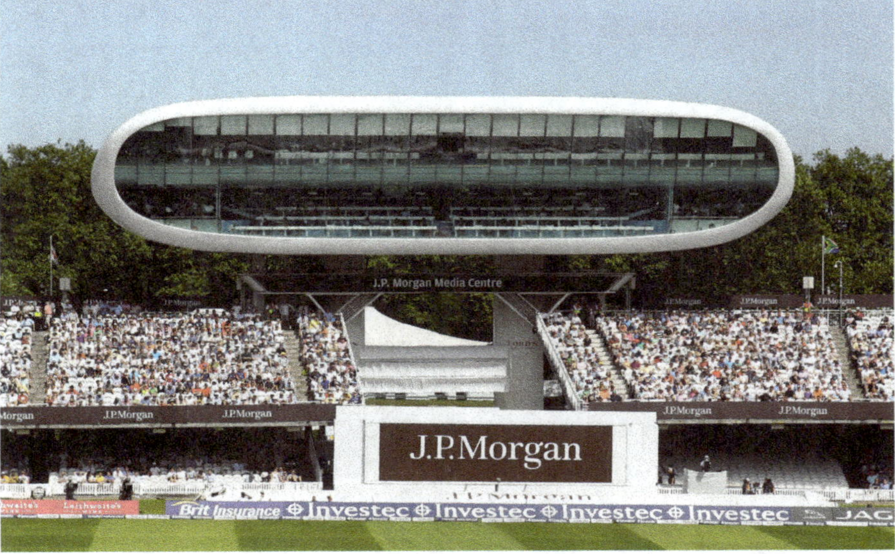

Figure 3.36 | Future Systems, J.P. Morgan Media Centre, Lord's Cricket Ground, London, 1999. Source: © Clare Skinner / MCC, reproduced by kind permission of MCC.

Is the composition of Future System's Lord's Media Centre symmetrical or asymmetrical? Is it decorated or undecorated? How does its colour and shape affect its appearance? Was it constructed on site or off site? We should also consider the extent to which these formal elements underlie the function of Media Centre as a private commercial space for the media to report on the ground's cricket matches.

and its aerodynamic form and fluid surface seem not just ship-like, but spaceship-like.

Described as the world's first all-aluminium building, undoubtedly the materials, techniques and processes of its construction have had a significant impact on the building's aerodynamic form and futuristic style. The building has also been described as **semi-monocoque** on account of its external skin being singular and load-bearing. Interestingly, the term is used in the aviation industry to describe fuselage construction and shipbuilding when the hull of a boat is made in one continuous piece. The building was designed to be prefabricated and largely assembled off site to avoid unnecessary disruption to the venue's cricketing fixtures.

Built to accommodate the media (journalists, radio and television broadcasters, etc.), the building's aluminium skin needed to fulfil both thermal and acoustic functions. These were aided by padded ceilings (a technique borrowed from the shipbuilding industry) and carpeting. The aluminium shell is coated in glass reinforced plastic (GRP) – a boat-building material – and its white colour maintains a lower surface temperature than alternative colours. Similarly functional, the use of pale blue in the building's interior absorbs rather than reflects the light.

As the exterior of the building warms up it swells, and as it cools down it contracts, but the entire structure is designed to accommodate this acclimatisation and even the shell meets its legs on bearings described by its creators as 'free-rolling'. The legs, sitting at the back of the building, were thought inadequate to carry their crowning biomorphic form but, despite its unbalanced appearance, the Media Centre is prevented from toppling forward because those same legs travel some 26 metres below ground level, functioning as **tension piles** that more than adequately cope with its cantilevered mass. The legs also function as a fire escape, power supply and lift housing. Made with reinforced concrete, they gain further strength from the steel staircases they house. The functionality of the Media Centre was noted by David Glover, engineer at Ove Arup Partners:

The final shape, size and volume came from the brief – putting the brief down and arranging it in a very functional form, which is what Future

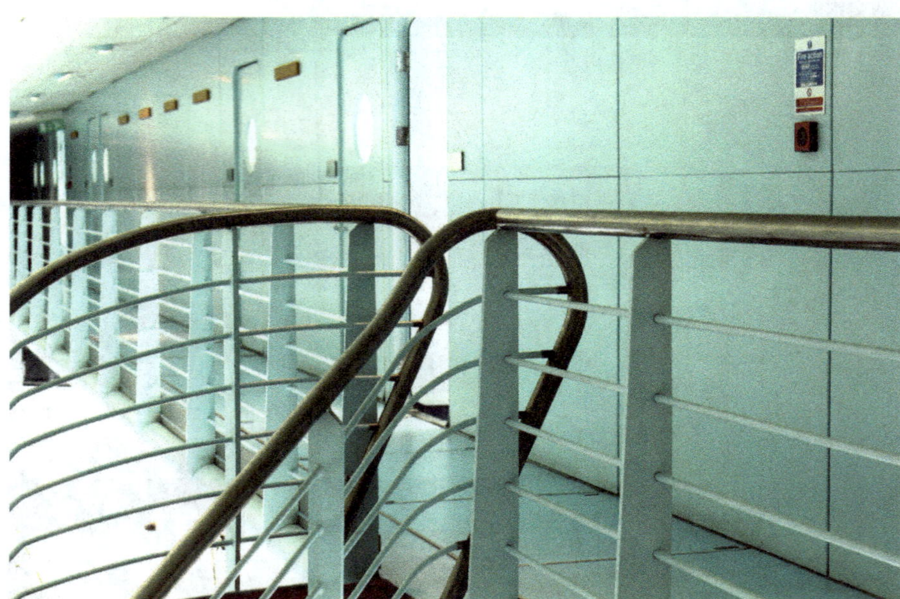

Figure 3.37 | Future Systems, J.P. Morgan Media Centre, Lord's Cricket Ground, London, 1999, interior handrail and balustrade on mezzanine. Source: © Clare Skinner / MCC, reproduced by kind permission of MCC.

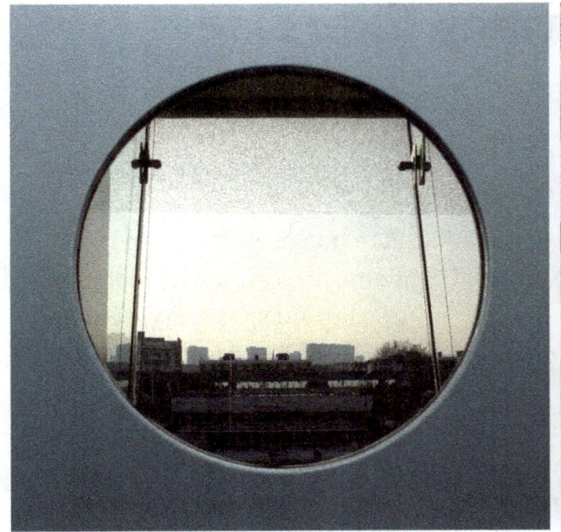

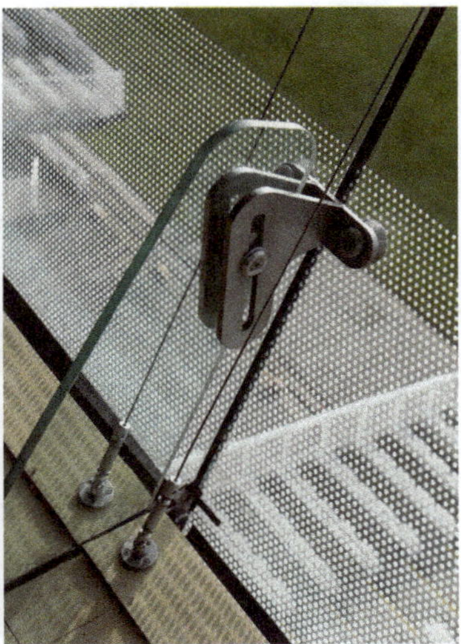

Left to right:
Figure 3.38 | Future Systems, J.P. Morgan Media Centre, Lord's Cricket Ground, London, 1999, porthole window. Source: © Clare Skinner / MCC, reproduced by kind permission of MCC.

Figure 3.39 | Future Systems, J.P. Morgan Media Centre, Lord's Cricket Ground, London, 1999, interior view of system for holding glass panes in place. Source: © Clare Skinner / MCC, reproduced by kind permission of MCC.

Systems are absolutely fantastic at. They will take all these obscure requirements and arrange them really functionally. You go in there and it's clear where the writers go – you don't have to ask. If you want to eat, you can see which area to go to. (Quoted in Kaplický, *Unique Building: Lord's Media Centre*, p. 77)

The sky-blue interior is coupled with nautical-style balustrade, handrails, **mezzanine** floor and porthole-style windows, all of which provide the feeling of being on board a boat.

Despite the Media Centre's modern style, it still responds to the more traditional elements of the site: its oval contours reflect the shape of the 'hallowed ground' it overlooks and, coupled with the fact that it rests at the same height as the Victorian Pavilion opposite, lends a harmonious feeling to the ground's composite parts. Cricket matches are conveyed globally and often simultaneously through its eye-shaped lens. This could, perhaps, be interpreted as a metaphor for the power of the media itself. The building is also functional: the expanse of glazing on the west façade is tilted at 25 degrees to avoid glare (a significant functional benefit given that glare has forced play to stop on other grounds), while simultaneously providing an unprecedented and uninterrupted view of play.

The enormous glass viewing façade is made up of a number of large glass panes, held together almost invisibly by interior alloy bolts (see Figure 3.39). Narrow rubber bands ensure almost seamless joints between the panes, aiding the fluid and **high-tech** appearance of the exterior façade.

Perhaps in its ultimate expression of functionality, the elevated position of the structure provides panoramic views of the ground for the newspaper journalists in its lower tier, and television and radio broadcasters situated in private commentary pods in its upper mezzanine tier; its purpose and navigation once inside are effortlessly communicated.

As well as the buildings examined in detail in this chapter, buildings discussed in other chapters, such as Philip Webb's Red House, 1859, and Richard Rogers' Lloyd's Building, 1978–1986, are equally worthy examples to study in terms of form, style and function. The choice of works of art and architecture available to consider under such a broad heading is innumerable, and you are encouraged to find your own examples through which to explore the ideas discussed here.

Chapter Summary Exercise

Using the words below complete the Chapter Summary. Each word or term should be used only once.

anatomical
movements
lightweight
content
light
free-planning
Classicism
colour
diagonals
simultaneously
aluminium
painterly
contrapposto
materials
texture
undecorated
pediments

Formalism looks at the form or appearance of an image, rather than its __________ or narrative. Formal elements of works of art include: line, shape, colour, tone, __________, scale and space. Style can be a complicated term to define; sometimes the collective styles of artists are associated with __________, such as Impressionism.

The Early Renaissance, in Italy, marked a new beginning in art history and became characterised by the revival of __________ and by the artists' greater understanding of __________ correctness and new ways to achieve realism. The figures of the High Renaissance twist in realistic __________, to create an unsurpassed level of realism.

The Baroque style, which emerged in the century after the High Renaissance, introduced __________ and raking light into scenes which gave them dynamism and theatricality.

Romanticism, unlike its Neo-classical antithesis, is characterised by loose and __________ brush strokes which communicate an intensity of feeling.

The Impressionist style is also characterised by free and visible brush work; although Impressionism largely ignores form, in pursuit of capturing the effects of the __________, which fragments it.

Cubism evolved through three stages. In the Analytical stage of Cubism subjects are viewed from multiple viewpoints __________.

Abstract art tends to rely on form and __________ alone to convey meaning.

The Classical style of architecture is recognised by columns, __________, and entablatures. The style of some architecture is also attributable to the __________, techniques and processes of its construction.

The Modern Movement can be described as minimalist, __________ and machine-age. Ferroconcrete walls afford the __________ of interior spaces and create highly functional and flexible accommodation.

New technologies borrowed from industries such as boat-building have been used to create __________ constructions from materials such as __________. The forms and styles of buildings in the future are likely to evolve with changing materials and technological advancement.

Checkpoint Answers

3.1 Identify three formal elements associated with the Renaissance style.
Anatomical correctness, linear perspective, foreshortening, contrapposto.

3.2 Identify three formal elements that are associated with the Baroque style of painting and/or sculpture and/or architecture.
In painting: dramatic lighting, compositional complexity such as the use of intersecting diagonals, severe tonal contrasts. In sculpture: compositional complexity, verisimilitude, hyperbolic gestures. In architecture: twinned columns, convex cornicing, highly decorated surfaces.

3.3 What kinds of formal elements are associated with the Modern Movement (International Style)?
Geometric shapes such as the rectangle or square, straight lines, hard edges and undecorated surfaces.

References

Chipp, H.B. *Theories of Modern Art*, University of California Press, 1984.

Frampton, K. *Modern Architecture: A Critical History*, Thames & Hudson, 2007.

Gage, J. *Colour and Meaning: Art Science and Symbolism*, Thames & Hudson, 2006.

Kaplický, J. *Unique Building: Lord's Media Centre*, Future Systems / John Wiley & Sons, 2007.

Murray, L. and Murray, P. *Dictionary of Art and Artists*, 7th ed., Penguin, 1998.

Vasari, G. *Lives of the Artists*, Vol. 1, Penguin, 1987. (First published 1550.)

Woodford, S. *The Parthenon*, Press Syndicate of the University of Cambridge, 2001.

Other Useful Sources

Cornell, S. *Art: A History of Changing Style*, Phaidon, 1983.

Denison, E. and Glancey, J. *30-Second Architecture: The 50 Most Significant Principles and Styles in Architecture, Each Explained in Half a Minute*, Ivy Press, 2013.

Piper, D. and Tressidor, J. *Understanding Art: Appreciation, Method and Technique*, Octopus Publishing, 1981.

Chapter 4

Social and Historical Contexts

Learning Outcomes

By the end of this chapter you will be able to:

- define the concepts of social and historical contexts in relation to painting, sculpture and architecture and show how these help to determine our interpretation
- describe the formal characteristics that comprise a response to particular social and/or historical contexts
- identify a broad range of influences that affect a work of art or architecture and provide a range of examples.

Thinking About Art: A Thematic Guide to Art History, First Edition. Penny Huntsman.

Chapter Map

This chapter map provides a visual overview of Chapter 4 – 'Social and Historical Context' – together with its key works.

Seventeenth Century: Baroque Rome and the Catholic Counter-Reformation

– Caravaggio (1571–1610), *The Entombment of Christ*, 1602–1604
– Gian Lorenzo Bernini (1598–1680), *The Ecstasy of St. Teresa of Ávila*, 1645–1652
– Artemisia Gentileschi (1593–1656), *Judith Slaying Holofernes*, c. 1620

Nineteenth-Century France: Transformation and Modernity

– Pierre-Auguste Renoir (1841–1919), *Bal du Moulin de la Galette à Montmartre*, 1876
– Edgar Degas (1834–1917), *L'Absinthe*, 1875–1876
– Gustave Caillebotte (1848–1894), *Paris Street; Rainy Day*, 1877
– *Édouard Manet (1832–1883), Olympia*, 1863
– Charles Garnier (1825–1898), Opéra Garnier (Paris Opera), 1862–1875

Mid-Nineteenth-Century England and Victorian Morality

– Augustus Leopold Egg (1816–1863), *Past and Present*, 1858
– William Holman Hunt (1827–1910), *The Awakening Conscience*, 1853

Mid-Twentieth-Century United States and the Depression Era

– Edward Hopper (1882–1967), *Nighthawks*, 1942

Twentieth-Century United States: The Boom Years

– Andy Warhol (1928–1987), *Marilyn Diptych*, 1962
– Jeff Koons (born 1955), *Michael Jackson and Bubbles*, 1988
– Barbara Kruger (born 1945), *Untitled (I Shop Therefore I Am)*, 1987

Class Fragmentation and the Urban Documentary

– William Powell Frith (1819–1909), *The Railway Station*, 1860–1862
– Richard Billingham (born 1970), *Untitled*, 1994

Introduction

This chapter introduces you to the theme of social and historical contexts and considers how works of art or architecture reflect the times in which they were made, or were influenced by a particular social or historical event, events or circumstances. *Historical context* means the political, cultural, economic and social circumstances in which a work of art or architecture was created. Relevant historical conditions or events may include wars, scientific or industrial developments (such as the Industrial Revolution), political revolutions, and economic booms and busts. Typically, social and historical contexts are closely inter-related and provide a broad perspective on 'what is going on' in society at a particular time in its history. *Social context* means the social conditions and popularly accepted beliefs in a society at a particular time, such as attitudes relating to **gender** or class.

Chapter 3 examined the formal features of works of art and architecture regardless of the subject matter and irrespective of the work's social and historical contexts. In contrast, this chapter prioritises the broader contexts in which the art was produced as the basis for its formal aesthetic or style, and considers the multitude of variables that may permeate a work's production and contribute to the meaning we assign to it.[14]

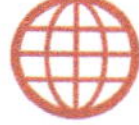

See the companion website for wider reading in relation to art in context.

Many of the works already discussed in previous chapters may be further scrutinised under the lens of social and historical contexts. For example, Jacques-Louis David's *Death of Marat*, 1793, first examined in *Chapter 1* as an example of the history and portrait genre, will be explored in relation to the social and historical contexts of the French Revolution and the political ideology of the National Convention that ruled France during the king's removal from power.

This chapter will illustrate the significance of context in relation to the seventeenth, nineteenth and twentieth centuries as a focus, although readers have the freedom to select examples from Western art and architecture from Classical Greece to the year 2000.

14 This chapter is designed to give readers a taste of the contextual information that surrounds chosen examples, and none of the examples examined is discussed comprehensively in terms of its social and historical contexts.

Seventeenth Century: Baroque Rome and the Catholic Counter-Reformation

The **Baroque** style that originated in Rome during the seventeenth century spread throughout Europe to Flanders, Spain, France, the Dutch Republic and England. **Secular** commissions were becoming more widespread, although the art of Spain and Italy (particularly Rome) was dominated by religious genres patronised by the church. Rome provides a logical starting point, given its artistic importance during the seventeenth century. See *4.1 Explore this example* if you want to move outside Italy in the seventeenth century to investigate the context of the Dutch Republic.

In the early sixteenth century, Protestantism was gaining a considerable following in northern Europe following a successful campaign against the Catholic Church led by German priest and professor of theology Martin Luther (1483–1546). Luther is commonly agreed to have initiated the Protestant Reformation in 1517. The charismatic leader of this tidal religious change visited Rome in 1510 and was shocked by the corruption he witnessed in the Catholic Church, particularly in relation to the sale of **indulgences**. Luther posted his Ninety-Five Theses (disputes with the church) on the church door at Wittenberg, Germany in 1517, an act that marked the beginning of the Protestant Reformation.

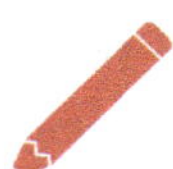

4.1 Explore this example
Meindart Hobbema's seventeenth-century landscape *The Avenue at Middleharnis*, 1689, with its low-lying land and panoramic view may be understood in the social and historical context of the Dutch Republic's Declaration of Independence from Spain (finalised in the Treaty of Münster, 1648). Hobbema's painting is examined as an example of the landscape genre in *Chapter 1*.

A further blow to the status of the Catholic Church was the sack of Rome and the pillaging of its churches in 1527 by Charles V's mercenaries, during which the then Pope, Clement VII, was forced to pay a ransom in order to escape. However, by the end of the sixteenth century, the city had been rebuilt to appear more resplendent than ever. Countless new churches, chapels and streets reasserted the authority of Catholicism and buried the memory of its past humiliation. Rome was transformed from a poor, ruined town to a vibrant city: the Catholic **Counter-Reformation** had arrived with the power of the Baroque style at its service.

On the theological front in the mid-sixteenth century, Pope Paul III (1468–1549) counteracted the threat from Protestantism by re-establishing the orthodox rules of Catholicism at the Council of Trent (a general church council established in the small Italian town of Trent). The Council of Trent convened over a 20-year period between 1545 and 1563. It issued instructions to educate the **laity**, enrolling the arts to strengthen the Roman Catholic faith. Crucially, it recommended that these instructions be communicated by artists as clearly as possible. According to art historian Rudolf Wittkower the Council of Trent laid down rules broadly under three headings:

1. 'Clarity, simplicity and intelligibility': many stories relating to saints deal with martyrdom, brutality, horror and truth, in the sense that Christ must be shown *afflicted, bleeding, spat upon, with His skin torn, wounded, deformed, pale and unsightly*, if needed. And yet, decorum should be maintained (e.g. no nudity).
2. 'Realistic interpretation': precise adherence to the Scriptures should be maintained.

3 'Emotional stimulus to piety': there was a new emphasis on martyrdoms to stimulate emotional responses from the faithful and new saints to celebrate: Ignatius Loyola, Charles Borromeo, Teresa of Ávila, Philip Neri and Francis Xavier were all canonised between 1610 and 1622.

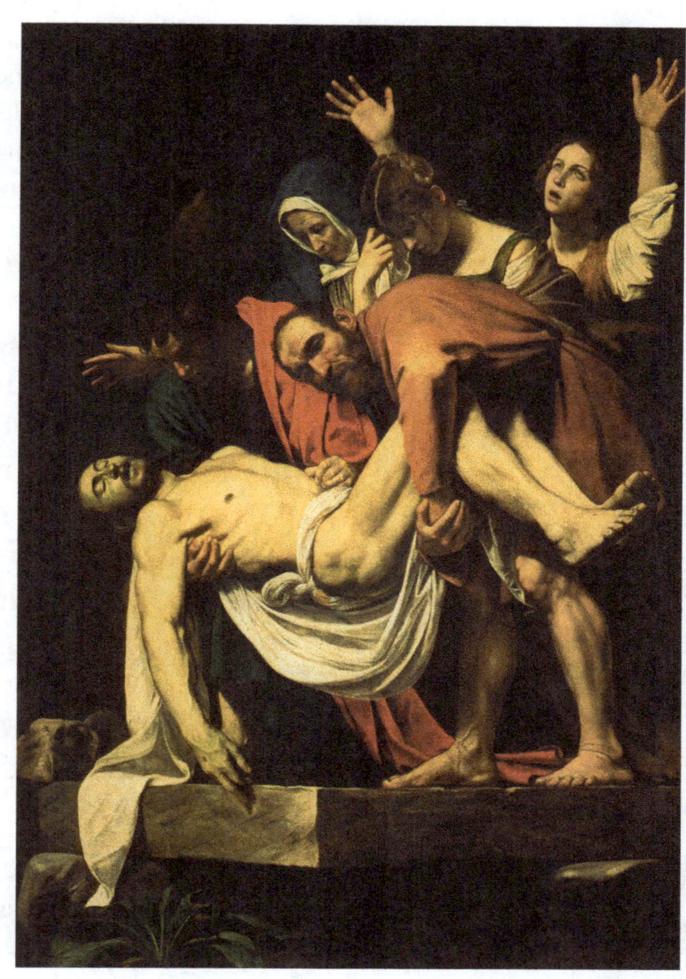

Figure 4.1 | Caravaggio, *The Entombment of Christ*, 1602–1604, oil on canvas, 300 × 203 cm, Rome, Pinacoteca Vaticana. Source: akg-images.

The Council encouraged the establishment of new religious orders of monks and nuns and heralded a religious transformation that led to a more triumphant Catholicism. The Council of Trent was convened numerous times, but its most significant meetings were in 1545 to discuss Luther's Theses and, in 1563, to recommend the employment of art as an integral part of the Counter-Reformatory process. The Council recommended that the power of the visual image be used to combat the austerity of the Protestant faith. It proposed that art should enable the observer to continuously remember the mysteries of our faith and Caravaggio (originally Michelangelo Merisi da Caravaggio, 1571–1610), the painter-cum-criminal, delivered upon the brief when he created some of the most memorable religious images ever painted.

Painted for a side chapel in Santa Maria in Vallicella, *The Entombment of Christ*, 1602–1604, is one of Caravaggio's less controversial works. Nevertheless, this sacred altarpiece risks breaching decorum, with Christ's slightly over-exposed buttock and Joseph of Arimathea's (sometimes identified as St. John) dirty fingers delving into Christ's open wound. Six religious figures emerge from a **tenebristic** void, illuminated by an artfully angled candlelight; the splayed fingers of Mary of Cleopas (sometimes thought to be Mary Magdalene, who is adjacent), at the top right, compete for our attention with the weathered-looking Nicodemus, on the central vertical axis, who insists upon returning our gaze, seemingly including us in the scene. The tale of Christ's body being lowered into his tomb is retold here with unprecedented realism for the time; but owing to the daring spatial composition, it almost seems as if he is also being lowered onto us, or the repentant laity of the time. Thus, it's not only the sprouting plant in the foreground that signifies life; we seem to be there too, breathing the same air. As art historian Ann Sutherland Harris points out, Caravaggio's painting seems to offer us as viewers the opportunity to 'receive' the body of Christ, just as the priest traditionally raises the host (the bread that symbolises the body of Christ) to bless it during the Mass. Harris also draws our attention to *Christ's left hand with its awkwardly contracted fingers frozen by* rigor mortis, an accurate observation of death by an artist intent on presenting the laity with the ugly truth and on bringing out the full meaning of the embodiment of God as man (Harris, *Seventeenth-Century Art and Architecture*, p. 47).

While the Council of Trent busied itself with the sanctity of the Bible, Caravaggio imbued Scriptures with perhaps a little too much **humanism**. Fortunately for him, his unique ability to reach out to all men – even the sinners – followed what had been declared a Holy Year, 1600, in Rome. A Holy Year or Jubilee is mentioned in the Bible, which describes God's mercy being granted on such an occasion. In what ways do you think Holy Year may have granted Caravaggio's often indecorous images a degree of immunity?

Caravaggio was not the only artist to greet the Baroque era with a hyperbolic sense of drama; the Italian painter, sculptor and architect Gian Lorenzo Bernini (1598–1680) would at least match Caravaggio's ability to create an almost cinematic experience for the viewer, exemplified in his *Ecstasy of St. Teresa of Ávila*, 1645–1652. St. Teresa of Ávila (1515–1582) was a Spanish nun who entered the Carmelite Order at the age of 21 and founded the order of the nuns of Teresa of Ávila. During her life she preached spirituality, modesty and poverty, and after her death she was made a saint. Her widely read autobiography describes her religious visions and gives an insight into the socio-religious context of seventeenth-century art.

In his hands I saw a great golden spear, and at the iron tip there appeared to be a point of fire. This he plunged into my heart several times so that it penetrated to my entrails. When he pulled it out, I felt that he took them with him and left me utterly consumed by the great love of God. The pain was so severe that it made me mutter several moans. The sweetness caused by this intense pain is so extreme that one cannot possibly wish it to cease, nor is one's soul then content with anything but God. This is not a physical, but a spiritual pain, though the body has some share in it – even a considerable share.

(Teresa of Ávila and Cohen, *The Life of Saint Teresa of Ávila by Herself*, p. 210)

Bernini brought one of her spiritual encounters with God vividly to life, bringing heaven down to earth in a moment of **transverberation**. The seraphim's drapery flutters with a heavenly lightness, while St. Teresa's billows dramatically, emphasising the materiality of the human realm.

Contained in an **aedicule** crowned with a broken **pediment** and flanked by polychromatic marble, the pair are 'illuminated' by natural light that filters through a concealed yellow-tinted glass lantern above the scene, reinforced by golden 'rays' made of coloured **stucco** that provide arguably the most theatrical and illusionistic backdrop in sculptural history. With this piece, Bernini has created a **bel composto**, a beautiful whole comprising component parts: painting, sculpture and architecture. It was a stage design, a theatrical performance and a sensory delight that chimed with Counter-Reformation propaganda.

The intensity and bodily character of St. Teresa's visions were in accord with Spanish Saint Ignatius Loyola's book of *Spiritual Exercises*. Loyola (1491–1556) believed that the re-enactment of scenes of mystical experiences, such as that of St. Teresa, would inspire devotion in all those who beheld the spectacle. The renewed significance of saints, martyrdoms and the mysteries of their faith became the papacy's most effective tool during the Catholic Counter-Reformation.

The Society of Jesus, known as Jesuits, was founded by Loyola in 1539. His own conversion experience inspired his book of *Spiritual Exercises*,

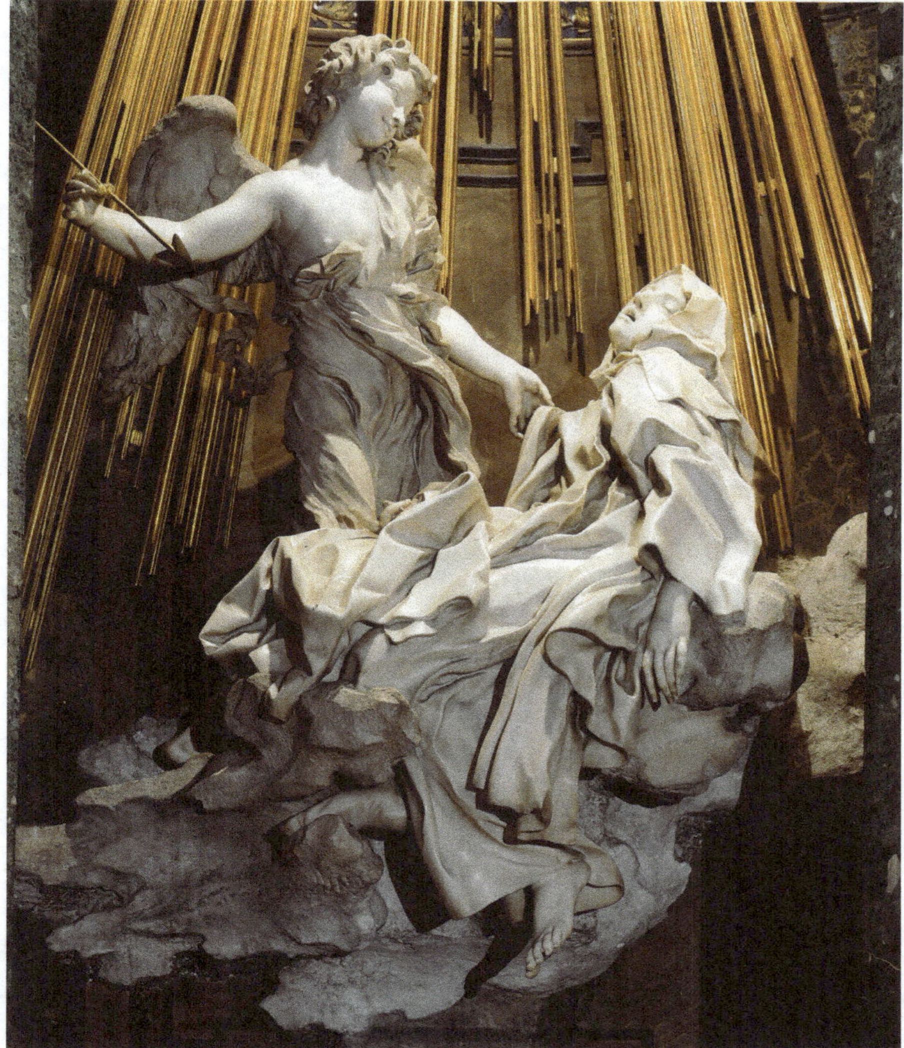

Figure 4.2 | Gian Lorenzo Bernini, *The Ecstasy of St. Teresa of Ávila*, 1645–1652, marble, height 350 cm, Rome, Church of Santa Maria della Vittoria. Source: akg-images / De Agostini Picture Library / G. Nimatallah.

1548. The society preached the upholding of the fundamental rules of the Catholic faith and aided the impetus of the Catholic Counter-Reformation. The *Spiritual Exercises* taught meditative prayer techniques and disseminated a strict obedience to the church. In the same way that a person's physical well-being is aided by walking or running, so their spiritual well-being was considered to be aided by spiritual exercises. For just as strolling, walking and running are exercises for the body, so 'spiritual exercises' were a way of preparing and disposing one's soul to rid oneself of all disordered attachments; once rid of them one might seek and find the divine will in regard to the disposition of one's life for the good of the soul (Loyola and Munitiz, *Saint Ignatius Loyola: Personal Writings*, p. 283).

As well as the broader social and historical contexts within which a work of art was produced, specific events in the life of an artist or **patron** may also have an influence on artistic output. For example, seventeenth-century artist Artemisia Gentileschi (1593–1656), whose Baroque style was examined in *Chapter 3*, may be re-examined here under the theme of social and historical contexts in two ways: firstly, as a visual manifestation of rhetorical art in a country fighting to preserve the Catholic faith; and, secondly, as a possible response to the artist's seduction and betrayal by a friend and fellow artist of her painter-father, Orazio Lomi Gentileschi. Gentileschi's treatment can be

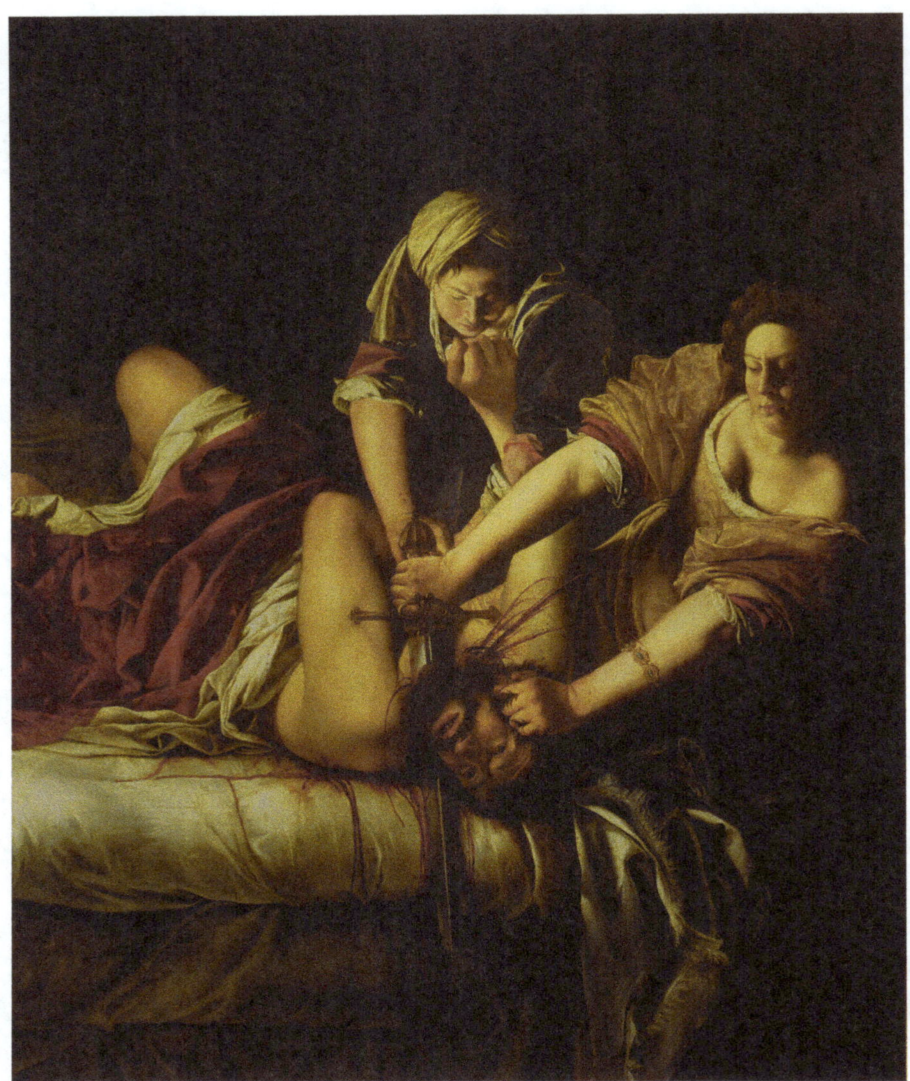

Figure 4.3 | Artemisia Gentileschi, *Judith Slaying Holofernes*, c.1620, oil on canvas, 199 x 162 cm, Florence, Galleria degli Uffizi. Source: © 2015. Photo Scala, Florence – courtesy of the Ministero Beni e Att. Culturali.

seen to reveal the relatively harsh attitudes towards sexual relations outside wedlock during this period, as well as the unequal treatment of women in a **patriarchal**, or male-dominated, society.

Gentileschi's *Judith Slaying Holofernes*, 1620, represents the biblical story of Judith, a Jewish widow, who, with her maid Abra, murdered the Assyrian general Holofernes. He had laid siege to the women's town Bethuliah, and this image depicts the two women killing the brute with his own sword. An incident in the artist's own life may account for the determination of the protagonists in this scene: the much older and more established painter, Agostino Tasso, seduced the young Artemisia in the guise of her teacher. A woman's virginity was a significant 'value' in **Renaissance** society, and Artemisia's father attempted to redeem her honour by accusing Tasso of rape. The trial, conducted during or just before this scene, subjected Gentileschi to humiliating physical examination and torture with thumbscrews.

Our knowledge of Gentileschi's endurance may lead us to a particular interpretation of the scene: as though about to butcher a side of meat, the female slayers push up their sleeves to conduct the task with an unhesitating zeal for its completion. The artist's literacy was both a Baroque trait and a characteristic response to the honest interpretation of the Scriptures in accordance with those rules laid down by the Council of Trent. Compare the following passage from the Book of Judith 13:4–9 with Gentileschi's visual interpretation of the act:

4 *So all went forth and none was left in the bedchamber, neither little nor great. Then Judith, standing by his bed, said in her heart, O Lord God of all power, look at this present upon the works of mine hands for the exaltation of Jerusalem.*
5 *For now is the time to help thine inheritance, and to execute thine enterprises to the destruction of the enemies which are risen against us.*
6 *Then she came to the pillar of the bed, which was at Holofernes' head, and took down his fauchion from thence,*
7 *And approached to his bed, and took hold of the hair of his head, and said, Strengthen me, O Lord God of Israel, this day.*
8 *And she smote twice upon his neck with all her might, and she took away his head from him.*
9 *And tumbled his body down from the bed, and pulled down the canopy from the pillars; and anon after she went forth, and gave Holofernes' head to her maid.*

The works of Caravaggio, Bernini and Gentileschi are bound by a similar commitment to vivid and intensely bodily interpretations of biblical stories, and their uses of dramatic and rhetorically persuasive artistic devices draw us deep into the Counter-Reformation propaganda of their particular historical period.

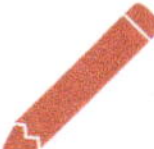

4.2 Explore this example
Research the context of Italian seventeenth-century Baroque architect Francesco Borromini's San Carlo alle Quattro Fontane, 1638–1646 (façade begun c.1665). In common with the paintings of Caravaggio and the sculptures of Bernini, previously examined, the church responded to its times, which was dominated by the philosophy of the Catholic Counter-Reformation. As a fitting example of the Baroque style in architecture, it may also be considered under the theme discussed in *Chapter 3*.

During these years, Catholicism in Europe regained its might by strategic means: it established the Council of Trent to support papal power and Catholic dogma; captured the hearts and minds of the laity with new religious orders; celebrated the lives of the saints and used art and architecture to make the Catholic faith and the mystical visions of Catholic saints accessible and inspirational to the masses. The propaganda machine was designed to transform as many people as possible: heretics, Protestants, wavering Catholics and agnostics.

Seventeenth-century Italian architecture was just as dynamic and theatrical as painting and sculpture. Richly ornamented and grandiose in scale, Baroque buildings spoke to the laity using the same energising language – a kind of counter-reformatory syntax – comprising bouncy-looking **volutes**, **raking cornices**, light and shade, convexity and concavity – all interplaying with characteristic theatricality. See *4.2 Explore this example*.

4.1 Checkpoint question
What kinds of formal devices did artists and architects employ to persuade viewers of the strength of the Catholic Church?

The art and architecture of mid-nineteenth-century France is just as richly infused with the social and historical circumstances of its time as was that of Italy in the seventeenth century. Paris, in particular, was undergoing tremendous social and technological changes.

Nineteenth-Century France: Transformation and Modernity

Emperor Napoleon III ruled France from 1852 to 1870, during which time he brought about an unprecedented renovation of Paris. The project was led by the Seine prefect Baron Georges-Eugène Haussmann, who conceived the wide boulevards, public parks and city facilities to create the Paris we know today. The period of upheaval caused by the modernisation and transformation of the city would become known as 'Haussmannisation'.

The housing Haussmann replaced had mostly been overcrowded and insanitary, carrying the constant threat of disease. Haussmann's grand improvement project was welcomed by some of the area's inhabitants, but the demolition of the old Paris also dismantled the social cohesion that had existed among its poverty-stricken inhabitants. Consequently, Haussmann has been remembered in the conflicting roles of both hero and destroyer. Works of art of the period provide evidence for both roles in equal measure.

How ugly Paris seems after a year's absence. How one chokes in these dark, narrow and dank corridors that we like to call the streets of Paris! One would think that one was in a subterranean city, that's how heavy is the atmosphere, how profound is the darkness!

(Vicomte de Launay quoted in Rice, *Parisian Views*, p. 9)

Reportedly, Haussmann had endured a sickly childhood, much of which was blamed upon the polluted Parisian air. Correlations have been drawn between his zeal to eliminate the old Paris and rebuild the new with his personal interest in clean air and water. Whatever the motivation, the new sewer system he initiated in the 1850s was clearly a positive contribution to the health and safety of its citizens.

The polarised experiences of Parisians during this period may be demonstrated if we juxtapose two contemporaneous nineteenth-century scenes: *Bal du Moulin de la Galette à Montmartre* by Pierre-Auguste Renoir (1841–1919) and *L'Absinthe* by Edgar Degas (1834–1917). Renoir's *Bal du Mou-*

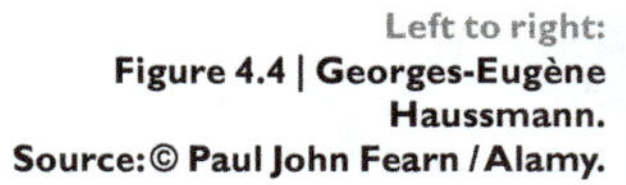

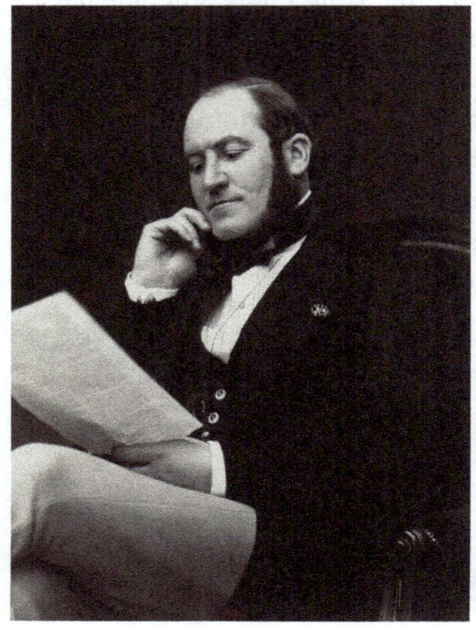

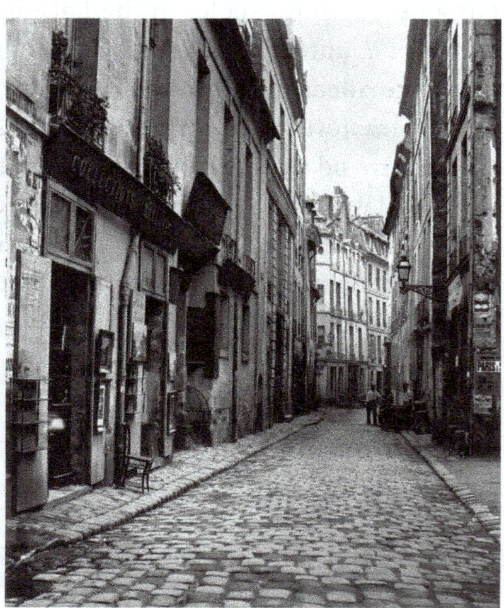

Left to right:
Figure 4.4 | Georges-Eugène Haussmann. Source: © Paul John Fearn / Alamy.

Figure 4.5 | Charles Marville, Rue du Jardinet, from passage Hautefeuille, Paris, 1858–1878, black and white photograph. Source: Musée de la Ville de Paris, Musée Carnavalet, Paris, France / Bridgeman Images. Haussmann destroyed dirty, narrow streets like these and replaced them with clean, bright, wide ones suitable for strolling along.

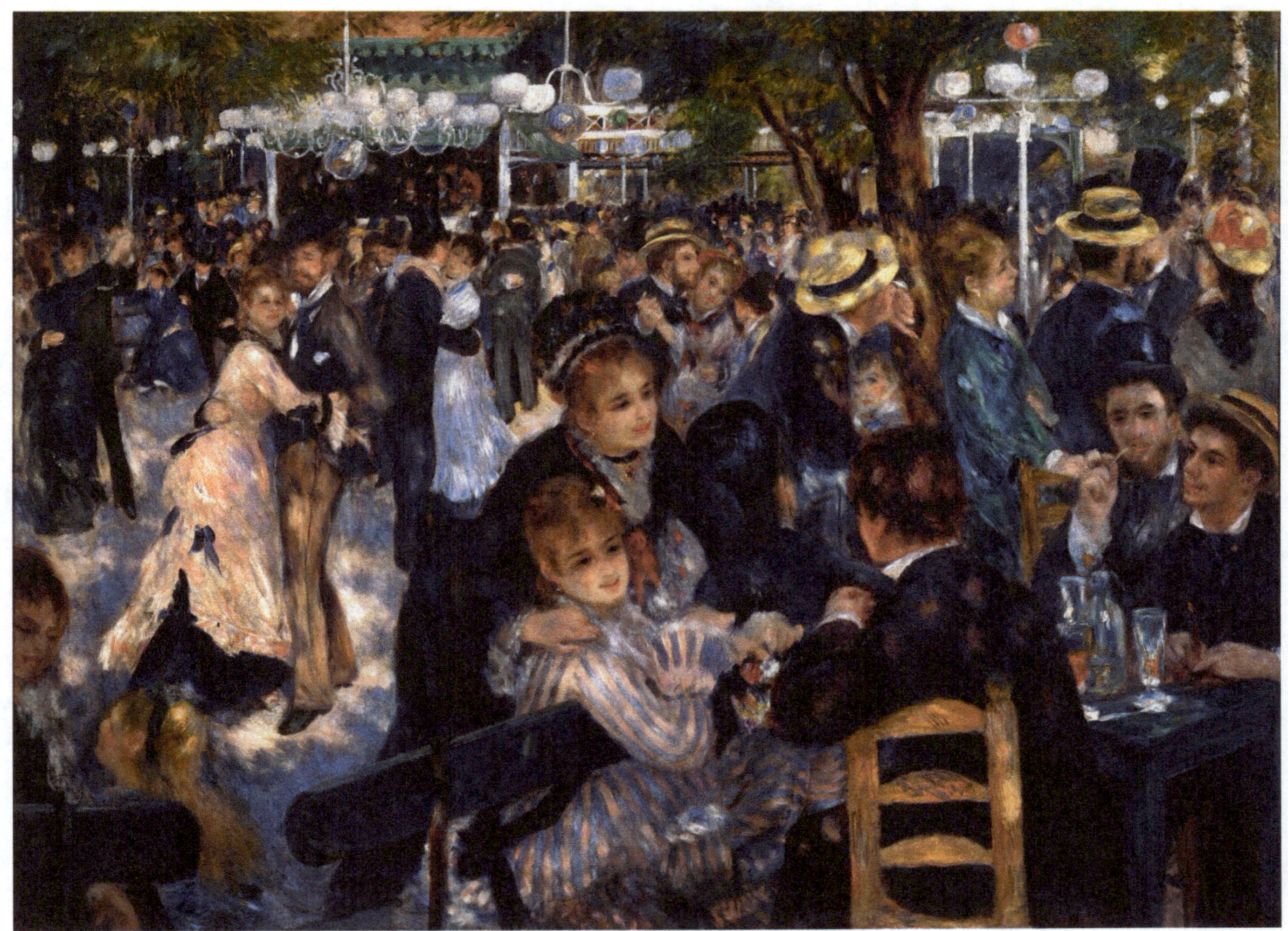

Figure 4.6 | Pierre-Auguste Renoir, *Bal du Moulin de la Galette à Montmartre*, 1876, oil on canvas, 131 × 175 cm, Paris, Musée d'Orsay. Source: © 2015. A. Dagli Orti / Scala, Florence.

lin de la Galette, 1876, shows a typically fun-filled late nineteenth-century scene in Montmartre. It captures the spirit of this highly sociable outdoor recreation space and well-known haunt of Parisian good-timers. However, beyond the brightly lit dabs of Renoir's brush there lurks evidence of a darker side to Parisian life: a crowd of excluded onlookers, emitting a sense of loneliness. Sexual favours and the drinking of absinthe (a very strong green alcohol) may be the sub-text in Renoir's painting, but the latter and all its societal ills are the explicit focus of Degas' baldly named *L'Absinthe*. According to a contemporary observer, H.P. Hugh, *The sickly odour of absinthe lies heavily in the air. The absinthe hour of the Boulevards begins vaguely at half-past five ... but the deadly opal drink lasts longer than anything else* (quoted in Adams, 'The Drink that Fuelled a Nation's Art').

The reaction to paintings such as Degas' was twofold: on the one hand, **avant-garde** artists, together with sympathetic critics such as the French poet Charles Baudelaire (1821–1867), felt invigorated by the new subject matter; but on the other hand, the more conservative artistic and critical establishment needed some time to catch up with the social change

We have sewn rags onto the purple robe of a queen; we have built within Paris two cities, quite different and quite hostile: the city of luxury, surrounded, besieged by the city of misery ... you have put temptation and covetousness side by side.

(Louis Lazare quoted in Clark, *The Painting of Modern Life: Paris in the Art of Manet and His Followers*, p. 29)

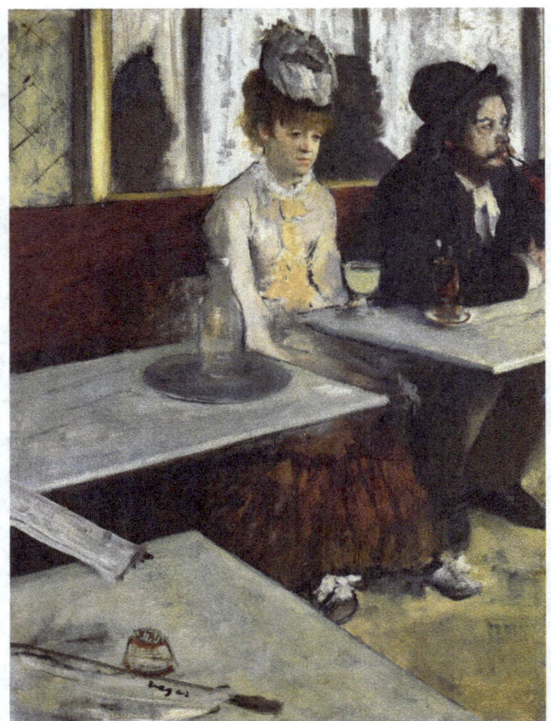

Figure 4.7 | Edgar Degas, *L'Absinthe*, 1873, oil on canvas, 92 × 68 cm, Paris, Musée d'Orsay. Source: Musée d'Orsay, Paris, France / Bridgeman Images.

to which it was increasingly bearing witness. Read the extract from *The Westminster Gazette*, 1893, for an insight into the painting's reception (see *4.1 Critical debates: one response to* L'Absinthe). Degas' absinthe drinkers may be seen as victims of the destruction of their homes and former neighbourhoods as Haussmann's workers built the new boulevards and apartments. Their looming sense of alienation is also to be found in works such as Manet's *Absinthe Drinker*, 1858–1859 and his *A Bar at the Folies Bergères*, 1882.

4.1 Critical debates: one response to *L'Absinthe*

Read the following response to *L'Absinthe* from Anon (J.S. Spender) in *The Westminster Gazette* on February 17, 1893:

The two works of Degas exhibited in this gallery bring so forcibly before us the artistic ideals of the 'new painters' that we really cannot forbear. One is called 'Absinthe'... A man and a woman, both of the most degraded type, are seated on a bench in a wine-shop, their backs reflected in a glass screen behind them ... the total effect ... is one which most of us will be anxious to banish from our minds as quickly as possible, and neither of them tells us anything about M. Degas' skill which we did not know about before. (Tate Gallery, 'Degas, Sickert and Toulouse-Lautrec')

What is it about Degas' subject and his Impressionist technique that so upset traditional/normative opinion at the time? What is your response to *L'Absinthe*?

Some writers have claimed that Napoleon III encouraged the building of long, wide and straight boulevards to deter insurgents from building barricades – indeed, even the installation of street lights might be seen as aiding the ruler's surveillance of his citizens. The streets of Paris had a history of revolution, which included the July Revolution (the so-called 'Three Glorious Days') of 1830, the June Rebellion of 1832 and the February Revolution of 1848. It may be that France's new ruler felt that this history of revolution had to be stopped in the streets.

The painting *Paris Street; Rainy Day*, painted in 1877 by Gustave Caillebotte (1848–1894), offers an almost photographic representation of Haussmann's newly built Paris. Various wide boulevards radiate from a central intersection, providing a panoramic view of new streets on an epic scale.

Perhaps Caillebotte's is a truthful description of the historical nature of the scene, or perhaps it celebrates the monumental achievements of Napoleon III and Baron Haussmann. The scene is populated by the **haute bourgeoisie**, and the approaching couple, far right, are certainly well-dressed members of its rank. Formally, it may depart from the Impressionist style but the painting certainly captures the transient feel of a modern, urban scene in a wealthy Parisian street. As the rain falls down, the main couple draw uncomfortably closer to us with each step.

Technological advances in photography (see *4.1 Let's connect the themes: materials and techniques – early photography*) had a significant impact on artists because the camera was able to quickly and accurately reproduce the natural world, placing greater pressure on artists to display creative ingenuity in order to match or surpass its achievements. Partly as a result of its invention, perhaps, the **Impressionists** of the latter half of the nineteenth century searched for new ways to capture their material world; a modern world characterised by the transient and the fleeting. An interest in the effects of light and a greater understanding of optics defined the **Zeitgeist**. Arguably, photography inspired the Impressionists both to aim to capture a moment in time and to 'crop' their compositions to create a 'slice-of-life' painting.

Figure 4.8 | Gustave Caillebotte, *Paris Street; Rainy Day*, 1877, oil on canvas, 212 × 276 cm, the Art Institute of Chicago. Source: © 2015. Photo Fine Art Images / Heritage Images / Scala, Florence.

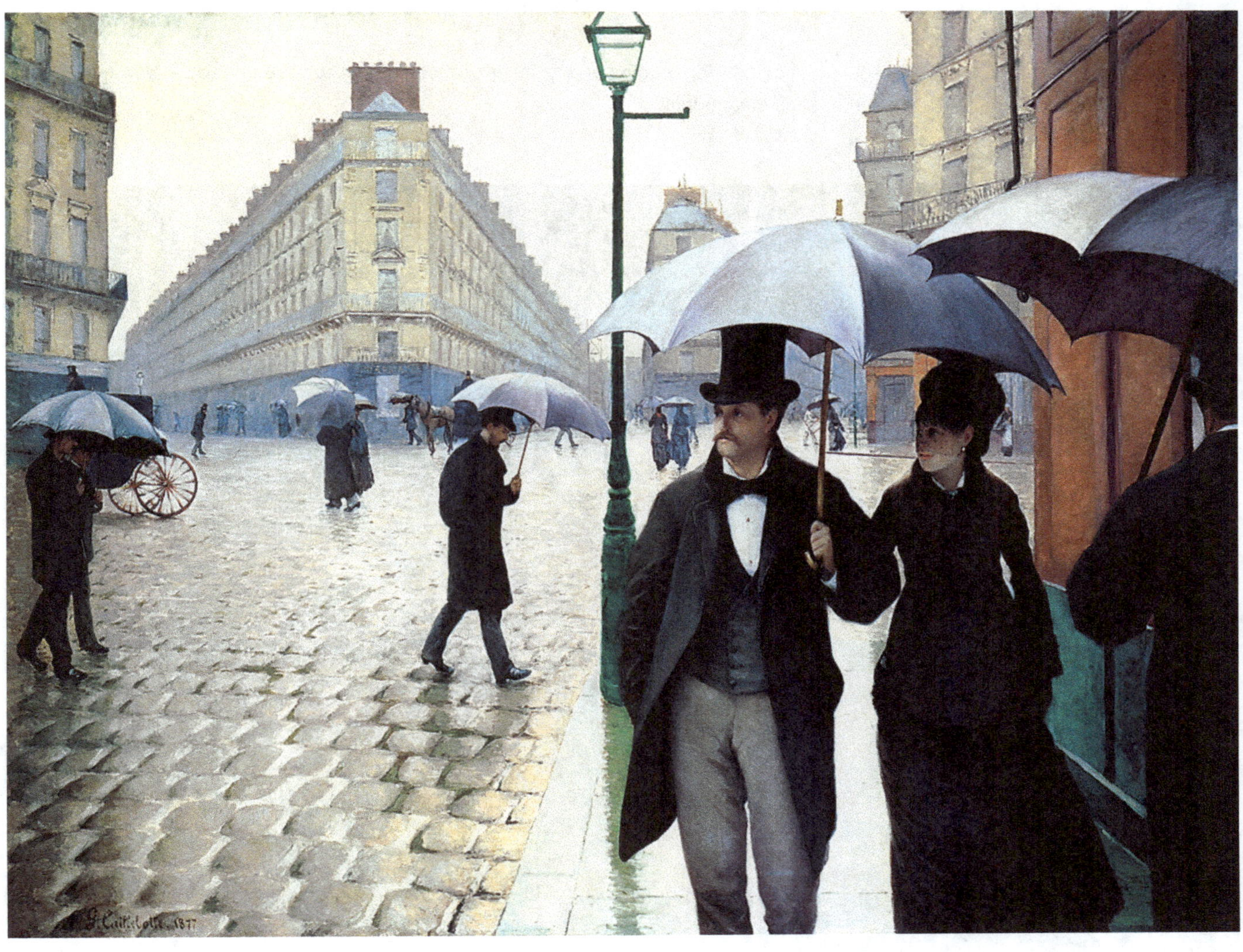

4.1 Let's connect the themes: materials and techniques – early photography

For centuries, artists had tried to recreate the world as precisely as their skill allowed; now the camera could capture that world, freeze-frame it and make copying an almost unskilled activity. The invention of the camera heralded new painting techniques – the rapid application of pigment would capture a new reality, a transient moment indicative of the modern times in which artists found themselves; blurred lines, soft-focus edges and cropped subjects were all a part of the painters' new toolbox. The invention of photography seems to have begun in France and England around the same time. Although Joseph Niépce had taken photographs in the mid-1820s, it was in 1839 when the Frenchman Louis-Jacques-Mandé Daguerre officially revealed his invention of the **daguerrotype** – a metal plate prepared with light-sensitive chemicals – that true photography was born. When placed in an unlit box with a small aperture, the plate records the scene outside the camera. Photographic technology was further advanced by the Englishman William Henry Fox Talbot, whose invention of a negative image allowed for multiple positive prints to be made.

For further reading on the invention of photography, see Frizot, *A New History of Photography.*

Figure 4.9 | Édouard Manet, *Olympia*, 1863, oil on canvas, 130.5 × 190 cm, Paris, Musée d'Orsay. Source: Musée d'Orsay, Paris, France / Bridgeman Images.

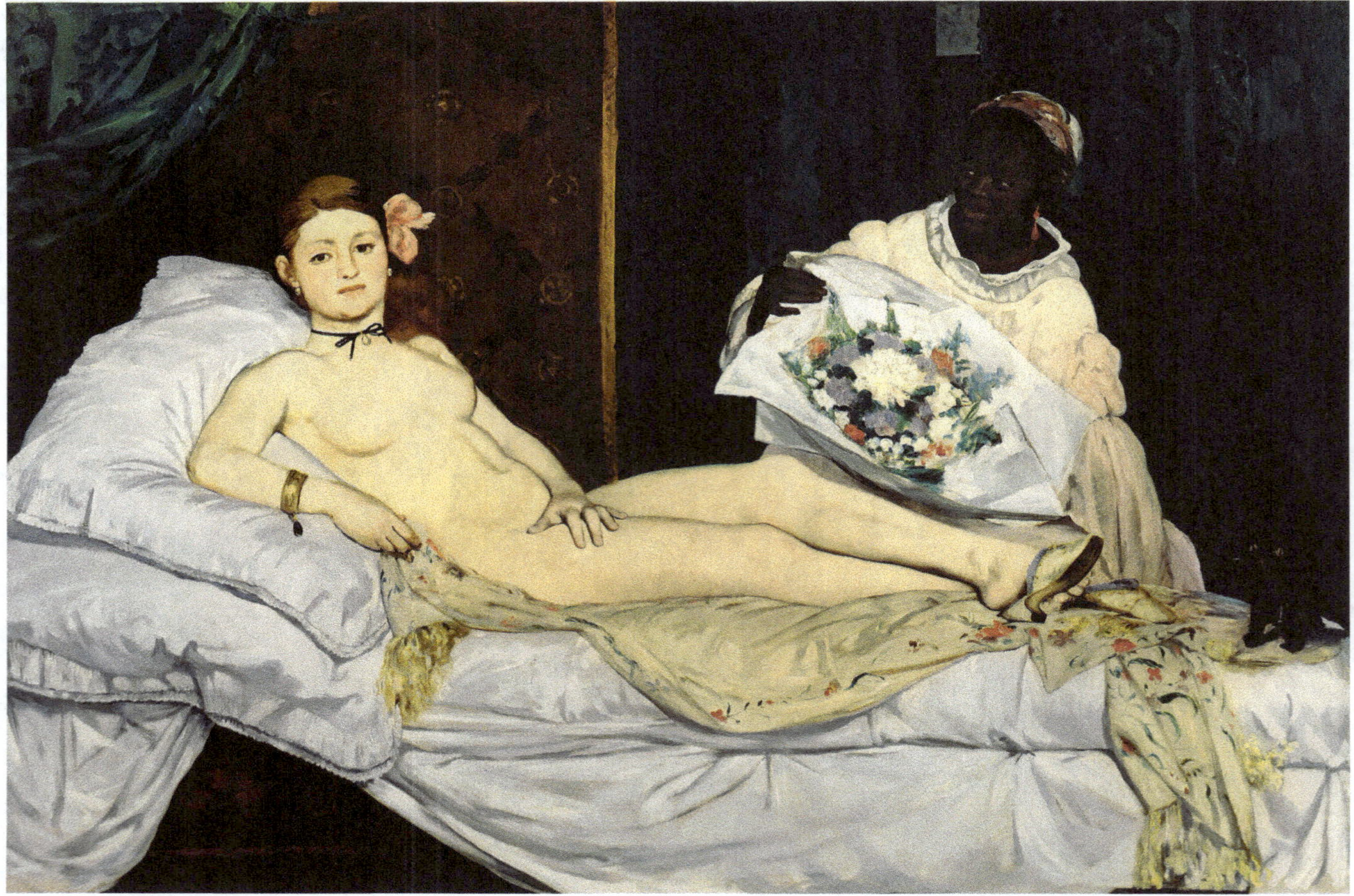

The train, the electric telegraph and photography were major inventions in the mid-nineteenth century and collectively they changed our perceptions of time itself. Photography managed to suspend a moment in time and the capture of the transitory moment became an important part of the Impressionists' new aesthetic. The Impressionists responded to a new and modern world – **modernity** – as did fellow French artist, and friend to the group, Édouard Manet. In fact, Manet was among the first to consciously respond to the change. The French poet Baudelaire (1821–1867) suggested that every period had its own form of beauty and that the mid-nineteenth century contained *an element of the eternal and an element of the transitory*. The modern hero, according to Baudelaire, had shed his antique cloak and donned the 'frock coat' instead; the top-hatted dandy, voyeur, or **flâneur**, was, for Baudelaire, the ultimate observer of modernity. According to French writer Antonin Proust, Manet was one such a character – the archetypal painter of modern life, and an artist who immortalised his times and their spirit. Proust wrote:

I have already said what a flâneur Manet was. We strolled together one day, along what was later to be the Boulevard Malesherbes, through the midst of the demolitions, intersected by gaping holes where the ground had already been levelled. The Monceau district had not yet been planned … Farther on, house-beaters stood out white against a wall less white, which was collapsing under their blows, covering them in a cloud of dust. For a long time Manet remained absorbed in admiration of this scene … A woman came out of a low tavern holding up her dress and clutching a guitar; Manet went straight up to her and asked her to pose for him. She began to laugh. (Quoted in Frascina et al., *Modernity and Modernism*, p. 95)

Olympia, 1863, by Édouard Manet (1832–1883) was so 'of the times' that, as we have seen in *Chapter 1*, the Salon couldn't cope with the furore she caused. Its initial reception devastated the artist – *The insults rain down on me like hail*, he complained to his supporter and friend, Baudelaire (Manet quoted in Krell, *Manet*, p. 67). Manet's modern nude was far too recognisable as a contemporary courtesan to sit comfortably with the prudish sensibilities of upper-middle-class Parisians. As Clark states:

The baron's demolitions had laid waste some famous streets of brothels near the Louvre and on the Ile de la Cité; the general rise in rents had obliged the owners of some brothels to move them out to the periphery, and many more to convert their establishments into hôtels garnis at the disposal of the individual streetwalker. The city had changed shape, and the usual places in which the prostitute sought her client – places where men danced, drank, took dinner, or were entertained – had multiplied and become more conspicuous. (Clark, *The Painting of Modern Life: Paris in the Art of Manet and His Followers*, p. 106)

For Manet, however, she was one of the outcast characters of Baudelaire's modernity. This reclining goddess was too 'modern' – she represented perhaps the first 'shock of the new'. The artists of the times couldn't wait to celebrate the new subjects of modernity, however: the prostitutes, the absinthe drinkers, the working women, the haute bourgeoisie, the dancers, the music halls, the cafés – all of these, the products of their social and historical contexts – were no longer hidden away but instead were paraded by these artists as symbols of modernity. In the words of Baudelaire, their first great literary ambassador: *The pageant of fashionable life and the thousands of floating existences – criminals and kept women – which drift about in the underworld of a great city; the Gazette des Tribuaux and the Moniteur all prove to us that we have only to open our eyes to recognise our heroism.* (Quoted in Edwards, *Art and Its Histories: A Reader,* pp. 195–196)

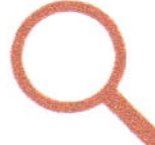

4.1 What can you see?

The Montmartre district assimilated some members of the underworld who were shunted out of the city centre as a result of 'Haussmannisation'. So did Haussmann unleash the 'underworld'? Or did he improve the life of the city's inhabitants? What do you think?

Look at Manet's equally famous work, *A Bar at the Folies Bergère*, 1882, and think about how the top-hatted dandy reflected in the right-hand side of the picture may relate to Baron Haussmann's newly created urban environment and artificially lit leisure spaces. The duality of Parisian society and its breathless transience is captured on film by director Baz Luhrmann in *Moulin Rouge*, 2001. The Moulin Rouge became a popular meeting place for Parisians to socialise and watch working girls in risqué performances. In the opening montage sequence of Luhrmann's film we are reminded of the Impressionist style of painting and the modernity it sought to capture, in all of its breathless transience. One of the film's central characters, the beautiful courtesan Satine, at one point says *We're creatures of the underworld – we can't afford to love*; a sentiment to be found also perhaps in the defiant eyes of Manet's *Olympia*.

Napoleon III's vision for the city's new structure included the erection of a number of leisure spaces, including a new opera house, designed by architect Charles Garnier (1825–1898). The Opéra Garnier was built between 1862 and 1875, and the uniformity and grandeur of its façade are particularly striking.[15] It is still one of the French capital's most admired buildings. Situated at the top of the Avenue de l'Opéra, it is a visual manifestation of the process of

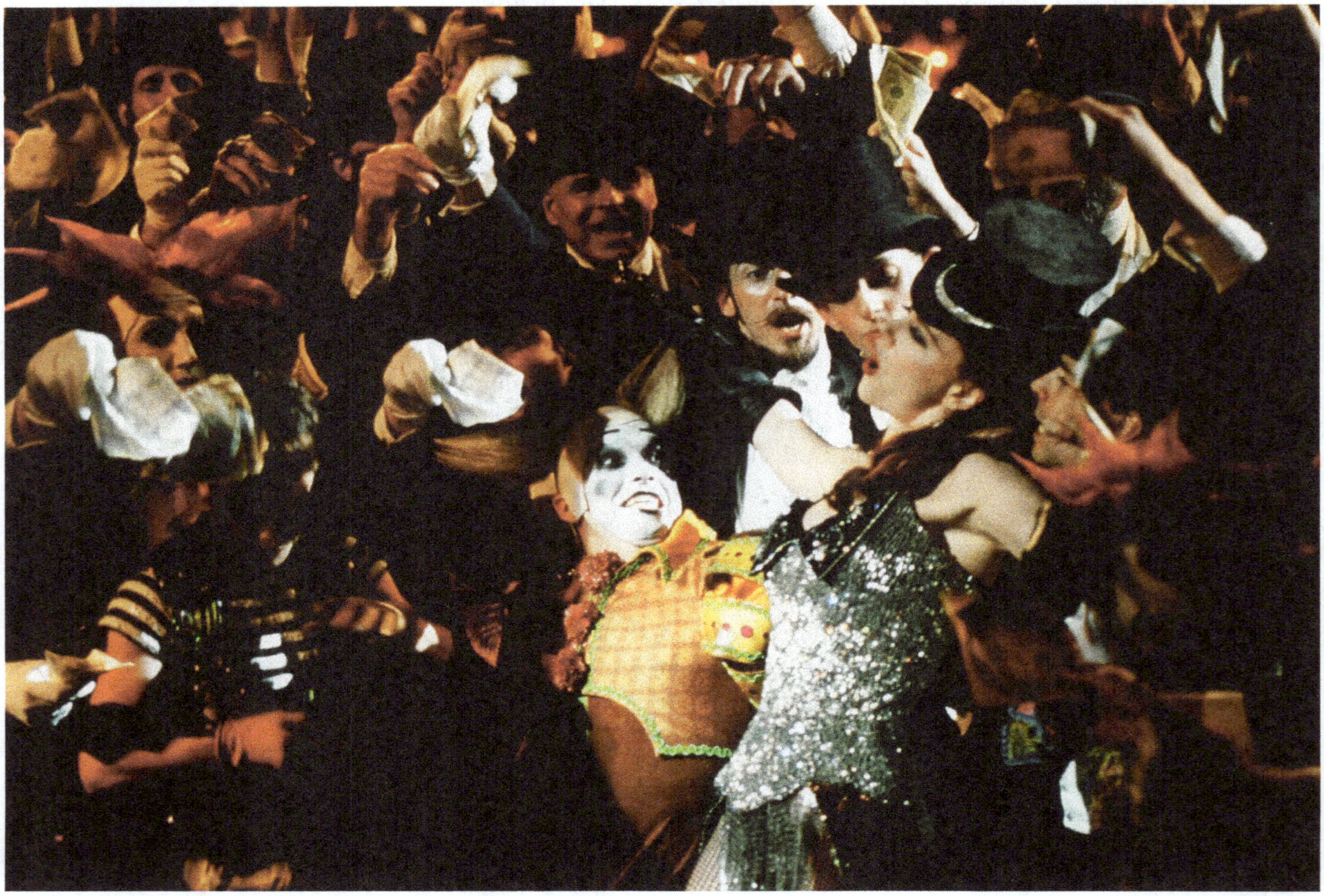

Figure 4.10 | *Moulin Rouge*, 2001, starring Nicole Kidman, directed by Baz Luhrmann. Dancing girls, courtesans, bright lights and dandies in frock coats capture a snapshot of Parisian modernity. Source: 20th Century Fox / The Kobal Collection / Ellen von Unwerth.

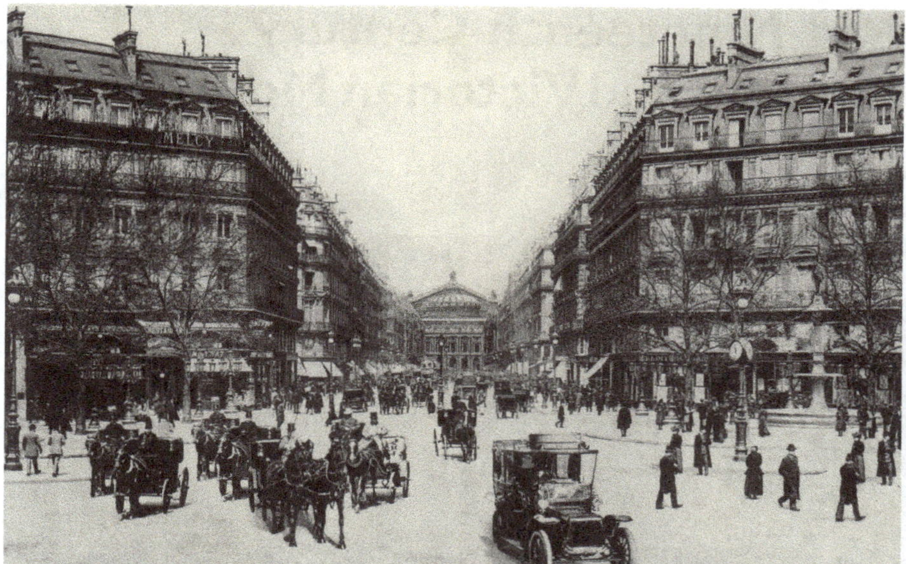

Figure 4.11 | Avenue de l'Opéra, Paris, 1904.
Source: © Mary Evans Picture Library / Alamy.

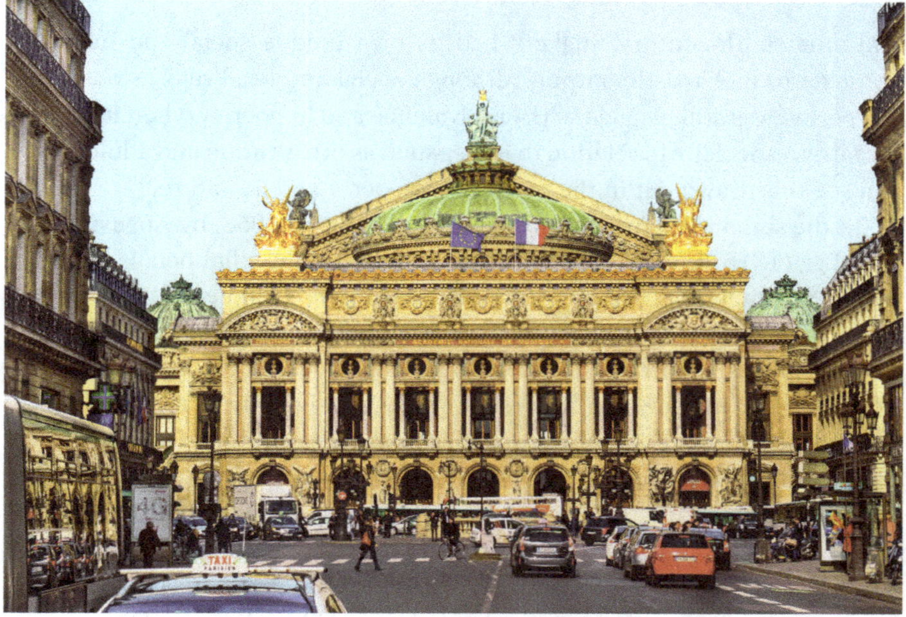

Figure 4.12 | Opéra Garnier (Paris Opera), Paris, 1862–1875.
Source: © Rainbow / iStockphoto.

'Haussmannisation' and a monument to Napoleon III's desire to place Paris on the world stage.

The Opéra Garnier, a theatre for the opera and the ballet, is a statement of Napoleon's power and authority. Its large-scale interior space, with impressive sweeping staircase, match its lavish façade, which is fairly eclectic, being heavily influenced by the Baroque style. Garlands, **bas-reliefs**, **gargoyle** masks and gilded sculptures symbolically reinforce the political rhetoric of the Second Empire.

Paris was not the only important European city of the nineteenth century. London, too, had a claim to historical importance at this time, and its own distinctive art soon arose to match this context.

4.2 Checkpoint question
How did artists of the nineteenth century convey a sense of modernity in France?

15 In 1989, when a new opera house was built in Paris at Bastille (Opéra Bastille), the former Paris Opera (which had also been known as the Palais Garnier) was renamed Opéra Garnier, in honour of its architect, to distinguish it from the newer opera house.

Mid-Nineteenth-Century England and Victorian Morality

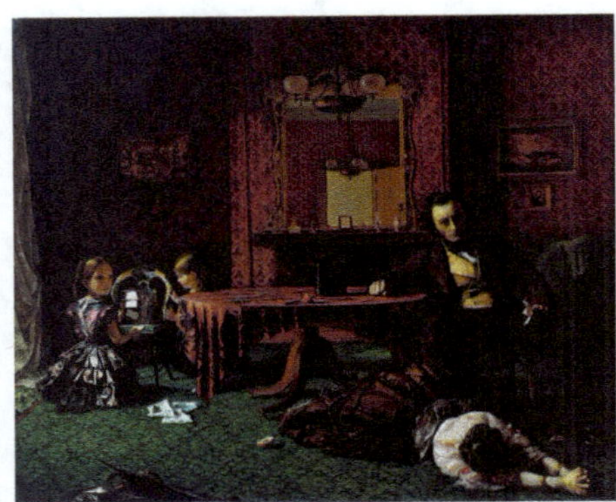

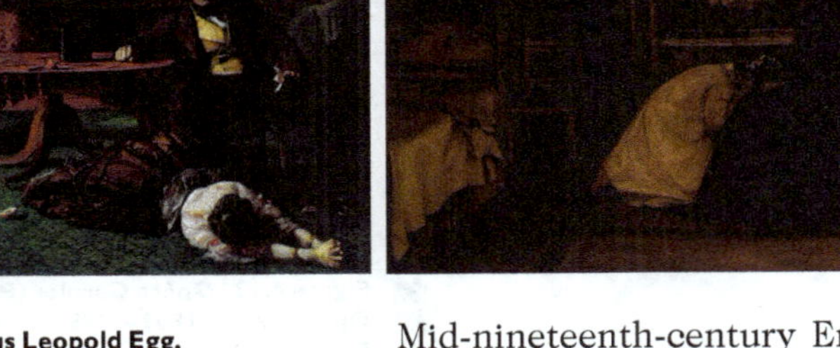

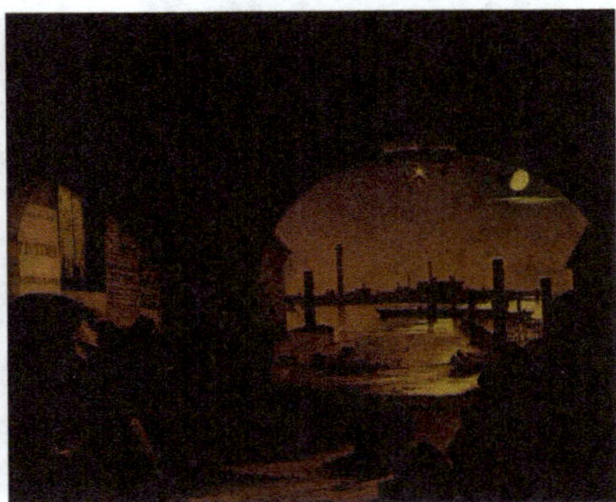

Left to right:

Figure 4.13 | Augustus Leopold Egg, *Past and Present 1*, 1858, oil paint on canvas, 63 × 76 cm, London, Tate Britain. Source: © Tate, London 2015.

Figure 4.14 | Augustus Leopold Egg, *Past and Present 2*, 1858, oil paint on canvas, 63 × 76 cm, London, Tate Britain. Source: © Tate, London 2015.

Figure 4.15 | Augustus Leopold Egg, *Past and Present 3*, 1858, oil paint on canvas, 63 × 76 cm, London, Tate Britain. Source: © Tate, London 2015.

See the companion website for links to the Married Woman's Property Act and suggested reading in relation to the Women's Rights Movement in Britain.

Mid-nineteenth-century England had its own unique social and historical contexts to fuel artistic output. Although social and legal reform was afoot, the period was still plagued with ambivalence and hypocrisy when it came to morality, especially in relation to issues such as prostitution and adultery. We can see this drawn out in the period's art, poetry and literature.

In the serial narrative painting *Past and Present*, 1858, by Augustus Leopold Egg (1816–1863), we learn about the terrible fate that befalls a woman who is an adulteress. We are reminded that we have choices in life, but are warned about making the wrong one. The first image in the series shows a woman collapsed, like her children's collapsing house of cards, shown in Figure 4.13. Her husband holds a letter which presumably presents evidence of her adulterous affair. The second and third images provide us with two simultaneous frames: the second image in Figure 4.14 shows the woman's children from her legitimate marriage praying for their mother's return, while the third (Figure 4.15), under the same moon, shows the mother alone near the banks of the Thames; she is utterly destitute with only her illegitimate child for company. This work was intended to be read like a book and its message mirrored the prevailing attitudes of the era.

Victorian legislation demonstrated institutionalised inequality between men and women, and the following two parliamentary acts may be read in conjunction with our interpretation of both the **Pre-Raphaelite** painter William Holman Hunt's *The Awakening Conscience* and Egg's *Past and Present*. The Matrimonial Causes Act (1857) reinforced gender inequality. Under this Act adultery was not sufficient grounds for a woman to divorce her husband, but it was for a man to divorce his wife. The Married Women's Property Act (1882) allowed a married woman to retain ownership of her own property. Before this Act, even property gifted to her by a parent would have become the property of her husband.

Victorian feminists, such as Barbara Leigh Smith, foremost founder of the Women's Rights Movement, challenged the Victorian idea of women's inherent weakness and subsequent domination. So too, perhaps, did Pre-Raphaelite painter William Holman Hunt (1827–1910) in his famous work *The Awakening Conscience,* 1853.

Hunt breaks with convention when he depicts both the perpetrator/seducer and the victim/seduced in his painting. We are given insight into the process of this woman's 'fall' from grace and respectability and, in so doing, Hunt challenges the idea that we are all responsible for our choices and moral improvement. In comparison with the paintings of his contemporary Augustus Egg, which charts the dire consequences of a woman's adultery, Hunt gives us a sense of the social injustice prevalent in Victorian England. Each work may therefore be read as alternative responses to 'the great social evil' – women's sexual immorality – which seemed to threaten the period's cherished morality. While we are led to believe that Egg's subject must inevitably die for her 'deviance', Hunt's subject is allowed to bathe for a moment in the light of her possible redemption, and we feel genuinely uplifted by the prospect.

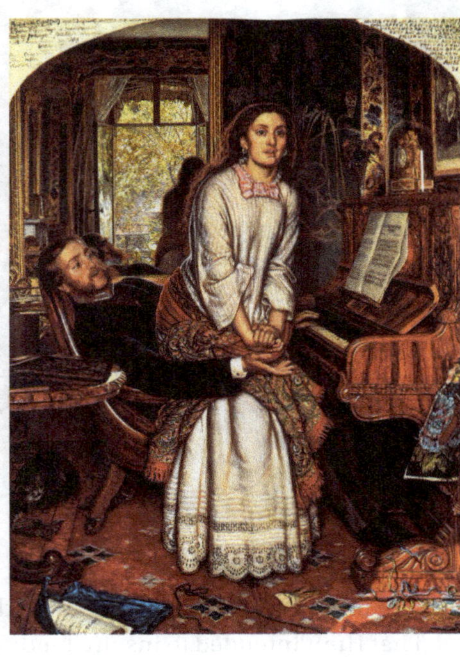

Figure 4.16 | William Holman Hunt, *The Awakening Conscience*, 1853, oil on canvas, 74.9 × 55.8 cm, London, Tate Gallery. Source: © 2015. DeAgostini Picture Library / Scala, Florence.

Being a kept woman could save a working-class girl from the stresses of the factory, but only for as long as she was still wanted. The seducer has already cast off one glove without a care, and we might read this as an indication of the woman's inevitable fate. The seducer's right hand extends to catch her hands – which are clasped together in a moment of untutored prayer – and the obvious lack of a ring on her finger reminds us that he's not offering his mistress betrothal – ever. Rising from her keeper's lap, she sees the light, towards which she seems to move as if in a spiritual trance, approaching ever nearer to the open window, a metaphor for her potential freedom and salvation. Indeed, the outdoors is every bit as significant as Hunt's meticulously painted interior: he's reflected it in the mirror on the back wall. However, we also see a cat toy with its prey, bottom left, an allusion to the way in which men might toy with their mistresses, in this context. Will the bird get away? Will she? Hunt makes us long for her escape.

There is some evidence that the times were beginning to change for the better in terms of social attitudes towards women. The towering figure of Victorian criticism John Ruskin wrote in a letter to *The Times* in 1854 about Hunt's *The Awakening Conscience*: *There will not be found one powerful as this to meet full in the front the moral evil of the age in which it is painted; to waken into mercy the cruel thoughtlessness of youth, and subdue the severities of judgement into the sanctity of compassion* (quoted in Golby, *Culture and Society in Britain 1850–1900*, p. 104).

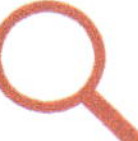

4.2 What can you see?

Hunt's startling colour palette and the hard-edged realism of his pictorial style draws us into the painting and causes us to examine every object in this cluttered room. Are the surfaces of things especially important? Is Hunt's lucid rendering of the piano's veneer somehow analogous to the materialism and superficial respectability of the times? Do these surfaces remind us of the material luxury afforded to the mistress of a wealthy man?

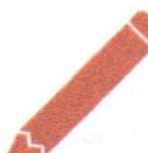

4.3 Explore this example

The idea of a woman trapped socially and politically is a recurrent theme in the Victorian era. You might like to compare Hunt's representation of moral failing to Oscar Wilde's poem *The Harlot's House*, c. 1883, which describes prostitution disparagingly. Similarly, Thomas Hardy's novel *Tess of the d'Urbervilles*, 1888–1889, tells how Tess' illegitimate child is baptised 'Sorrow' before he dies, as though his death is a redeeming sacrifice for *her* sin. This is despite the fact that the baby was born as a result of her being raped.

Left to right:
Figure 4.17 | William Holman Hunt, *The Light of the World*, 1853, Oxford, Keble College. Source: akg-images.

Figure 4.18 | William Holman Hunt, *The Awakening Conscience*, 1853, oil on canvas, 74.9 × 55.8 cm, London, Tate Gallery. Source: © 2015. DeAgostini Picture Library / Scala, Florence.

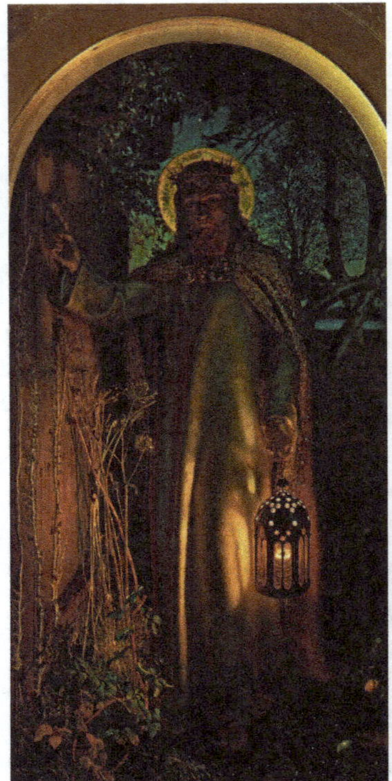

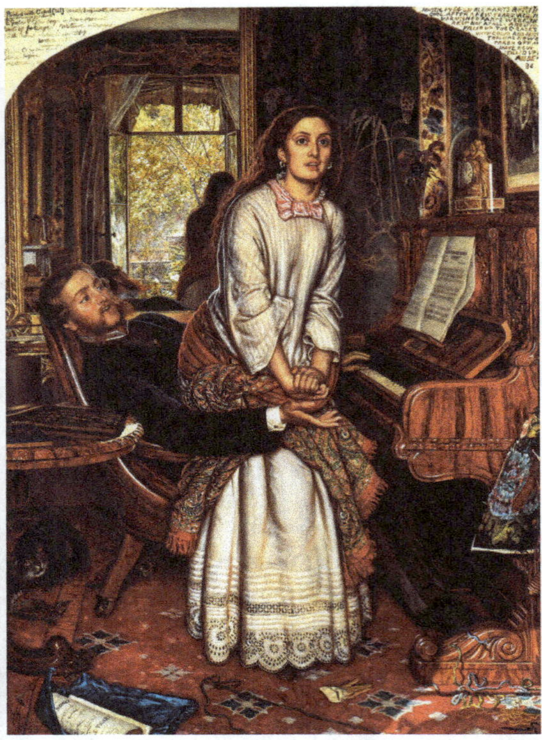

Ruskin urges the reader not to judge this 'poor' young woman too hastily, despite her kept status characterising the 'moral evil' of the age.

That Hunt intended to inspire kindness and forgiveness towards those less fortunate is further supported by another of Hunt's paintings, *The Light of the World*, 1853. Viewing these paintings together, we are reassured that our protagonist has heard Christ's knock on the door and that in *The Awakening Conscience* we are shown the moment she finds her path to salvation.

The idea that society should accept a certain moral responsibility towards the underprivileged, the downtrodden and the destitute is one which grows slowly in strength and commitment during this period, although arguably Hunt's painting retains a notion of *individual* conscience as the most important agent of change. The strictly hierarchical class system prevalent during the Victorian era was another form of social entrapment. The fate of the working-class prostitute was usually a sad one, but that of the middle-class adulteress was also likely to be bad; society at the time simply could not find any justification for it. See *4.4 Explore this example* for a contemporary focus on an altogether different kind of moral evil.

The tragic plight of those less fortunate seems to be a timeless occurrence. In the following century, the United States suffered a crisis that would have a lasting effect, not just on its lower classes, but on the majority of its citizens.

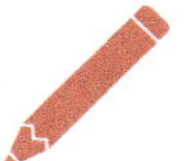

4.4 Explore this example
Joseph Mallord William (J.M.W.) Turner's *The Slave Ship* (also known as *Slavers Throwing Overboard the Dead and Dying – Typhoon Coming On*), 1840, reveals in its delicate riot of swirling colour the inhumane practice of the eighteenth-century slave traders, who threw the dead or dying overboard mid-Atlantic to claim the 'lost cargo' on their insurance. Research will reveal possible sources of Turner's inspiration. Turner's *The Slave Ship* was exhibited at the Royal Academy shortly before the first World Anti-Slavery Convention met in London. Do you think the painting had any impact on subsequent British laws to supress slavery?

Mid-Twentieth-Century United States and the Depression Era

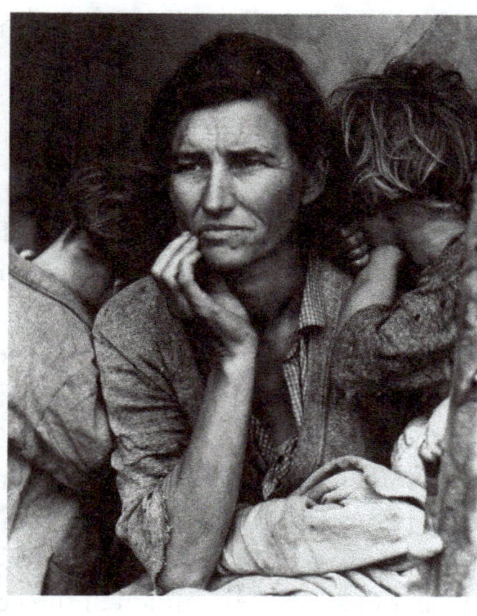

Figure 4.19 | Dorothea Lange, *Migrant Mother*, 1935, Nipomo Valley, 28.2 × 21.6 cm. Source: Library of Congress.

The Great Depression of the 1930s was a defining period in the history of the United States, as it was in many countries whose economy and financial system were dependent on that of the United States. During the 1920s the United States had appeared to be booming, with factories turning out consumer products and share prices rising. But all that changed in 1929. Quite why it did so is a matter of debate among economists, but it seems that an over-supply of goods led to falling prices, people lost confidence in the financial system and the stock market tumbled, finally crashing on 29 October 1929. Mass panic ensued as people rushed to withdraw their savings from the banks. Some banks collapsed, leaving many major investors and ordinary people bankrupt. People who had thought their savings were secure were left with no money and no job, and many became reliant on soup kitchens and handouts. Similar hardship was felt across the Western world, but artists in the United States in particular produced some of the most iconic images of these economically difficult times.

Photographer Dorothea Lange (1895–1965) was commissioned by the US Government's Farm Security Administration to record the devastation being wreaked on the agricultural economy of the country's Mid-West. But her photographs turned out to be something more than simply 'records'; she captured the pain and despair of the farm labourers in photographs that have strong aesthetic qualities. The weight of the world is clear upon a woman's face in *Migrant Mother*, one of Lange's many images of migrant labourers in California. This iconic image was published in a San Francisco newspaper and brought the plight of the rural community into the consciousness of every American. It even led to practical help from the government, who were alerted to the plight of the migrant workers in the camp Lange had photographed and sent food aid.

The stock market crash of 1929 was felt particularly badly in the Mid-West, where falling prices for agricultural products were compounded by the impact of over-farming and the use of grazing fields for crops, which left the soil infertile. This was exacerbated by drought, and the ensuing dust storms led to the term 'Dust Bowl' being used. Whole families left their farms and took to the roads in search of work, experiencing intense suffering due to the lack of food and clean water along the way.

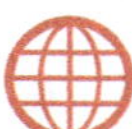

See the companion website for suggested reading on novelist John Steinbeck's novels and documentaries as well as films which relate to the Depression era in America.

Lange's photographic portrayal of the human condition embodies a depression that resonates in the **oeuvre** of the artist Edward Hopper (1882–

1967). Hopper provides us with a sense of the impact of the Depression on city dwellers. With images rendered every bit as still as the photographer's, Hopper conveys a sense of people's self-reliance amid a hopelessness with a pigment-loaded brush.

Hopper's *Nighthawks*, 1942, which was discussed as a 'genre' painting in *Chapter 1*, is also a powerful illustration of the social and historical contexts from which it grew – life in the United States during the Depression. The usual frivolity associated with a leisure space is absent, and the dark palette is perhaps a metaphor for the hopelessness of America's unemployed. Light is possibly the most significant formal device in Hopper's oeuvre, and in *Nighthawks* light structures the composition and creates mood. We get the impression that the light from this all-American diner shines alone in an otherwise vacant street and does little to illuminate its characters. In common with the 1940s **film noir** that influenced Hopper's visual style, the scene is arranged like a set; the **mise-en-scène** provides the signifiers: the only sense of movement is the presumably recent departure of the customer who left the unaccompanied tumbler on the bar. Their departure provides a sense of relief that somebody has shifted in this space, but it also allows us to scrutinise the couple on the other side of the counter: both are deeply reflective. Perhaps the dolled-up woman in the red dress is checking the bill, or perhaps we are in danger of reading too much of the economic context into the painting. What do you think would happen in this scene if this frozen image came to life?

The context of *Nighthawks* is one in which the government and the banks were perceived to have failed their citizens, and Hopper's paintings seem to be implicitly loaded with the heroism of individual self-reliance in such harsh times. In the same way that Manet and Degas observed and commented on the social upheavals of their time, Hopper observes the scene with the detached gaze of a modern flâneur. He uses windows in his scenes to offer the viewer access to the human condition – a technique probably borrowed from cinematography. We are drawn closer and closer to the scene, but always kept at a distance, behind the viewing pane.

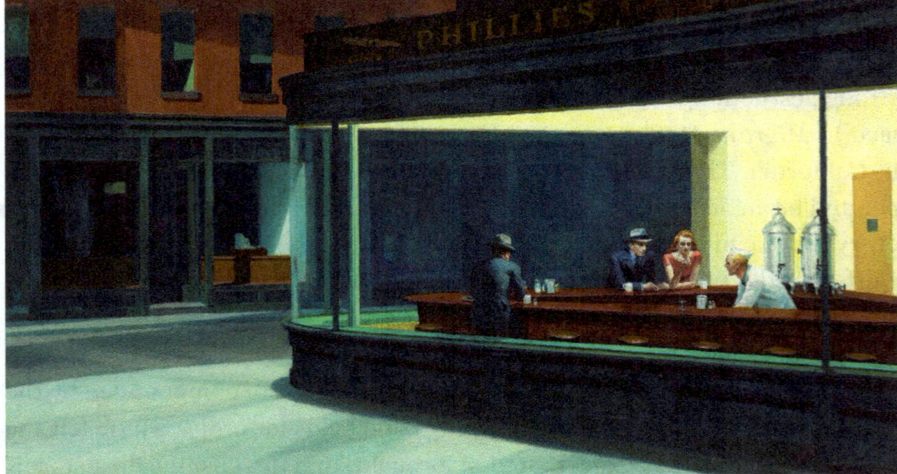

Figure 4.20 | Edward Hopper, *Nighthawks*, 1942, oil on canvas, 84.1 × 152.4 cm, Friends of American Art Collection, 1942.51, the Art Institute of Chicago. Source: Photography ©The Art Institute of Chicago.

Twentieth-Century United States: The Boom Years

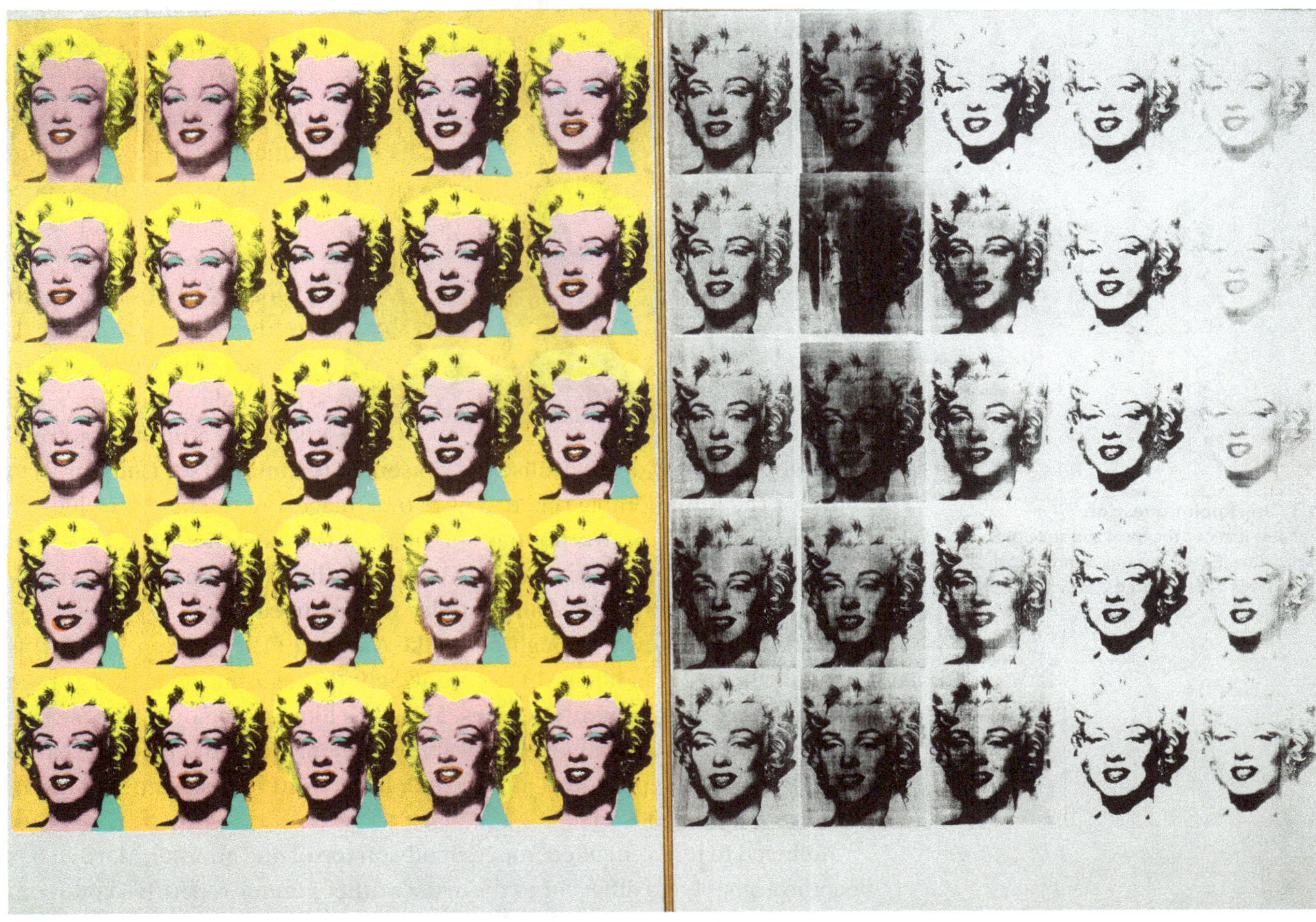

Figure | 4.21 Andy Warhol, *Marilyn Diptych*, 1962, acrylic paint on canvas, each panel 2054 × 1448 × 20 mm, 1962, London, Tate. Source: ©Tate, London 2015 / © 2015 The Andy Warhol Foundation for the Visual Arts, Inc. / Artists Rights Society (ARS), New York and DACS, London.

What is the effect of the technique of repetition on our interpretation of Warhol's Marilyn Diptych?

The entry of the United States into the Second World War in 1941 brought the Great Depression to an end. During the immediate post-war period, the country experienced an economic boom, most clearly evident in domestic **consumerism**. By the time of John F. Kennedy's presidency (1961–1963), the work of some American artists reflected this and the term **Pop Art** was used to describe it.

There is some debate about whether Pop Art images were a celebration of American life, a neutral commentary upon its consumerism or a satirical criticism of the **commodification** of everything. Most Pop Art is not explicitly critical of American society, but its representations of banal subjects have led to it being viewed as critiquing the culture that produced it. When Pop artists such as Andy Warhol and Roy Lichtenstein borrowed motifs from advertising, comics and magazine images – dispassionate, popular culture mediums – they exaggerated consumer identity and heightened our awareness of its superficiality.

Commercially trained Pop artist Andy Warhol (1928–1987) subverted elitism in the art world with the language of mass culture and, according to

Figure 4.22 | Marilyn Monroe, publicity photo for film *Niagara*, 1953. Source: 20th Century Fox / Photofest.

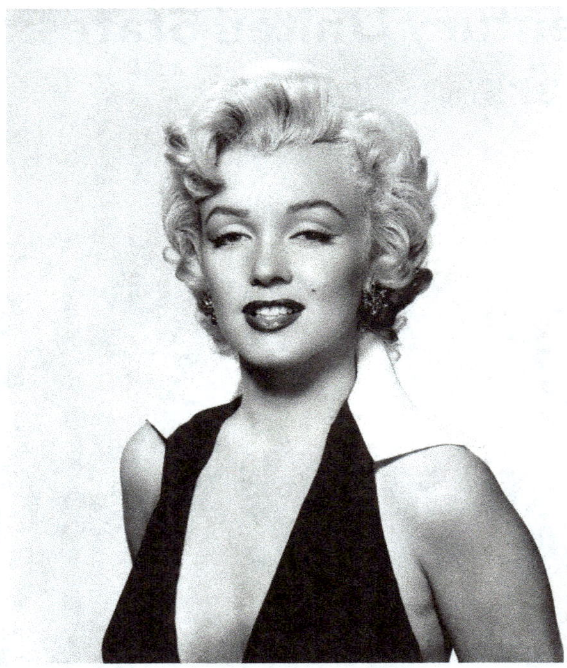

the German cultural historian Andreas Huyssen, conflated the 'great divide' between high art and mass culture (Huyssen, *Introduction: After the Great Divide, Modernism, Mass Culture, Postmodernism*, pp. vii–x). Warhol was also acutely aware of the significance of celebrity and the idea of tragedy as spectacle in modern times.

In *Marilyn Diptych*, 1962, Warhol's 50 similar (although not identical) images of movie icon Marilyn Monroe, produced shortly after the actress' tragic and untimely death, utilise the silkscreen technique (see *Chapter 2*) to allow for the innumerable repetitions of one image and the mass production of an iconic celebrity. Warhol has summed up the existence of Norma Jean Baker (Marilyn Monroe's real name) in the mask-like face of her pseudonym – her consumer identity, and all that she was reduced to.

4.3 Checkpoint question
What is it about the form and style of Pop Art that reflected the social and historical conditions of the United States in the 1960s?

Marilyn was known through films like *Niagara* (1953), from which this particular image was taken, but more widely through images of her screen persona reproduced countless times. Marilyn's likeness is not Warhol's creation, but one schematically recognisable as belonging to the media because it's appropriated, reproduced and re-sold. If *we* want her, *we* can buy her in the form of cheap posters.

Reduced to units, stacked impersonally on top of one another, Marilyn has become arguably no different to the artist's other famous repetitive commodities: soup cans and Coca-Cola bottles. Warhol fostered a mechanical style well suited to the **mechanisation** of American society and perhaps symptomatic of the repetitive labour processes of **Fordism**. This commodity philosophy seemed to be embodied in the impersonal touches of Warhol's assistants, who worked in the studio that he rather aptly named The Factory. It was at The Factory where Warhol developed his **screen printing** technique and met with his celebrity friends, such as Lou Reed, Bob Dylan and Mick Jagger. Warhol's Pop Art, with its unsigned, assembly-style 'signs' of the era, was certainly of the times – and those times were marked by consumerism, commodification and celebrity.

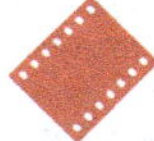

The film *Factory Girl* (2006) provides an interesting insight into life at Warhol's Factory.

In the 1960s Warhol was good at finding images that fed society's consumer fascination with the 'human interest' story, but a more recent sculpture by contemporary American artist Jeff Koons (born 1955), *Michael Jackson and Bubbles*, reminds us that our fascination with celebrity and tragedy persists.

This sculpture almost doesn't need an identifying inscription, since Michael Jackson, the celebrity singing icon, is recognised the world over as a pop music legend. In 1988, when Koons produced this work, the singer was still enjoying universal success; however, since his unexpected death, he has

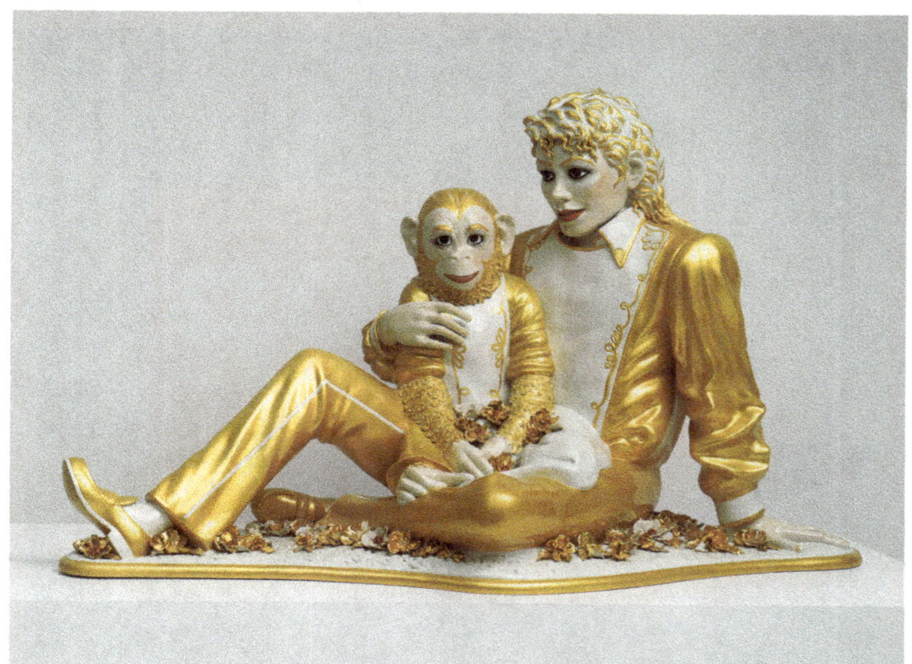

Figure 4.23 | Jeff Koons, *Michael Jackson and Bubbles*, 1988, porcelain, 106.7 × 179.1 × 82.6 cm, San Francisco Museum of Modern Art. Source: © Jeff Koons.

become a tragic figure in a way that makes him comparable perhaps with Marilyn Monroe. Jackson and Bubbles, the performing duo, may be anatomically correct but they also seem excessively fake and doll-like. Their matching gold outfits, oversized black pupils and lips, painted in the same shade of red, render them stylised and cheaply 'touristy'.

The medium of porcelain is delicate and fragile, which may be interpreted as alluding to the fragile and temporary adulation enjoyed by celebrities like Michael Jackson. This richly embellished duo appears to have their venerated status mocked by the artist. Jackson envelops his surrogate baby in a way we might think we recognise from Renaissance paintings of the Madonna and Child (and indeed, the chimpanzee, with its fixed and knowing stare, seems to know more than his keeper, just as the Christ Child seems to have an adult presentiment of his fate). This can hardly be described as a portrait of Michael Jackson: it's a portrayal of his marketable and consumer-loved persona – celebrity as the ultimate commodity. Unsettling in its superficiality, it may be read as a scathing attack on consumerism.

Jeff Koons is a mega-artist, rivalled only by Damien Hirst in commercial success and fame. He is also underrated as a fantastic chronicler of the modern world.

(Jones, 'Jeff Koons: Not Just the King of Kitsch')

Fittingly, Jeff Koons was a commodities broker before he became an artist. Moreover, he did not craft this sculpture himself but rather had it made for him by professional craftsmen, something which makes his referencing of the mass-produced object of popular culture all the more ironic. Such mass-produced objects are the epitome of **kitsch**, which the American art critic Clement Greenberg (associated with **Modernism**)[16] identified as cheaply entertaining and therefore threatening to the arts.[17] In referencing this kitsch, Koons is arguably drawing our attention to the superficiality and banality of American culture.

Cultural identity in terms of consumption occupied a range of artists in the latter half of the twentieth century. *I Shop Therefore I Am*, 1987, by

16 See the extensive definition of modern, modernist and Modernism (with a capital M) in Pooke and Whitham, *Understand Art History*, pp. 37–44, 200.

17 See Greenberg, 'Avant-Garde and Kitsch'.

Figure 4.24 | Barbara Kruger, *Untitled (I Shop Therefore I Am)*, 1987, photographic silkscreen/vinyl, 282 × 287 cm, New York, Mary Boone Gallery, MBG#4057. Source: Copyright: Barbara Kruger. Courtesy: Mary Boone Gallery, New York.

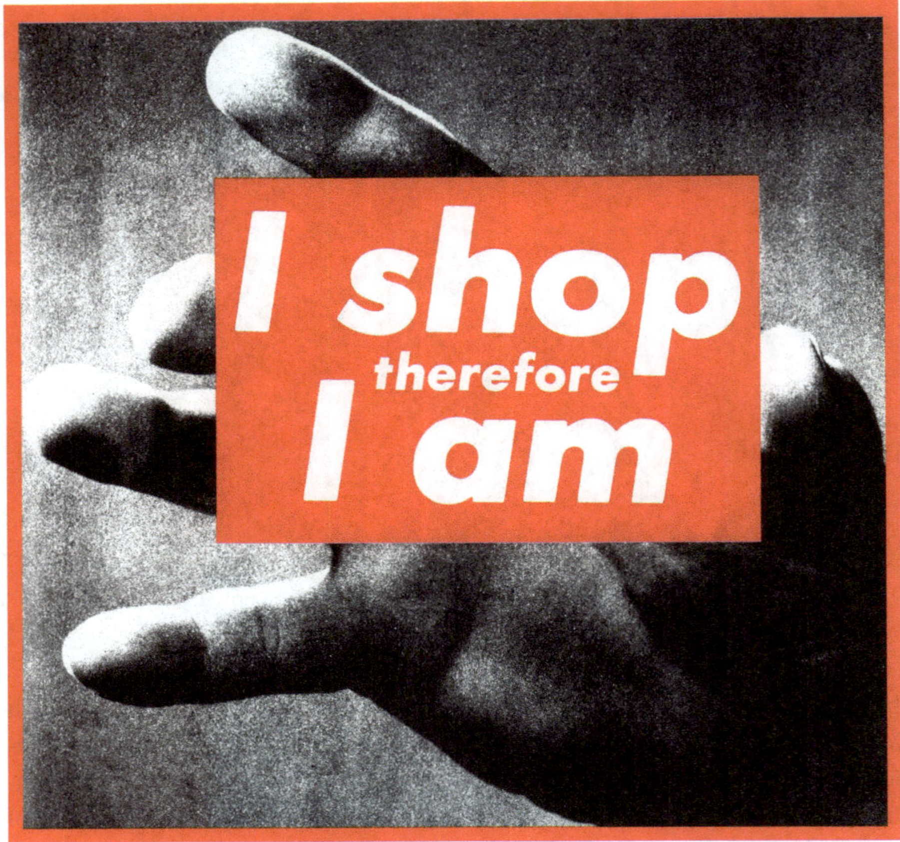

American conceptual artist Barbara Kruger (born 1945) plays satirically on seventeenth-century French philosopher René Descartes' famous axiom 'I think therefore I am' (*Cogito ergo sum*).

Kruger's statement draws attention to the fact that we used to *think* in order to know that we existed, but now we *shop* instead – the implication being that the latter is a meaningless substitute. Kruger's bold type, assimilated from the media itself, strikes a familiar and authoritative tone. Her oeuvre features the juxtaposition of imagery and text, a common device of social critique.

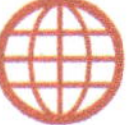

See the companion website for more information about the contexts of Postmodernism.

The work of Warhol, Koons and Kruger poses the question: is consumerism the defining feature of our times? In his book *The Ecstasy of Media Communication*, French philosopher and cultural critic Jean Baudrillard argues that the media plays an 'essential' role in defining Western culture. He suggests that the traditional distinctions between 'reality' and 'imitation' no longer exist because the media produces images that are neither one nor the other, but are rather a mixture of both, creating what he calls a 'hyperreality'. For example, Michael Jackson was 'real' but our knowledge of him through his portrayal in the media is 'hyperreal' – a simulation which is characteristic of our times.

The collapse of previously defined categories – a distinctly postmodern feature – casts an interesting light on the issue of social class. Strictly hierarchical in Victorian England, there is some evidence that class distinctions have fragmented in **postmodern** times.

Class Fragmentation and the Urban Documentary

Victorian morality paintings, such as those featured previously by Augustus Leopold Egg and William Holman Hunt, pivoted around the issue of class-based norms. Social class features once again, at least as a sub-text, in *The Railway Station*, 1860–1862, by William Powell Frith (1819–1909). Frith's painting of a busy platform at Paddington Station provides a microcosm of the hierarchy in Victorian society and an insightful commentary on the period's technological advances. The changes brought about by the Industrial Revolution, which had started in the UK in the mid-eighteenth century, were felt in every facet of the epoch, and the railway in particular became an emblematic sign of modernity.

What appears to be a rather chaotic scene on the station platform of Paddington is, upon closer inspection, a highly structured documentary of Victorian life: the crowds are organised compositionally in accordance with their social class, as art historian Andrew Graham-Dixon observes: *The crowd has been organised as if in alignment with the train's compartments, third class, second class and first class, so that to read the painting from left to right is to ascend smoothly from the lowest level of society to the highest* (Graham-Dixon, *A History of British Art*, p. 160).

The image is imbued with the middle-class values that have come, perhaps stereotypically, to define the Victorian era: self-improvement, respectability and social position (or at least the outward appearance of such), and Frith's restrained brushwork and recording of minutiae echo the political conservatism of the era and meticulously observed Victorian mores. Ironically, in an age when **meritocracy** was more of a myth than a reality, many individuals in Victorian England aspired to climb the social ladder. The preoccupation with an individual's social standing was a common theme in literature, as well

Figure 4.25 | William Powell Frith, *The Railway Station*, 1860–1862, oil on canvas, 117 × 256 cm, Royal Holloway, University of London. Source: © Royal Holloway, University of London / Bridgeman Images.

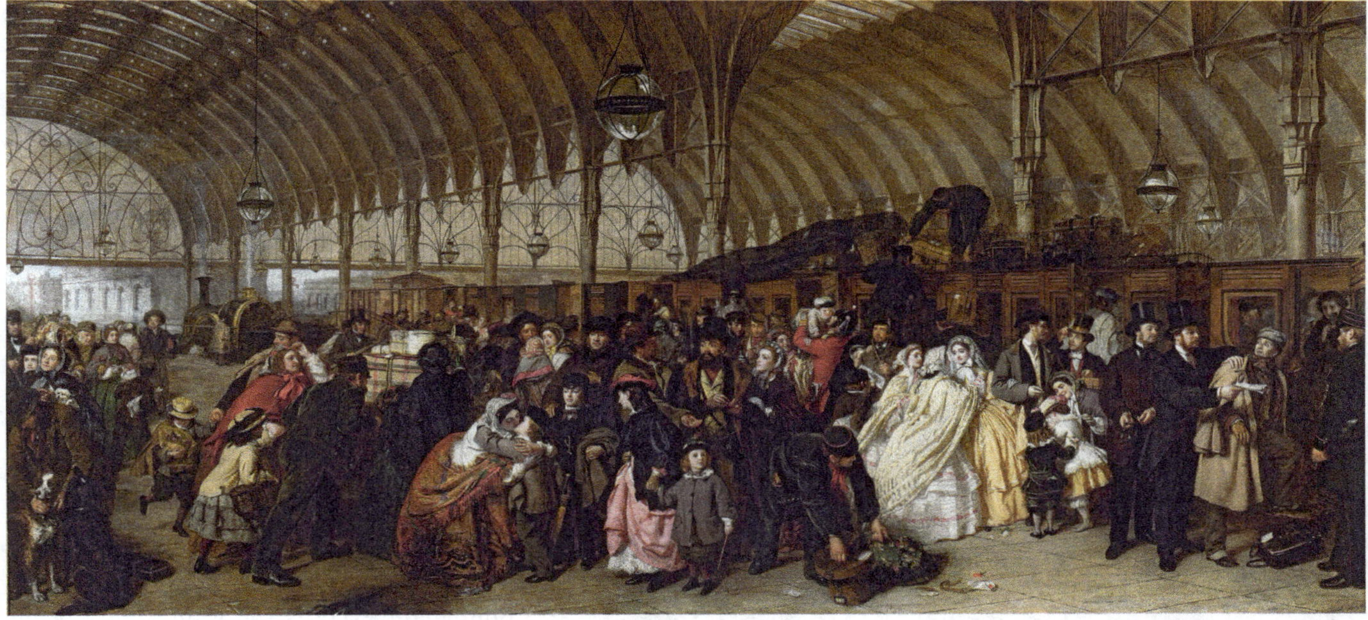

as painting; Thomas Hardy's novel *Jude the Obscure*, 1895, is just one illustration of the rigid social scale that prevailed. Frith's travellers are all dressed in clothing that reveals their class; every bonnet, top hat and crinoline tells a social story.

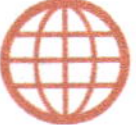

See the companion website for more information about the impact of the railway on Victorian society.

Along with a changing social landscape, this was the time of technological progress and the train and its station illustrate this. Indeed, the railway seemed to have an almost religious significance for Britain's most famous painter of the period, J.M.W. Turner; his *Rain, Steam and Speed – The Great Western Railway*, c.1844, captures the new technology's essence in an ephemeral, light-saturated landscape.

The railway had a huge social and economic impact on mid-nineteenth-century Britain. By the 1860s the country was criss-crossed with a network of rail tracks, and many towns and villages had a local station. Trains enabled people to move out of their rural farming communities to seek employment in the cities, and they provided a cheap and fast method for transporting both industrial and agricultural products.

Quick and relatively affordable travel allowed day trips to the coast, with even poorer people able to afford this by travelling in open-topped carriages. Not everybody thought that this was a positive prospect. The Duke of Wellington – famous for his victory at the Battle of Waterloo, and subsequently a Tory prime minster – was afraid that trains would encourage poor and socially undesirable people to come to London.

The impoverished classes were often represented as '**other**' in Victorian England, their social failures used as moral warnings to the masses or their lives documented like grotesque spectacles of the era. Nevertheless, in earlier times, eighteenth-century satirist William Hogarth (1697–1764) sympathetically depicted the plight of the poor in images such as *Gin Lane*, 1751. Gin drinking was used as a means of escape from the harsh lives many of the poor in London and other cities experienced. Hogarth's subjects were usually low-life and often syphilitic, but always bore resemblances to the characters of contemporary urban living, in common with so many artists who documented the times in which they lived.

Figure 4.26 | William Hogarth, *Gin Lane*, 1751, copper engraving and etching, 35.8 × 30.2 cm. Source: akg-images.

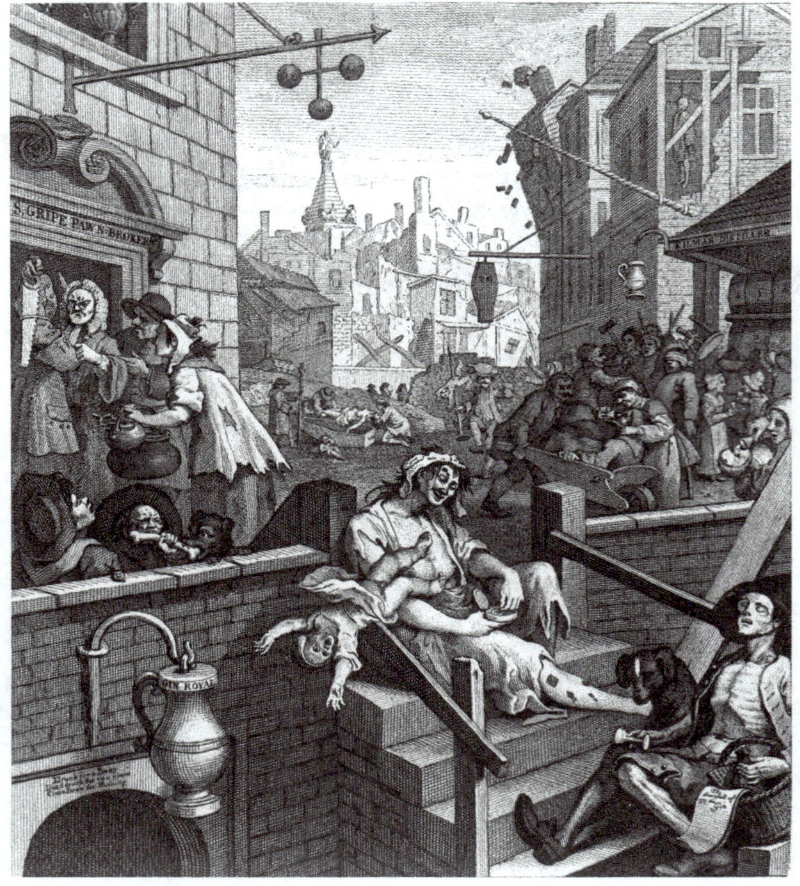

Stereotypical depravity and drunkenness both shocked and gratified the rigidly hierarchical Victorians, but when contemporary artist Richard Billingham (born 1970) turned a camera lens on his own parents it was the fact that he, the class-conscious product of his subjects, was now a part of the establishment that prompted the question: have traditional class distinctions really collapsed in the twenty-first century? The idea of the death of social class resonated with 1980s individualism and **Thatcherite** values of free enterprise and social mobility.

Billingham exposes the grim reality of his

family's social conditions with almost unthinkable candour. Candour is a commodity, or so it seems, in recent times and, unsurprisingly, Billingham's photographic confessions caught the attention of that most famous backer of the class-conscious, maverick and patron of the arts Charles Saatchi. Billingham's commercial success arguably demonstrates meritocracy in operation and a distinct vogue, even celebrity prestige, in having climbed out of the Hogarthian gutter. In an extract from 'We Are Family' in *Genius of Photography* (*Wall to Wall*), Billingham states:

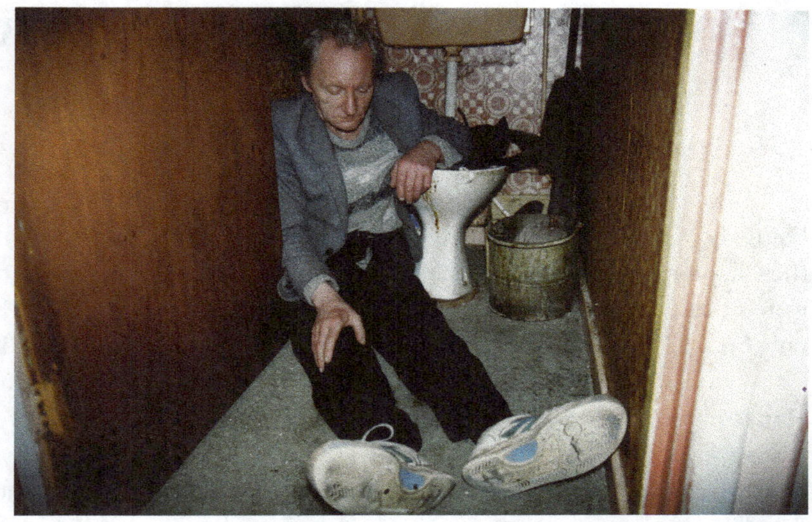

Figure 4.27 | Richard Billingham, *Untitled*, 1994, colour photograph mounted on aluminum, 75 × 50 cm, Edition of 10 + 1 AP. Source: Copyright the artist, courtesy Anthony Reynolds Gallery, London.

I was living in this tower block; there was just me and him. He was an alcoholic, he would lie in bed, drink, get to sleep, wake up, get to sleep, didn't know if it was day or night. But it was difficult to get him to stay still for more than say 20 minutes at a time so I thought that if I could take photographs of him that would act as a source material for these paintings and then I could make more detailed paintings later on. So that's how I first started taking photographs. (Billingham, 'We Are Family')

Of course, contemporary artists such as Tracey Emin and Richard Billingham have been famously proud of their 'in-your-face' working-classness: their work is gritty, raw, confessional and immediately accessible to the masses. Both artists' works have met with critical acclaim, perhaps because it suits our lay-everything-bare times. Since the 1990s the media has been saturated by voyeuristic glimpses of abject and dysfunctional families. Private lives unfold in TV programmes such as *Celebrity Big Brother* and *My Big Fat Gypsy Wedding*. Yet, however unnerving Billingham's 'fly-on-the-wall' portraits are for the viewer, their authenticity makes them deeply poignant and brimming with social class narrative; even if Billingham's example supports the idea that it is possible to move beyond a working-class background. There is certainly an irony in the fact that many of these 'working-class' artists enjoy levels of wealth that match or exceed that of their patrons.

The social and historical contexts of architecture have only been touched upon in this chapter because key buildings examined in *Chapter 2* and *Chapter 3*, are considered there in terms of their wider social and historical contexts. Considering that no work of art or architecture appears in a social and historical vacuum, and that every object is born of its times, the choices under this theme are as limitless as the works themselves.

Chapter Summary Exercise

Using the words below complete the Chapter Summary. Each word or term should be used only once.

Haussmann
transitory
consumerism
Baudelaire
popular
Catholic
photography
Matrimonial
Great Depression
fallen woman
Trent

The most important historical and contextual factor affecting Italian Baroque art and architecture of the seventeenth century was the ______ Counter-Reformation. The Council of ______ convened over a 20-year period and their instruction sought to strengthen the Catholic faith.

In nineteenth-century France Napoleon III ordered Baron Georges ______ to modernise and transform Paris. The invention of ______ during the 1820s had a significant impact on artists who found new ways to depict the modern world. Poet and art critic Charles ______ suggested that every epoch had its own form of beauty and the nineteenth century's was the '______'.

In nineteenth-century Victorian England, the theme of the subjugation or redemption of the ______ became well worn. Moral dualism characterised the period and even Victorian legislation supported a patriarchal society: The ______ Causes Act, 1857, reinforced gender inequality.

In October 1929, the American stock market crashed and marked the beginning of the ______. Conversely, the 1950s and 1960s in America were boom years, and the country's commercial successes led to a level of ______ that became emblematic of American identity. Pop art capitalised on the prevailing commodification of society and borrowed motifs from ______ culture to comment on cultural conditions in a celebratory and satirical way.

Checkpoint Answers

4.1 What kinds of formal devices did artists and architects employ to persuade viewers of the strength of the Catholic Church?
In painting: tenebristic backgrounds, emphatic gestures and expressions, striking colour palettes, dynamic compositions.
In sculpture: emphatic gestures and expressions, dynamic compositions, deeply carved drapery and facial expressions.
In architecture: undulating façades, interplay of light and shade, volutes, abundance of architectural decoration.

4.2 How did artists of the nineteenth century convey a sense of modernity in France?
Painterly application, cropped compositions, modern characters as new subject matter, depiction of new, urban leisure spaces.

4.3 What is it about the form and style of Pop Art that reflected the social and historical conditions of the United States in the 1960s?
Serialisation, popular culture motifs, celebrity, relationship to cheaply produced goods and middle-class consumerism, economic prosperity.

References

Adams, J. 'The Drink that Fuelled a Nation's Art', *Tate Etc.*, 1 September 2005, http://www.tate.org.uk/context-comment/articles/drink-fuelled-nations-art.

Billingham, R. 'We Are Family', 2014, http://www.bbc.co.uk/photography/genius/gallery/billingham.shtml.

Clark, T.J. *The Painting of Modern Life: Paris in the Art of Manet and His Followers*, rev. ed., Princeton University Press, 1999.

Edwards, S. *Art and Its Histories: A Reader*, Yale University Press / Open University, 1999.

Frascina, F., Blake, N., Fer, B., Garb, T. and Harrison, C. *Modernity and Modernism*, Yale University Press / Open University, 1993.

Frizot, M. *A New History of Photography*, Konemann, 1998.

Golby, J.M. *Culture and Society in Britain 1850–1900*, Oxford University Press, 1986.

Graham-Dixon, A. *A History of British Art*, BBC Worldwide, 1999.

Greenberg, C. 'Avant-Garde and Kitsch', *Partisan Review*, 1939.

Harris, A.S. *Seventeenth-Century Art and Architecture*, 2nd ed., Laurence King, 2008.

Huyssen, A. *Introduction: After the Great Divide, Modernism, Mass Culture, Postmodernism*, Macmillan, 1986.

Jones, J. 'Jeff Koons: Not Just the King of Kitsch', *The Guardian*, 30 June 2009, http://www.theguardian.com/artanddesign/2009/jun/30/jeff-koons-exhibition-serpentine.

Krell, A. *Manet*, Thames and Hudson, 1996.

Loyola, I. and Munitiz, J. *Saint Ignatius Loyola: Personal Writings*, Penguin, 2004.

Pooke, G. and Whitham, G. *Understand Art History*, Hodder, 2010.

Rice, S. *Parisian Views*, MIT Press, 1999.

Tate Gallery, 'Degas, Sickert and Toulouse-Lautrec', 2005–2006, http://www.tate.org.uk/britain/exhibitions/degas/absinthe.htm.

Teresa of Ávila and Cohen, J. *The Life of Saint Teresa of Ávila by Herself*, Penguin, 1957.

Wittkower, R., rev. by Connors, J. and Montagu, J. *Art and Architecture in Italy, 1600–1750*, Vol. 1. Yale University Press, 1999.

Other Useful Sources

Appignanesi, R. and Garratt, C. with Sardar, Z. and Curry, P. *Introducing Postmodernism*, Icon Books, 1999.

Cachin, F. *Manet: Painter of Modern Life*, Thames & Hudson, 1995.

Colquhoun, A. *Modern Architecture*, Oxford University Press, 2002.

Fischer, D.H. *The Great Wave: Price Revolutions and the Rhythm of History*, Oxford University Press, 1997.

Johnson, P. *A History of the American People*, HarperCollins, 1997.

Lange, D. 'The Assignment I'll Never Forget' in Newhall, B. *Photography: Essays and Images*, Secker & Warburg, 1981. (First published 1960.)

Partridge, E. *Restless Spirit: The Life and Work of Dorothea Lange*, Viking Juvenile, 1998.

Robinson, D. and Garratt, C. *Introducing Descartes*, Icon Books, 1999.

Treuherz, J. *Victorian Painting*, Thames & Hudson, 1997.

Troyen, C. and Barter, J.A. *Edward Hopper*, Thames & Hudson, 2007.

Whitham, G. and Pooke, G. *Understand Contemporary Art*, Hodder, 2010.

Wilson-Bareau, J. (ed.) *Manet by Himself*, Time Warner, 2004.

Chapter 5
Patronage and the Social and Cultural Status of the Artist

Learning Outcomes

By the end of this chapter you will be able to:

- define the concepts of patronage and social and cultural status and understand their inter-relatedness
- consider different forms of artistic patronage and their effect on art and architecture
- explain how artistic patronage influences the appearance, interpretation and meaning of art and architecture
- distinguish the relationship between patronage and the social and cultural status of the artist
- describe how artistic status contributes to the interpretation of works of art and architecture.

Thinking About Art: A Thematic Guide to Art History, First Edition. Penny Huntsman.

Chapter Map

This chapter map provides a visual overview of Chapter 5 – 'Patronage and the Social and Cultural Status of the Artist' – together with its key works.

Private Patronage in the Fifteenth and Sixteenth Centuries

Glorification of the patron and self-glorification by the artist

– Sandro Botticelli (1445–1510), *The Adoration of the Magi*, c.1475
– Jan van Eyck (c.1390–1441), *The Arnolfini Portrait*, 1434
– Donatello (c.1386–1466), *David*, 1440
– Albrecht Dürer (1471–1528), *Self-Portrait*, 1500

Public Patronage in the Fifteenth and Sixteenth Centuries

The importance of guilds and the rise of the 'artist-genius'

– Filippo Brunelleschi (1377–1446), Dome of Florence Cathedral, c.1420–1436
– Michelangelo (1475–1564), *David*, 1501–1504

Papal and Church Patronage in the Seventeenth Century

The glory of God?

– Gian Lorenzo Bernini (1598–1680), *The Ecstasy of Saint Teresa of Ávila*, 1645–1652
– Juan Martínez Montañés (1568–1649), *Christ of Clemency*, 1603

Patronage in the Eighteenth Century

Worldly motives

– Jacques-Louis David (1748–1825), *The Death of Marat*, 1793
– George Stubbs (1724–1806), *Whistlejacket*, c.1762

The Modern Artist and the Market in the Nineteenth Century

Solitary and against society?

– Vincent van Gogh (1853–1890), *Self-Portrait with Bandaged Ear*, 1889

Twentieth Century

Collectors and critics

– The patron: Peggy Guggenheim (1898–1979)
– The artist: Jackson Pollock (1912–1956), *Mural*, 1943
– The critic: Clement Greenberg (1909–1994)

The Contemporary Artworld

The artist as celebrity and the rise of the supercollector

– Tracey Emin (born 1963), *I've Got it All*, 2000
– Tracey Emin, *My Bed*, 1998
– Damien Hirst (born 1965), *A Thousand Years*, 1990
– Damien Hirst, *The Physical Impossibility of Death in the Mind of Someone Living*, 1991
– Marcus Harvey (born 1963), *Myra*, 1995
– Jake (born 1966) and Dinos (born 1962) Chapman, *Zygotic Acceleration, Biogenetic, and De-sublimated Libidinal Model*, 1995

Architectural Landmarks in the Twentieth and Twenty-First Centuries

Enhancing corporate 'brands' through association with 'star' architects

– Richard Rogers (born 1933) and Renzo Piano (born 1937), Pompidou Centre, 1971–1977
– Richard Rogers, Lloyds Building, 1978–1986

Introduction

This chapter introduces you to two important and inter-related themes:

1. patronage
2. the social and cultural status of the artist.

Patronage and the status of the artist have evolved a great deal over the centuries, and this extended Introduction provides a brief overview of the history of both themes and considers how the form and motives of patronage have changed in accordance with the wider social and economic contexts. Throughout this chapter, we will address the ways in which artistic patronage and its motivation have influenced both the appearance and our interpretation of art and architecture.

A brief history of patronage

Patronage is the commissioning or purchasing of works of art by an individual, group or state. There are many different possible motives for becoming a **patron**. These include:

- private patronage for pleasure, commemoration, investment, prestige
- group patronage for power and corporate identity, commemoration, assertion of status, competitiveness, devotion, civic pride, nationalism
- church patronage for the glory of God, private devotion, didacticism (a focus on the instructional qualities of works), power and the status of the church as a political force
- monarchy and state patronage for reasons of connoisseurship, national status, dynasty-building, commemoration, propaganda.

The history of patronage runs in parallel with the history of ascendant monarchs, religions, merchant classes and the artist as individual, even celebrity. Needless to say, the role and nature of patronage has changed over the centuries. During the period known as **Classical Antiquity** the state was the chief patron of the arts; in the **medieval period** patronage was dominated by the church, the papacy and powerful individuals. It was during the **Renaissance** that a new form of patronage emerged: lay patrons increasingly exerted their influence over artistic production, and **donor portraits** were common.

During and after the Renaissance, the middle classes began to emerge across Europe, alongside a rise in merchant and banking families. In Florence, **guilds** competed to commission the greatest artists, as did **confraternities** of lay people. During the High Renaissance, patrons came to recognise the artist as an intellectual and even a genius.

During the seventeenth century the church was the dominant patron of the arts, which it invariably employed for propaganda to fuel the Catholic **Counter-Reformation**. Royal court painters flourished, as did private patronage and collections were amassed, such as that of Charles I in England.

In the eighteenth century a new commercial patronage emerged with the expansion of trade and the opening up of the New World. Academies were founded all over Europe, and ready-painted works – not commissioned by patrons but made to sell to whoever might like them – were sold by artists themselves or via the middlemen of the expanding **art market**: the **dealers**.

The nineteenth century saw the resurgence of more traditional patronage from the church, the state and the monarchy, although the trend for works made to sell to any willing buyer also continued. New industrialists bought art to demonstrate their *nouveau riche* prestige. This was the century in which the dealer emerged as someone who could broker a mutually beneficial relationship between individual artists and rich would-be collectors.

The twentieth century saw the role of the dealer increase and the artist-dealer relationship flourish. While the role of the critic was felt in the nineteenth century – for example, **Pre-Raphaelite** artist Dante Gabriel Rossetti vowed never to exhibit in public again, following a bad review of *The Annunciation* (1849–1850) – twentieth-century critics, perhaps as a consequence of the power of the media, became increasingly significant and could make or break an artist's reputation. **Collectors** turned into supercollectors and artists found the technical means to promote their ready-painted work without the need for a patron, dealer or even a physical exhibition space.

The changing status of the artist

The social and cultural status of the artist relates to the rank or position of artists in society in relation to others, and so reflects the importance accorded to art in a given society. How important is art considered to be? Is it considered a reflection of a society's highest values or merely useful decoration? You also need to consider the individual success or otherwise of particular artists. Did they achieve fame and riches in their lifetime, or did celebrity and adulation only occur posthumously? The social and cultural status of an artist or architect is often inextricably linked to the quality and quantity of patronage they enjoyed, and both themes are examined jointly, when appropriate, in this chapter.

The factors to be considered when assessing the status of art and artists in general in society are:

- Autonomy: how much freedom does an artist have at any particular historical period over the choice of subject matter and style? Conversely, how much influence do patrons – or the market – wield over artists?
- Education or training: do artists have special institutions dedicated to their training? Are artists members of guilds or academies or other professional associations? Have they trained with others of artistic status?
- Economic rewards: how well rewarded are artists monetarily? Has the economic value of an artist's work increased since his or her death?
- Social marks of status: what indicators of social status do successful artists in a particular society receive? Do they receive knighthoods or other honours? Do they socialise with the richest in society or the poorest? Are they expected to act as critics of society or to support it?
- Institutional prominence: how far do works of art, and therefore artists, benefit from being exhibited in gallery or museum collections? How influential are art critics? How much money is made by selling works of art at

auctions and by dealers?

The factors to consider when assessing any individual artist's degree of personal success include:

- Critical renown: what do art critics and art historians say about the artist? How much is published about the artist and his or her work? Is their work taught in schools and universities, and if so is it considered to be part of the art-historical '**canon**'?
- Financial rewards: has the artist achieved wealth through his or her work?
- Popular reputation: has the artist become well-known to a general, non-specialist audience? What degree of promotion does the artist receive through publicity, self-publicity (**self-portraits**, autobiography), marketing, discussion by critics, art historians, press, curators, patrons?

The ancient Greeks, and later the Romans, differentiated between the **liberal arts** for educated classes and the **mechanical arts** for tradesmen. During these times, artists – as we know them today – were treated like labourers and worked for daily rates; although some were valued and financially successful, most were still of a relatively low social status.

In the medieval period, most art was made for the glory of God and the individual artist was not celebrated. Artists worked with their hands and, on the whole, were seen as no better than skilled labourers. A painting was more valued for its use of expensive materials than for the artist's creativity and skill.

It was only during the Italian Renaissance that a change in the status of the artist took place, fuelled both by the emerging philosophy of **humanism** and by larger economic changes and the rise of a merchant class. **Secular** patronage and the emergence of wealthy merchant-patrons changed demand, and the artist became a creative ally to the patron. For the first time, artistic skill was believed to be God-given and the artist's fame was promoted in treatises and biographies, such as Giorgio Vasari's *Lives of the Artists* (1550).

In the seventeenth century, artists and architects in Italy, for example, enjoyed a high status as they helped the Catholic Church to rebuild Rome; conversely, the fame of some artists increased the prestige of their patron. In the late eighteenth and early nineteenth centuries European nation-states placed increasing importance on art collections and, accordingly, on museums as treasure-houses and display vehicles of a nation's wealth and prestige. The rise of national institutions and museums – such as the Royal Academy (founded 1768) and the National Gallery (founded 1824) in England, and the Louvre (founded 1793) in France – helped to bring about the rise to international fame of individual artists, as well-heeled European travellers visited the collections of courts, popes and noblemen, and returned from the Grand Tour determined to purchase works by some of the artists they had seen.

The nineteenth century saw artists creating and selling works independently and it is therefore at this point that the figure of the struggling artist emerges. Many artists depicted their poverty and challenged, rather than accepted, the political status quo. Artistic rules and **genres** were likewise broken and dissolved and, in the process, individual artists came to prominence as the latest scandalous sensation, or leader of a new artistic tendency or school. Arguably, art lovers, patrons and publics in the nineteenth century increasingly cared less for the richness of an artwork's materials than for the reputation of the artist who had made the work.

The twentieth century saw this trend intensify, with **avant-garde** artists disregarding traditional **mediums** and adopting such forms as the **ready-made**, an everyday object selected by the artist and displayed as art with little or no modification. Such a development appeared to confirm that the rules of art had all but disintegrated. Anything could become art, or so it seemed, if a famous artist said it was art. The artist as celebrity emerged with gusto, fuelled by the media-saturated times. At the same time, however, this era has seen the museum become even more important, as it is arguably institutional acceptance that now marks a work as 'art'. Having charted a brief history of the changing status of the artist, let us now examine more closely each phase in this story, using individual artistic examples.

Private Patronage in the Fifteenth and Sixteenth Centuries

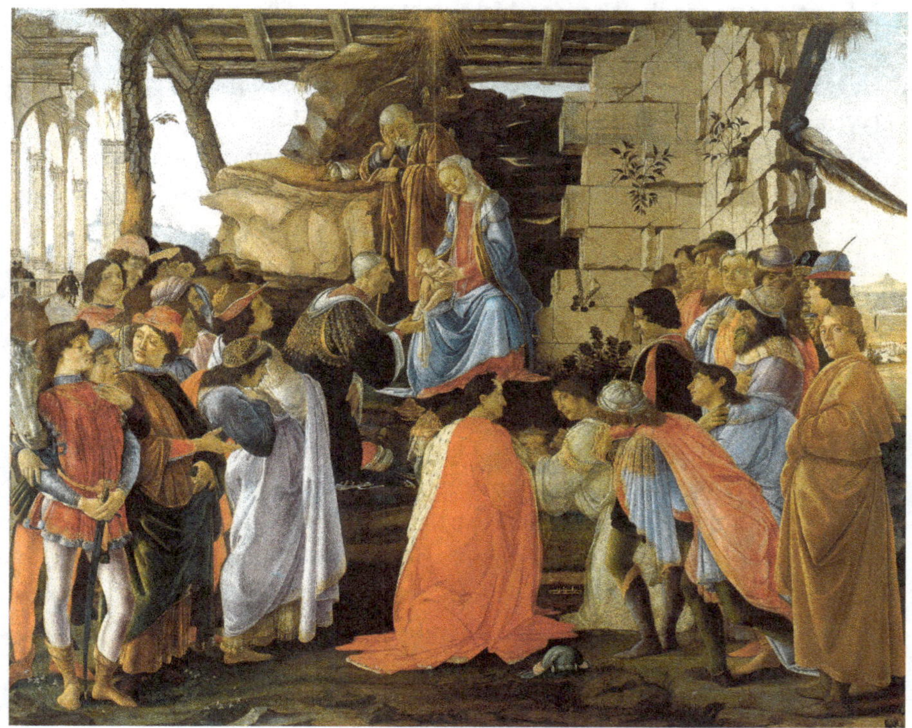

Figure 5.1 | Sandro Botticelli, *The Adoration of the Magi*, c.1475, tempera on wood, 111 × 134 cm, Florence, Galleria degli Uffizi. Source: akg-images / De Agostini Picture Library / G. Nimatallah.

Glorification of the patron and self-glorification by the artist

In the Renaissance, the Italian city of Florence was a self-governed, independent state. From around 1434, however, the Medici banking family unofficially ruled the city. The dynasty that they formed commissioned a vast array of paintings, sculptures and architecture, and their generosity and competitive nature ensured the city's status as the artistic centre of Europe during the fifteenth century and beyond. Florentine Renaissance artist Benozzo Gozzoli (1421–1497) was commissioned by the Medici family to make a fresco for the private chapel of the Palazzo Medici. As was common practice, it included a representation of his patrons in *The Procession of the Magi*, c.1459–1461. But as an indication of the relatively high status of the artist, Gozzoli also included a self-portrait with the words *opus benotti* (work of Benozzo).

The Medici family was so powerful that its members even appeared in paintings they had not directly commissioned. Guasparre di Zanobi Del Lama commissioned *The Adoration of the Magi*, c.1475, from Sandro Botticelli (originally Alessandro Filipepi, 1445–1510), which features several members of the Medici family. Why did Guasparre pay Botticelli to depict so many members of the most powerful banking family in Florence? The answer may lie in Guasparre's dubious past. The lowly patron had been convicted of embezzlement in 1447 but made his subsequent fortune as a broker and money changer. This wealth allowed him to commission Botticelli to paint this altarpiece in a chapel of Santa Maria Novella. Bearing in mind that the Medici were enrolled with the Guild of Money Changers (Arte di Cambio) it is little wonder Guasparre wanted to secure a favourable association with them. The *Adoration* was the only artistic product of Guasparre's brief social elevation. In 1476 he was convicted of fraud again and banned from trading (Deimling, *Botticelli*, p. 22).

5.1 Let's connect the themes: historical perspectives

Guasparre probably commissioned a work depicting the adoration of the Magi (Wise Men) precisely because he was named after the first of the Magi, Caspar, who was thus considered to be his patron saint. It was common practice in medieval and Renaissance times for people to commission artworks depicting their patron saint in the hope that this saint would intercede on their behalf at the Last Judgement, when the dead are resurrected and separated into the righteous and the damned (Deimling, *Botticelli*, p. 21).

As well as including the portrait of his patron Guasparre, the grey-haired merchant in a light blue robe on the right-hand side, and portraits of the Medici, Sandro Botticelli also unashamedly seized the opportunity to paint his own portrait among the group. The artist (far right, in a yellow robe) positioned himself as compositional counterpart to no less a figure than the Florentine ruler Lorenzo de' Medici, who was known as 'the Magnificent' (far left, wearing white stockings). Both have rather self-satisfied expressions, and together they frame the painting.

Despite ostensibly being a religious painting, the Holy Family is accorded less importance than a whole series of contemporary portraits. This painting was commissioned for personal gain, self-promotion and to gain favour; forget the Magi, it is the Medici – the *de facto* rulers of Florence – who are the most important potential givers of gifts in this scene. They include Cosimo the Elder, founder of the Medici dynasty, who is kneeling directly before the Virgin and Christ Child, and his son Pietro (Lorenzo's father), centre stage in vibrant red. They appear crownless, a deliberate omission given the family's need to present a humble image in a city that was, after all, a republic. There is some dispute over the identity of some of the people in the painting. Use your online research to find out more about Medici dynasty and which of them might be shown here.

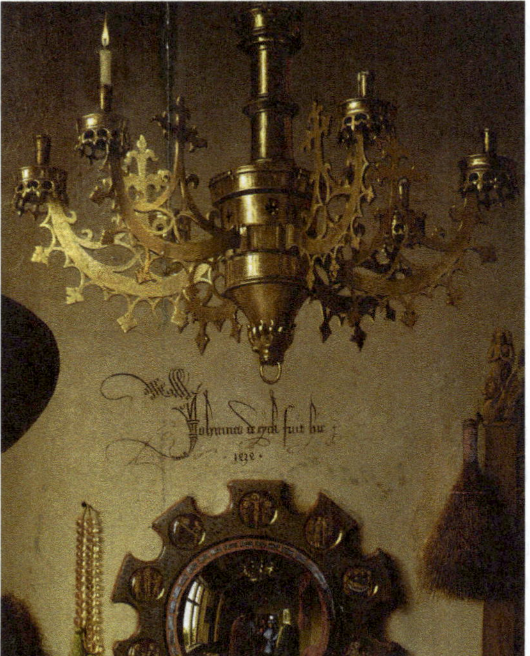

Figure 5.2 | Jan van Eyck, *The Arnolfini Portrait*, portrait of Giovanni (?) Arnolfini and his wife Giovanna Cenami (?), 1434, detail of chandelier and van Eyck's signature on back wall, oil on oak panel, 82.2 × 60 cm, London, National Gallery. Source: National Gallery, London, UK / Bridgeman Images.

There are countless other examples of Renaissance painters appearing in cameo roles in their own paintings.

Jan van Eyck (1395–1441) unapologetically included 'Jan van Eyck was here, 1434' on the central vertical axis of his *Arnolfini Portrait*, 1434 (examined in *Chapter 1*, as an example of double-portraiture, and in *Chapter 2*, as an example of oil painting). In relation to the portrait's patron, Giovanni di Arrigo Arnolfini (an often contested identity) the commission was a status symbol not only in its schematic depiction of wealth and success but also as evidence of the material ability of the client to commission such a well-regarded artist.

The meaning of this painting is that wealth – the wealth to hire Van Eyck – can purchase immortality, even if no one can be quite sure what your name was.

(Journalist Jonathan Jones quoted in Graham-Dixon, *Art: The Definitive Guide*, p. 144)

Jan van Eyck enjoyed the constant patronage of Philip the Good (Duke of Burgundy), and records show that the artist was highly valued and handsomely paid as a court painter to the Duke. Indeed, since Van Eyck was in receipt of an annual salary from the court when he painted the private double portrait of the Arnolfinis, it seems highly likely that **ducal** permission was sought and granted. This fact heightens the status of the Arnolfinis and validates the size and prominence of the artist's signature – everybody's cachet is enhanced by the deal. Unlike many of the artists featured in this chapter, much of Jan van Eyck's biographical detail remains unknown, even though he did have a biographer – Karel van Mander – itself a sign of status. In fact, Van Mander, who wrote *The Painter's Book*, 1604, falsely attributed the invention of oil to Van Eyck (as had Italian Renaissance biographer Vasari in the previous century). In truth, the artist's technical innovation was the perfection of oil painting, and not its invention.

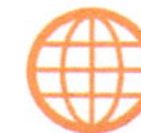

See the companion website for recommended reading in relation to every facet of Van Eyck's portrait.

5.2 Let's connect the themes: historical perspectives

The **Early Renaissance** period witnessed the growing status of the artist and biographies were a response to this new interest in them as individuals. Giorgio Vasari's *Lives of the Artists*, in particular, helped to turn artists – previously considered by society only as skilled artisans – into something more like modern celebrities when it was published in 1550.

Vasari, who was himself a painter and architect, publicised the trials, tribulations and idiosyncrasies of many Renaissance artists and architects. His evaluation of their work helped to shape critical opinions for generations and is still a rich source of information about key Renaissance artists.

The famously androgynous bronze *David*, 1420–1440 (examined briefly in *Chapter 3*) was commissioned by Cosimo de' Medici from Renaissance sculptor Donatello (originally Donato di Niccolò di Betto Bardi, c.1386–1466). According to the story from the Old Testament, David is the young shepherd boy who, against all odds, defeats the giant Goliath with a single stone to the head. He then beheads Goliath in a final act of triumph. For the Florentines, this story was of great importance as it reflected their own political position as a small state, which would nevertheless triumph against adversity.

However, Donatello's rendering of the subject was radical and new in a variety of ways: the figure's nakedness – heightened by his flamboyant hat

Figure 5.3 | Donatello, *David*, 1440 (before restoration), bronze, height 158 cm, Florence, Bargello Museum. Source: © 2015. Photo Scala, Florence – courtesy of the Ministero Beni e Att. Culturali.

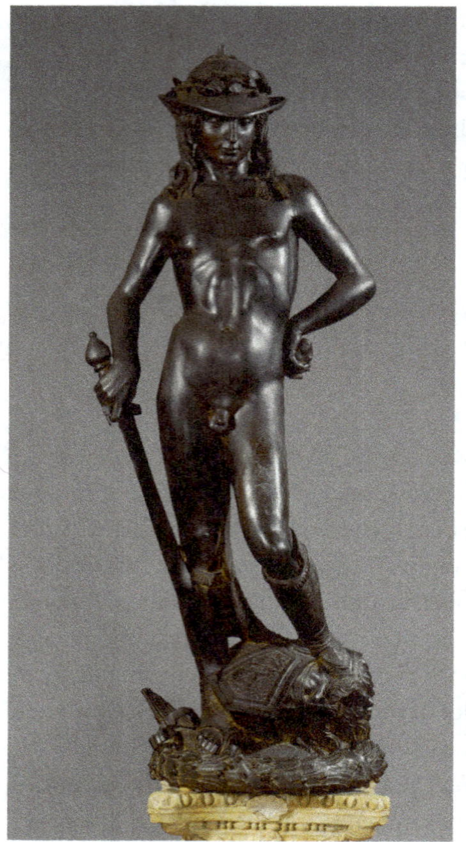

and boots – set him apart from other fifteenth-century depictions of the same subject. The hat itself was a deviation from the usual iconography of the young shepherd boy, and the way the toes on David's left foot caress Goliath's heavy beard lend a sensuality that also broke with the past. Cosimo de' Medici's acceptance of this break with tradition reveals the family's liberal attitude towards the arts. The Medici wanted to be known as intellectual leaders and despite the religious subject matter, this commission was certainly evidence that their interest in humanism and **Neo-Platonism** meant more to them than the furore this particular *David* caused.

See the companion website for more details about the Medici and their motives for commissioning works such as Donatello's *David*.

Furthermore, as the first free-standing nude bronze since Antiquity, *David* was capable of being seen as an emblematic new man – a naked and individual figure, breaking completely with medieval tradition. Its placement, too, is revealing. This particular symbolic defender of the city was tucked away in the private courtyard of the Medici palace – perhaps because it was considered too shocking to be shown in public, or perhaps because this placement would allow it to serve as a symbolic gesture for its patron. In appropriating *David* – who represented the Florentine Republic – the Medici expressed a quiet ambition, but only in the safety of their own home.

The status of the artist had increased exponentially since the medieval period, and the success of Vasari's *Lives of the Artists* was testament to public interest in the individual characters and achievements of artists. For example, Vasari describes the day when the grouchy Donatello pushed his own bronze handiwork over a parapet wall onto the street below, and, rather than punishing him, Cosimo de' Medici declared *[o]ne must treat these people of extraordinary genius as if they were celestial spirits, not as if they are beasts of burden* (Vasari, *Lives of the Artists*, p. 107).

5.1 Checkpoint question
What do you think Cosimo de' Medici's motives were for commissioning Donatello's *David*?

The Medici, self-made financiers and well-read connoisseurs, respected artists as individuals and recognised the artist's ability to propagate the dynasty's power all over Florence and beyond. As such, they were typical of powerful citizens from wealthy banking and merchant families who during this period commissioned art and architecture on an unprecedented scale. Many of these citizens were self-made and, arguably, valued those artists who matched their ambition. One notable example in the north of Europe was the painter Albrecht Dürer (1471–1528), who seemed to aspire to Florentine panache and whose *Self-Portrait*, 1500, is an extraordinary image of artistic self-righteousness.

Dürer's *Self-Portrait* demonstrates the changing status of the artist during the Renaissance and the emerging importance of the artist as a gifted individual. In the painting, Dürer shamelessly presents himself in the guise of Christ, perpetuating a self-image and status in the north of Europe somewhat akin to that which Vasari was perpetuating in the south for the artists he wrote about in his *Lives of the Artists*. Dürer's monogram hints at the persona he was actively creating for himself, and the skilful depiction of his fur collar would not have been lost on his audience either. Its black background establishes a certain gravitas – he is an intellectual artist. This famous image is probably one of the earliest examples of the artist as 'celebrity' in Western art.

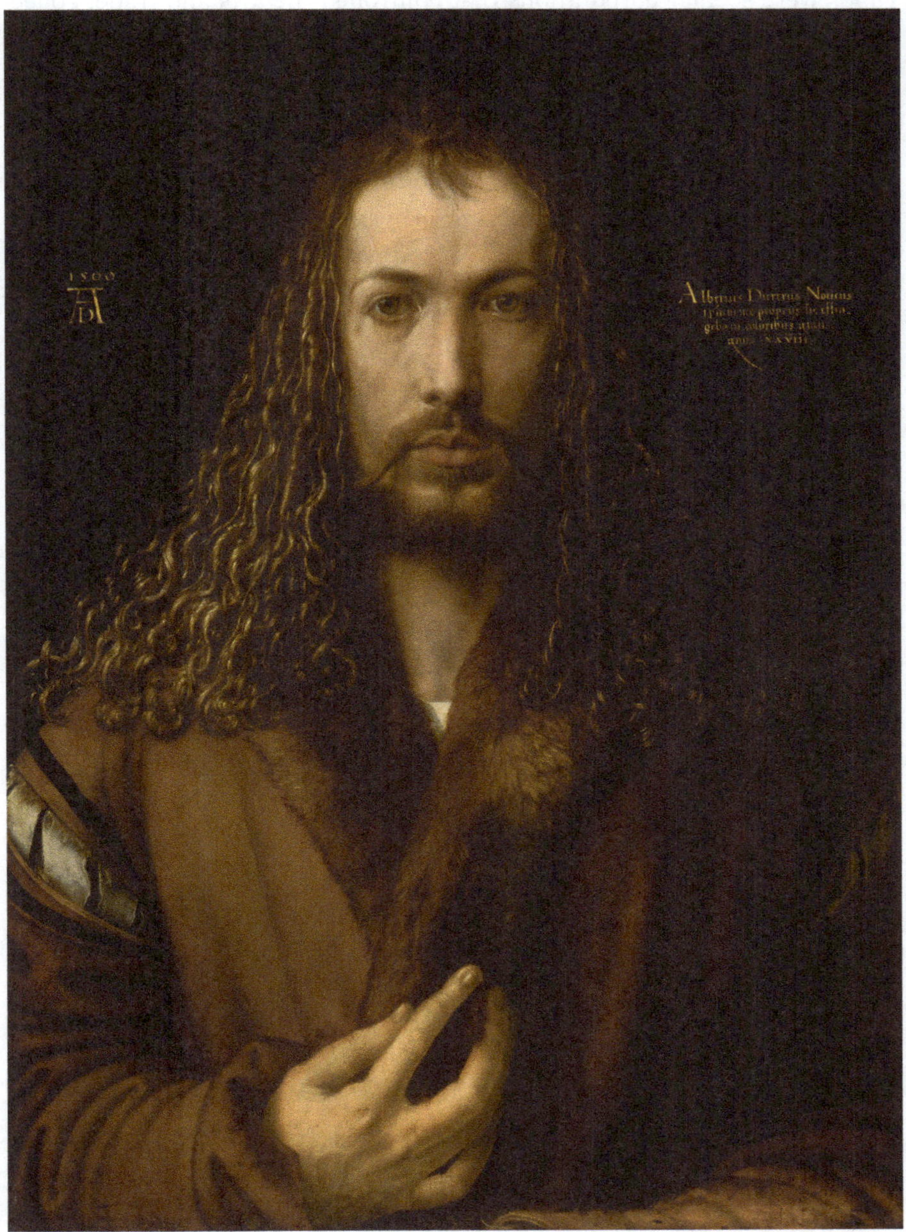

Figure 5.4 | Albrecht Dürer, *Self-portrait*, 1500, on limewood, 67 × 49 cm, Munich, Alte Pinakothek. Source: akg-images.

Public Patronage in the Fifteenth and Sixteenth Centuries

The importance of guilds and the rise of the 'artist-genius'

Much of Florence's wealth depended on the manufacture and trading of wool and cloth and, of course, the commercial success of banking. Florentine guilds were secular corporations that controlled the arts and trade; collectively, they influenced the artistic legacy of Florence. During the Renaissance in Florence there were seven major guilds (collectively known as the *arti maggiori*), five middle guilds (*arti mediane*) and nine minor guilds (*arti minori*) which competed with each other to gain commissions and status. The rivalry between guilds extended to the status of the artists they employed. A notable example is the competition set up by the Cloth Importers' Guild (*Calimala*) – one of the wealthiest guilds in Florence – in 1401 for the commission to decorate the bronze North Doors of the Baptistery. The competition was won by Lorenzo Ghiberti (1378–1455), with Filipo Brunelleschi (1377–1446) as runner-up. Another major guild was the Wool Merchant's Guild (*Arte della Lana*). It took charge of commissioning a dome for the cathedral of Santa Maria del Fiore (Florence Cathedral) in 1418. This time, Brunelleschi beat Ghiberti to the prize.

5.3 Let's connect the themes: materials and techniques

We learnt in *Chapter 2* about the materials, techniques and processes associated with Filippo Brunelleschi's dome of Florence Cathedral. The works relating to the *Opera del Duomo* – as it is known – were overseen by the Wool Merchant's Guild (the city's most powerful guild) who, in announcing the competition for the construction of the huge dome, established an architectural challenge that would help define the achievements of the city, its architect and the epoch.

The *Opera del Duomo* put up an exceptionally large sum of money – 200 gold florins – to the person capable of vaulting what is still the largest **masonry** dome in the world. The 'greatest architectural puzzle of the age' could be solved by only one man – Brunelleschi (1377–1446) (King, *Brunelleschi's Dome: The Story of the Great Cathedral in Florence*, p. 3). He is credited with mapping the rules of **linear perspective**, recognising the Classical **Orders** of architecture, engineering a hoist to carry incredible weights for the dome's construction and spanning the **drum** with the dome itself. The completion of the dome secured his fame and fortune, not only as a master mason – like his medieval forebears – but also as an innovative engineer with mathematical ingenuity and aesthetic vision. The dome is an enduring monument to the civic pride of the city and, arguably, still creates the most magnificent silhouette in Italy. It would revolutionise dome construction, and a commission for the Medici family church, San Lorenzo, predictably followed.

Figure 5.5 | Filippo Brunelleschi, Dome of Florence Cathedral, 1420–1436.
Source: © santof / iStockphoto.

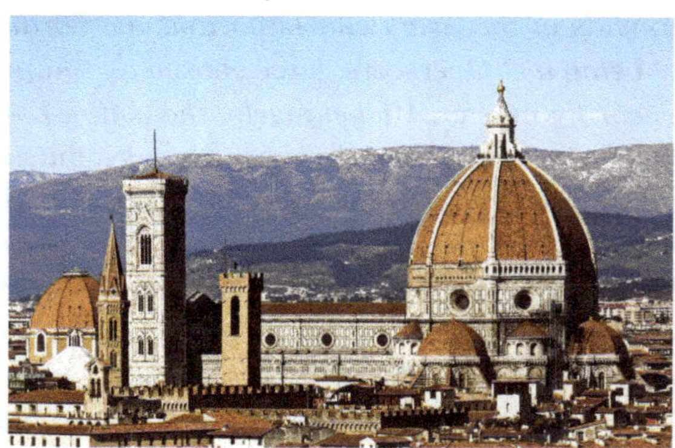

Brunelleschi's dome may be examined in relation to a number of themes in this book. Already scrutinised for the materials, **techniques and processes** related to its construction in *Chapter 2*, the dome's monumental scale (testament to the domination of religion during the fifteenth century and the competition between neighbouring Italian cities, particularly Pisa and Siena) reveals a great deal about its social and historical context. In the context of this chapter, its very existence not only demonstrates the importance of commercial patrons such as the Wool Guild, but also reveals the tremendous status some Renaissance artists enjoyed in their own lifetimes.

Brunelleschi's body lies in the crypt of Florence Cathedral, a great honour for a great Renaissance man and a mark of the changing status of the artist in this period. Thousands of mourners paid their respect at his funeral held in Santa Maria del Fiore (the actual name of Florence Cathedral) itself, and on his marble slab is the inscription *CORPUS MAGNI INGENII VIRI PHILIPPI BRUNELLESCHI FIORENTINI* (Here lies the body of the great ingenious man Filippo Brunelleschi of Florence) (King, *Brunelleschi's Dome: The Story of the Great Cathedral in Florence*, p. 156).

Brunelleschi's dome for Florence Cathedral was not only a symbol of civic pride, but a symbol of the Renaissance itself. Similarly, High Renaissance giant Michelangelo (originally Michelangelo di Lodovico Buonarroti Simoni, 1475–1564) created a world-famous emblem of the city with his iconic sculpture *David*, 1501 a few decades later. Michelangelo's stone subject was the same Old Testament figure that Donatello had forged in bronze for the Medici around 60 years earlier, although the comparison ends there.

Michelangelo was awarded the commission for the colossal figure of *David* by the Arte della Lana (Guild of Wool Merchants), which was also responsible for the decoration and maintenance of the cathedral. As this example shows, patronage is sometimes difficult to classify: Michelangelo's *David* was commissioned by a Florentine guild – making the commission a work of corporate patronage – but the statue itself was intended for the cathedral, which means the commission exemplifies both religious and civic patronage. By this time, Michelangelo's status as a sculptor had already been established by works such as his serene *Pièta*, examined in *Chapter 1* as an example of a religious subject. However, with *David*, he was widely held to have surpassed the skill and beauty achieved by the sculptors of Classical Antiquity.

Michelangelo achieved these supreme artistic results despite being given

And without doubt this figure has put in the shade every other statue, ancient or modern, Greek or Roman.

(Vasari, *Lives of the Artists*, p. 339)

a second-hand block of marble from which to create his masterpiece. (Agostino di Duccio had tried and failed with the same block four decades earlier.) The following is an extract from the **contract** for Michelangelo's *David*, dated 16 August 1501:

Spectabiles ... viri, the Consuls of the Arte della Lana and the Lords Overseers [of the Cathedral][18] *being met Overseers, have chosen as sculptor to the said Cathedral the worthy master, Michelangelo, the son of Lodovico Buonarroti, a citizen of Florence, to the end that he may make, finish and bring to perfection the male figure known as the Giant, nine braccia in height, already blocked out in marble by Maestro Agostino*[19] *grande, of Florence, and badly blocked; and now stored in the workshops of the Cathedral.*

The work shall be completed within the period and term of two years next ensuing, beginning from the first day of September next ensuing, with a salary and payment together in joint assembly within the hall of the said of six broad florins of gold in gold for every month. And for all other works that shall be required about the said building (edificium) the said Overseers

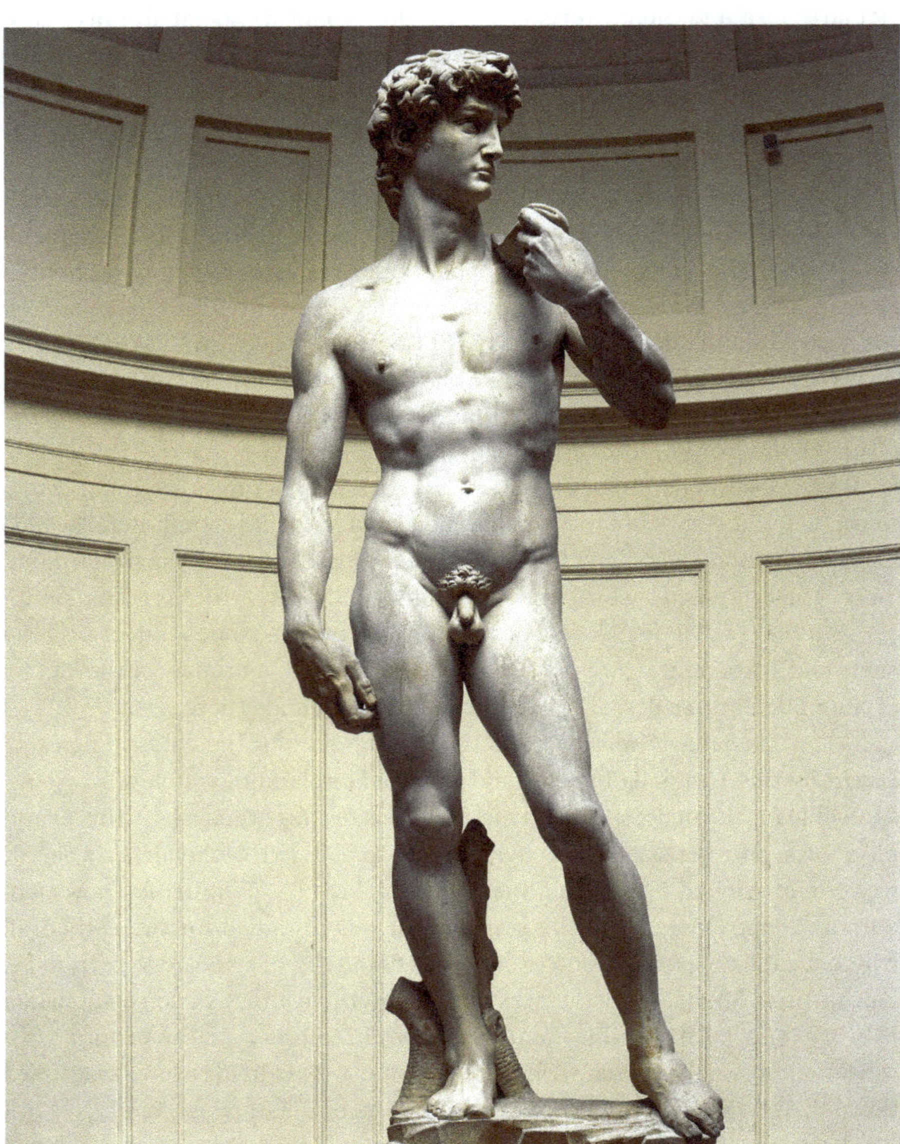

Figure 5.6 | Michelangelo, *David*, 1501–1504, marble, height 434 cm, Florence, Galleria dell'Accademia. Source: akg-images / Andrea Jemolo.

18 The *Operai*, or committee in charge of a building.

19 Agostino di Duccio.

bind themselves to supply and provide both men and scaffolding from their office and all else that may be necessary. When the said work and the said male figure of marble shall be finished, then the Consuls and Overseers who shall at that time be in authority shall judge whether it merits a higher reward, being guided therein by the dictates of their own consciences. (Holt, *A Documentary History of Art*, pp. 4–5)

The timescale within which Michelangelo had to work – and for which he would be supplied with the necessary practical and financial support – was clearly specified, as were the limitations imposed by the poorly blocked out piece of marble he was commissioned to carve. There was thus no margin for error – or space for significant **contrapposto** in the figure. Nevertheless, Michelangelo achieved a forceful and warrior-like effect through a subtle distribution of weight in the figure and a determined expression. Blood seems to pump visibly down his arms into his oversized hands, reinforcing his virility and readiness for battle.

Michelangelo's status during the Renaissance was unsurpassed. We learn from Condivi's authorised *Life of Michelangelo*, 1553, that the Pope treated the artist like a 'brother' and Vasari positively swooned over the artist's apparently divinely inspired creations, describing him as a 'Tuscan genius'. Vasari also recalls how Michelangelo was invited into the Medici household to live and how Lorenzo the Magnificent wanted to *keep him as one of his own sons* (Vasari, *Lives of the Artists*, p. 331).

Michelangelo's status may be measured by the fact that his death was marked by an elaborate funerary procession. The Florentine Academy of Painters and Sculptors stated their wish to pay tribute to *the greatest artist of their profession that has perhaps ever lived.*

Despite his unprecedented status and well-tolerated bad temper, in a letter to his biographer, Vasari, he wrote *Messer Giorgio, Dear Friend, – God is my witness how much against my will it was that Pope Paul forced me into this work on St. Peter's in Rome ten years ago* (Holt, *A Documentary History of Art*, p. 19). He was referring to the *Last Judgement* wall **fresco** which, against his passion and his wishes, he painted in the Sistine Chapel for his authoritative patron Pope Paul III. (He had painted the ceiling three decades earlier for Pope Julius II.)

Michelangelo may have angered popes but he also charmed them – not least because they regarded his artistic skill as invaluable in securing their long-lasting reputations. Of Pope Paul III, Vasari said, *God ensured future renown for his holiness and for Michelangelo. How greatly are the merits of the Pope enhanced by the genius of the artist?* (Vasari, *Lives of the Artists*, p. 337).

Considering that an artist has enjoyed such powerful patronage, and such long-lasting fame, does the fame of the artist still affect our interpretation of his work? Should it? It is easy to conflate the value of a work with the artist's status, especially in the case of Michelangelo. His works have become famous the world over. He has become a transnational brand.

5.2 Checkpoint question

What impact do you think biographies, such as Vasari's *Lives of the Artists*, 1550, have on the status of artists or architects?

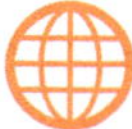

See the companion website for details on a variety of sources relating to Michelangelo's life and works.

Papal and Church Patronage in the Seventeenth Century

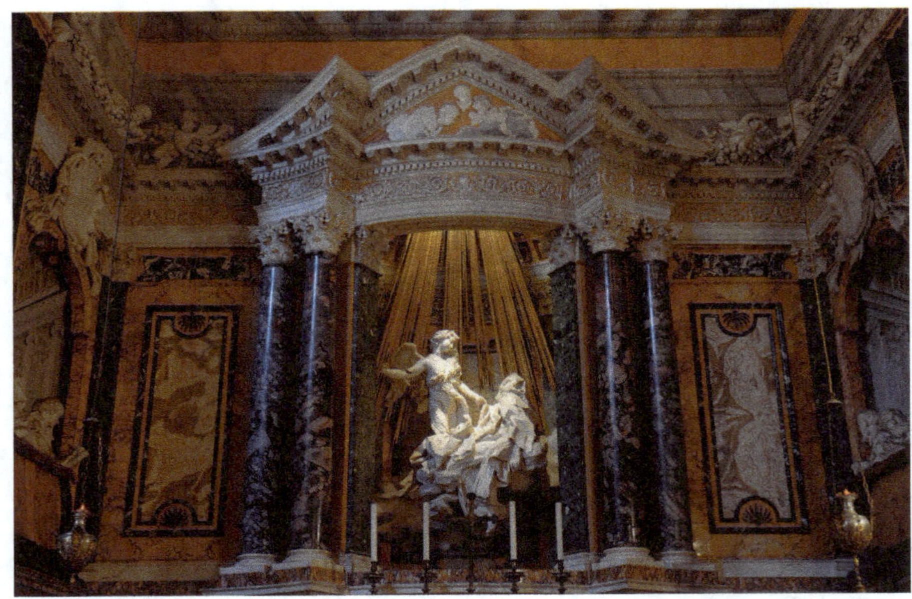

Figure 5.7 | Gian Lorenzo Bernini, *The Ecstasy of St. Teresa of Ávila*, 1645–1652, marble, life-size, Rome, Church of Santa Maria della Vittoria, Cornaro Chapel. Source: © Adam Eastland Art + Architecture / Alamy.

The glory of God?

By the seventeenth century Florence had lost its artistic dominance, and Rome became the major cultural centre of Italy. Rome's supremacy during this period is partly attributable to powerful and visionary papal patrons but also to their relationships with the artistic masters of their time. The **High Baroque** masters of the mid-seventeenth century, Gian Lorenzo Bernini (1598–1680), Pietro da Cortona (1596–1669) and Francesco Borromini (1599–1667), enjoyed constant papal patronage. When Urban VIII became Pope in 1623 he was alleged to have said to the young and precociously gifted Bernini: *It is your great good luck, Cavaliere ... to see Matteo Barberini Pope; but we are even luckier in that the Cavaliere Bernini lives at the time of Our pontificate* (Wittkower, *Art and Architecture in Italy 1600–1750*, p. 2).

With the help of their favourite artists, the **Baroque** popes – Urban VIII Barberini (ruled 1623–1644), Innocent X Pamphili (ruled 1644–1655) and Alexander VII Chigi (ruled 1655–1667) – set about rebuilding Rome's magnificence during the Catholic Counter-Reformation. (See *Chapter 4* for more details on the social and historical context of the seventeenth century.) St. Peter's in Rome, the heart of Christendom on earth, was their main focus, but a multitude of smaller projects, nearly as majestic, gained significant fame for their creators. The favoured prodigy of popes, Bernini was all too aware of his talents and the high status they afforded him. As historian Simon Schama points out, *[f]alse modesty was definitely not one of Gian Lorenzo Bernini's failings. But since there had never been a time when he has not been hailed as a human marvel, it's surprising he wasn't more swollen-headed* (Schama, *The Power of Art*, p. 82).

However, under the pontificate of Innocent X, the golden boy of Urban's empire predictably fell out of favour. A new Pope was always keen to make his own competitive mark on the city and, in addition, Bernini's devout life had suffered a sinful episode: he'd hired a servant to slash his mistress' face upon the discovery that she'd also been sleeping with the artist's brother. It was at this point, suffering a dip in both patronage and pride, that Bernini was given one of the most memorable commissions of his entire career. Cardinal Federico Cornaro became patron to one of Bernini's most important works when he commissioned him to create a private family chapel in the left **transept** of the church of S. Maria Vittoria in Rome. Cornaro paid 12,000 scudi, a very sizeable sum indeed, for his spectacular **aedicule** and, in so doing, allowed Bernini to create a masterpiece of both self-promotion and piety – probably in that order.

St. Teresa is modelled here as the patron's intercessor between heaven and earth, and even to modern eyes Bernini's illusionism is spectacularly effective. Bernini has incorporated the patron's family into the side walls in the same way that some painters incorporated their donors into altar paintings. Cardinal Cornaro is joined by deceased members of the Cornaro family to watch the mystery of their faith unfold. Set high in their theatre-style boxes, they discuss the event – a composition, one would assume, that was inspired by Bernini's set-designing past. The chapel's patron is distinguished from his deceased companions by his glance beyond the mystical sphere towards ours, which is earthly; and in so doing helps to draw us into the scene. Whatever its spiritual success, this altarpiece certainly helped to redeem Bernini's tainted social status and still serves to showcase his genius today; it remains a monument that innovatively fuses painting, sculpture and architecture.

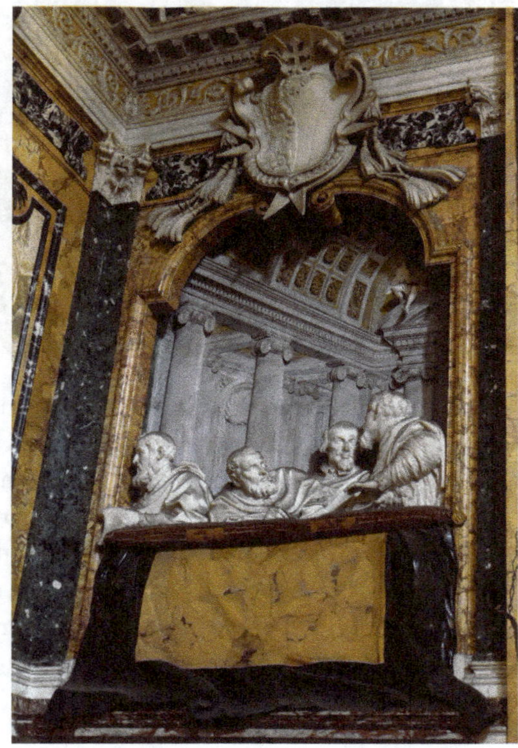

Figure 5.8 | Gian Lorenzo Bernini, Cornaro family sculpted into lateral walls of *The Ecstasy of St. Teresa of Ávila*, 1645–1652. Source: © Stefano Ravera / Alamy.

Art historian William Barcham has suggested that Cardinal Cornaro commissioned the *Ecstasy of St. Teresa* because he aspired to climb the papal hierarchy himself – he was the son of a Venetian Doge after all. The entrepreneurial Cardinal must have known that his choice of high-profile sculptor and dramatic multi-figure composition would keep him in the public eye (Harris, *Seventeenth-Century Art and Architecture*, p. 108).

Cardinal Cornaro fulfilled his personal need to make manifest his success and provide himself with a marble bridge to his place in heaven, but he also afforded Bernini artistic freedom to create a scene from St. Teresa's life as he, the artist, imagined it.

Not all artists were allowed the same degree of freedom by their patrons. One notable example of the control that could be exerted by patrons is provided by the wooden sculpture *Christ of Clemency*, 1603, made in the neighbouring country of Spain by Juan Martínez Montañés (1568–1649).

Christ of Clemency was commissioned for the private chapel of Mateo Vázquez de Leca (archdeacon of Carmona). Despite his presumed religiosity, Vázquez de Leca had consorted with prostitutes; supposedly, one memorable night, however, he was pursuing a woman who turned around to appear as a ghostly skeleton. This vision halted Vázquez de Leca's ungodly behaviour and prompted him to commission the aptly named *Christ of Clemency*. The patron saw to it that the representation of Christ was manipulated sufficiently to grant him the forgiveness he so desperately sought. Accordingly, the patron afforded very little artistic licence to Montañés; the contract stressed that Christ was *to be alive, before He had died with the head inclined towards the right side, looking to any person who might be praying at the foot of the crucifix, as if Christ Himself were speaking to him* (Bray et al., *The Sacred Made Real*, p. 25).

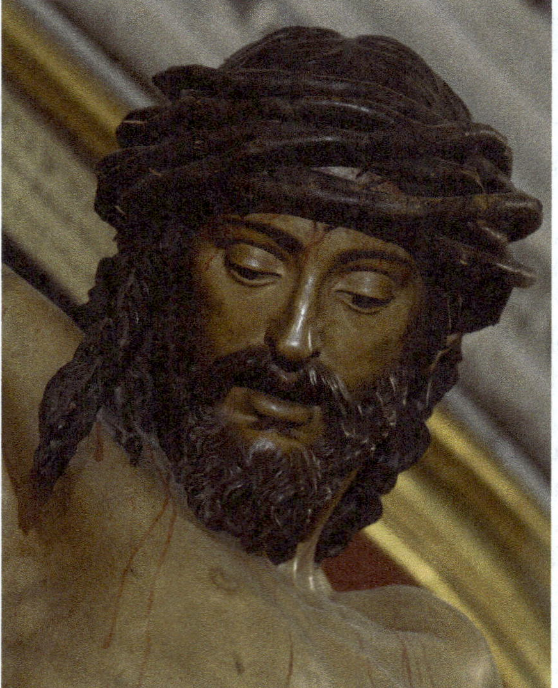

Figure 5.9 | Juan Martínez Montañés (polychromer unknown), *Christ of Clemency*, 1603, detail, polychromed wood, height 190 cm, Seville Cathedral. Source: akg-images / Album / Oronoz.

The stipulations set down in the contract have been adhered to: Christ's flesh is indeed still pink with the warmth of life so that he can grant forgiveness to the sinner at his feet. You may remember that we examined another seventeenth-century **polychrome** sculpture – Gregorio Fernández's, *Dead Christ*, c.1625–1630 – in *Chapter 2*, paying particular attention to the materials, techniques and processes involved in its creation. *Christ of Clemency* is also polychrome, and the painter's use of **chiaroscuro** only heightens the figure's realism and further suspends our disbelief. Three-dimensional tears roll down Christ's face, appearing as if about to fall through real space to reach the patron in a moment of forgiveness. In Christ's eyes there is an incredible alertness; in his raised eyebrows the knowledge of a significant moment; in his open mouth a message of forgiveness. This is an example of artists breaking with traditional depictions of Christ on the Cross in response to the specific demands of a patron, a patron who in this instance commissioned a work to fulfil his private need for redemption.

Patronage in the Eighteenth Century

Worldly motives

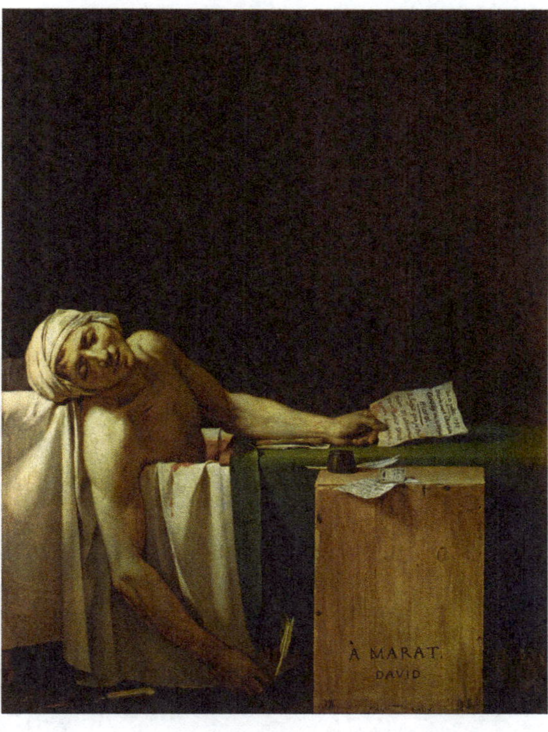

Figure 5.10 | Jacques-Louis David, *The Death of Marat*, 1793 (stabbed in his bath by Charlotte Corday, Paris, 13 July 1793), oil on canvas, 165 × 128 cm, Brussels, Musées Royaux des Beaux-Arts. Source: akg-images / André Held.

The relationship between an artist and his patron can be a fickle affair, and political allegiances may alter it over time. You may remember Jacques-Louis David's masterful 'history' painting *Oath of the Horatii*, 1784, examined in *Chapter 1*. The story is from Antiquity and was a royal commission for King Louis XVI. It was not long, however, before the artist would turn his back on his royal patron and, in 1792, sign the king's death warrant. During the French Revolution, David (1748–1825) joined the Jacobins, led by Robespierre (the man responsible for the Reign of Terror), and found himself as deputy in the Republican National Convention. It was during David's involvement with the Jacobins that he painted another image with which you will be familiar from *Chapter 1*, *The Death of Marat*, 1793.

According to historian Simon Schama, when David presented *Marat* to the Convention he said: *Citizens, the people ... yearn to see once more the features of their faithful friend. David, they cry, seize your brushes, avenge our friend. Avenge Marat ... I heard the voice of the people. I obeyed* (Schama, *The Power of Art*, p. 224).

The motive for David and the Convention was thus political propaganda: to promote the Jacobin, Jean-Paul Marat, and to perpetuate pro-revolutionary zeal. However, the **idealised** image of Marat, the journalist and co-conspirator of the Terror, would eventually haunt David: Robespierre, the revolutionary leader behind the execution of tens of thousands of civilians, was put to death, and David, lucky to be alive, was disgraced by his association with these two figures.

Not all patrons are religiously or politically motivated, however, and throughout history works of art have been commissioned for a variety of reasons. George Stubbs (1724–1806) painted *Whistlejacket*, c.1762, for the Marquess of Rockingham, the owner of this chestnut stallion. What motive did the Marquess have for commissioning such a painting of his horse? Using the Toolbox provided at the start of the book, what is it about this particular representation of a horse that indicates the patron's feelings towards it?

The eighteenth century was the epoch of the horse, and racing and breeding were the pursuit of the aristocracy. Whistlejacket is depicted as though he is an individual sitting for a portrait. Painted life-size on a monumental canvas, he is a testament to the wealth and élite social class to which his owner belonged. In this sense, the message of *Whistlejacket* is similar perhaps to that of Gainsborough's painting *Mr and Mrs Andrews* (examined briefly in *Chapter 1*): both were painted as manifestations of their patrons' successes. The motive was personal, egotistical and competitive.

The sheen of Whistlejacket's well-groomed coat, his confident rearing posture and the dynamic flash of white in his eye all convey his character but also his patron's status. Depicted with anatomical perfection, he conveys an image of athletic health. Compositionally isolated against a plain background, this chestnut stallion leaves the viewer in little doubt that they are looking at a 'champion' – as was certainly intended.

Figure 5.11 | George Stubbs, *Whistlejacket*, c.1762, oil on canvas, 292 × 246.4 cm, London, National Gallery. Source: The National Gallery, London / akg-images.

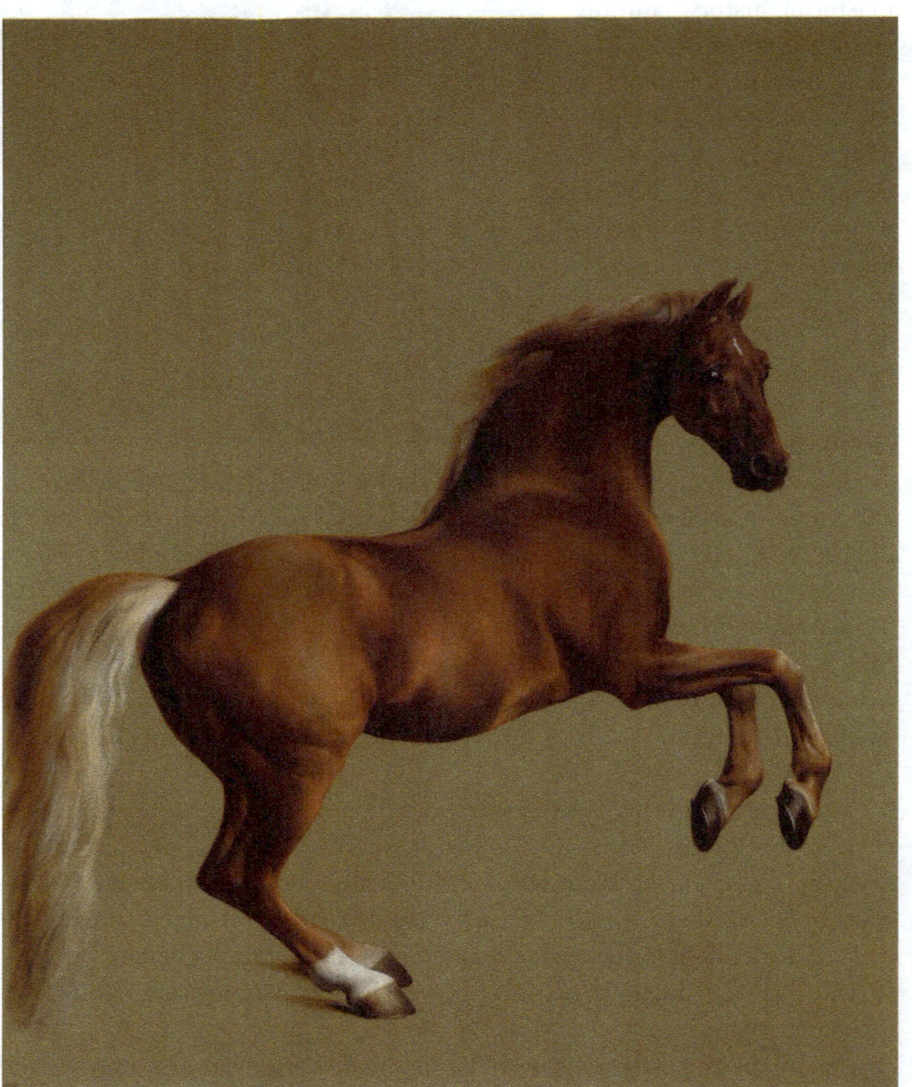

The Modern Artist and the Market in the Nineteenth Century

Solitary and against society?

Patronage and the status of the artist are concepts that evolve over time (as outlined in the Introduction to this chapter). Art was largely commission-based from the medieval period to the eighteenth century, at which point people began to be interested in acquiring works of art for their homes. The founding of auction houses, such as Sotheby's in 1744 and Christie's in 1766, to sell art commercially is evidence of this new development – something that strengthened in the nineteenth century with the rise of wealthy industrialists and a strengthening middle class. As Jonathan Harris puts it:

> *In the late nineteenth and twentieth centuries this dominant patronal relation broke down and artists began to produce works increasingly for what was (and still is) called the 'free market': a system or network of now largely socially unconnected artists, buyers, sellers, and influential intermediaries (such as dealers, agents, and critics).* (Harris, *Art History: The Key Concepts,* p. 229)

As the control that patrons typically had over artists was gradually relinquished, artists began to enjoy the freedom to express themselves more subjectively than ever before. The role of art critics became increasingly significant. Their judgements, published in newspapers and journals and widely disseminated, soon demonstrated the power to ruin or launch an artistic career. Art critic and poet Charles Baudelaire was an early champion of Manet and the Impressionists. Twentieth-century art critic Clement Greenberg not only championed the **Abstract Expressionists**, particularly Jackson Pollock, but, as we shall see, even attempted to define **Modernism** itself. Before exploring these developments, let us first examine the roots of the myth of the modern artist as a solitary and heroic individual.

Dutch artist Vincent van Gogh (1853–1890) exemplified the expressive qualities that may be seen in landscape painting, as we saw in the discussion of *Wheatfield with Crows*, 1890, in *Chapter 1*. In *Self-Portrait with Bandaged Ear*, 1889, the artist confronts us with the image of the artist as a solitary individual, while his bandaged ear, supposedly the result of a self-inflicted injury, tells, perhaps, of the personal cost at which such radical individualism was sustained (Figure 5.12).

5.1 What can you see?
Look at Van Gogh's *Self-Portrait with Bandaged Ear*, 1889. How has the artist's application of paint and use of colour contributed to our understanding of his status as a lonely and mentally tormented figure?

The image is unnerving because a lonely and possibly mentally disturbed man looks back at us, but at the same time the image can be placed in a tradition of heroic artistic self-portraits, going back to the Renaissance. Remember the *Self-Portrait*, 1500, by Albrecht Dürer? The artist was daring enough to portray himself as unmistakably Christ-like. Arguably, Van Gogh is following artistic tradition here in presenting himself as an isolated figure with piercing eyes and an aura of martyrdom.

In 1888, he travelled to Arles in the south of France in the hope of collaborating with artist friends, especially Paul Gauguin. Unfortunately, the trip didn't end well. The story goes that Van Gogh attempted to attack Gauguin with a razor which predictably precipitated Gauguin's premature departure.

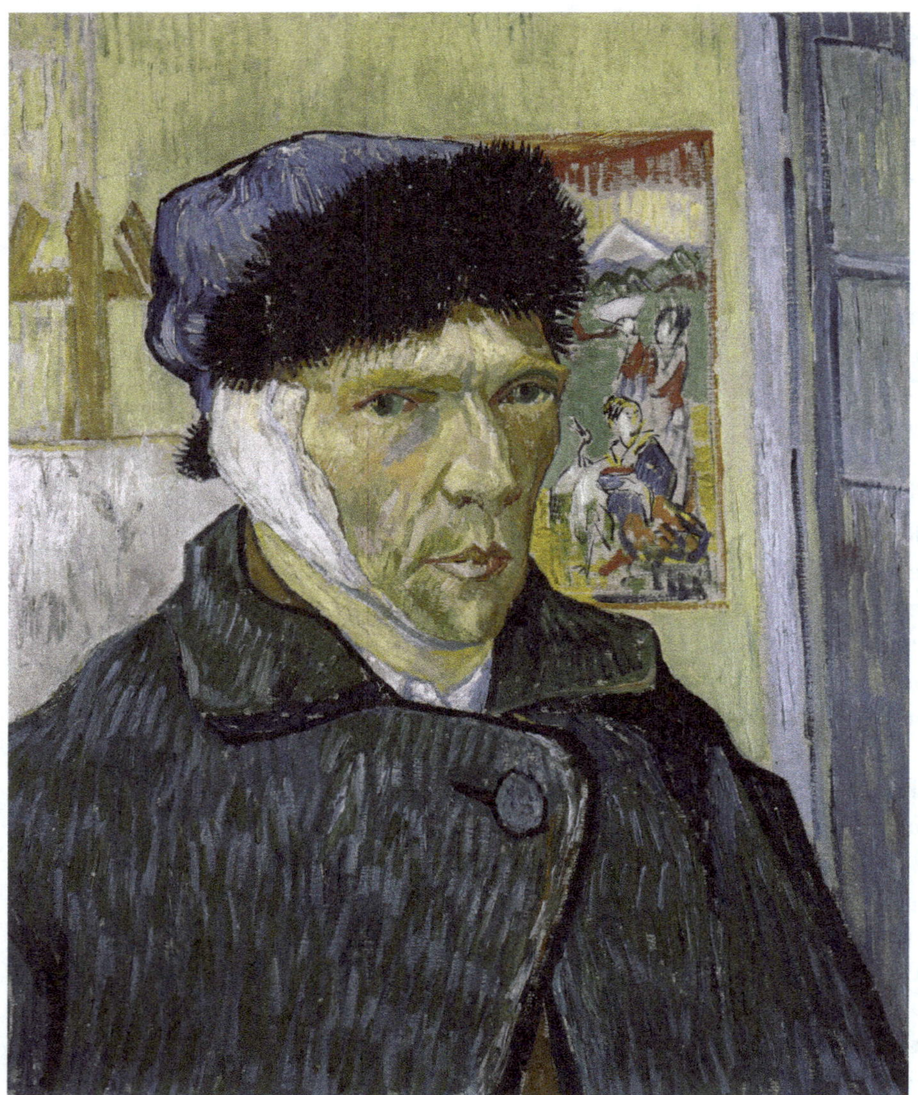

Figure 5.12 | Vincent van Gogh, *Self-Portrait with Bandaged Ear*, 1889, oil on canvas, 60 × 49 cm, London, Courtauld Institute. Source: The Art Archive / Courtauld Institute London / Superstock.

Supposedly in remorse for his attack on his friend, Van Gogh cut part of his own ear off, cementing his mythological notoriety as a mad artist. Recently, however, the self-inflicted slice-wound to the ear has been disputed by academics Hans Kaufmann and Rita Wildegans. In *Van Gogh's Ear: Paul Gauguin and the Pact of Silence* the suggestion is that Gauguin inflicted the injury on his friend in a violent exchange and the pair then made a pact to remain silent on the issue (Kaufman and Lustig, 'Van Gogh's Ear').

Van Gogh's life has been endlessly dissected and we're bound to be fascinated by suggestions such as that he went without food, or even ate his own paints in periods of paranoid depression. The fact that he died after apparently shooting himself only sets the seal on his fame. However, scholars insist that in the months leading up to his death, he had been enjoying one of his most prolific periods of artistic output. He was not drinking at this time and his sobriety probably heightened his artistic creativity. Historian Simon Schama also attempts to dispel the black clouds from our interpretation of the artist's work and convincingly disputes the myth that the artist's demise was inevitable:

In May 1890, the last springtime of his life, everything seemed to be going right for Vincent van Gogh. He was no longer neglected ... In Brussels his paintings had been shown alongside works by Cézanne, Renoir and Toulouse-Lautrec. One of them, The Red Vineyard, 1888, had even been sold for 400 francs ... In the Mercure de France an influential young critic, Albert Aurier, had praised him to the skies. (Schama, *The Power of Art*, p. 298)

In truth, we will never really know the reason why Van Gogh pulled the trigger on himself in the wheatfield that day (if indeed he did). The gun shot wasn't fatal: it was aimed below the chest, missing all his vital organs. In fact it seems very likely to have been the subsequent mismanagement of his care by homeopathic practitioner Dr. Gachet that ultimately killed him. We can only speculate about the success he might have enjoyed in his own lifetime had it not been cut short.

Financial worry almost certainly contributed to his malaise; and the lack of secure patronage contributed to this. **Feminist** art historian Griselda Pollock points out that it is not strictly true that Van Gogh did not have a patron, because in 1883 he entered into a dealer's contract with his brother Theo, who provided him with a fixed monthly income. Poverty seemed to beckon, however, when Vincent overspent on costly **pigments** such as **ultramarine**. In a letter to his beloved brother, Theo, the artist wrote:

I dare hope the burden will be a little less heavy for you, I even hope much less heavy.

I realize, to the point of being morally crushed and physically drained by it, that taking all in all, I have absolutely no other means of ever recovering what we have spent.

I cannot help it that my pictures do not sell well.

The day will come, however, when people will see they are worth more than the price of the paint and my living expenses, very meagre on the whole, which we put into them. (Van Gogh, 'To Theo van Gogh')

It is sad to reflect on the way that money worries haunted Van Gogh during his life, given the astonishing sums that his works fetch now. Van Gogh's *Vase with Fifteen Sunflowers*, 1888, was unsold during the artist's impoverished lifetime but more than 100 years later, in 1987, it sold for £24.75 million ($39.7 million). This astonishing price tripled the previous record and heralded a new era of super-priced art works in the twenty-first century. Cynically, it is in the commercial world's interest to perpetuate the myth surrounding artists like Van Gogh – his personal life makes him very saleable.

What the case of Van Gogh shows us is that in modern times, tremendous market value, recognition and success are dependent not necessarily on a patron but rather on powerful and wealthy collectors and museums vying for the most saleable commodity. Less than eight months after the sale of Van Gogh's *Vase with Fifteen Sunflowers*, 1888, its record price was topped by the sale of another of Van Gogh's flower paintings:

Van Gogh's glowing 'Irises' – painted in 1889 during the artist's first week at the asylum at St.-Remy – was sold at Sotheby's in New York last night for $53.9 million, the highest price ever paid for an artwork at auction. The sale of 100 artworks, in which 75 were sold, totalled $110 million, a record total for an art auction.

The fierce bidding for the Van Gogh masterpiece was witnessed by an international gathering of about 2,200 collectors, dealers, museum curators and officials, a standing-room-only crowd that watched the proceedings in person and over closed-circuit television. (Reif, 'Van Gogh's "Irises" Sells for $53.9 Million')

Van Gogh did not work to commission. A patron, other than his brother, might have been his financial saviour but undoubtedly his unpredictable temperament would have made a patronal relationship difficult. Indeed, patronage of the kind we encountered early on in this chapter seemed a thing of the past by the nineteenth century.

Twentieth Century

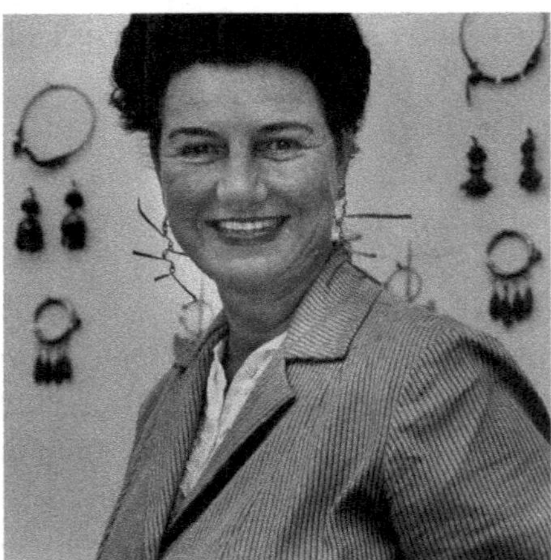

Figure 5.13 | Peggy Guggenheim. Source: Photo by Frank Scherschel / The LIFE Picture Collection / Getty Images.

Collectors and critics

In the twentieth century, the system by which artists derived a living changed. Rather than patrons commissioning specific works of art, it was increasingly the case that artists created works according to their own expressive and compositional decisions, which were then sought out and purchased by collectors. It was therefore the collectors who enhanced the status and commercial fortunes of particular artists, but they were, in turn, influenced by the judgements made in print by prominent critics. This can be seen, for example, by studying the way in which Jackson Pollock (1912–1956), the famous mid-century Abstract Expressionist, rose to prominence. Pollock was the *enfant terrible* of the art world, a womaniser and an alcoholic. His untimely death in a car accident at the age of 44 made him a media icon. Unlike Van Gogh, however, he enjoyed tremendous fame and fortune during his own lifetime, thanks in part to the efforts of the critic Clement Greenberg and the collector Peggy Guggenheim.

Peggy Guggenheim (1898–1979) was an American art collector and **gallerist**, the niece of the well-known art collector Solomon R. Guggenheim. During the 1930s she lived in France and collected largely European works, principally by **Cubist** and **Surrealist** artists. After the Second World War, she became a champion of American painting. Countless mid-twentieth century American artists received her patronal support. She lived a privileged life and gained an international reputation for serious collecting in a male-dominated profession. With no papacy or royal family, America relied on collectors like Guggenheim to form the basis of their collections. She is credited with discovering the iconic American Abstract Expressionist painter Jackson Pollock, and her significant private collection in Venice continues to draw visitors from all over the globe.

In 1943 Peggy Guggenheim commissioned Pollock to create *Mural*, a vast painting (on canvas) for her new house in New York. Apart from the enormous scale of the canvas, she left its style and content up to the emerging new 'genius' she had just discovered. The freedom this modern patronal relationship accorded the artist, which Pollock himself described as having 'no strings' attached to it, was unrecognisable by comparison to those in previous centuries (see the article on the University of Iowa Museum of Art website 'More about *Mural*').

Pollock's status was partly attributable to his innovation, which was acknowledged by fellow Abstract Expressionist Willem de Kooning: *Every so often, a painter has to destroy painting. Cézanne did it. Picasso did it with*

20 He was called this by *Time* magazine: *Time*, 'Art: The Wild Ones'.

Cubism. Then Pollock did it. He busted our idea of a picture to hell. Then there could be new paintings again (quoted in Hatje Cantz, 'Action-Painting').

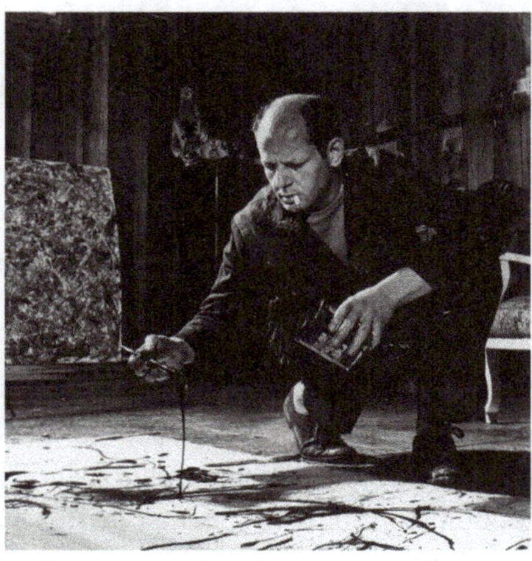

Figure 5.14 | Artist Jackson Pollock painting in his studio.
Source: Photo by Martha Holmes / The LIFE Picture Collection / Getty Images.

He was the 'bad-boy' genius, a heady commercial combination. And the involvement of the media perpetuated the myth, giving him the nickname 'Jack the Dripper'.[20]

Guggenheim's patronage was certainly important, but it was also Clement Greenberg's critical support that helped ensure lasting and iconic success for Pollock. Famously, and at a very early point in Pollock's career, Greenberg hailed him as the 'greatest painter of the age'. Equally importantly for our purposes in this chapter, the terms in which Greenberg hailed Pollock helped to establish a new appreciation of the formal qualities of an artwork rather than what it might represent – and this led to a new value being given to art as a cultural activity.

Greenberg's theory of Modernism hinges on the importance of formal properties of artworks such as colour, line, space and composition. He claims that modernist painting remains true to its medium and that modern artists focus on the effects of their chosen medium alone. Thus, modern painting draws attention first and foremost to its pigment, its flatness, rather than seeking to trick the viewer into reading illusionistic properties in an object. Greenberg saw a linear progression in the history of art to the point where painting had 'purified' itself by concerning itself only with its own medium. He saw this as, in effect, a march towards abstraction and 'flatness'. For him,

Figure 5.15 | Jackson Pollock, *Mural*, 1943, oil on canvas, 247 × 605 cm, Iowa City, University Museum of Art. Gift from Peggy Guggenheim.
Source: akg-images / ©The Pollock-Krasner Foundation ARS, NY and DACS, London 2015.

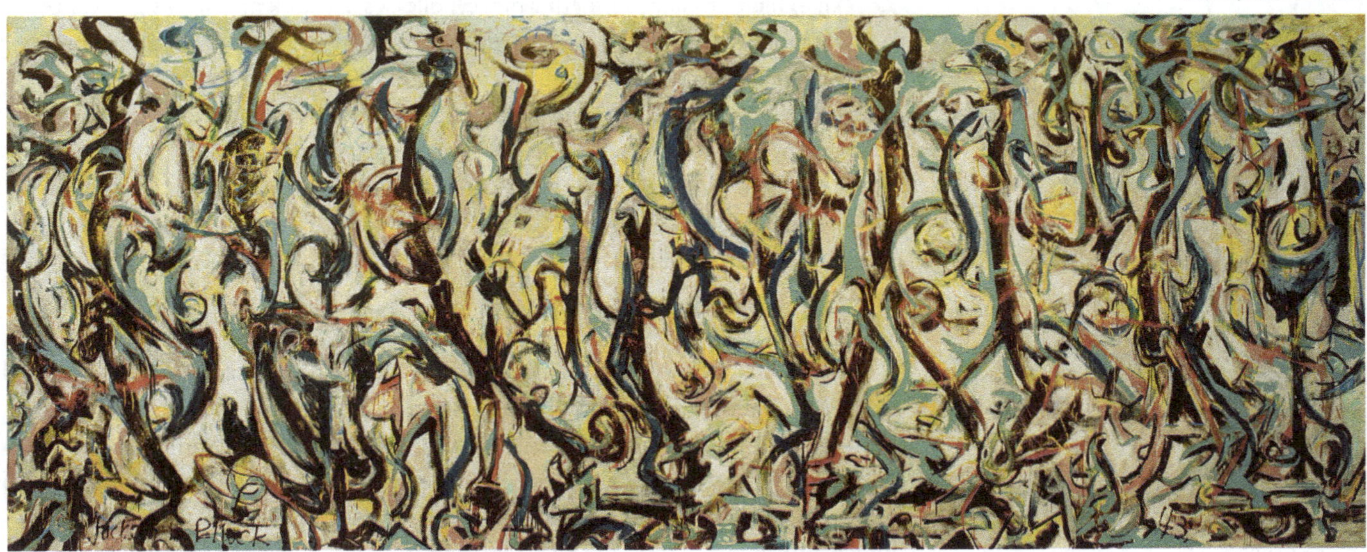

Figure 5.16
Art critic Clement Greenberg.
Source: Photo by Leonard Mccombe / The LIFE Images Collection / Getty Images.

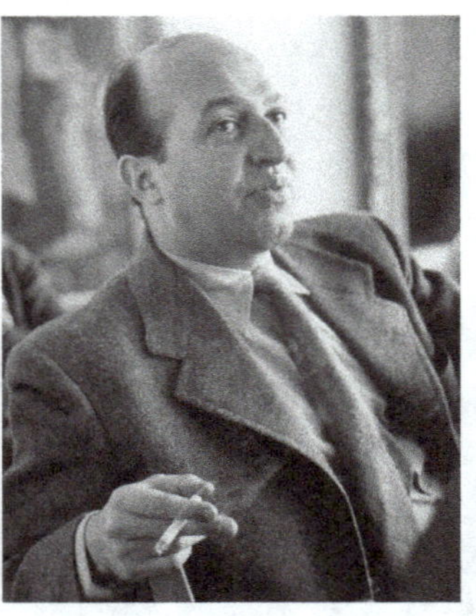

Pollock's use of paint represented a real **truth to medium** – brown, white, grey and black, dripped from a can in as unmediated a way as possible. Accordingly, he saw Pollock as the most important painter of his age – the one who captured the modern experience – the **Zeitgeist**. In 1948 Greenberg wrote:

Isolation, or rather the alienation that is its cause, is the truth – isolation, alienation, naked and revealed unto itself, is the condition under which the true reality of our age is experienced. And the experience of this true reality is indispensable to any ambitious art. (Quoted in Wood, Frascina and Harrison, *Modernism in Dispute: Art Since the Forties,* p. 153)

Greenberg championed the Abstract Expressionists as Charles Baudelaire had championed the Impressionists nearly a century earlier. Baudelaire's prime value was 'the transitory'; Greenberg's was 'medium-specificity'. The belief, shared by modernist critics a century apart, that art's chief value is in its ability to capture and express its moment, was a new and significant claim concerning the status of art in society.

5.1 Critical debates: critical analysis versus artistic intention

Although Clement Greenberg developed theories about the development of art, these did not necessarily match the ways in which artists themselves understood or spoke about their work. In a statement Greenberg conveniently ignored, Pollock gives us an insight into what he intended his art to be about: *'I don't care for "abstract expressionism"... and it's certainly not "non-objective", and not "nonrepresentational" either. I'm very representational some of the time, and a little all of the time.'* (Quoted in Wood, Frascina and Harrison, *Modernism in Dispute: Art Since the Forties,* p. 155)

How does this statement from Pollock refute Greenberg's claims about the artist's place in the progression of Western art?

In exhibitions abroad, furthermore, Pollock's art took on a new significance. It was assimilated into the United States' Cold War politics as an example of the creative freedom enjoyed by its citizens in contrast to their Soviet counterparts under Communism. The exhibitions of Abstract Expressionist work partly funded by the CIA, though unknown to the artists, to promote the idea of art's freedom in the West as opposed to the communist world's control of art, was a form of political propaganda.[21] Why do you think Greenberg chose to ignore these contextual details?

During his lifetime, Pollock's paintings made the artist hugely famous and earned him a feature article in the magazine *Life* in the 8 August 1949 issue, with the title, 'Jackson Pollock: Is He the Greatest Living Painter in the United States?' Nevertheless it was only after his death that his works began to reach the astronomical values they claim today. In 2006 Sotheby's sold Pollock's *Number 5*, 1948, for $140 million.

21 See Cockcroft, 'Abstract Expressionism: Weapon of the Cold War' and Saunders, 'Modern Art was CIA Weapon'.

The artist as celebrity and the rise of the supercollector

Pollock didn't particularly seek self-promotion and, arguably, the pressure he felt as a result of his fame contributed to his unhappiness before his untimely death. Nevertheless, self-promotion and the technological means with which to do it is arguably the hallmark of the media-saturated twentieth and twenty-first centuries.

We have already examined the changing status of the artist from the **Middle Ages** through to the Renaissance, and witnessed the birth of the artist as celebrity, but in modern times this celebrity has taken on almost epoch-defining proportions. The contemporary British artist Tracey Emin (born 1963) has received a series of institutional honours and been granted a number of solo exhibitions. Yet her high profile and newsworthy status could arguably be ascribed to her representation of taboo subjects, her sensational autobiographical subject matter and her former 'bad girl' lifestyle, as much as to serious critical and public admiration of her art. Perhaps the most significant factor that helped shape her success was the relationship that was made over many years with the collector Charles Saatchi.

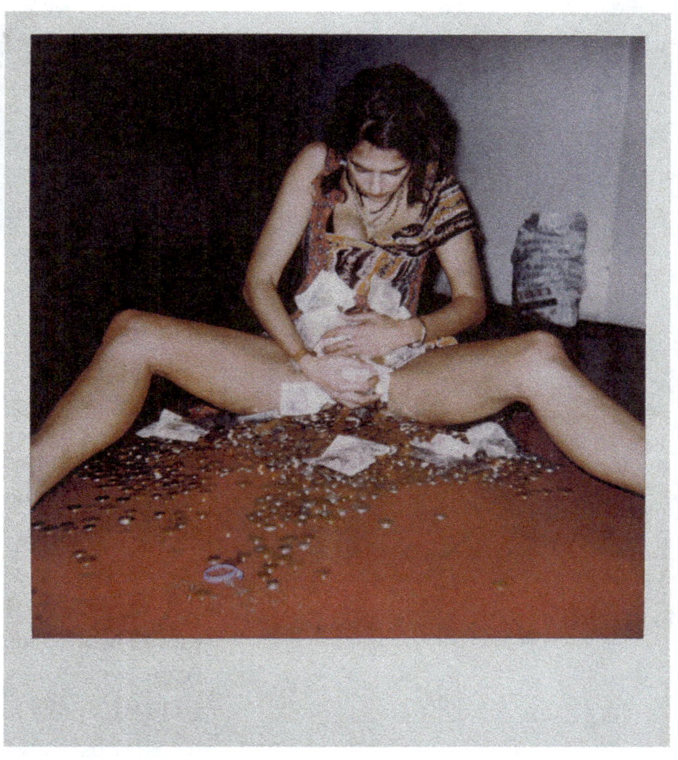

Figure 5.17 | Tracey Emin, *I've Got It All*, 2000, ink-jet print, 124 × 109 cm. Source: ©Tracey Emin. All rights reserved, DACS 2015. Image courtesy White Cube.

As well as taking part in iconic group exhibitions such as 'Sensation', 1997, and the Turner Prize, 1999, the artist has enjoyed a number of solo exhibitions including: 'My Major Retrospective (1982–1992)', 1994; 'I Need Art Like I Need God', 1997; 'Tracey Emin Museum, 1995–1997'; 'Sagacho Space', 1998; 'Everyone's Bleeding', 1999; 'You Forgot to Kiss My Soul', 2001. She also represented Britain in the Venice Biennale and collaborated with the internationally acclaimed artist Louise Bourgeois in the exhibition 'Do Not Abandon Me', 2010.

Emin's distinctive persona and commercial success have provided her with the opportunity to model for controversial clothes designer Vivienne Westwood. *I've Got It All*, 2000, features Emin sitting on the floor with open legs framing and almost consuming her independently earned wealth. Its blatant vulgarity is characteristic of the artist's **oeuvre**. The money, together with the artist's designer dress, is thought to relate to Emin's recent financial success and public recognition, but they jar with the basement-style space in which she sits. Professor Peter Osborne describes the work's connotations in terms of:

> *a certain tabloid triumphalism of the 'loadsamoney' variety. (Pictures of pools/lottery winners covered in cash – sometimes posed naked on beds – are a staple of British tabloid journalism.)*
>
> *... The artist is wearing a Vivienne Westwood dress ... Designer cloth-*

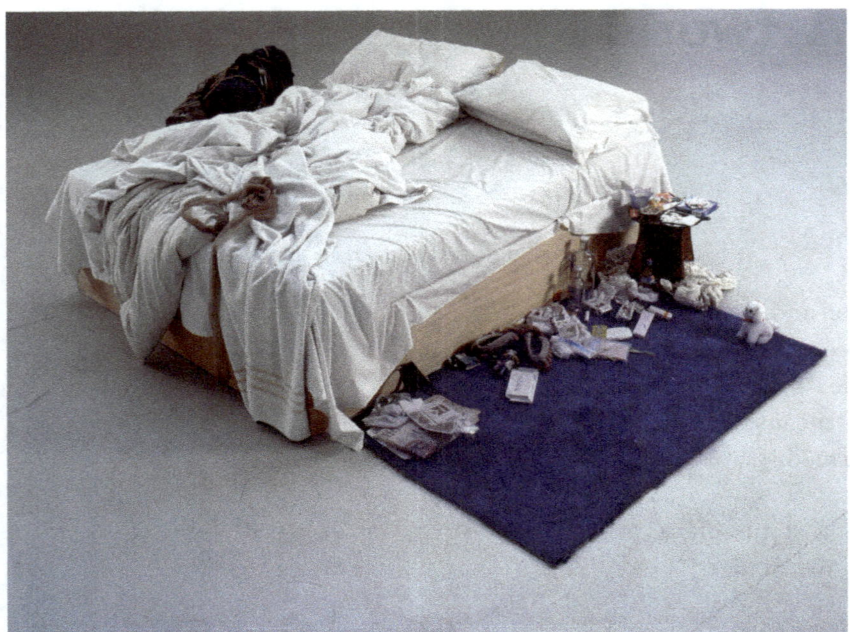

Figure 5.18 | Tracey Emin, *My Bed*, 1998, mixed media (mattress, linens, various memorabilia), maximum width 234 cm. Source: ©Tracey Emin. All rights reserved, DACS 2015. Image courtesy Saatchi Gallery, London. Photo: Prudence Cuming Associates Ltd.

ing was at the forefront of the consumer booms of the 1980s and 1990s ... Emin's dress, then, is a sign of success ... she has crossed the divide from the ordinary (the world of that carrier-bag, the high street) to the extraordinary (the dress and the occasions to wear it) and both must be present in order to see it. (Townsend and Merck, *The Art of Tracey Emin*, pp. 45, 55)

The **installation** *My Bed*, 1998, shown at Tate Gallery in 1999 as part of Emin's Turner Prize-nominated exhibition, is a confessional work with a supposedly autobiographical representational value. It stems, apparently, from a dark episode in the artist's life and is said to represent four days she spent under the covers, contemplating suicide. The installation had no patron, but it sold to art collector and gallery owner Charles Saatchi for £150,000 on the **secondary art market**; Emin's bed became Saatchi's bed overnight.

Saatchi – who supposedly out-bid Tate to acquire *My Bed* for his collection – represents the continued ascendency of private enterprise and commerce in the face of the continuing demise of state patronage. He was born in Baghdad in 1943 but his family left their native Iraq and arrived in London in 1946. He made his fortune from the advertising firm Saatchi & Saatchi, which he established with his brother, Maurice, in 1970. In 1978, Saatchi & Saatchi changed political advertising with their epoch-defining poster 'Labour isn't working'; its sub-title read 'Britain's better off with the Tories'. Their campaign helped to bring the Conservatives, led by Margaret Thatcher, to power. In turn, the agency itself became a super-brand and the Saatchi brothers were propelled to the international forefront of advertising.

5.1 Explore this example
Examine the work, persona and status of the Mexican painter Frida Kahlo. Can you draw any similarities between Kahlo's work and Emin's?

It is not the case that Saatchi has shaped the contemporary art world entirely in his image. Rather, it seems that his interest was piqued by a generation of young artists, Emin and Damien Hirst among them, who already seemed to share his interests (not least in making money) and his market-orientated world-view. Saatchi's first serious art collection was housed in the Saatchi Gallery in Boundary Road, London, and one of its first exhibits was the installation *A Thousand Years*, 1990 by British artist Damien Hirst (born 1965). Until their professional relationship ended in 2003, Saatchi was Hirst's most constant patron and is widely believed to have been responsible for the young maverick's fame and fortune. Hirst was shortlisted for the Turner Prize in 1992, winning the competition in 1995 with *Mother and Child, Divided*, 1993. His diamond-encrusted skull *For The Love of God*, 2007, is reported to have sold for £50 million – a breath-taking testament to materialism.

The rise of Hirst demonstrates the flowering of the kind of celebrity status found in seed form in the Early Renaissance. Furthermore, in Hirst was born the idea of artist *as* curator: in 1988, while still a student at Goldsmiths College, he conceived and curated the critically acclaimed 'Freeze' show in London's Docklands. Saatchi visited the exhibition and a famous collaboration between the pair ensued, leading to multi-million pound success and lasting celebrity. The relationship could be considered analogous to that between the High Renaissance master Michelangelo and Pope Julius II; certainly both were self-promoting, celebrity-making, tempestuous and historically significant in terms of creating an artistic legacy.

It is not so much the mansion he owns or the hundreds of millions he is worth that matter, says Damien Hirst, it is the recognition they bring that counts.

(Brooks, 'It's the Fame I Crave, Says Damien Hirst')

Unlike in the **quattrocento**, however, the twentieth- and twenty-first-century art markets are aided by 'the dealer'. In the early 1990s Hirst was represented by dealer Jay Jopling and one of the most famous triangles in the art world was in operation: Damien Hirst, the shock-tactic artist; Charles Saatchi, the patron/supercollector; Jay Jopling, the charismatic dealer. An amalgam of artistic controversy, marketing might and the power to set trends was a fortune-winning formula, as gallerist and writer Gregor Muir describes:

> *As the nation's economy staggered through the Nineties, Saatchi found an explosion of talent on his own doorstep. What was more, the artists were producing reasonably priced work. As his attentions turned from New York to London, Saatchi started to buy up the block. Enter Jay Jopling, the perfect dealer for the Saatchi era – and what better artist to take on than Hirst? The Holy Trinity had arrived: artist, dealer, and collector, all destined to become key figures in the history of young British art.* (Muir, *Lucky Kunst: The Rise and Fall of Young British Art,* p. 36)

The relationship between Hirst and Saatchi was also shaped through a series of eye-catching public exhibitions, indicating the increasing influence that such public displays had on the status of both art and individual artists in this period. In 1990 Hirst co-curated 'Gambler', a show from which Charles Saatchi acquired *A Thousand Years*, 1990, a double-chambered glass case which enclosed the severed head of a cow in one compartment, maggots, flies and an insect-o-cutor in the other. The stench from the rotting head made the artwork notorious but it also necessitated its prosthetic substitute. It was one of many of the artist's identity-defining animal installations. Hirst would win the Turner Prize five years later with an animal-based artwork, demonstrating once more the brevity of life and the inevitability of death.

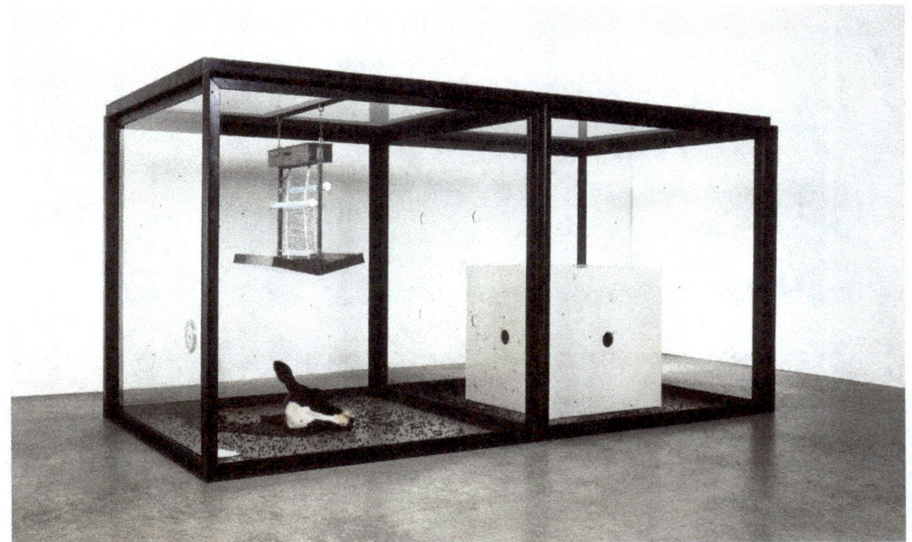

Figure 5.19 | Damien Hirst, *A Thousand Years*, 1990, glass, steel, silicone rubber, painted MDF, insect-o-cutor, cow's head, blood, flies, maggots, metal dishes, cotton wool, sugar and water, 207.5 × 400 × 215 cm. Source: © Damien Hirst and Science Ltd. All rights reserved, DACS 2015. Photo: Roger Wooldridge.

Falling under each other's spell, Saatchi offered to purchase whatever Hirst chose to create for the Saatchi Gallery's exhibition 'Young British Artists' in 1992. Saatchi's large north London space allowed for large-scale installations in a wide range of media. The show featured Hirst's *The Physical Impossibility of Death in the Mind of Someone Living*, 1991, and *A Thousand Years*, 1990. The former, the show's signature work, became an international art icon, an emblem of the **YBA** (Young British Artists) and synonymous with its patron. Saatchi had secured the 'bad boy' of art – and newsworthy visuals to match. A 14 foot Australian tiger shark suspended in a vitrine of formaldehyde was the ultimate, updated **memento mori**.

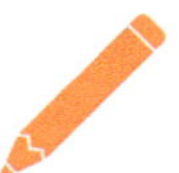

5.2 Explore this example
Compare the seventeenth-century Dutch genre painting by Steenwyck, *Still Life: An Allegory of the Vanities of Human Life*, c.1640, featured in *Chapter 1*, with either of Hirst's works examined in this chapter, or his diamond-encrusted skull *For the Love of God*, 2007.

Gregor Muir sums up well the notoriety and critical dismissal of Hirst's shark:

Everyone knows Hirst's 'The Physical Impossibility of Death in the Mind of Someone Living', the tiger shark in a glass tank filled with water and formaldehyde. Otherwise known as 'the shark', it has embedded itself in the public imagination to such a degree that it might be said to be the contemporary equivalent to the 'Mona Lisa'. Commissioned by Charles Saatchi for £50,000, it caused a public outcry when it was finally unveiled at the Boundary Road Gallery. This wasn't art! At best, it was inhumane. More importantly, how much did it cost? 'The Sun' newspaper paraded the headline '£50,000 for Fish without Chips'. Needless to say, thanks to the ensuing furore, Hirst broke through the barrier of an otherwise clandestine art world and became a household name. (Muir, *Lucky Kunst: The Rise and Fall of Young British Art,* p. 44)

Hirst's rise to fame, and the rise to prominence of the Saatchi artists more generally, were aided by two further key artistic institutions of the 1990s, both of which chimed with the mood of the times: The Turner Prize and Goldsmiths College. The Turner Prize, sponsored by Channel 4 Television, was founded in 1984. In a bid to enthuse the collectors of the future, the organisers enlisted the media to raise the profile of contemporary British art, which

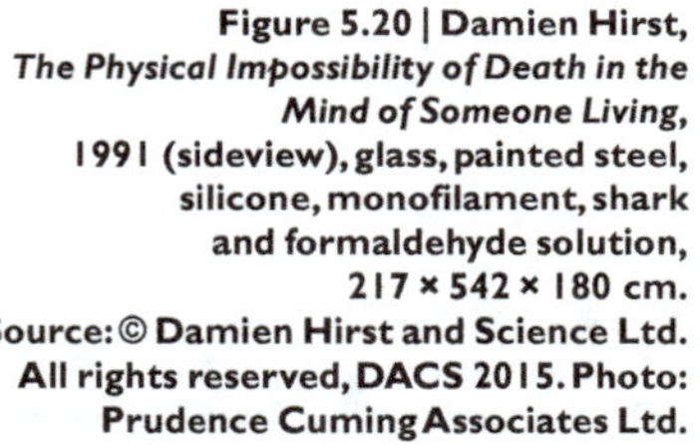

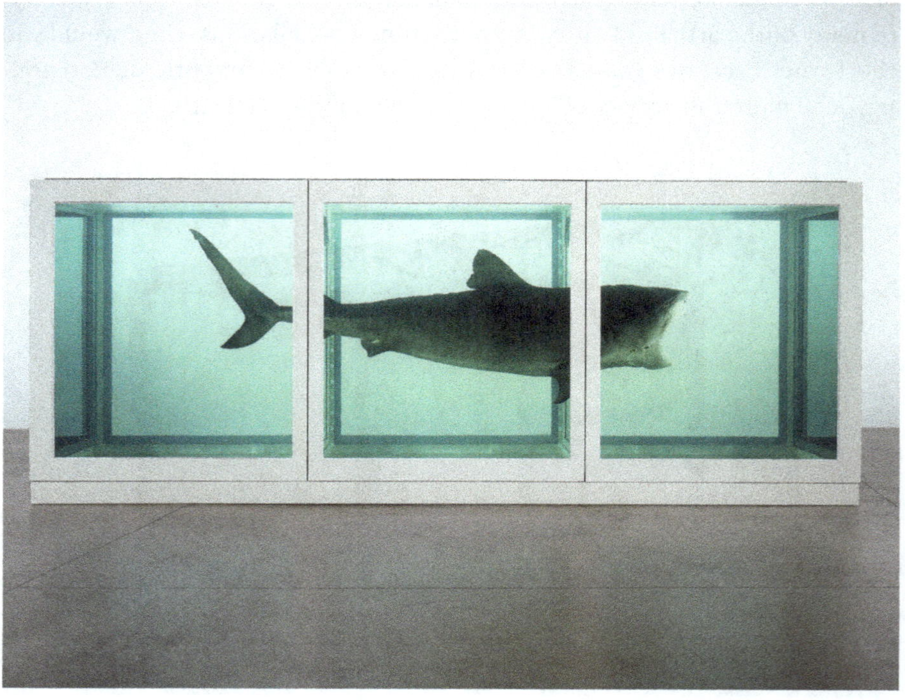

Figure 5.20 | Damien Hirst, *The Physical Impossibility of Death in the Mind of Someone Living*, 1991 (sideview), glass, painted steel, silicone, monofilament, shark and formaldehyde solution, 217 × 542 × 180 cm. Source: © Damien Hirst and Science Ltd. All rights reserved, DACS 2015. Photo: Prudence Cuming Associates Ltd.

22 The full title of the exhibition was: 'Sensation: Young British Artists from The Saatchi Collection.'

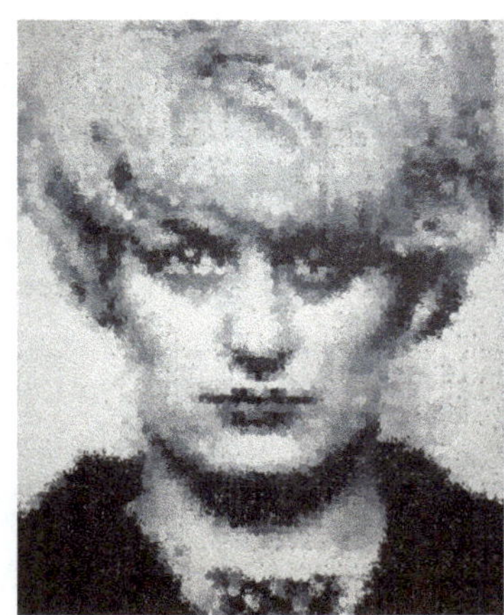

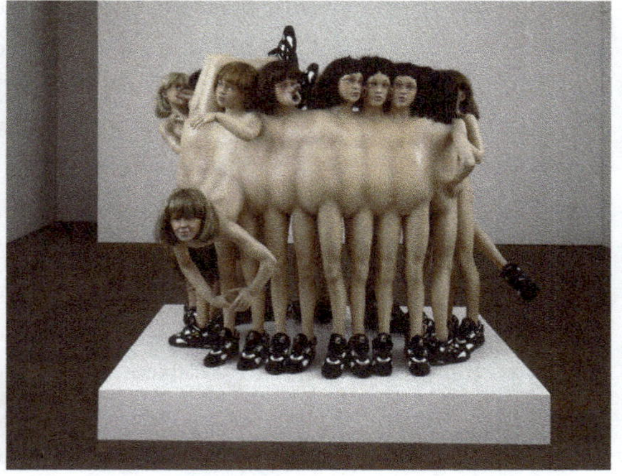

Left to right:
Figure 5.21 | Marcus Harvey, *Myra*, 1995, acrylic on canvas, 396 × 320 cm. Source: Image courtesy of Marcus Harvey and Vigo Gallery. © Marcus Harvey. All Rights Reserved, DACS 2015.

Figure 5.22 | Jake and Dinos Chapman, *Zygotic Acceleration, Biogenetic, and De-sublimated Libidinal Model* (Enlarged × 1000), 1995, fibreglass, resin, paint, wigs and trainers, 150 × 180 × 140 cm. Source: © Jake and Dinos Chapman. All Rights Reserved, DACS 2015. Image courtesy White Cube.

had always courted controversy and media attention. The 1995 Turner Prize exhibition attracted unprecedented numbers of visitors who queued daily to see the work of the shortlisted artists. Many were curious to see Damien Hirst's *Mother and Child, Divided* which created a tidal wave of tabloid excitement: *Have they gone stark-raving mad? The Turner Prize for Modern Art (worth £20,000) has gone to Damien Hirst, the 'artist' whose works are lumps of dead animals* (Button, *The Turner Prize: Twenty Years*, p. 112).

The influence of Goldsmiths College, the equivalent of an educational super-brand for artistic impresarios, cannot be underestimated. Its art department is recognised internationally as fostering many of the generation of artists who became known as the YBA, and who dominated the Turner Prize nomination lists during the 1990s and beyond.

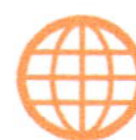

See the companion website for more information on the status-saturated competition that is the Turner Prize.

In addition to these institutions, the next important exhibition in this story was the non-Saatchi-curated, but wholly Saatchi-influenced 'Sensation', held at the Royal Academy in 1997.[22] This show displayed 110 works by YBA from the Saatchi Collection, and it attracted both high levels of media coverage and public outrage. Indeed, it was probably its transgressive nature that made it commercially successful.

In the UK, it was Marcus Harvey's *Myra*, 1995, juxtaposed with the Chapman Brothers' sexually mutant children that caused a storm. The overtly paedophilic associations of the latter made a latent connection with Myra Hindley's role in the sickening murder of five children. According to lecturer, writer and curator Julian Stallabrass: *In a curatorial strategy that Saatchi was very likely to have influenced, the child murderer Myra was hung adjacent to the Chapman Brothers* Zygotic Acceleration, Biogenetic, and De-sublimated Libidinal Model (Stallabrass, *High Art Lite: The Rise and Fall of Young British Art*, p. 213).

5.2 What can you see?
Describe the factors that combine to make Harvey's portrait of Myra Hindley so shocking. How has Harvey's use of the **acrylic** medium, application technique and choice of colour palette (discussed in *Chapter* 2) affected our interpretation of his work? Frequently attacked for being hideously perverse, the Chapman Brothers' *Zygotic Acceleration, Biogenetic, and De-sublimated Libidinal Model* is itself an attack on the sexualisation of children by the fashion industry; but, how does the work's **fibreglass** medium, mannequin appearance and addition of the readymade trainers contribute to its meaning?

Artist Jenny Saville (born 1970), examined in *Chapter 1* and *Chapter 6*, has enjoyed seven solo exhibitions since 1996, and her commercial success has been largely attributed to Saatchi; she was one of his early protégés. He is said to have first spotted her work at the 'Critics' Choice' show in 1993, whereupon he commissioned 15 of her paintings for the Saatchi Collection and put her on the road to financial security and wider recognition. In the 'Sensation' exhibition, Saville's controversial nudes fuelled media interest and perpetuated the success of Saatchi's new acquisitions. Artist and collector became inextricably linked. Was it the case that Saville had to relinquish a degree of control as a result, however:

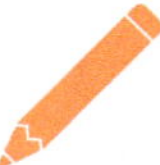

5.3 Explore this example
In 2003, the Saatchi collection moved from Boundary Road to London's old County Hall, then in 2008 from County Hall to Duke of York's Headquarters in Chelsea. All these spaces have shared the capacity to exhibit large mixed-media installations, and all have featured Richard Wilson's *20:50*, 1987. Research an image of this installation and work out what makes it so spectacular.

I just heard today that Saatchi has put frames round most of my paintings ... Now that's not the point – the figures are supposed to challenge the edges of the canvas. Putting a boundary around them just gets them wrong ... I want to make an installation out of this painting [that is, 'Strategy', 1994] – put a mirror across the gallery so the viewer can read the reversed text. But I'm having to really fight to make that happen. (Hatton and Walker, *Supercollector: A Critique of Charles Saatchi,* p. 154)

As we established at the beginning of this chapter, a patron's motivation for commissioning a work of art or architecture is an important issue. So, what are Saatchi's motives for patronage and collecting? Gordon Burn indirectly asked Saatchi this very question:

First question [from Burn]: Would he describe his collecting as: (a) a hobby; (b) an obsession; (c) a dalliance; (d) an investment opportunity; (e) a bid for immortality?

And the message came back [from Saatchi]: all of the above apart from (e). (Burn, *Sex & Violence, Death & Silence,* p. 290)

Like the Medici family in Renaissance Italy, who were businessmen with ambition to rule a city and invest in their cultural legacy, Saatchi is both increasing his private fortune and making his own impact on the history of British art. While a patron supports an artist financially and may have some influence over the work as a result, a collector buys work indirectly on the secondary market via auctions and galleries. Nevertheless, when a collector is wealthy enough to out-bid the competition, and to buy (and then sell) *en masse* many or all of an artist's works, he or she exerts comparable influence to that of a traditional patron. According to Hatton and Walker, because Charles Saatchi is both patron and collector, he is classed as a 'supercollector'.

Saatchi's purchasing strategy has been of great importance both to individual artists in establishing their careers and in helping to establish the status of British art as at the forefront of international trends and the international market. If Saatchi had not provided this support, would anyone else have done so? And would British art today be as internationally successful as it is?

Whatever you think of Charles's taste for dots, unmade beds, discarded condoms, pickled sharks, bisected cows, frolicking child mannequins with penises for noses, there's no doubt that, under his patronage, London has become Europe's – perhaps the world's – modern-art capital. (Aldridge, 'Ad You Like It: The Bloody Battle Between the Saatchis').

However, according to late journalist and author Gordon Burn, Saatchi not only has the ability to 'make' an artist, but also to 'break' them:

[b]eing taken up by Charles Saatchi has become one of the conditions of success for an artist in recent years. Being dropped by him, it is now becoming clear, can have equally devastating repercussions. (Burn, *Sex & Violence, Death & Silence,* p. 291)

Charles Saatchi, the supercollector of the twentieth century, presumably reflects upon his status, and, as Hatton and Walker point out in their **socialist** critique of him, his purchase of Ashley Bickerton's *The Patron*, 1997, is perhaps *a sign of growing self-awareness and a willingness to tolerate criticism* (Hatton and Walker, *Supercollector: A Critique of Charles Saatchi*, p. 186).

It is certainly unlikely that Julius II would have purchased such a damning critique of his own monumental cultural investment.

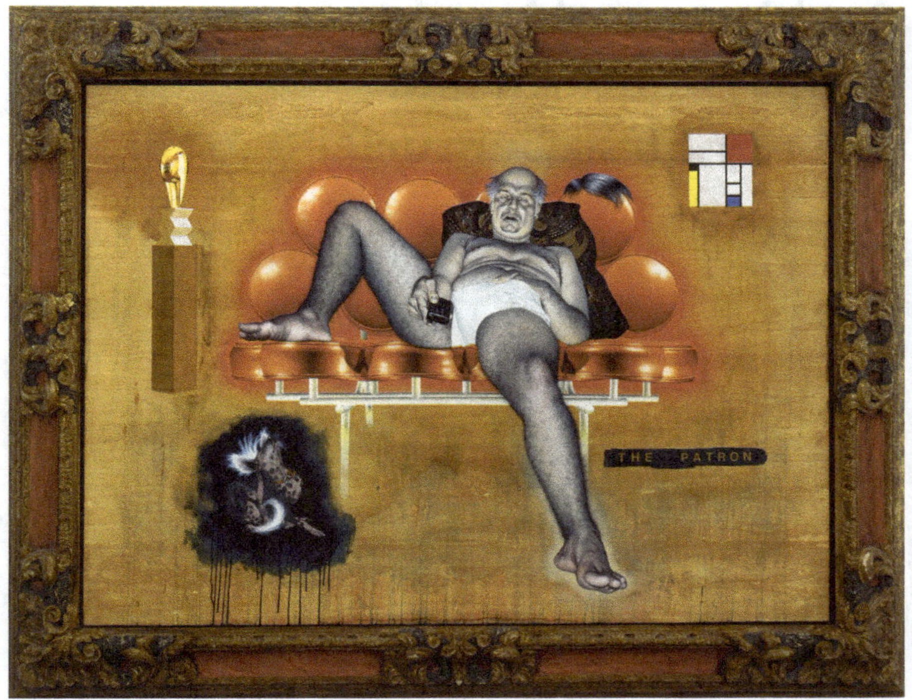

Figure 5.23 | Ashley Bickerton,
The Patron,
1997, oil, acrylic, pencil and aniline dye on wood, 167.5 × 228.5 cm.
Source: Courtesy the artist and Lehmann Maupin, New York and Hong Kong.

In July 2010 Saatchi announced that he was donating his gallery's collection to the nation. What are we to make of this philanthropic contribution? Recently, he has created new ways for artists to show their works for free, online, via his website. His facilitation of a free exhibition website allows over 100,000 artists to sell their work directly without incurring commission fees.

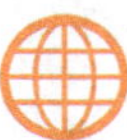

See the companion website for details on Saatchi's facilitation of a free exhibition website, which allows over 100,000 artists to sell their work directly without incurring commission fees.

Saatchi appears to consider this kind of direct, artist-to-audience – and potentially artist-to-buyer – viewing as enabling artists to escape potentially constraining relationships to patrons, collectors or dealers. He also appears to view it as indicating the obsolescence of art criticism. On the role of the critic, Saatchi, perhaps ironically, comments as follows:

[N]o one critic matters that much, whatever their credentials ... The days when critics could create an art movement by declaring the birth of 'Abstract Expressionism', Clement Greenberg-style, are firmly over. (Saatchi, *My Name Is Charles Saatchi and I Am an Artoholic,* p. 97)

In seeming confirmation of this viewpoint, Saatchi has diversified not only via his website, but also onto television. The BBC TV reality show *The School of Saatchi*, screened in 2009, was a talent competition strangely reminiscent of that staged by the guilds in Renaissance Florence for the Baptistery doors. Artists competed for the chance to be exhibited at the Saatchi Gallery and to have a studio space for three years. Suddenly, the trail from the Medici to Saatchi seems less obtuse.

5.3 Checkpoint question
Does an artist have to have a patron's support in order to achieve status and success?

Many of the factors arising from and influencing patronal relationships, and the intersection of and potential tensions between the interests of the public, specialist critics, private patrons and state institutions, can also be seen in the case of architectural commissions.

Architectural Landmarks in the Twentieth and Twenty-First Centuries

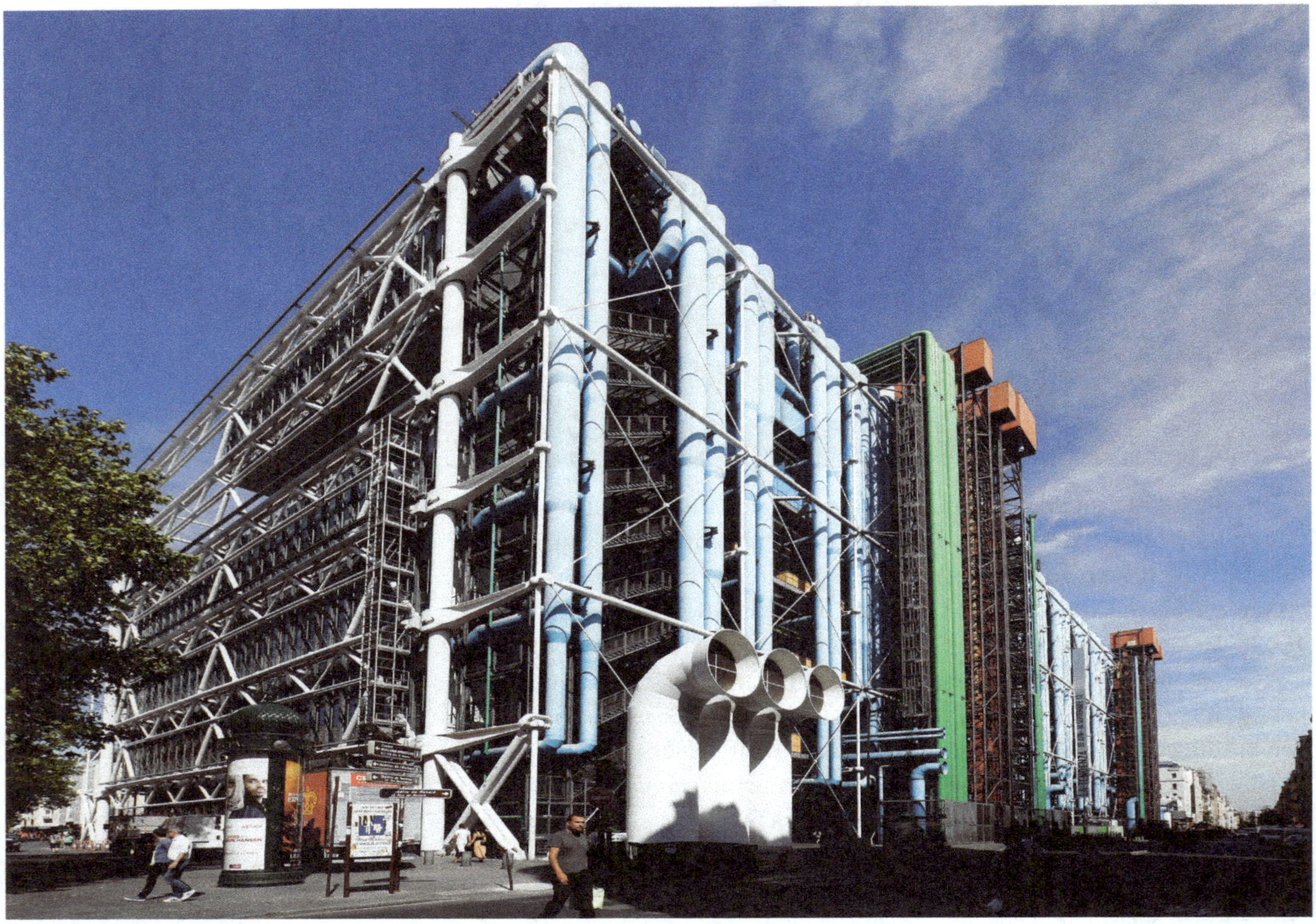

Figure 5.24 | Rogers and Piano, Pompidou Centre, Paris, 1971–1977. Source: © digitalimagination / iStockphoto.

Enhancing corporate 'brands' through association with 'star' architects

Several of those buildings already discussed in other chapters in this book can be looked at in terms of patronage and the social and cultural status of the architect. For example, the close patronal relationship between architect Philip Webb and patron William Morris in the Red House; between Le Corbusier and the Savoye family in Villa Savoye; between Frank Lloyd Wright and Edgar Kauffmann Snr. in Fallingwater, and between Richard Rogers and Lloyd's of London in the Lloyd's Building, to name but a few. For the purpose of illustration, let's take a closer look at the patronal relationship that existed between Richard Rogers and his client, Lloyd's of London, and the extent to which Rogers' social and cultural status helped him to secure the commission.

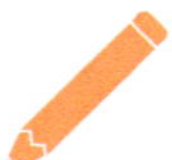

5.4 Explore this example
Gerrit Thomas Rietveld's Schröder House, 1924, is examined in relation to its form, style and function in *Chapter 3*; however, you may like to revisit the house in relation to the unique patronal relationship that developed between the patron, Mrs. Truus Schröder, and the architect.

British architect Richard Rogers was knighted by Queen Elizabeth II in 1981, and became Baron Rogers of Riverside in 1996. His awards include: RIBA Gold Medal 1985; Thomas Jefferson Medal 1999; Stirling Prize 2006, 2009; Minerva Medal 2007, and Pritzker Prize 2007. When insurance giant

Lloyd's commissioned Rogers to redevelop the existing Lloyd's site, he had already achieved a degree of fame for his work with Renzo Piano on the Pompidou Centre in Paris, 1971–1977; many more accolades were to follow the Lloyd's commission.[23] The Pompidou Centre is an iconic landmark today, but back in the 1970s its **high-tech** design was given the derogatory label 'Bowellism' by its critics because they said the many pipes on the outside of the building looked like intestines. Rogers developed this style (not that he labelled it high-tech himself) further to make his famous London landmark. Lloyd's, a powerful corporate brand and risk-taking business, adopted a very effective PR campaign when they hired such a well-known and risk-taking architect.

On the role of the architect in relation to the patron, Rogers states:

Buildings are not idiosyncratic private institutions: they give public performances both to the user and the passer-by. Thus the architect's responsibility must go beyond the client's program and into the broader public realm. Though the client's program [sic] offers the architect a point of departure, it must be questioned, as the architectural solution lies in the complex and often contradictory interpretation of the needs of the individual, the institution, the place and history. (In Campbell Cole and Rogers, *Richard Rogers + Architects*, p. 19)

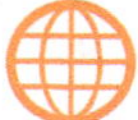

See the companion website for more details about the status of Rogers and the patronal relationship Rogers enjoyed with Lloyd's.

In conclusion, our interpretation and understanding of any given work is dependent on a number of related factors. *Chapter 3* focused on the formal aspects of works of art, paying very little attention to the artist's biography or the social and historical context of their creations; *Chapter 4*, meanwhile, focused specifically on the social and historical context of art and architecture, often at the expense of **formal analysis**. Art history involves learning about all of these, often inter-related, factors and asking how they affect our interpretation of works. In this chapter the themes of patronage and the social and cultural status of the architect have been examined separately yet, inevitably, in close relationship with one another.

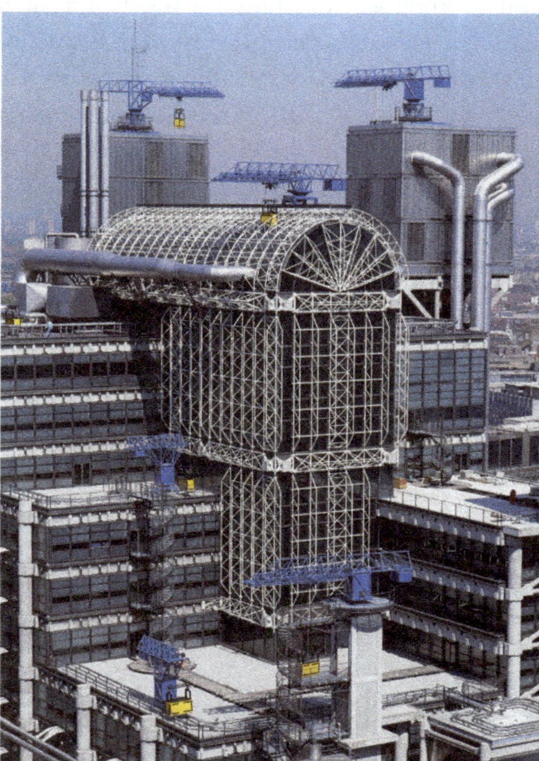

Figure 5.25 | Richard Rogers, Lloyd's Building, City of London, 1978–1986, façade with atrium. Source: © Robert Harding Picture Library Ltd / Alamy.

23 Rogers has also designed the Bordeaux Law Courts, 1998; Millennium Dome, 1999; Madrid-Barajas airport Terminal 4, 2005; and London Heathrow Airport, Terminal 5, 2008.

Chapter Summary Exercise

Using the words below complete the Chapter Summary. Each word or term should be used only once.

Medici
critic
celebrity
supercollector
biography
civic
propaganda
dealer
skill
church
collector
motives
guilds
Abstract Expressionism
internet

A patron may commission work for a variety of reasons: for pleasure, commemoration, devotion and __________. These are just a few of the possible __________ a patron may have when he/she decides to support a work of art or architecture.

During the medieval period the chief patron was the __________ but during the Renaissance new patrons emerged including powerful banking families like the __________.

In Italy during the Renaissance __________ such as the Arte della Lana were powerful __________ associations responsible for commissioning some of the most significant works of the period.

In the nineteenth century the __________, who acted like an intermediary, buying and selling works of art, emerged and continues to flourish today.

The authoritative published opinion of the __________ made an impact in the nineteenth century with individuals like Baudelaire, who championed the Impressionists and, in the twentieth century via voices such as Clement Greenberg, who championed __________.

The twentieth century saw the role of the __________ take more prominence, and influential gallerists and collectors like Charles Saatchi have been labelled as a __________ today.

Most recently, you could argue that increased technology and mass use of the __________ has afforded artists the ability to exhibit, promote and sell their work without the need for a patron or dealer.

An artist's status is often linked to the degree of patronage and support he or she has received. Status may be measured in a number of different ways: economic success, critical recognition and artistic __________.

The status of the artist may be enhanced by a __________ of their lives or media interest in their personality and lifestyle.

In these so-called media-saturated times we have seen the artist as __________ emerge, and some become household names – famous for being famous, if you like.

Checkpoint Answers

5.1 What do you think Cosimo de' Medici's motives were for commissioning Donatello's *David*?

Commissions like the sculpture *David* demonstrated Medici intellect and forward-thinking interest in humanism. The Old Testament David was capable of defending himself and his territory – so were the Medici. He symbolised their personal ambitions too.

5.2 What impact do you think biographies, such as Vasari's *Lives of the Artists*, 1550, have on the status of artists or architects?

Vasari chronicled the lives of Renaissance artists and publicised the details of their characters and achievements. Vasari's *Lives*, arguably, sold their achievements to his readers and perpetuated their status. He described Botticelli as both 'beautiful' and 'competent' and Michelangelo as a 'Tuscan genius'.

5.3 Does an artist have to have a patron's support in order to achieve status and success?

This was true of artists many centuries ago, but in the nineteenth-century artist Vincent van Gogh, who survived on the dealer's income provided by his brother, achieved unprecedented posthumous fame.

However, 'Saatchi artists', as they have become known, provide evidence for the continuing need for patronal support in order to achieve significant status and success.

References

Aldridge, J. 'Ad You Like It: The Bloody Battle Between the Saatchis', *Sunday Times Magazine*, 5 September 2010, http://www.thesundaytimes.co.uk/sto/Magazine/Features/article380951.ece.

Bray, X., Ceballos, R.G. de, Barbour, D. and Ozone, J. *The Sacred Made Real*, Yale University Press, 2010.

Brooks, R. 'It's the Fame I Crave, Says Damien Hirst', *Sunday Times*, 28 March 2010, http://www.thesundaytimes.co.uk/sto/news/uk_news/People/article251988.ece.

Burn, G. *Sex & Violence, Death & Silence*, Faber & Faber, 2009.

Button, V. *The Turner Prize: Twenty Years*, Tate Publishing, 2003.

Campbell Cole, B. and Rogers, R.E. (eds.) *Richard Rogers + Architects*, Academy Editions, 1985.

Cockcroft, E. 'Abstract Expressionism: Weapon of the Cold War', *Artforum*, 12 June 1974. (Reprinted in Frascina, F. (ed.) *Pollock and After: The Critical Debate*, Harper & Row, 1985.)

Deimling, B. *Botticelli*, Taschen, 1994.

Graham-Dixon, A. *Art: The Definitive Guide*, Dorling Kindersley, 2008.

Harris, A.S. *Seventeenth-Century Art and Architecture*, 2nd ed., Laurence King, 2008.

Harris, J. *Art History: The Key Concepts*, Routledge, 2008.

Hatje Cantz, 'Action-Painting', 2008, http://www.hatjecantz.de/action-painting-5031-1.html.

Hatton, R. and Walker, J.A. *Supercollector: A Critique of Charles Saatchi*, 4th ed., Institute of Artology, 2010.

Holt, E.G. *A Documentary History of Art*, Vol. 2, Doubleday Anchor, 1958.

Kaufmann, H. and Lustig, R. 'Van Gogh's Ear', *The World Tonight*, 2009, http://www.bbc.co.uk/archive/van_gogh/10928.shtml.

King, R. *Brunelleschi's Dome: The Story of the Great Cathedral in Florence*, Vintage, 2008.

Muir, G. *Lucky Kunst: The Rise and Fall of Young British Art*, Aurum Press, 2010.

Reif, R. 'Van Gogh's "Irises" Sells for $53.9 Million', *New York Times*, 12 November 1987, http://www.nytimes.com/1987/11/12/arts/van-gogh-s-irises-sells-for-53.9-million.html.

Saatchi, C. *My Name is Charles Saatchi and I Am an Artoholic*, Phaidon, 2009.

Saunders, F.S. 'Modern Art Was CIA Weapon. Revealed: How the Spy Agency Used Unwitting Artists such as Pollock and de Kooning in a Cultural Cold War', *The Independent*, 22 October 1995, http://www.independent.co.uk/news/world/modern-art-was-cia-weapon-1578808.html.

Schama, S. *The Power of Art*, Bodley Head, 2006.

Stallabrass, J. *High Art Lite: The Rise and Fall of Young British Art*, Verso, 2006.

Time, 'Art: The Wild Ones', 20 February 1956.

Townsend, C. and Merck, M. (eds.) *The Art of Tracey Emin*, Thames & Hudson, 2002.

University of Iowa Museum of Art, 'More about *Mural*', n.d., http://uima.uiowa.edu/mural.

Van Gogh, V. 'To Theo van Gogh. Arles, on or about Thursday, 25 October 1888 (Letter 712)', 1888, http://vangoghletters.org/vg/letters/let712/letter.html.

Vasari, G. *Lives of the Artists*, Vol. 1, Penguin, 1987. (First published 1550.)

Wittkower, R. *Art and Architecture in Italy 1600–1750*, Vol. 2, Yale University Press, 1999.

Wood, P., Frascina, F. and Harrison, C. *Modernism in Dispute: Art Since the Forties*, Yale University Press / Open University, 1993.

Other Useful Sources

Strathern, P. *The Medici: Godfathers of the Renaissance*, Vintage, 2007.

Chapter 6
Gender, Nationality and Ethnicity

Learning Outcomes

By the end of this chapter you will be able to:

- define the concepts of gender, nationality and ethnicity
- examine the representation of gender, nationality and ethnicity in art and architecture, and consider how this aids meaning and interpretation
- consider how the gender, nationality and ethnicity of artists and architects may influence the creation and appearance of art and architecture
- compare and contrast different works of art and architecture that address a similar subject.

Thinking About Art: A Thematic Guide to Art History, First Edition. Penny Huntsman.

Chapter Map

This chapter map provides a visual overview of Chapter 6 – 'Gender, Nationality and Ethnicity' – together with its key works.

Gender: The Representation and Subversion of Gender Stereotypes

A 'woman's place' and the 'male gaze'

- Paul Jamin (1853–1903), *Brenn and his Share of the Plunder*, 1893
- Jan van Eyck (c.1390–1441), *The Arnolfini Portrait*, 1434
- Louise Bourgeois (1911–2010), *Femme Maison*, 1994
- Cindy Sherman (born 1954), *Untitled Film Still #3*, 1977

Woman as 'other'

- Jacques-Louis David (1748–1825), *Oath of the Horatii*, 1784
- Barbara Kruger (born 1945), *Untitled (We Don't Need Another Hero)*, 1986
- Pierre-Auguste Renoir (1841–1919), *La Loge*, 1874
- Mary Cassatt (1844–1926), *In the Loge*, 1878
- Jean-Auguste-Dominique Ingres (1780–1867), *La Grande Odalisque*, 1814
- Guerrilla Girls (born 1985), *Untitled or Do Women Have to Be Naked to Get Into the Met. Museum?*, 1989
- Jean-Auguste-Dominique Ingres, *The Turkish Bath*, 1862

Subverting the 'male gaze'

- Sylvia Sleigh (1916–2010), *The Turkish Bath*, 1973
- Jenny Saville (born 1970), *Hybrid*, 1997

The 'masculine' prototype, the sensuous male and gender duality

- *Laocoön*, first century BCE
- Auguste Rodin (1840–1917), *The Age of Bronze*, c.1876/1877
- Antonio Canova (1757–1822), *Psyche Revived by Cupid's Kiss*, 1793

Who is victimised here?

- Alberto Giacometti (1901–1966), *Woman with Her Throat Cut*, 1932 (cast 1949)
- Louise Bourgeois (1911–2010), *The Destruction of the Father*, 1974
- Louise Bourgeois, *Maman*, 1999

The celebration of woman's work

- Judy Chicago (born 1939), *The Dinner Party*, 1979
- Tracey Emin (born 1963), *Everyone I Have Ever Slept With 1963–1995*, 1995

Gender and the built environment

- Iktinos and Kallikrates, Parthenon Temple, 447–438 BCE
- Ludwig Mies van der Rohe (1886–1969) and Philip Johnson (1906–2005), Seagram Building, 1958
- Frank Gehry (born 1929) and Vlado Milunić (born 1941), Netherlands National Building or 'Dancing House', Prague, 1996

Nationality

Emblems and monuments to national identity

- Eugène Delacroix (1798–1863), *Liberty Leading the People*, 1830
- Frida Kahlo (1907–1954), *Self-Portrait on the Borderline Between Mexico and the United States*, 1932
- Alexandre Gustave Eiffel (1832–1923), Eiffel Tower, 1887–1889
- Frédéric Bartholdi (1834–1904), Statue of Liberty, 1886
- Charles Garnier (1825–1898), Opéra Garnier (Paris Opera), 1861–1875
- Jørn Utzon (1918–2008), Sydney Opera House, 1973

Ethnicity

Through the eyes of an empire: hybridity and the mythologised 'other'

- John Nash (1752–1835), Royal Pavilion, Brighton, 1815–1822
- Sir Joshua Reynolds (1723–1792), *Portrait of Omai*, c.1776
- Henry Matisse (1869–1954), *Blue Nude*, 1907

Twentieth-century stereotypes and discrimination

- Rasheed Araeen (born 1935), *The Golden Verses*, 1990–1991
- Chris Ofili (born 1968), *No Woman, No Cry*, 1998

Gender, nationality and ethnicity symbiotically linked

- Guerrilla Girls (born 1985), The Advantages of Being a Woman Artist, 1988, poster on college campuses, 1990

Introduction

This chapter introduces you to the important concepts of gender, nationality and ethnicity and considers how they may be significant for the interpretation of works of painting, sculpture and architecture. These themes have been explored in a variety of different ways by artists, both consciously and unconsciously, and very often the different themes overlap in a particular work.

In the discussion of **gender**, the ideas of pioneering female artists and art theorists are examined in relation to gender relations in art-historical discourse and in relation to the representation of male and female bodies. Issues of power in relation to gender and art are also examined in terms of their **symbiotic** relationship with ethnicity, especially in early twentieth-century Europe.

The concepts of **nationality** and **ethnicity** are inextricably linked; both may be understood in the context of European exploration and **colonial** expansion. Nationality is examined primarily in relation to national monuments and the conscious decision of artists, sculptors and architects to create iconic emblems for their states.

In relation to ethnicity, the legacy of the colonial past is examined in terms of the unequal relationship that existed between the colonisers and the colonised in the early twentieth century, namely, White Europeans assuming supremacy over people from 'other' lands. Such discrimination was challenged later on in the century and different ethnicities were in some cases embraced by artists proud to claim a non-White identity. The label '**other**' was considered to be a disadvantage, especially where White artists tended to assume no label at all.

While works are studied primarily for their content in terms of gender, nationality and ethnicity, their formal elements and materials, techniques and processes are, more often than not, inextricably linked to their meaning.

Gender: The Representation and Subversion of Gender Stereotypes

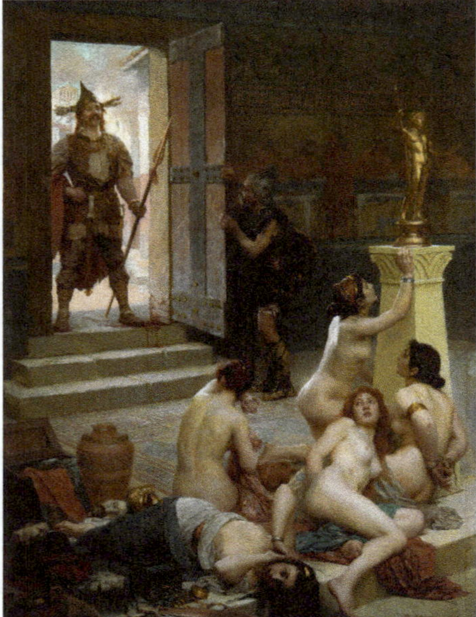
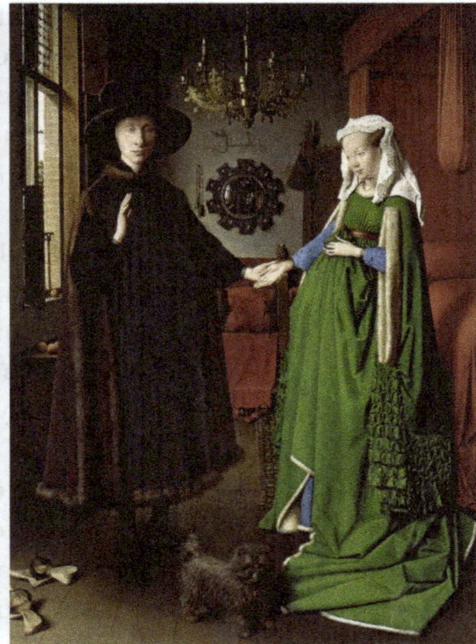

Left to right:
Figure 6.1 | Paul Joseph Jamin, *Brenn and his Share of the Plunder (or Spoils)*, 1893, oil on canvas, 162 × 118 cm, La Rochelle, Musée des Beaux-Arts. Source: akg-images.

Figure 6.2 | Jan van Eyck, *The Arnolfini Portrait*, 1434, portrait of Giovanni (?) Arnolfini and his wife Giovanna Cenami (?), oil on oak panel, 82.2 × 60 cm, London, National Gallery. Source: National Gallery, London, UK / Bridgeman Images.

Gender is a complex issue and best understood in relation to its difference from sex. What is the difference between sex and gender? What do we mean by femininity and masculinity? Gender commonly relates to what we understand as being either 'masculine' or 'feminine'. In this sense gender is socially and culturally constructed rather than biologically determined. For this reason, gender is often treated stereotypically. For example, women have often been shown in passive and subordinate positions in visual media, while men have typically been portrayed in active and powerful roles. This contrasts with a person's sex, which is fixed; sex is a biological term used to classify human beings as either male or female. Our sex is determined by our physical difference at the level of our genitals and hormones.

A 'woman's place' and the 'male gaze'

Brenn and his Share of the Plunder, 1893, by Paul Joseph Jamin (1853–1903) epitomises the stereotypical portrayal of the sexes at its most basic. This work lends itself to what British **feminist** film theorist Laura Mulvey described as the '**male gaze**': the conquering Gaul warrior stands erect and, having seized the palace, he is about to claim his prize: the semi-naked women within. In the canon, this work was celebrated as a history painting, but what is its real **subject** – eroticism, voyeurism and/or fetishism? The 'male gaze' controls the women as objects of desire and enables the spectator vicariously to share in the enjoyment of the spoils – provided, however, that the spectator imaginatively identifies with the male figure. How does the composition of this work help us to read the social and cultural status of the sexes at the time of its painting? What does this tell us about the perceived intended audience of such works?

Jan van Eyck's *The Arnolfini Portrait*, 1434, previously examined as an example of double-portraiture in *Chapter 1*, is revealing of the figures' respective gender status. Art historians have determined that the woman, believed to have become Mrs. Arnolfini, is not depicted as pregnant, but the work seems to foreshadow her pregnancy with the abundance of fabric gathered boastfully around her middle. The oranges ripening on the window-sill serve as a symbol of her expected fertility, and St. Margaret (the patron saint of women in childbirth), whose image is carved on the chair positioned against the back wall (right), is a further symbol of her child-bearing role. The little dog, almost camouflaged against the wooden floor, stands between the couple apparently as an emblem of fidelity, a trait expected to characterise her marriage.[24] A marital contract would ensure that Mr. Arnolfini's wealth passed to his rightful heirs in the future. The shoes, however, are perhaps the most interesting of all in the context of gender; their positioning is, arguably, far from incidental. Her delicate little slippers find themselves trapped adjacent to the bed, barely distinguishable from their surroundings; Mr. Arnolfini's, in stark contrast, find themselves almost illuminated in the foreground of the work, still slightly muddied from his recent excursion outdoors, demonstrating he has access to the public sphere of existence. The art historian Carola Hicks, noted a range of oppositions in relation to Mr. Arnolfini's and Mrs. Arnolfini's respective headdresses alone: *black/white, cosmopolitan/local, up-to-date/old fashioned, dashing/demure* (Hicks, *Girl in a Green Gown*, p. 28). Hicks also noted that Mr. Arnolfini's tabard is lined with 'marten fur': hers from 'cheaper squirrel' (Hicks, *Girl in a Green Gown*, p. 23).

It would hardly win us respect if our wife busied herself among the men in the marketplace, out in the public eye. It also seems some-what demeaning to me to remain shut up in the home among women when I have manly things to do among men.

(Leon Battista Alberti quoted in Wigley, 'Untitled: The Housing of Gender', pp. 334–335)

From a feminist perspective, *The Arnolfini Portrait* can be read as a telling document of the inferior position of women in fifteenth-century Europe, although *Chapter 1* notes the more recent reading of this work as Mrs. Arnolfini signing a business transaction that requires witnessing. Whichever our perspective, it is fair to say that **patriarchy** prevailed at this time across Europe and beyond. However, any reading of a work made so long ago, so far removed from the context in which we read it, cannot be treated as wholly accurate or finite.

6.1 Explore this example
Chapter 1 examined Thomas Gainsborough's painting *Mr and Mrs Andrews*, 1750, as an example of the landscape **genre** and also as a double portrait. In the context of this chapter, consider how the structure of the composition could reflect the structure of society at the time. What signs are there of Mr. Andrews' authority in this painting?

The idea that a woman may feel trapped by domesticity is a common one, thought-provokingly described by feminist architectural historian Leslie Kanes Weisman:

A homemaker has no inviolable space of her own. She is attached to spaces of service. She is a hostess in the living room, a cook in the kitchen, a mother in the children's bedroom, a lover in the bedroom, a chauffeur in the garage. The house is a spatial and temporal metaphor for conventional role playing. (Quoted in Weisman, 'Prologue', p. 2)

It was made manifest in marble five centuries after *The Arnolfini Portrait*

24 Reflectogram technology proves that the dog in *The Arnolfini Portrait* was a late addition, despite all of the investment in its symbolism that art historians have made over the centuries. This finding may alter a straightforward reading of the image in terms of gender.

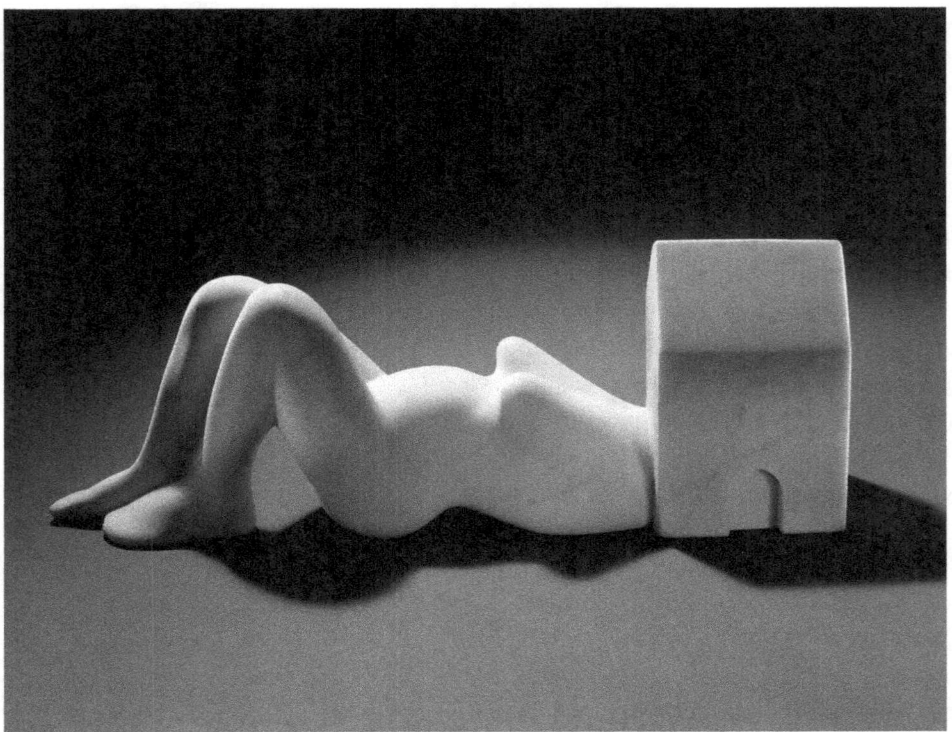

Figure 6.3 | Louise Bourgeois, *Femme Maison*, 1994, white marble, 11.4 × 31.1 × 6.6 cm. Source: Photo: Christopher Burke, ©The Easton Foundation /VAGA, New York / DACS, London 2015.

in the work entitled *Femme Maison*, 1994, by French artist Louise Bourgeois (1911–2010).

A female form without arms lies trapped and anchored under that timeless symbol of domesticity – the house. Specifically, her head, the part of her anatomy most strongly associated with her personal identity, is trapped in the home; a fitting response to the axiom 'a woman's place is in the home'. American photographer and film director Cindy Sherman (born 1954) has based much of her work on the roles assigned to women in a 'man's world'. Her black and white film stills are specifically based on the **stereotypical** roles of women in old Hollywood movies. In each one of Sherman's 69 black and white photographs that form her iconic *Untitled Film Stills* series, the artist masquerades as every conceivable cliché of constructed femininity. In *Untitled Film Still #3*, 1977, she's the kind of wife 'a man might long to come home to': literally behind the kitchen sink, locked in the domestic sphere, all the while looking delectable and wanton; her self-embrace anticipating the touch of the male. The whole **mise-en-scène** is planned as meticulously as a film director's. Every element, including the camera angle, the lighting, the make-up, the hair and the clothes, signifies its role in creating the myth of the feminine. Another in the series, *Untitled Film Still #6*, 1977, features the artist with deeply coloured lips, open mouth, carefully combed hair, and body sprawled in a state of undress across a bed. Together these features imply some sort of narrative we feel we should work out. The camera looks down on the figure from above, heightening her objectification. Look up *Untitled Film Still #6*. What persona is Sherman adopting here? The *femme fatale*? The starlet? Whichever the role, we feel we know the character, and we have certainly seen her type in films.

Despite Sherman's role as the main character in these film stills, seldom does the artist reveal anything of herself – her *actual* rather than her *constructed* identity. Rather, she focuses on the way in which make-up, pose and costume help to construct a variety of socially acceptable identities for women, particularly in visual culture, where women have tended to be particularly objectified. Do you remember Jenny Saville's *Branded* examined in *Chapter 1* as an example of self-portraiture? Does Saville's painting conform to or reject the 'male gaze'? Do you think there

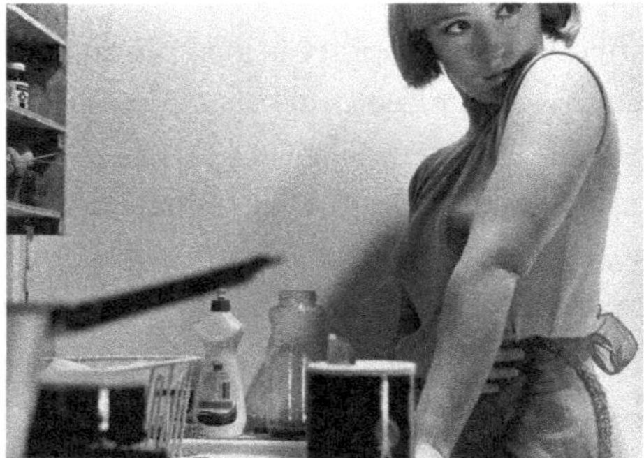

Figure 6.4 | Cindy Sherman, *Untitled Film Still #3* 1977, gelatine silver print, 18 × 24 cm. Source: Courtesy of the artist and Metro Pictures.

is a corresponding 'female gaze' in recent times? And, is it necessarily liberating?

British film theorist Laura Mulvey, coined the term 'male gaze' in her 1970s critiques of visual culture and specifically of film. In her seminal work 'Visual Pleasure and Narrative Cinema', 1975, she used psychoanalysis to examine the way film, through its editing and shot selections, constructs gender roles so that male characters are shown to gaze at and derive pleasure from the sight of female characters, noting that these roles are rarely reversed.

6.1 Checkpoint question

In relation to gender, what is meant by the 'domestic' sphere?

In a world ordered by sexual imbalance, pleasure in looking has been split between active/male and passive/female. The determining 'male gaze' projects its fantasy onto the female figure, which is styled accordingly. In their traditional exhibitionist role women are simultaneously looked at and displayed, with their appearance coded for strong visual and erotic impact so that they can be said to connote 'to-be-looked-at-ness' (Mulvey, 'Visual Pleasure and Narrative Cinema', 1975).

Women are constructed as 'objects' of the 'male gaze', and male and female viewers alike must assume the imaginative position of the heterosexual male character in order to take pleasure in the sights the image offers. This is a gaze that women then internalise, as they learn to objectify themselves and turn a critical gaze on their own appearance and behaviour, seeking to bring it into conformity with the on-screen women. Sherman's *Untitled Film Stills* show the artist taking on and exploring this internalisation of the 'male gaze'.

Woman as 'other'

Oath of the Horatii, 1784, by Jacques-Louis David (1748–1825) (examined in some detail in *Chapter 1* as an example of the 'history' genre) is a highly gendered image of the noble defence of pride and territory. The men, about to go to war, stand with tensed muscles, outward gaze and grounded feet. Even the colour palette selected to depict them is vibrant in contrast to the paler, more insipid hues of the women's robes. The female group is depicted as sedentary, home-bound, with downcast eyes and weeping. Part of the tension in this work lies in the knowledge that one of the Horatii wives is the sister of a Curiatii enemy, and one of the sisters of the Horatii is soon to be married to one of the Curiatii, and so many of their tears are harbingers of lost love. Despite the emotional torment of the women, the men still go to war at the command of their father. David's **Neo-classical** style conveys their impressive musculature with an almost photographic level of precision and polish, while their emphatic stances convey their readiness for battle.

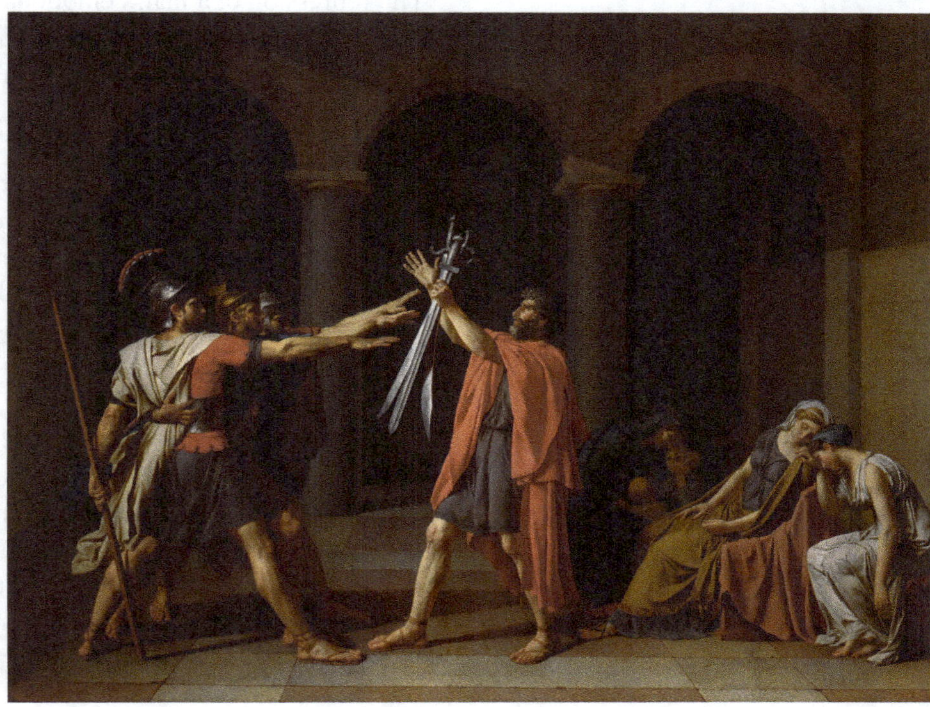

Figure 6.5 | Jacques-Louis David, *Oath of the Horatii*, 1784, oil on canvas, 330 × 425 cm, Paris, Musée du Louvre. Source: akg-images / Erich Lessing.

The machismo in the *Horatii* is almost palpable; these brothers-in-arms will proudly die in defence of

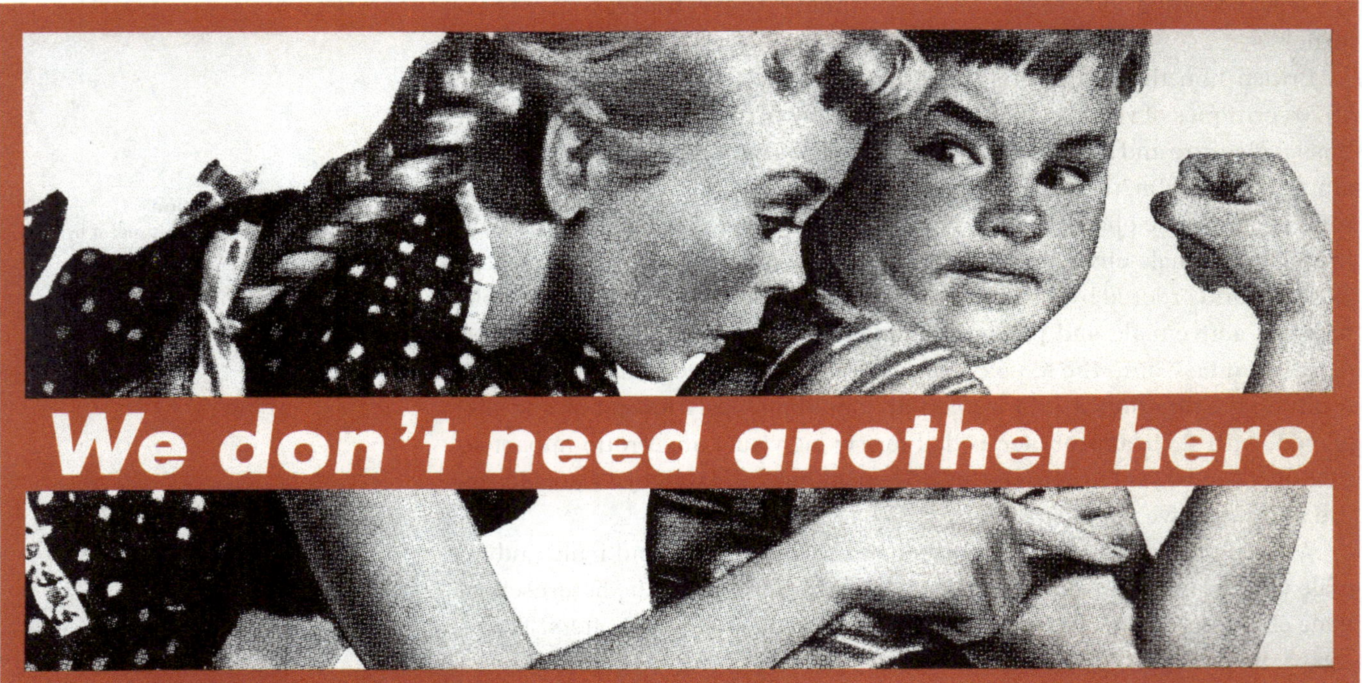

Figure 6.6 | Barbara Kruger, *Untitled* (*We Don't Need Another Hero*), 1987, photographic silkscreen/vinyl, 228.6 × 297.2 cm, New York, Mary Boone Gallery, MBG#4186. Source: Copyright: Barbara Kruger. Courtesy: Mary Boone Gallery, New York.

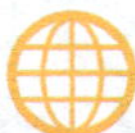

See the companion website for more information about Artemisia Gentileschi's life as a female painter and her masterful depiction of *Judith Slaying Holofernes*.

their city. The masculine stereotype is a familiar one, and the modern tendency to ridicule it is not lost on American artist Barbara Kruger (born 1945). Kruger's *Untitled* (*We Don't Need Another Hero*), 1986, makes a playfully powerful statement about the polarity of gender in terms of the stereotypically assumed strength of men over women. The artist's depiction of the youthful boy with cheeks about to burst with bravado indicates the historical socialisation of children into gender stereotypes and a 1980s' critique of it. Kruger stated, *I work with pictures and words because they have the ability to determine who we are, what we want to be, and what we become* (Barbara Kruger quoted in Stedelijk Museum, 'July 23: Appropriation').

The repression of a man's emotions and the injunction upon him to provide for all of his dependants are as potentially problematic for men as the more commonly discussed restraints have been for women. Perhaps the recently emerged '**crisis of masculinity**' may suggest that the pendulum has now swung too far.

The issue of gender in relation to art history relates both to the portrayal of the sexes and the different fortunes of male and female artists. Women artists have historically been subjected to discrimination, for example. Nevertheless, there have been some notable exceptions. Feminist scholar Germaine Greer describes seventeenth-century Italian artist Artemisia Gentileschi (the artist who painted *Judith Slaying Holofernes*; see Figure 4.3) as *the exception to all the rules* (Greer, *The Obstacle Race: The Fortunes of Women Painters and Their Work*, p. 207).

La Loge, 1874, by Pierre-Auguste Renoir (1841–1919), depicts the prettiest of women and the dandiest of men in a box at the Paris Opera – one of Paris' newly built entertainment spaces in the mid-nineteenth century. The woman looks at us with sorrowful eyes; the man, meanwhile, looks at another woman, certainly not at the entertainment on stage (which would be below). His binoculars are practical and powerful; hers, in contrast, are decorative, and powerless.

Renoir's subject matter was approached from a different angle by American artist Mary Cassatt (1844–1926) in her painting *In the Loge*, 1878. Cassatt appears to have consciously subverted the 'male gaze' in her take on a theatre-box scene. By putting herself into the position of the male artist she actually subverts the 'male gaze'. This lady has no frills, no pretty bonnet or flowers; she is a lone spectator of the show, buttoned up to the neck with emphatic control of the gaze – she is empowered – her vision is active not passive. As feminist art historian Linda Nochlin observed:

[The] woman ... artist is merely ridiculous, but I feel that it is acceptable for a woman to be a singer or a dancer.

(Renoir (1888) quoted in Clark, *Women and Achievement in Nineteenth-Century Europe*, p. 82)

Cassatt ... associated femininity and the active gaze. Her young woman in black, armed with opera glasses, is all active and aggressive-looking. She holds the opera glasses, those prototypical instruments of masculine specular power, firmly to her eyes, and her tense silhouette suggests the concentrated energy of her assertive visual thrust into space. (Nochlin, *Representing Women*, p. 194)

Cassatt was ahead of her time in achieving a measure of success as a woman artist. She was aided in her efforts by her independent wealth – poorer women had far fewer chances. Nevertheless, she used her position to explore the definition of bourgeois femininity with all of its contradictions. She said she wanted to *be someone rather than something* (Nochlin, *Representing Women*, p. 215).

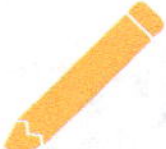

6.2 Explore this example
Compare Renoir's *Woman Breastfeeding her Child*, 1886, with Cassatt's *Baby's First Caress*, 1891. Consider how the artists' respective genders may have influenced the representation of the subject.

Look again at Cassatt's *Lydia at her Tapestry Frame* discussed in relation to its form and style in *Chapter 3*. This time examine the scene through the lens of gender.

Cassatt's *In the Loge* repositioned the nineteenth-century female subject as the one who can and is able to look for herself; Cassatt also affirmed the position of the female as independent professional artist. It may be surprising, therefore, to learn that almost a century later, the American feminist activist group known as the Guerrilla Girls (see later discussion) felt it necessary to launch a scathing attack on the art world for its continuing subjugation of women, and on some of New York's Museum of Modern Art's best-loved male artists. The nineteenth-century French Neo-classical painter Jean-Au-

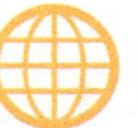

See also the companion website for a fuller discussion on Cassatt.

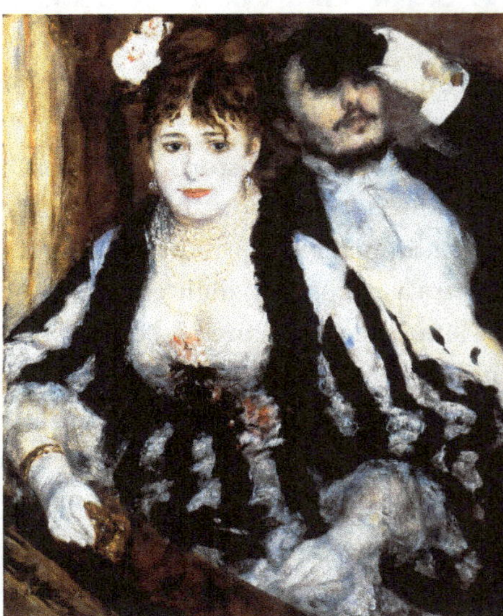

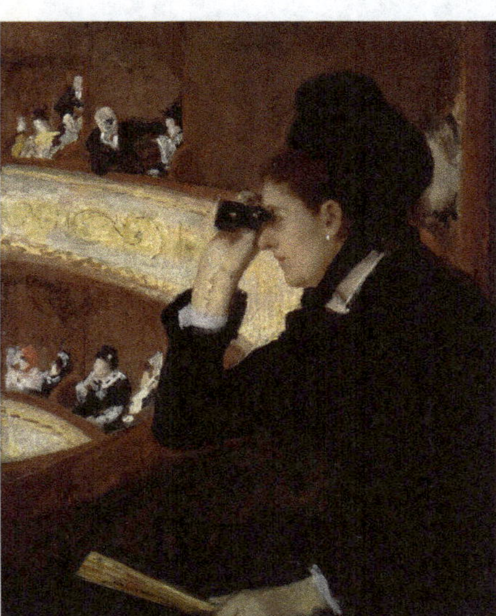

Left to right:
Figure 6.7 | Pierre-Auguste Renoir, *La Loge*, 1874, oil on canvas, 80 × 63 cm, London, Courtauld Institute of Art Gallery.
Source: akg-images / De Agostini Picture Library.

Figure 6.8 | Mary Cassatt, *In the Loge*, 1878, oil on canvas, 81.28 × 66.04 cm, Museum of Fine Arts, Boston, the Hayden Collection – Charles Henry Hayden Fund 10.35.
Source: Photograph © 2015 Museum of Fine Arts, Boston. All rights reserved / Bridgeman Images.

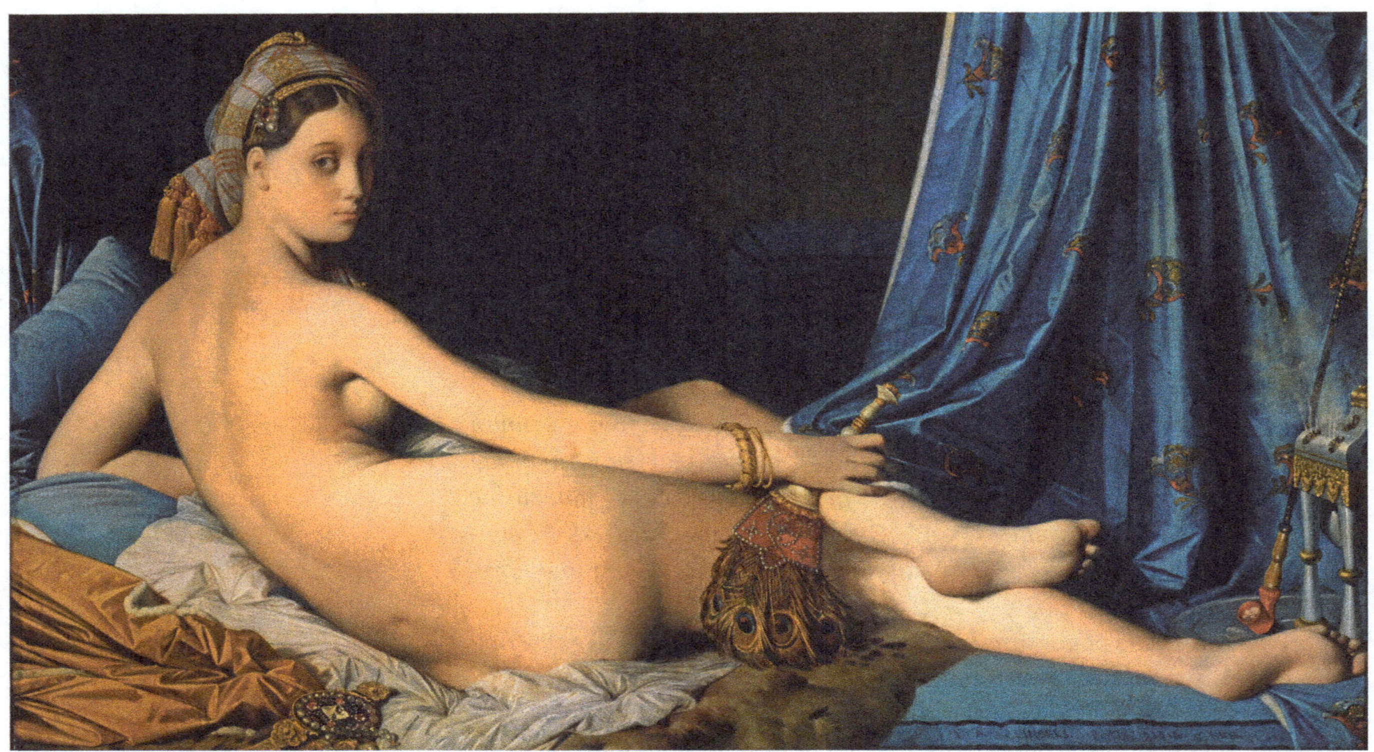

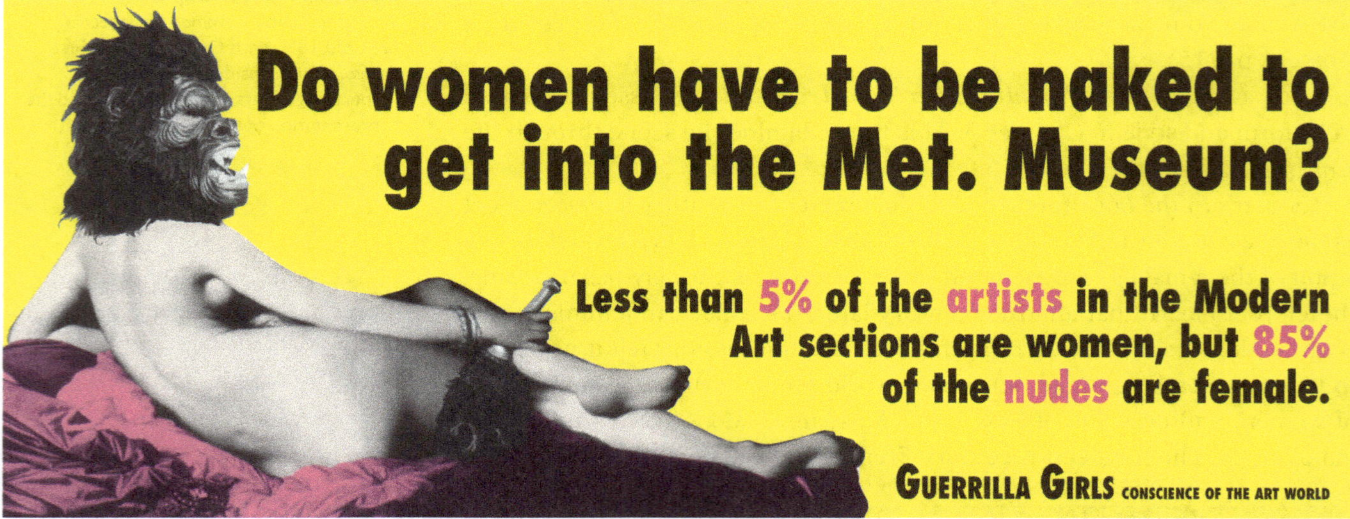

Top to bottom:
Figure 6.9 | Jean-Auguste-Dominique Ingres, ***La Grande Odalisque*****, 1814, oil on canvas, 91 × 162 cm, Paris, Musée du Louvre.** **Source: © 2015. A. Dagli. Orti / Scala, Florence.**

Figure 6.10 | Guerrilla Girls, ***Untitled*** **or** ***Do Women Have to Be Naked to Get Into the Met. Museum?*****, 1989 (from the series 'Guerrilla Girls Talk Back: The First Five Years', 1985–1990).** **Source: Copyright © Guerrilla Girls / Courtesy www.guerrillagirls.com.**

guste-Dominique Ingres (1780–1867) came under their satirical spotlight, for example.

Ingres' *La Grande Odalisque*, 1814, epitomises the distortions imposed on women's bodies by the imposition of idealised 'perfection'. Ingres' women are deeply sensuous to the point of being anatomically incorrect. The woman in this painting appears to have three extra vertebrae, which elongate the spine and help her back seem even more sinuous, so enhancing her unblemished appearance. Arguably we see a similar technique in today's airbrushed models, whose legs are lengthened and skin made to appear flawless to help sell films, cosmetics and magazines. (Most recently, however, male models are as much a victim of the **idealisation** treatment as female models; consumerism does not appear to discriminate as easily anymore.)

The Guerrilla Girls, in their *Untitled* from the series 'Guerrilla Girls Talk Back: The First Five Years', parody Ingres' **odalisque** model and ridicule the objectification of women and women's constructed role as passive muse rather than active artist.

The **semiotics** associated with sexual desirability is frequently used in today's media. For example, in the advertising campaign for a Dolce and Gabbana fragrance, 'The One', the mise-en-scène, the knowing flick of the hair (in place of Ingres' caressing feather), and the invitation to the male voyeur, are as potent as ever.

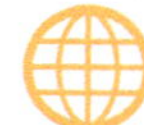

What's changed in a couple of centuries regarding the concept of the male versus the female gaze? See the companion website.

In The Turkish Bath, 1862, also by Ingres, the artist presents, whether intentionally or not, the ultimate male fantasy in this pile-up of fleshy, wanton females. This **tondo** adds to the feeling of glimpsing into a secret cavern of Oriental eroticism as though peeping through an illicit keyhole. The scene is intended to appear as set in a Middle Eastern country, and its titillating subject is made just about acceptable by virtue of its 'otherness'. Ingres' work is a fruitful subject for examination in terms of gender and ethnicity.

Subverting the 'male gaze'

The Turkish Bath, 1973, by the artist Sylvia Sleigh (1916–2010) playfully mimics Ingres' objectifying viewpoint, but here Sleigh positions male models languidly, seductively and nakedly in front of the viewer. She also makes a decorative feature out of body hair and tan lines. The mise-en-scène is a little less alluring than in Ingres' painting and the men look more confrontationally at us. The image makes us question why this should seem more surprising than Ingres' representation. Indeed, the very fact of the production of such a work may seem to us indicative of changing power relations in society as well as evidence of the rising numbers of women able to train and achieve success as artists. Contemporary American feminist writer Whitney Chadwick states:

Sylvia Sleigh's male nudes combine portrait genre with the nude as a representational type. In Philip Golub Reclining (1971), The Turkish Bath (1973), and other paintings of the 1970s, Sleigh reverses a history in which men contemplate the naked bodies of women. (Chadwick, *Women, Art and Society*, p. 370)

Sleigh replicated the objectifying gaze, only reversing its gender roles, but contemporary British artist Jenny Saville (born 1970, discussed in *Chapter 1* and *Chapter 5*) challenges and repels objectifying spectatorship with her

Left to right:

Figure 6.11 | Jean-Auguste-Dominique Ingres, *The Turkish Bath*, 1862, oil on canvas, 108 × 108 cm, Musée du Louvre, Paris. Source: © 2015. Photo Scala, Florence.

Figure 6.12 | Sylvia Sleigh, *The Turkish Bath*, 1973, oil on canvas, 193 × 259.1 × 5.1 cm (framed: 203.2 × 266.7 × 12.7 cm), The David and Alfred Smart Museum of Art, The University of Chicago; purchased by Paul and Miriam Kirkley Fund for Acquisitions. Source: Photograph 62014 courtesy of The David and Alfred Smart Museum of Art, The University of Chicago.

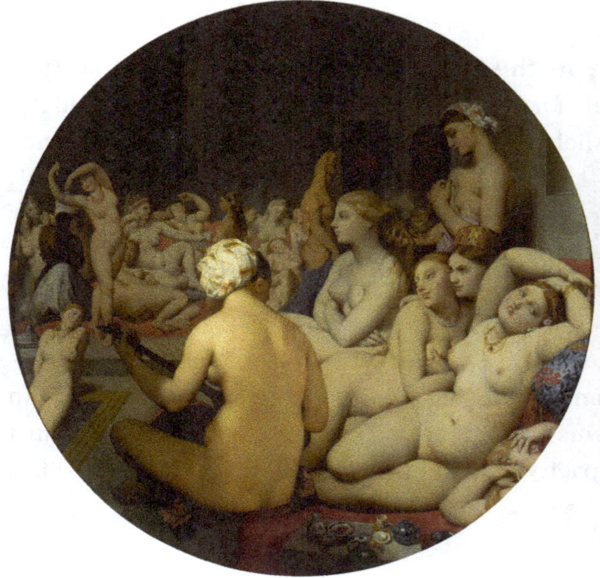

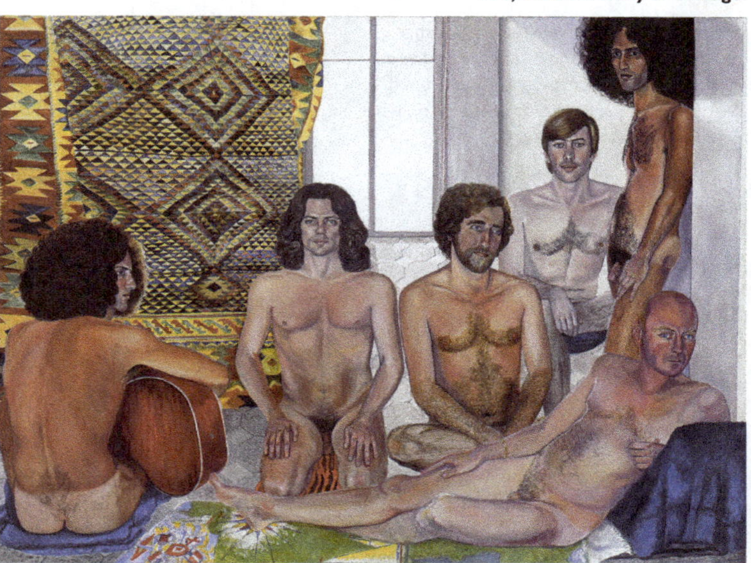

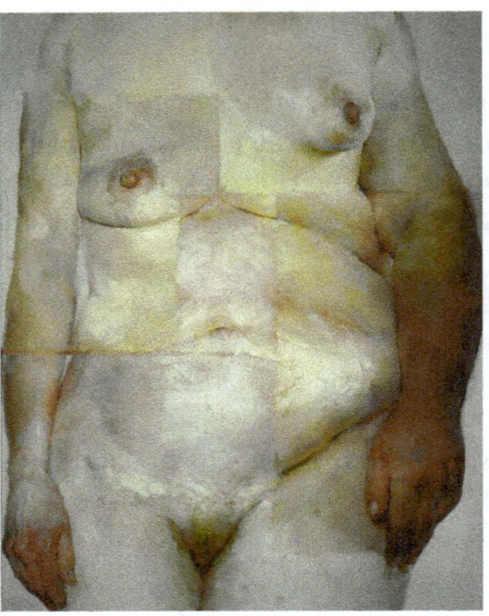

Figure 6.13 | Jenny Saville, *Hybrid*, 1997, oil on canvas, 274.3 × 213.4 cm. Source: Photo courtesy Gagosian Gallery. © Jenny Saville. All rights reserved, DACS 2015.

monumental female nudes made so fleshy they loom over the spectator.

In utter contrast to the idealised nudes painstakingly depicted by Ingres, Saville presents us with another entirely modern take on the female nude. Saville's *Branded*, 1992, was examined as an example of self-portraiture in *Chapter 1* and we may remember her painterly assault on society's view of fat women as 'folk devils'. *Hybrid*, 1997, is so wrong, it's right: it takes the 'constructed' female body, mythologised over the centuries and, by way of patchwork flesh, shows the very act of that construction as unnatural and pernicious. Saville removes us from **mythology** into the real world and forces us to confront the consequences of desiring perfection. It would appear that, from Saville's perspective, women diet, exercise and learn to hate themselves to the point where they become their own enemy. The implication is that women are supposed to cut themselves into pieces under the surgeon's knife to be reborn beautiful. In the same way that Saville confronted us with prejudice towards fat people in *Branded*, she presents us with the damaging unnaturalness of perfection in *Hybrid*. Can Saville's *Hybrid* be viewed as a reaction to eighteenth-century artist and writer Sir Joshua Reynolds' lectures on what makes a body beautiful in art?

Women persecute themselves with a desire to retain adolescent figures ... Plastic surgeons use computers to create the perfect face, but it will achieve such blandness. What would beauty be, if everyone looked the same?

(Jenny Saville quoted in Kent, *Shark Infested Waters: The Saatchi Collection of British Art in the 90s*, pp. 83–84)

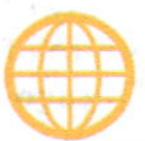

See the companion website for guidance on how Saville's *Hybrid* can be viewed as a reaction to eighteenth-century artist and writer Sir Joshua Reynolds' lectures on what makes a body beautiful in art.

The 'masculine' prototype, the sensuous male and gender duality

Representations of the male form have tended to be powerful, erect and noble. Look, for example, at Michelangelo's (originally Michelangelo di Lodovico Buonarroti Simoni, 1475–1564) **High Renaissance** sculpture *David*, 1501, which served for generations as an emblem of ideal masculinity: gracefully poised, powerfully muscled and victorious in combat. Of course this stereotype can be just as imprisoning for men as female stereotypes can be for women. Accordingly, representations of men in art often display men as possessing strength; however, such power is threatened by the pressure of keeping the stereotype intact and repressing elements perceived as weak. To an extent, this sometimes seems beyond the conscious control of the artist, just as it may be beyond the capacity of an individual to live up to the gender-ideal of their time.

6.2 Checkpoint question
Identify two female artists whose work attempts to subvert what feminist art historians have described as the 'male gaze'.

6.1 Critical debates: masculinity in question

Art historian Norman Bryson has argued that Théodore Géricault's faulty depiction of the man's anatomy and the insecurity of the figure's position in space in his painting *The Wounded Cuirassier*, 1814, produces a representation of 'heroic' martial masculinity as uncertain and potentially under threat (Bryson, 'Géricault and "Masculinity"', pp. 228–59). He argues that this reflects the unconscious difficulty felt by male subjects in successfully performing the gender role required of them. Look at this painting for yourself. The horse was often a powerful military accessory to war, but how has Géricault depicted the Cuirassier's horse? What do you make of the fact that this solitary soldier's 'wound' is not visible?

The central figure of the **Hellenistic** sculpture *Laocoön*, appears to demonstrate a very early sense of 'masculinity' – a rippling musculature that has, arguably, been matched but never surpassed in stone.

In this marble masterpiece, the priest *Laocoön* is encoiled by a deadly serpent as punishment for warning the Trojans against accepting a wooden horse as a gift from the Greeks. He is flanked by his sons and together they

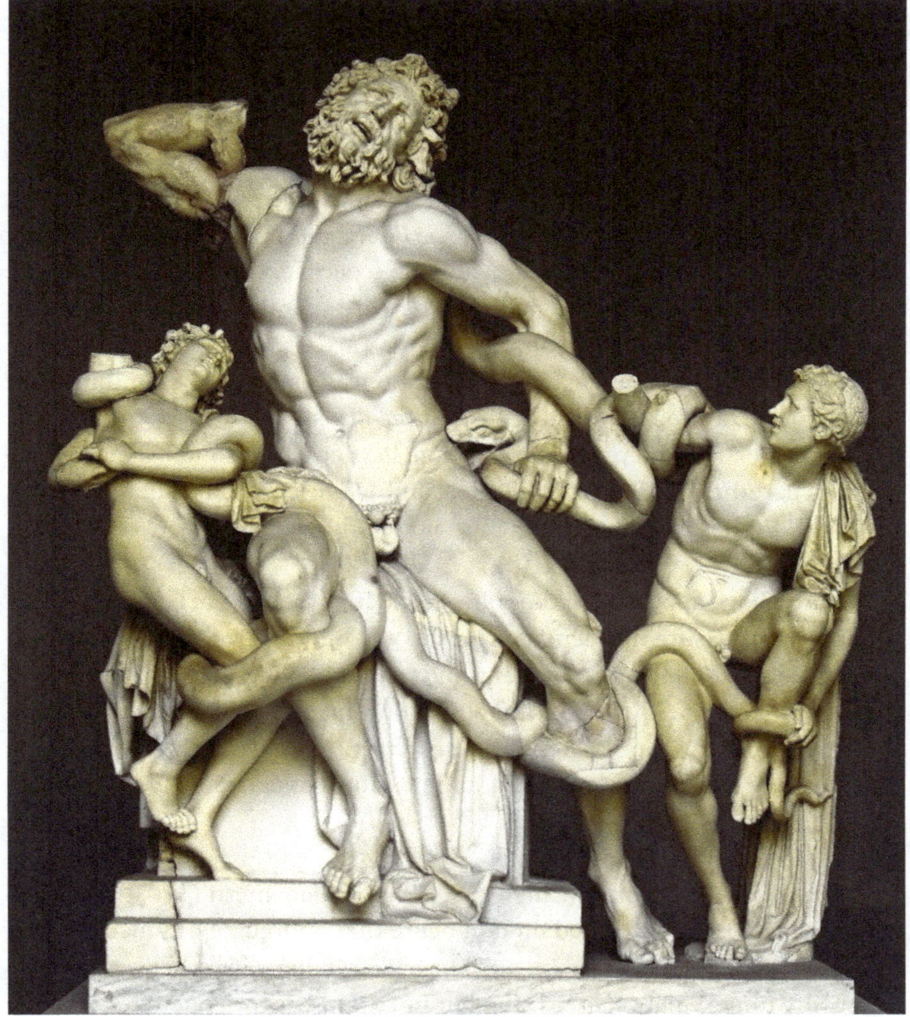

Figure 6.14 | *Laocoön*, group from the Hellenistic period, first century BCE, marble, height 208 cm. Source: © Zaharov / iStockphoto.

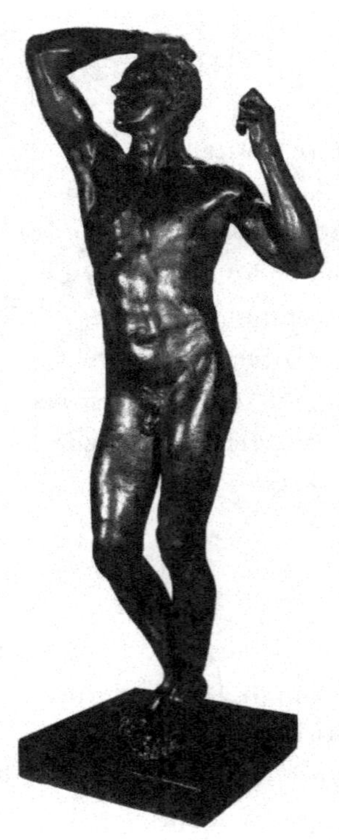

Figure 6.15 | Auguste Rodin, *The Age of Bronze*, c.1876/1877, bronze, height 182.9 cm, Paris, Musée Rodin.
Source: Musée Rodin, Paris, France / Photo ©AISA / Bridgeman Images.

fight their certain deaths in vain. In wrestling the coiling monster, *Laocoön's* body twists in stunning **contrapposto** and every sinewy tendon and muscle-bound limb is accentuated in the throes of battle. The central protagonist becomes an archetypal powerhouse of 'masculinity'; and yet, maybe what the statue really shows us is the figures' own struggle to maintain an impossible ideal of strength and mastery. What might a psychoanalyst say about the gender-symbolic significance of the serpent? You may like to compare *Laocoön* with its 'feminine' Hellenistic counterpart the *Venus de Milo*, third to first centuries BCE.

The relationship between gender and art is too often over-simplified and categorisation can be unhelpful and misleading. The figure in *The Age of Bronze*, c.1876/1877 by Auguste Rodin (1840–1917), seems to melt rhythmically and gracefully from the top of his odalisque-like elbow to his toe, and he is poised on one foot with his hips tilted out in a typical posture of physical display. The **patinated** surface of the statue appears wet with a sensuous sheen and this male figure, while standing erect with a wealth of impressive musculature on show, is effeminate to the point that he seems to confront both 'masculine' and 'feminine' stereotypes.

In what sense can the sculptures described above be discussed in terms of gender? A rigid classification is sometimes impossible, although some works do function primarily in this way. *Psyche Revived by Cupid's Kiss*, 1793, by Antonio Canova (1757–1822) is a notable example. Ask yourself how the sculptor has represented the figures. They are certainly graceful and captured in a moment of loving embrace, but they are also very sensual: the male figure touches the female figure's breast, their eyes meet and an imminent kiss becomes our focus within their framing arms.

In terms of its gendered representation, Psyche is horizontal, languid, passive and bare-breasted; Cupid is vertical and active, controlling her head with his hand. He has the power of flight – notice the way he pivots on his feet, wings still not yet rested.

Women have appeared in the role of seductress, object of beauty and victim in equal measure throughout art history. While Canova's eighteenth-century marble exemplifies a reverent and masterful Neo-classical beauty, in which woman appears as the ideal object of romantic love, Alberto Giacometti's twentieth-century bronze, *Woman with Her Throat Cut*, depicts the female figure as victim of physical, and possibly sexual, violence.

Who is victimised here?

In *Woman with Her Throat Cut*, 1932, Alberto Giacometti (1901–1966) depicts a violated and murdered mutant figure that is, arguably, denied identity other than as an object of desire and abuse. Part female, part insect, her fragile legs are unnervingly splayed, and her torso appears torn open to reveal the

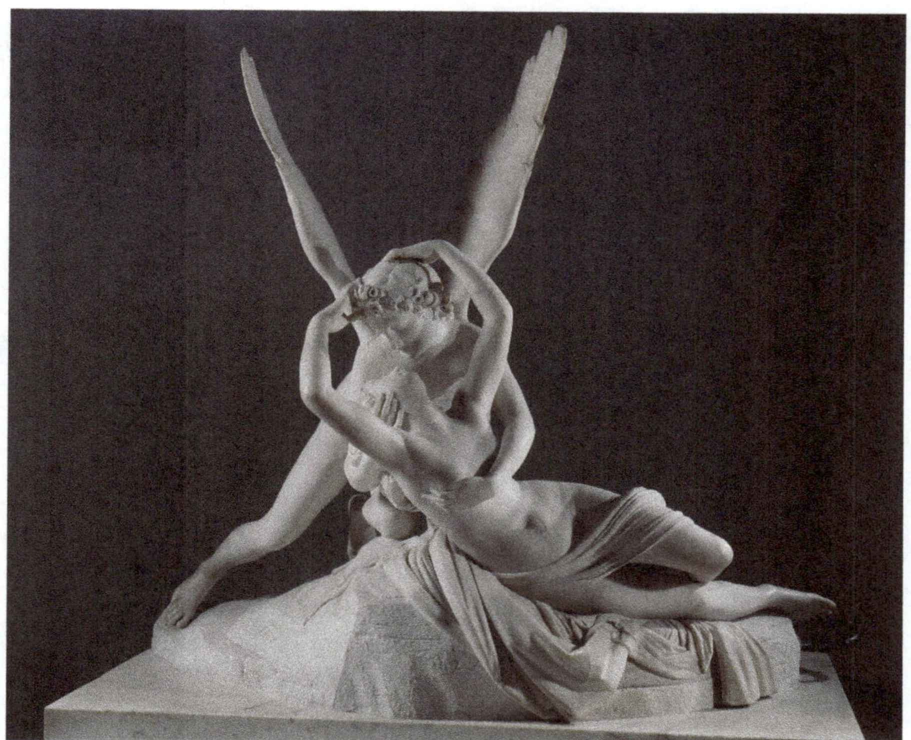

Figure 6.16 | Antonio Canova, *Psyche Revived by Cupid's Kiss*, 1793, marble sculpture, height 155 cm, Paris, Musée du Louvre. Source: The Art Archive / Musée du Louvre Paris / Gianni Dagli Orti.

curvature of her abdomen; two tiny breasts between twig-like arms enable us to identify her sex. Spoon-shaped hands anchor her helplessly to the floor. An arched and extended trachea terminates with a tiny head and an open mouth that belies her silence; she is anonymous and without voice. Typically displayed on the floor without a plinth, the sculpture suggests an invitation to walk over the hybrid figure. We look down on the work, its battered surface capturing the light as we watch her convulse in the throes of death and suffering.

This work could be understood as representing a hideously misogynistic depiction of the female nude, but this reading may be too simplistic. Her torment is unnerving enough to subvert the voyeurism attached to the history of the nude. The themes of sex and violence surface more immediately

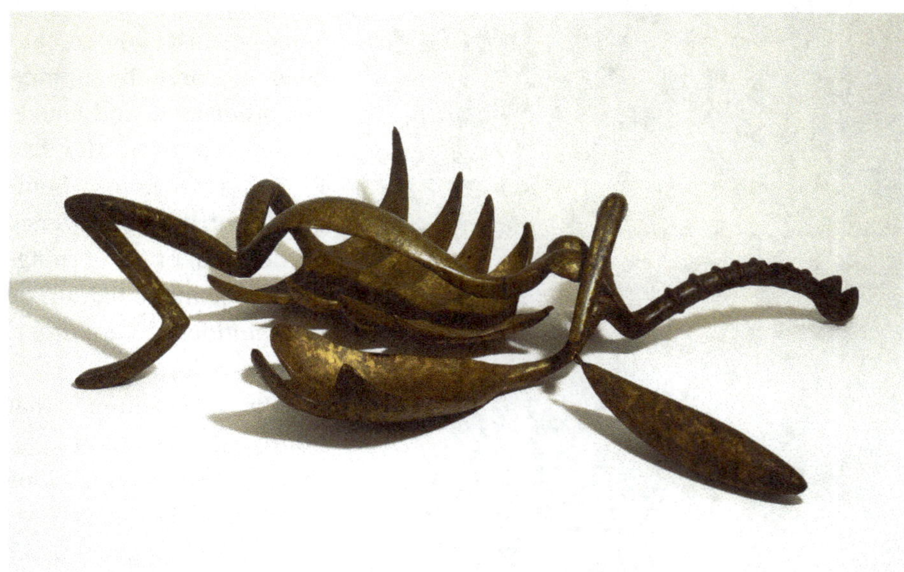

Figure 6.17 | Alberto Giacometti, *Woman with Her Throat Cut*, 1932, bronze (cast 1949), 20.3 × 87.6 × 63.5 cm, New York, Museum of Modern Art (MoMA). Purchase. Acc. n.: 696.1949. Source: © 2015. Digital image, The Museum of Modern Art, New York / Scala, Florence / © The Estate of Alberto Giacometti (Fondation Giacometti, Paris and ADAGP, Paris), licensed in the UK by ACS and DACS, London 2015.

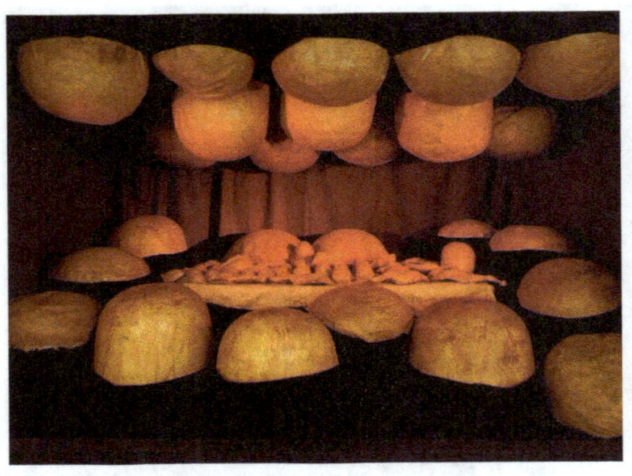

Figure 6.18 | Louise Bourgeois, *The Destruction of the Father*, 1974, latex, plaster, wood, fabric and red lighting, 237.8 × 362.3 × 248.6 cm. Source: Photo: Rafael Lobato, ©The Easton Foundation / VAGA, New York / DACS, London 2015.

than issues of gender; or do they? As the gallery label at the Museum of Modern Art (MoMA), New York, puts it:

Giacometti originally intended Woman with Her Throat Cut to rest directly on the floor, part of the 'real' world, distanced from the lofty realm of art. A hybrid animal, insect, and human, the female figure's body appears to be simultaneously in the throes of sexual ecstasy and in the spasms of death – embodying the phrase petite mort (little death), a French term for orgasm. The sexual drama and violence in this work is a powerfully discomfiting example of the misogynistic imagery frequently present in Surrealism. (Exhibition label 'The Erotic Object: Surrealist Sculpture from the Collection', Museum of Modern Art, New York, 2009–2010)

You may recall the grisly murder scene *Judith Slaying Holofernes*, painted by the female Baroque artist Artemisia Gentileschi, c.1593–1652 (examined previously in *Chapter 3* and *Chapter 4*). Gentileschi, herself the victim of torture by the authorities following her seduction by her tutor, sought revenge in the only way she could – painting the brutal decapitation of Judith's enemy – Holofernes.

The recurring role of woman as sexual victim throughout the centuries found a particularly critical voice in the work of contemporary feminist artist Jenny Holzer, who brought the idea of female vulnerability home with her series of 'Truisms' (a statement that is obviously true), particularly the work *Murder has its Sexual Side*, 1993/4.

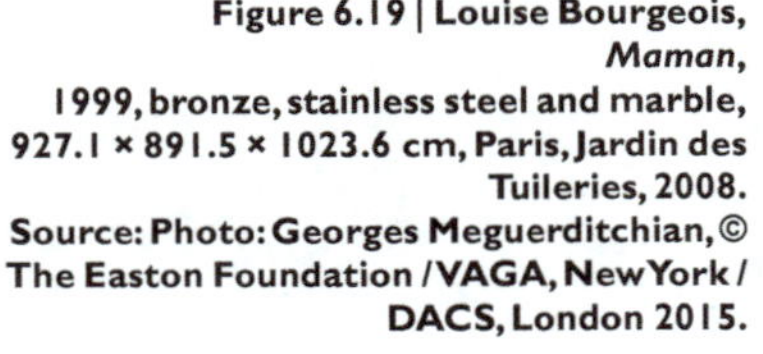

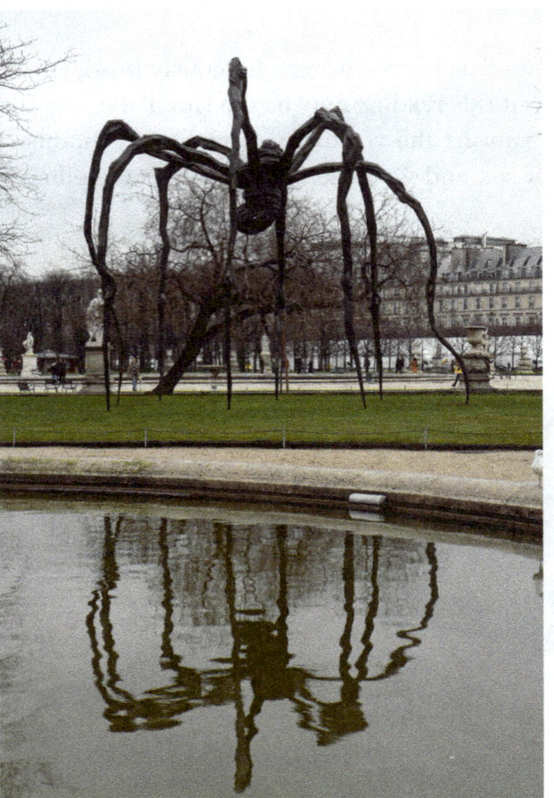

Figure 6.19 | Louise Bourgeois, *Maman*, 1999, bronze, stainless steel and marble, 927.1 × 891.5 × 1023.6 cm, Paris, Jardin des Tuileries, 2008. Source: Photo: Georges Meguerditchian, © The Easton Foundation / VAGA, New York / DACS, London 2015.

The theme of violence, and often sexualised violence against women, has been explored by numerous other male and female artists. However, the late French artist Louise Bourgeois contributes a reversal of the usual order of things in her seminal work *The Destruction of the Father*, 1974.

The revelation that Bourgeois' philandering father had been having a long affair with her governess had a lasting impact on her and her subsequent work.

The Destruction of the Father is usually interpreted as a confessional and Freudian exploration of her father's dominance over her mother and his offspring; the womb-like **installation** in mixed-media glows with the expectant consumption of the dominating father. The children, featured as abstract blobs, murder their father in an unthinkably cannibalistic crime. Bourgeois described the 'event':

He is unbearably dominating although probably he does not realize it himself. A kind of resentment grows and one day my brother and I decided, 'the time has come!' We grabbed him, laid him on the table and with our knives dissected him. We took him apart and dismembered him, we cut off his penis. And he became food. We ate him up … he was liquidated the same way he liquidated the children. (Louise Bourgeois quoted in Conn, 'Delicate Strength')

Bourgeois' **oeuvre** tends to be characterised by issues relating to parenthood, the male form and childhood. *Maman*, 1999, is a monumental sculpture of a giant female spider and Bourgeois has said it represents the power, protection and strength she associates with the figure of the mother:

The Spider is an ode to my mother. She was my best friend. Like a spider, my mother was a weaver. My family was in the business of tapestry restoration, and my mother was in charge of the workshop. Like spiders, my mother was very clever. Spiders are friendly presences that eat mosquitoes. We know that mosquitoes spread diseases and are therefore unwanted. So, spiders are helpful and protective, just like my mother. (Tate Gallery, 'Tate Acquires Louise Bourgeois's Giant Spider, Maman')

Bourgeois broke down masculine barriers in the art world with her mastery of the 'masculine' **medium** of sculpture, and subverted typical representations of the victimisation of the female. American artist Judy Chicago caused similar controversy in the male-dominated museum world of the 1970s with her famously explicit form of female **iconography**. At this time in Britain and the United States, a consciously feminist art was emerging and gaining support from a range of feminist publications that included *Spare Rib* in Britain and *The Feminist Art Journal in the United States*.

The celebration of woman's work

The feminist installation *The Dinner Party*, 1979, by Judy Chicago (born 1939) was first exhibited in 1979 and comprises 39 multi-media place settings (13 on each side of an equilateral triangle). Its triangular formation references an ancient symbol of femininity, while its equilateral nature represents the ideal of gender equality. Each elaborately decorated place setting celebrates an important woman in history and place settings include sensuously shiny dinner plates shaped to evoke the form and delicacy of female genitalia. Chicago describes these open, petal-like ceramics as *a central core, my vagina, that which made me a woman* (Chadwick, *Women, Art and Society*, p. 358).

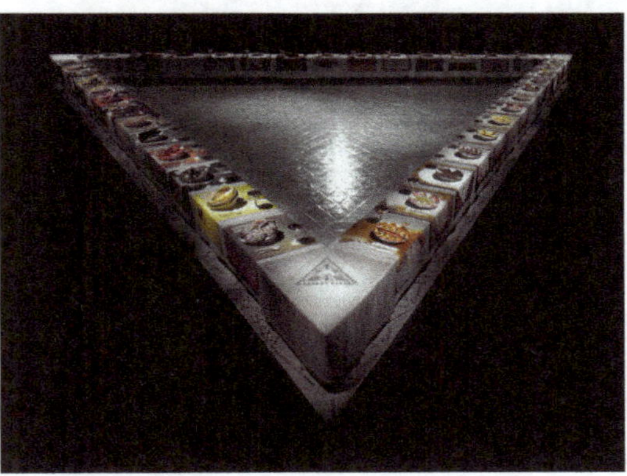

Figure 6.20 | Judy Chicago, *The Dinner Party*, 1979, mixed media, 1463 × 1463 cm, New York, NY, USA, Brooklyn Museum. Source: Photo: © Donald Woodman, courtesy of Judy Chicago / Art Resource, NY / © Judy Chicago. ARS, NY and DACS, London 2015.

6.2 Critical debates: feminism in conflict

Many women, both in the late 1970s and since, have criticised Judy Chicago's *The Dinner Party* for appearing to reduce important female artists and historical figures represented in the work to their genitals. However, as Whitney Chadwick points out, Chicago warned from the beginning that the celebration of femaleness should not simply be viewed as 'womb art' but, in Chadwick's words, *It should be understood by providing a framework within which to reverse devaluations of female anatomy in patriarchal culture* (Chadwick, *Women, Art and Society*, p. 359). The oversized female genitalia were a reverential celebration of that which made a woman female, intended to confront and reverse the typical social evaluation of the male form as superior.

There is obviously scope for debate about this. Was it helpful to the feminist cause to point out biological female difference and to suggest that women should celebrate and affirm their difference from men, rooting these differences in their bodies? Or does this strategy risk reaffirming discrimination and prejudice?

British feminists Griselda Pollock and Roszika Parker (1981) criticised Chicago's installation because *it is easily retrieved and co-opted by a male culture because [it does] not rupture radically meanings and connotations of woman in art as body, as sexual, as nature, as object for male possession* (Chadwick, *Women, Art and Society*, p. 379). What do you think?

Patriarchy, according to feminists, has also been responsible for the separation of 'high' and 'low' art. Typically, craft work has been considered 'low', 'feminine' and devalued in comparison to the so-called 'high' arts of painting and sculpture, which for centuries restricted training to men and so have been male-dominated. Chicago, and other feminist artists like her, resurrected craft skills and elevated 'low' – and by extension female – art to the status of 'high' art by exhibiting it in the San Francisco Museum of Modern Art.

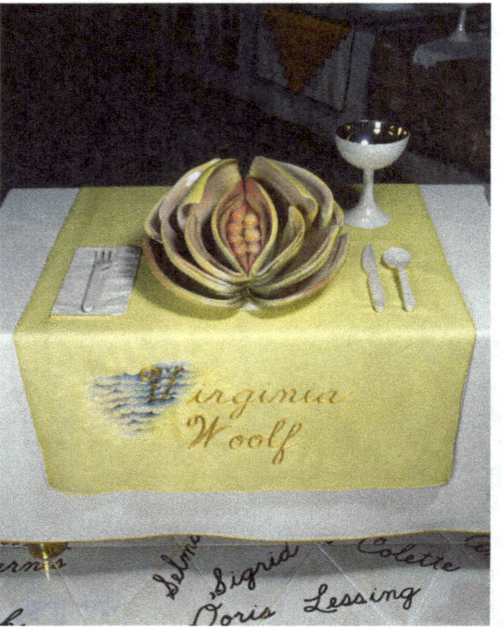

Figure 6.21 | Judy Chicago, *The Dinner Party*, 1979, detail, Virginia Woolf place setting, mixed media, 1463 × 1463 cm, New York, NY, USA, Brooklyn Museum. Source: Photo: © Donald Woodman, courtesy of Judy Chicago / Art Resource, NY / © Judy Chicago. ARS, NY and DACS, London 2015.

In *The Dinner Party*, decorative needlework records the names of honoured women, who include artists Georgia O'Keeffe and Frida Kahlo, and the writer Virginia Woolf. Butterflies are scattered in various stages of evolution (from larva to fully winged) as symbols of emancipation. Two decades later, contemporary British artist Tracey Emin (born 1963) drew on needlework skills (although her work is deliberately rough and ready in appearance) to create her infamous tent, *Everyone I Have Ever Slept With 1963–1995*, 1995. Unfortunately, this

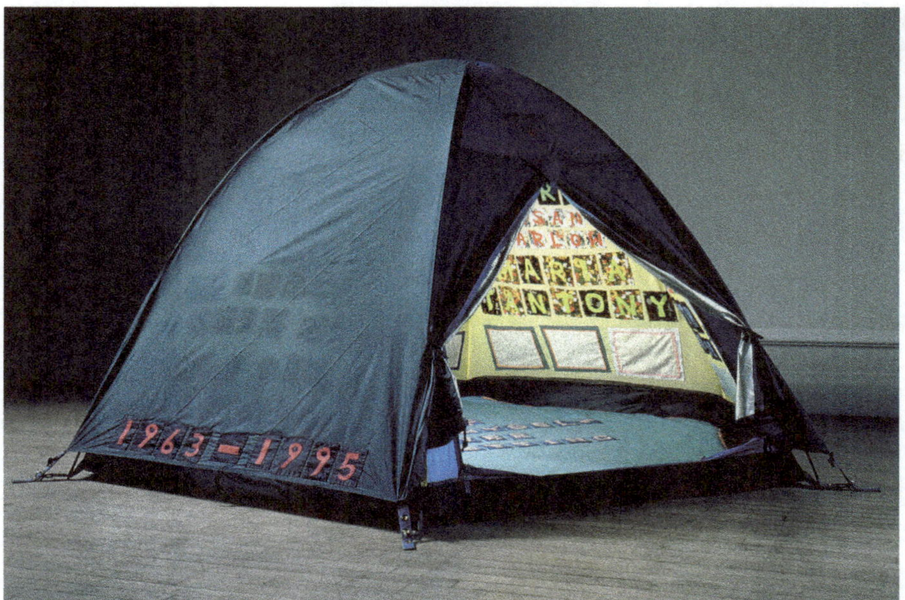

Figure 6.22 | Tracey Emin, *Everyone I Have Ever Slept With 1963–1995*, 1995, fabric appliqué, mattress, light. Source: © Tracey Emin. All rights reserved, DACS 2015. Image courtesy White Cube.

work was destroyed in a warehouse fire in 2004.

As the title suggests, Emin embellished this tent – a shop-bought **ready-made** – with the names of everyone she had ever slept with (meaning this term in the sense of sleeping, not sexual relations). The names include Emin's grandmother as well as the words 'FOETUS I' and 'FOETUS II', referring to two lost pregnancies. This embellished object subverts 'high' art once again through its use of craft techniques – a historically relegated and 'feminine' practice. Emin's tent stands unapologetically as a monument both to the artist's subjective feelings and to the elevation of the craft of appliqué in a contemporary canonical context. Emin's social and cultural status as an artist is discussed in *Chapter 5*.

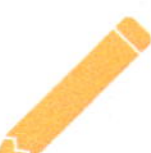

6.3 Explore this example

Take a look at the work of American artist Jann Haworth (born 1942). She is the real pioneer of **soft sculpture**, a type of sculpture associated with **Pop Art**. Does Haworth appear in any of the art history books you have found featuring American Pop Art? Soft sculpture tends to be associated with the American male artist Claes Oldenburg (born 1929). Interestingly, many of his works were stitched together by his wife, Coosje van Bruggen.

Gender inequality is not simply found in relation to the artist, subject or technique of the work of art; it is also to be found in an under-representation, or complete omission, of women's art work from galleries, collections, exhibitions and art history books. The latter was the subject of Linda Nochlin's essay 'Why Have There Been No Great Women Artists?' In this article, Nochlin explored why the status of artistic 'greatness' has been reserved for male artists such as Michelangelo and argues that the social expectations were historically against women pursuing art as a career, and so there were restrictions on women's art education and ability to exhibit and sell art works. These factors precluded the emergence of great women artists.

Gender issues in painting and sculpture are widely discussed, and an enormous body of literature exists to provide the reader with myriad related perspectives. However, the examination of gender and architecture is a path less worn, although no less interesting in scope.

Gender and the built environment

According to architectural historian Beatriz Colomina, *[t]he politics of space are always sexual* (Colomina, 'Introduction'). The following discussion seeks to examine architecture in relation to gender difference and so to navigate a complicated area of evolving discussion.

At the beginning of this chapter, Jan van Eyck's *Arnolfini Portrait* was dis-

The active production of gender distinctions can be found at every level of architectural discourse: in its ritual of legitimation, hiring practices, classification systems, lecture techniques, publicity images, canon formation, division of labor, bibliographies, design conventions, legal codes, salary structures, publishing practices, language, professional ethics, editing protocols, project credits etc.

(Wigley, 'Untitled: The Housing of Gender', p. 329)

cussed in association with ideas regarding the association of women with private domestic spaces and the association of men with outdoor, public spaces. These associations arose because of the different kinds of work done by men and women and the different social roles they were supposed to take historically. In his essay 'The Housing of Gender', architectural historian Mark Wigley identifies women's supposed propensity to immorality if granted freedom outside the home as a belief dating back to ancient Greece. He argues that the consequent effort to restrain women inside the home has had a lasting legacy in architecture, through the construction not only of architectural discourse but also of physical architectural spaces: *Unable to control herself, she must be controlled by being bounded* (Wigley, 'Untitled: The Housing of Gender', p. 335).

Architecture, in this sense, has been used historically to help regulate the social behaviour of men and women, and in particular to help reinforce the idea that a woman's place is in the home.

Gender symbolism has been attached to particular formal features of architecture since **Antiquity**; the ancient Greeks developed three **Orders**: **Doric**, **Ionic** and **Corinthian**, and the former two have been personified as 'male' and 'female', respectively (architectural Orders are most easily distinguished by their **capitals**). Roman writer, Marcus Vitruvius Pollio on the character of the Doric and Ionic Orders, stated: *Thus two orders were invented, one of a masculine character, without ornament, the other bearing a character which resembled the delicacy, ornament, and proportion of a female* (Vitruvius, *De Architectura*, Book IV, Chapter 1:7).

The Parthenon, the Temple of Athena Parthenos, in Athens is considered to be the finest example of the Doric Order ever built. The Doric Order, named after the Dorians, an ethnic Greek tribe, was thought to display stereotypically 'masculine' attributes on account of its proportions: larger diameter **columns** with a plain, strong design. The Doric Order also carried the

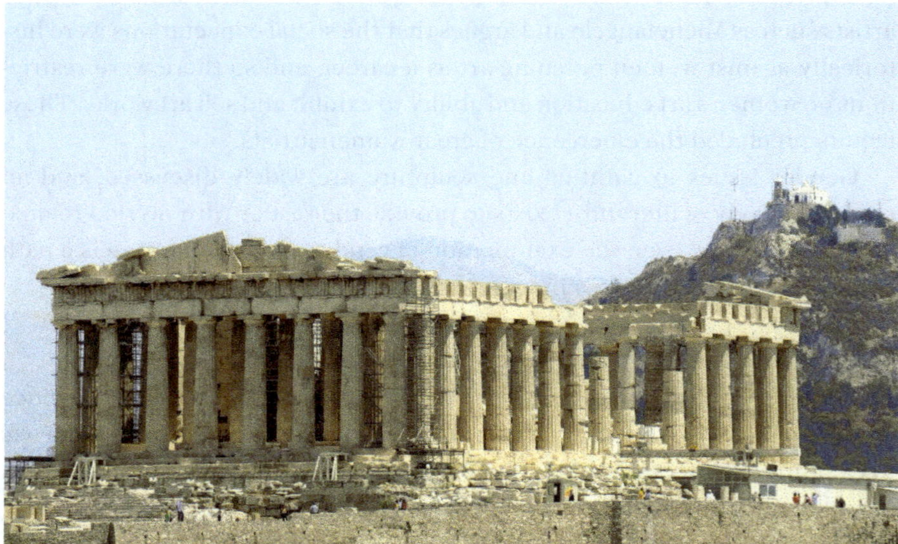

Figure 6.23 | Iktinos and Kallikrates, The Parthenon Temple, 447–438 BCE. Source: © krechet / iStockphoto.

heaviest **entablature** and became a metaphor for power and strength. While the Parthenon is built primarily in the Doric Order, its inner **colonnade** comprises Ionic columns supporting a continuous **frieze** – an ambivalent hybrid that its architect Iktinos had made his own. Despite its primary masculinity, the Parthenon was built to house the goddess of wisdom and war, Athena. However, the **mythological** story of Athena brings a level of complexity to our analysis of her as the 'feminine' aspect of the 'masculine' Parthenon. Born not from her mother but from her father's head, Athena appears from the very first instance in full armour and remains an unmarried virgin and goddess of war, no less.

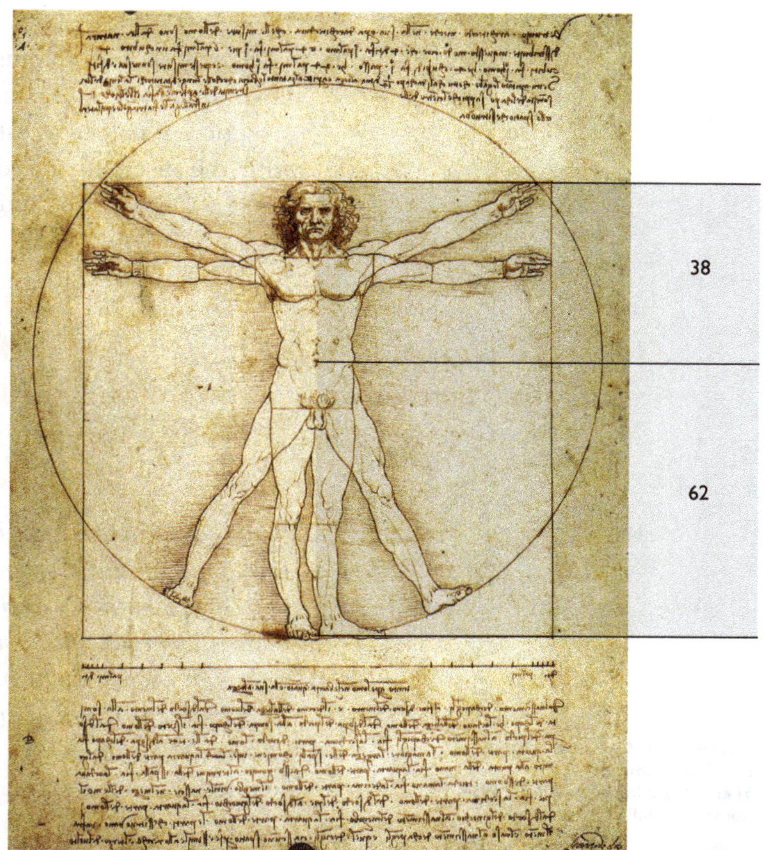

Figure 6.24 | Leonardo da Vinci, *Vitruvian Man*, 1490, pen and ink, Venice, Gallerie dell'Accademia. Source: © Dennis Hallinan / Alamy.

Compare the Doric Order of the Parthenon with the Ionic Order of the Temple of Athena Nike in Athens, late fifth century BCE. What are their technical differences? How do their differing proportions and decorative treatments support an analysis in terms of their 'masculinity' or 'femininity'? Since Antiquity, the **Golden Section** (discussed in *Chapter 3*) has been regarded as the perfect proportion. Expressed as ϕ, it is also known as the 'divine proportion' and is found in nature and mathematics and used in art and architecture. The Golden Section is a ratio of 1:1.618, regarded as the most ideal proportion not just aesthetically but also because it occurs in nature, in such things as seed spirals in sunflowers and shells. In seeking the ideal, artists and architects applied geometrical proportions, including the Golden Section, to the human body.

Leonardo da Vinci based his drawing *Vitruvian Man* on some tentative correlations of ideal human proportions with geometry in Book III of the treatise *On Architecture* (*De Architectura*) by the ancient Roman architect Marcus Vitruvius Pollio. According to architectural theorist Diane Agrest, the patriarchal **Renaissance** discourse that symbolically excluded women at professional and built level was considered normative after a while:

Architecture in the Renaissance establishes a system of rules that is the basis of Western architecture. The texts of the Renaissance, which in turn read the classic texts from Vitruvius, develop a logocentric and anthropomorphic discourse establishing the male body at the center of the unconscious of architectural rules and configurations. The body is inscribed in the system of architecture as a male body replacing the female body. (Agrest, 'Architecture from Without: Body, Logic and Sex', p. 359)

In the mid-twentieth century, German architect and dominant figure in skyscraper design Ludwig Mies van der Rohe (1886–1969), created strictly functional, non-decorative, glass-walled structures that punctuated the American skyline with a 'masculine' authority and scale. The Miesian prototype answered the need for corporate office spaces and delivered the acme of the modernist aesthetic in the process. Arguably, the vertical force, competing height and sleekly engineered **façades** sat comfortably in a city. How do these vertical forms symbolise male power and authority?

The Seagram Building, 1958, was designed by Mies van der Rohe in collaboration with the American architect Philip Johnson. At the time of its construction, it helped to establish the lexicon of skyscraper design and chimed with the disciplined and commercial demands of New York City. In what sense is the Seagram Building gendered? What formal characteristics are you identifying to justify your response?

The twentieth-century skyscraper, a pinnacle of patriarchal symbology, is rooted in the masculine mystique of the big, erect, the forceful – the full balloon of the inflated masculine ego.

(Weisman, 'Prologue', p. 1)

According to architectural theorist and writer Jane Rendell, the male-dominated profession of architecture affects women in a number of different ways:

Women's exclusion from the architectural profession and education is not only a historical problem but also one critical to the role of women architects practising today. For example, in the United Kingdom, although many women start architectural courses – an average of 27 per cent of all architectural students are women – only 9 per cent of women complete their studies and practise architecture. In the profession, although there has been an increase in the number of women registered as architects, from 5 per cent in 1975 to 11 per cent in 1997, the figure still shows that only one in ten of practicing architects is female. (Rendell in Rendell, Penner and Borden, *Gender Space Architecture: An Interdisciplinary Introduction*, p. 228)

Figure 6.25 | Mies van der Rohe and Philip Johnson, Seagram Building, New York, 1958. Source: © Philip Scalia / Alamy.

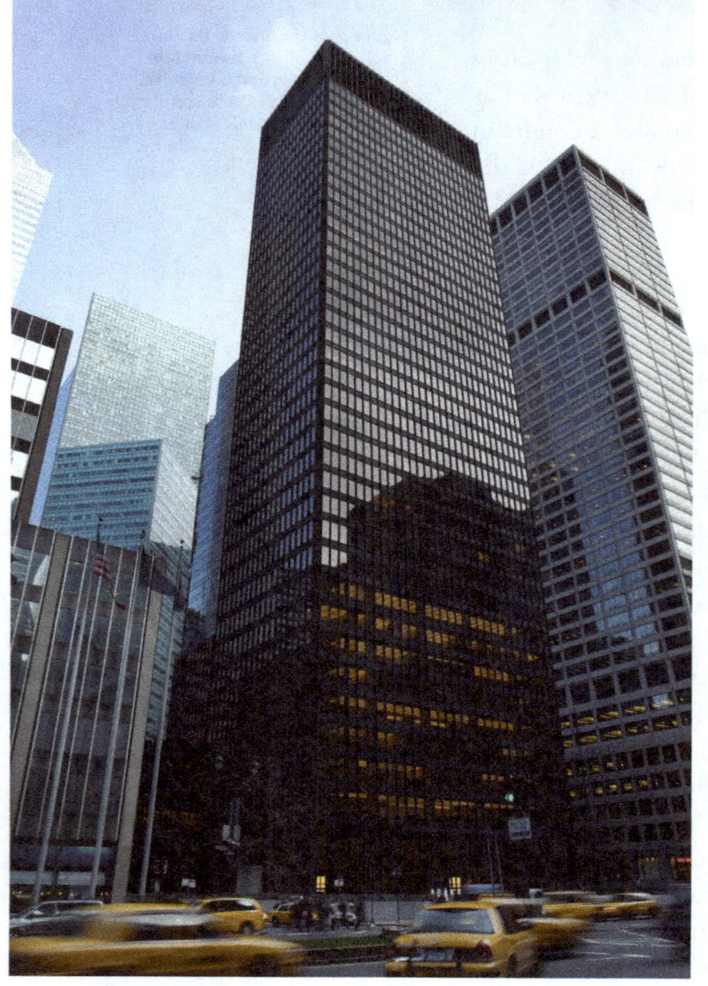

Women may have been excluded from practising architecture historically, but recently some female architects have been responsible for creating some of the world's most famous buildings. Amanda Levete collaborated with her husband Jan Kaplický to create the Media Centre at Lord's Cricket Ground, examined in *Chapter 4*. Award-winning architect Jane Drew triumphed in a male-dominated profession to design and co-design numerous buildings all around the world, including ones in Milton Keynes for that bastion of inclusive learning the Open University. In 2004, Zaha Hadid became the first female in the world to win the Pritzker Architectural Prize – the profession's highest award – and has most recently received tremendous media attention in relation to her Al-Wakrah Stadium in Qatar, on account of it looking far too female in form. What do you think?

Architect Barbara Kuit worked with Mark Hemel to create the Canton Tower, Guangzhou, China, 2009 – the world's tallest TV tower – and designed a building so female in form it's been dubbed the 'Supermodel': the structure's two ellipses tighten in the middle to form 'her' waist. How does her nipped-in form defy the 'masculine' prototype for skyscraper functionality?

Another building whose idiosyncratic form confers gender stereotypes is that created by Canadian-born architect Frank Gehry (born 1929) and Croatian-born architect Vlado Milunić (born 1941) in Prague for the giant insurance company Nationale-Nederlanden. The architects eschewed Canadian, Czech and Dutch identities to create a structure for which there was no precedent in Prague's historic centre. Known officially as the Netherlands National Building, and playfully as the 'Fred and Ginger' building – after twentieth-century dancers Fred Astaire and Ginger Rogers – the structure's form lends itself readily to a discussion of gender and architecture, just as much as it serves to defy nationalism. The left-hand structure of this building mimics the female form; its glass sheathing is fragile, and its dress-like frame appears delicate and corseted. Together, these structures combine to appear dancing and highly gendered. It also has a dancing **fenestration**: geometric windows on rhythmically decorated walls.

Gehry and Milunić created a **Deconstructivist** icon for Prague, debunking modernist aesthetics and pulling apart old formulae. Their **postmodern** caricaturing smacks of an 'anything goes' **Zeitgeist** and puts any discussion of gender identity into an uncomfortable state of flux. Similarly, the Netherlands National Building also has an interesting and unexpected contribution to make to the theme of nationality. Former Soviet occupation and dominance necessitated a need to reassert Czech architecture in order to heal old wounds and Gehry's and Milunić's creation was viewed by some of its critics as more American and less Czech than had been hoped for. Academic writers Sibelan Forrester, Magdalena Zaborowska and Elena Gapova stated:

In this context, as the most visible and widely publicised contemporary building in Prague, the Netherlands National Building will continue to represent an important moment in the ongoing debate over Prague's architectural future. For many, the transposition of the signature style of an important American [sic] architect into the centre of Prague connotes Western cultural imperialism. However, for many Czechs, the building also symbolises renewed cultural and economic links to the West. While an American critic may see another prestigious sculptural building that functions primarily as [a] monument to itself and its maker, many Czechs see a new symbol of creativity and freedom regained. (Forrester, Zaborowska *and Gapova, Over the Wall/After the Fall: Post-Communist Cultures Through an East–West Gaze,* p. 123)

It seems that Frank Gehry himself was well aware of the nationalist associations his building could elicit. His co-architect, Vlado Milunić, was asked in 2003: *In the beginning it was more commonly known as the Fred and Ginger Building, now everyone seems to call it the Dancing Building – did the Fred and Ginger name just disappear?* To which he answered: *That was Frank's idea but then he was afraid to import American Hollywood* ***kitsch*** *to Prague* (Willoughby, 'Architect Recalls Genesis of Dancing Building as Coffee Table Book Published').

Top to bottom:

Figure 6.26 | Frank Gehry, and Vlado Milunić Netherlands National Building or 'Dancing House', Prague, 1996. Source: © age fotostock / Alamy.

Figure 6.27 | Frank Gehry, and Vlado Milunić Netherlands National Building, Prague, 1996, detail of dancing window. Source: © Andrea Visconti / Shutterstock.

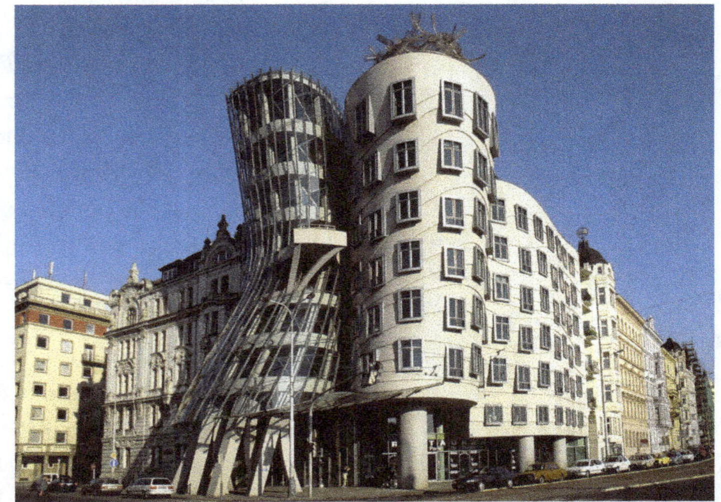

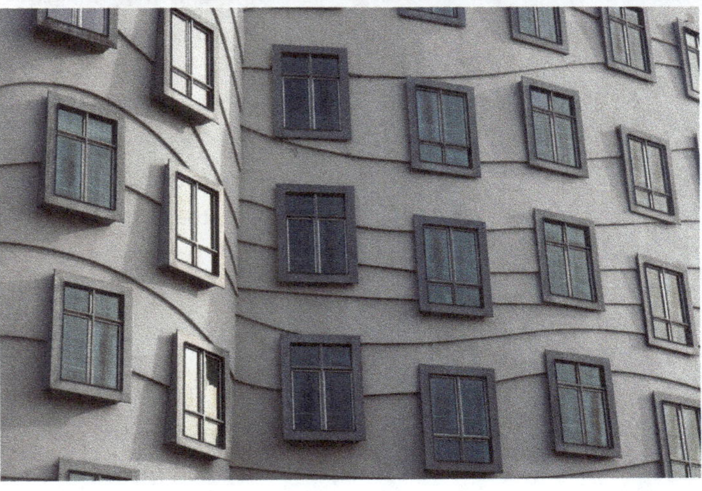

Nationality

So much of art history is viewed through the lenses of national and geographical difference and the history of nations competing for dominance. Trends in international trading and the recent phenomenon of globalisation may have led to the erosion of distinct national identities. Despite these changes, nations across the globe have erected monuments that assert their national supremacy to the world.

Emblems and monuments to national identity

Famous for its depiction of the people's revolution against the monarch Charles X, *Liberty Leading the People*, 1830, by Eugène Delacroix (1798–1863) is a useful example to study in relation to the topic of 'nationality'. Liberty, the embodiment of the fight for freedom, strides towards us, the tricolour flag (ultimate emblem of French nationality) held high and emphatically on the central vertical axis. There had been fighting in the capital since the previous day and the citizens of Paris and the king's troops had formed ranks on opposite sites. Barricades had been erected. Shots had been fired. People had been killed. Early that morning, the senior commander of the royal troops informed the king: *This is no riot. This is a revolution* (Hagen and Hagen, *What Great Paintings Say: From the Bayeux Tapestry to Diego Rivera*, p. 567). The citizens of Paris united, and the 27th, 28th and 29th of July 1830 were 'Three Glorious Days' of revolution (the second major revolution after the French Revolution of 1789). Insurgents from every class revolted against the policies of Charles X. Among the king's decrees was censorship of the press, and the citizens of Paris fought hardest in defence of this freedom. The insurgents were triumphant and the king was forced to abdicate.

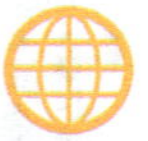

See the companion website for reference to a detailed discussion of this painting.

6.1 Let's connect the themes: form and style

In *Liberty Leading the People* by Eugène Delacroix, the freedom the people are shown fighting for can be interpreted as being reflected in Delacroix's loose brushwork and the colours of the nationalist tricolour that permeate the canvas. The sabre-wielding proletarian ties his pistol around his waist with a red, white and blue cloth, while a smaller tricolour is visible through gun powder grey plumes on the cathedral of Notre-Dame in the distance to the right of the figures. The red, white and blue of the nation's flag even appear in the air down the right-hand side of this atmospheric canvas.

In these ways, colour unites the image compositionally, just as the classes are shown – the poor, the proletarian, and the bourgeois – uniting politically.

Liberty Leading the People may allude conveniently to nationality, but the centrality of its female warrior has also attracted feminist analysis. Linda Nochlin concedes that Delacroix's Liberty *is not a conciliatory peacemaker*

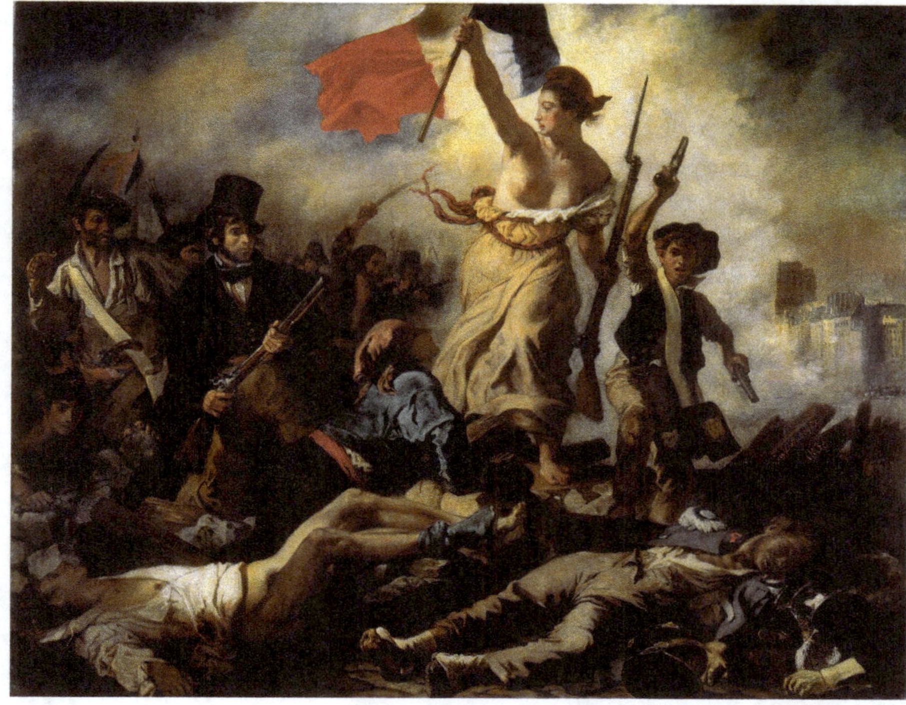

Figure 6.28 | Eugène Delacroix, *Liberty Leading the People* (Allegory of the July Revolution 1830, with self-portrait), 1830, oil on canvas, 360 × 225 cm, Paris, Musée du Louvre. Source: akg-images.

but a bellicose leader; however, she also notes that Liberty's active and emphatic lead is *only by virtue of the fact that she is neither a historical personage nor a contemporary member of the crowd she leads but, rather, an allegorical figure* (Nochlin, *Representing Women*, p. 49).[25] Delacroix wrote to his brother, *If I haven't lived for my country, at least I shall paint for it!* (Hagen and Hagen, *What Great Paintings Say: From the Bayeux Tapestry to Diego Rivera*, p. 569).

In the same way that the revolution of 1830 inspired Delacroix to paint, the Mexican Revolution of 1910–1920 inspired the work of the fervently nationalistic Mexican painter Frida Kahlo. Following the revolution, and after many years of colonialism, Mexico fostered a proud national culture pertaining to all things Mexican, known as *Mexicanidad*. No one celebrated *Mexicanidad* more than Mexico's most famous female artist, Frida Kahlo (1907–1954). Such was Kahlo's sense of national pride that she changed her birth date to 1910 (she was born in 1907) to coincide with the Mexican Revolution (see *6.2 Let's connect the themes: historical perspectives*), thus realigning herself more fully with its cause. Kahlo also developed what could be described as a national style: naive and folk-like with references to popular culture, but also reminiscent of traditional Catholic colonial Mexican **ex-voto** and **retablos** paintings, some alluding to ancient gods, native flora and fauna, Mexican costume and produce.

25 Nochlin relates the dilution of woman's power by mythology to what Simone de Beauvoir meant by 'woman-as-other' in de Beauvoir's seminal feminist text *The Second Sex*, 1949.

6.2 Let's connect the themes: historical perspectives

Mexico gained independence from Spain in 1813 and immediately embraced its ancient pre-colonised, **pre-Columbian** ancestry. Despite the nation's freedom from colonisation, a culturally repressive and authoritarian regime soon grew up to replace the old colonial administration, and it was not until the 1910–1920 revolution that Mexican people were fully free to find their true Mexican identity.

The authoritarian regime was led by the Mexican dictator Porfirio Díaz, who was ousted from power by Francisco Madero. While Díaz had been considered a ruthless autocrat, Madero appeared to champion liberal reform, but he was assassinated in 1913 and Mexico was thrown into a bloody power struggle. By 1920 the revolution had all but come to an end and, with Álvaro Obregón as president, the country settled into a comparatively peaceful period. During this time there was an unprecedented call to nationalism known as *Mexicanidad* and the artist Frida Kahlo, who had felt bound up with and loyal to the revolution all her life, turned to pre-Columbian culture as one way of reconstructing her indigenous Mexican identity. This was associated with negating Mexico's Western colonialism and its subsequent autocracy. See the companion website for more detail.

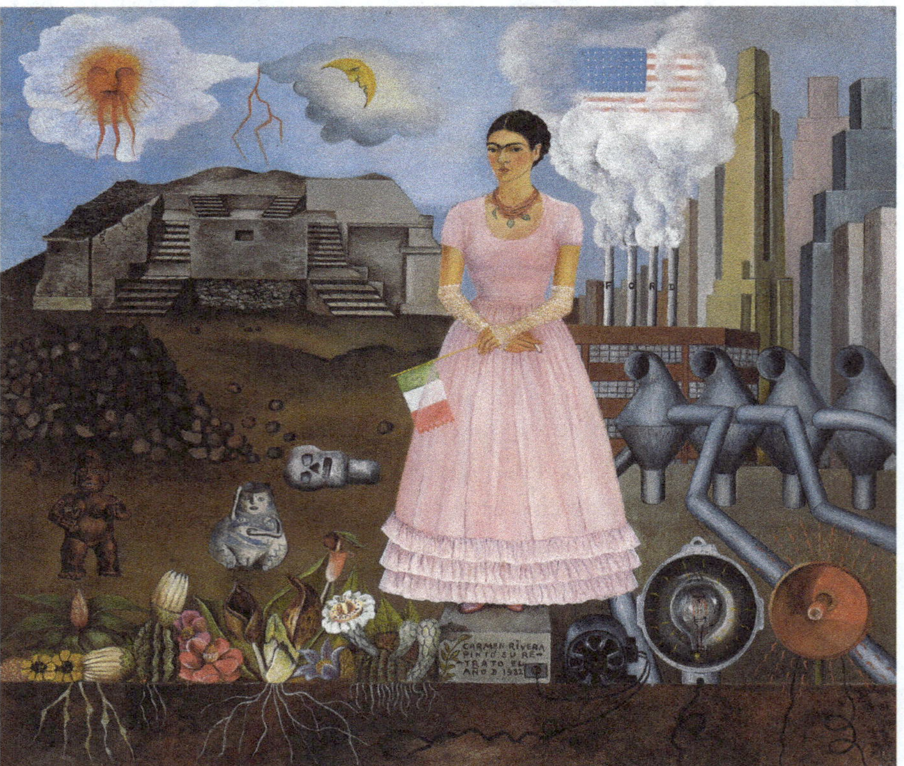

Figure 6.29 | Frida Kahlo, *Self-Portrait on the Borderline between Mexico and the United States*, 1932, oil on canvas, Private Collection. Source: Private Collection / Photo © Christie's Images / Bridgeman Images / © 2015. Banco de México Diego Rivera Frida Kahlo museums Trust, Mexico, D.F. / DACS.

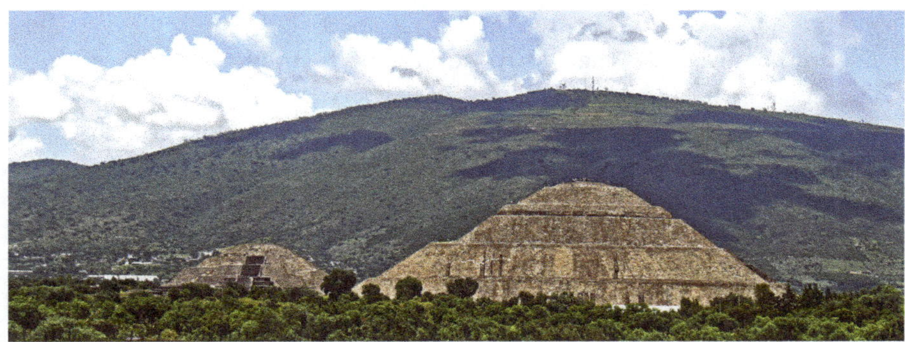

Figure 6.30 | Pyramid of the Sun, Teotihuacan.
This site is believed to date from the second century BCE and its position as central to ancient Mexico is revered.
© Lazcanini / iStockphoto.

Kahlo conveyed her Mexican nationality throughout her oeuvre (her painting *Viva La Vida*, examined as an example of still life in *Chapter 1*, is a notable example), but *Self-Portrait on the Borderline Between Mexico and the United States*, 1932, is the most explicit indication of how she felt about her ancient homeland, which is on the left of the painting, and the comparatively grey and industrialised United States, on the right. Kahlo stands in the middle of the composition on the fault-line of their polarised divide. She is holding the Mexican flag in her left hand and shifting her body on its pedestal towards home – an outward indication of nationalistic loyalty. This painting is political: it represents Kahlo's post-revolutionary, left-wing national identity. She paints the United States as the bastion of capitalism and Mexico as a cultural heartland rejuvenated by the post-revolution transformation of the nation.

Apart from the painting's title and composition, Kahlo expresses her affiliation with Mexico in a number of other ways: dressed in an indigenous Tehuana dress with pre-Columbian beads around her neck, the artist stands over remnants of the ancient Aztec culture she often referenced in her work. In the left-hand foreground, vibrant colours and lush native flowers spring from the fertile soil, which nurtures (solid roots have taken hold) regeneration. On the right, monochromatic factory parts feed from electric cables, which appear lifeless in comparison (although they represent the air-conditioning, heat and light Americans enjoyed and Mexicans aimed to achieve). The mechanised production in the background spells out 'FORD', ex-voto style, perhaps as though this brand-name were a kind of industrial god that supports the Stars and Stripes above it. White vertical puffs of polluted air belch out from Ford's pipes and find their opposite – or perhaps their parallel – in the horizontal clouds on the left that drift above an ancient ruined Aztec temple. Beneath the temple are fertility dolls and a skull to remind us of the cycle of life, in contrast to the anthropomorphic ducts – a continuing duality that pervades the entire canvas. Does the painting represent the superiority of one culture over another, or their equivalence?

Does the fact that Kahlo was a woman mean that critics automatically assume she privileges 'nature' over technology in her work?

Kahlo's pride in her nation was expressed in small-scale works that took decades to reach a worldwide audience. Expressions of nationality in architecture tend to make their impact more instantaneously, however.

Alexandre Gustave Eiffel (1832–1923) was a French structural engineer who founded his own engineering office in 1866 and designed and built bridges all over Europe. He is best known, however, as the architect of the world-famous Eiffel Tower, 1887–1889, which was built for the 1889 'Universal Exposition' in Paris, France. (see Figure 6.31)

> **6.3 Let's connect the themes: materials and techniques**
>
> The new technologies and materials heralded by the Industrial Revolution had a tremendous impact on art and architecture across Europe. All-metal machine tools were developed early on in the nineteenth century, and Eiffel's own expertise in metal facilitated construction on grander and more complicated scales than had ever been achieved before. Eiffel gained a reputation for the construction of bridges, the demand for which had increased as a result of new opportunities to travel.

The Eiffel Tower took centre stage at the 'Exposition Universelle' in 1889 to celebrate the hundredth anniversary of the French Revolution, and drew unprecedented numbers of people to the capital. The tower is now recognised as a national symbol of France the world over. At 301 metres high, it was the tallest structure in the world at the time of its completion.

Across the Atlantic, the monumental and equally iconic Statue of Liberty

Left to right:
Figure 6.31 | Alexandre Gustave Eiffel, The Eiffel Tower, Paris, 1887–1889, wrought iron, height 301 m. Source: © carterdayne / iStockphoto.

Figure 6.32 | Frédéric Bartholdi, Statue of Liberty, 1886, copper. Source: © Nikada / iStockphoto.

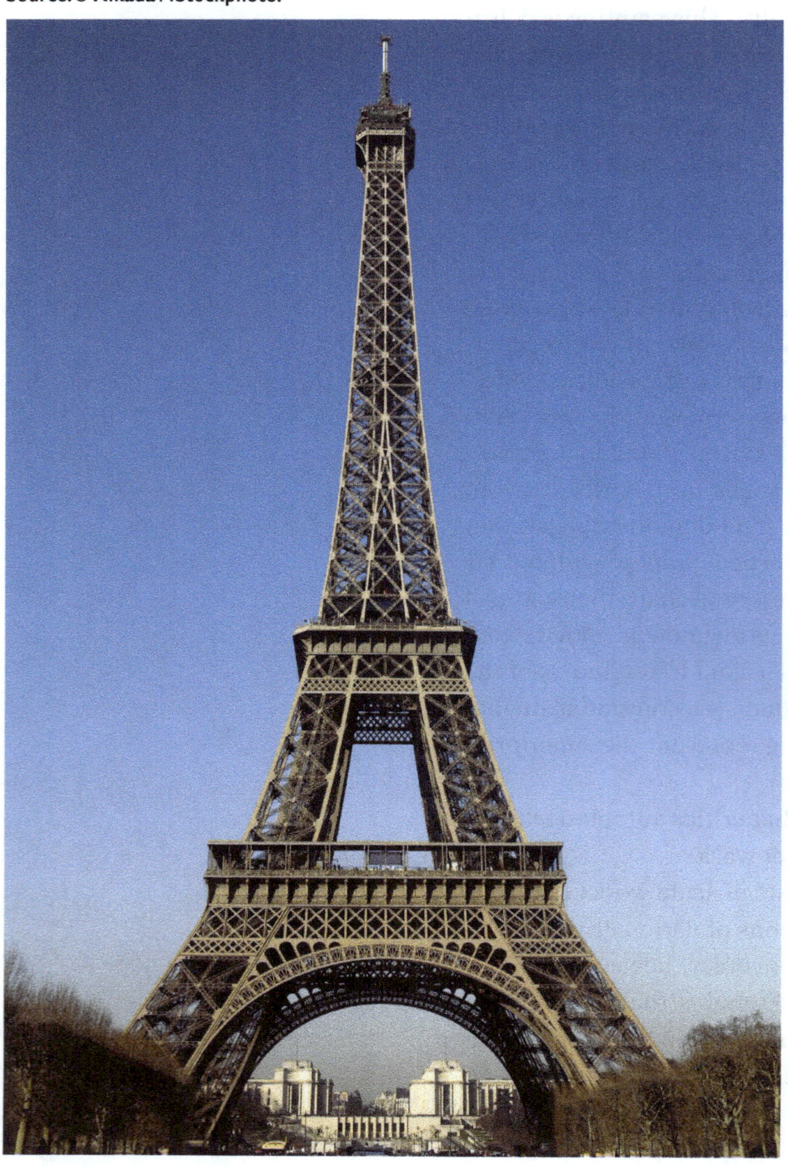

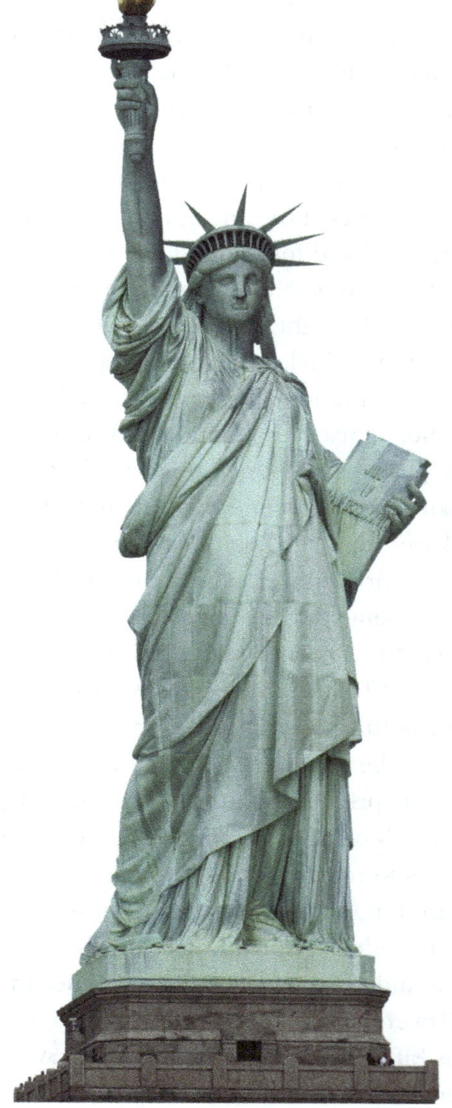

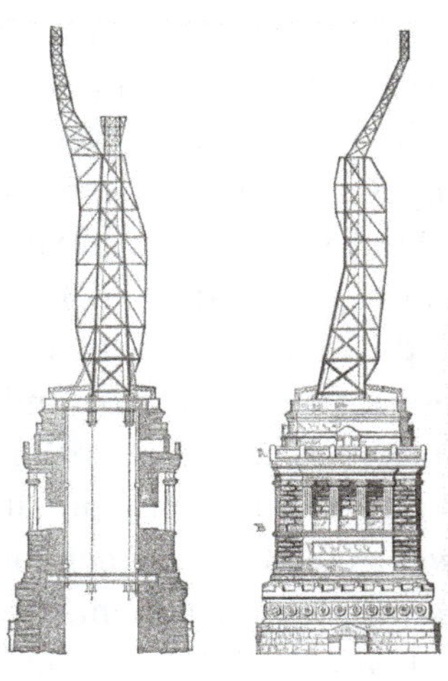

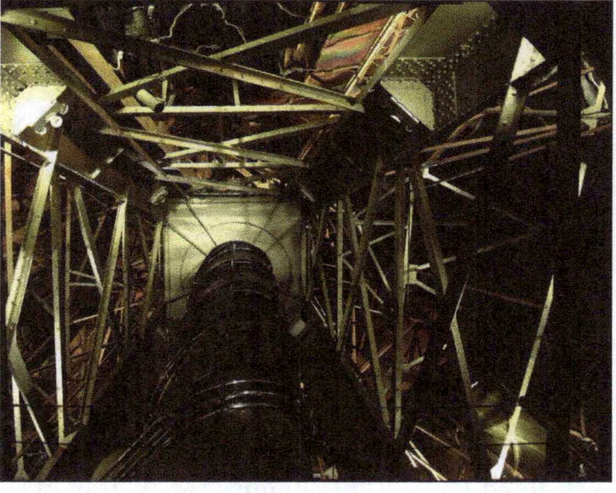

Left to right:
Figure 6.33 | Frédéric Bartholdi, Statue of Liberty, drawing of the internal armature designed by Gustave Eiffel, from *Scientific American*, 13 June 1885. Source: *Scientific American*.

Figure 6.34 | Frédéric Bartholdi, Statue of Liberty, internal armature by Gustave Eiffel. Source: © debstheleo / iStockphoto.

took up residence on Liberty Island at the entrance to New York Harbour in 1886, a gift from France to its friend and fellow Republican nation, the United States of America. Liberty was born from the collaborative efforts of the sculptor Frédéric Bartholdi (1834–1904) and the engineer Eiffel. Eiffel designed the interior **armature** for the statue, which became a universal symbol of freedom as well as a national emblem of the United States. Immigration to the United States was unparalleled during the second half of the nineteenth century, and the Statue of Liberty was placed so as to be the first figure new immigrants would see as they arrived by sea, extolling the virtues of a free country to its foreign arrivals.

Including its base, the statue stands a colossal 93 metres high, the classical goddess Liberty is represented here as a colossal sculpture holding aloft a torch in her right hand and a tablet that evokes the law in her left. The tablet is inscribed with the date of the American Declaration of Independence: *JULY IV MDCCLXXVI* (4 July 1776). The broken chain at her feet and the torch in her hand represent freedom and enlightenment, respectively. The Statue of Liberty was classified as a World Heritage Site in 1984 on the basis of a number of criteria, of which the following is an example:

***Criterion VI**. The symbolic value of the Statue of Liberty lies in two basic factors. It was presented by France with the intention of affirming the historical alliance between the two nations. It was financed by international subscription in recognition of the establishment of the principles of freedom and democracy by the U.S. Declaration of Independence, which the Statue holds in her left hand. The Statue also soon became and has endured as a symbol of the migration of people from many countries into the United States in the late 19th and the early 20th centuries. She endures as a highly potent symbol – inspiring contemplation, debate and protest – of ideals such as liberty, peace, human rights, abolition of slavery, democracy and opportunity.* (UNESCO, 'Statue of Liberty')

Such is the affinity between architecture and nationality that the establishing shot of many films uses landmark buildings, such as those examined here, to indicate the location (and country) of a particular scene; for example, Big Ben or the London Eye for London, the Eiffel Tower for Paris, the Sydney Opera House for Australia and the Statue of Liberty for New York.

The Opéra Garnier, 1861–1875, examined briefly in *Chapter 4*, was commissioned by Emperor Napoleon III as part of a monumental renovation of the city of Paris supervised by Baron Georges-Eugène Haussmann. De-

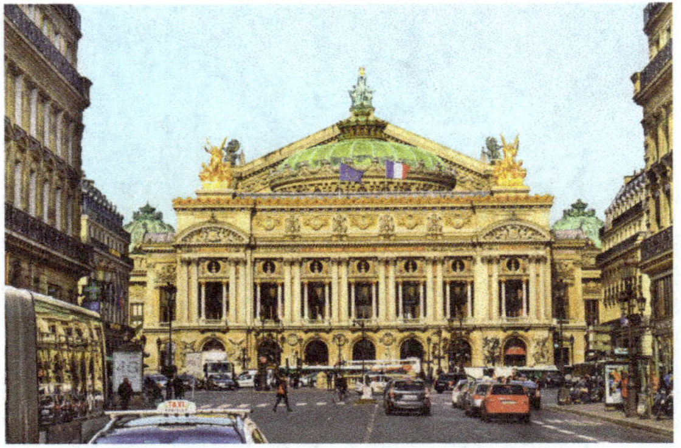

Figure 6.35 | Charles Garnier, Opéra Garnier (Paris Opera), Paris, 1861–1875. Source: © Rainbow / iStockphoto.

signed by Charles Garnier (1825–1898), and located at the top of the Avenue de l'Opéra, it was intended to be one of the capital's most admired buildings and emblematic of the nation's power, culture and influence. As well as being a theatre and a museum, it was a political statement of the authority of the Second Empire and remains a national monument. We examined Baron Haussmann's renovation of central Paris in *Chapter 4*, and the opera house was a majestic sight in a wondrous new townscape.

Opera houses have, for centuries, been associated with learnt cultures and powerful people. While Napoleon III's Paris Opera provided an exemplary node in a nexus of the capital's rebuilding, the Sydney Opera House became Australia's most famous icon, despite being conceived and built by Danish architect Jørn Utzon (1918–2008). When awarding him the Pritzker Prize, architecture's highest honour, in 2003, Thomas J. Pritzker, president of the Hyatt Foundation, said, *Jørn Utzon has designed a remarkably beautiful building in Australia that has become a national symbol to the rest of the world* (Pritzker Architecture Prize, 'Danish Architect Jørn Utzon Becomes 2003 Pritzker Architecture Prize Laureate').

6.4 Explore the example

To what extent can Herbert Baker's Bank of England (examined previously in *Chapter 3* in relation to its form and style) be said to embody a sense of the British nation? Has it borrowed from any other nations? You may also like to explore Niels Møller Lund's painting, *The Heart of the Empire*, 1904. Lund's cityscape also provides a financial landscape of London, before iconic financial buildings such as the Bank of England moved its headquarters to the capital.

This status is confirmed by the Australian government, which features it on its visa site with the accolade: *as representative of Australia as the pyramids are of Egypt and the Colosseum of Rome* (Visas Australia, 'Sydney Opera House').

The sail-like silhouette of its concrete roofs has become synonymous with the Australian nation itself and the material seems to belie the delicacy of its airborne form. The most striking and most photographed landmark in Australia, this unique building can be seen from miles around.

6.3 Checkpoint question

How can works of art convey the nationality of their maker or designer?

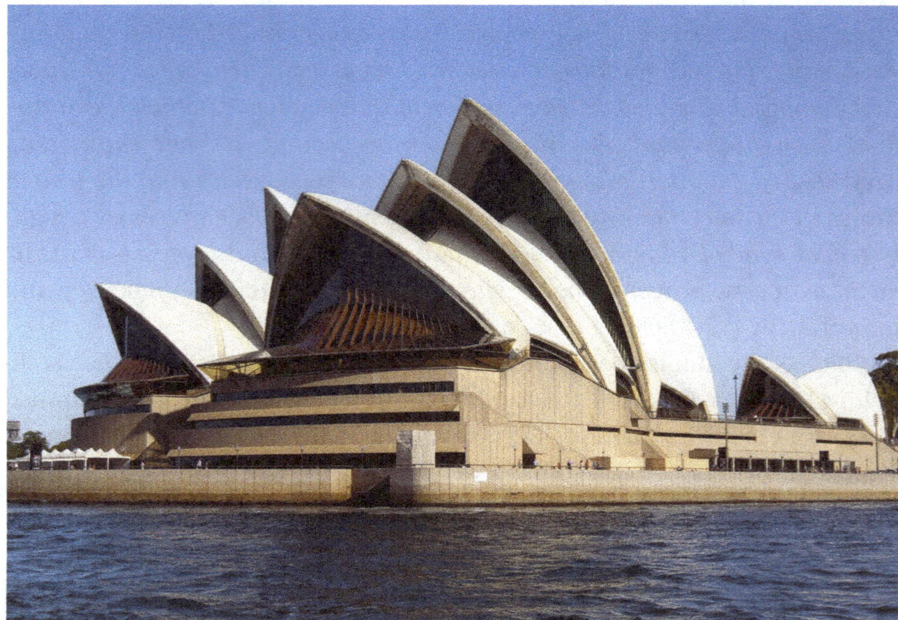

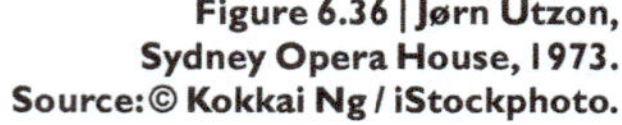

Figure 6.36 | Jørn Utzon, Sydney Opera House, 1973. Source: © Kokkai Ng / iStockphoto.

Ethnicity

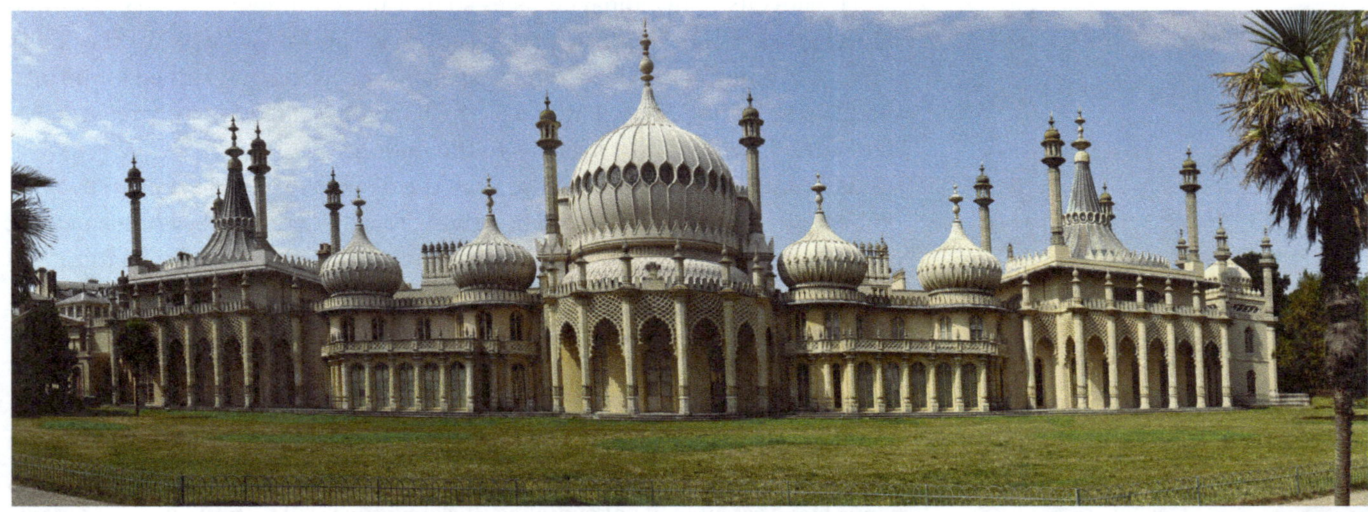

Figure 6.37 | John Nash, Royal Pavilion, Brighton, 1815–1822. Source: © Lovattpics / iStockphoto.

Ethnicity is a term used to describe a person's cultural heritage and/or racial identity, and this includes a shared language, food, style of dress and so on. To have an ethnic identity involves having a sense of pride and union with others of the same culture, which is why the term is inextricably linked with nationality. In fact, the following example relates to gender, nationality and ethnicity.

Through the eyes of an empire: hybridity and the mythologised 'other'

The Royal Pavilion in Brighton provides an interesting example of the kind of cultural and ethnic **hybridity** that is often thought to characterise modern times. It is also a good example of a building that can stimulate discussion in terms of all three of the themes of this chapter: gender, nationality and ethnicity.

The Pavilion, a former royal residence commissioned by George IV when he was Prince Regent, is today owned by Brighton & Hove City Council and is open to the public. It began as a Neo-classical structure designed by Henry Holland and was transformed into its present, iconic Oriental style between 1815 and 1822 by architect John Nash (1752–1835). The Pavilion's refashioning under Nash was achieved using an elaborate iron framework to which stone and **stucco** were attached. Its exterior has a distinctively Islamic style, although its interior is dominated by Chinese influences. Its iconic status can be attributed to its ethnic hybridity and its fantastically exotic punctuation of the skyline in an otherwise **Regency**-style environment.

George IV (1762–1830) was the king of the United Kingdom of Great Britain, Ireland and Hanover from 1820 until 1830. From his youth, he had been known for his extravagance and pleasure seeking. He loved Brighton and sought to ensure that his Royal Pavilion would become one of the world's most talked-about buildings. As Jessica Rutherford notes in her book about the monarch, *A Prince's Passion*, the king made such an impression on the seaside town of Brighton that the *Sussex Weekly Advertiser*, 24 April 1820, reported: *the King is to this town what the sun is to our hemisphere – universal cheerfulness is presented when the rays of Royalty sparkle upon the picture of our local sociabilities and interests* (Rutherford, *A Prince's Passion: The Life of the Royal Pavilion*, p. 19).

The novelty of his idiosyncrasies soon waned, however, and many viewed his reign with contempt. In its long history, the Royal Pavilion, the king's homage to empire, has been admired for its innovation and vilified for its mismatched vulgarity. Now a landmark, the Pavilion is affectionately regarded as one of the king's greatest legacies to the nation.

As Britain's empire grew in the East, the discourse of **Orientalism** became embedded in the West, and Nash, striving to satisfy the wishes of his patron, created an ethnic hybrid before the concept of cultural hybridisation had been coined. The Pavilion says more about the British nation's enchantment with the East than about the East itself, however.

On the outside, the style would have been regarded as unmistakably exotic: Indian, **Mogul** and Oriental – a melting pot of its patron's favourite flavours of the East. Richly decorated surfaces, **horse-shoe arches** and **minarets** are characteristically Islamic, while the Pavilion's idiosyncratic **crenellations**, reminiscent of an iced cake, makes this structure quite a fantastical spectacle to behold in its setting of an English seaside town.

Gazing at the Pavilion, our eyes seldom find a place to rest; the façade appears to pop in and out and up and down with such regular irregularity that harmony is finally achieved. The central pavilion, crowned by a large onion dome with a band of eye-shaped windows around its exotic belly, is flanked on either side by striking minarets and subsidiary domes. Together, these fleshy rounded forms bulge voluptuously, perhaps like coded promises of the pleasures awaiting the visitor within.

Consider the composition of this building for a moment: the central pavilion is echoed by the side pavilions to form a **tripartite** composition overall. A repetition of rounded forms unifies the whole: the façade is predominantly curved, with rounded domes, double-bowed side pavilions, rounded central pavilion, circular motifs on subsidiary domes and so on. The 'femininity' of its organic bulges is relieved by the 'masculine' verticality of its towers.

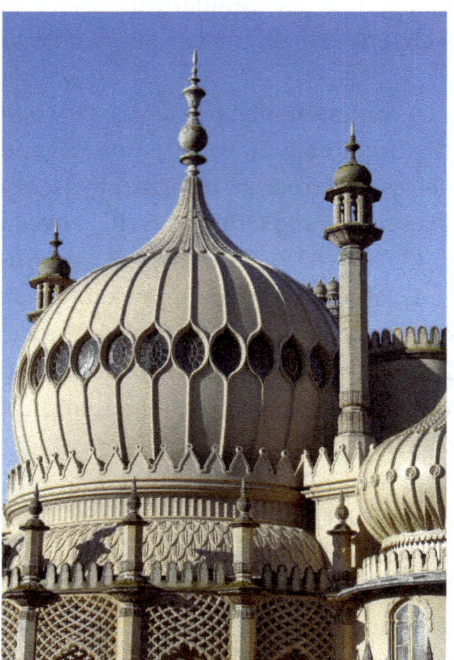

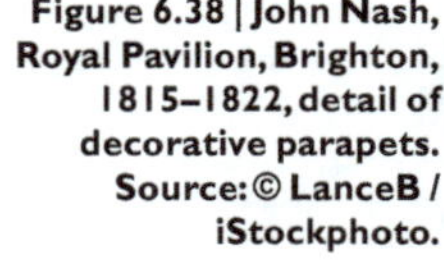

Figure 6.38 | John Nash, Royal Pavilion, Brighton, 1815–1822, detail of decorative parapets. Source: © LanceB / iStockphoto.

The interior maintains its patron's fascination with the East, but evokes China this time, via the decorative trend known as Chinoiserie. This is a term used to describe a European interpretation of Chinese art and decorations, producing an exotic stereotype. The whole building provides a theatrical viewing experience: mythical creatures bulge, leap and coil from every corner, and a riot of colour bedazzles in every de-

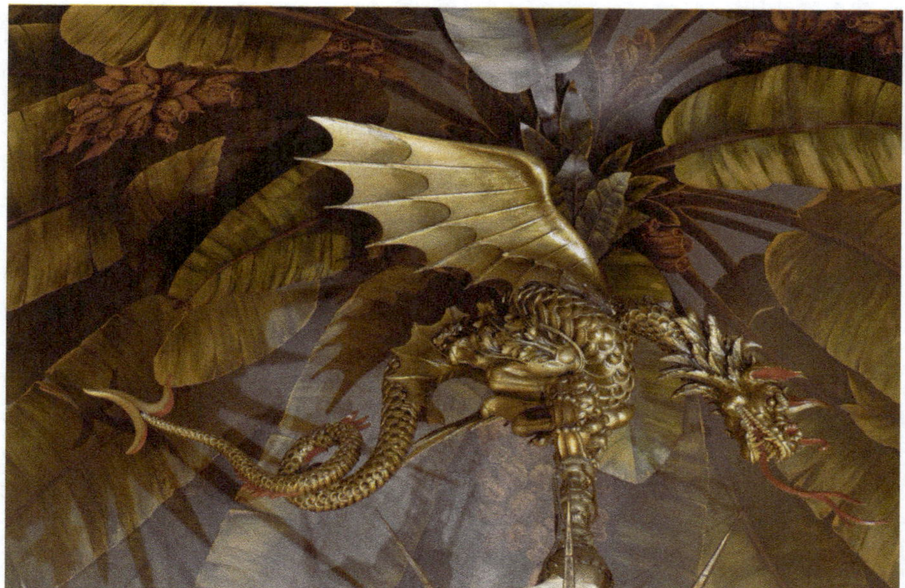

Figure 6.39 | John Nash, Royal Pavilion, Brighton, 1815–1822, elaborate dragon ceiling rose which supports the colossal chandelier in the centre of the Banqueting Room.
Source: © Angelo Hornak / Alamy.

tail. The furniture and stucco is gilded and even the cast-iron **balustrade** that guides you from one fantastical floor to the next has been given a bamboo-effect treatment that suspends disbelief. Everything evokes the Orient or, more precisely, the Western perception of Eastern myth and its associated exoticism.

The Royal Pavilion lends itself to an analysis in terms of both gender and ethnicity. The Pavilion's ethnic hybridity is obvious, particularly when the entire building, inside and out is viewed as a whole; however, less obvious is its 'femininity', which, as the Pavilion's keeper, David Beevers, confirmed, was largely attributable to its Chinese-inspired interior at the time:

Satirised and criticised, associated with female sensibility and rapacity, Chinoiserie allowed a welcome injection of the exotic into the classical mainstream. The number of surviving Chinese rooms in country houses testifies to its appeal in providing a sensual aesthetic based on irregularity, fantasy and 'otherness'. (Beevers, *Chinese Whispers: Chinoiserie in Britain 1650–1930,* p. 24)

In her essay 'What's in a Chinese Room? Twentieth Century Chinoiserie, Modernity and Femininity', Sarah Cheang points to John Galsworthy's novel *The White Monkey*, 1924, from his series, The Forsyte Saga, as exemplifying Chinoiserie's association with iniquitous morality and femininity in the British imagination. In this tale, Galsworthy presents the character of Fleur as an insatiable femme fatale, delectably fashionable and desirable, placed in the midst of a Chinese-style interior, complete with Pekingese dog. Fleur's transformation from vixen to 'dutiful' mother is matched by the change in her taste in interiors, which becomes 'Louis Quinze', and her new dog a 'Dandie Dinmont terrier' (Beevers, *Chinese Whispers: Chinoiserie in Britain 1650–1930*, p. 76).

A sense of 'Britishness' so often associated with the monarchy and all its accompanying symbols was at the very least diluted by King George IV's ethnically mixed Pavilion. However, the British fascination with the East had started long before the king's reign. *Portrait of Omai*, c.1776, by British artist Sir Joshua Reynolds (1723–1792), provides an eighteenth-century insight into the West's preoccupation with civilising the exotic 'other'.

Figure 6.40 | Sir Joshua Reynolds, *Portrait of Omai*, c.1776, oil on canvas. Source: Courtesy of Sotheby's Picture Library.

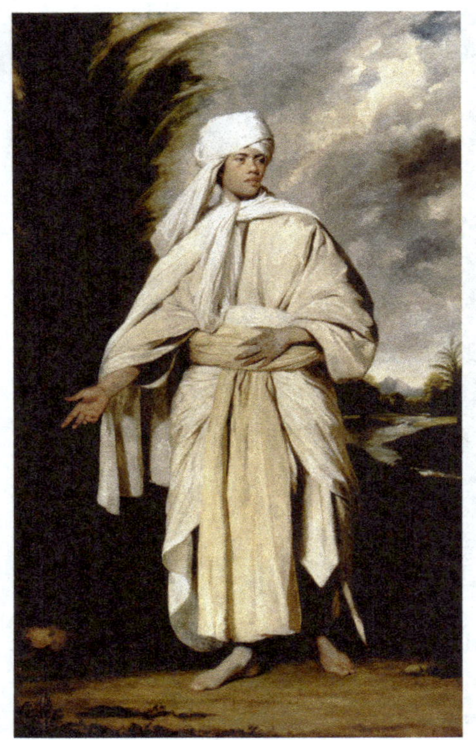

Omai was brought to England in 1774 from the Polynesian island of Huahine in a ship that took part in Captain Cook's second voyage of discovery. He is presented by Reynolds in the garb and posture of an antique statue, as a '**noble savage**' who has been 'civilised'. During his two-year stay in Britain, Omai became a celebrity, a spectacle deeply revealing of the West's attitude towards 'other' cultures, and this painting arguably tells us more about British imperialism than it does about Omai as a historical individual.

In her essay 'Portrait of a Nation', 2003, Patricia Fara stated: *The latest scientific theories still assumed that white men lay at the summit of God's creation, and Europeans regarded Pacific islanders as inferior primitives who were dirty, uncivilised and far closer to animals than themselves. But at the same time, they referred to the Pacific region as though it were a new Arcadia, and admired its inhabitants for living in an innocent, uncorrupted state, untainted by the depravity of modern civilisation and unburdened by the necessity of earning their living.* (Fara, 'Portrait of a Nation')

6.1 What can you see?

We might see Omai, represented in formal costume and carefully posed, as given a certain dignity. Or we might feel that the painting leaves us with an unnerving sense of his exploitation, a sense of him being dressed-up as a symbol of the British Empire? What do you think? How does the background of the painting contribute to our interpretation?

Fara draws upon a duality of opinion that marked the period; polite society chose to focus on the romantic aspect of such transracial exchanges, while more enlightened critics drew attention to the exploitative and unnecessary expansion of empire in an elitist game of world dominance.

Some have suggested that the Arcadia, or idealised landscape, glimpsed in Reynolds' background is typical of the way that people perceived ethnic 'others' as somehow identified with the realm of nature rather than the realm of reason, culture or science. We see similar Arcadian backgrounds in paintings by countless other artists, up to and including the twentieth century. Look at the work *Blue Nude* by French artist Henri Matisse (1869–1954), for example.

Blue Nude, 1907, may be interpreted as providing a male European's imperialist perspective of an ethnic 'other'. The system of beliefs at work both in Matisse's painting and in its critical reception is sometimes known as '**primitivism**': describing the racist prejudice that non-Western cultures are more 'primitive', meaning less developed, and perhaps closer to animal nature, than Western societies. This was a belief that permeated the language of European colonisers and the art that was produced in European societies during the colonial period. African, Oceanic (now known as Polynesian), Native American and other non-Western people and their cultures were all represented in this 'primitivising' way, indicating that they were considered to be inferior, albeit exotic and exciting, alternatives to the West. Matisse's image presents us with a 'primitive' subject painted in a 'primitive' way: she reclines in an odalisque pose, her abundant breasts, accentuated buttock and shortened thighs connote her otherness. Naked and framed by exotic flora and fauna, she also signifies replenishment, an 'oasis' for the traveller, or perhaps a decorative and escapist vision of the artist's personal Arcadia. The artist's use of bold black outline and non-naturalistic colour defied the conventions of the traditional nude in Western painting and helped secure his status as leader of the artistic movement aptly labelled the **Fauves** (wild beasts). Despite this, or indeed because of this, the painting received damning reviews when it was first exhibited on account of its ugly deviation from academic standards. Many early twentieth-century European artists were inspired by so-called primitive art. According to Jonathan Harris,

[t]he production of these works was also dependent upon the imperialistic relation modern French artists had with the tribal societies and cultures of the Pacific islands and northern Africa that the western European nation-states had invaded, conquered, colonised, and exploited. (Harris, *Art History: The Key Concepts,* p. 252)

Thus, primitivism was adopted by **avant-garde** European artists as a device that helped them to reject the perceived corruption of the West and conventional **academicism** in art. The perceived 'wildness' of the subject matter and non-Western decorative styles and motifs helped European artists find the vivid and forceful means they needed to represent their rejection of tradition. In the bold and escapist vision of riotous colour and flattened form represented in *Blue Nude*, Matisse, perhaps unwittingly, both perpetuates colonial **ideology** and fuels the notion of the people of North Africa as 'other'. At the same time, however, he produces a daring and innovative work by the standards of French painting at the time, and paved the way for future generations of artists to come.

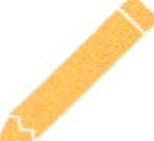

6.5 Explore this example

At the beginning of this chapter we examined two paintings by Jean-Auguste-Dominique Ingres: *Grande Odalisque*, 1814, and *The Turkish Bath*, 1862. We looked at these works in the general context of gender, and specifically of woman as 'other'. However, these women are twice 'othered': once in terms of their gender and again in terms of their ethnicity. Examine them again in the light of the mythologised Orientalism.

Edward Said coined the term 'Orientalism' in his seminal book *Orientalism: Western Conceptions of the Orient*, first published in 1978. The book examines the disparity between Said's experience of being an Arab and the West's mythologised representation of the Orient. Said asks why some people have preconceptions about the East, even though they may never have been there themselves. His readers are made to consider the West's view of the East as a distorted one, and the distortion – the stereotype – is called 'Orientalism'.

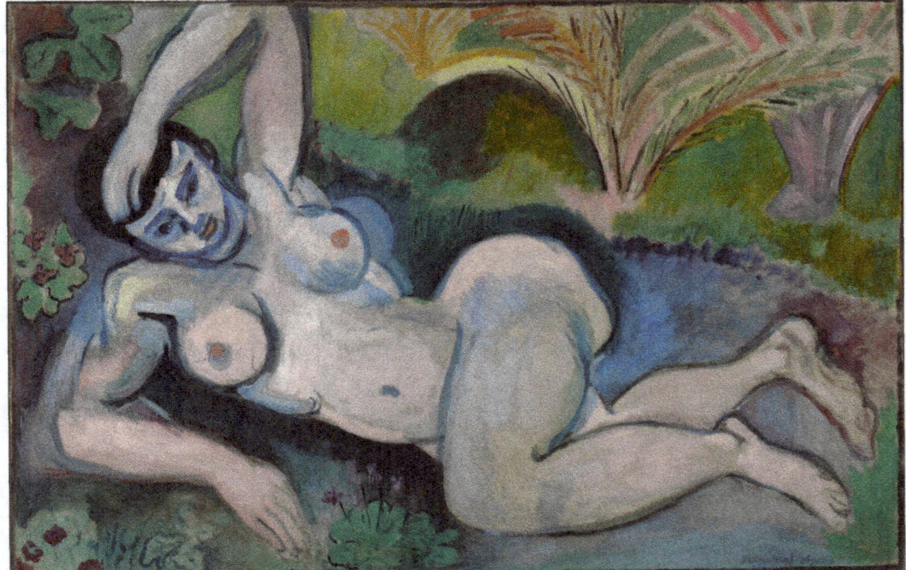

Figure 6.41 | Henri Matisse, *Blue Nude*, 1907, oil on canvas, 92.1 × 140.3 cm, Baltimore Museum of Art: The Cone Collection, formed by Dr. Claribel Cone and Miss Etta Cone of Baltimore, Maryland, BMA 1950.228. Source: Baltimore Museum of Art. Photography by Mitro Hood. Artwork: © Succession H. Matisse/ DACS 2015.

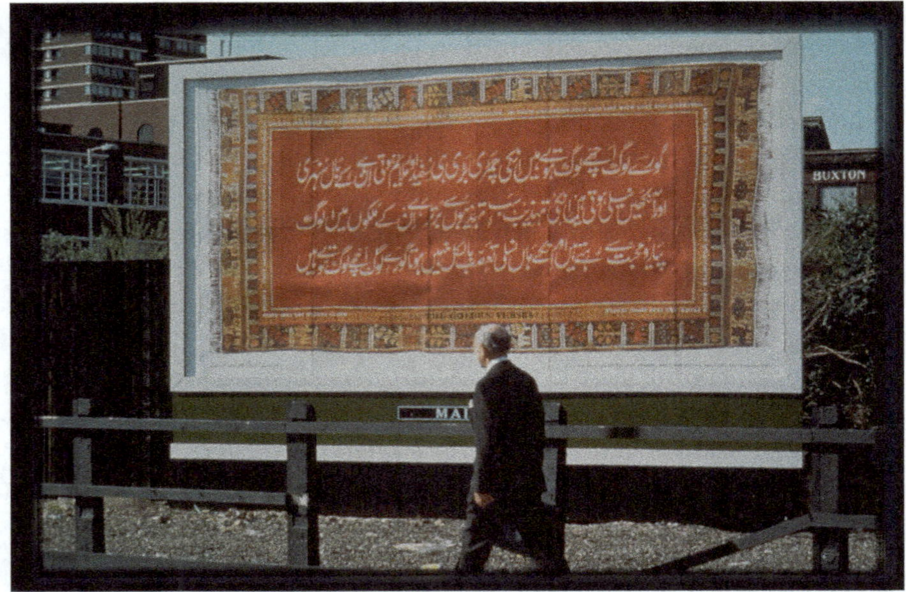

Figure 6.42 | Rasheed Araeen, *The Golden Verses*, 1990–1991, billboard poster, 300 × 600 cm. Source: Commissioned and produced by Artangel.

In *Orientalism* Said stated, *The Orient is not only adjacent to Europe; it is also the place of Europe's greatest and richest colonies, the source of its civilisations and languages, its cultural contestant, and one of its deepest and most recurring images of 'Other'* (Said, *Orientalism*, pp. 1–2).

The 'ism' of Orientalism, according to Jonathan Harris, signals both its constructed nature and association with *imperialism, colonialism and economic penetration* (Harris, *Art History: The Key Concepts*, p. 222). Do you think that our focus on the label 'Orientalism' is in fact an act of Orientalism itself?

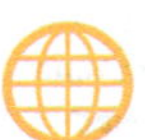

See the companion website for web links to documentary footage of Edward Said discussing his text.

Twentieth-century stereotypes and discrimination

While Ingres represented the Orient as 'other' in the nineteenth century, and Matisse represented colonial subjects as 'primitive' in the early twentieth century, many contemporary artists have used their art to expose the inaccuracies of such prejudicial judgement. British Afro-Caribbean artist Sonia Boyce addressed the issue of discriminatory constructions of identities in her *From Tarzan to Rambo: English Born 'Native' Considers her Relationship to the Constructed/Self Image and her Roots in Reconstruction*, 1987; and contemporary Pakistan-born, British-based artist Rasheed Araeen (born 1935) sought to liberate the post-colonial artist from the chains of the 'otherness' that defined them in the West.

Pasted to a London billboard, Aareen's commercial print installation *The Golden Verses*, 1990–1991, is Urdu calligraphic text on an Oriental carpet. Its translation belies its Islamic appearance:

White people are very good people. They have very white and soft skin. Their hair is golden and their eyes are blue. Their civilisation is the best civilisation. In their countries they live life with love and affection. And there is no racial discrimination whatsoever. White people are very good people.

The text discusses 'White people' in a language few White people would be able to read. What do you think the artist's intention is here?

In his essay 'The Artist as a Post-colonial Subject and This Individual's Journey Towards the Centre', Araeen discusses the barriers post-colonial artists have upon entering the so-called 'centre' of the West from the periphery of the 'other'.[26] Araeen views the recent celebration of multiculturalism as a smokescreen for the continuing **ethnocentrism** present in mainstream art. Rather than being defined by an 'other' culture, post-colonial artists need to be freed from their cultural identification and afforded the same degree of individual recognition as their Western counterparts. Araeen seeks to break down dominant Western ideology and the 'White' discourse that has prevented non-White artists from gaining recognition in their own right without the need necessarily to associate their art with their ethnic identity or supposed cultural otherness.

Contemporary British artist Chris Ofili (born 1968), born to Nigerian parents, incorporates a variety of cultural references in his works, ranging from scripture to **blaxploitation** and pornographic magazines. Ofili seems to be interested in deconstructing powerful discourses on ethnicity that form the ideological frameworks in which we think. Writer and art critic Stuart Morgan noted the way in which Ofili's work is *caught between the Black arts movement in Britain – urging a return to African roots – and the multiculturalism of borderline positions* (Morgan 'The Elephant Man: An Interview with Chris Ofili'). Ofili's work may offer an experimental enquiry into his sense of 'Blackness' in a White-dominated art world but it does so from a personal and individual perspective. Ofili demonstrates an awareness of ethnic categorisation which expects a Black artist to paint in a certain style, an expectation Ofili questions in his paintings. Africa is a foreign place to Ofili, the British artist.

6.4 Let's connect the themes: materials and techniques

No Woman, No Cry, 1998, in common with others in Ofili's distinctive oeuvre, is characterised by a broad range of borrowings. In 1992 Ofili visited ancient caves in the Metobo Hills in Zimbabwe and has described the multiple dot decorations he saw there as analogous to musical rhythms. The experimental layering of media and colour in his work relate to the layered compositions of 'hip-hop' music, which originated in the Afro-Caribbean, Afro-American and Latino communities in New York. The complicated weaving of different elements acts like a visual identity metaphor – both are stable only in so far as their fragmentation is certain.

While a great deal of Ofili's works examine 'Africanness' playfully, albeit with a serious sub-text, *No Woman, No Cry* leads its audience into a serious discussion about racism and prejudice. Stephen Lawrence was a young Black man murdered in the street and – in a landmark case – the Metropolitan Police Force admitted to the mishandling of their investigation. Ofili's painting is dedicated to, and represents the maternal grief of, Stephen's mother Doreen Lawrence. Every tear contains a tiny portrait of her murdered son. The claustrophobia of grief may be indicated by the delicate pattern of dots that veil her. A tribal fire of colour rages near her heart and yet she is still strong and dignified; the pyramidal composition, even the colour palette, reminds us of another work by Ofili and the ultimate racial stereotype debunker: *The Holy Virgin Mary*, 1996, examined in *Chapter 2*. The title *No Woman, No Cry*

26 In this essay, Araeen explains the term post-colonial, and discusses his work from his personal perspective as a Pakistani-British artist. He describes himself as a post-colonial subject who is still faced with a dominant colonial ideology. It is a serious and thought-provoking read in relation to the theme of ethnicity.

is taken from the 1974 hit by Jamaican singer-songwriter Bob Marley:

No woman, no cry
No woman, no cry
Oh my Little sister, don't shed no tears
No woman, no cry. (Bob Marley)

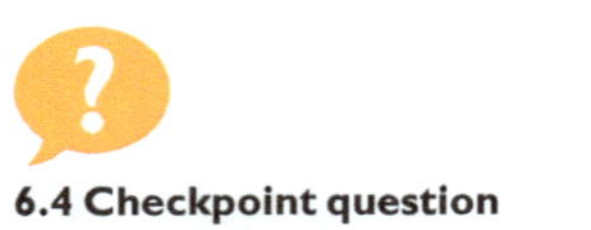

6.4 Checkpoint question
How have artists either embodied or reacted to ethnocentrism in their art?

The words 'No Woman No Cry' are picked-out in coloured pins stuck into the balls of elephant dung at the painting's feet. Dung, symbolic of African pride, elevates the painting, but also defiantly so, in its Western context. We find ourselves questioning not only what counts as an artistic medium but also society's prejudice. This portrait is both a tribute to Stephen's family and a political statement about racial discrimination. Ofili was clearly moved by the case, and the Africanness of his image emanates Black African pride; it is a poignant statement about the reality of institutional racism. The words 'RIP Stephen Lawrence' are written in phosphorescent paint barely discernible by day but glowing by night. The multi-media nature of this work makes it a particularly rich example to analyse in relation to *Chapter 2*.

Gender, nationality and ethnicity symbiotically linked

This chapter has examined issues of gender, nationality and ethnicity as sep-

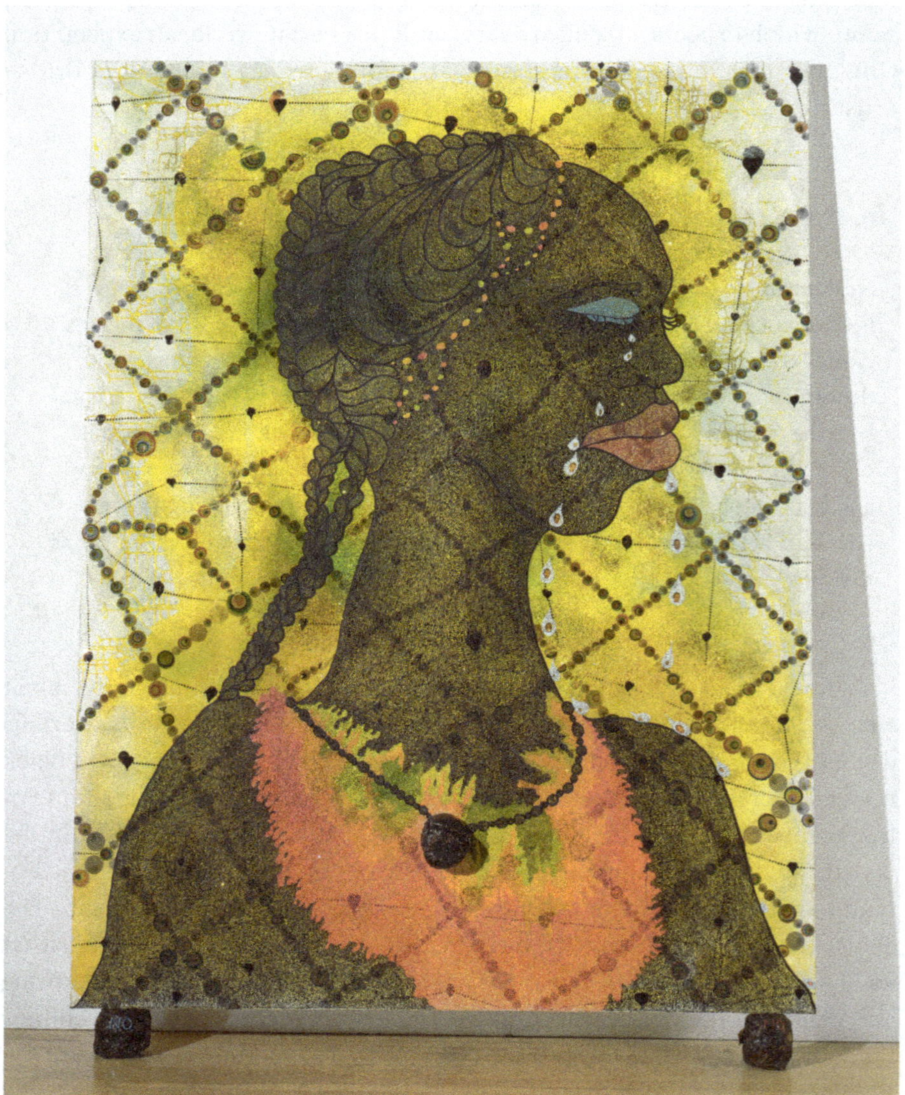

Figure 6.43 | Chris Ofili, *No Woman, No Cry*, 1998, oil paint, acrylic paint, graphite, polyester resin, printed pap, 243.8 × 182.8 × 5.1 cm, London, Tate (on loan to New Museum, New York, NY). Source: Photo ©Tate, London 2015. Reproduced courtesy of the artist and Tate, London. © Chris Ofili.

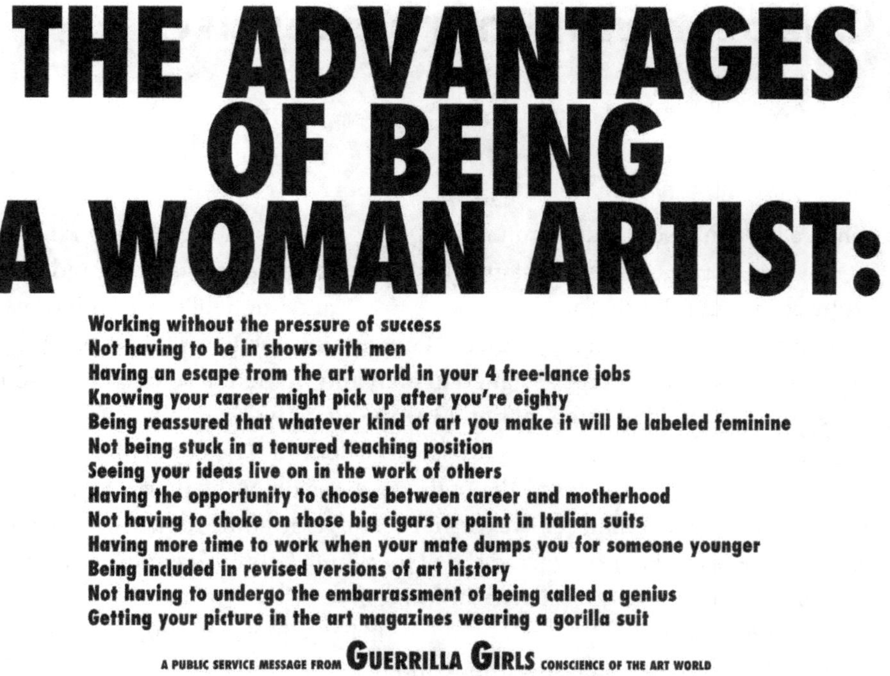

THE ADVANTAGES OF BEING A WOMAN ARTIST:

Working without the pressure of success
Not having to be in shows with men
Having an escape from the art world in your 4 free-lance jobs
Knowing your career might pick up after you're eighty
Being reassured that whatever kind of art you make it will be labeled feminine
Not being stuck in a tenured teaching position
Seeing your ideas live on in the work of others
Having the opportunity to choose between career and motherhood
Not having to choke on those big cigars or paint in Italian suits
Having more time to work when your mate dumps you for someone younger
Being included in revised versions of art history
Not having to undergo the embarrassment of being called a genius
Getting your picture in the art magazines wearing a gorilla suit

A PUBLIC SERVICE MESSAGE FROM **GUERRILLA GIRLS** CONSCIENCE OF THE ART WORLD

Figure 6.44 | Guerrilla Girls, *The Advantages of Being a Woman Artist*, 1988, poster on college campuses. Source: Copyright © Guerrilla Girls / Courtesy www.guerrillagirls.com.

arate themes; however, these areas of stratification, or difference, are too often bound to one another, as the work of the Guerrilla Girls demonstrates.

The Guerrilla Girls is an anonymous group of feminist activists devoted to fighting against **sexism** and racism in the art world. They formed in the United States in 1985 and became famous for maintaining their anonymity behind gorilla masks and fighting social injustice with tenacity and wit. In an interview in 1995, an anonymous Guerrilla Girl adopted the pseudonym of artist Käthe Kollwitz:

Q. How did the Guerrilla Girls start?

Käthe Kollwitz: In 1985, The Museum of Modern Art in New York opened an exhibition titled 'An International Survey of Painting and Sculpture'. It was supposed to be an up-to-the-minute summary of the most significant contemporary art in the world. Out of 169 artists, only 13 were women. All the artists were white, either from Europe or the United States. That was bad enough, but the curator, Kynaston McShine, said any artist who wasn't in the show should rethink 'his' career. And that really annoyed a lot of artists because obviously the guy was completely prejudiced. Women demonstrated in front of the museum with the usual placards and picket line. Some of us who attended were irritated that we didn't make any impression on passersby. (Guerrilla Girls, 'Guerrilla Girls Bare All')

Issues relating to gender, nationality and ethnicity have tended to be issues relating to marginalisation, '**symbolic exclusion**' and 'otherness'; together these issues create a nexus of ideas that all pivot on the axis of power relations in society. It is not just a question of difference, but of imposed inferiority too. This chapter has provided an interface for the discussion of multiple forms of 'otherness'. From a twenty-first-century perspective, the imperialist grip has loosened; identity is less compartmentalised, and discrimination, which is widely legislated against – although still operating covertly – has been brought into the bright light of public debate, not least by artists for whom 'the personal is *still* political'.

Chapter Summary Exercise

Using the words below complete the Chapter Summary. Each word or term should be used only once.

identity
stereotypes
patriarchy
biologically
Primitivism
male gaze
other
belonging
uncivilised
social construct
cultural
indoor

While a person's 'sex' is determined ____________, their 'gender' is a ____________. Feminist art historians examine works of art and architecture in relation to ____________ and unequal power relations in society between men and women. Many feminist artists have focused on the separate social spheres assigned to men and women in society and used their art to express their feelings of injustice about woman's identity as one trapped in the domestic, ____________ sphere. The concept of the '____________' relates to the male's possession of the power to actively look at the passive female. However, in recent years some female artists and theorists have actively subverted the objectifying lens of the male look and challenged the historical passivity of women.

Nationality means ____________ to a particular nation and may involve a sense of national sentiment and pride.

Ethnicity is a term used to describe a person's ____________ or racial ____________. Positively, it relates to a feeling of unity; however, the West has historically referred to people from different ethnicities as '____________'.

____________ refers to African, Oceanic and tribal art, motifs and cultures but in the colonial past it was particularly associated with cultures deemed '____________' and sometimes inferior to the West.

Many artists have challenged inaccurate ____________ used to refer to non-Western peoples.

Checkpoint Answers

6.1 In relation to gender, what is meant by the 'domestic' sphere?
The 'indoor', limited space traditionally occupied by women. It contrasts with the 'outdoor', unlimited space traditionally occupied by men.

6.2 Identify two female artists whose work attempts to subvert what feminist art historians have described as the 'male gaze'.
Cindy Sherman's constructed identities as numerous made-up personas forces our questioning of the objectification of women by men, and Jenny Saville's *Branded* and *Hybrid* repels the desirous intentions of the 'male gaze'. There are countless other examples, including those that raise issues of the 'female gaze', a new and under-researched counter-phenomenon.

6.3 How can works of art convey the nationality of their maker or designer?
In the style and content of their work, as is the case in Mexican artist Frida Kahlo's *Self-portrait on the Borderline Between Mexico and The United States*, 1932. It is painted in a Mexican ex-voto style, and it contains representations of indigenous flora and fauna and symbolic references to Mexico's pre-colonial Aztec history (holding the Mexican flag and using the vibrant colours of Mexico are an overt statement of national loyalty).

Eugène Delacroix's *Liberty Leading the People*, 1830, relates directly to the freedom of the French nation not only in its revolutionary scene but also in the symbolic use of Liberty herself. Liberty holding the French flag dominates the painting and the colours of the tricolour permeate the entire canvas.

6.4 How have artists either embodied or reacted to ethnocentrism in their art?
Reynolds' *Portrait of Omai*, c.1776, can be read as a patronising portrait of a native as spectacle, which reveals no trace of awareness from the artist as to its moral implication. Later, early twentieth-century works such as *Blue Nude* by Henri Matisse displayed the 'native' as 'other', positively from their perspective, a perspective that sought to escape from an industrialised and corrupted Europe. But *Blue Nude* is nonetheless shown as exotic 'other' and just as ethnocentric a depiction as *Omai*, more than a century earlier. Recent artists such as Sonia Boyce have confronted the assumed superiority of the West and challenged commonly held assumptions relating to 'other' cultures. Rasheed Araeen's *The Golden Verses*, 1990–1991, is an ingenious affront to the West's ethnocentricity and the stereotypes of 'other' it has perpetuated over the centuries.

References

Agrest, D. 'Architecture from Without: Body, Logic and Sex' in Rendell, J., Penner, B. and Borden, I., *Gender Space Architecture: An Interdisciplinary Introduction*, Routledge, 2000.

Araeen, R. 'The Artist as a Post-colonial Subject and This Individual's Journey Towards the Centre' in King, C. (ed.) *Views of Difference: Different Views of Art*, Yale University Press / Open University, 1999.

Beevers, D. *Chinese Whispers: Chinoiserie in Britain 1650–1930*, Royal Pavilion Libraries & Museums, 2009.

Bryson, N. 'Géricault and "Masculinity"' in Bryson, N., Holly, M.A. and Moxey, K. (eds.) *Visual Culture: Images and Interpretations*, Wesleyan University Press, 1994.

Chadwick, W. *Women, Art and Society*, 4th ed., Thames & Hudson, 2007.

Clark, L. *Women and Achievement in Nineteenth-Century Europe*, Cambridge University Press, 2008.

Colomina, B. (ed.) 'Introduction' in *Sexuality and Space*, Princeton Architectural Press, 1992.

Conn, C. 'Louise Bourgeois: Delicate Strength', 2012, http://cyndiconn.com/wp-content/uploads/2012/03/Cyndi-Conn-Louise-Bourgeois.pdf.

Fara, P. 'Portrait of a Nation', *New Statesman*, 6 October 2003, http://www.newstatesman.com/node/146422.

Forrester, S., Zaborowska, M.J. and Gapova, E. *Over the Wall/After the Fall: Post-Communist Cultures Through an East–West Gaze*, Indiana University Press, 2004.

Greer, G. *The Obstacle Race: The Fortunes of Women Painters and Their Work*, Tauris Parke, 2001.

Guerrilla Girls, 'Guerrilla Girls Bare All', 1995, http://www.guerrillagirls.com/interview/index.shtml.

Hagen, R.-M. and Hagen, R. *What Great Paintings Say: From the Bayeux Tapestry to Diego Rivera*, Vol. 2, Taschen, 2005.

Harris, J. *Art History: The Key Concepts*, Routledge, 2006.

Hicks, C. *Girl in a Green Gown: The History and Mystery of the Arnolfini Portrait*, Chatto & Windus, 2011.

Kent, S. *Shark Infested Waters: The Saatchi Collection of British Art in the 90s*, I.B. Tauris, 1994.

Morgan, S. 'The Elephant Man: An Interview with Chris Ofili', *Frieze*, 15 April 1994, http://www.frieze.com/issue/article/the_elephant_man.

Mulvey, L. 'Visual Pleasure and Narrative Cinema', Screen, Vol. 16, No. 3, 1975, imlportfolio.usc.edu/ctcs505/mulveyVisualPleasureNarrativeCinema.pdf.

Nochlin, L. *Representing Women*, Thames & Hudson, 1999.

Pritzker Architecture Prize. 'Danish Architect Jørn Utzon Becomes 2003 Pritzker Architecture Prize Laureate', 2003, http://www.pritzkerprize.com/2003/announcement.

Rendell, J., Penner, B. and Borden, I. *Gender Space Architecture: An Interdisciplinary Introduction*, Routledge, 2000.

Rutherford, J. *A Prince's Passion: The Life of the Royal Pavilion*, Royal Pavilion Libraries & Museums, 2003.

Said, E. *Orientalism: Western Conceptions of the Orient*, Penguin, 1995. (First published 1978.)

Stedelijk Museum. 'July 23: Appropriation', n.d., http://www.theslideprojector.com/art1/art1tuesthurslectures/art1lecture25.html.

Tate Gallery. 'Tate Acquires Louise Bourgeois's Giant Spider, *Maman* (Press Release)', 11 January 2008, http://www.tate.org.uk/about/press-office/press-releases/tate-acquires-louise-bourgeoiss-giant-spider-maman.

UNESCO. 'Statue of Liberty', n.d., http://whc.unesco.org/en/list/307.

Visas Australia, 'Sydney Opera House', 2008, http://www.visas-australia.com/visas/sydney_opera_house.asp?country=1&requestid=&visa.

Weisman, L. 'Prologue' in Rendell, J., Penner, B. and Borden, I. (eds.) *Gender, Space Architecture: An Interdisciplinary Introduction*, Routledge, 2000.

Wigley, M. 'Untitled: The Housing of Gender' in Colomina, B. (ed.) *Sexuality and Space*, Princeton School of Architecture, 1992.

Willoughby, I. 'Architect Recalls Genesis of Dancing Building as Coffee Table Book Published', 11 July 2003, http://www.radio.cz/en/section/arts/architect-recalls-genesis-of-dancing-building-as-coffee-table-book-published.

Other Useful Sources

Billinge, R. and Campbell, L. 'The Infra-Red Reflectograms of Jan van Eyck's Portrait of Giovanni(?) Arnolfini and his Wife Giovanna Cenami(?)', *National Gallery Technical Bulletin*, No. 16, 1995.

Colquhoun, A. *Modern Architecture*, Oxford University Press, 2002.

Kettenmann, A. *Kahlo*, Taschen, 2003.

Nochlin, L. 'Why Have There Been No Great Women Artists?' in Nochlin, L. *Women, Art, and Power and Other Essays*, Thames & Hudson, 1989. (First published 1971.)

Parker, R. and Pollock, G. *Old Mistresses: Women, Art and Ideology*, Pandora, 1981.

Sharwood Smith, J. *Temples, Priests and Worship (Greek and Roman Topics)*, Allen & Unwin, 1975.

Wagenaar, M. 'Townscapes of Power', *GeoJournal*, Vol. 51, No. 1, 2000.

Glossary

abstract A term associated with early twentieth-century art which communicates meaning through lines, shapes, colours, forms, textures, rather than imitating material objects in the real world.

abstracted Taken from something we can recognise but not represented in a realistic manner.

Abstract Expressionism American painting movement of the 1940s and 1950s associated with abstraction and self-expression.

abutment In architecture, a solid block, usually made from masonry placed to counteract the lateral thrust of a vault or arch.

academicism (*ac-a-dem-i-cism*) Relating to traditionalism and a formal rule-bound appreciation, especially in the arts.

acrylic paint A synthetic, quick-drying and versatile **medium**, capable of being applied thickly or thinly, but perhaps best suited to areas of flat, unmodulated colour.

additive process Adding one thing to another, such as adding clay to a model.

aedicule (**ee**-*di-kyool, or* **ed**-*i-kyool*) A small structure containing a statue framed by **columns** supporting an **entablature** and a **pediment**. Used more frequently to describe a framed opening.

alloy A metal made by combining two or more metallic elements. Bronze is an alloy of tin combined with copper. The combination provides greater strength.

Analytical Cubism The phase of **Cubism** dating from c.1909 to c.1912, characterised by a dissolution of form. It involved an analysis of a **subject** by its fragmentation and reassembly, the inter-penetration of **planes** in a shallow space and a virtually monochromatic colour palette consisting of ochres/browns/grey.

anthropocentrism A belief that human beings are the central or most significant species on the planet.

Antiquity Referring to the classical past, before the **Middle Ages**. See **Classical Antiquity**.

applied arts Arts such as ceramics, furniture construction, decorative objects (such as jewellery) and so on, that are not considered 'fine arts'. In this sense, applied arts are associated with crafts and design. Applied arts is also referred to, more pejoratively, as the 'minor arts'.

applied plaster Applying wet plaster, layer by layer, to an **armature** when making a sculpture.

armature A frame used to support the modelled sculpture. It is usually made from wire or more substantial metal manipulated into the sculptor's chosen form.

art market The art market is subdivided into two broad categories: the primary and the secondary. The primary market refers to when an artwork comes to market for sale for the first time at a gallery or exhibition; if the purchaser (**collector** or **dealer**) then decides to sell the work it enters the secondary market (often at auction).

Arts and Crafts Movement Initially, a British movement of the nineteenth century which advocated skilled craftsmanship and the 'honest' use of traditional **materials** and techniques.

assemblage A form of sculpture comprised of objects being assembled (put together) to create a work of art. The objects are often **found objects**.

atmospheric perspective or **aerial perspective** A term that describes the changes in **tone** and colour that occur when objects recede towards the horizon line. Colours tend to fade and appear bluish at their furthest point from the viewer. Atmospheric/aerial perspective refers to the effect of an object being viewed in the distance through atmosphere.

atrium In architecture, a sky-lit central court or cavity, often rising through several floors.

automation A workerless system of production consisting of machine or computer-controlled manufacture. A concept relating to the displacement of human skill and involvement in the production process.

avant-garde Art and artists regarded to be at the

forefront of artistic development because their work challenges established conventions and norms.

azurite A mineral that produces a blue **pigment**. It performs best with a water-based paint, such as **tempera**, rather than with oil.

balustrade A series of posts supporting a handrail on a staircase.

Baroque Derived from the Spanish *barrueco* or the Portuguese *barroco* meaning 'deformed pearl', the term describes mainly Catholic art and architecture in Europe of the seventeenth century. It is characterised by dynamism and theatricality. Baroque **naturalism** may be related to the illusionary realistic art achieved by Caravaggio and his followers.

bas-relief or **basso-rilievo** A low-relief sculpture in which the figures never project more than half their depth from the background.

bel composto A synthesis of architecture, sculpture and painting.

binder Any material that binds (holds together) other **materials** (e.g. linseed oil in oil paint).

biomorphic Used to describe **abstract** forms which derive their form from organic shapes, rather than geometric ones.

blaxploitation A term comprised of the words 'black' and 'exploitation' to refer to a film **genre** that emerged in the United States in the 1970s. Blaxploitation films such as *Shaft*, 1971, tended to feature funk and soul music as well as a primarily Black cast in stereotypical roles.

buon fresco Meaning 'true fresco', is painting in which paint is applied directly onto the surface of wet plaster.

Byzantine mosaics Wall (and floor) art, mainly pictorial, made from tiny pieces of brightly coloured or sparkling glass or stone (tesserae). This art form reached its peak in Western art during the time of the Byzantine Empire (fourth century to 1453), which developed from the Eastern Roman Empire, whose capital was the city of Byzantium (now Istanbul).

canon Authoritative rule or criterion; accepted standard.

canonical Included in a group of officially recognised and accepted works.

cantilevered In architecture, a term to describe horizontal forms projecting from a wall or central core capable of carrying loads without support along its projection.

capitals The head or crowning feature of a **column**. See **Orders** for illustration of the **Doric**, **Ionic** and **Corinthian** capitals.

Caravaggisti A term to describe artists who followed in the style of Italian **Baroque** artist Caravaggio.

caryatid (*kar-ee-***at***-id*) Carved standing female figures used as a load-bearing **column** to support an **entablature**.

celestial Heavenly, or of the sky.

centring In building, wooden framework used in construction of arches and vaults which is removed once the mortar is dry.

chasing The tooling of a metal surface by denting or hammering to create pattern, texture or a smoothing effect following the **lost-wax process**.

chiaroscuro (*kee-ahr-uh-***skyoor***-oh*) From the Italian meaning 'light-dark'. The treatment of light and shade to achieve a three-dimensional representation, or **modelling**. The term is generally applied to a dramatic use of extreme light and dark in a painting.

Classical Antiquity Also known as the Classical period, comprising the interconnected civilisations of Ancient Greece and Ancient Rome from the sixth century BCE to the fall of the Roman Empire in the fourth century CE.

Classical Orders See **Orders**

collaged From the French *coller* to 'gum' or 'glue'; a technique in which pasted paper or other materials are stuck down as part of or to create a whole pictorial composition.

collectors People who collect things of interest, in this context, art. A collector's item is an object associated with monetary value and/or beauty.

colonial Relating to a colony or colonies, and/or inhabitants of a colony – for example, British colonisation (control) of a place foreign to itself.

colonnade A row or series of **columns** at regular intervals carrying an **entablature**.

columns Free-standing, usually supporting, upright architectural members. In Classical architecture each column consists of a shaft, **capital** and (except in **Doric**) a base.

commodification Turning everything into a commodity – to be bought and sold.

complementary colours Pairs of colours which, when placed next to each other, create a strong contrast. The optical strengthening of such combinations was explored by the chemist, Michel Eugène Chevreul. He wrote *The Principles of Harmony and Contrast of Colours, and Their Applications to the Arts*, 1839.

confraternities Civic societies comprising lay people who dedicated themselves to a particular saint and usually devoted themselves to charitable causes. Due to their collective nature and wealth from subscriptions, they were often able to commission important artists to work for them. For example, Gentile Bellini's *Procession in the Piazza San Marco*, 1496, was commissioned for the confraternity of the Scuola Grande di San Giovanni Evangelista in Venice.

Constructivism A post-revolutionary (after 1917) Russian art movement characterised by **abstract** angular forms and the use of 'non-art' **materials** (metal, glass, wire, wood, etc.). Some constructivists questioned the role and purpose of art in the new socialist state and applied constructivist forms to architecture and design; others developed Constructivism as an **abstract** art movement that subsequently spread to Western Europe and the United States.

consumerism A term relating to a high rate of buying (consuming) goods and/or services.

continuous narrative Multiple scenes from a narrative, all contained within a single frame.

contract A written or spoken agreement between two parties intended to be a binding commitment enforceable by law. Contracts between artists and **patrons** often dictated the content, **materials** and timescale of the work to be produced.

contrapposto (*kohn-truh*-**pos**-*toh*) An Italian term, meaning 'set against' and used to describe one part of the body twisting away from another, usually identified by the turn of the shoulders and the hips in opposite directions.

contre-jour French photographic term used to describe photographs taken into the light. The effect is often a rim of light around the objects of the camera's lens. In painting, the term is used for an object seen against the light.

corbels In architecture, a block of stone, wood or metal jutting from a wall to carry a weight, such as an **oriel** window.

Corinthian One of the five Classical **Orders** of architecture, characterised by a slender fluted column with a flared capital decorated with florid acanthus leaves.

cornice From the Italian, meaning 'ledge', a horizontal and decorative moulded projection of a building that forms the uppermost part of an **entablature**. See also **raking cornices**.

Counter-Reformation A period of revival for the Roman Catholic Church, prompted by the rise of Protestantism. It started with the Council of Trent (1545–1563) and ended in the mid-seventeenth century.

crenellation A parapet (low wall) with indentations or raised elements, also known as a battlement.

crisis of masculinity A sociological term used to describe the feelings of some men at the loss of a traditional masculine role.

critic Someone who writes and publishes their opinions on art and artists. They can be very influential, raising or lowering an artist's status.

cross-hatching Crossing lines of **hatching** to denote shading and tonal **modelling**.

cruciform Cross-shaped.

Cubism An early twentieth-century movement in art (c.1907–c.1914), invented by Georges Braque (1882–1963) and Pablo Picasso (1881–1973), which abandoned single-point perspective in favour of interlocking or **faceted planes**. Cubism is understood to have developed in three distinct phases: **Proto-Cubism**, **Analytical Cubism**, **Synthetic Cubism**.

curtain wall A non-load-bearing wall of a building. Its non-structural function allows it to be made from lightweight **materials** such as glass and it is frequently used in skyscrapers where the structure is an internal steel or **ferroconcrete** (**reinforced concrete**) frame.

daguerrotype The first widespread photographic process introduced in 1839. A chemical reaction on a highly polished silver surface formed an image. The process was invented by Louis-Jacque-Mandé Daguerre (1787–1851).

dealer An art dealer is a person or company who buys and sells works of art. Some have become well known for their relationships with certain artists, such as Daniel-Henry Kahnweiler with Pablo Picasso and Jay Jopling with Damien Hirst. Some dealers have been able to influence buying trends in the **art market**.

Deconstructivist A late twentieth-century approach to architecture (also known as deconstruction/ deconstructivism, following its literary origins) that uses dislocated and fragmentary effects, creating a sense of disharmony and instability. It may be viewed as a reaction to the geometric regularity and harmony of **Modern Movement** buildings.

delineating Describing something precisely (e.g. drawing using line to create a crisp, hard-edged finish).

De Stijl (*duh-stahyl*) A Dutch artistic movement which literally translates as 'The Style'. It proposed a pure geometric and **abstract** style.

donor portraits Donors are the **patrons** of religious works of art in **Renaissance** paintings, and a portrait of them would typically appear somewhere in the scene.

Doric One of the five Classical **Orders** of architecture, distinguished by heavy fluted **column** and plain **capital**.

drum An upright and circular or polygonal–shaped base which supports a dome.

ducal Relating to a duke.

Early Renaissance The period c.1400–1490 in Italian art, principally used in relation to art and architecture in Florence. See also **Renaissance**.

engaged column A column that is attached to a wall, having between half and three-quarters of its shaft exposed. Its curvature distinguishes it from a **pilaster**.

entablature In Classical architecture, the continuous horizontal section supported by **columns** which comprises: architrave (main beam), **frieze** (horizontal decoration) and **cornice**.

essentialism A focus on the fundamental truth and basic elements of a person or thing.

ethnicity Used to describe a person's cultural heritage and/or racial identity. Culture includes a shared language, food, style of dress and so on. To have an ethnic identity involves having a sense of pride and union with others of the same culture.

ethnocentric Judging other cultures by criteria specific to one's own, usually implying inferiority.

Expressionism When used with a capital 'E' it relates specifically to two early twentieth century German movements: Die Brücke (The Bridge) and Der Blaue Reiter (The Blue Rider). Both groups employed a non-naturalistic use of colour and presented the world from a subjective and emotional viewpoint. When the term is used with a small 'e' it refers more generally to art which expresses emotion or to the works of forerunners to Expressionism such as Edvard Munch and Vincent van Gogh. See also **Neo-Expressionism**.

ex-voto An object, such as a picture, presented as a votive offering, often at a shrine.

façade In architecture, the front of a building.

faceted Small **planes** meeting at sharp angles; in **Analytical Cubism** they suggest a simultaneous viewpoint.

Fauves Early twentieth-century European **avant-garde** movement characterised by bold, disharmonious colour palettes and dark outlines for expressive effect. Henri Matisse (1869–1954) was their leading figure. The 'Fauve' label was applied derogatorily by **critic** Louis Vauxcelles at the Salon d'Automne, 1905, where the Fauves exhibited.

feminist A person who advocates the rights of women on the grounds of equality of the sexes.

fenestration Arrangement of windows on a building.

ferroconcrete (or **reinforced concrete**) Concrete with steel rods set inside; this reinforcing gives a **high-tensile** strength that concrete alone does not have.

fibreglass Glass in a fibrous form. Plastic reinforced by glass fibre is a strong and lightweight material.

film noir Literally 'black film', it relates to movies of the 1940s and 1950s, often featuring a private detective in a fictitious crime story.

flâneur A man who strolls around and observes his surroundings, from the French noun meaning 'stroller'.

flying buttress In architecture, an arched structure generally on the exterior of a building that carries the outward thrust of a wall to the ground. In this way, it acts like a buttress by supporting the wall but is only fixed to it at its upper point.

Fordism The manufacturing system initiated by Henry Ford to produce standardised goods efficiently and at low cost. It initially related to the manufacture of Ford's low-cost car, but the term is now used to refer to mass-produced goods generally.

foreshortening An aspect of **linear perspective** where the depiction of an object on a two-dimensional surface creates the illusion of its projection or extension in space.

formal analysis A consideration of an artwork in terms of the following elements: composition, line, colour, shape, scale.

formalism An artistic and critical approach which stresses form (line, colour and shape) over content. In early twentieth-century Britain, leading Formalist **critics** were Clive Bell and Roger Fry, and in the United States the critic Clement Greenberg.

found object A natural or human-made object used in an artwork.

fresco Water-based painting applied onto wet lime or gypsum plaster.

frieze A broad horizontal band of sculpted or painted decoration. In architecture, it is the central horizontal section of an **entablature**.

gables In architecture, the triangular shape at the end of a pitched roof.

gallerist Someone who owns an art gallery or who exhibits artworks in galleries in order to attract potential buyers.

gargoyle Grotesque-style carvings of human or animal form. Used often as water spouts from gutters as symbols to spew evil away from buildings.

gender Relates to being either 'masculine' or 'feminine'. Gender is socially and culturally constructed rather than biologically determined.

genre French term meaning 'kind', 'type' or 'category'. In painting a genre might be 'still life', 'landscape', 'portrait', 'history painting' and, rather confusingly, 'genre' (see next entry).

genre-genre A painting depicting an 'everyday' scene.

German Expressionism See **Expressionism**.

gesso Italian meaning 'gypsum'. A smooth white surface (ground) on which to paint, achieved by applying a mixture of ground gypsum (a natural mineral used to make plaster), chalk and some kind of glue.

giornate Italian for 'a day's work'; sections of new plaster that a painter can complete in a day.

glaze A thin and transparent layer of paint applied over the top of an opaque layer.

gold leaf Real gold which has been beaten into a very thin layer, like foil, before it is applied decoratively.

Golden Section A proportional ratio, believed to be ideal or perfect, that relates to the division of a unit into two parts such that the ratio of the shorter (B) to the longer (A) equals the ratio of the longer (A) to the whole (C). The ratio is approximately 1:1.618 (often expressed as Φ) and originated in the sixth century BCE (at the time of Pythagoras). It is believed that we are inherently drawn to the aesthetic harmony of objects/building made in accordance with the Golden Section.

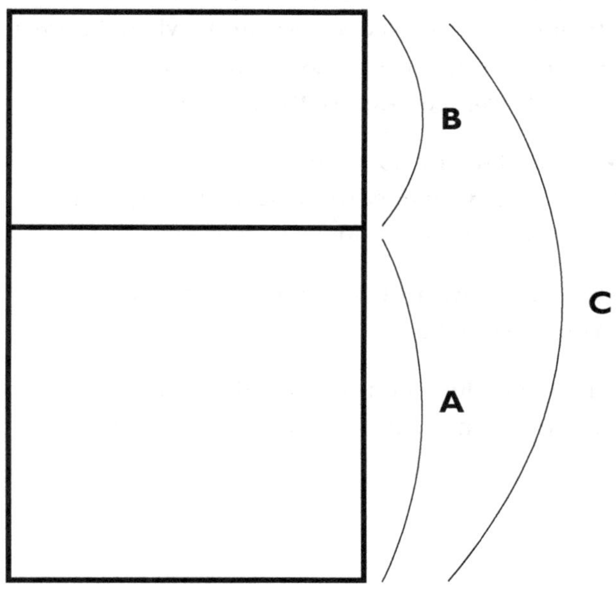

Gothic A style of art and architecture which prevailed from the twelfth to the fifteenth centuries.

Gothic Revival A nineteenth-century style, principally architectural, that copied **Gothic** forms from the twelfth to sixteenth centuries, such as pointed arches, ribbed vaulting and stained-glass windows.

graffito Drawing on the surface of walls; plural 'graffiti'.

guild Civic association of artists or craftsmen that originated in the **medieval period**. They were often associated with a patron saint.

hatching A technique which uses closely spaced parallel lines to achieve tonal **modelling** and suggest depth. See **cross-hatching**.

haute bourgeoisie The upper middle classes.

Hellenistic A period ranging from the death of Alexander the Great in 323 BCE to the emergence of the Roman Empire following the defeat of Cleopatra by Octavian in 31 BCE. Hellenistic art is more decorative and opulent than that of preceding periods.

herringbone brickwork Describes bricks laid at an angle to one another.

hierarchical scale A hierarchy of size or proportion is a technique used by artists to manipulate scale to show the relative importance of **subjects**.

High Baroque A style dating from c.1625 to c.1660 when the drama of the style was at its height. See also **Baroque**.

High Renaissance A name given to developments in the late fifteenth and early sixteenth century when the great **Renaissance** masters Leonardo da Vinci, Raphael and Michelangelo worked. See also **Renaissance**.

high-tech High-technology architecture characteristically imitates the style of industry and its **materials**: steel, glass, plastic.

high-tensile Strength and resistance to breaking when drawn out or stretched.

hoop-tie In building, stone and wooden chains locked together with iron to act as a belt around the base of a dome.

horse-shoe arches Characteristic of Islamic architecture, they are also called Moorish or keyhole arches. They resemble horse-shoe shapes and can be rounded or pointed in form.

humanism A cultural movement associated with the **Renaissance**, relating to the belief in human progress by human efforts. Inspired by Ancient Greek philosophy and thought.

hybridity/hybridisation The term is used broadly today, although it is often used to refer to the blending of cultures.

hyperrealism A detailed, accurate, life-like manner. With a capital 'H', a movement in painting in the late 1960s and 1970s that is an accurate and detailed imitation of the real world much like a photograph. Also referred to as **Superrealism** or Photorealism.

icon Literally 'image', but in the Eastern Christian tradition an image of a holy being or object that might be used as a focus for veneration.

iconography The study of the symbolic meaning of images in a work of art, such as particular objects, animals, plants, physical gestures, etc.

idealisation The representation of things in an ideal or perfect way.

ideology A sociological concept that refers to a set of ideas (that of the dominant class) that are presented as the only way of seeing things and therefore accepted despite their being based on a partial truth.

impasto Thickly applied paint (usually oil) that stands up above the surface to which it has been applied.

Impressionists Members of the French movement Impressionism. Fifty different artists exhibited in the eight Impressionist exhibitions, but of these Monet, Pissarro, Sisley, Renoir, Morisot, Cassatt and Degas are now considered to be the core group. Their work is characterised by bright palettes, painterly (loose) brushwork, and scenes of contemporary Parisian life and landscapes.

indulgences In Catholic theology, an indulgence is the remission of punishment on earth or in purgatory (although not in Heaven) for sins that have already been forgiven through Confession. Luther criticised the Catholic practice of allowing priests to sell indulgences (to raise money for the church, or even for themselves) and the assumption that priests possessed the power to grant the **laity** eternal earthly happiness in the transaction.

infra-red reflectogram Data captured from reflectology. Infra-red reflectology (IRR) is a technique used to look through paint layers, using wavelengths of infra-red radiation to reveal underdrawings.

installation A work of art created for a specific location, which then becomes an integral aspect of the work experienced by the viewer. This may be indoor (in a gallery or a non-art setting) or outdoor. Sometimes the viewer must physically enter the installation.

International Gothic A style prevalent in the late fourteenth to early fifteenth centuries, characteristically decorative and showing attention to detail.

International Style A term derived from the 1932 Museum of Modern Art (MoMA), New York, exhibition of that name. It is an alternative style label to **Modern Movement**. See **Modern Movement**.

Ionic One of the five Classical **Orders** of architecture, distinguished by a more slender **column** than in the **Doric** Order and **capital** with **volutes**.

istoria A term used by Leon Battista Alberti in his treatise *About Painting* (1435) to describe a generally complex and uplifting figure composition that conveys a biblical, **mythological** or historical narrative.

Japonisme A French term relating to the nineteenth-century European interest in Japanese art. In Western art this was manifest in the use of dark outline, stark pattern and areas of flat, unmodelled paint derived from Japanese woodblock prints.

kitsch A German term for 'trash'. It has come to be associated with vulgarity, poor taste and popular culture. Its style is epitomised in garish tourist souvenirs.

laity Ordinary people, as distinct from the clergy.

lancet In architecture, a tall narrow window terminated in a pointed arch. A **Gothic** feature.

lapis lazuli A semi-precious blue mineral used to make a bright blue **pigment** which, in the **Middle Ages** and the **Renaissance**, was more expensive than **gold leaf**.

liberal arts Considered to be more intellectual and therefore superior to the **mechanical arts** (practical craftsmanship). Art was considered more liberal than mechanical during the **Renaissance**.

lime-proof pigments Colours (pigments) that can withstand the chemical effects of the lime mortar into which they are incorporated during the **fresco** process. For this reason **fresco** has a limited colour palette.

linear perspective The method of representing solid, three-dimensional objects on a two-dimensional surface using the optical impression that parallel lines converge as they recede to a vanishing point on a horizon or eye-level line. This geometry allows the artist to plot the relative size of objects.

loggia (*loh-jee-uh*) In architecture, a **colonnade** or arcade that is roofed and open to the air, usually on one side only.

lost-wax process (in French *cire perdue*) A bronze casting method in which the wax model is melted and 'lost', leaving a cavity into which molten metal is poured.

low-tensile Weakness and susceptibility to breaking when drawn out or stretched.

maestà An Italian word for 'majesty', which refers to paintings of the Madonna enthroned as the Queen of Heaven.

male gaze Used in relation to psychoanalytic theory and relating to the gendered gaze in terms of male desire or destruction. Feminist theorist Laura Mulvey examined the exclusively male gaze in terms of patriarchy. See **patriarchal**.

Marxist A follower of the beliefs of German social theorist Karl Marx (1818–1883). Marxism explores the concept of man's alienation: the lack of control an individual has over the product of their labour.

masonry Stonework in architecture and building.

material The type of material used by artists (such as oil, **acrylic**, bronze) and architects (such as brick and stone). Also referred to as **medium**.

mechanical arts Practical skills such as weaving and blacksmithing. The mechanical arts complemented the **liberal arts**, which were considered to be more intellectual.

mechanisation The use of machines for production, communication, transport, etc. The term is generally applied to developments in Western society during and after the Industrial Revolution (from the mid-eighteenth century) and suggests a decline in hand production, direct human interaction, travel using natural means, etc.

medieval period A period in history from the fifth century to the early fifteenth century, also referred to as the **Middle Ages**. The medieval period followed the fall of the Western Roman Empire in the fifth century and preceded what is called the Early Modern Era, beginning with the **Renaissance**.

medium The type of **material** used by artists (such as oil, **acrylic**, bronze) and architects (such as brick and stone).

memento mori Objects designed to remind people of their own mortality, sometimes included in a type of still life known as a **vanitas**.

meritocracy A system in which people are selected or promoted according to merit.

mezzanine The partial storey or floor between two main storeys in a building.

Middle Ages A term first used in the **Renaissance** for the period in European history dating from about the fifth to the fifteenth century. So-called because **Renaissance** scholars regarded it as a middle period between two 'great' periods – the Classical of ancient Greece and Rome, and their own, which they called 'modern'.

minarets In architecture, tall, slender and circular towers which are usually attached to an Islamic mosque, from which the faithful can be called to prayer.

miniature A term associated with minute portraits, small enough to be worn or carried.

mise-en-scène (*meez-on-sen*) The arrangement of a scene in a film, photograph or advertisement. Elements include lighting, make-up, props, facial expression, etc.

modelling In two-dimensional work, the way artists achieve volume and a sense of three-dimensional realism by shading from light to dark. It is often used interchangeably with the more technical term **chiaroscuro**, although this implies a dramatic use of extreme light and dark. It can also refer to the making of a sculpture in clay, plaster or wax by adding and forming material to create form.

Modernism A very broad term relating to modern thought and a break with the past, and, more specifically, Modernism with a capital 'M' relates to the ideas of twentieth-century American art **critic** Clement Greenberg.

modernity The condition of being modern, up to date, but used by the French writer and art critic Charles Baudelaire to describe a particular aspect of the modern – the fleeting experience of life in the urban city of Paris in the nineteenth century.

Modern Movement In architecture, the term relates to angular, undecorated buildings in modern **materials** with an emphasis on functionalism. Also known as the **International Style**.

Mogul The decorative art and architecture of the Mogul dynasty (Muslim rulers of India) from the sixteenth to the eighteenth centuries. The Taj Mahal is the most well-known example of this kind of Indian Islamic architecture.

monochromatic A term referring to objects or images with a narrow range of colours. The term is often applied when black and white is used.

mythological Concerning a body of myths from Greek and Roman **mythology**.

mythology Stories relating to superhuman beings (gods and goddesses) from **Antiquity**.

nationality The status of belonging to a particular nation. Nations often believe themselves to possess their own characteristic qualities, and people belonging to a nation often demonstrate national sentiment.

naturalism In art, depicting the natural appearance of things as closely as possible.

Neo-classical Describes a style in European art of the eighteenth and nineteenth centuries that drew inspiration from the art, architecture and ideas of ancient Greece and, especially, Rome; sometimes expressed as Neo-classicism. It was considered to offer a 'pure' style.

Neo-Expressionism A revival of **Expressionism** in the second half of the twentieth century, one exponent of which was George Baselitz.

Neo-Plasticism A term coined by Dutch artist Piet Mondrian (1872–1944) to describe a severe **abstract**

aesthetic typically using straight lines and primary colours with white, black and grey.

Neo-Platonism A new (neo) Platonism derived from the philosophy of Plato, which suggests that perfection can only exist in the immaterial or transcendental realm. Neo-platonic beauty suggests that which is beyond the imperfections of the material realm.

noble savage The term expresses the concept of a romanticised native or non-Western '**other**'; deemed to be uncorrupted by civilisation and born gentle and free.

odalisque (*o-da-leesk*) A Turkish female slave or concubine. The **subject** was popular in nineteenth-century art. The pose of the model is often indicative of sexual availability. Typically, one arm or both arms are raised above the shoulder to enable a fuller view of the upper body.

oeuvre (*oeu-vre*) The collective works of an artist; their entire body of work.

opacity Describes being unable to see through, lacking transparency.

Orders In Classical architecture, the features of a **trabeated** structure, such as a temple. There are five main orders in Classical architecture: **Doric**, Tuscan, **Ionic**, **Corinthian** and Composite. Each order has a **column**, **capital** and (apart from **Doric**) a base, and above it a particular style of **entablature**, consisting of architrave (main beam), **frieze** (horizontal decoration) and **cornice** (moulded projection).

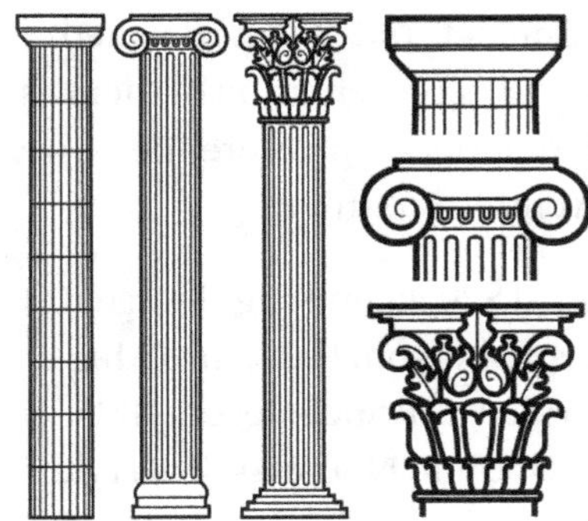

oriel In architecture, a projecting window usually built out from an upper storey and supported by **corbels**.

Orientalism A term most commonly used to describe the depiction of the East by Western artists. The term, which became synonymous with the exotic in Western usage, was critically examined by scholar Edward Said in his seminal text *Orientalism: Western Conceptions of the Orient*, 1978, which examined the West's fascination with the East as '**other**'.

other A term that denotes difference or divergence from norms established by ruling or controlling authorities in relation to ethnicity, culture, **gender** or other groupings.

painterly Brushstrokes that are clearly visible.

patina The colouring that may occur on metal sculptures naturally as a result of age and environmental conditions or which may be encouraged artificially using chemicals.

patriarchal Denoting a society dominated by men.

patrons Patrons commission, support or collect works of art and architecture (they are the clients). In commissioning a work they may exert influence over its creation and specify what they want, what **materials** should be used and the timescale for its completion.

pediment A Classical architectural feature. A low-pitched **gable** on top of a portico (entrance), door, window or the end of a building following the roof slope. Most pediments are straight-sided (triangular) although they can be curved.

piano nobile An Italian term used to describe the 'noble floor', or main living floor, usually raised above ground level and frequently the first floor. Larger windows often indicate its status as a principal reception floor.

picture plane The **plane** of a picture from which the illusory three-dimensional space appears to recede.

pietà (*pi-e-tà*) Italian term for 'pity', and a **subject** of paintings and/or sculptures of the Virgin Mary holding the dead body of Jesus on her lap.

pigment A substance, usually dry, used as colouring when mixed with a liquid **binder**.

pilasters A shallow pier or rectangular **column** projecting from the wall and, in Classical architecture, conforming one of the **Orders**.

piloti A thin **column** that acts as a support.

plane A flat surface.

plein air A French term meaning 'open air' used to describe painting outdoors.

polychromatic Many-coloured.

polychromer An artist who painted wooden sculpture in a variety of colours.

polyptych (*po-lyp-tych*) A work, usually an altarpiece, on more than three panels.

Pop Art An art movement of the early 1960s that challenged traditional **subjects** and forms of art, often employing imagery from mass culture such as comics, consumer goods and advertising, and using **collage** and **found objects** in combination with painted imagery.

Post-Impressionism A term used to describe the work of a generation of painters who came after the **Impressionists**. It is an imprecise and umbrella term for a wide variety of styles.

Post-Impressionists Artists painting in a variety of ways, expressively or symbolically, after Impressionism.

postmodern A twentieth-century concept which represents a move away from **Modernism** and its accompanying ideologies. Encompasses a range of artistic and architectural styles, often in a playful manner. The term first came into use in the 1960s with reference to architecture, but is now commonly used in relation to all of the arts.

Prairie Style American architectural style characterised by long, horizontal buildings with low-pitched roofs and over-hanging eaves. Frank Lloyd Wright's Robie House, Chicago, 1908–1909, is typical of the style.

precisionist Generally suggesting accuracy and exactness. With a capital 'P', it is an art style in America from c.1910s–1940s characterised by clean-cut, immaculate representations of features of the urban landscape. Originally called the 'Immaculate School', they were later dubbed Cubo-Realists, then (in 1960) Precisionists.

pre-Columbian Relates to the history of the indigenous Americas cultures before the arrival of Christopher Columbus in 1492 (who is traditionally credited with their discovery). It therefore tends to denote the period prior to European influence. Pre-Columbian art is made by indigenous peoples (e.g. the Mayan, Aztecs and Incas).

prefabricated Parts/units (often in building) manufactured off site and brought together for assembly.

Pre-Raphaelites The Pre-Raphaelite Brotherhood was formed in 1848 by a group of English painters who took their inspiration from art which preceded that of the Italian **Renaissance** painter Raphael. They admired such art for its simplicity and apparent moral content. The principal founding members of the group were John Everett Millais, Dante Gabriel Rossetti and William Holman Hunt.

primary colours In pigments, red, yellow and blue are the colours from which all other colours are derived.

primitivism Influence of primitive art, in the early twentieth century principally from Africa and the Pacific Islands.

Prix de Rome Literally 'Rome Prize', this was an art scholarship introduced by the French Royal Academy in 1663. The winner took up a student scholarship to study Classical and **Renaissance** art at the Académie de France à Rome at the King's expense for a period of three to five years.

Proto-Cubism Early, pre-Cubist phase that preceded mature **Cubism**. Mature **Cubism** comprised **Analytical** and **Synthetic Cubism**.

quattrocento (*kwah-troh-***chen***-toh*). A term (relating to the one thousand four hundreds) used to refer to the fifteenth-century period of Italian art during the **Renaissance**.

raking cornices **Cornices** which follow the slopes of a **gable** or **pediment**.

raking light A light applied to the **picture plane** at an acute angle.

readymade Everyday manufactured objects deemed to be art by virtue of the artist's presentation of them as such. A concept of art Marcel Duchamp is credited with perfecting in the early twentieth century.

Regency The period 1811–1820 when King George III was deemed unfit to rule and his son, the future King George IV (1820–1830), ruled as Prince Regent. It is used more loosely to describe late **Neo-classical** style furniture and architecture in England.

reinforced concrete See **ferroconcrete**.

Renaissance A French term meaning 'rebirth' used to describe arts in Italy from the early fourteenth to the mid-sixteenth centuries.

retablos Literally means 'behind the altar'. In Mexico, retablos are small oil paintings on tin, zinc, copper or wood principally for use in the home and usually venerate Catholic saints. They are deeply rooted in Spanish and Mexican culture and distinctively folk-art in style.

rib In architecture, a moulding which projects from the surface of a ceiling or wall. Often with a rounded profile and found especially in Gothic church architecture where they define and decorate the vaults of naves and **transepts**. They are also found on the outside of domes.

ribbon window In architecture, a continuous horizontal strip of windows.

Rococo A term to describe the elegant style of interior decoration, probably derived from the French *rocaille* (stone) and *coquille* (shell). It is used to identify painting, sculpture and other visual arts in the early eighteenth century.

rustication Cutting stone in a way that sinks the joints to create a channel. **Façades** can often look powerful and solid as a result.

Salon Refers to annual or biannual art exhibitions held in Paris under the auspices of the French Royal Academy from 1725 and, in the nineteenth century, sponsored by the French government.

screen printing Also known as silkscreen printing and serigraphy. A method of printmaking which places a cut, painted or photographically applied stencil design on a screen of polyester or other fine mesh. In areas not blocked out by the stencil, printing ink is forced through the mesh (screen) onto the printing surface. A separate stencil is required for each colour printing. The technique is said to have originated in China during the Song Dynasty (c.960–1279) where silk was used. Nowadays, cheaper, modern and more durable **materials** (such as nylon filament fibre) are used.

secco fresco Painting on a plaster wall where the plaster is dry. In order for the paint to adhere to the wall, egg yolk is added to the pigment as a **binder**.

secondary art market The re-sale art market. A sale achieved after the original (primary) sale.

secondary colours Colours made by mixing two primary colours to form green, orange and purple in pigments.

secular Not religious.

self-portrait A representation of the artist drawn, painted, printed, sculpted or made in some way using other media by the artist.

semi-monocoque Monocoque (mon-*uh*-kohk,-kok) is from the French word *mono* (single) *coque* (shell) that relates to a construction type where the shell carries the stress/load. A structure which has its load supported partly (semi) by its single shell is semi-monocoque.

semiotics The study of signs and symbols in various fields, especially language (e.g. a rose is a sign of love).

sexism Assumption that one sex is inferior, or discrimination based on this assumption or a presupposition based on a fixed notion of **gender** (e.g. images that degrade women or turn them into sex objects for the gratification of men are said to be sexist). Discrimination can be overt or covert.

silicone resin An adhesive synthetic organic polymer containing silicone and oxygen.

size Usually animal-skin glue used as a **binder** or for priming canvas.

socialist Someone who follows the philosophy or doctrine of socialism, which is an economic and political system based on collective ownership and the collective rights of man. Socialists value liberty and equality.

soft sculpture A type of sculpture made using soft **materials** such as fabric, wool, foam and other natural or man-made non-rigid **materials**.

stereotype/stereotypical A pejorative term to describe the way people or things are viewed in certain fixed and often unjustified and exaggerated ways.

stigmata The nail wounds pertaining to Christ's Crucifixion.

stucco A plaster-coated decoration or wall coating.

stylus A small and pointed metal tool used for incising and marking.

subject Refers to the literal and visible topic or theme of a work. This can be almost anything, but common examples include the nude, war and animals.

sub-text An underlying theme and/or meaning.

subtractive A sculpture technique in which material is reduced and taken away (as in carving).

Superrealism A movement in painting in the late 1960s and 1970s that is an accurate and detailed imitation of the real world much like a photograph. Also referred to as **hyperrealism** or Photorealism.

Suprematism A term coined by the artist Kasimir Malevich about 1915 to describe his **abstract** art of coloured geometric forms.

Surrealism A twentieth-century **avant-garde** movement in art and literature that aimed to release the creative potential of the unconscious mind. Founded by the French poet André Breton with the *First Surrealist Manifesto*, 1924, the diversity of the group's artistic style tended to be united by a Freudian interest in liberating the mind from rationality and control. Despite his eventual expulsion from the movement, its most famous exponent was the Spanish artist Salvador Dalí.

symbiotic A close association or relationship between two interdependent objects, people, ideas, etc.

symbolic exclusion A sociological term used by Parveen Akhtar (2005) to describe the way Muslims in the UK have been made to feel excluded from wider society on account of their **ethnicity** and faith. The term 'symbolic annihilation' was used by feminist theorist Gaye Tuchman (1978) in a similar way to describe the under-representation of individuals based on **gender** and **ethnicity** in the media. Both terms can be understood as relating to the marginalisation of the '**other**' and social inequality.

Symbolism A late nineteenth-century art movement embracing a variety of styles but with the common aim of rejecting literal representations in favour of images that evoke, suggest or symbolise **subjects** and meanings. A good deal of Symbolist art is anti-materialistic, anti-rational, mystical and, sometimes, associated with decadence, eroticism and the perverse.

synaesthete Someone who experiences synaesthesia, in which the stimulation of one sense leads to the involuntary stimulation of another, such as an auditory sound stimulating the visual experience of a corresponding colour.

Synthetic Cubism A style dating from c.1912–c.1914 in which the image was built up from sections of the **subject** as a series of **planes**. **Collage**, or simulated collage in paint, was frequently used.

techniques and processes Describes the various ways artists and architects handle the **materials** they use.

tempera A permanent and fast-drying **medium** also known as egg tempera because **pigment** is mixed with egg yolk, which acts as a **binder**.

tenebristic (tenebrous, tenebrism) From the Italian word *tenebroso*, meaning 'obscure', it describes a work which is predominantly dark. Typified by the seventeenth-century work of painter Caravaggio.

tension piles In architecture and building, large upright posts hammered deep into the ground to support a superstructure.

Thatcherite A follower of the political policies advocated by Margaret Thatcher, who was UK Prime Minister from 1979 to 1990. It includes an emphasis on the free market and individual enterprise.

thinner A liquid used to dilute paint, making it flow more easily. In oil-based paint, this is generally turpentine, which can also be used as a cleaning agent.

tondo An Italian word for 'round', used to describe a circular painting or relief sculpture especially common in the fifteenth century.

tone Relating to the quality of brightness; a shade of colour.

tooled Tooling can refer to removing blemishes to smooth stone and metal, or decorating a surface by punching or marking to create indentations.

trabeated Having horizontal beams rather than arches; a post and lintel system of construction.

transept A section of a building, usually a Christian church, that lies across the main body of the building.

transverberation The moment of spiritual rapture when experiencing God's presence in one's own body. This is symbolised in art and literature by the piercing of the heart with a spear or arrow.

tripartite An arrangement/composition in art and architecture which is divided into three parts/sections.

truth to medium Responding to and taking advantage of the natural and inherent properties of the **medium**.

tympanum (*tym-pa-nem*) Triangular or segmental face of the **pediment** (the space within the pediment), or the arched area (frequently decorated with sculpture) above an entrance (usually to a Christian church).

ultramarine From Latin meaning 'beyond the sea'. It is a deep-blue coloured **pigment** derived from ground **lapis lazuli**. During the **Middle Ages** and **Renaissance**, **lapis** was mined in Afghanistan and imported to Europe where, because it was an extremely expensive **pigment** and also because it symbolised the blue of Heaven, it was used to depict the robes of the Virgin Mary. A synthetic version of ultramarine was first made in 1826.

Usonian A term coined by Frank Lloyd Wright to describe architecture and town planning of the United States, as distinct from America (which included Canada and Mexico). Wright built about 60 Usonian houses from 1936 until his death in 1959. Designed for middle-income families, they were intended to epitomise a singularly US architecture independent of European influence. They were also to suggest an egalitarian culture and an idealistic vision of a new civilisation.

vanitas Latin for 'vanity'; taken from Ecclesiastes 1:2 'Vanity of vanities' and commonly an allegorical still life painting in which objects become symbolic of the transience of human life.

verdigris A green coloured **pigment** obtained from the residue formed after applying acid to copper.

verisimilitude Extreme realism and meticulous attention to detail.

vernacular Indigenous and local, derived from the Latin *vernaculus*.

volutes From the Latin for 'scroll'. In architecture, a spiral scroll feature found at the top, the **capital** of an **Ionic Order** (also found as part of the **capital** on a **Corinthian** and Composite Order).

wet-on-wet A painting technique in which wet paint is applied onto layers of wet paint or wet ground. For the technique to be effective, the paint must be applied quickly before the first layers have dried out. Known in French as *au premier coup* and in Italian as *alla prima*.

YBA An abbreviation of Young British Artists used to identify a number of artists chiefly supported by the **patron** and **collector** Charles Saatchi. They include Damien Hirst, Rachel Whiteread and Tracey Emin.

Zeitgeist (*zight-guise-t*) German word meaning the spirit of the age (an outlook specific to a particular period in history).

Other Useful Sources

Clarke, M. *Concise Dictionary of Art Terms*, Oxford University Press, 2010.

Curl, J.S. *A Dictionary of Architecture and Landscape Architecture*, Oxford University Press, 2006.

Fleming, J., Honour, H. and Pevsner, N. *The Penguin Dictionary of Architecture*, 4th ed., Penguin, 1991.

Harris, J. *Art History: The Key Concepts*, Routledge, 2008.

Murray, P. and Murray, L. *Dictionary of Art and Artists*, Penguin, 1997.

Pooke, G. and Whitham, G. *Understand Art History*, Hodder, 2010.

Index

References to illustrations are in italics. References to notes are given as follows: 32n (for marginal comments) or 32n1 (where the note is numbered and refers back to the main text). References to glossary definitions are given as follows: 275g. Illustrations and notes are indexed separately only if there is no other information on that subject in the main text on that page.

Printed in the USA
CPSIA information can be obtained
at www.ICGtesting.com
LVHW081921301024
795287LV00008B/173

9 781118 904978